CRIME, POLICING AND I
IN ENGLAND, 1660–1914

CRIME, POLICING AND PUNISHMENT IN ENGLAND, 1660–1914

Drew D. Gray

This book is supported by a companion website, which includes an extended bibliography and seminar exercises.

Website materials can be accessed at
www.bloomsbury.com/crimeinengland.

Bloomsbury Academic
An imprint of Bloomsbury Publishing Plc

B L O O M S B U R Y
LONDON · OXFORD · NEW YORK · NEW DELHI · SYDNEY

Bloomsbury Academic

An imprint of Bloomsbury Publishing Plc

50 Bedford Square	1385 Broadway
London	New York
WC1B 3DP	NY 10018
UK	USA

www.bloomsbury.com

BLOOMSBURY and the Diana logo are trademarks of Bloomsbury Publishing Plc

First published 2016

British Library Cataloguing-in-Publication Data
A catalogue record for this book is available from the British Library.

ISBN: HB: 978-1-4411-3563-6
PB: 978-1-4411-1765-6
ePDF: 978-1-4725-7929-4
ePub: 978-1-4725-7928-7

Library of Congress Cataloging-in-Publication Data
Gray, Drew D.
Crime, policing and punishment in England, 1660-1914 / Drew D. Gray.
pages cm
Includes bibliographical references and index.
ISBN 978-1-4411-3563-6 (hb) – ISBN 978-1-4411-1765-6 (pb) –
ISBN 978-1-4725-7929-4 (ePDF) – ISBN 978-1-4725-7928-7 (epub)
1. Criminal justice, Administration of–England–History.
2. Crime–England–History. 3. Police–England–History. I. Title.
HV9960.G72G73 2016
364.94209'03–dc23
2015017471

Typeset by Integra Software Services Pvt. Ltd.
Printed and bound in Great Britain

CONTENTS

Contents

Contents

LIST OF ILLUSTRATIONS AND TABLES

Figures

Tables

ACKNOWLEDGEMENTS

This textbook has been the result of continual study over the period of my teaching and research at the University of Northampton and would not have been possible without the grounding in the history of crime I received from my PhD supervisor Peter King. More than that Pete has remained a good and close friend, and he and his wife Lee have always been there with a glass of wine and sympathy when I have needed them. The network of historians of crime is a close one, and I am indebted to them for all the advice I have had over the years from many sources, too numerous to list here. The reviewers who looked at my drafts have helped reshape this study in several ways, and I am grateful for their suggestions. The mistakes are, of course, all my own.

I must pause also to thank my mother, Diana, for once again taking the time to read over my drafts. As a former probation officer, she brought an interested perspective to some of our discussions and an ever-present level of support. Thanks also to Emma Johns who provided a critical and encouraging eye and ear. My colleagues at Northampton are owed thanks, particularly Dr Cathy Smith who always has time to listen to me, even when I know she is running out of minutes let alone hours for herself. The students I have taught have all contributed in their way to this book by engaging in discussion, challenging me and my ideas and undertaking the seminar and assessment tasks I have set them. Finally, my thanks to the editorial team at Bloomsbury who have been more than patient with me and professional in everything they do.

This book is for Charlie and Curtis Spencer as they embark upon their undergraduate careers; I am very proud of both of you.

SECTION I
KEY THEMES IN THE HISTORY OF CRIME

CHAPTER 1
INTRODUCTION – METHODS, THEMES AND DEBATES IN THE HISTORY OF CRIME AND PUNISHMENT

This is a book about the history of crime and punishment and is intended for undergraduates as well as those more broadly interested in the topic. However, it is not and never was intended to be a comprehensive guide for the student. This study references some of the vast and growing historiography that surrounds this topic, and there is no substitute for engaging directly with the arguments and debates that historians of crime have contributed to.[1]

Within this introduction is a brief guide to the contents of this book, but before going any further, it is important to set some limits as to what is (and is not) covered here. This is primarily a study of the history of crime and punishment in England from c. 1660 to c. 1914; Scotland, because it had a separate legal system, is excluded completely, and Wales is largely ignored or included as a part of the whole. Nor is Ireland a part of this story. These omissions partly reflect not only the reality that most of this history focuses on England but also a pressure on space. In order to try and cover such a wide chronological period, it has been necessary to concentrate on particular areas. This is also reflected in the particular topics that I have chosen to cover. This textbook is new in offering such a detailed overview of the operation of the court system across three centuries and unique in analysing the role of the Justice of the Peace and the evolution of Magistrates courts. This has meant, however, that certain topics have been omitted; there is, for example, no discussion of the crime of witchcraft beyond a short mention of its importance later in this introduction. Likewise, I have largely avoided rioting (although this is touched on briefly in a section on 'social crime').

It will also be apparent that while in some areas (such as juvenile offending, punishment and policing) there is a wide chronological reach, from the late seventeenth to the early twentieth century, in others change is not so pronounced, and the primary focus of study will be on the period 1700–1900. No book is perfect, but hopefully this one will offer a strong overview of the subject with plenty of space for further reading and research.

The final section of this introduction will precede the chronological evolution of the court system, policing and punishment by providing a short reflection on the criminal justice system of the late medieval and early modern period and the legacy that it bestowed on Restoration England. Before that, there will be a discussion of the importance of understanding crime rates, the uses of source material in historical research and first, a justification for studying the history of crime.

Reasons for studying crime and punishment history

It may seem unnecessary to explain the reasons for studying the history of crime and punishment; after all if you are reading this book, it is probably because you have decided to do so anyway. Nevertheless a brief introduction is useful. The history of crime is still a relatively new discipline, growing as it did out of the broader area of social history or 'history from below'. Historians in the 1970s began to use research into crime and punishment as part of wider research into social relations, class and power relationships. Much of this research was rooted in Marxist social history and in the concept of 'social control'. As F.M.L. Thompson observed, throughout the 1970s,

> [M]any social historians have approached a whole range of the activities of power groups as exercises in devising mechanisms of social control which conditioned and manipulated the propertyless masses into accepting and operating the forms and functions of behaviour necessary to sustain the social order of an industrial society.[2]

This manifested itself in studies of the rise of the prison, most notably by the French historian/philosopher Michel Foucault and by Michael Ignatieff.[3] Historians of eighteenth-century society, such as Edward Thompson and Douglas Hay, used the study of crime to look at the operation of power in Hanoverian England, in particular focusing on the selective use of the growing body of capital statutes after 1688: the so-called 'Bloody Code'.[4] Hay's seminal essay 'Power, Authority and the Criminal Law' (in his edited volume *Albion's Fatal Tree*) laid the cornerstone for future research into the history of crime.[5]

However, much of what has been written about the history of crime prior to the intervention of Thompson and Hay and their followers can be largely described as either administrative history (Sir Leon Radzinowicz's history of the criminal law, for example[6]) or 'popular history' (often gleaned from individual memoirs). Very few of the latter try to take an analytical view or use primary source material and statistical evidence for their conclusions. Others tend towards the sensational or 'true crime' genre.

Hay and his collaborators were more interested in presenting histories of crime that stressed the clash of classes in the wake of changing economic relationships in the eighteenth and nineteenth centuries. Thus, *Albion's Fatal Tree* contains essays that consider what historians have termed 'social crimes' (smuggling and poaching, for example). Instead of being simply regarded as criminal actions, social crimes are linked with popular forms of protest (such as the food riots that E. P. Thompson analysed elsewhere[7]) and have transformed the working-class offender into a sort of class warrior against the march of capitalism.[8]

Since the early 1980s then, the history of crime has developed from this largely ideological beginning. Historians, many inspired by the work of Thompson and Hay, have undertaken detailed case studies of prisons, policing and transportation to Australia as well as developing new and related themes such as the relationship between gender and crime and the history of interpersonal violence. However, the fundamental question of class and social control has not gone away. Indeed, as Vic Gatrell pointed out in an important essay in 1990:

> Historians might profitably remind themselves that the history of crime is a grim subject, not because it is about crime, but because it is about power.[9]

Thus, the question that continues to exercise historians of crime is therefore how useful was the law in the eighteenth and nineteenth centuries to those at the bottom of society? This debate will be addressed later in this volume but remains a crucial area for historical analysis and research.

It is also important to understand that the criminal law does not exist in isolation; it is a part of the social fabric of society, a crucial element in social relations. Therefore, the study of crime and punishment reveals much about a society and its attitudes and fears. This is very clear today with media concerns about violent crime, anti-social behaviour, gangs and terrorism, and these concerns are nothing new. The changing criminal justice system is therefore a useful prism through which to study the changing nature of society across the periods covered in this volume. Arguably, we can see a move from a society that is deeply concerned about the protection of private property (or perhaps more properly, individual wealth and privilege) to one that places much more importance on the preservation of human life and the public peace. In crude terms, a violent street robber in the eighteenth century would have been prosecuted and condemned for the theft, while by the end of the nineteenth it would have been the violence he used that caused him to appear before a court. Twenty-first-century Britain is most exercised by violence and anti-social behaviour, and this is partly because we have sophisticated alarms, locks and insurance to protect our property, but less means to protect our persons.

The history of crime is also very much a history 'from below'. What we mean by this is that it looks at the lives of 'ordinary' people: the working classes or labouring poor – in short, those who have previously been neglected by historians concerned with the exploits of kings and queens, generals, politicians and discoverers. History from below developed from the 1950s and 1960s from its beginnings at Ruskin College, Oxford, to a wider movement that has embraced gender history, the history of working-class struggle and oral history. The history of crime is an ideal vehicle for this sort of history because while hitherto the voices of the poor have rarely been heard in historical sources, within the records of criminal justice (for example, trial accounts, prison records, logs of transported felons) plebeian lives are frequently illuminated.

This process has continued into the twenty-first century and has been very much helped by new developments in technology and new approaches to history. The digitization of datasets such as the *Old Bailey Proceedings* and the advent of gender and cultural history have allowed writers and researchers to explore all sorts of new areas.[10] The former is not without its difficulties; increasingly, archives are looking to digitize records as a means both of disseminating them more easily electronically and as a way of conserving the original material. However, while electronic resources are (generally) easy to use, it is rare that they are free to all. The *Old Bailey Online* is a notable exception, but resources such as the *Eighteenth Century Collections Online* (ECCO) and *Early English Books Online* (EEBO), or the British Library's (growing) newspaper archive, are often restricted by cost. The National Archives has also reacted to the growth of genealogy (family history) as a popular pastime by making a considerable amount of primary material accessible, but at a price.

The digitization of old newspapers (and some other sources) has also created an additional problem: the ability to search them by keyword means that we no longer read old newspapers in the way that they were intended. Keyword searching encourages the reader to hunt within sections of documents rather than seeing them as they were presented in the past. There is a danger then that a modern researcher, using this method, might not discover the text in the context of how it was printed. The search mechanisms (especially for some of the earlier iterations of digested collections) are often so crude and inaccurate that researchers are apt to miss things and gain a far from accurate picture of the reporting of events in history. Finally, the *Old Bailey Online*, useful as it undoubtedly is, now means that a tremendous amount of research is conducted using its database of criminal trials. However, the Old Bailey only served London and its environs and is not representative of England as a whole. Indeed, recent work by Peter King and other researchers at Leicester has revealed how unique London and the Home Counties were in the long eighteenth century.[11] One might also add that the fact that the *Old Bailey Proceedings* are now available, in easy to read transcripts, has a tendency to render all other forms of contemporary text 'difficult' and less attractive to students of history. That said, new process such as data mining (as pioneered by Tim Hitchcock and others) opens up new possibilities for the way we 'do' history.[12] We might add to this the excellent mapping project *Locating London's Past* and similar work on the criminal corpse at Leicester University.[13]

In recent years, historians of crime and criminal justice have looked at a variety of themes, many of which will be dealt with in this textbook. These have included the criminal law and how it changed; crime rates and their relationship to periods of dearth and war; gender (the position of women under law and the newly emerging history of masculinity and its effect on understanding male violence); youth and delinquency; the operation of the courts (and at the emergence of the legal profession); particular types of crime, such as assault or forgery; the changing nature of punishment and the decline in the use of hanging and torture; violent crime (in particular, the nature and extent of homicide and whether this is affected by regionality or national culture); and finally, the role of the magistrate and the increased use of summary justice throughout the eighteenth and nineteenth centuries. Many of these, however, are still connected to the key question of what is the law and whom does it serve.

So hopefully all of this gives us ample justification for studying the history of crime, as if we needed it. After all crime and punishment is a fascinating subject in its own right; one only needs to switch on a television, radio or peruse the shelves of a bookshop to know that there exists an enduring passion for the stories of famous crime and criminals. Most of us have a vicarious interest in criminals partly because they represent 'the other' in society. They represent, to some extent at least, our 'dark side'; the lives of men such as the Krays, 'Mad Frankie' Fraser, as well as older villains such as Jack Sheppard, Dick Turpin, Charles Peace and the ubiquitous 'Jack the Ripper' hold our attention in a way that even great heroes such as Nelson and the Duke of Wellington fail to do. This book is designed to help students explore the histories of crime, through the writings of historians and the documents that the criminal justice system has left us.

How this book is organized

Part of the problem in writing any textbook is in trying to decide what exactly to cover. It is clearly impossible to offer a comprehensive study of any aspect of history because the subject is not static; our understanding of history is developing with every new piece of research and with each new source that is discovered and analysed. Even as I write this introduction, I am aware of new research being undertaken on gender and summary process, on the criminal corpse, murder and its contexts in London, the patterns of female criminality in nineteenth-century Liverpool and a host of other fascinating projects.

In consequence, this study is broken into two broad sections: the first of which provides a guide to several key themes in the history of crime and the second offering an introduction and overview of the criminal justice system.

The first theme is concerned with the role of the media and with changing attitudes towards crime and the criminal. We are so used to the ubiquity of media in the modern world that we are apt to forget what a fundamental role it plays in the shaping of attitudes and misconceptions. This is dramatically the case with regard to the history of crime and punishment, as this chapter will show. Many of us are now familiar with the notion of the 'moral panic' as outlined by Stanley Cohen in his seminal study, but how can we apply this to earlier episodes than the Mods and Rockers beach fights of the 1960s?[14] Chapter 2 will therefore look at the evolution of print media and its relationship with crime and the image of the criminal. This important topic also touches on the changing nature of attitudes towards the criminal across the 250-year period covered by this volume. The idea of the criminal changed in this time, from that of an individual *criminal* who had chosen the wrong path – a 'sinner' to use the language of the medieval or early modern period – to a more collective understanding of *criminals*: a subsection of the working class who were a product of the degraded environment which they inhabited. This change in the conceptualization of the criminal had a concomitant effect on the treatment of offenders, and so, we need to place the representation of the criminal at the heart of debates about crime. The effect of the media, while it has been considered in some key articles and a handful of recent monographs, has not usually featured at the heart of previous survey volumes on the history of crime. I think that as a topic it is fundamental to our understanding of how the criminal justice system has developed in the past, and that is why I have chosen to focus on this subject from the outset.

Closely linked to representations of crime is the form of offending which excites the most visceral emotional reaction: murder and violence. Chapter 3 will therefore analyse the debates around homicide and explore other forms of interpersonal violence. However, given that there is considerable danger of overlap between topics, I have chosen to deal with domestic violence and rape elsewhere for reasons which are hopefully understandable to the reader. Chapters 4 and 5 look in some detail at property crime because it was the illegal appropriation of other peoples' possessions that so exercised society for most of the period between 1660 and 1914. The first of these two chapters examines the nature of theft in its various forms, while Chapter 5 interrogates the reasons why individuals stole and explores the concept of 'social crime'. To separate a study of property offending from the other themes covered here is, of course, quite impossible; the 'Bloody Code', policing, juvenile offending, female crime and prosecution at all levels are ultimately bound up with theft. But, most histories of crime have avoided looking at property crime as a topic in its own right, and this study will therefore offer something new here.

This book will then go on to look in turn at gender (in Chapters 6 and 7) and at juvenile crime in Chapter 8. Both of these are topics that overlap with several of the other themes in the book, but this is inevitable and unavoidable. Where possible I have tried to place discussions within the most appropriate section or chapters and avoid duplication; for example, domestic violence is considered within Chapter 6 rather than in Chapter 3 (which deals with violence) because the subject is so closely linked to themes of gender and power. Similarly, while Chapter 13 considers the evolution of the prison (as a part of a wider analysis of changing punishment policies), the rise of the Reformatory and the development of separate courts for juveniles are situated within Chapter 8.

The second section follows the path of the offender through the criminal justice system and so will start by looking in detail at the summary process and at the changing nature and role of the magistrate (or justice of the peace – JP); this is an area which had been seriously neglected by historians but has been opened up considerably in recent years. Most people who are accused of an offence (a 'crime') today will not face trial before a judge and jury but will instead be required to attend at a magistrates' court and have their action judged before a bench of three JPs. This was also true for most defendants in the eighteenth and nineteenth centuries and so deserves some consideration in order to redress the balance of most previous studies of crime and punishment. Part of the role of the justice was to investigate crime as well as being responsible for keeping the peace. However, this role was gradually assumed by the professional police forces that emerged in the early 1800s, and the move towards a professional police force is the subject of Chapter 10. As will be shown, the development of professional policing was a gradual, not a revolutionary, process. There was plenty of amateur policing in England in the early modern period that continued well into the 1800s, beyond Sir Robert Peel's reforms in 1829. Much of this policing has been dismissed as inefficient, corrupt or frankly incompetent, but one of the successes of the discipline of the history crime has been a much more nuanced understanding of historical forms of policing. We now know that early eighteenth-century society had some very dedicated 'crime fighters' and, more interestingly perhaps, a more collective societal attitude towards crime prevention. One of the characteristic changes in the criminal justice system (noticeable particularly in policing and prosecution) has been the gradual removal of the public and the victim from the process. In the late twentieth century, this has been recognized as the police and court system strive to make the voice of the victim heard and to consider issues such as reconciliation and restorative justice. Arguably, both of these were an integral part of the justice system in early modern and eighteenth-century England. Modern Britain might therefore have much to learn from the way in which society was policed in the past.

Following from arrest and the gathering of evidence (both tasks now associated with policing), it is logical to see the defendant take his or her trial before a judge and jury. Therefore, Chapter 11 considers the changing nature of prosecution in the long eighteenth century (usually recognized as the chronological period from c. 1688 to c. 1815) at a time when the victim of crime was perhaps the key figure in the process. This changed significantly from the late eighteenth century to the nineteenth (which saw the gradual emergence of a more professional system of legal representation or what one historian has termed the 'lawyerisation' of the criminal trial).[15] Having established how the court system and the process of prosecution, trial and sentencing evolved from the late seventeenth to the early twentieth century, the study moves on to explore changing forms and ideologies of punishment (Chapters 12 and 13). The early modern and eighteenth-century property criminal faced a grim choice if convicted: death or exile from the country. Notwithstanding these, he (or she) would have had to endure imprisonment in conditions that at best might render him unfit to stand trial bad at worst were almost a death sentence in themselves. The nineteenth century saw the virtual abandonment of execution (and most forms of corporal punishment) for all crimes excepting murder, but transportation (to the new Australian colonies) and the inexorable rise of the prison still represented considerable challenges for those caught up in the process. Modern politicians and social commentators who are quick to demand tougher sentences for convicted criminals might usefully study the history of punishment in England; they will likely discover that most options have already been attempted without any noticeable improvement in the prevention of crime. This is such a large topic that I have, as with the study of gender and crime, split it into two complementary sections.

The book is completed by a conclusion which will contain some suggestions for future research and a select bibliography.[16]

Before we go very much further, we need to think about exactly what constitutes a crime, and how this affects the study of crime and punishment in the past. There is a considerable debate in modern (and past) society around rising and falling levels of crime or 'crime rates'.

Lies, damn lies and statistics: What are 'crime rates' and why do they matter?

It might seem obvious to most people that a crime is simply an action that breaks the law of the land, but in reality, it is much more complicated than that. Laws (like rules) are broken all the time, but relatively, few of these result in prosecutions, much less the full sanction of the criminal justice system. And some lawbreaking activity is not considered serious (or even criminal) by large swathes of the populace, while others are widely broken on a regular basis, seemingly without anything happening. Examples here might include not only offences such as underage drinking, the consumption of illegal drugs, speeding on the roads and using mobile phones while driving, but also some amount of tax fraud, benefit fraud and insurance fraud; in fact plenty of types of fraud go unpunished. So, when is a crime not a crime and vice versa?

The criminal justice system has four key elements, and this was the case throughout the period 1680–1914 (although how they operated or were delivered saw considerable change). The four key elements are:

1. The criminal law
2. Policing and prosecution
3. The courts
4. Punishment

The criminal law defines what is a crime – the lawbreaking act: the system of policing and prosecution exists to detect, apprehend and bring an offender into the criminal justice system; the role of the courts is to determine guilt or innocence and then pass sentence; and finally the function of punishment is to administer an appropriate penalty or form of rehabilitation commensurate with the crime committed. *Crime rates* are generated or created from an interaction between these four elements. Thus, lawbreaking and its prosecution create *prosecution rates*, and the courts and sentencing produce *punishment rates*. Crime rates, then, are a combination of these two sets of data. Crime rates leave records that historians can use to try to understand crime in the past. However, there is a fundamental problem here, one best illustrated by a modern example.

Like many people, I own a bicycle that I use to get to and from the local railway station when I am travelling to work and back. Let us say that one day I leave my bike in the designated spot at the station, making sure I have secured it with a standard bike lock. When I get home in the evening, my bike is missing, the lock lies broken nearby and I have a long walk home! It is, unfortunately, a fairly familiar scenario as in 2010 the Home Office estimated that around 500,000 bikes were stolen annually. The question now arises, what should I do about this? I *could* ring my local police and report it, but I am aware that it is highly unlikely that they will do anything about it as it is not a priority property crime, and the chances of them making an arrest (or recovering my property) are small. However, my bike is insured via my home contents insurance, and if I wish to claim on it, I will need a record of my crime – a *crime number* – which is obtained from the police. As the bike cost me £500 and I need to replace it, I am obliged to report it. If it had been a less valuable bike, it is likely that the claim would have been swallowed by the excess on my insurance policy, and so it may not have been worthwhile claiming for it.

However, having decided to claim, I call the police to report the crime. It is now a *statistic*. But no one is caught, no bike recovered; there is no trial and no punishment. This happens thousands of times a year, to thousands of people. And, this also must have happened in the past, particularly in an age before professional full-time policing and before insurance. In addition for certain crimes, such as domestic violence and rape, which are very hard to prosecute and which involve considerable courage on the part of the victims to come forward, we can be sure that many more incidents of lawbreaking occurred (indeed continue to occur) than the records reveal. Historians refer to this as the 'dark figure' of unrecorded or unprosecuted crime.

Trying to determine exactly how much crime occurred in the past is therefore fraught with difficulty. As a result, the issue of crime rates and how useful they are has exercised a number of historians of crime and punishment. Some, like J.J. Tobias, argue that statistics of crime are singularly unhelpful and untrustworthy.[17] They claim that we would be much better studying what contemporaries said about crime than trying to analyse the limited material we have about the numbers of crimes committed or the consequences of that lawbreaking. Other scholars, notably Vic Gatrell, have suggested instead that crime rates (or prosecution rates) can be a useful tool for researchers, arguing that we can identify short- and long-term trends and patterns from the recorded levels of crime in the past.[18] Between these pessimistic and optimistic positions are those, like Chris Williams, who believe that as long as we consider the whole of the criminal justice system (and not simply one or other set of resources), the records of crime can tell us a lot about crime in the past.[19]

Why does any of this matter? Well, the statistics of crime have been continually manipulated (by government, the media, the police and penal reformers) to justify, excuse or otherwise influence policy decisions and procedural innovations. And, it is important to recognize that crime rates are affected by a number of factors including legislative and policy changes, economic and social upheavals, national and international events and societal fears over a variety of issues. To be more precise, crime and its prosecution are affected by war and peace (soldiers going off to, or returning from, war affected the levels of prosecutions) changes to economic practice (the decline of customary 'rights' and the rise of capitalism), population and industrial growth (especially in the period after 1750) and increased urbanization (notably in the early nineteenth century), and these in turn created 'moral panics' which placed pressure on legislators to reform or otherwise adjust the criminal justice system. Legislative change (the creation of new laws, institutions or the operation of the justice system) also undoubtedly led to changes in crime rates. For example, the creation of the 'New Police' in London in 1829 undoubtedly led to more arrests of juveniles and others for street-related offences, simply because of the increased presence of a new force and their need to justify their new position in society. Moreover, crime rates are affected by policing practice and by the ways in which certain offences are labelled. Thus Howard Taylor argued that in the middle of the nineteenth century 'most murders and suspicious deaths went uninvestigated'. It is a staggering claim and is certainly open to discussion, but Taylor was arguing that the police effectively 'rationed' what offences they investigated to demonstrate their efficiency and to minimize the levels of unsolved crime (which impact their budgets and undermined the justification for their existence).[20]

So crime rates, however they are created, are not neutral; they are political ammunition, and they have been used for centuries in a variety of ways to justify (among other things) increased powers for police, longer sentences, new forms of punishment and greater surveillance. For the historians, they can provide information about crime but not necessarily *levels* of crime: that will always be an elusive prize.

Methods of study: Primary materials for the history of crime

What we do have is a tremendous body of primary source material for the history of crime[21]: the institutions that together create the criminal justice system (police, courts and prisons) have all left records of their activity. While survival of records is not complete or universal, county archives up and down the country hold the records of the courts of assize and quarter sessions as well as some material from the summary process as well. Court records usually contain set of documents bound together in a roll, as well as ledgers that record what has happened in court. The best sources are probably depositions, because these usually contain detailed information about offences. Depositions (and examinations) are witness statements, given under oath and full of information about the crime but recording information such as location, occupation and (if it is signed) evidence of literacy. Indictments have also been used extensively by historians; these are small formal documents which record the name of the accused and the offence he was *indicted* for. Indictments survive in much larger numbers than depositions or examinations. There are also copies of many of the county assize circuit records as well as calendars of prisoners facing trail at assize and quarter sessions.[22]

The records of London's central criminal court, the Old Bailey, are held by the London Metropolitan Archives (LMA) and contain the same information (indictment and depositions) as those held for the English and Welsh counties. However, in addition, the trial reports of the Old Bailey were recorded and published throughout the period 1674–1911 as the *Old Bailey Proceedings*. These have been digitized and are available online, thanks to a major research project undertaken by the universities of Hertfordshire and Sheffield.[23] While the *Proceedings* are not the complete record of every trial held at the Old Bailey (and indeed are not verbatim records of what was said in court), they do represent probably our best source of material for the history of crime in the period covered by this study.

The National Archives (TNA) is also the home of archival material created by the police and prison service, as well as related material on crime and punishment from earlier periods. From 1805, criminal registers of prisoners tried across the country were kept and published and these are held at the National Archives.[24] The information is formulaic but lists names, the nature of the offence, where they were tried, verdict and sentence. After 1834, there is some recording of ages. The records are not exhaustive, but they do allow researchers to get a feel for the nature and extent of those prosecuted for a variety of crimes in the nineteenth century. There are also records from 1869 onwards listing those deemed to be Habitual Offenders.[25]

For sources on punishment, there are useful records from the prison service. These include license for early release[26] or transfer to other prisons[27] (so individual convicts can be followed through the prison system), plus administrative material about the running of particular prisons such as Pentonville.[28] The records of county gaols, the hulks and those set for transportation overseas can also be found at the National Archives, so a very wide-ranging set of material is available for researchers and students interested in the history of crime.[29]

Some of the more interesting and early records for the history of punishment can be found among the Sheriffs' Cravings for individual counties.[30] Using these sources, historians have been able, for the first time, to accurately calculate the number of executions that took place throughout the long eighteenth century.[31] This has enabled an important revaluation of a key debate within the historiography of crime and punishment which shows us that there is still much to be discovered, over forty years later.[32]

Finally, there are the records produced by the police. There are the records from several county forces in England to 1900 and those from the Metropolitan Police in London. Possibly the most famous entry of all is MEPO 3/142 which holds the so-called 'Ripper' letters; hundreds of items of correspondence received by the police regarding the infamous (and unsolved) Whitechapel murders of 1888/9. In addition, the MEPO series has a lot of largely mundane material relating to the policing of the Ripper case but sadly little that sheds any light on who the murderer was.

Non-official records such as newspapers, other forms of popular print culture, songs, pictures and personal diaries and letters, as well as official records such as the reports of parliamentary committees, legislation and debates, can all offer an insight into the history of crime. There are some areas of the history of crime where archival material is harder to find: summary court records, by their very nature, are few and far between. These were produced by and for individual justices of the peace and many only survive in private collections, if at all. It is also hard to get very good information about juvenile crime before the late eighteenth century. This is because for most of the period before the 1780s, there was little attempt to distinguish between offenders on the grounds of age, so ages are rarely listed. Sometimes, it is possible to ascertain if a young offender is involved by the language used ('youthful', for example), but there is no real systematic recording of ages in criminal registers until the early 1800s. Gender, while rarely specified before the nineteenth century, is much easier to see simply because of the use of names. It is probably worth saying that historical records were created for contemporary administrative reasons and not for the benefit of future generations or their historians! Nevertheless, there is plenty for us to work with.

Before we start to tell the story of the evolution of the English criminal justice system in Section I, there needs to be an acknowledgement that much of what existed in 1660 had been long established in the early modern and medieval period. Some of this is covered in Chapter 12 (the first of two on punishment), but there are three broad themes that are worth mentioning here.

The early modern legacy

First, many of the punishments that were in use at the start of our time period would have been familiar to inhabitants of late medieval and Tudor England: hanging, the pillory, whipping, the stocks, ducking and imprisonment were all used to discipline or punish offenders. Likewise, many of the offences that were prosecuted from the late 1600s onwards had been prosecuted in previous centuries: murder, highway robbery, burglary, coining and several other forms of property crime all brought miscreants to court and to the gallows.[33] Third, the nature of prosecution was victim led, and the players involved in the merry-go-round of criminal justice were, for the most part, ordinary citizens and not paid professionals. In English towns and villages, the onus was on individuals to catch and prosecute criminals and this meant that reactions to crime could be sporadic at best, especially in less populated areas.[34]

This participatory system of prosecution developed from the medieval period; it allowed individuals (at least for those men of some means) to confront those that had 'wronged', and the law gave them an arena in which to settle their differences.[35] Individuals and communities also took an active involvement in punishing those that transgressed accepted norms or broke the law. The overriding nature of punishment in medieval and early modern England was that it was public, painful and shaming. The early modern world appears to have had a broader concept of 'honour' and 'honesty', and so, thieves, sexual deviants and fraudsters were all lumped together as offenders against the commonweal. Such punishments as the pillory, stocks and ducking stool were all clearly intended to shame offenders and warn others not to follow their example. Offenders were also ritually maimed, whipped and executed, close by the scenes of their crime so that the consequences of offending was visible to all.[36] But we should not fall into the trap of characterizing early modern punishments as merely physical; this was the society that introduced the house of correction and hard labour as a method to reform bad behaviour.[37]

So, in prosecution, policing and punishment, we can see clear continuities between the early modern state and that of the long eighteenth century. By the end of the 1800s, however, most of the seemingly brutal physical punishments had been swept away, as had the supposedly shambolic forms of private policing. In the courts, for example, private prosecution had largely been taken over by the legal profession, but all of these reforms happened gradually as we shall see. So, what was different about late medieval and early modern England? Historians tend to view history from their own particular era and often fail to appreciate the continuities with previous (or later) ones. However, it seems reasonable to suggest that England after the Glorious Revolution of 1688 *was* a different country to that which had been ravaged by the Reformation and then by several years of civil war. The state (and I accept that scholars will argue about what that term means historically) was on the rise in the early years of late Stuart and Hanoverian England but was far from being as fully formed as it was by the time Victoria celebrated her diamond jubilee.

Along with the rise of the state perhaps, the other striking difference was the declining role of the Church along with a changing view of God. As one historian has put it, 'In the early modern period, a transition occurred between two paradigms: on the one hand, community, custom, faith, rumour and the omnipotence of God; on the other hand, the state, law, certainty, proof and surveillance and the intervention of man.'[38] Post Restoration England was becoming a more secular and a more *rational* place and this was reflected in a changing criminal justice system.[39]

In terms of the criminal justice system itself, we might note that witchcraft had effectively ceased to be an issue for the courts by the last decades of the 1600s, perhaps itself an illustration that a more rational mentality was gaining ground. The criminalization of the poor – something which was very much a part of eighteenth- and nineteenth-century England – had begun, as had the prosecution of those that attempted to alter or counterfeit the currency of the realm. In general terms, crime rates (for what they are worth) had been falling from a high in the Tudor period, and historians have identified clear connections with periods of economic unrest and poor harvests. Broadly speaking then, the legacy of the medieval and early modern period is that they laid the foundations both for the way in which crime was characterized and dealt with in the 1700s and for the ways in which the criminal justice system changed or rather evolved, over the next 200 or so years.

CHAPTER 2
MEDIA AND CRIME: CHANGING ATTITUDES TOWARDS THE CRIMINAL AND MEDIA REFLECTIONS ON CRIMINALITY

Early attitudes towards the criminal

Medieval scholars such as St Thomas Aquinas argued that 'natural law' derived from God which meant that people would naturally do good rather than commit acts of evil. Thus, those that broke the law were doing something *unnatural*. Moreover, these lawbreakers were also 'sinners' and therefore not only hurting others but damaging their own spiritual well-being. This spiritual explanation of crime was underpinned by the belief that offenders were possessed by demons – or led astray by the devil – rather than acting from their own free will. The sinner who failed to atone for his crimes would end up damned to Hell and everlasting torment. As a consequence, the medieval and early modern authorities legitimized the use of torture and harsh physical punishments to purify the body of the criminal and to drive out the demons that possessed them. So, sin and crime and church law and secular law were interwoven. The power of the medieval church on everyday lives cannot be overemphasized, and the sense that criminals and murderers had offended God as well as their victims persisted well into the early modern period.

The effect of the Enlightenment: Classicism and the social contract

The seventeenth century saw a tremendous change in politics, religion and society. Religious wars blighted the European continent, and Britain was ravaged by the civil wars between King Charles I and parliament. What emerged from this tumultuous period was a new way of looking at the world: a view based on reason rather than superstition, on the 'here and now' rather than the hereafter, the so-called Enlightenment within which there was a general questioning of early modern beliefs about religion, politics and society with an emphasis on rational enquiry and empiricism.

At the heart of the Enlightenment lay a desire to better understand and explain human nature. In the wake of the British civil wars, the English philosopher Thomas Hobbes (1588–1679) concluded that in order to preserve the rights and liberties of society, individuals had to be prepared to surrender a degree of control over their lives to some form of authority. John Locke (1634–1704) took a slightly less pessimistic view of human nature to Hobbes, but both agreed that in order for individuals to enjoy freedoms, their rights – especially property rights – had to be protected by a set of agreed laws that would be upheld by institutions that operated with authority.[1] In France, Jean-Jacques Rousseau (1712–1778) developed the idea of a collected communal interest of well-being.

Thus, the Enlightenment represented a move away from medieval and early modern concepts that were deeply rooted in obedience to God and the fear of damnation, and towards the evolution of the application of reason in all avenues of life. Enlightenment thinkers believed in the importance of free will and the ability of individuals to regulate and control their own behaviour, while society retained the right, by the application of a rational code of laws, to punish those that failed to do so. Thus, the Enlightenment introduced the idea of the 'rational actor', someone who could make decisions based upon the consequences that might result from them.

In essence, the influence of rational thinking in the long eighteenth century altered the way in which the criminal was viewed by society. This was an age in which the emphasis was placed upon individual actions and motivations, and so, it followed that crime could be seen through the same vector. The Italian criminologist Cesare Beccaria believed that anyone had the potential to be a criminal, but not everyone would commit criminal acts. Beccaria argued that crime was 'an act undertaken by a rational being', by which he meant that a criminal's action were logical; those committing crime did so out of choice and after assessing the associated risks involved.[2] Therefore, if society was going to protect itself from thieves and murderers, it had to impose sanctions upon offenders in order to deter them from criminal activity. Beccaria argued that any sanctions imposed on criminals had to be applied consistently and fairly. Justice had to be done and to be seen to be done. The English 'Bloody Code' treated petty thieves and murderers with little distinction, applying death penalty to both alike, something Beccaria profoundly disagreed with. Moreover, in eighteenth-century England, the criminal justice system was 'shot through with discretion'[3] which militated against the worst excesses of the gallows but equally left offenders unsure of the consequences of committing crime. Classicists like Beccaria were uncomfortable with discretion, arguing that punishments should be determined by law and not by individuals, and the punishments handed down for crimes should also be appropriate and imposed to counterbalance any reward that had been gained by the criminal action in the first place. Thus, punishment was about deterrence through sanction, and not simply retribution which had informed penal policy in the early modern period. It followed then, for Beccaria, that the death penalty was both an unnecessary and inefficient way of ensuring that offenders compensated society for their depredations. He also insisted that the *prevention* of crime was much more important than the punishment of offenders. This classicist viewpoint was a key factor in the reform of the 'Bloody Code' and development of the prison in the late eighteenth and early nineteenth century and also underpinned the drive towards the creation of professional police forces.

In England, the philosopher Jeremy Bentham (1748–1832) also rejected any idea that criminals were somehow predetermined or 'born'. Instead, he viewed offenders as those members of society who lacked the self-discipline to control their offending behaviour. He made an important distinction between crimes against society and what we might term 'moral' crimes. Immorality such as adultery was routinely punished in the early modern period at the church courts, but Bentham argued that the law was there to protect society and property not to regulate morality. Bentham's 1791 design of the panopticon, based on 'the inspection principle', represented the apogee of classicist and utilitarian criminological thought. Bentham advocated a system of surveillance coupled with rewards and sanctions that would bring about the reformation of prisoners. He himself described it as a 'mill for grinding rogues honest'.[4]

The move towards an environmental view of the criminal

However, as the nineteenth century progressed and industrialization drew more and more of the population of Britain away from the countryside to swell the growing numbers living in urban areas, concerns about crime continued. With an ever-growing bureaucracy, the forces of order now possessed an armoury of weapons with which to combat criminality. However, despite the introduction of a professional police (1829–1856) and the building of more local and national prisons, crime persisted. The explanations of the classicists clearly needed some revision, as the deterrents of capture and imprisonment were not preventing some people from turning to crime.[5] In addition, continental criminologists were convinced that scientific empirical study represented the key to understanding deviant behaviour. What developed from the emerging science of criminology was the concept of the 'pre-destined actor'. Building upon what was to some extent a misreading of evolutionary biology, a theory developed that rejected the notion of free will and replaced it with determinism. Charles Darwin had published his controversial *Origin of Species* in 1859 which had outlined the principle that species evolve through interaction with their environment. However, Darwin's thesis also allowed for the possibility of 'degeneration' whereby men might de-evolve and become 'beasts'.[6] This is apparent in some of the apelike caricatures of late Victorian criminals. Herbert Spencer (1820–1903), whose ideas developed independently of Darwin, argued that 'human beings develop as a part of a process of interaction with the social world they inhabit'.[7] Spencer has possibly unfairly been closely associated with the worst excesses of Social Darwinism, but the idea that criminals are in some ways biologically different from non-criminals has its roots in evolutionary theory. The investigative journalist and social commentator, Henry Mayhew (1812–1887), categorized the inhabitants of London in the 1850s into two distinct 'races': the 'vagabond and the citizen – the nomadic and the civilized' with the latter distinguished by heavy jowls and high cheek bones that demonstrated a less well-developed brain.[8]

The most celebrated advocate of the predestined actor model was the Italian theorist Cesare Lombroso (1835–1909). Lombroso has been described as the father of criminology and was certainly responsible for driving forward debates about criminality from the 1870s onwards. In 1876, he published *The Criminal Man* which set out the model of the 'born criminal'. He argued that rather than crime being a choice – the rational perspective of Beccaria and Bentham – it was a natural compulsion, something that was a part of the human condition. He viewed criminals in evolutionary terms, as 'throwbacks', and to support this undertook a study of criminals within Italy's gaols. From this, he built up a picture of the 'criminal type', one that bore striking similarities to many negative presentations of the working class. His theories broke the causes of crime down into four categories: some criminals were born, others were criminal as a result of mental defects, there were occasional offenders and others that simply committed crimes of passion. Lombroso's ideas chimed with prevailing concerns about the rise of crime in the late 1860s and with more general worries about the state of society, fears of revolutionary socialism and the growth of the 'dangerous classes'.[9] It followed from Lombroso's thesis that some criminal could not be reformed, but only identified early, so that the risk they posed to society could be minimized. The 'born criminal' was becoming a central figure in discussions of deviance and crime.

However, the extent to which Lombroso's ideas carried any real influence in Britain is much less apparent. In Britain, positivist criminology developed through a study of criminals within penal institutions. Psychiatrists in England were intent on creating a classification system for identifying inmates, so saw some criminals as 'feeble-minded' and others as 'insane' or 'degenerate', for example, but they did not conceive the 'criminal as a psychological type'. Early work by the psychiatrist Henry Maudsley (1835–1918) and the prison medical officer J. Bruce Thomson (1810–1873) had suggested that deviance was a product of heredity and environment.[10] Indeed, while they later qualified and largely reworked their theories, both men argued in the 1860s that criminals belonged to a separate 'class'. George Wilson (1808–1870) had used phrenology (the study of the shape and size of skulls) to measure the heads of prisoners, and from 1865 onwards, the Prison Act ensured that all convicts were subject to medical examinations. In the early twentieth century, Dr Charles Goring published his study of convicts, *The English Convict* (1913), which drew different conclusions from Lombroso. Goring did not identify a criminal type, but he did discover that convicts had 'significant physiological differences'. They were less intelligent and 'less able to cope with the demands of life' than the average person.[11] While this was in some way reassuring in suggesting that criminals were not inherently 'bad' or their crimes inevitable, it did at the same time present the possibility that previously law-abiding citizens might descend into a path of criminality if a set of negative circumstances presented themselves.

In the long period covered by this book, the idea of the criminal changed. From someone who offended God and needed to be cleansed, to a 'fallen' individual at the mercy of God's forgiveness; and thence to a 'rational actor' who calculated his chances of evading 'justice' in the pursuit of personal gain; to the 'habitual criminal' – a member of a 'criminal class' – who was the product of the environment in which they were born. All these tropes or types reflected changing contemporary attitudes towards crime, attitudes and conceptions that were shaped less by personal experience of crime but more often by the shared discourses presented by social commentators, moral entrepreneurs and the publishers of printed popular culture and the newspapers. So having looked briefly at the changing understandings or interpretations of criminality in religious, philosophical and scientific thought, we can now move on to explore the ways in which this was reflected and, in some ways driven, by a developing print media.

The role of the media in presenting crime and constructing criminality

Much of what we call 'history' is of course a construction of the past. In the words of James Sharpe, controlling the past 'can be an important element in controlling the present and the future'.[12] This is a truism for all periods and peoples but is perhaps especially the case for those that have left little or no record of their existence in their own words. Indeed, social historians have embraced the history of crime and punishment so wholeheartedly because it offers an opportunity to peer into the lives of the poor and otherwise neglected majority of the population. Even today, relatively few of us are unfortunate enough to experience crime directly and so mostly develop our knowledge about it through the vector of the media.

The modern reader or viewer is bombarded with a tremendous volume of 'crime news' as well as fictionalized accounts of criminals, law enforcement agencies and courtroom dramas. The British national and local press carry regular stories of petty and serious crimes as well as comment on social problems (such as the outbreaks of rioting and looting in English cities in the summer of 2011), and these are often highly influenced by the political 'colour' of the newspaper concerned. The internet has allowed a faster and more interactive vehicle for crime news to develop with organizations such as the police embracing social media such as Facebook and Twitter. Television crime news exists in a variety of forms for both entertaining and information. The BBC's *Crimewatch* series has been running since 1984 and offers a diet of crime news, warnings and information about stolen goods. *Crimewatch* is part of a long tradition of public service criminal justice broadcasts which have encouraged the public to become involved in the hunt for wanted criminals. As we shall see, such programmes have their antecedents in much earlier examples of print media that spread information about crime and punishment. However, much of what appears on television and in film at best distorts the public's view and understanding of crime and at worst simply offers a sensationalized fabrication of reality. The modern crime drama will often focus almost exclusively on murder, a crime that is much rarer than would seem to be the case from watching television. In addition, the widespread use of CCTV cameras has enabled TV producers to produce cheap and sensational documentaries about crime and law enforcement that can give the impression of a society that is almost overwhelmed with crime and criminals. These help to set the police and courts up as heroic warriors against this tide of deviant behaviour.

The media, then, plays a very important role in forming attitudes towards crime and about those people that break the law, and this role has a very long history. The media's role is important because it has the power to fill in the gaps in our knowledge of events we have not experienced ourselves. Several historians of crime have suggested that contemporaries in eighteenth-century England formed their understanding of the extent of crime and its associated problems from the print media, and that this contributed to early forms of moral panic.[13] There has been one discordant voice: Norma Landau has argued that individuals' experience of crime in eighteenth-century London was much higher than Peter King allows,[14] but her subject sample – sixty-five justices of the peace – has failed to convince the most recent scholar of print culture, Richard Ward. Ward accepts that previous research has not always recognized the myriad ways (other than print) by which people could find out about crime and welcomes Landau's intervention. However, this does not, he continues, change the fundamental premise of King's 'assumption that relatively few contemporaries would have been a victim of crime, certainly not the more serious forms of lethal violence, robbery and burglary which were [and remain] the primary focus of printed crime reporting and which generated considerable anxieties'.[15] The debate continues, and hopefully, this new focus on what are rich sources for the history of crime will allow future research to interrogate the contrasting views of Landau and King further. In particular, we need more work that looks (as Snell's work has) at the effect of the provincial press on attitudes towards crime.[16]

For now though, let us leave the newspapers and look instead at two ways in which other forms of print culture represented the criminal and contributed to contemporary notions of criminality.

Criminal biography and the last dying confessions

The late seventeenth and early eighteenth centuries gave birth to what we might understand today as 'true crime' literature. Some 2,000–3,000 biographies of criminals (often published in collections dubbed *Newgate Calendars*)[17] survive from the period with some particularly notorious individuals having multiple editions of their life and crimes.[18] These biographies, along with the Ordinary of Newgate's (the chaplain of Newgate prison in London) *Accounts of the Behaviour, Confession, & Dying Words of the Condemned Criminals*, and the published *Proceedings of the Old Bailey* provide social historians with a rich source of information about crime and punishment from the late seventeenth century onwards.[19] The biographies and *Accounts* were supposedly accurate stories of the lives of felons told to the authors by the subjects themselves. The Ordinary was ideally placed to hear the last confessions of those about to be hanged at Tyburn and to witness their behaviour as they were executed. For this, he took a fee and earned a good living from the proceeds. Biographies were sold cheaply by London printers and could be read (for a small fee) in the capital's many coffee houses, reaching a largely middle-class audience.[20] Both the *Proceedings* and the *Account* flourished in the 1730s, but the *Account* began to lose its semi-official status after 1744 and then disappeared in the 1760s before briefly reviving in the early 1770s. Convicts were also expected to make a full confession and repent of their sins in a speech given at the gallows just before they were executed. These speeches were published as short pamphlets or broadsheets, often including accounts of the behaviour of the condemned just before the execution.

Figure 2.1 Detail from *Industry and Idleness: The IDLE PRENTICE Executed at Tyburn*, by William Hogarth (1747).

Prominent in the foreground of this scene from William Hogarth's *Industry and Idleness* series (see Figure 2.1) is a woman who is already selling Tom's 'last dying speech'. These were often published before the execution even took place, and on the hanging day, the condemned criminal would endorse one particular version of the story. The Ordinary's *Accounts* were highly moralized sermons on the fall from grace of certain individuals and the perils of idleness, gambling, drink and loose women. Many were edited and published by the newspaper magnate John Applebee, who published many newspaper stories about crime in the period, including one of the most celebrated criminals of his day, the thief and prison breaker Jack Sheppard (more of whom later).

As well as preparing the criminal to meet his maker, these speeches also served to legitimize the criminal justice system to the spectators, since the speaker (by making a confession of his guilt and an appeal for his soul) supposedly accepted the legitimacy of the trial verdict and the death sentence. But, convicts did not always follow the expected conventions, and the writers of the pamphlets could not control how audiences received them. So, while 'printed criminal lives were [often] touted as appropriate moral instruction for the young in particular',[21] some felt they might be a bad influence on young minds.

In addition, criminal biographies can also be viewed as a cheap form of plebeian entertainment. However, we should be wary of seeing the *Newgate Calendars* and their ilk as being aimed solely at the lower classes; McKenzie argues that the readership was much wider than this, and that criminal biographies were a staple of coffee-house culture in the mid-1700s.[22] The *Proceedings* were not cheap; each session was divided into parts, and the cost of these would have 'required a significant sacrifice' in the budgets of labouring men and women. The adverts contained in the *Proceedings* and the comments of at least one publisher suggest that they were produced for a middle-class and 'respectable' audience, not a plebeian one.[23] The more notorious criminals (like Sheppard) attracted more than one biography, and since some of the (often competing) biographies went through multiple editions, it is likely that the texts were heavily edited by publishers. Criminal biographies, along with newspaper reporting of crime, also served to give readers the low down on how to avoid falling victim to crime. Thus, the readership could learn about the techniques criminals used and the places that were most frequently associated with crime. Articles about crime might advise readers and warn them of how to avoid falling victim to crime, but some commentators 'worried that the publication of trial counts [...] particularly accounts of acquittals – might also provide offenders with "tricks and alibis that would allow them to avoid conviction"'.[24]

At the same time, printed 'lives' and other forms of 'crime news' gave social commentators (such as the novelist and magistrate Henry Fielding) interested in improving law enforcement a vehicle with which to get across their warnings about the state of crime and the dangers faced by society.[25] According to Andrea McKenzie, the Ordinary's *Accounts* allowed convicted criminals to assume the role of 'Everyman' by preaching to the crowds that gathered to watch them hang, and through them, the writers of the biographies invoked the appropriate scripture to demonstrate that the individual about to hang was, while repentant, there because he had sinned.[26] We cannot know how people read these works in the past; the contemporary diarist James Boswell (1740–1795) seems to have taken them at face value while others note in their diaries that they read them for entertainment. In reality, we might expect different audiences to view them differently.[27] There were complaints about inaccurate reporting of trials in the *Proceedings*, and we should not assume that readers believed everything they read.

The biographies and *Accounts* also influenced other forms of popular culture. The most obvious example is that of the popular play, *The Beggar's Opera*, which will be examined shortly, but first let us examine the careers of two of the period's most notorious criminals, both of whom owe much of their fame to print culture.

By the middle of the nineteenth century, two particular villains had established their place in history and had earned reputations that were, in some ways, quite different from the reality of their lives. Both had passed into popular mythology and, such was the blurring of fact and fiction, had taken on the guise of romantic heroes. Both remained famous over 150 years after they had died. Why this was and what do we know about these notorious Hanoverian crooks?

Jack Sheppard: Prison breaker extraordinaire

Jack Sheppard was a minor London criminal living in the 1720s. Jack was a burglar and a street thief who repeatedly got caught but just as frequently managed to escape from prison. He escaped three times from a variety of London gaols before he was tried and sentenced to death in 1724 for burgling the home of his former master, William Kneebone.[28] Jack had been born in Spitalfields in the East End of London but had not taken well to his apprenticeship. Fulfilling the popular trope as illustrated by Hogarth in his *Industry and Idleness* series, Jack neglected his work and fell into bad company, whoring and drink. His master attempted to contain him, but Jack's carpentry skills enabled him to come and go as he pleased. Eventually, he left his place and took up with an older woman, Elizabeth Lyons, better known as 'Edgeworth Bess'. Jack's is a well repeated tale of petty criminality and a rather inept attempt to stay out of trouble.

Jack also fell foul of Jonathan Wild, the capital's self-styled 'Thief-taker General' (see Chapter 10), and was in and out of several of the city's gaols. Having been convicted of burglary and sentenced to death, he was placed in Newgate's condemned cell, manacled and chained to the floor. The situation, for most people, would have seemed helpless, but Jack knew how the prison operated. Newgate was not like modern gaols (or those that were to be constructed in the nineteenth century); here, people could come and go, and there was drinking, prostitution and gambling going on all day and night.[29] When the Old Bailey (which was connected to the prison) was in session, the gaolers were busy ferrying convicts to and from between the court and the gaol and therefore far too occupied to keep an eye on Jack.

Somehow Jack managed to slip the manacles on his wrists and the locks that held him chained to the floor of his cell; he wrapped the chains around his legs and secured them with his stockings. Then, he dragged his bedding over to the fireplace on one side of the cell and set about escaping up the chimney. Jack made his way through several locked door to the roof of the prison before having to retrace his steps to collect his bedding (which ne heeded to make a rope ladder).

No one heard or saw him. He grabbed his bedding and made his way back up again to the roof and made good his escape and, in doing so, secured his place in history and myth.

This is not a story with a happy ending however; after a brief spell of laying low in the villages north of London he returned to the centre, was quickly rearrested and sent back to gaol. He now became the centre of intense media attention, with newspapers writing about his daring escapes and crimes and even the king commissioning his portrait in prison. Jack was a celebrity criminal, and everyone seemingly wanted a piece of him. The authorities took no chances this time, and a special execution was arranged for Jack just to make sure nothing went wrong. When it came to the hanging day, it is estimated that an incredible 200,000 people lined London's streets ready to cheer their hero. There are stories of a plot to free him before he was executed, but sadly, Jack was not rescued; he died at Tyburn like so many other young men at the time but became, in that moment, something of a popular hero.

Jack Sheppard was a celebrity in the eighteenth century and remained famous well after his death (partly as a result of his notoriety, the number of column inches written about him and because of Gay's *Beggar's Opera*). Jack featured in several *penny dreadfuls* in the nineteenth century, but (despite his appearance in a Tommy Steele film of 1969[30]) he has been eclipsed by another infamous eighteenth-century villain, Richard, or 'Dick', Turpin.

Richard 'Dick' Turpin and the ride to York

I grew up not far from Hampstead in the north London and the heath was a favourite destination for family excursions when I was a small child. Hampstead Heath has long associations with highwaymen given its location on one of the main transit routes into the capital. The Spaniard's Inn, a pub close to the old toll house, has erroneously been claimed as the birthplace of Turpin, and my father once told me that holes in the whitewashed walls of the building were made by musket balls fired by the eponymous highwayman as he escaped the clutches of the law! Needless to say, none of this is true.

Turpin's story has become even more mired in myth than Jack Sheppard's, to the extent that the traditional story of England's most famous highwayman bears very little resemblance to the truth. This is what most people know about Dick: Turpin was a handsome and brave highway robber who rode a horse called 'Black Bess' and terrorized the turnpike roads in and out of London in the early 1700s. He held up coaches and separated the nobility from their riches, while always treating his female victims with courtesy and gallantry. Eventually, he was run to ground by a gang of thief-takers (the entrepreneurial police of their day) and was surrounded somewhere near the Heath. However, he outwitted his assailants and escaped north, riding overnight to York (a journey of some 200 miles). Within sight of York Minster, Black Bess, collapsed and died. Turpin was arrested, put on trial and executed. However, very little of this is based on actual truth, and the story of Turpin the highwayman is actually much darker and less glamorous.

Turpin was not born in the Spaniard's Inn on Hampstead Heath, but at Hempstead in Essex in 1705, the son of a butcher named John Palmer and his wife Maria. His father ran the Bell Inn at Hempstead (where Dick was born), so it is possible to see how these mistakes were made.[31] Turpin was supposedly apprenticed to a butcher in Whitechapel in the East End of London (so shared a location with Sheppard and its association with crime and criminality) before returning to Essex to set himself up as a butcher in Thaxted. What is clear is that Turpin became connected with a gang of deer thieves that operated in the area in the early 1730s; Turpin's trade (as a butcher) was useful to the gang as an outlet for selling the meat that they stole. The gang, about two dozen strong and dubbed the Gregory Gang (after their leader, Samuel Gregory and his brother Jeremiah or Jasper), soon escalated to robbery and burglary and carried out a series of ruthless and brutal attacks on the homes of local farmers and landholders, subjecting them to physical violence, threats, robbery and criminal damage. On at least one occasion, the gang threatened to put an elderly woman over a fire to force her reveal where her valuables were, and in February 1735, Samuel Gregory raped a maidservant at gunpoint.[32]

Turpin and his exploits have often been compared to the activities of the elusive Robin Hood, and he has been characterized as lovable rogue, a romantic hero and friend of the poor, while both he and the Gregory gang were nothing of the sort. These were, Sharpe notes, 'vicious criminals, with no respect for property or for the right of people to enjoy the safety of their own homes, who had no reservations about using violence, even potentially fatal violence.'[33] The notoriety of the gang led to attempts to capture them, and eventually, several of them were rounded up, and one, the youngest John Wheeler, agreed to save his own life by giving up his companions and turning king's evidence. Turpin and two others, Thomas Rowden and John Jones, remained at liberty and took to highway robbery. Jones was soon caught, and Rowden was taken after he switched to counterfeiting money. This left Turpin as the sole remaining member of the Gregory gang yet to be in custody.

It is largely a myth that highwaymen operated alone. Robbing a stagecoach or other travellers was fraught with danger. Most people carried side arms of some sort in the period, and coaches routinely employed guards or at least equipped the driver with a weapon. The romantic notion of the dandy highwayman springing from the shadows and crying 'Stand and deliver!' needs to be treated with some caution.[34] Turpin found two new accomplices, Mathew King and Stephen Potter, robbers who worked together on the roads around the capital. Having stolen a horse in Leytonstone, King and Turpin were tracked by the victim and some hired associates, to the Red Lion pub in Whitechapel. King was captured and called upon Turpin to shoot his captor dead, declaring that 'we are taken by G-d'.[35] However, Turpin shot and wounded King instead. Whether Turpin intended this or not is a matter of conjecture, but with King dead, there would have been no one to turn evidence against him in court. However, before he died King was able to give information against his companion, and Turpin went into hiding.

Turpin was followed into Epping Forest there by Thomas Morris who hoped to capture the wanted man, but Turpin shot him dead. A proclamation was issued offering £200 reward for the capture, prosecution and conviction of Turpin for the committal of 'several notorious felonies and robberies'.[36] Turpin's exploits made the pages of the London press (particularly his murder of Morris in Epping Forest) and some papers suggested that he was responsible for a number of robberies in and around London, but there is no contemporary mention of a ride to York, or any association with a horse called Black Bess.

In reality, Turpin moved to Lincolnshire to evade the law and changed his name to Palmer (his mother's maiden name) to disguise his identity. He was unable to give up his criminal lifestyle though and went back to animal theft. He kept moving and ended up near Brough in Yorkshire, using that as a base from which to raid Lincolnshire for horses which he then sold on.

Palmer became well known among the local landowners, although no one was very sure of how he made his money. He hunted and dined with them, but apart from being some sort of 'dealer' in livestock, his history was hardly known. When he got into an altercation with a labourer, the wheels of justice began to turn against him. Palmer shot a chicken and when he was challenged by a witness, John Robinson, he threatened to shoot him too. Robinson complained to the local justices of the peace who came to Brough to hear the case. Palmer refused the justices' request to provide sureties against his failure to attend court, and so, they sent him to the nearby Bridewell at Beverley. In the meantime, the justices made some enquiries about John Palmer and the mystery of how he came by his living started a chain reaction that was to have fatal consequences for Turpin.

Palmer told the justices he had been a butcher in Long Sutton, Lincolnshire (where he claimed his father lived), but he had left there after his business had failed in an attempt to avoid his debts. The justices followed this up and instead discovered the truth: namely that Palmer's father had never lived there and, moreover, that Dick had been suspected of stealing sheep and horses. Now, the JPs of the East Riding asked Palmer to provide sureties for his appearance at York assizes, and when once again he refused, they committed him to York Castle dungeon.[37]

While incarcerated at York, Turpin needed help to get himself off the capital charge of horse theft that was due to be prosecuted at the next assize. Turpin – as a first offender – faced only a limited risk of being executed, but he needed to mobilize some character witnesses to speak on his behalf. He wrote to his brother-in-law back in Essex, and this turned out to be another mistake. Turpin's brother-in-law refused to accept the letter at the post office, either because he did not want to pay the fee or that he realized it was from Dick and wanted nothing to do with him. Unfortunately, for Turpin, however, a local man named James Smith *did* recognize the handwriting as he had taught the outlaw to read and write. As Sharpe notes, Smith's 'presence in Hempstead post office was a piece of massive bad luck for the highwayman'.[38] Smith was required by the local JPs to travel to York where he identified John Palmer as Richard Turpin in February 1739.

Prime Minister Robert Walpole's government was informed that the prisoner in York Castle was none other than the infamous highwayman, someone who still had a £200 price tag on his head. He might have been tried in London but that was risky, as he might have escaped or evaded conviction. Turpin was tried in March 1739 for stealing two horses. The indictment was incorrectly drawn up, and so, the case should, under eighteenth-century procedure, have been thrown out by the grand jury. Turpin's protestations that he had not had time to put together a defence were ignored. When convicted, he again claimed the process was unfair, that he should have been tried in Essex, and that he had no time to prepare. The judge waived away his protest and sentenced him to death.

Turpin was executed on 7 April 1739 and, according to witnesses, he died well (see Figure 2.2). He had paid for new suit of clothes and for mourners to walk behind his cart as he was led to the gallows. This 'good death' probably helped his reputation, but it did not 'make' his legend,[39] that was to come later and involved the intervention of print culture.

In 1834, Harrison Ainsworth wrote a gothic romance novel entitled *Rookwood* which detailed (at some length) the historical saga of a West Yorkshire family and their rather unfortunate lives. Within it was the rather minor character of Dick Turpin the highwayman. Ainsworth embellished the Turpin story, added bits and wrote a highly romanticized account of his ride to York and the death of Black Bess within the sight of York minister. The real Turpin was hidden beneath a meshing of stories that included an even older highway robber called Claude Duval. In *Rookwood*, the Turpin character

THE

TRIAL

7.

Of the Notorious Highwayman

𝕽𝖎𝖈𝖍𝖆𝖗𝖉 𝕿𝖚𝖗𝖕𝖎𝖓,

At *York* Affizes, on the 22d Day of *March*, 1739, before the Hon. Sir WILLIAM CHAPPLE, Knt. Judge of Affize, and one of His Majefty's Juftices of the Court of *King's Bench*.

Taken down in Court by Mr. THOMAS KYLL, Profeffor of Short-Hand.

To which is prefix'd,

An exact Account of the faid *Turpin*, from his firft coming into *Yorkfhire*, to the Time of his being committed Prifoner to *York* Caftle; communicated by Mr. APPLETON of *Beverley*, Clerk of the Peace for the *Eaft-Riding* of the faid County.

With a Copy of a Letter which *Turpin* received form his Father, while under Sentence of Death.

To which is added,

His Behaviour at the Place of Execution, on *Saturday* the 7th of *April*, 1739. Together with the whole Confeffion he made to the Hangman at the Gallows; wherein he acknowledg'd himfelf guilty of the Facts for which he fuffer'd, own'd the Murder of Mr. *Thompfon's* Servant on *Epping-Foreft*, and gave a particular Account of feveral Robberies which he had committed.

The SECOND EDITION..

Y O R K:

Printed by WARD and CHANDLER Bookfellers, at their Printing-Office in *Coney-Street*; and Sold at their Shop without *Temple-Bar, London*; 1739. (Price Sixpence.)

Figure 2.2 *A contemporary account of Turpin's Execution*, by Thomas Kyall (1739).

talked up the social credentials of the highwayman arguing that 'it is as necessary for a man to be a gentleman before he can turn highwayman, as it is for a doctor to have his diploma, or an attorney his certificate'.[40] And so, Ainsworth helped to create the idea of the highwayman as a heroic figure.

Rookwood sold well, as did Ainsworth's other novels at the time, and they were copied and diluted by mid-nineteenth-century *penny dreadfulls*.[41] So, while aspects of Turpin's life have survived, they have been amalgamated with the lives of other notorious highwaymen to produce an archetype, and one that probably never existed in reality. The same is true to a lesser extent for Sheppard: his life story has been told and retold, and the reality of his existence as a fairly ignorant and mundane criminal who was particularly good at escaping (but particularly bad at staying out of trouble) has been confused and mythologized. To some extent, this a common problem for histories of crime; as I have argued elsewhere, it will not be very long before more recent criminals such as 'Jack the Ripper' become completely detached from the reality of history.[42]

Both of these characters were launched into infamy by the interaction of print culture and a contemporary fascination with, and concern about, crime and criminality. This is most obviously illustrated by the *Beggar's Opera*, which was first performed in 1728.

John Gay's *Beggar's Opera* (1728) and other forms of popular biography

In 1728, just a few years after Jack Sheppard was hanged at Tyburn, the *Beggar's Opera* opened on the London stage. Jack was supposedly the inspiration for the play's central character and eponymous hero, MacHeath, a highwayman locked up in the condemned cell of Newgate.

The 'opera' – perhaps the earliest musical in the English language – boasts a cast of low-life characters including Captain MacHeath (a highwayman who attempts to remake his own history as a romantic gentleman while at the same time struggling to keep a string of mistresses); Lucy Lockitt and Polly Peachum (the daughters of a thief-taker and a jobbing lawyer); prostitute pickpockets (Jenny Diver and Betty Doxy); and members of MacHeath's gang (Crook-fingered Jack and Mat of the Mint).

The *Beggar's Opera* was a major hit with all classes in the eighteenth century. It was described by contemporaries who disapproved of it as the 'Thief's creed and common prayer book', and there are several examples of criminals being captured with a copy in their pockets or going to the gallows vowing to die 'like MacHeath'.

Despite its connections to real and infamous criminals, the play is actually a wider satire on corruption in public life. Mr Peachum is a thief-taker who buys stolen property from thieves but then impeaches them (in other words, he gives them up to the authorities) when they fail provide him with enough stolen goods to sell on in the black market. Peachum is clearly a parody of the real-life character of Jonathan Wild – so, this is a 'portrait of the criminal as businessman and it implies a portrait of the businessman as criminal', eighteenth-century audiences would also have seen this as an attack on politicians and in particular on Sir Robert Walpole 'the greatest criminal of all'.[43]

The *Beggar's Opera* was not the only manifestation of print culture to embrace crime and criminality. The eighteenth-century audience had several different outlets for their interest. There are surviving examples of criminal biographies in collections such as Captain Alexander Smith's *History of the Highwaymen* (1714) and Captain Johnson's *History of the most notorious Pirates* (1724), and the *Newgate Calendars* also presented the histories of infamous criminals as did the anonymous *Tales of the most remarkable criminals* (1735). All carried partly invented, and certainly embellished, stories of men and women like Jack Sheppard, Dick Turpin, the Golden Farmer and Sarah Malcolm – all of whom would have been household names at the time. These stories, of which between 2,000 and 3,000 have survived, would have been copied and shared, performed as plays and ballads and passed on by word of mouth. While we need to be aware that they will contain plenty of inaccuracies, at the same time they also provide a useful commentary of attitudes towards crime and criminality and the justice system of the day. Whether they actually reflect a true picture of crime and punishment in the late seventeenth and eighteenth centuries is much more debatable. McZenzie suggests they might, at least as far as the *Newgate Calendars* were concerned; they appear to have been seen as 'more reliable and more reputable than earlier publications'.[44] Richard Ward is clear that 'printed crime reporting offered a heavily distorted image of crime as prosecuted in the courts and, by extension, the nature of criminality as a whole'.[45] His research suggests that the eighteenth-century press placed a greater emphasis on crime news than had been the case previously and, in doing so, helped formulate public views about the problem of crime.[46] As we will see, this process may have started in the early 1700s, but it was not unique to the period. Indeed, it would be wrong to think that print culture either remained static or was unaffected by changing attitudes towards crime. As with modern crime dramas, crime reflects wider concerns within society, and so, in the later eighteenth century, the nature of the criminal biography also began to change.

The changing nature of the criminal biography

Lincoln Faller has also offered an analysis of the criminal biography, concentrating on the earlier, late seventeenth-century period.[47] He outlined a duality of functions for the genre: one that attempted to reintegrate the offender within society and the other set him apart and exaggerated his 'otherness'. The purpose appears to have been to deter others from committing crime or into falling for the same temptations that led the subjects of the biographies astray in the first place (neglect of religion, work, a propensity to consume alcohol and connections with women of 'easy virtue').[48]

Faller noted the contrast between the heroic highwayman of popular literature and the reality of most highway robbers. Most highwaymen were sole 'not mounted horsemen', as the mythology would have it, but many operated on foot and were far less glamorous. Gangs of robbers were much more common, but gangs do not generally feature in the popular literature of crime.[49] The notion of the highwayman as hero or social critic is therefore problematic but still allows us to look carefully at the ways in which contemporary print culture informs our understanding of attitudes towards criminals.

Over time, the nature of biography and its use changed. As the eighteenth century wore on, the notion of criminal as 'everyman' became less and less applicable.[50] After 1744 (when the Ordinary of Newgate dispensed with the editorial assistance of John Applebee), an emphasis was placed on producing true and accurate confessions rather than fabricated and heavily 'political' ones. The real words and misspellings of criminals were printed, and criminals came to be seen as very different from the often middling sort readership of the *Account*. No longer were criminals being portrayed as 'just like us', but increasingly, they were being seen as 'the other'. With this, there seems to have been a movement away from seeing crime as something committed by the 'fallen' individual and towards an activity pursued because of what McKenzie calls 'environmental and class-specific factors'. We can see just how important this distinction was as we move into the later eighteenth and early nineteenth centuries, because this shift from individual acts of criminality by 'sinners' is quite different to viewing an entire section of society as 'criminal' or as part of a 'criminal class'.[51]

By 1775, the Ordinary's *Account* had gone, and 'newspapers reported briefly on only the most remarkable crimes', and within pamphlet literature, there was a move towards the stories of highly selective criminals such as 'the occasional eminent murderer or gentleman highwayman or genteel forger'. As for the more common 'street-robbers, housebreakers and pickpockets' that had filled the pages of the *Newgate Calendars*, 'their lives were repackaged and effectively refurbished for a class of readers who viewed them as exotic relics of a "gross and brutal" and "bloodthirsty" age, long since thankfully consigned to the proverbial dustbin of history'.[52]

So, the lives of criminals such as Jack Sheppard were in many ways constructed by a variety of narrative forms that used these individuals for different purposes throughout the first half of the eighteenth century. Clearly, one of those purposes was to entertain, but perhaps more importantly, the reporting of crime and criminal 'lives' served to validate the criminal justice system. But, the idea of criminal biography and people's fascination with crime did not go away. The nineteenth-century public were enthralled by crime news, and this was extended to a wider, working-class readership. The criminal biography evolved into the penny broadside, and these vignettes on the lives of those about to hang, 'sold in vast numbers, particularly on the days of executions, offered the reader a potted history of the crime, the trial and the formulaic redemption of the accused in the condemned cell'.[53] But perhaps the most enduring manifestation of crime news as popular culture was the penny dreadful, the forerunner of the twentieth-century graphic novel or comic.

The penny dreadful and nineteenth-century popular culture

Penny dreadfuls were a manifestation of cheaply printed stories, often featuring notorious criminals or fantastical creatures. They were aimed at a young working-class audience, and the stories were simplistic and formulaic. They echoed or copied stories from stage melodramas or borrowed heavily from bestselling novels of the time. They had their heyday in the middle of the nineteenth century but owe their origins to the chapbooks that were printed and sold in the seventeenth and eighteenth centuries.[54] The penny dreadful, although much maligned by contemporaries, represented 'what most late Victorian and Edwardian juveniles actually chose to read, as opposed to the improving "reward book" literature which adults in power over them felt they should read'.[55] John Springhall advises us that the term 'penny dreadful' should itself be used with care; it was a derogatory label used by those that disapproved of the content of these publications, and who felt they were having a negative effect on the morals and behaviour of the young people that were reading them. Instead, we should more properly refer to earlier manifestations as 'penny bloods'. These told the stories of Dick Turpin and Jack Sheppard alongside less corporeal characters such as Sweeney Todd and Spring-Heeled Jack and were aimed at a predominantly adult readership (although the same subject matter eventually appeared in the dreadfuls). By the 1870s, perhaps two-thirds of English children were receiving some sort of basic education, and so, the market for these cheap fictions was growing. With serialized stories such as *The Wild Boys of London* (1864–1865), the penny dreadful 'held a vicarious appeal for young metropolitan readers seeking a romantic escape from uneventful daily lives'.[56]

In the later nineteenth century, dreadfuls developed and spread across the Atlantic to appear as American dime novels and eventually to evolve into the comic and graphic novel.[57]

The rise of the popular newspaper

Newspapers first began to appear in England in the late seventeenth century. There had been a vibrant pamphlet trade, which had started in the turmoil of the British Civil Wars (1642–1651) with both sides using print to conduct propaganda campaigns. Up until 1700, all newspapers had been printed in the capital but the new century saw the appearance of papers in Norwich and Bristol in 1701–1702. Experimentation followed quickly, and by 1760, some 130 different papers had been started (although many soon failed), and hundreds of thousands of copies were being printed weekly. By 1760 London, by far the most populated and commercial city had more than a dozen papers alone. By the late eighteenth century, the newspaper had become an essential part of the English gentleman's daily life.

The 1780s saw weekly, thrice weekly and daily newspapers in circulation, while the early 1800s saw the arrival of the political weekly and the Sunday newspaper. The eighteenth-century provincial press took their news from London, steered clear of controversy and filled their columns with advertising, but by the early nineteenth century, increased competition led to change here as well. Local papers began to report local issues and became more prepared to use editorials to voice concerns and make political statements, and this led to the emergence of some of the more important and in some cases more radical papers such as the *Manchester Guardian*. Nevertheless, these local papers were not as influential as the London press which was growing in power and reach.

The most dominant of all was *The Times*. Steam printing of *The Times* began in 1814 and with faster production came faster distribution (with the advent of the railways) and lower prices, which helped the so-called 'respectable' press to outstrip and outsell the competition. As a result, the nineteenth century saw the popularization of the press with a much increased readership; newspapers were now an established part of British culture and not something reserved for the elite.

With this growing popularity came a change in political attitudes towards the press. Once seen as dangerous and independent, politicians now began to realize that the press could be a useful ally in the campaign to gather as many votes as possible in a changing electoral landscape. There was a growing feeling, expressed by men such as Palmerston and Gladstone, that the press could help to bring the nation together. This view of the press, as an agent of social control, recognized the role it could play in inculcating accepted norms of behaviour and standardizing opinions about state institutions. The police believed it could help cut crime and educators believed it could increase knowledge in a positive way, and so, it became an 'essential component of an educated democracy'.[58] Between 1855 and 1861, various duties and taxes were abolished, and this helped make newspapers even more affordable. These reforms dovetailed with technological breakthroughs such as the invention of the rotary printer (1843) and linotype machine (1884). Thereafter, mass production allowed for cheap prices which ensured that the popular newspaper was 'securely implanted in to the cultural landscape as an essential reference point in the daily lives of millions of people'.[59] The newspaper had now developed into a huge industry, and this had important consequences for the way that crime news was disseminated and consumed.

Accompanying the development of more prosperous, newspaper industry was a new sort of journalism that was aimed at the lower middle and working classes. At the heart of this lay the reporting of crime. For example, *Lloyd's Weekly Newspaper* devoted 50 per cent of its content to crime in 1866 as did the *Daily Telegraph*. Press coverage shifted from the world of politics to the world of crime and sensation and the birth of what was termed 'new journalism'. As the readership of the popular press grew, so too did its influence, an influence that some journalists and editors were keen to exploit for social reform purposes.

New journalism was also stylistically different from the traditional form that was epitomized by *The Times*: the increasing use of the telegraph to deliver news fast affected the way in which journalism developed; there 'was a gain in simplicity and lack of padding, the use of shorter sentences, the over-simplification of complicated issues and the greater distortion caused by increasing use of the emphatic key word'.[60] As recent scholars have put it, the 'Victorian press served an ever widening readership and therefore adopted a popular language, tone and layout in which sensation and fact intertwined to generate and arouse interest, fear and concern in equal measure'.[61] In effect, this was the birth of what we understand as the modern 'tabloid' newspaper, with an emphasis on sensational headlines rather than a careful and balanced exposition of complex news items.

One of the results of the development of the press in the nineteenth century was increased newspaper competition and increased influence over society and social issues. This led to what Stanley Cohen has famously termed the rise of the media-led 'moral panic'.[62]

Moral panics: The garrotting scare of 1862

In 1972, Stanley Cohen developed his theory of the 'moral panic' which is probably best left to him to outline:

> Societies appear to be subject, every now and then, to periods of moral panic. A condition, episode, person or groups of persons emerges to become defined as a threat to societal values and interests; its nature is presented in stylised and stereotypical fashion by the mass media; the moral barricades are manned by editors, bishops, politicians and other right-thinking people; socially accredited experts pronounce their diagnosis and solutions; ways of coping are evolved or (more often) resorted to; the condition then disappears, submerges or deteriorates and becomes more visible.[63]

Cohen's model outlines five stages for a moral panic, and while these have been slightly revised in recent years, I think they hold true. There is an unfortunate tendency to see almost everything as a moral panic as soon as the media gets a hold of it, but this theoretical framework allows us to investigate instances of 'panic' more carefully. Instead of outlining Cohen's thesis in full here, I will use one nineteenth-century example of a moral panic as an illustration of how the paradigm can be used. In doing so, I will be drawing heavily on the work of Jennifer Davis, who first brought this particular panic to our attention.[64]

On 17 July 1862, while on his way to his club from the House of Commons, Hugh Pilkington MP was 'garotted'. The unfortunate politician had been attacked from behind, choked and the thieves stole his watch, or in modern terminology, he was 'mugged'. This represented the first stage of a moral panic (as described by Cohen); here was an initial incident, or 'act of deviancy',[65] that would spark a reaction from the press, public and authorities. Sparks need fuel to generate fire and, as Davis pointed out, there was plenty of contextual material in which this particular panic could thrive.[66] The attack was widely reported in the press and led to the reporting of dozens of similar incidents in London.

The press were quick to pick up the story and started to publish similar accounts of garrotings as well as offering a commentary on those responsible for the attacks. After just two reported attacks (that of Pilkington and an antiquarian named Hawkins),[67] the *Spectator* stated boldly that, 'Highway robbery is becoming an institution in London and roads like the Bayswater road are as unsafe as Naples. Case after case has been reported this week'.[68] The culprits were characterized as dangerous members of a subspecies of humanity, a 'criminal class', and depicted as animalistic, simian, with heavy brows and crooked legs and bodies. *The Times* called them 'the profound enemies of the human race', while the *Observer* dubbed them 'brutal ruffians'.[69] The press soon began to offer explanations for this outbreak and to suggest solutions, to act, as Sindall has argued, as 'moral entrepreneurs'.[70] Prisons were too soft, and the end of transportation with an increased use of the ticket-of-leave system had allowed offenders licence to operate almost without impunity. As was (and is) so often the case with the press, the cry was 'something must be done'.

The media met the second criteria for Cohen's model of a moral panic, and by exaggerating the threat posed by this seemingly new form of street crime, they helped create, in the minds of the public, the image of a dangerous 'folk devil' (the garrotter). By making the public, the police and the authorities increasingly aware of a new crime threat, they increased the amount of such crime reported. This then forced the authorities to respond and can be seen in the actions of the police. Standing orders were issued to the police on the beat to keep an eye on those sites that had the potential for garrotting attacks: dark alleys, dimly lit areas of open spaces, doorways and other places where thieves could hide themselves. Plain-clothed police were put on the streets, and ticket-of-leave men were subjected to close inspection and interview. While all this might seem like sensible precautions by professional police, Davis argues that they went well beyond this remit. She accuses them of manipulating the panic for their own purposes (such as the tighter surveillance of those released on licence) and of arresting large numbers of men 'on suspicion'.[71]

The courts also reacted in a draconian manner. Simple thefts were redefined as violent 'garrottings' and offenders sent for trial at the higher courts instead of being dealt with summarily. One petty criminal received a ten-year sentence for stealing £2 from a drunk in the street. A policeman had supposedly seen him knock his victim down, but it emerged that the victim himself had been quite reluctant to prosecute, only doing so under pressure from the police.[72]

The press played a role in exaggerating the extent of the problem and as a result, the public were increasingly sensitized and alarmed. The papers now carried genuine advertisements for anti-garrotting devices and clothing as well as satirical columns which poked fun at the panic that had been generated. Stage five of Cohen's model was reached when the government took long-term measures to combat the so-called threat offered by street robberies. These took place, as Davis describes, within a climate of concern about crime and the punishment of offenders. Transportation had been abolished in 1857 (although it had been dwindling for some time because of a marked reluctance of the colonies to continue to receive unwanted criminals from British Isles), and there was growing concern about issue of tickets-of-leave that allowed prisoners to be released from sentences early. Finally, there was increasing criticism of prison regimes that were seen as too soft. The garrotting panic offered social commentators, penal reformers, police and government the opportunity to toughen up on criminal justice policy, and this is exactly what they chose to do.

The 1863 Security against Violence Act (the 'Garrotters' Act' as it became known) reintroduced whipping for offenders. The broad thrust of penal reform in the nineteenth century had been to move away from corporal punishment and towards incarceration, and so, this act was something of a *volte-face*. The following year parliament passed the Penal Servitude Act (1864) which had much deeper consequences for those convicted of crimes. Second offenders now faced a minimum sentence of five years imprisonment. Perhaps more important was the prescription that those released on license would now have to report to a police station monthly, on threat of being prosecuted as suspicious person and liable to three months imprisonment, awarded without the need for a jury trial. Prison regimes were also toughened up under the terms of the Prisons Act (1865) with the widespread use of controlled diets, mechanistic punishments and labour, and solitary confinement for those that failed to comply with them.

But, it was the final piece of legislation that followed the garrotting panic that probably had the most long-term effect on criminal justice in the last quarter of the nineteenth century. The Habitual Criminals Act (1869) took a giant leap towards 'defining and controlling a particular group of lawbreakers as distinct from the rest of the population', creating what Davis (and others) have termed a separate 'criminal class', although arguably no such class actually existed.[73] This act decreed that any convicted felon caught for a second offence had on release to undergo seven years of police surveillance and re-arrest for trivial offences. Summary conviction for a host of minor offences could be secured on the unsubstantiated word of a single police constable. A register of prisoners was created, and the new science of photography employed to record their features. Thus, the moral panic that resulted from the media's reporting of a handful of street robberies in 1862 had very real consequences for thousands of people convicted of crime in the ensuing decades. This was a very real example of the power of the press to influence government policy and police practice.

Garrotting was not the only media-driven panic in the nineteenth century, there were concerns about attacks on the new railways,[74] which might in part reflect wider fears about the mingling of social classes on these new methods of transport. In the 1880s, a new terror, one arguably more real and threatening than the garrotting panic, hit the streets of the capital and garnered considerable column inches in the London press. The Whitechapel (or 'Jack the Ripper') murders were followed, in 1911, by one of the most celebrated 'true crime' stories of the day. Both these cases, and their media impact, will be briefly addressed towards the end of this chapter, but before that, let us examine a phenomenon that first surfaced in the later 1800s but has continued to dominate media coverage of crime ever since: antisocial youth and gang crime.

Hooligans and 'roughs': The problem of youth gangs

Geoffrey Pearson argued that there is continuity in the way in which youth offending has been characterized as a societal problem throughout history.[75] Young people have been pictured as lawless, antisocial and disrespectful to their elders and out of control. This study will consider the problems surrounding youth crime, and the way in which it has been characterized in Chapter 8, but since Pearson is most concerned with antisocial behaviour rather than property crime (which occupied contemporaries in the early nineteenth century), let us look at his arguments here. Pearson starts his study with the summer of 1981 when youth ran amok in London, Bristol and Liverpool in a series of riots during the premiership of Mrs Thatcher. He then goes back through time via the Teddy Boys (1950s); 1930s razor gangs; the Hooligans (1890s); before turning his attention to the street urchins of the 1820s (famously described by Dickens in *Oliver Twist*) and the Mohawks, who terrorized London in the early 1700s.[76] If we were to update Pearson's thesis for the twenty-first century, it would be necessary to include 'punk rock' (1970s), football hooliganism (1970s/1980s) and the emergence of gangs of 'hoodies' and 'postcode gangstas'[77] in the 2000s.

However, there is a problem with Pearson's continuity thesis. The gangs of 'artful dodgers' that infested the streets of London in the early nineteenth century cannot be characterized in the same ways as late-century hooligans or modern youth gangs. Fagin's 'gang' of pickpockets were thieves who stole from unsuspecting passers-by; they dressed to conceal their purpose not to stand out from the crowd, and they did not appear to have a sense of a distinctive youth culture. Modern youth, from Teddy Boys and Mods, Punks, Goths and Skinheads, to New Romantics, Casuals and Emos all have a distinctive, recognizable group identity and style. In addition, modern criminal gangs (as opposed to the youth groups listed above) are associated with violent crime, drug dealing and prostitution and not simple street robbery or pickpocketing (as Fagin's gang of thieves was). Modern gangs are described as territorial and are often associated with specific locations (postcodes); as a result, they come in to conflict with other, rival, gangs or groups. While their offending and antisocial behaviour does spill out and affect their neighbourhoods, the main targets of their criminality are not generally ordinary members of the public.

It is the violence associated with present-day gang members that concerns society, whereas in the early nineteenth century, contemporaries were more agitated about street robbery and pocket picking. However, it is possible to argue (as I have elsewhere[78]) that there is some continuity in the way that violent street gangs have been characterized by the media since the 1870s, although even here there are clear discontinuities as well. So, let us look in more detail at the phenomena of street gangs in the second half of the nineteenth century, and at the so-called 'hooligan panic' of the 1890s, because this was largely a product of media attention.

The Hooligan scare came to prominence in 1898 as the press reported the activities of large groups of youths in a number of British cities. However, as John Archer, Heather Shore, Stephen Humphries and Andrew Davies have all shown, there were earlier manifestations of gang violence in Britain.[79] Liverpool's 'Cornermen' gathered at the intersections of certain streets in the working-class slums close to the docks and came to national prominence in 1874 when an innocent passer-by was murdered in Titheburn Street. Richard Morgan was accosted and asked for money for beer by a member of the notorious 'High Rip' gang. When he refused (and suggested that his assailant might like to earn the money instead), he was knocked to the ground and beaten to death. As a result, two gang members were executed and another sent to prison for life. Archer has associated the outbreaks of gang violence in Liverpool in the 1870s with a small group of individuals who had close links to semi-organized crime rather than as evidence of the emergence of 'gang culture' in any modern sense. Davies has studied the 'scuttling gangs' of Manchester and Salford in a similar period. These gangs dressed alike and wielded belts studded with horse brasses as weapons, and again the scuttlers came to the attention of the press for their violence, not their relationship with petty crime. London had a plethora of street gangs in the decades before the emergence of the hooligan, while Birmingham had the 'peaky blinders' (so-called because they concealed razor blades in their caps).

There are some continuities between nineteenth-century gangs and those of the present day, but it is quite hard to establish this comprehensively; in part, this is because we still have relatively little research on modern-day gangs in the UK.[80] Humphries, Pearson and Davies all noted that Victorian and Edwardian gangs had a loose structural organization and tended to dress alike. So, Birmingham's 'peaky blinders', Manchester's scuttlers and London's hooligans adapted contemporary fashions, sporting bell-bottomed trousers, peaked caps and large belts and had their hair cut short with a 'donkey fringe'. In this, they seem to be forerunners of modern fashion-conscious youths (such as the Mods, Casuals and other contemporary gangs who wear labels conspicuously). By contrast, Liverpool's cornermen were far from fashionable; indeed, they were among the most poorly dressed inhabitants of the city.[13] Today, fashion is an important driver of youth culture, and modern influences extend beyond the local to the global, with much 'street' fashion heavily influenced by American culture. Today's street gangs are influenced by (and indeed influence) popular street music (rap and hip hop) as well as film and television, and Victorian street gangs took their cultural links from the proliferation of 'penny dreadfuls' and the music hall: the popular culture of their day. In nineteenth-century London, gangs had names such as 'Monkey Parade gang', the 'Gang of Roughs' and the 'Jovial Thirty-Two', the 'Marylebone gang', 'Fitzroy Place gang' and the 'New Cut gang' from Lambeth (soon to become the home of the 'hooligan'). Many twentieth-century and contemporary gangs have also adopted names that associate them with areas of the cities they claimed territorial rights over. The Hoxton Mob fought the Sabini gang for dominance in Soho between the world wars, and the Tottenham Mandem emerged on the notorious Broadwater Farm estate in north London in the 1980s.

Victorian and early Edwardian gangs also had strong geographical ties and would fight over territories and girls, even if some of these 'fights' were little more than symbolic gestures to establish 'ownership' and as a 'ritualistic expression of aggression and masculinity'[14]. The fights took place on the streets but also in out of the way places or at night. London's Embankment was the scene of a number of clashes in the 1880s, and Regent's Park was a notorious arena for gang disputes, petty crime and prostitution. In the north-west of England, gang fights were frequent and court appearances a regular occurrence. Attacks on, or insults to, females connected to gangs were seen as attacks on the honour of the gang itself.

It was rare, however, for fights to result in fatalities. The Regent's Park murder of 1888 (when a young man was stabbed to death by York Gates) was very much an exception.[81] However, when such incidents did occur, they garnered a tremendous amount of press coverage. The Regent's Park case ran for several weeks in the London and national press, and even made the newspapers in India. While gang crime was certainly a real concern for those that encountered it, it was neither as prevalent nor as destructive as the contemporary Victorian and Edwardian press made it out to be. The identification of the youth gang is a part of the rhetoric of the 'criminal class' in a similar way that modern street gangs are associated with an 'underclass'.[82]

It is also important to recognize that much of the concern about youth gangs in the later 1800s was bound up with other, deeper concerns about the state of the nation, Empire and a changing and rapidly growing society. Britain's population was rising rapidly, its cities were expanding, and – towards the end of the century – she had become embroiled in an imperialist war in southern Africa. Pearson noted that media hype has frequently fuelled past panics about young people behaving badly, and he recognized that this often related to periods of economic or political unrest when the state of the nation was a matter for debate. This was certainly the case in the 1880s and 1890s when tensions at home and abroad were manifest. It was true of course in the 1980s when the Thatcher government was attempting to impose a new and harsh economic strategy on British society, and trades unions and others were attempting to resist this. Humphries and Davies have both associated gang violence with expressions of impotent masculinity in the face of declining industry or opportunities for traditional male employment, and this would seem to be an interesting area for future study in a historical and contemporary context.

Finally, it is also worth pointing out that concerns about youth crime or youth offending have almost exclusively been focused on working-class youth. The excesses of middle-class youths were seen as 'a healthy expression of a spirit of adventure and manliness'.[83] In the late Victorian and early Edwardian period, groups of middle-class and elite youths travelled to London for fun and frolics at the music halls and pubs and reportedly wreaked havoc on occasions. Instead of this behaviour being condemned, it was actually widely praised as a demonstration of masculinity and a necessary part of the passage to adulthood. This is also evident in the ways in which some elite men justified the use of physical violence against others. For example, Edward Parker wrote to his sister about his violent encounter with working-class youth on the streets while an undergraduate at Cambridge in 1842. Parker was clearly proud of his efforts in fighting off a 'mob' of armed 'fellows', and such examples of heroism 'and physical strength were increasingly emphasized in the nineteenth-century concepts of elite virtue'.[84] Class was therefore an important aspect of the rhetoric of youth offending in the nineteenth century and remains so to this day.

The treatment of youth gangs and concerns about their antisocial and criminal behaviour is one clear way in which the media manipulates 'crime news' for its own ends. These are in part political (either to show support for a favoured political party or philosophy or to criticize an incumbent government or opposition position).

Newspapers are, by their very nature, *populist* and thrive on telling their readership what it wants to hear and thereby reaffirming widely held misconceptions about society. We can see this is the reportage that produced the early modern and eighteenth-century narratives of crime and then continued throughout the nineteenth century. By the later 1800s, the newspaper had become a commonplace accessory of everyday life, with a vastly increased readership. There was fierce competition for readers, and newspaper editors recognized that one clear way to drive sales was to exploit the public's appetite for stories about scandal and murder.

The 'invention' of murder?[85]

From the murder of the Marrs family on the Ratcliffe Highway in 1811 to the arrest of Dr Crippen a century later, we can see an increasing interest in the murder story. This interest was not necessarily new; as we have seen print culture has used crime (and homicide in particular) to shock, entertain and moralize from at least the seventeenth century. Recent scholarship has questioned how 'civilised' we can claim to be, given our continued consumption of a variety of forms of popular culture that have violence (often extreme violence) at their core, and it is certainly a question worth asking about the second half of the nineteenth century.[86] Until 1868, executions were held in public and drew large crowds with plenty of broadsides telling the stories of the condemned. There was also a lively trade in the memorabilia of infamous murders and murderers such as William Corder and his victim, Maria Marten. Famous cases were transported to the stage as melodramas or made into songs and ballads. Rosalind Crone's research demonstrates the link between the rapid urbanization of nineteenth-century England and this new enthusiasm for the consumption of narratives of violence[87]; so, were the Victorians trying to make sense of this new world that was changing before their eyes?

After 1868, convicted killers were executed behind closed doors, and murder was actually a rare and fairly mundane affair. Judith Flanders suggests that the more that Victorian society became distanced from death, the more fascinated it became with it.[88] Murder, because it is such an unusual crime (even at its height in 1862, it never rose beyond 2 murders per 100,000 people and usually remained at 1.5), was both scary *and* fascinating. The ideal murder in the nineteenth century had to have three key elements: the *crime*, the *trial* and the *hanging*. After 1868, the trial became the single most important element in this process because crowds were now robbed of the opportunity to see the guilty parties meet their end on the scaffold.

At the trial, all the (hopefully gruesome) details of the crime emerged. The daily and weekly newspapers would carry reports of the trials, and these were consumed avidly by a growing and widening readership.

The murder of Patrick O'Connor in 1849 by Maria Manning and her husband Frederick was sensational and gripped the attention of the public. Maria had planned the killing and hoped to profit by selling off O'Connor's shares in a railway company. But she and her subordinate husband bungled their escape and were quickly captured.

Maria, a foreign lady's maid, played the part of the wronged woman to perfection in court, screaming abuse at Frederick, the jury and the public gallery. Both were executed at Horsemonger Lane Gaol in front of a huge crowd.

The execution of the Mannings was manipulated by those opposed to such public displays of violence, such as Charles Dickens, and the subsequent move after 1868 towards private hangings within prison walls has been seen as a victory for the 'civilizing process'.[89] Hereafter, violence was increasingly associated with a newly identified 'criminal class', and other violent pastimes were toned down or legislated out of existence. Crone shows, for example, how the Punch and Judy sideshow moved from a form of violent street theatre to a (relatively) sanitized children's seaside entertainment. Mr Punch did not entirely clean up his act, but his character was redrawn to reflect middle-class concerns about violence in society.[90]

But it is in the presentation of poisoning that the nineteenth-century press was fully able to exploit new public fears of the murderer *within* rather than the criminal class itself. Poisoning was a secret crime, hard to detect and therefore seemingly more sinister and dangerous.[91] It had been a feature of court intrigues and popular imaginings of murder in the Tudor and Jacobean period but had largely disappeared from the public consciousness in the seventeenth and eighteenth centuries. It returned, in a dramatic form, in the Victorian period, reaching its apogee with the conviction of William Palmer in 1856. The nineteenth century witnessed a growth in the reporting of poisoning cases in the newspapers, a level of reportage that was out of all proportion to the relative number of incidents that occurred. Poisoning cases allowed the papers to present this type of murder in particular ways, as predominantly female, for example, or later as a way of uncovering popular fears about the medical profession.[92]

Newspaper reports of poisoning cases (especially those with working-class protagonists) followed a set format which focused on the interior – the homes and habits of ordinary people – which contrasted with reports of homicides that involved physical violence (where the focus was on disruption to the public sphere). In doing so, they offered the reading public a 'window on to the underside of Victorian domesticity'.[93] Reportage revealed the base motives for murder by poison, namely the desire of wives or mothers to be rid of their offspring or husbands, so they could benefit from the proceeds of burial clubs or insurance. This alerted the public to baby farmers and other forms of child abuse and murder and increased the pressure on government to reform laws surrounding childcare and the sale of poisons or food additives. As one contemporary noted, poisoners wanted something, 'money, or a lover, or a house, or to be free of the trouble of an infant; and they put out the life which stands in the way of what they want'.[94]

By the early years of the twentieth century, poisons had almost been legislated or regulated out of the hands of the ordinary killer, and so, the poisoner became synonymous with corrupt or 'evil' medical practitioners, as these were the only people that could easily get hold of dangerous toxins. Medicine also had an important role to play in the conviction of poisoners, and this feature of murder trials involving poison also allowed the media a new angle to offer their readership. One feature of the nineteenth-century trial was the emergence of 'expert' witnesses who were 'allowed to give an opinion on matters [...] without being personally acquainted with the facts'.[95] In poisoning cases, this meant the toxicologist who now took centre stage as he described the nature of poisons and the effects they had to an enthralled audience well beyond the confines of the courtroom.

The late nineteenth and early twentieth century provided the press and public with a number of grisly murders and 'whodunits', none more appealing than the Whitechapel murders of 1888 and the manhunt for Dr Crippen in 1911.

Later crime news: 'Jack the Ripper' and Dr Crippen

Media-driven moral panics play on a rather simplistic difference between 'good' and 'evil' in human nature and then exploit such differences to make explicit the suggestion that there is a moral decay in society.[96] It helps to set up murderers as very different from 'ordinary' people: more vicious, criminal and animalistic. This sort of reporting sells papers – as the industry saying goes: 'if it bleeds, it leads'. This was to be brought to bear in the dramatic and sensationalized reporting of the Whitechapel murders in the late summer and autumn of 1888.

The later 1800s saw the emergence of a group of individuals who pioneered what has been called the 'golden age of English journalism'; these were men such as George Reynolds (*Reynold's Newspaper*), Edward Lloyd (*Lloyd's*), Henry W. Lucy of the *Daily News*, Henry Labouchere of *Truth*, Frederic Greenwood and William Stead of the *Pall Mall Gazette* and Sir William H. Russell of *The Times*. W. T. Stead was the most compelling of these characters, partly because he had very clear ideas about the power of the press and the extent to which he could manipulate news stories to tackle social problems. A campaigning journalist, Stead believed in the principle that the ends justifies the means and in 1885 was embroiled in scandal and found himself on trial at the Old Bailey for his involvement in the abduction of a 13-year-old girl for prostitution.[97] Journalists such as Stead went in search of stories about poverty, crime, prostitution, child abuse and health both as a way of raising public awareness *and* to keep one step ahead of their rivals. The Ripper murders offered an opportunity to combine this interest in social problems with the age's most celebrated unsolved murder case.

It is vital that we consider the reporting of the Whitechapel murders in the context of Victorian journalism and 'sensation' news. Writers such as Matthew Arnold and Oscar Wilde were quick to condemn newspapers for printing lurid accounts of murder, but as we have seen, these sensational accounts of crime and murder were not new; the *Newgate Calendars* had been publishing the daring exploits and wicked crimes of notorious criminals throughout the eighteenth century. Penny dreadfuls had titillated popular tastes since the 1840s, and in the 1880s, these were augmented by the new and colourful 'sixpenny wonderfuls' that gave their readership illustrated thrillers and romances. These threats to the newspapers' market prompted editors to give over more space and 'bigger headlines to any murder that contained even modest amounts of mystery or gore'.[98] Most newspapers had to rely on words to convey the drama of their stories, since photographs and illustrations were the preserve of the weekly magazines such as the *Illustrated London News* and the *Illustrated Police News* which also featured emotive illustrations of crime scenes and murders.

Victorian sensation covered human disasters (such as the sinking of boats); human 'freaks' (such as the 'Elephant Man', Joseph Merrick); and tales of foreign bandits, misdoings in convents and the discoveries of new and exotic species. So-called 'sensation' novels (such as Wilkie Collins's *The Woman in White* and *The Moonstone*) used the familiar themes of crime, scandal, horror, sex and violence. Victorians also enjoyed the theatre and melodrama where sensation played a crucial part and contemporary audiences expected to be thrilled with dramatic reconstructions of disasters and other shocking events. Thus, the theatre, music hall and penny dreadfuls all formed a part of a growing popular culture in the nineteenth century, with linking themes within them that reflected society's wider interests in crime and punishment, sex and violence and human tragedy and heroism. The graphic description of injuries in the Victorian press suggests that there was a voyeuristic element to these reports; readers were 'enabled by such detailed reports to watch the drama unfold, to view the victim as she fell down the stairs or was knocked senseless to the floor by a poker'.[99]

So, how did all this affect the reporting of the Whitechapel murders? Michael Diamond describes the Ripper murders as the 'greatest murder sensation of the Victorian era' because the brutality, the serial nature of the killings and the failure of the police to catch anyone all contributed to making it the biggest story of its day.[100,101] Much of the press reporting was second-hand and repetitious, since they all bought information from the same news agencies or stole it from each other. Disjointed articles were cobbled together as pressure from deadlines forced papers to go to press before the stories could be more carefully presented. Some reporters ventured out to investigate the Whitechapel area and talked to residents, while others made up stories from their comfortable offices. Reporters often got key facts wrong in their reports, even basic details such as the names of the victims or times of death.

The most interesting thing about the reportage surrounding the Whitechapel murders is the differences in style adopted by the papers. The *Times* reported the death of Polly Nichols under the headline; ANOTHER MURDER IN WHITECHAPEL; the reporter mentioning the arrival of the police surgeon, and alluding to the 'terrible' wounds she had suffered. The *Star*, whose circulation was one of the success stories of the Ripper affair, took a quite different approach, giving the story a much more sensationalist twist. The headline read: A REVOLTING MURDER/ ANOTHER WOMAN FOUND HORRIBLY MUTILATED IN WHITECHAPEL/GHASTLY CRIMES BY A MANIAC. There were subheadings such as 'Her throat cut from ear to ear' and 'the deed of a maniac' linking her death to two previous murders (not always associated with the 'Ripper'). The papers, with the exception of the East End local press, painted a picture of Whitechapel's degraded state – helping build an image of a netherworld. Other papers echoed these themes, imagining the whole of the East End and its inhabitants as degraded and immoral. The killer emerged as a kind of supernatural being; whose ability to evade capture was a combination of his rude cunning, police incompetence and the geography of poorly lit alleys and courts. The press (particularly the *Pall Mall Gazette* under William Stead) attacked the Commissioner of the Metropolitan Police (Sir Charles Warren) and printed hundreds of letters from members of the public offering advice or confessions related to the murders. They interfered with witnesses, polluted crime scenes and generally undermined the police investigation. At the same time, they created most of the myths and falsehoods that surround the Ripper case to this day.

While he was not in the same league as the 'Ripper', Hawley Harvey Crippen was also the subject of massive press interest towards the end of the period covered by this book. His case is also worth a brief analysis for the way in which the press interact with, and to some extent influence, real-life crime stories.

Dr Crippen was an American medical practitioner who had moved to London at the end of the nineteenth century with his second wife, Cora, a music-hall performer. In 1905, the Crippens took a house at Hilldrop Crescent in north London, and Hawley worked in a medical centre for the deaf nearby. Here, he met Ethel Le Neve with whom he was later to have an affair.

It would be fair to say that the Crippens had a strained marriage. Cora had several affairs and seems to have treated her husband with some contempt; whether this was what led him to murder her, we are unlikely to discover. In January 1910, Cora disappeared and soon afterwards Ethel moved in and set herself up as Crippen's mistress. Crippen claimed that his wife had left him and returned to the United States with one of her lovers. However, he also told the police that she had died, so Crippen clearly had something to hide, even if it was simply his embarrassment that he had been made a cuckold. The police made a brief search of the house on Hilldrop Crescent before leaving, presumably satisfied by Crippen's explanation. However, on the next day, the couple fled to the Continent and boarded a ship for Canada and the police, led by Chief Inspector Walter Dew (who had been a junior detective on the Whitechapel murder case), returned. Dew's team found the remains of a human body buried under the floor of the basement. Several parts were missing, but the celebrated Home Office pathologist, Bernard Spilsbury, was able to identify traces of scopolamine (or hyoscine), a drug that was sometimes used as an anaesthetic or to assist births. More importantly, it was a substance Crippen was known to have purchased in the days before Cora's disappearance. This fact, the body parts and the couple's flight all added up to something very suspicious and had the makings of a sensational news story.

There is plenty of doubt surrounding Crippen's guilt, especially as the human remains have never been proved to be Cora's. But, this is not what really interests us here, nor is it the reason that the case became such a media sensation at the time. It was the sordid nature of the killing and the Crippen's scandalous relationship, coupled with seemingly romantic escape attempt, plus the fugitives' eventual capture via the new technology of the wireless telegraph that made it such a sensational story. Dew travelled to Canada and intercepted the boat carrying Crippen and Le Neve. The pair were returned to England and put on trial; Ethel was acquitted but her lover was found guilty, sentenced to death and hanged at Pentonville prison in November 1910. The press carried detailed descriptions and photographs of the pair as they attempted to sail across the Atlantic and covered the subsequent trial for their readers. Photos of the pair in the dock at the Old Bailey as well as the more familiar sketches of those involved helped bring the sensational case into the homes of Edwardian England.

The press were able to cover every twist and turn in the case as it unfolded, as the telegraph and the fully fledged newspaper industry built on the solid base they had constructed from the late 1800s. The *Hull Daily Mail* reported the discovery of buried remains 'in a Camden Town cellar' and offered descriptions of the fugitives (noting that Ethel may 'or may not be dressed as a boy') as well as line drawings of Hawley and Cora. It commented that the crime had shocked London and declared that the remains were those of Cora Crippen (despite this being far from proven).[102] The press explored Crippen's history, contacting his former associates abroad, to investigate the death of his previous wife. They reported the police search, and one regional paper noted that the heart of the victim had been found.[103] This sort of detailed (and highly speculative) reportage is now often largely omitted from modern crime news because it is recognized that it might prejudice any possible court case and undermine the police investigation; no such qualms appear to have existed in the late nineteenth and early twentieth centuries. On 29 July, the news that Crippen was on board the liner *Montrose* was relayed to its readership by the newspapers, along with the story that Walter Dew was about to arrive and intercept them. The 'Cellar Murder' or the 'North London Mystery' had become what modern journalists would term a 'rolling news' item.[104] The press followed his arrest, return to England and even his telegram exchanges with his defence counsel en route.

All this attention on Crippen provoked *The Times* into complaining that such 'interest in murders becomes perverse when it is treated as a mere source of pleasure', suggesting that people enjoyed looking at pictures of Crippen because he gave them 'a pleasant feeling that they are in the movement'[105] (or perhaps somehow fashionable). This again was nothing new; *The Times* had complained about the sensational coverage of the Whitechapel murders and had often pointed out that the consumption of 'murder news'

Figure 2.3 Crippen and Le Neve at Bow Street magistrates' court (1911).

by the masses was at best a distraction from work and at worst represented a threat to their morals and those of the nation. Unfortunately, for the well-heeled readership of the 'quality press', the genie was out of the bottle, and the popular newspaper was here to stay.

Conclusions: The impact of the media, mythmaking and the future of crime histories

This chapter started by looking at the ways in which the criminal has been characterized in history; from a 'fallen' individual to a product of a degraded society. Today criminologists are well aware of the complex and overlapping personal, psychological, economic and environmental factors that propel certain individuals into patterns of offending. Much of this science has developed over the last 200 years as a result of an ongoing discourse about crime and criminality. Print culture and the news media have played an important role in this process, but it is also responsible for a considerable amount of distortion and manipulation for multiple ends. As Clive Emsley noted, 'crime stories were exciting and possibly increased reporting of crime helped to generate increased fears which, in turn, generated decisions to launch prosecutions against offenders as a warning to others.'[106] In the early to mid-eighteenth century, debates about the 'crime problem' were conducted in, and encouraged by, the London newspapers who were interacting with their readership. This interaction continued in to the Victorian period and continues today. Now, we have blogs and a variety of forms of social media that allows readers and commentators to offer instant feedback on opinion and crime news.

In the early modern period, far fewer people had direct access to news in the way we are so accustomed to and so print culture and crime literature in particular, 'constituted an important point of contact between official ideas on law and order and the culture of the masses.'[107] And, this connection is important because once newspapers became an established part of daily lives, the 'moral entrepreneurs' identified by Robert Sindall were increasingly able to utilize crime news to drive agendas about penal policy. Newspapers printed stories of crime for all sorts of reasons and crime reporting, Ward suggests, might in part be influenced by the 'format of publication itself'.[108] In the 'Ripper' case, the 'Sundays' were at a distinct advantage in that they had more time, and more 'news' to draw from. However, the presentation of crime news is also influenced by the nature of the paper itself; whether it has particular political allegiances or a particular readership. Newspapers are organs not only of information but also of discussion and criticism, and exaggerating the problem of crime is a well-established vehicle for criticizing government and police. This was clearly evident in 1888 but equally, if less obviously, the case in the 1740s, and remains a pertinent consideration today.

The past informs us that print culture, while offering periodic critiques of elements of the criminal justice system, presented a vindication of the law and the methods of enforcing it. It also helped to establish who the perpetrators of crime were and helped to define them as deviant and as belonging to a separate 'class' or section of society.

This has remained one of the key functions of the modern popular press and can be seen in the way in which modern 'enemies of society' (such as terrorists, paedophiles and violent criminals) are portrayed and characterized. Ward argues that 'the substantial developments in the nature of printed crime reporting which took place in late seventeenth and eighteenth-century London were crucial in cultivating heightened fears about crime and in promoting hard-line policies as the best response to the criminal threat'.[109] I would strongly agree with Ward, and we can look to the aftermath of the garrotting panic to see exactly how the police, moral entrepreneurs and the government manipulated that scare.

Jennifer Davis argued that the garrotting panic helped to fix the notion of a 'criminal class' in the public consciousness, and I would suggest this then allowed society to abrogate its responsibility for the crime problem. Instead of tackling the underlying social and environmental causes of crime (poverty, inequality, poor housing, inadequate education and training, unemployment and so on) the blame could be placed squarely at the feet of the habitual criminal. The media was fundamental to this process because of the ways in which it has consistently closed down debate and reinforced stereotypes about crime, deviance and society. Print media and much of its modern multi-platform equivalents delight in reducing the most complex issues to headlines, sound bites and crude generalizations. Investigative journalism has had its moments of success (the outcome of the 'Maiden Tribute' was the raising of the age of consent, for example), but these are relatively few and far between.

For the historian, printed crime literature and crime news offer a fascinating opportunity to look at the way in which society digested stories about criminals, and for sure, it tells us a lot about the techniques felons like Jack Sheppard used or the attempts of policing agencies to catch them. But, it is also almost as unrepresentative of actual crime as the modern TV drama or soap. This is because what we want to read about is the extraordinary: the brutal murder, the serial killers, the daring robbery and death on the gallows. The reality of crime is, of course, that it is much more mundane. The so-called 'heroes' of the criminal biographies, penny dreadfuls and their modern equivalents (the confessional true crime narratives from former felons such as 'Mad' Frankie Fraser and Bruce Reynolds[110]) are not *at all* representative of the majority of those who came before the criminal justice system in the period covered by this book. Crime is much more run-of-the-mill, much less exciting or glamorous than the media and various forms of popular culture would have us believe.

Which brings me to my closing remarks for this chapter on media and its role in the (mis) representation of crime and criminals. Some histories of former criminals are so mired in legend that it has become almost impossible to agree as to whether they existed at all. Did Robin Hood rob the rich to feed the poor? Were the unsuspecting clients of the barber Sweeney Todd turned into meat pies by his willing partner on Fleet Street? Did Spring-heeled Jack terrorize the women of mid-nineteenth-century London? At what point will the character of 'Jack the Ripper' become as fantastical as these three celebrated 'legends'? We might collectively believe that in our modern society with its highly developed technology we can offer concrete proof of crime. After all, we have discovered

DNA and offender profiling and cameras watch our every step on a daily basis. The reality is, however, that technological advances, while they have helped convict criminals, have also created more opportunities for crime and for greater distortion of facts. So, while we might not be able to trust a printed image from the 1700s, are we any more confident about a photoshopped picture in our own period? Some of these questions need to be discussed further, but for now, I think we can conclude that the media has had (and continues to have) an extremely important place in the representation of crime and in debates about criminal justice policy. As such, it underpins much of what follows in the rest of this study.

CHAPTER 3
VIOLENCE: THE DECLINE OF HOMICIDE AND A GROWING INTOLERANCE TOWARDS ASSAULT

Of all crime, the one that promotes the most fear and alarm is the crime that involves violence towards the person. Successive governments and home secretaries are continually at pains to say that violent crime is on the decrease, while their opposite numbers are quick to point to any leap in the numbers of reported crimes involving violence. For at least the last 150 years, newspapers have filled their pages with stories about murder and violent robbery, and this fascination with violence extends to other areas of the media with nearly all TV and film detective or crime dramas being centred around murder and serial killings. This is despite the fact that violent crime represents only a very small percentage of all recorded crime. For example, according to figures released by the Office of National Statistics (ONS) in July 2013 while 14 per cent of adults are likely to have been a victim of a crime against the household (i.e. burglary, vehicle theft, vandalism), only 5 per cent were at risk of being the victim of a crime against the person.[1] One of the questions this chapter will try to answer then is why are we so disproportionately concerned about violent crime?

We might also ask ourselves: how violent is modern Britain compared to the period 1660–1914? There is a tendency to believe that the late seventeenth and eighteenth centuries were quite violent by comparison and that the nineteenth century witnessed a process of pacification of our violent tendencies. In particular, it has been argued that the 1800s saw a widespread growth in intolerance of male (and particularly working-class male) violence.[2] How accurate is this viewpoint, and how can we measure this? The decline in violence has been attributed to a much earlier move towards manner and politeness, something that the sociologist Norbert Elias identified as a 'civilizing process' at work in continental Europe and England from the early modern period onwards.[3] This thesis has been used and critiqued by a number of historians and criminologists who have explored the decline in homicide rates from the medieval to the modern period.[4]

As we saw with the discussion of crime rates, trying to measure or map patterns of crime (violent or otherwise) is fraught with difficulty. As this chapter will demonstrate, mapping petty or non-lethal violence (particularly domestic violence) is especially problematic as it is often underreported. Let us start by attempting to define what we mean by violence before going on to look at lethal violence (homicide) and the debate concerning its supposed decline. We will then move on to discuss assault and how the prosecution of such non-lethal violence has changed over the period of this study and how historians have explained this.

Defining violent crime

As John Carter Wood has noted, any attempt to define 'what is violence' is problematic. This is because it refers to 'two distinct things: particular kinds of acts and the interpretative frameworks used to define and understand' them.[5] We tend to think of violent crime as attacks upon people: homicide, assault or rape. But, in legal terms, violence can cover a much wider range of offences. Highway robbery is robbery with violence (either actual violence or the threat of violence), but it is usually categorized under 'property crime'. Terrorism is clearly violent, but it is better viewed as a politically or ideologically inspired crime. Rape has been considered within the chapter on gender. This is not intended to ignore the reality that men can be and are victims of rape, just that in the period of this book, the victims of rape were invariably female. Similarly, the issue of domestic violence is perhaps best dealt with elsewhere as it is so bound up with contemporary attitudes towards women and their place within a male dominated (patriarchal) society. Therefore, this chapter will concentrate on homicide (murder and manslaughter) and assault.

Before we move on, it is worth setting the study of violence and crime in the context of the wider study of the criminal justice system of the past.

Historians of crime have tended to pay less attention to violent crime than to property crime, and there are a number of reasons for this. The first explanation is simply that violent crime has rarely formed more than 10–15 per cent of all the crimes that have reached the jury courts. And, as we have seen, it is from these courts that records commonly survive for historians to examine. A considerable amount of petty violence (assault and threatening behaviour) was dealt with by magistrates (Justices of the Peace) at summary level in the eighteenth and nineteenth centuries, and many of these records are lost to us. It is only in recent years that scholars have looked seriously at assault and its prosecution and punishment.[6]

The second underlying factor behind the neglect of violent crime is that interpersonal violence has a much less clear *class* dimension. Most violent crimes were committed between members of the same social group – and indeed often involved combatants drawn from the same household. Whereas property crime, by contrast, was usually, or at least often, committed by the poorer members of society (the 'labouring poor' or working class, dependent upon which period we are discussing) on the propertied or better off. As a result, violent crime was therefore much less interesting to those Marxist historians who turned to court records in the 1970s and 1980s to study the nature of authority and class conflict. This is because apart from riot and arson (the latter of which is usually deemed to be a property crime), which were extensively studied, violent crimes could very rarely be seen as deliberate expressions of class conflict.

As a result, early interest in the history of violence tended to be fuelled mainly by contemporary concerns about riot and about fluctuations in homicide rates.

Violent crime and the decline of homicide in England and Europe[7]

Historians have searched for evidence about whether violence had been more or less prevalent in the past and to see if violence patterns were rising or falling. Violence can of course cover a wide range of actions from minor assaults (such as pushing and shoving) to major assaults (what might be termed 'full-scale fights') and then to more serious incidents such as potentially lethal assaults (which often involved weapons) and to attempted murder (where the aim was to kill but the attack did not succeed). Finally, there are those acts of violence that ended in death: manslaughter (which is the killing of someone without intention) and murder. Even murder can be subdivided into premeditated murder, unpremeditated murder and serial murder (the killing of more than one individual).

Until recently, historians have had to limit their studies because reliable figures on levels of violence are almost impossible to obtain except in relation to assaults that led to death (manslaughters and murders). Most historical work on violence has therefore been formed around a long-running debate about homicide rates and about murder and the contexts in which it occurs (something addressed later in this chapter). This is because homicide is the type of violent crime that is most *likely* to be reported and is also the crime that most preoccupies contemporary and current concerns.

There is now a well-established consensus that there was a long-term decline in homicide rates in England and Europe from the late medieval period to the modern. The fall began sometime in the 1400s and accelerated in the late seventeenth and early eighteenth centuries. One of the arguments given for this fall is the growth of politeness and rationality and a retreat from barbarism and incivility during Europe's 'Enlightenment' period. Thus, the decline in homicide is situated neatly within the period of study of this book. Let us now look at this debate in more detail.

John Beattie's work on Surrey is perhaps our best guide to homicide rates in England. His Table 3.1 shows a clear fall in murder and manslaughter prosecutions between the Restoration of King Charles II and the dawn of the nineteenth century.

So what happened to homicide rates in England in the long eighteenth century, and what effect did location have on these statistics? Overall, there is a clear decline in homicide rates, from 6.2/100,000 in 1660–1679 to just 0.9/100,000 in the period 1780–1802. The rate of fall for Sussex is less dramatic, from 2.6 to 0.6, but still follows the general pattern. What is also apparent is that the homicide rate was notably higher in urban areas (i.e. those parishes close to London) for most of the late seventeenth and the first three quarters of the eighteenth century.

Figures for Essex also suggest similar changes in the seventeenth century; moreover, Ted Gurr's important and influential 1981 study appears to offer conclusive proof of a long-term decline in homicide in England from the thirteenth to late twentieth centuries.[8]

Table 3.1 Homicide indictments in urban and rural Surrey and in Sussex, 1660–1800.

	Approx. Rate Per 100,000		Population	
Period	*Urban*	*Rural*	*Total*	*Sussex*
1660–1679	8.1	4.3	6.2	2.6
1680–1699	5.0	4.7	4.9	1.9
1700–1719	3.9	2.9	3.5	1.2
1720–1739	2.8	0.9	2.0	1.1
1740–1759	2.0	1.6	1.8	1.9
1760–1779	1.7	1.1	1.4	0.5
1780–1802	0.9	0.9	0.9	0.6

Notes: Note that homicide rates are measured per 100,000 people. This is important because it allows us to analyse murder and manslaughter indictments regardless of changing population size. As populations grow, it is likely that the number of homicides will increase, but this system measures the rate, not the number of cases.

Source: J. M. Beattie, *Crime and the Courts in England, 1660-1800*, (Princeton UP, Princeton, NJ, 1986).

If we look at the data from Figure 3.1 it is evident that there has been a long-term decline in homicide rates in England from the medieval period. The early numbers show us that the homicide rate was ten times that of the modern period, and that by the sixteenth and seventeenth centuries, this had halved to around five times modern figures. From the seventeenth/eighteenth centuries, it is possible to track a rapid fall to the modern level of less than 1/100,000.

How accurate is this scale? Part of the problem here is that for some areas we have very good records, while in others little survives; once again historians are hamstrung by the inconsistent survival of court records and so are naturally drawn towards counties (such as Essex and Kent) where materials exist across long periods.[9] We should also take account of periods of civil war or strife that may affect these statistics – in the thirteenth and sixteenth centuries for example, where indicators appear to rise sharply, or during the wars between king and Parliament when the normal infrastructure of law and order was effectively suspended. Finally, two other issues emerge with homicide rates: how do we know that we are measuring like-for-like, and (more crucially perhaps) can we assume that the recorded figures we have are an accurate representation of the number of unlawful killings? The answer to both is probably a resounding 'no'. Homicides can be recorded by the number of deaths or by prosecutions. So, if a man kills five people, it could be recorded as one murderer or five murders, meaning that one serial killer might artificially inflate statistics. As for accurate measurements, we know that in the years following the introduction of the 'New Police' chief constables sometimes chose not to record those homicides that might be impossible to solve (i.e. to bring a successful prosecution).[10] Nevertheless, even with all these caveats the trend is clearly downwards; the question is why did this happen?

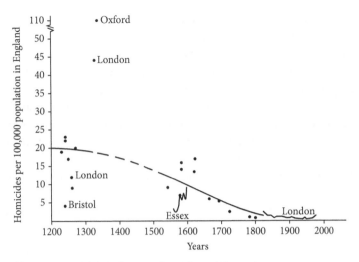

Figure 3.1 Ted Gurr historical trends in violent crime.

Explaining the decline of homicide: Stone and Sharpe's debate

In 1982, Lawrence Stone used the work of Norbert Elias to argue that the long-term decline in homicide rates was a result of a 'cultural softening of manners' in European society.[11] Elias had declared that a 'civilizing process' was at play in the early modern period whereby European states enjoyed a period of stability which allowed the power of the state to flourish. This led to a development of manners and rules that helped to create a capitalistic economy and smooth the interactions between people. Thus, neighbours, strangers and foreign traders found less aggressive ways of settling disputes and 'over time, societal norms became internalised.'[12] So, we became more rational, reflective and responsible citizens of an increasingly civilized world.[13] This process has been summed up by one leading academic thus:

> The centralization of state control and its monopolization of violence, the growth of craft guilds and bureaucracies, the replacement of barter with money, the development of technology, the enhancement of trade, the growing webs of dependency among far-flung individuals, all fit into an organic whole. And to prosper within that whole, one had to cultivate faculties of empathy and self-control until they became, as he put it, second nature.[14]

The need for violence was lessened and made less legitimate, and this manifested itself in a number of ways. As one historian has put it:

> The ['civilizing process'] suggests that people became increasingly sensitized to violent behaviour, becoming more likely to see certain kinds of behaviour as violence as well as finding it increasingly abhorrent. At the same time, social and state pressures drove the development of more restrained, self-controlled personalities, making the use of violence less likely.[15]

According to Stone, then, society had become less violent overall, and this was related to the way we interacted with each other.

His justification for this view is that homicide creates a strong emotional response in us (one of disgust) and is therefore better reported than non-lethal or indeed other forms of offending. The notion that people were much more likely to report a murder to the authorities is a position that historians generally accept.[16] In addition, Stone argued that criminal homicide is very difficult to conceal and is the only crime for which an official – a coroner – is responsible. Therefore, homicide prosecutions represent an accurate guide to homicide levels. This is deeply problematic however given the way that the criminal justice system worked in the past and what we know about crime rates, something I shall return to later.

Having argued that the decline in homicide rates was representative of a *real* fall in murder and manslaughter, Stone went on to explain that this decline was related to a broader shift in social and cultural attitudes. Stone used Elias's 'civilizing process' thesis to show that there had been a gradual taming of violent instincts among the upper classes in sixteenth-century England and Europe. This was followed by new emphasis placed on civility, politeness and property and on the settlement of disputes without recourse to violence.

Stone tried to explain that this change in attitudes was partly the result of the changing economic character of early modern Europe. As the continent moved from a feudal to a bourgeois economic system, he argued, there was a discernible change in behaviour. Society moved from recognizing honour and status as the prime male attributes, to a society where money and market relationships formed the axis of relationships and social organization. As society moved to a greater emphasis on property, it witnessed 'a growing rebellion to physical cruelty'.[17] Thus, Stone's main conclusion was that deep social and cultural changes were the underlying reason for the declining homicide rate – which was also a real reflection of the falling levels of violence. However, a number of scholars have taken issue with Stone.

James Sharpe, while accepting that there had been a fall in levels of homicide, disagreed with Stone's methodology and his explanations. In his response to Stone,[18] Sharpe challenged the suggestion that it is possible to see falling homicide rates as an indicator of falling wider levels of violence. Sharpe pointed out that coroners had considerable discretion in labelling deaths as suspicious or not, and more recent work has noted that the police could also affect homicide rates by labelling them differently or not recording them at all. [19] Coroners had the power to decide if a death was labelled accidental or not, and coroners varied in their approach to indictments across time. This continued with the involvement of the police and has led Howard Taylor to argue that 'budgetary limitations caused an under-investigation of murders and other crimes by coroners and the police during much of the nineteenth century and beyond'.[20] Second, we should be wary about Stone's complacency in believing that the emotional connection to death meant that all unlawful or suspicious deaths were necessarily reported. What was the role of the community in reporting a death? As Peter King's recent study of homicide in Britain has noted, rural communities might have chosen to deal with homicide informally while the 'relative anonymity of many urban areas' might also have allowed suspicious deaths to go unreported or unprosecuted.[21] If a community decided a death did not need a coroner's involvement, it might reduce the number of murders that were prosecuted; if a coroner was not situated in the locality (and this may well have been the situation in the more rural or peripheral areas of Britain), might locals have decided to deal with the problem themselves? These are hard questions to answer satisfactorily, but we should certainly consider the possibility that certain murders or acts of manslaughter could have been effectively concealed from the authorities. Emmerichs has argued that the homicide rate in London was 'artificially low' given the reality that coroners often recorded deaths as accidental that were clearly cases of deliberate homicide. In many cases examined by Emmerichs in the records of the London Metropolitan Archives, the coroners had simply returned a verdict of 'found drowned' after which there was no police investigation. Many of these might well have been murders, and identified as such, if modern methods of forensic science had been available. For example, one staggering case of poisoning from 1803 was dismissed as 'accidental' when it is clear that the perpetrator's actions were deliberate. It is reasonable to ask how many more instances of 'accidental death' or 'drowning' were actually homicides?[22] Emmerichs and Sharpe are not alone in suggesting that we need to be sceptical of the records; King and Ian Archer have also questioned the reliability of official records. King noted that in London many bodies went undiscovered, and some murders were not detected as such (especially those involving poison). As King says, 'Even when bodies could be identified, the circumstances of their deaths were often impossible to reconstruct'.[23] Archer used a variety of sources, but by looking in particular at newspaper reports of 'suspicious' or 'mysterious' deaths in nineteenth-century Liverpool, he has been able to 'identify deaths which were regarded as suspicious at the time, but which do not appear to have been recorded by the police or coroners as murders or even as homicides'. For example, when coroner's inquests recorded 'open verdicts' because the cause of death was uncertain, the police frequently stopped investigating. Moreover, if the police believed they had little or no chance of arresting and prosecuting a suspect, then the case could simply drop off the official record, meaning that historical murder rates are artificially deflated.[24] It seems clear then that the nineteenth-century murder rate has, for several reasons, been underestimated. Wiener, Wood and Emsley have all 'suggested that nineteenth-century society tolerated violence less and less' and that 'violent actions were increasingly prosecuted'.[25] However, we need to be clear that while the growing historical consensus – that there was a decline in homicide – is not challenged by Archer, Emmerichs or King's work on murder rates, we need to acknowledge that the level of homicides was probably much higher in the nineteenth century than historians have previously accepted. As a result, the decline is probably much less dramatic than it might appear.

Moreover, the decline of homicide could not, Sharpe argued, be simplistically linked to a feudal and market economic transition (i.e. to modernization), and this point has been taken by others who have contributed to the debate.[26] The transition from feudalism to capitalism was a gradual one and not something that either happened overnight nor equally in all areas of Britain or indeed Europe. Manuel Eisner suggested there was a correlation between levels of violence and modernization, and his research showed that homicide rates fell first and fastest in the emerging industrial economies of Britain and the Low Countries.[27] Moreover, when he extended his research to use figures from the last decades of the nineteenth century, he made strong links between urbanization and falling levels of unlawful killing, something that jarred with more modern research that has identified large urban centres as being synonymous with violence.[28] Sharpe, while offering a rigorous critique of Stone, did not really offer us an alternative viewpoint. Likewise, Stone, in his rejoinder to Sharpe, merely restated his case without really addressing the former's criticisms; fortunately, in subsequent years the debate has moved on.

Understanding the decline in homicide post-Stone/Sharpe

James Cockburn's detailed long-term study of Kent and King's study of England and Wales in the eighteenth and nineteenth centuries both offer fresh perspectives on the debate on falling homicide rates.[29] Robert Shoemaker's research into changing notions of masculinity and male honour has also refined it.[30] All of these studies point to an explanation that involves understanding why men (because overwhelmingly violence was perpetrated by males) committed homicides, and what effect a rapidly urbanizing society had on levels of unlawful killing, because most of the recorded violence that reached the courts of England and Wales (and indeed Scotland) was carried out in towns and cities.[31] Broadly speaking, Cockburn's data showed the same pattern of decline in homicide rates (at least until the 1970s) as Gurr's, and so, he could argue (for Kent at least) that the wider narrative (of a decline in homicide) was a reality. Of course, we should be wary of taking Kent as typical of England as a whole, but it is a mixed county (with both rural and urban centres) and is not peripheral to the centre (London). Thus, while it may not be *typical*, it is not *atypical* either. Cockburn casts doubt on Stone's view that falling homicide rates reflect real changes in levels of violence. This is, I would argue, self-evident for a number of reasons, and Cockburn's study reflects this.

Let us consider Cockburn's argument that medical changes mean that modern statistics for homicide badly *underestimate* previously murderous acts. From the second half of the twentieth century, advances in medical science have allowed us to save lives that might previously have been lost in violent altercations. The development of antibiotics (from Fleming's discovery in 1928 to the first successful use in treating wounds after 1945) transformed medicine. Before then, even relatively minor injuries could become infected, and patients were exposed to high levels of risk rather than recovery. We have also witnessed tremendous improvements in hospital A&E and the creation of the ambulance service and mobile paramedics, all of which have served to prevent deaths from injuries that would undoubtedly have killed our ancestors prior to the end of the Second World War. Again, as we have seen with the early discussion of crime rates, it is important to be precise about exactly *what* it is we are measuring; so, if we included attempted murder cases modern homicide statistics would look much higher.

Thus, while the long-term decline in homicide exists, the dramatic nature of that decline might be overstated. Cockburn's work also offers a more nuanced explanation for the decline, an explanation which minimizes the importance of the mono-casual, meta-narrative explanation offered by Stone. Cockburn provides evidence of more complex and overlapping factors, such as the fact that soldiers accused of unlawful homicide were tried by military courts till around 1800 and so are not included in previous statistics. Moreover, the regular involvement of England in domestic and European wars between 1600 and 1815 offered the authorities an alternative strategy for dealing with violent men. These might seem like minor fluctuations to the pattern of homicides, but they show that determining the actual rate of homicides is problematic. Most importantly for Cockburn was a change in attitudes to the use of weaponry, and this is echoed in Shoemaker's work on dueling.[32] Both downplay the importance of 'modernization' as an explanatory framework in understanding the decline of homicide and suggest more pragmatic or individual reasons for the fall.

In the sixteenth and seventeenth centuries, people routinely carried blunt or sharp instruments about their persons, and these were used for all manner of purposes (many of them quite benign and harmless such as cutting food or eating a meal). Naturally, when arguments flared, it must have been quite common to reach for a weapon. In the early modern period, Cockburn found that two-thirds of killings involved the use of sharp implements such as swords and knives (fuelled in part by the cult of dueling with rapiers). By the later eighteenth century, this figure had fallen to about a quarter. In the eighteenth and the early nineteenth century, as technology improved, killings involving firearms increased; the nature of the duel (from something involving displays of swordsmanship to 'pistols at dawn') had been transformed. However, during the nineteenth century, shooting and the carrying of guns declined. By 1841, hitting and kicking were responsible for 40 per cent of homicides (while in the sixteenth century, this figure was just 5 per cent). This is not to suggest that there was an increase in people being killed in this way, but rather that the decline in the use of weapons was reflected in a proportional rise in the use of fists or boots.

Naturally, when we consider the topic of homicide and in particular that of fighting, we need to take gender into account. Most violence is male violence; most murderers are men and while women do kill, fewer women use traditional weapons to do so. And so, as Shoemaker has argued, we need to look in detail at changing patterns of masculinity if we are to better understand the nature of homicide and its decline.[33] In his 2001 study of homicide rates in London, Shoemaker noted that in 93 per cent of homicide cases, the person accused of killing was male, and he argued that homicide is directly linked to masculinity. Perhaps even more importantly, his data showed a crucial causal link between street brawls and unlawful deaths.

Shoemaker tied this propensity towards violence to notions of male honour. In the seventeenth and early eighteenth century, masculinity and honour were intrinsically linked; a man's honour and reputation was uppermost. If a man's reputation was impugned, they had to be prepared to use violence to defend it (and this was particularly the case for gentlemen and military officers). Therefore, very trivial disputes could easily escalate into major fights or duels.[34] By the later eighteenth century, these attitudes were changing. New understandings of masculinity were emerging, and violence was no longer perceived by men as the best way of demonstrating their manhood; male violence was increasingly felt to be unacceptable and unnecessary. Therefore, Shoemaker argues, over 'the course of the eighteenth century the fundamental link between masculine honour and violence weakened'.[35] So, killings provoked by insults and jostling all fell because there was less need for men to respond when insulted, and consequently dueling accounts for a third less deaths than it did in earlier periods.

But, while it may have been these changes that primarily caused the decline of homicide in London, it is less easy to use the decline of dueling as indicative of a more widespread retreat from violence in the later eighteenth century. Shoemaker's explanation draws upon Elias's and Stone's in equating a 'cultural softening of manners' to the declining homicide rate, so while he is surely right to stress the importance of looking at men, I am not convinced that the answer is simply to be found in changing attitudes and to definitions of masculinity. What I find most problematic here is that dueling was largely an elite pastime and means of settling disputes.[36] Indeed, the literature on dueling would seem to suggest that it became less fashionable in the early nineteenth century as members of middling sorts and soldiers of lower ranks engaged in it.[37] This might indicate a desire for gentlemen to distance themselves from those that sought to ape their behaviour rather than a conscious retreat from violence per se.

This is the problem with explaining a decline of homicide over such a long time frame; we have limited ability to track change or even to determine if there was a real decline. Eisner found evidence of similar trends in Europe and made links between modernization and levels of homicide.[38] He suggests that those states that moved towards a system of mercantile capitalism based upon trade and industry (such as England, Germany and the Netherlands) saw a commensurate fall in levels of unlawful homicide, while those that remained largely agrarian and decentralized (such as Italy) retained high levels of violence. Eisner draws conclusions similar to Stone and Shoemaker, notably about the connection between notions of honour and violence. There was no longer a need for violence to protect individual or collective 'honour'. Self-scrutiny and reformation, individualization and the growing market economy meant that individuals were increasingly guided by personal ideals about proper behaviour. Individual violence fell because of a cultural diffusion of modern ideas of the self. There was no longer a need for violence to protect individual or collective 'honour'. The problem for Eisner is that while he mapped these patterns in Europe, King's work on Britain appears to show the reverse: that violence was less likely to occur (or at least less likely to be recorded) in more rural and agricultural areas. The areas with the highest density of homicide indictments were not places like west Wales, Cornwall or northern England, but instead the highest rates were in counties which had 'rapidly developing industrial and urban centres' (such as Cheshire, Lancashire and Staffordshire) or areas with a mixed industrial/agricultural economy (i.e. Leicestershire and Warwickshire).[39] This suggests that alongside Elias, we should also be looking at the work of Emile Durkheim, the French sociologist. While Elias equated a fall in violence with changing attitudes towards individual behaviour,

Durkheim suggested that it was actually the decline of 'collectivist societies' that mattered more. Within a tribal- or clan-based society, individuals are more likely to be prepared to put their own lives 'on the line in order to defend the integrity and honor of the group'.[40] So, as the state gradually emerged in the early modern period to assume power and authority, bonds of kinship (which had previously compelled individuals to defend the honour or interests of the group) were diluted or marginalized.[41]

Of course, alongside industrialization and urbanization, Europe (including Britain) experienced a rise in the centralized state with increased measures of control over individual behaviour. The state is central to Durkheim because it was the ability of the state to play a moral role in individual lives that affected change in society.[42] This is manifested through education and other institutions, or what Foucault would call 'social control'. Eisner has argued that when the state began to be seen as a force that could deliver justice, it was increasingly accepted as the main arbiter of disputes, thus negating the need for individuals to rush to take revenge or seek 'justice' (through violence) for themselves. Randolph Rolf studied homicide rates in the United States and noted a 'massive decline' in the nineteenth century. He also attributed this fall to an increasing belief in the legitimacy of government and confidence in the rule of law, as well as a growing sense of national identity, patriotism and 'fellow feeling'.[43] This echoes Max Weber's concept of *Lebensführung* or 'conduct of life' which argues that a cultural belief system (such as self-restraint) is reinforced via institutions such as the 'school, families and the church, and bureaucracies'.[44]

Eisner also argued that culture, 'more specifically the ideas of Protestantism and modern moral individualism', is an important factor in the decline of homicide. It follows then that societies that 'emphasize duty, sobriety and frugality, a methodic conduct of life, inner-directedness and consciousness as major principles of conducting one's life' would see a retreat from violence[45]; this could be summarized as the emergence of a culture of self-control (something that Wiener has also recognized).

However, we keep returning to the problem that the long-term decline in unlawful homicide began well before this. Neither developments in medicine nor improvements in mechanism of social control were in place early enough to materially affect a fall in lethal violence. We are left then where we started, with Stone and Elias and the somewhat nebulous concept of a 'civilizing process', and while these arguments are somewhat unsatisfactory and unconvincing, they remain the best explanations we have at present. Recent work on the nature of murder and manslaughter and the contexts in which it occurs may help to offer a new perspective in future years, and we should encourage work that attempts to combine studies of homicide with those of non-lethal violence. It may be that determining just how violent our current society is by comparison to those of the past is a futile and rather self-serving exercise anyway. We like to characterize the past as a violent and lawless place when in reality we have sanitized violence and removed ourselves from the necessity of confronting it on a daily basis. Everyday casual and unnecessary physical violence towards strangers, family members, colleagues and animals remains a part of twentieth-century living despite legislation, education and a whole host of other social control mechanisms.

Historians have already discovered that measuring unlawful homicide is problematic, even with the not unreasonable assumption that most suspicious deaths are reported to the authorities. Stone has also suggested that a long-term decline in homicide rates from the early modern period can be used as a proxy indicator of an increasingly less violent society. However, most of the violent acts committed in the past did not result in homicide, and historians have been presented with even more problems when they have attempted to calculate levels of non-lethal violence, as sources here are much less rich than those for murder and manslaughter. What is clear, however, is that non-lethal violence was very prevalent in past societies, and that attitudes towards it gradually moved from toleration to condemnation. This topic will be discussed in due course, but first let us continue to look at lethal violence and the nature and context of homicide in the past. What follows is an analysis and typology of murder from the late seventeenth to the early twentieth centuries.

A typology of homicide: From 1660 to 1914

Murder comes in many forms, as anyone who has watched a contemporary TV drama will be aware. Some forms of murder are relatively mundane, while others can be quite bizarre. Throughout all of the period covered by this book, murder was punished by death, but the lesser offences of attempted murder or manslaughter only brought with them a spell of imprisonment at worst (and sometime less than this). In addition for most of the period discussed, the police (or previous policing agents) had very little forensic intelligence they could draw upon to help them catch killers. The infamous Whitechapel murders of 1888 demonstrated the inherent difficulties in catching murderers who struck at victims with whom they had no prior known relationship. Likewise, while there may have been hundreds of serial killers in English history, the deficiencies in detection means that 'Jack the Ripper' has emerged from history as England's first such phenomenon.

Serial killing is a peculiar and thankfully very rare offshoot of homicide, and I do not intend to discuss it here; if murder has anything to tell us as historians of crime, it is in the more everyday killings that we should search for enlightenment.

Defining what murder is would seem to be a quite straightforward thing; after all, it is one of the most fundamental building blocks of human society set out in *The Bible* that 'thou shall not kill'. But of course it is not that simple. Killing can be legitimized (by the state, e.g. in war or as a punishment), or where it can be justified. As a result, then, homicide (as with all other forms of crime) is 'socially constructed. Unlawful homicide is not an absolute.'[46] This means that murder is really 'a legal definition of a criminal event that can only be applied at the conclusion of a trial', or after all attempts at appealing that judgement have been exhausted.[47] Murder, then, is bound up with statute law and practice, and these have changed and developed over hundreds of years.

Under the terms of the Offences Against the Person Act (1861) murder is when,

a man of sound memory, and of the age of discretion, unlawfully killest within any county of the realm any reasonable creature in rerum natura [in existence] under the King's peace, with malice aforethought, either expressed by the party or implied by law, so as the party wounded or hurt etc. die of the wound or hurt etc. within a year and a day after the same.[48]

Murder implies an intent to kill (which distinguishes it from manslaughter), and from that it is generally important for a court to establish that the defendant had a motive for doing so, as this helps to establish the intent. However, while establishing a motive might assist juries to determine guilt, English law is not framed to discriminate around motive; it was generally unlawful to kill regardless of motive, nor, with a couple of notable exceptions, did the status of the victim affect this.[49] Murder is one of the few crimes in which the nature of prosecution has changed relatively little since the seventeenth century. While there have been important changes, in essence, murder remains a crime that is prosecuted by the Crown and carries the severest sentence available in law. For all of the time period covered by this volume, the sentence for those convicted of murder was death, usually by hanging, but in some cases (for example, women convicted of killing their husbands) a more extreme form of capital punishment (burning) was employed.[50]

Early English society also viewed murder as abhorrent, and the state acted against it. After all, murder 'usurped God's right to take life, symbolizing rebellion against providence, nature, authority and Christian society'.[51] Laws surrounding unlawful homicide were tightened in Tudor England to make it easier for suspected murderers to be caught and put on trial, and penalties were imposed on individuals and communities that failed to take action to catch and prosecute murderers. The office of the coroner had been established in the twelfth century, but until the early modern period, the coroner was more of a 'revenue officer than [a] policeman or prosecutor'.[52] The position became more official and regulated in the late sixteenth century, but coroners remained amateur and open to accusations of corruption. This situation was little changed in the seventeenth and early eighteenth centuries, and while there is no hard evidence of foul play in the coroner's examination of the body of George Linnell (who was killed while attempting to serve a warrant on the father of Thomas Gordon in 1788), it is highly likely that a local coroner sided with local people to ensure that the Gordons (all outsiders) were held responsible for the constable's murder despite there being considerable cause for an alternative view of events.[53] There were attempts to make the office of coroner more effective and to remunerate them properly for investigating all suspicious deaths, but they were only awarded independent salaries in the second half of the nineteenth century. Even then, it would seem that coroners remained largely amateur, untrained and open to the influences of others. As we have seen, Emmerichs's work has suggested that the costs of inquests may have meant that coroners in nineteenth-century London were under pressure from JPs *not* to investigate suspicious deaths unless there were clear signs that foul play was evident. There was no obligation for coroners to have any formal medical training until well into the twentieth century, and so many of them 'simply guessed at the causes of death'.[54]

Is murder ever justifiable? The law recognizes that there are defences against a charge of murder that work even when it is admitted that the accused killed his or her victim. The first of these is self-defence; the second is provocation; and the third is diminished responsibility. The principle is that these forms of defence 'centre on a limited and formally structured range of mitigating reasons for killing, out in issue at trial by the accused with a view to being convicted of manslaughter rather than of murder'.[55]

Under law, a plea of justifiable homicide might work if the accused could demonstrate that they were protecting their home, family or person from attack from intruders or were otherwise in danger of their lives. But self-defence could be quite hard to prove, especially if the majority of those giving evidence had sided against the defendant and there was no independent evidence to support such a claim.[56]

Provocation is equally hard to prove, and judges periodically ask jurors to think about what they might have done in the same situation, what indeed is 'reasonable'? Do years of domestic abuse, for example, justify the murder of the abuser? In 1902, Kitty Byron was convicted of killing her abusive partner but drew considerable sympathy for the beatings she had suffered at his hands. Provocation, while not accepted as a defence, was beginning to affect outcomes and the punishment of victims. The twenty-first century has finally recognized that serial abuse can provoke individuals to commit murder, and an amendment to legislation in 2009 introduced a new defence of 'loss of control' accorded by a fear of 'serious violence'. Does finding your wife in bed with her lover constitute grounds for provocation? Juries may well have taken circumstances into account, but historical records, even though they are considerably richer for homicide than for many other crimes, rarely allow us to get inside the minds of those sitting in judgement on defendants.

As for diminished responsibility, this technical defence was introduced in 1957, but there had been previous attempts to reform the law around the use of an insanity plea. In 1843, Daniel M'Naughten was found not guilty, by reason of insanity, of the murder of Edward Drummond, secretary to Sir Robert Peel the sitting Prime Minister. The case created a precedent, and parliament called for a ruling from Queen's Bench which established that the insanity plea worked if it could be shown that the accused was unable (on mental health grounds) to determine right from wrong.[57] Charles Westron was recommended for mercy by the jury at his trial in 1856, even though they found him guilty of murdering a solicitor he accused of 'ruining' his life. Westron's defence claimed he suffered from 'delusions', *not* that he was insane, but that these delusions affected his judgement and that he 'did not know it was wrong to kill a person'.[58] In 1863, Broadmoor Prison opened its gates to the criminally insane as the law increasingly recognized that some murders were caused by 'diseases of the mind' rather than base motives such as personal gain or jealousy.

Murder was also quite hard to prove. While police today have a sophisticated armoury of forensic techniques and equipment, most of this dates from the period after the Second World War. Even something that we tend to take for granted – fingerprint technology – did not make an impact until the twentieth century. The first successful use of fingerprinting in England was the conviction of Alfred and Albert Stratton for robbery and murder in 1905, and this 'well-publicized case paved the way for the routine adoption of the fingerprint technique'.[59] The attempts to catch 'Jack the Ripper' in 1888 were hampered by even more basic deficiencies in forensic knowledge such as the inability to tell the difference between animal and human blood, something modern police detectives are routinely able to do. While we begin to see medical expertise being used to assist investigations and in trials from the early nineteenth century onwards (particularly in accusation of infanticide), the science of forensic pathology was not established until well into the 1900s.

In fact, most of the detection or discovery of homicide in the early modern period was conducted by amateurs; so barber surgeons, constables and midwives all contributed in attempts to determine cause of death and possible signs of murder. Coupled with this was the fact that popular or folk methods of detection prevailed; so '[m]uch was read into the appearance and position of the corpse when it was discovered', and the bodies of victims were often publically displayed in the hope that guilty persons would reveal themselves by their reactions, even the 'facial expression of a corpse was believed to hold clues about the killer'.[60] This might sound ridiculous to modern ears, but even late Victorian society was prepared to believe that the retina of murder victims carried the imprint of their assassins.[61]

The murder victim had other ways in which they might help apprehend their killer. If they survived the initial assault, they could name their assailant and, until the later 1700s, coroners and inquest jurymen regularly attended the bedsides of those that were dying of mortal wounds. In 1874, dying declarations were further undermined, and in the 1870s, they were finally ruled inadmissible in court. At the same time, medical evidence offered by professionals became more important both in determining the cause of death and in speculating on the guilt of the accused. Even after death, early modern society believed the victim might 'speak' and name his or her assassin. The appearance of ghosts (as in Shakespeare's *Macbeth*, or the Duke of Hamilton, killed by Lord Mahon in a celebrated duel in 1712) allowed accusations to be made. The popular belief from the medieval period was that 'murder will out', and as one tract from the early decades of the eighteenth century demonstrates, this belief continued into the 1700s: 'Such is Heinousness of this Sin above all other transgressions, except what is immediately directed against God himself', it argued, 'that it ordinarily meets with the severest Punishment, and Vengeance always treads upon the Heels of the Guilty'. The author then went on to list the unfortunate ends that had met murderous actors in history.[62] A similar pamphlet, authored by Henry Fielding, provided further 'examples of interposition of providence in the discovery and punishment of murder'.[63] However, while Fielding's curious narrative continued to be published long after his death in 1754, this is probably a reflection of a popular market for publications that exploited unusual crime stories to excite and entertain as, by the later eighteenth century at least, more faith was being placed in less divine forms of apprehending or exposing murderers.

An area which has seen development in recent years is an attempt to distinguish first-degree from second-degree murder, perhaps to placate public opinion which is particularly outraged by horrific or multiple murders. While both first-degree and second-degree murder involve a deliberate intent to do serious injury to someone with the risk of death, the former implies that death was the ultimate aim. This was understood as early as the fourteenth century, but judges 'did not routinely consider whether murder was premeditated or not until the mid-sixteenth century'.[64] There was an attempt, in 1867, following a Royal Commission report, to draw a line between first-degree murders (those that should be awarded a capital sentence) and second-degree homicides (those for which life imprisonment was appropriate) and so do away with judicial or ministerial discretion, but it never reached the statute book.[65] In his 1883 history of the criminal law, Sir James Stephen asked 'Is there anything to choose morally between the man who violently stabs another in the chest with the definite intention of killing him, and the man who stabs another in the chest with no definite intention at all as to his victim's life or death, but with a feeling of indifference whether he lives or dies?' He concluded that there was not.[66] Motive remains at the heart of all murders (and indeed, all good murder novels and dramas).

Towards a typology of murder: Whodunit and why?

So how can we study murder in the past? A useful way is to consider its context and the motivations behind it. As this reveals, murder and its related lesser crimes of attempted murder and manslaughter show considerable continuity across 450 years of history.

Professor Fiona Brookman (a recognized expert on homicide) has attempted to provide working typology of homicide that goes some way (within the restrictions that she identifies) towards understanding the motivations of killers. Her list is necessarily modern (she used data from the period 1999 to 2001), but it remains a useful jumping off point for historical analysis.[67] Let us look at her typology below:

1. Domestic Homicide
2. Homicide in the course of other crime
3. Gang homicide
4. Confrontational homicide
5. Jealousy/revenge (unrelated individuals)
6. Reckless Acts (unrelated individuals)
7. Racial violence
8. 'Other' unspecified circumstances
9. Context/motive unknown
10. Unusual cases (such as serial murder, terrorism, mass homicide, homicide among children)

Not all of these categories work especially well for the early modern to the early-twentieth-century periods, however, so, for our purposes, we can dispense with racial violence and terrorism. Gang murder is also problematic because while incidents certainly occurred (as my own research and that of others has shown[68]), they were rare and much less easy to quantify than they are today. One of her categories – domestic homicide – is depressingly consistent. Domestic homicide is the most common form of murder in modern Britain, and this holds true for the past. It is also overwhelmingly a male crime, so while women did kill their partners, they did so in much lower numbers than men. As a consequence of this, and of prevailing attitudes towards women which saw them as subordinate to men, murder by women engendered a higher level of condemnation in the period 1660–1914. Therefore, women that killed children were a negation of their role as mothers, and those that killed their husbands were seen as subverting the 'natural order' of patriarchy.

Men who killed women (*femicide*) were much more likely to be closely connected to them than in other scenarios of murder. Today wives and partners are much more likely to be murdered by a current or former lover, or by someone connected to them, and there is little reason to doubt that this was the case in the eighteenth and nineteenth centuries. The problem historians have is in determining the relationship between killer and victim given the quality of recorded material that has survived. We might suppose that jealously, possessiveness, control and rage (all identified by Brookman as motives for femicide) are applicable to murders in the past.[69]

Likewise, murders that arise out of other forms of crime (which can more accurately be termed 'instrumental homicides'[70]), such as robbery or burglary, show a clear continuity between the past and the present. Here, the victims are not so obviously gendered and will often include policing agents or those otherwise involved in catching criminals or preventing crimes. Men were frequently the victims of homicides that occurred as the result of arguments or disputes, many after angry exchanges in public and often associated with drunkenness. Men were much more likely than women to engage in *confrontational homicide* – killings that arise from face-to-face conflict or argument – often related to contemporary notions of honour or masculinity. This is most obviously illustrated by the duel, where two men (usually elite or military men) settled an argument or defended their honour by resorting to a controlled fight with swords or pistols. While dueling began as a formal encounter between members of the aristocracy, it developed to embrace combatants from lower down the social ladder before it eventually declined or was suppressed.[71] The 'fair fight' continued in to the later nineteenth century but was largely considered to be a working-class device for settling disagreements.[72] Brookman found that most men that killed other males in the twentieth century were 'relatively young' (33 or younger), with most victims being equally young (under 36). Offenders were most likely to use knives, blunt instruments or their fists or feet to kill, and strangers or acquaintances of the accused were the most frequent victims.[73]

Such disputes could flare up easily, especially when they involved alcohol, and easy access to bladed weapons could result in deaths in the past that might be avoided from the later twentieth century. Disputes could also be the result of prolonged or sustained disagreements. Revenge murder, as its name suggests, refers to killings which involved disputes that had festered over a long time period, or where culprits acted in reaction to an incident or series of events that had unfolded over time. Revenge killings have a greater degree of premeditation, and this can often make them appear more serious or heinous. It was also more likely that victim and aggressor would be known to each other. In early medieval England, the archetypal revenge killing was the product of feud between rival families, some of which could last for decades. In Anglo-Saxon England, those committing homicides were 'required to bear the feud, or else hand over a sum of money amounting to the worth of the dead man (the wergild)' in compensation.[74] So-called 'blood feuds' (or vendettas), such as that described by Richard Fletcher,[75] were recognized as destructive to the public peace and were instrumental in medieval attempts to establish the rule of law.

Investigating the context of homicides offers us the opportunity first to look for motives in killing and second, to see how past societies depicted murder. While we might expect to find that murder in all its forms was considered as something to be condemned, societies often exhibit variations in the particular sorts of murders they find most disturbing or worthy of the most severe punishment. In modern Britain, it is probably the murder of children that garners most opprobrium from the popular press. This reflects both the innocence that we associate with infants and young people and the premium that our society places on youth. Given that in 2014 the average life expectancy is 81, the death of a child appears particularly tragic. When we consider that in Hanoverian England average life expectancy was around 35–40 years (and by the Victorian period perhaps 43–45), we can see that attitudes might be different, especially as so many children died in infancy. Death is a much rarer occurrence today and our lack of familiarity with it might be expected to colour the way we view mortality.

This is not to suggest that our ancestors were unconcerned about homicide; they were, but at different times, they exhibited particular anxiety about certain forms of murder such as the killing of masters by their servants and murders that happened in the course of street robberies. The 1752 Murder Act is an example of legislation being passed in an attempt to offset widespread public fears about unprecedented levels of highway robbery and murder, while in 1531 poisoning was made punishable by boiling (although this extreme sentence was later repealed under Edward IV). It was the secrecy of poisoning that made it such a serious offence, an attitude that was revived in the nineteenth century as the newspapers reported with alarm on a series of murders carried out using arsenic and other substances that were hard to detect (and to defend against).

There is not the time or space to investigate historical murders at length here, but two short dips into the archives allow us to look at some of the contexts for homicide in the past. First, we can explore the evidence of murder from the popular print culture produced in the late seventeenth and eighteenth centuries before looking at a selection of homicides prosecuted at the Old Bailey in 1888.

The sample of cases from the earlier period is necessarily selective because they are all taken from the printed broadsides and 'last confessions' of executed offenders that were sold at, or soon after, the execution of offenders for a variety of crimes. Many of these were bound and sold in volumes such as *The Lives of the Most Notorious Criminals*.[76] One of the most famous of these narratives was that of Catherine Hayes (1722) who conspired with her illegitimate son, Thomas Billings, and another man to murder her husband.

Hayes and her accomplices had killed John and cut up his body. His head was discovered by a watchman and exhibited in public as a means of identifying it (and possibly to entrap the culprits). In her confession, made just before her public execution by burning, Hayes claimed provocation. She declared that Hayes 'beat me, he abus'd me' and 'he almost starv'd me'. Even more dramatic was the confession of Lady Aberga15ney who also met her end by burning in 1712. She had killed her son ('by roasting him, till his bowels burst out of his body') and her husband by the use of poison. Her apparent motive was the protection of her daughter who had been left no provision in her husband's will.[77] Both women had transgressed contemporary mores surrounding female character and behaviour, and little emphasis was placed on any possible justification for their crimes.

Charles Slaughter and John Allen both conformed to recognizable tropes surrounding homicide by murdering their 'sweethearts'; Slaughter beat Jane Young and threw her body in a pond while Allen cut Mary Finch's throat and left her to die in a ditch. Allen, a 17-year-old merchant's son, was hanged near to the scene of the crime in Holloway, north of London. In Allen's case, the motive was rejection as Mary had refused his offer of marriage; others also killed out of jealousy or rejection. George Dingler had been separated from his wife for a year and had singularly failed to persuade her to return. When she finally agreed to come home, it took him less than a couple of hours to stab her and attempt to cut her throat. Her cries alerted the neighbours, but while a rescue was effected, she later died of her wounds. James Cluff killed a fellow servant, Mart Green, who was carrying his child, again because she may have rejected his advances. John Clarke killed his fellow servant after getting her pregnant; here the motive seems to have been to prevent his wife and children finding out about his adultery.

Another man (simply referred to as Mr C......) hanged his wife at home following an argument and tried to pretend she had taken her own life. Elizabeth Osborn, a young woman of 19, cut her stepmother's throat while she slept because she had refused to let her marry her lover. In another sorry tale, Ann Graham, a blacksmith's wife, killed two of her own children by strangling them and attempted to take the life of a third, before cutting her own throat and leaving her husband to discover the tragedy. The inquest jury was told that she was 'labouring under strong mental derangement' and returned a verdict of insanity. Mental health issues that might have afforded a plea of diminished responsibility in a modern court may have saved John Sparke from the noose. He strangled his own mother to death during a drunken argument but he was widely known to drink and to use 'out of the way language' which indicated that he was not fully in command of his senses.

Thomas Douglas and William Sparks were shipmates and drinking companions, but after a bout of excessive consumption, Douglas became 'rash and inconsiderate', and he stabbed his mate to death. Thomas Johnson was murdered by his close friend, another John Clarke, because he had been seen out with his friend's common law wife. Finally, there is the celebrated case of Elizabeth Jeffrey and John Swan who, like Catherine Hayes, hatched a conspiracy to murder her uncle Joseph in 1752. Elizabeth was having an adulterous affair with Swan, and her uncle disapproved; the pair hoped to profit from his death as Elizabeth was the main beneficiary in his will.

What these cases reveal are some of the basic motives for murder: jealousy, rejection, greed and revenge, and these can be seen again in a selection of trials that reached the Old Bailey in the late nineteenth century. I have chosen 1888 because that year will be forever associated with a spate of unsolved murders in London's East End that have been dubbed the Whitechapel Murders perpetrated by 'Jack the Ripper'. While the 'Ripper' murders have commanded the attention of researchers and the public, they actually have relatively little to tell us about homicide in the nineteenth century. Partly, this is because we have no idea who committed these crimes or why. But, there were many other murders in 1888, and for some, we know quite a lot about the circumstances in which they occurred and the individuals that carried them out. So, as with our earlier example, we can attempt to understand the context of these homicides and the motives of those that committed them, this time by studying the records of the trials of those accused.

There were thirty-two trials for murder or manslaughter heard at the Old Bailey between January and December 1888, and these were equally divided between murder and manslaughter. There were also seven cases of infanticide or concealing the birth of child that had subsequently died. There were a further eighty-two cases of wounding: in different circumstances some of these might have ended up as murder or manslaughter charges. While men accused of homicide outnumbered women by a factor of three (76–24 per cent), the proportion of victims in its gender was much closer (seventeen men/fifteen women). This would support modern statistics for homicide and everything researchers have argued for the historical record; simply put, men are much more likely to kill and women are more likely to be victims.

In the manslaughter trials, only three defendants were fully convicted. Lawrence Sullivan killed John Hart after a fight in Seven Dials, but Hart had survived long enough to give a statement in hospital and at least one witness described the fight between the two men as 'fair'. Sullivan was convicted of manslaughter and sent to prison for three months.[78] Robert Hodges and William Walker, who roomed together in Finsbury, had been drinking when they fell out with each other over the ownership of a shilling and, in the words of one witness, 'went out to fight'. Again, it was a so-called fair fight with 'rounds', but when Hodges struck his fellow lodger 'in the third', he fractured his skull in the fall and died a few days later in hospital. Hodges also received a three-month sentence.[79] Alfred Winwood caused the death of Elizabeth Gibbs, the 68-year-old wife of an estate agent, when his van hit her and her husband as they were crossing the road. Mrs Gibbs was badly injured and lost an arm but died a few days later, while her husband only suffered cuts and bruises. Winwood had not stopped – it what was we would now deem a 'hit and run' – but he was apprehended by a passer-by soon afterwards who had seen the incident. He had been driving fast and on the wrong side of the road, and he was sent to gaol for six months hard labour.[80] Today, it is unlikely that such an event would have landed Winwood on a manslaughter charge or even a prison sentence, which reminds us of Cockburn's analysis in the decline of homicide debate.[81]

There were eleven guilty verdicts in the murder trials. Two other men and four women were found to be guilty but 'insane at the time' the murder was committed. As a consequence, they were ordered to be 'detained during Her Majesty's pleasure'. One example of the female defendants is indicative of the sort of murders that resulted in a guilty but insane verdict. Emma Aston killed her two small children because it seems that she could just not cope with supporting them without the help of her absent husband. She owed money to her landlady and various shopkeepers and suppliers, and while her husband, a commercial traveller, had previously been sending her money, this had gradually dried up. Emma was suffering from severe headaches, and presumably at some point, her troubles overwhelmed her, and she cut the oldest boy's throat and smothered the infant with a pillow. She told her landlady that 'I was mad, I was mad; I felt such a weight on the top of my head, something impelled me to do it'. The court agreed that she was insane at the time she committed the crime.[82] John Brown had been a patient in the Westminster hospital for several months and then lived in a convalescent home for six weeks until his discharge at the end of September 1888. Brown had been suffering from pneumonia and pleurisy, but the doctors there also noticed the signs of melancholia or what modern psychology would understand as a form of depression. When he returned home, his wife complained that he made excessive sexual demands on her, even when she was pregnant. He grew suspicious of her and accused her of inviting other men into the house, striking matches to look for them and exhibiting several other signs of increased anxiety. After an argument, Brown confronted his wife and cut her throat. Several witnesses testified to his bouts of insanity, including the surgeon at Holloway Prison who told the court that 'he is under the delusion that he heard many voices speaking to him, neighbours and friends to his wife, saying that she ought to be ashamed of herself, that she ought to be killed'.[83]

Of the others who were tried for murder, some, like Ernest Vickery, were found guilty of the lesser offence of manslaughter. Vickery killed Robert Maxwell, an engineer's foreman who was married to his sister. By all accounts, Maxwell was a violent man, especially when he had been drinking, and on this occasion, he had arrived home drunk and knocked his wife and child about. Vickery intervened and a fight ensured. In the process, Maxwell was hit with piece of wood, and Ernest admitted he had had his 'revenge' on his brother-in-law. However, the jury decided that it had not been Vickery's intention to kill and convicted him of the lesser offence of manslaughter; he received five years imprisonment.[84]

Three of those convicted fully of murder were recommended to mercy by the court. George Galletly killed Joseph Rumbold in a gang-related murder in Regent's Park, but the jury recommended mercy on the grounds of his youth (he was only 17). While the judge passed sentence of death upon him, he was later reprieved by the home secretary.[85] Age was also one of the reasons that the jury felt that James White did not deserve to die for the murder of his wife Margaret. James was 65 and scraped a living as a shoemaker. He and his wife had been out with family drinking, and after they returned home, an argument started about alcohol and money (or the lack of it). James hit her with a poker and pushed over Margaret's chair; she fell off, hit her head and died. James apparently told the doctor that it was 'a bloody good job, too' when he was told she was dead. James told the policeman that arrested him: 'My God, I settled her; she would not do as I wanted her, so I hit her three times on the head with the *soft end* of the poker; that is the knob', and while he was on the way to the police station he added, 'We have lived happily together for 41 years, but if she had done as I told her I should not have killed her; I suppose the Old Bailey will be my lot'. The jury decided that while it was murder, it was not 'wilful'.[86] William Pierrepoint benefitted from the sympathy of the jury and court not because he was notably young or old (he was 31), but because they could appreciate the extreme stress that he was under when he killed his son. Pierrepoint and his small family were being evicted from their home in Camberwell because they were behind with the rent, he was out of work and they were 'in a starving condition' according to his landlord who gave evidence in court. A small crowd had gathered as they left and William was clearly upset, angry and, in a rage at something said to him, he held his youngest child up and threw him to the ground crying 'Patty, you shall be the victim!' Possibly the child simply slipped out of his arms, evidence from witnesses was not always clear. He was arrested later that night and had been drinking; he claimed it was an accident not intentional and while the jury found him guilty, they recommended he be spared the rope.[87] In fact, only a handful of cases involved guilty verdicts which were likely to result in a hanging, so what contexts led to these crimes?

Henry Bowles murdered his wife, Hannah, and her younger brother Edward with poison. Bowles worked as a gardener and told the doctor he called when his wife and nephew were taken ill that she had a heart condition, and he feared they may have eaten poisonous mushrooms by mistake. But this was a subterfuge. Bowles had poisoned them using a small amount of strychnine, and this was eventually discovered after a careful post-mortem. The motive was greed; Bowles had insured both of their lives (Edward's more than once as was common with children) and had intended to cash in on the life assurance. As this was a deliberate and calculated murder, he received a death sentence without mercy.[88] Levi Bartlett also killed his wife, smashing her skull with a hammer. The pair frequently argued, witnesses deposed, and more often than not when they had been drinking. Threats were quite commonly made but laughed off when they sobered up. There was some debate as to Bowles's state of mind, and another jury might have found him insane as well. This one did not, and he was sentenced to death.

In fact, death sentences for killing were remarkably rare in the later nineteenth century. From 1 January 1880 to 31 December 1889, of 202 persons found guilty of unlawful killing only forty-one were given a capital sentence. Most were sent to prison for life or detained at Her Majesty's pleasure. What this analysis of homicide cases from early eighteenth and late nineteenth century shows us is that most murder was domestic; the victims were wives and children and occasionally husbands. The motive was rarely anything other than a drunken rage or fit of jealousy. Increasingly, the mental state of the accused became a key element in determining culpability and thence punishment. Ordinary people appear to have committed murder, not extraordinary ones. And, they did so in ordinary circumstances. Victims were stabbed or had their throats cut and were clubbed to death or smothered. More elaborate forms of killing, such as beheading or poisoning, were rare. As we might expect, when blazing rows were the catalyst for homicide, the weapons used were those that were easy to handle. It is a depressingly mundane catalogue of murder and not one that would provide the media with the necessary sensation that it required to entertain its readership. As a result, the Victorian press, like the eighteenth-century print culture that preceded it, chose to focus on murders that excited most fear or disgust.

Assault and changing attitudes towards interpersonal violence

Non-lethal violence is not only hard to quantify, it is also hard to define. In law, non-lethal violence has a number of definitions, and these have been redefined and codified in a handful of key pieces of legislation (notably the Offences Against the Person Act 1861[89]). The 1861 Act (and its predecessor in 1828[90]) essentially attempted to simplify the laws surrounding interpersonal violence. The significance of these two acts will be addressed shortly, but first it is necessary to look at the nature of the law that applied to petty violence throughout the long eighteenth century.

The offence most often associated with non-lethal violence in early modern and eighteenth-century England was assault. According to the 1785 version of Richard Burn's handbook for eighteenth-century magistrates, an assault was:

> An attempt or offer, with force and violence, to do a corporal hurt to another; as by striking him with or without a weapon; or presenting a gun at him, at such as distance to which the gun will carry; or pointing a pitchfork at him, standing within the reach of it; or by holding one's fist up at him; or by any other such like act, done in an angry, threatening manner.[91]

In addition to assault, there was battery, which involved actual injury, however trivial it was. Both descriptors are suitably vague, and even the great law writer William Blackstone struggled to be more precise. Writing in 1765, he declared assault was:

> An attempt or offer to beat another, without touching him: as one lifts up his cane, or his fist, in a threatening manner; or strikes at him, but misses him; this is an assault.[92]

Assault was a breach of the peace, and maintaining the peace was uppermost in the duties of the magistrate (or Justice of the Peace). This is evident from Michael Dalton's *Countrey Justice* in which he stated that 'peace is taken for an abstinence from actual and injurious force, and offer of violence' and could include threatening words or behaviour as well as actual physical harm to another's body.[93] Assault was therefore a vague term that could cover a wide range of actions from punching someone, to slapping their face, or pushing, tripping or waiving knife at them. It could even involve threatening words or public insult. But, it was an offence that was treated very much as a matter for the individuals concerned *not* as a criminal action. Those accused of assault were most commonly dealt with at the lower reaches of the criminal justice system because, as Dalton's explanation demonstrates, assault represented the breakdown in good social relations, and that was a matter for the magistrate to sort out.

In consequence, assault was frequently dealt with at summary level, without recourse to a jury. This gives historians a further problem because so few records survive, either from petty sessions or from individual magistrates. If a case could not be resolved before a justice (because it was more serious or the complainant wanted to take the matter further), it was likely to be heard at the quarter sessions. However, it appears that only a tiny proportion of assault cases were sent up to the quarter sessions by eighteenth-century magistrates. In the City of London, for example, the figure for the last quarter of the century is a mere 6 per cent, so here 94 per cent of assault accusations were dealt with at summary level.[94] For northern Essex, in the same period, a sample of 100 assault-related examinations before the JPs shows 'only one [that] appears to have led to formal indictment at the Essex quarter sessions'.[95] More serious violence could result in a trial at the assizes, but this was an even rarer occurrence. The assaults that reached the assizes courts were usually those involving actual harm or the use of weapons. Only a very small number of crimes fell into this latter category – between 1674 and 1800, only forty-three cases of assault were tried at Old Bailey of which fifteen resulted in a 'not-guilty' verdict.[96] By contrast, on average, 1,000 cases of assault were being presented annually to the City of London magistracy in the last quarter of the eighteenth century.[97]

The reason so few cases reached the jury courts is clear to see: assault was a very wide term which could mean anything from threatening behaviour to actual violence, the shaking of fists to the use of weapons. As Peter King has written, 'It is not difficult to imagine the customers in a crowded alehouse jostling, pushing, threatening, and hitting each other often enough in one evening to keep the local quarter sessions busy for weeks, if all such acts ended in an indictment.' [98] Of course most of them refrained from formal methods of resolution, opting instead to ignore the insult, take their own revenge later or accept an apology from their aggressor. As a result, the figure for unreported and unrecorded acts of petty violence is vast. The first problem historians have then is in attempting to quantify the extent of non-lethal violence in past societies, and the task is, to all intents and purposes, pretty much impossible for early modern period and the long eighteenth century.

The situation does get better in the nineteenth century, as records improved and the Police Court system was formalized after 1848. But the pattern remains the same, and Abraham's recent study of Northampton and Nottingham shows that nearly all assault cases were dealt with by the magistrates, without recourse to a full jury trial.[99] Indeed, the vagaries of the term 'assault' remained despite attempts to consolidate the law in 1828 and 1861. Thus, according to the Police Code book for 1870, 'A common assault is the beating, or it may only be the striking, or touching of a person or putting him or her in fear'.[100] Beat officers had considerable discretion in interpreting the law of assault when they dealt with acts of interpersonal violence.

The Offenses Against the Person Act of 1861 contained a number of offences such as *grievous bodily harm* (GBH) and *wounding* that allowed action to be taken by the police, but *common assault* was still extremely vague and was punished with a fine or a small term of imprisonment in a house of correction. Minor assaults were not indictable and so were only dealt with summarily. Under the 1861 Offences Against the Person Act, any assault that caused harm – and this could mean merely bruising or minor breaks – could result in more serious punishment. Actual bodily harm (ABH) carried a prison sentence, as did the more serious offence of GBH. Wounding carried a maximum sentence of five years imprisonment, whereas GBH could be punished by life. Furthermore, if a court believed that there was an intention to kill the victim, then a charge of *attempted* murder could be levelled. These broad definitions of interpersonal violence have to some extent survived into current legislation, the most recent reclassification being in 1998.

Almost inevitably, then, a large degree of discretion was involved in the prosecution of assaults. An assault without a weapon (or without an associated attempt to steal) was not indictable and so did not involve a jury trial, but add one of these elements and it became more serious. Note the comment of the Criminal Registrar in 1909:

> There is no… clear rule, and (it may be said) no uniform practice as to the degree of violence which makes it proper to prosecute an assault as an indictable offence…. Many of the common assaults and still more of the assaults on police constables, now disposed of summarily, amount in reality to malicious wounding, causing grievous bodily harm, or even felonious wounding, and if they were sent for trial, would swell the number of indictable offences against the person.[101]

Given the vagaries of the legislation and the civil nature of assault, it is perhaps not surprising that historians have generally shied away from studies of it in preference for the more reliable area of homicide. However, there has been a growing body of work in recent years that has considered the prosecution of assault at the summary level. Most of this research has concentrated on the eighteenth century with a small amount touching the nineteenth. While more work is necessary, it is now possible to comment upon a couple of themes relating to non-lethal violence in the period 1700–1900. The first of these is the nature and context of assault – or who assaults who and why? The second is the way in which assault prosecutions were dealt with in the eighteenth and early nineteenth centuries, and what has been seen as the gradual criminalization of assault.

The nature of assault charges brought before the eighteenth-century magistracy

The first observation to be made about the prosecution of assault at summary level in the eighteenth century is that it was a very common offence. In all studies of the Georgian magistracy, assault (and related offences such as threatening behaviour) constitutes a very high proportion of all offences heard by JPs. Overall, assault accounted for approximately one-third of all business conducted at the City of London magistrate courts in the last quarter of the eighteenth century.[102] In Essex, in the period 1770–1813, of the 1,200 sampled cases 325 (27 per cent) were for assaults.[103] In rural Wiltshire, between 1744 and 1748, assaults made up 29 per cent of the business brought before William Hunt.[104] The figure was even higher in Boldon in the north east of England where 43 per cent of offences heard were assault prosecutions.[105] The amount of prosecutions for assault was also notably higher in urban areas; offences involving 'interpersonal violence, threat or defamation' accounted for 64 per cent of justices' caseloads in urban Hackney in 1730–1741, and 51 per cent for the City of London in 1729–1730.[106] In his study of petty crime in London and rural Middlesex for an earlier period, Shoemaker also noted that assault was among the most commonly prosecuted of offences.[107] So, the picture we have is of magistrates spending a considerable amount of their time dealing with accusations of assault brought by a range of different individuals from all sorts of social backgrounds.

We might expect the levels of prosecution to be higher in the towns and cities of England, for a couple of reasons. First, and this is particularly true of London, magistrates were simply much closer at hand and available in the period. In Middlesex, there were competing justices who operated as businesses sometimes touting for business in the streets in a way not dissimilar to present day 'No win, No fee' legal firms who offer to represent anyone who stubs their toe on the pavement.[108] The City of London's magistracy sat in rotation for much of the eighteenth century, and after 1752, there were two summary courts that sat six days a week, 52 weeks of the year, making the law at this level very accessible. By contrast, in rural areas, aggrieved victims of petty violence may well have had long distances to travel to find a magistrate to complain to. They may also have felt less of an inclination to prosecute given the close communities that are associated with rural areas; instead of taking legal action, victims might have opted to resolve the matter themselves. The second factor was the nature of the urban environment and increased tensions that may have arisen as a result of large populations of people living together in close proximity. This is best illustrated by examples – all of these drawn from the records of the City of London's summary courts (or from London press reporting of them).

In 1789, Josiah Simmonds complained to the incumbent Lord Mayor about Joseph Cooper at the Mansion House justice room. Cooper had run into him and smashed the sheet of glass that he had been carrying. In his defence, Joseph Cooper said he had turned a corner too fast and, in stepping aside to avoid a passing horse and cart, had collided with Simmonds.[109] In another example, a German visitor to the capital, unhappy about the careless way in which a local drunkard was barging into people as he staggered along a busy street, chose to retaliate when he was shoved. He punched his assailant who fell down and cracked his skull on the wheel of a passing cart. This resulted in the German's appearance before a magistrate on a charge of assault. These sorts of incidents, along with hats being knocked off, pails of water (or worse, chamber pots) being thrown, fists waived and punches landed, were the reality of assault charges in the City.

There were clear associations between petty violence and alcohol, and London's many pubs and taverns were often venues for assaults. In 1815, an Irishman named Thomas Cobham, rather the worse for drink, was refused more beer by the landlord. Cobham complained and insisted that as a 'gentleman' he was entitled to do as he pleased and vowed to remain in the parlour until he was served. The landlord, not wanting the peace of his quiet room shattered by such a boorish character, threw him out. Cobham picked himself up and after shouting verbal abuse from the street inveigled his way back inside. He went straight up to the landlord and attacked him while his victim tried to restrain him. The fight escalated into a barroom brawl, and Cobham went on to 'destroy every article of glass, china, delft, etc. in the bar, independent of which he smashed several panes of glass, a patent lamp, and other articles' before he was eventually subdued and arrested. At his examination, he made a public apology, which he agreed to publish in the papers, and paid the landlord compensation for the damage done to his establishment.[110]

Not only is the link to alcohol well established, it is also evident that most (but not all) of this petty violence was committed by men. This statistic is supported not only by the records of the City summary courts but also by work elsewhere. In London, in the late eighteenth century, around 65 per cent of violence was perpetrated by males (in fact possibly as high as 70 per cent if assaults on watchmen, constables and other officials are included).[111] This is almost identical to Morgan and Rushton's figure of 69 per cent for Boldon in the north east of England.[112] In his study of eighteenth-century Bath, R.S. Neale found that over three-quarters of assailants were men[113], and so, as Shoemaker noted, when we come to consider violence, it is impossible to separate it from contemporary notions of masculinity.[114]

In the City of London, men hit men (41 per cent), men also hit women (24 per cent) and a significant number of women hit other women (22 per cent), and a very similar statistic (23 per cent) emerges for rural Essex in the late eighteenth century.[115] However, it seems that very few women attacked men (5 per cent), and this might actually reflect the fact that men were unlikely to prosecute a woman who assaulted them because it could be seen as a slight to their reputation.[116] Assaults on officials were a small but important occurrence (at 7.5 per cent of all assaults) because assaults on constables and watchmen were much more likely to be taken seriously by the courts.[117] This pattern continued into the nineteenth century when assaults on policemen drew stiffer penalties from the capital's stipendiary magistrates.

If male violence was gendered (in that fights erupted in ale houses and on the streets), women also fought in circumstances and spaces that reflected their own gendered spheres of influence. So, women fought in market places, in and around homes and in shops. They were also less likely to resort to formal weapons, and in consequence, the violence between women was generally less serious and less likely to lead to serious injuries. Thus, in 1794, Mary McIntyre was prosecuted for spitting in the face of Ann Bird, and in 1788, Mary Clark was 'very much beat and scratched' after she was assaulted by Jane Satchell. The records do not reveal the causal factors behind these assaults but two other women fell out over hair ribbons in 1794, while an ongoing feud between neighbours Elizabeth Hemmings and Sarah Pipkin resulted in the latter hurling a chamber pot at her neighbour after several other incidents of insult and injury.[118] Women and men both acted to protect their reputations, and for women this meant reacting to slights on their chastity or fidelity. The eighteenth-century summary court was therefore an important arena within which women could challenge cries of 'whore' or 'harlot' in much the same way that the consistory (or church) court had been used in the early modern period.[119]

Assault was characterized, therefore, as a *civil* offence throughout much of the period covered by this book. As a consequence of this, assault actions at law often took the form of an arbitration process. When individuals such as those we met earlier came before the magistracy, they were urged to reconcile their differences. As Wiener outlined, 'in its 1814 edition, Burn's Justice of the Peace, the standard handbook for magistrates, instructed that in assault cases "the court frequently recommends the defendant to talk with the prosecutor, that is to make him amends for the injury done him," and thereafter impose a small fine.'[120] This is not to argue that the courts did not take assault seriously or, more importantly, that the victims of assault were content for little punishment to follow. We need to see assault prosecutions instead as an important part of the mechanism of maintaining good social relations in the growing metropolis of London. Sometimes, it would seem that the main point of prosecution seems to have been simply to have the grievance aired and to obtain an apology. The small fine was often intended either as a form of compensation or was used to cover the cost of the warrant that brought the case to the presence of the justice. Other forms of compensation might not necessarily involve money at all. In May 1794, two combatants agreed to settle their dispute with a gallon of ale, which the sitting magistrate observed as being 'the practice with these fellows'.[121]

Settlements were very much the norm for cases heard at summary level; 46 per cent of assault cases heard by the summary courts of the City were settled between the victim and the defendant. In a further 35 per cent of cases, the magistrate simply dismissed the case, deciding that the offence was either trivial (particularly so when the protagonists were female) or that there was guilt on both sides, and sometimes because the victim failed to turn up. For more serious assaults, or when no agreement could be reached between the parties, the JP could bind over the assailant and order them to produce sureties against their future behaviour. Failure to produce sureties could mean a spell in prison, but imprisonment was not generally used as a punishment for assault in the eighteenth century at the summary court level. However, this situation began to change in the nineteenth century and historians have argued that assault began to be considered less as a civil and more as a criminal offence as the century unfolded.

From *civil* to *criminal*? The changing nature of assault prosecutions

A useful way to look at the prosecution and punishment of assault is to explore the outcomes of cases that reached the quarter sessions. Most offenders that reached a trial before a quarter sessions jury were likely merely to be fined a shilling or less. A small number were imprisoned, while a few received a higher fine, and a sizeable number were found 'not guilty'. In fact, it has been suggested that the main motive of those victims of petty violence that went to law at this level was to secure some financial compensation.[122] In late seventeenth and early eighteenth-century Westminster, some women who sued the court system emphasized that they were 'bigg with child' as part of a strategy to gain the sympathy of the magistracy,[123] and it is likely that there were multiple and overlapping reasons for taking assault cases to law. However, by looking at outcomes for the Essex bench from the middle of the eighteenth century, we can begin to notice a change.

From 1748 to 1821, there was a marked shift in attitudes by the quarter sessions court.[124] While in the middle of the eighteenth century, the Essex bench were most likely to fine those they found guilty of assault, and by the early nineteenth century, imprisonment was increasingly being used to punish offenders. This move was accompanied by a concomitant decrease in confessions as more of the accused entered 'not guilty' pleas, presumably to avoid what they considered to the more severe sanction of incarceration. In King's view, it was the increasing availability of imprisonment as a viable sentencing option that determined this. This may have been coupled with growing concerns about lawlessness in the mid-1780s following the 1783 Treaty of Paris (which ended the American War of Independence) and before the outbreak of war with revolutionary France (in 1793). Instead of being simply dismissed or fined, more and more violent men (and some women) whose cases reached the quarter sessions were being sent to prison for short periods. In part, this was because the prisons were increasingly available to be used for this purpose. But, the availability of prisons also reflects changing attitudes towards offenders – that there was an increased belief in the early nineteenth century that these sorts of offenders could be reformed, and that prison was an appropriate way of dealing with them.

It is also possible that the civilizing process that we have discussed earlier with regard to lethal violence can be applied to non-lethal forms. Emsley has declared that it 'was in the early nineteenth century that violence began to be described in England as a social problem'.[125] Wiener and Wood have both argued that there was a 'civilizing offensive' at work in nineteenth-century Britain that may have affected attitudes towards violence.[126] Again, this is critically linked to notions of masculinity; while less emphasis was being placed on males fighting to preserve their status and honour, there was a new focus upon self-control and dignity. As we have seen, Shoemaker touched upon this in his work on weapon carrying, dueling and the decline in insult.[127] As the century progressed, the opportunities for demonstrations of acceptable violence diminished, and where once men might have resorted to their fists 'civilized male honor could [now] be won and maintained in ways unconnected to violence and physical prowess'.[128] This civilizing process may also have influenced attempts to reduce the severity of the criminal code in relation to physical punishments. However, the shift away from punishing property offenders with death heralded a move to tackle violence more seriously. While property crime had been the focus of attention in the eighteenth century, the richer elements of society in the second half of the nineteenth increasingly felt threatened by the mass of humanity below them, and while the law protected their property, it did not seem to offer much protection for their bodies. As Wiener puts it, they feared a new 'barbarism'.

> Economic growth seemed to most to do nothing for the security of the person (indeed perhaps diminishing it by, for example, making it more affordable for more people to drink themselves into belligerent intoxication). A new 'modern' form of barbarism [now] seemed possible.[129]

The period after the Napoleonic Wars saw fewer deaths from dueling and working-class fights, and as a result, Spierenburg argues, the 'image of residual murder darkened'[130]; in other words, the more distant violent death became, the more society was concerned about it. This might seem counter intuitive, but actually it makes a great deal of sense. We tend to inflate our concerns around subjects that we are less familiar with, and so, murder, which is an extremely rare occurrence, occupies a disproportionally high position of fear in our collective consciousness, that is, to our actual risk of being murdered. This fear – a top-down middle-class fear of the underclass – influenced punishment policy. While penalties for property criminals were being 'reduced in the 1830s, maximum sentences for various kinds of assault were actually raised, both in law and in practice.'[131] And this change is reflected in the edition of Burn's handbook for 1825, where the emphasis was placed on *punishing* assault rather than on brokering an agreement between the victim and accused. Under the terms of the 1828 Offences Against the Person Act, assault became a more serious offence, one worthy of greater sanction from the state. By 1837, the maximum penalty for common assault was increased to three year's imprisonment. As Wiener has argued, as Queen Victoria came to the throne 'the transition from "civil" to "criminal" treatment of assault was almost complete.'[132]

The Victorians' underlying fear of violence and violent offenders was brought into sharp focus in the 1850s and 1860s as London was gripped by the garrotting panic. This caused a huge upsurge in reported incidents of violent street robbery and led to police actions against habitual offenders and legislation to toughen prison regimes. A similar panic about the lower orders and their propensity for violence occurred when Chartism was at its height in the 1840s; so-called 'outrages' such as these undoubtedly affected attitudes towards violence and possibly increased prosecution rates in the short term. Once again, measuring the extent of violent crime is far from an exact science. However, it is possible to argue that contemporaries in the nineteenth century *believed* that their society was becoming more violent, if we believe the number of articles penned in the newspapers, popular magazines and popular literature. But were they right to be so worried?

The decline of violence in the nineteenth century

Vic Gatrell noticed a rise in the prosecution of violent offences from 1857 to around 1880 and then a decline. Assaults rose gradually from 408.2 per 100,000 to 424.6 before falling to 226.2 by the end of the century. How do we explain these figures? Gatrell argued that the fall in prosecutions for violence reflects a real fall in violence in the period to the outbreak of the First World War. This is indicated not only by a fall in homicide and wounding, but also more broadly in assaults and (importantly in his view) a fall in assaults upon the police.[133] But, there are several ways to look at this. As he himself admitted, an interpretation of the statistics of violent crime (indeed any crime) is bound up with attitudes towards crime, and these are in turn affected by events (such as the garrotting panic). More recently, research has questioned whether a fall in the statistics of violent crime actually constituted a broader fall in violence.[134]

One explanation for falling indictments might be related to alcohol and attitudes towards drunkenness. In 1872, the Licensing Act tightened up the laws surrounding drinking. Initially, this brought landlords and bar staff into conflict with drunken clients who refused to go home, something John Archer has termed 'a power struggle for drinking space.'[135] The arrests of drunks often resulted in assaults upon the police and fears about drunken behaviour may well have caused people to report more crimes, but, as the licensing laws took effect, and public drunkenness declined, so did incidents and therefore the fear they engendered. Thus, as Gatrell says, 'the possibility has to be admitted that a relaxation of anxieties about drunkenness might have relaxed anxieties about drink-related violence as well, thus reducing the urge to prosecute for petty assaults, and thus in turn reducing the visible rates.'[136] A recent government survey found that 47 per cent of violent offences committed in 2011/12 were directly related to the consumption of alcohol.[137] The correlation between alcohol consumption, deviance and violence (in addition to health issues) has prompted calls for minimum pricing of alcohol by unit. This is fuelled by a perception that our society is blighted by a 'binge-drinking' culture.[138] Part of this debate reflects a broader concern not only about youth culture (something that was looked at in Chapter 2) but also about the state of Britain's cities at night.

This emphasis on control (or indeed a lack of control) echoes social commentary from both the eighteenth and nineteenth centuries and played a part in the gradual acceptance of a need for a professional police force. It was the emergence of the 'New Police' in English cities and towns from the 1840s onwards that Gatrell points to as the second-causal factor in the decline of violence. While at first they struggled to establish their authority, by the last quarter of the century their presence was largely accepted by the population. Not only this but they 'were increasingly sought out when violence erupted, and more workers began turning to the authorities rather than to direct, physical retribution.'[139] Thus, the role of the police, as the nineteenth-century 'keepers of the peace', was crucial both in curbing 'bad behaviour' on the streets and in persuading the working classes that they were an appropriate conduit to use in the resolution of interpersonal disputes.

For an assault to become a criminal statistic, there had to be a chain of events: a victim must report the incident, the police had to take action and a court had to hear the case and adjudicate. Discretion was available throughout this process, and many assault cases were settled without any need for a court hearing. If the police chose to deal with assaults without formal prosecution, this would have caused the recorded crime rates to fall. The police, whose role was largely to deter potential criminals and those who would resort to antisocial behaviour, walked a thin blue line. They could use other forms of punishment such as semi-official (or 'legitimate') violence against violent members of the community. Godfrey's research in the late nineteenth century suggests that more often than not the police chose not to prosecute assaults.[140] Assault carries a particularly difficult problem of proof, especially if little or injury is actually caused. Witnesses can be suspect, and often it comes down to one person's word against another's. The actions of the nineteenth-century Police court were also prejudiced on class lines. A working-class man that assaulted an employer was far more likely to be convicted than if an assault had taken place between equals. The word of a prostitute who was a victim was unlikely to carry much weight with a magistrate, while the word of a police constable assaulted by a drunk was unlikely to be disbelieved. So, we need to be aware of these procedural and legislative effects on crime rates as well as the effects of public opinion. Godfrey is certainly sceptical that there was a real fall in violence, commenting that the 'national and local statistics are simply not credible as a mirror of a real decline in violence'.[141] If there *was* a fall in public violence, are there other ways in which we can try and explain this?

Wood has used Elias's notion of the 'civilizing process' to explore the nineteenth century and the male experience of violence, and Wiener has identified a process whereby male violence was criminalized in the Victorian period as part of a wider reconstruction of gender that had been going on from the late eighteenth century. Let us look in more detail at these arguments.

As society became less violent, its citizens supposedly became more rational, reflective and responsible. The need for violence was lessened and made less legitimate, and this manifested itself in a number of ways. Thus, we see the gradual decline in public physical punishment from the late eighteenth century, and the gradual withering away of the 'Bloody Code' (e.g. the end of whipping for women and then for most men, in public if not completely). More serious punishments for major interpersonal violence were introduced (under the 1828 and 1861 acts), and there was a related decrease in the severity of punishments for crimes against property. As Gatrell has pointed out, 'when a man was flogged for robbery with violence [at mid-century], he was flogged for the robbery and not for the violence'.[142] This had begun to change but there was still a sense that punishing violent men was somehow pointless; since violence was considered an impulsive act, deterrents were unlikely to work.

Instead, the emphasis was increasingly placed upon self-restraint and self-discipline. Spierenburg has noted the connection between masculinity, honour and violence and has argued that men take pride in attacking men and react to insult with violence or the threat of violence.[143] Most violence was male-on-male violence, and men rarely reported it 'for reasons which are, in part, historical and bound up with notions of masculinity'.[144] In fact, Archer notes that far from behaving badly, men who resorted to violence were actually behaving 'normally'.

This debate needs to recognize that there were competing masculinities in the later 1800s and the early twentieth century. One of the effects of the 'civilizing offensive' that Wiener and Wood have highlighted was the way in which illegitimate violence was increasingly associated with the working-class male. So, for the late Victorians, '[v]iolence was identified as working class, and working class reciprocally identified as violent'.[145] This is an important corollary and fed into the wider discourse of the 'criminal class' and the so-called 'residuum' or underclass. Violence (and the excessive consumption of alcohol) was sharply juxtaposed with 'respectability', and so the growing intolerance to violence has to be seen within this contemporary discourse.

For the working classes, violence was very much a part of daily life, and for men, violence was a way to resolve disputes. Working-class fights adhered to rules and 'codes of honour', they had to be 'fair fights' and had a degree of formality about them. One Liverpool magistrate commented that if the two men that had been brought before him for fighting each other had merely contended themselves with using their fists, he would have let them off, but as they resorted to weapons, he was bound to apply the law.[146] Bare knuckle fights were bound up with notions of Englishness; while foreigners carried knives, it was argued that 'real men' used their fists. As Wood argues, for working-class men 'violence remained an integral part of their daily lives' as they had fewer opportunities to demonstrate the new 'spiritualized sense of honor' that was being practised by middle-class men.[147] Nevertheless, organized fist fights by pugilists – the precursors of modern boxing – became increasingly formalized in the 1800s and were eventually regulated under the rules devised by the Marquis of Queensbury in the 1860s.

In reality, many fights got out of hand, and the weapons used were those that came easily to hand – bottles, tools, furniture and so on. In Manchester and Salford, 'scuttling gangs' used highly decorated belts to injure their victims; boots and clogs were also employed to kick in heads and break limbs, as did London gangs, and Liverpool's 'corner men' were not averse to inflicting real injury on their rivals and passers-by. The myth of the 'fair fight' was often just that – a myth.

The reasons for violence were multiple and often overlapping. Workplace violence resulted from overused 'banter', bullying or intimidation as a consequence of industrial action, while domestic squabbles and drink-related disputes all preceded minor assaults and actual violence with injury. Wood described the use of what he calls 'customary violence' as a way of settling disputes between social equals. These were fights in which 'public space was deliberately manipulated to maximise the openness of the fight'.[148] My mind immediately thinks back to the playground and the ring of small boys surrounding two kids scrapping. And just as the teachers would step in to break up these fights, such displays of overt masculinity were increasingly at odds with the demands and intentions of the state, who acted to try and control them – usually in the person of the 'bobby' on the beat. Instead of protecting one's honour with his fists, a real man was expected to use his head. The 'man of honour' in the Victorian view was equated with the 'man of dignity'. The male gender was being, in Wiener's view, reconstructed:

> The newer expectation for men, well established among gentlemen by the end of the eighteenth century, was extended in the following century in two directions: from gentlemen to all men, and from public, male-on-male violence to 'private' violence against subordinates, dependents and the entire female gender.[149]

Wood warns us against complacently accepting that the Victorian period ushered in a new civility and an absolute intolerance of violence. Moreover, we need to understand that the civilizing offensive was not simply orchestrated by the middle classes as this fails to recognize the reality that many working class people strove to adopt their own interpretation of 'respectability'. There is also the hoary subject of domestic violence which, rooted as it was in 'ideals of male dominance and female passivity that had strong cross-class agreement, reinforced by liberal notions of non-interference in private life', was able to resist 'change until late in the nineteenth century'.[150] The high levels of domestic violence that were reported and prosecuted in late Victorian Northampton and Nottingham bear witness to the durability of male violence towards women.[151] Violence may have been moved off of the streets, but it did not disappear.[152]

Violence: Some concluding remarks

The prosecution of assault changed over the long period of this study. From being an offence punished in both the civil and criminal courts by a small fine at most, it came to be punished as an offence against society. Violence always provokes fear within society and is played upon by the media and government agencies as in the moral panics surrounding the garrotting panics of the 1860s, the clashes between mods and rockers a century later and the current concern about knife-wielding teenagers in hoods. Assault in the eighteenth and nineteenth centuries covered a wide variety of interpersonal violence, from pushing and shoving to actual violence with or without weapons. Intolerance towards violence grew alongside growing urbanization and economic change and the growth of empire. The extent of a civilizing process can be questioned but not dismissed. The growth of imprisonment and the development of policing may also have impacted the treatment of violent offenders. We should be equally wary before we dismiss the pragmatic explanations for changes in the criminal justice system. But, while we remind ourselves that Lawrence Stone suggested that falling homicide rates could be seen as an indicator of falling levels of violence in society, Peter King sounds a warning to those who see a decline in homicide as a reflection of a growing sensitivity to violence: 'Unlike murder rates, which were in long-term decline during this period, assault indictments were rising fairly rapidly from 1750–1820, providing a cautionary note to those who wish to use murder rates as a guide to more general changes in levels of interpersonal violence.'[153] Godfrey recommends that historians make use of personal life histories of violent offenders and their victims, and where this is possible (for the late nineteenth and early twentieth centuries, for example) scholars are beginning to do so.[154] Not that this is without its problems of course; offenders like Arthur Harding, who have left us a detailed history of their activities, cannot be taken at face value while plenty of testimony has been rendered through the coloured lens of the researcher or interviewer.[155]

So, while we may not be able to account entirely for the fall of homicide (or even to agree about when that fall was or where it occurred), we can look at the nature of and context of interpersonal violence in history.

In the early twentieth century, Dr Crippen provided the press with the ultimate murder case. Crippen became a fixture in Madame Tussauds' *Chamber of Horrors* and an iconic figure in British criminal history out of all proportion to the extent of his crimes. This is because murder occupies a special place in the popular imagination, far beyond the reality of the crime. In this chapter, we have seen that violence has been, relatively speaking at least, somewhat neglected by the early historians of crime. Fortunately, this omission has started to be addressed in recent years. The debate surrounding the long-term decline in homicide has rumbled on, and I think that we are now in a position to start to address some of the key points that Stone and Sharpe's earlier exchange raised. Reported homicide cannot be a prism through which to observe all societal violence because scholars have categorically shown that recorded crime is only *one* measure of levels of offending. Nor, in my view, can we be complacent about the extent to which a decline in elite and middle-class fighting necessarily led to a fall in working-class violence. Violence may have become more regulated and public displays of force increasingly subject to sanction, but, as Wood and Wiener have shown, this merely meant that generations of working-class women ended up with broken limbs and blackened eyes, or much worse, as male brutality went indoors. Historians have completed extensive work on domestic violence across the period from 1660 to 1900 and have started to explore all forms of 'petty' violence in work on the JP and police magistrate, but there needs to be much more research into how violence was used (as a form of control) and at attitudes towards it and its toleration within working-class communities.

Murder has tended to be presented and researched from a more 'popular history' or 'true crime' perspective. The tales of infamous killers, from the seventeenth-century folk tale of 'Bluebeard' to 'Jack the Ripper', and from the horrors of the Ratcliffe Highway to the use of technology to the capture of Crippen, have been tackled by publications of varying quality. Indeed, our collective appetite for murder news has been fed by popular print culture for well over 300 years and shows no sign of abating anytime soon. Murder is good box office, and violence, the bloodier the better, remains a staple of popular entertainment. Crone's excellent study of the Victorian fascination with the darker side of life also ends with an observation that we have hardly become less obsessive or mawkish in the twenty-first century, and can we really make great claims for being civilized as a result?[156] We now need for the work Crone has carried out on London in the nineteenth century to be rolled out across the country and perhaps extended into the early 1900s.

We lack a big history of murder; there are some useful studies of particular forms of homicide and some important articles around murder rates and the variety of punishments used for murderers.[157] There is also information about race and gender and its effect on homicide within wider studies of criminality, but to my knowledge, there is no complete dedicated study of homicide in Britain for the eighteenth and nineteenth centuries.[158] It is hard to tell the story of murder without descending into a 'true crime' narrative; even here, I have been unable to avoid looking at individual cases from the archives. But, murder needs to be treated to a statistical analysis in just the same way that other, lesser, crimes have been. Most homicide it would seem is predicated on very similar motives to other forms of offending: greed, jealousy, desperation and opportunity. Murderers, by contrast, are more likely to be separated out and treated as if they are quite distinct from the rest of society, as dangerous 'others', irredeemable and somehow alien. In my experience, the murderers I have met (and it is only a handful I admit) or have studied seem to be very ordinary people, quite like you and I. The reasons they had for murder might seem shocking to us, but perhaps that is because we have never stood in their shoes or made the choices they made. The dawning realization that mental health affected the way that people acted in the later nineteenth centuries is now much better understood, and we could do with more studies that look at the motives behind murder and at the circumstances in which the killer found themselves. This might provide factual historical evidence to counter the arguments in favour of a reintroduction of capital punishment.

CHAPTER 4
THE NATURE OF PROPERTY CRIME

The importance of property in eighteenth- and nineteenth-century England

It might seem obvious that private property and its protection mattered to the Georgians and Victorians, after all it matters to us. But, it is possible to argue that the criminal justice system, throughout the long period covered by this book, placed a markedly stronger emphasis on the protection of property than the modern system does. Twenty-first-century law and order legislation and practice is more easily identified with the protection of the individual's person, rather than their personal property.

This is perhaps most clearly demonstrated by the growth in the late seventeenth and early eighteenth centuries of the number of statutes that prescribed the death penalty for seemingly trivial appropriations of property. In effect, the theft of goods valued at one shilling or more could lead to death by hanging.[1] This so-called 'Bloody Code' has come to characterize the Hanoverian justice system, and while the code was considerably less 'bloody' in practice, there were still over 200 individual acts of parliament that attempted to protect the property of the privileged few from the grubby fingers of the lower classes. While the period from the 1820s saw a dramatic falling away of the use of the death penalty and the removal of capital penalties from all property offences, this was replaced by a less discretionary use of transportation and imprisonment which meant that petty thieves and more serious robbers and burglars were exiled to Australia or confined under harsh conditions in ever greater numbers.

John Locke and property rights

Underlying the principle of private property is a wider concept of property rights and property usage, much of which we take for granted. Today, for example, if we buy something from a shop, we take ownership of it and understand that. The shop 'owns' that item until we exchange money for it, and it then becomes 'ours'. The underlying concept of 'theft', therefore, is the taking of goods or items that are owned by someone else. But, this simple understanding of property rights has evolved over centuries and is blurred by the fact that some goods are manufactured while others appear naturally. In the early seventeenth century, a Dutch jurist, Hugo de Groot, drew a distinction between usage and ownership of property; *dominium* in Latin 'originally meant the power to make use of what was not privately possessed' rather than *private* property (as the term came to be understood later). This philosophical nuance matters because, as de Groot noted, 'When property or ownership was invented, the law of property was established to imitate nature'.[2] The English philosopher most often associated with theories of property is John Locke (1652–1704), and his ideas about government and individual rights had considerable influence on the eighteenth century. I do not have space to engage in a thorough discussion of Locke's writings, but a brief understanding of his views on property will be useful in the context of property crime in the long eighteenth century.

Locke worked for the Board of Trade after 1688 and argued that every man was entitled to a basic level of subsistence: namely food, drink, clothing and heat. He therefore supported the idea of a Poor Law that protected people from the perils of destitution and starvation. Locke also understood the concept of property ownership, and how it had changed over centuries. Working from Biblical principles (as was natural in late seventeenth-century society), he argued that God had given the earth and all its bounties to mankind to use. At first, this meant that man used just what he needed and that anyone taking more than his share, to the detriment of his neighbour, was in effect breaking *natural* law. Gradually, as a largely agricultural and then an emerging commercial society developed the principle of monetary exchange, this allowed for profit and the accumulation of wealth. As long as those at the bottom were able to benefit from this system (or at least were not impoverished by it), Locke believed it existed for the good of mankind as a whole, because it preserved the Earth and its natural resources for future generations.

However, at this point, it became necessary to create laws to protect private property because disputes surrounding ownership were, in Locke's view, a major cause of conflict between people and, subsequently, monarchs and nations.[3] Locke tied property ownership to labour and property that was the result of labour (whether this was the cultivation of crops or the manufacture of goods) and so gave a greater value to it. In essence, men had a right to property they had created or 'earned'. Following on from this, the invention of money allowed men to own more property than they needed to simply survive. For Locke, the duty of government was to protect 'human entitlements' (what we might call 'rights'), and property was one of those 'rights'.[4] This of course involved protecting the rights of property owners through law.

It is very doubtful that Locke would have approved of the draconian 'Bloody Code' however; he believed that even the poorest had rights and would presumably have sympathized with those that stole to feed or clothe themselves or their families from those that possessed surplus wealth (a practice historians have termed 'social crime' and discussed in Chapter 5). But, the principle of property ownership was reasserted after the British Civil Wars (when radical groups such as the Diggers and Levellers challenged the notion of individual property rights and asserted that God had made the Earth 'a common treasury for all'[5]). The importance of property was also noted by William Blackstone, the eighteenth-century jurist and law writer, who stated that the 'third absolute right, inherent in every Englishman, is that of property', and maintained that the laws of the land were primarily conceived to protect that property.[6]

Property ownership was also interlinked with voting rights and parochial duty and so became very much a mark of social standing. Even after the first reform of the electoral system in 1832, a very small minority of men were entitled to vote, and the ownership of property above a certain value (or the payment of certain rates or taxes based upon wealth) was a qualification for jury duty and a host of other privileges or obligations. Ownership of property was therefore *fundamental* to eighteenth- and nineteenth-century society in a way that is no longer so much the case in modern Britain. Having established the underlying importance of property (aside of course from the emotional and practical attachments people have to 'things'), this chapter will now go on to explore the nature of property crime in the period between 1660 and 1914.

A typology of property crime

The nature of this crime has not changed that much since then of course; robbery, burglary and shoplifting are all crimes under law today, although they are punished very differently. Nor has the general demographic of the criminal changed significantly; most eighteenth- and nineteenth-century property offenders were young, male and working class. Property crime was (and to some extent remains) gendered; so women and men stole slightly different items and in different ways. This will all be explored below, but since some areas (such as shoplifting) have been covered in some depth elsewhere, they will only receive scant attention here. Nor will this chapter dwell too long on the punishments available for property crime; in part, this is because until the early nineteenth century, there was little real distinction in law between serious and less serious property crime, and more practically, because Chapters 12 and 13 deal with punishment and penal histories at length.

So what follows is an examination of the nature of property offending in the period we are interested in but one that relies quite considerably on London and the prosecution of offences at the Old Bailey. This is partly because the printed reports of trials at the Old Bailey (the *Proceedings*) offer us such a rich archive over a long period of time. However, we should recognize that property crime outside of the capital was similar but different, notably in its scale. London drew all manner of people to it and presented a tempting array of goods that could be stolen in an ever more consumerist society. We should not neglect county or regional studies that have looked at property offending in other parts of England, but this chapter will focus for the most part on the capital.[7]

The importance of property crime in criminal statistics

There are over 200,000 trials listed on the *Old Bailey Online* website, and these only represent a partial figure of crimes prosecuted at the Central criminal court between 1674 and 1913.[8] Furthermore, these were only the crimes that reached trial before a jury (many being dealt with at quarter session or summary level, or which were thrown out by the grand jury as 'no true bills'). However, even with these qualifications 211,112 is a large body of data to work with.

As Table 4.1 demonstrates, of those 211,112 trials more than 85 per cent were concerned with some form of property offending. Indeed, despite society's collective obsession with violence, murder (including infanticide) and manslaughter account for only 2.33 per cent of all prosecuted crime at this level. This demonstrates the heavy emphasis on property crime in the criminal justice system.

It is harder to measure property offending at the lower levels of the criminal justice system because we are not blessed with a database as user-friendly as the *Old Bailey Online* for the lower courts, but we can use the recorded crime rates that were published each year from 1805 onwards to get a national picture of property crime compared to other offences. Here, we will concentrate (as the Home Office did) on indictable crime and use the data provided in V. A. C. Gatrell's important essay from 1980.[9] Gatrell's article looks at change over time – specifically 1836–1913 – and ranges across cases brought before assizes, quarter sessions and the magistracy. Using Home Office definitions, Gatrell arranged offences under the following categories: offences against the person, offences against property with violence, offences against property without violence, malicious

Table 4.1 All trials at The Central Criminal Court (Old Bailey), 1674–1913.

Offence	Number	Percentage
All non-property	31,171	14.77
Grand Larceny (until 1827)	41,265	19.55
Simple Larceny (after 1827)	30,640	14.51
Theft from specified place	15,344	7.27
Pocket picking	13,655	6.47
Stealing from Master (employer)	10,927	5.18
Burglary	10,450	4.95
Coining	10,213	4.84
Forgery	7,046	3.34
Fraud	6,910	3.27
Receiving stolen goods	5,664	2.68
Embezzlement	4,950	2.34
Robbery	4,846	2.30
Animal theft	4,230	2.00
Highway Robbery	4,169	1.97
Housebreaking	4,006	1.90
Shoplifting	3,454	1.64
Mail Theft	1,767	0.84
Extortion	405	0.19
Total property	179,941	85.33

Source: www.oldbaileyonline.org

offences against property, offences against the currency and miscellaneous offences. He also compared change over time by using a rate of offences per 100,000 people; this enabled a comparison that allowed for a rising population. So what did he find?

Not surprisingly, property crime again dominates, and within this, non-violent property crime was by far the highest category. In the period 1836–1840, there were 139.6/100,000 larcenies (offences against property without violence) compared to just 12.3/100,000 offences against the person (and 9.9/100,000 violent property crimes). The rate moved across the century (to a high of 257.7 in 1861–1865), but the difference between violent offending and property crime remained considerable.[10] So, with this in mind, we can now turn to a deeper exploration of the sorts of property offences that were regularly prosecuted in the long eighteenth and nineteenth centuries.

Here, it is worth using those same Home Office definitions of violent and non-violent crimes. However, violence here includes the threat of violence (often a feature of highway robbery) and violence as a *violation* (as in burglary). For simplicity's sake, I have grouped property offences into 'major' (robbery, burglary, housebreaking and coining) and 'minor' (other indictable thefts), as well as including a later section on non-indictable property crimes that were prosecuted at the summary level.

Major property offences

Highway robbery and robbery

As we saw in Chapter 2, the archetypal eighteenth-century criminal was the highwayman. Personified in popular culture and reinvented in later centuries, characters such as Claude du Vall, the Golden Farmer and Dick Turpin have come down to us as romanticized anti-heroes representing a time when crime was somehow disconnected from the mundane and every day.[11] Notwithstanding the reality of the lives of men like Turpin, we persist in seeing seventeenth- and early-eighteenth-century highwaymen as latter-day Robin Hoods rather than the often violent and ruthless criminals many undoubtedly were. Here, we need to look at the reality of robbery rather than the image that has been presented in popular fictions.

Robbery was defined as violent theft, although the level of violence employed could vary considerably. The Old Bailey provides a useful entry point for considering the nature and extent of robbery as from 1674 to 1913 there were over 9,000 trials for violent theft reported in the *Proceedings*, and these can be represented in Table 4.2.

Table 4.2 shows a dramatic falling away of highway robbery from the 1830s, and the explanation for this will be considered later. What is also noticeable are the high numbers of trials for highway robbery in the 1770s and 1780s, a period when public disquiet about crime was at its peak.

So, what exactly was the difference between robbery and any other form of theft? Robbery referred to a theft that involved the forcible separation of a victim from his property and included an element of threat or peril. As one late-seventeenth-century pamphlet put it, robbery was as 'the felonious taking of any thing from the person of

Table 4.2 Trials for violent theft at the Old Bailey, 1674–1913, counting by decade.

| Decade | Highway Robbery | | Robbery | |
	Number	Percentage	Number	Percentage
1670s*	28	76.00	9	24.00
1680s*	56	55.00	45	44.00
1690s*	146	77.00	43	23.00
1700s*	24	86.00	4	14.00
1710s*	144	75.00	48	25.00
1720s	311	88.00	44	12.00
1730s	338	82.00	76	18.00
1740s	269	79.00	72	21.00
1750s	260	86.00	43	14.00
1760s	199	87.00	31	13.00
1770s	480	93.00	36	7.00
1780s	639	90.00	75	11.00
1790s	264	78.00	74	22.00
1800s	206	79.00	54	21.00
1810s	425	85.00	76	15.00
1820s	373	79.00	99	21.00
1830s	6	2.00	266	98.00
1840s	0	0.00	298	100.00
1850s	0	0.00	382	100.00
1860s	0	0.00	674	100.00
1870s	1	0.00	520	100.00
1880s	0	0.00	713	100.00
1890s	0	0.00	583	100.00
1900s	0	0.00	468	100.00
1910s*	0	0.00	113	100.00
Totals	4,169	46.00	4,864	54.00

Note: *Incomplete decades.

Source: www.oldbaileyonline.org

another against his will, whereby the person is put in fear; though the thing taken be but to the value of a peny [sic], for which the Offender shall be hanged'.[12] Robbery was a bold and open crime and involved some degree of violence. If you were robbed without force or without noticing you had been robbed, then it was deemed a different (or less serious) kind of theft. Highway robbery had to take place on the king's highway but this did not restrict it to the roads outside England's towns and cities as eighteenth-century laws designated many thoroughfares as 'highways'. Highway robbers were often (but not always) mounted and the romantic image of the highwayman many have developed out of the reality that robbers on horseback were able to be gentler with their victims. The footpad had little choice but to disable his victim if he wanted to escape with his spoils, whereas the mounted robber was at a distinct advantage in that he could strike quickly and ride away.

Seventeenth- and eighteenth-century society was greatly concerned with robbery, especially highway robbery because, as Beattie points out, it 'threatened not only the safety of individuals but also the freedom of travel and commerce'.[13] The highwayman – mounted or otherwise – was therefore the antithesis of England's 'polite and commercial people'.[14] The author of a 1683 guide for travellers was in no doubt that the so-called 'gentlemen of the road' (who 'glory in their invention of the most Gentile Trade of Ruining Mankind'[15]) were an unwanted nuisance who needed to be dealt with severely. Moreover, he argued, it was the responsibility of everyone to help catch them. The Hue and Cry, an ancient institution that predated traditional forms of policing, obliged all fit and able men to join in the hunt for robbers, under pain of a fine and/or imprisonment.[16] Early in the eighteenth century, the anonymous writer of 'Hanging, not Punishment Enough' argued that the severest punishments had to be used to deter robbers or English roads would become as dangerous to travel on as the 'Deserts of Arabia'.[17] Highway robbery had been removed from benefit of clergy (making it more likely for those convicted to be sentenced to death) under the reign of Henry VIII and robbery followed in 1692.[18]

In 1751, the novelist and magistrate Henry Fielding wrote a long polemic on the problem of robbery in and around the capital. Addressing his remarks to the Lord High Chancellor of England (the head of the judiciary), Fielding offered a series of observations on the causes for what he called the 'late increase of Robbers'. He blamed the poor habits and morality of the 'Lower Kind of People' and their pursuit of luxury over industry. Drunkenness and gambling led to poverty and crime in his opinion; arguing that 'few Persons, I believe, have made their Exit at Tyburn, who have not owed their Fate to some of the Causes before mentioned'.[19] The Poor Law itself was at fault for it was, he argued, badly administered.

But Fielding offered other explanations as well, and these reflected his interest in policing (he was the creator of the Bow Street 'runners' and an advocate of government-funded policing). Fielding pointed an accusatory finger at the network of receivers that allowed robbers to easily dispose of their ill-gotten gains and at jurors who were too ready to downgrade the value of goods taken to restrict the use of hanging. His pamphlet noted that:

Among the great Number of Brokers and Pawn-brokers several are to be found, who are always ready to receive a gold Watch at an easy Rate, and where no Questions are asked, or, at least, where no Answer is expected but such as the Thief can very readily make

He added that victims (by advertising their stolen goods with rewards for their return) were merely creating a situation in which robbers could flourish.[20] Henry Fielding was writing at a time of heightened tension around crime, something we have noted before as being a catalyst for knee-jerk reactions from legislators. So, it is no surprise that a worried government passed the Murder Act in 1752, an act that included the prescription that convicted highway robbers should be hanged in chains as an example to deter others from crime. The moral panic of 1744 that preceded the act and extent to which robbers were actually gibbeted has been the subject of recent research that suggests that the fear of robbery far outstripped the reality.[21] Indeed, Table 4.2 shows that robberies were no higher (in fact a little lower) in the 1740s than they were in the preceding decades. However, as Beattie notes, robbery was often the benchmark by which the state of law and order was measured in the 1700s and arguably violent street crime has remained at the top of debates about crime and criminality ever since[22]; it only took a relatively small increase or a particularly heinous crime to propel robbery to the forefront of concerns.

In order to explore robberies, I have used data that has been collected from the *Old Bailey Online* and *Locating London's Past* to illustrate what the crime of robbery actually looked like in an eighteenth-century context.

A case study: Robbery in London, c.1750–1800

Of forty-four cases where we can be sure of a location, the majority (24 or 55 per cent) took place within what is described as a 'dwelling house'. One other occurred in 'a certain house near the King's Highway', two in an alehouse and seventeen on the streets or routes in and around the metropolis. Twenty-five women were indicted for being involved in robberies in dwelling houses as against sixteen men, while men were far more likely to be accused of committing robberies on the streets (eighteen men and just two women).

Some of street crimes could be seen as classic 'highway' robberies with victims being stopped in their vehicles as they made their way across London, while the others involved daring footpad attacks. A gang of three men stopped and attacked a watchmaker as he was on his way to Islington (then on the outskirts of the capital) to meet with four friends. He was knocked down by a group of men who were later apprehended by a patrol. The evidence was shaky, and two of the accused were acquitted with the other being forcibly enlisted in to the East India Company's army. Many robbers such as these must have escaped, but in two other cases, the patrols sent out from Bow Street caught the hapless criminals red-handed. John Parry was being watched by five or six Bow Street 'runners' as he tried to rob a man on Piccadilly, and Thomas Mayo was captured before he could even demand 'your money or your life!' Both Parry and Mayo were armed but so were the Bow Street officers, who routinely carried many more weapons than the nineteenth-century police.[23]

Thomas Tobin stopped a coach on Cheapside and robbed Beatus Savell (a teacher of French) of his watch and chain; the alarmed tutor fell out of the coach and received a nasty bang on the head. Thomas Wilts had an even closer call; his attackers knocked him down from behind and then one stood on his throat while they rifled his pockets. Fortunately for him they failed to search him properly and went off without his money.[24]

There are a couple of cases here where travellers in London are quite careful to conceal their possessions or place them in places that are hard to get at. This demonstrates an awareness of the dangers of the capital's streets where valuables were exposed to the deft fingers of pickpockets or more direct opportunistic thieves. Although some prosecutors successfully resisted when attacked, Thomas Darkis was caught because his intended victim battered him with a stick he carried with him (no doubt to afford some protection against just this eventuality).[25]

The one street robbery that involved a woman, Catherine Field, took place on the Mall. The victim was the wife of a soldier who was barracked nearby and was attacked by four people wearing disguises. She recognized them as soldiers (although one was a woman dressed as a man) from their 'regimentals' and pleaded with them not to harm her as she was a soldier's wife. They ignored this and punched her in the face, making her nose bleed. They took her cloak and handkerchief and warned her to keep her mouth shut. Possibly because they were disguised, identification was hard, and only one of the male assailants, John Groves, was indicted and convicted, and Field herself was acquitted.[26]

The majority of the robberies took place not on the street but inside properties. However, several of these crimes *started* on the streets, and here, the narrative is much less clear than it was for the more straightforward 'street' crimes. Again, most of the victims were male, but many more of the defendants were women. It would seem that a large proportion of the robberies that took place indoors had connections to London's sex trade.

In one instance, this is fairly unequivocal; a Welsh drover who had successfully discharged his responsibility for taking cattle to Smithfield market had enjoyed a few drinks and gone in search of one of the capital's many whores. He met Sarah Loft and agreed to go into a house with her in Sharp's Alley in St Sepulchre's. Once there Loft tried to pinch his purse and when he tried to stop her, she called in her friends who overpowered him, biting him several times in the process. With a little more foreknowledge of London, the drover might have avoided trouble. Sharp's Alley is part of network of back streets west of Smithfield in an area that had a poor reputation.[27]

In other cases, the prosecutors all claimed that either they had no intention of ending up in the place where they were robbed, or that they went there for some other more legitimate purpose than the purchase of illicit sex. Some of their narratives seem hard to believe but almost invariably they were enough to convince the juries of the defendants' guilt.

Christian Anderson was strolling along New Gravel Lane, in Upper Shadwell near the notorious Ratcliffe Highway when Mary Burke pinched his hat and ran into a nearby house. Anderson followed her – to retrieve his hat – and then was inveigled into a bedroom and separated from his money (twenty-two guineas if he is to be believed). Burke was convicted of the theft, but as no violence appeared to have taken place, she was spared the noose and transported.[28] Was Anderson an innocent here, or was he actively seeking sex in an area where he would be very likely to find it? Given that he carrying so much money, it seems likely that he was a recently discharged sailor newly arrived in the capital and as such presented an opportunity too good to pass up.

The court was very sceptical of Joseph Clark's claim that he had been overpowered and forced into a house of 'bad repute' at 45 Cable Street in Whitechapel. Could he not resist, they asked? Clark replied that he was trying to keep hold of the cheese he was carrying and had only been peering in at the windows, being newly arrived in the area and curious. His curiosity cost him his watch, several coins and two banknotes with perhaps a value of as much as £2,000 in today's money; it may well have cost his assailants their lives as they were sentenced – as so many of these defendants were – to be hanged.[29]

In all of these cases, the defendants were women, but in 1766, we can see a slight variation in the narrative. Elizabeth Webber persuaded a grocer to come back to her home for sex while her husband was at work. He obliged, but as soon as he was in her bedroom, her husband appeared and started making wild threats to his life and demanding money. The poor grocer was forced to hand over two guineas at knifepoint. Was this a clever conspiracy or a genuine case of an adulterous wife discovered by the cuckold-to-be? Elizabeth, possibly benefitting from the discretionary use of coverture, was acquitted while her husband (whose directions she may have been following) was sentenced to death.[30]

Thus, we can see that nine of the twenty-two cases (or 41 per cent) that took place inside a dwelling house involved men being lured or propositioned into properties for sex and then being overpowered and robbed. The areas where these crimes took place had established reputations for being associated with crime and prostitution, in districts such as Whitechapel and St Giles. For the most part, these robberies took place at night, between 8 pm and 11 pm, and the victims had been drinking after a day at work. The drover was robbed around midday, and the grocer who fell for the charms of another man's wife was robbed at 11 am in the morning, when the angry husband was supposedly going to be absent. All the rest occurred much later, and this suggests to me at least that some of these victims had actively sought out the liaisons that ultimately cost them their property. Indeed, while the accusations of theft might well be genuine, it is quite possible that the allegations of force were exaggerated and the circumstances contrived to protect the reputation of the victims. When looking at summary cases before the City magistracy in the same period, I came across hearings where embarrassed men complained of having been robbed by women they had seemingly accidentally ended up in bed with.[31] Not all of these cases were subsequently sent for trial with the City magistrates opting on occasion to reprimand the women and advise the men to be more circumspect in future.

Given the circumstances (men, slightly the worse for drink, and out on the town after work), it is not surprising that most of these victims lost personal valuables such as money and watches. Mary Bond tried to swallow the ten guineas she had stolen but was thwarted by her captors and one man, William Whitnell, who presumably had little else to steal, was struck over the head with a poker and parted from his outer clothing. Money and silver jewellery (watches, chains and shoe buckles) could be easily disposed of, exchanged in the second-hand market or pawned. Henry Fielding was well aware of the ease at which thieves could find a ready market for their stolen property. As we noted earlier, the Bow Street justice condemned receivers and pawnbrokers alike. Fielding wanted receiving to be made an offence in and of itself, as that would allow the thief to turn witness (i.e. give king's evidence) against the receiver, which he thought would be fitting given that 'many of the younger Thieves appearing plainly to be taught, encouraged and employed by the Receivers'.[32]

Fielding also argued that very nature of London made robbery a relatively risk-free activity for the opportunistic thief. The geography of the metropolis enabled criminals to strike and make their escape secure in the knowledge that they were very unlikely to get caught or be prosecuted if they were.

At night London's streets were patrolled by the watch, a much maligned body of men. From the 1750s onwards the Watch were sometimes supported by officers from Bow Street (the 'runners'), who were sent out to patrol particularly vulnerable areas or who were dispatched to track down gangs and individuals known to be involved in street robbery.[33] This is how Thomas Mayo and John Groves were arrested before they could complete their attacks. Of course, the Runners could not be everywhere at once and relied on their information networks just as modern police forces do. The fact that the government from the reign of William and Mary onwards offered rewards for the successful conviction of robbers encouraged thief-takers and informers to investigate crimes or give evidence in court. On more than one occasion, the court asked witnesses whether they had been prompted to offer evidence in the expectation of financial gain. Given that the reward for convicting a robber in the 1700s was £40 (or a figure between £2,500 and £3,500 today; about a year's wage for an eighteenth-century craftsman), it is likely that many of those giving evidence were tempted by the prospect of a reward and therefore happy to embellish or indeed entirely fabricate their testimony. But, let us return to the sample of trials where we have some idea of locations, what other robberies took place in dwelling houses and what circumstances accompanied them?

There are a handful cases that demonstrate thieves acting with some degree of planning or at least prior intent or knowledge. These are in contrast to most of the robberies in dwelling houses that appear to have been relatively spontaneous or opportunistic. Planned robbery can be seen as more heinous and perhaps more reflective of societal fears about crime in general. After all, numerous pamphleteers and commentators from the late 1600s through the eighteenth and nineteenth centuries have complained about the depredations carried out by members of a distinct 'criminal class'. Highwayman might be the elite members of this criminal fraternity, but the footpads and other robbers could be just as daring as can be seen in the following examples.

Abraham Danford and William Newton put a deposit of a half-guinea down to rent a property Blackfriars. The house was close to Lombard Street where the firm Smith, Wright and Gray had a compting (or counting) house. The plan was quite well conceived. Danford visited the counting house with a bill that was to be paid out to his new address. Meanwhile, he and Newton made some alterations to the rental property. When the bank clerk, James Watt, knocked on the door a few days later, Danford grabbed him and hauled him inside. The intention seems to have been to lock him up while one of the pair set off with the clerk's wallet of bills to collect on the payments. Unfortunately for our enterprising crooks, a neighbour, Anne Boucher, had seen Watts enter the house and heard a cry of 'murder!' Having failed to persuade two dustmen to help her break in, she shouted through the keyhole and spooked the robbers. When they ran out of the property, Anne caught Danford and a passing carman secured Newton. Both defendants – who had stood to make up to £4,000 from the robbery – were duly convicted and sentenced to death.[34]

Lawrence Jones was responsible for an even more elaborate attempt at robbery and fraud. Jones, who features in the *Newgate Calendar*, also rented a property in Hatton Garden (as he had done several times before in his criminal career) and set it up as a false counting house. When John Campbell arrived there, at ten in the morning, with a leather case containing a number of money bills, he was seized: a green baize cloth was thrown over his head and he was tied up, taken downstairs and chained to a heavy copper container in the kitchen. It took him until four in the afternoon to free himself. The culprits were rounded up by Carpmeal, Jealous and Kennedy, all well-known Bow Street Runners. The evidence they presented was enough to convict Jones, but the others were acquitted. Lawrence Jones cheated the hangman by committing suicide in Newgate three days before his execution; his dead body was paraded through the streets of Hatton Garden with, according to contemporary reports, an escort of City Marshals and over 500 constables. He may have avoided a public execution, but the state was not to be cheated of its opportunity to make an example of those that attempted to interfere with the precious business of banking.[35]

Some of the remaining incidents involving thefts from within dwelling houses were much more mundane. One young woman was asleep in the kitchen when another lodger crept in and stole some of her possessions, and when she protested, the thief waived a knife at her. A servant was stabbed in the stomach when a pair of thieves broke into his master's house in Bedford Row in the fashionable Gray's Inn area. In June 1780, while the Gordon rioters were terrorizing London William Brown, a former soldier who had been discharged wounded from the navy a year before, used a knife to extort money from a householder in Bishopsgate Street. It was merely a shilling, but it was enough, at this time of heightened anxieties about crime and disorder, to get him hanged.

There were also a couple of robberies in which the location given was an alehouse. Alehouses and public houses were frequently used as geographic references in Old Bailey trials. Hugh Harding was already quite drunk when he entered the Marquis of Granby pub in Chick Lane. The landlord refused to serve him because he was staggering about, and landlords had a care to their license not to allow wanton drunkenness in their establishments. Harding was angry and claimed his watch had been stolen. While he leant at the bar, Tamasin Allen helped herself to the contents of his pockets. The indictment accused her of taking several diamonds and other precious stones as well as a silver pencil case and a £10 note, a very serious theft. The theft had not involved violence, and Allen, who declared herself too ill to speak in her own defence, was sentenced to transportation. William Garrow offered a withering verdict on the prosecutor as he attempted to undermine his evidence by suggesting that he was incapacitated and unaware of what was happening at the time of the crime, stating that his reputation had it that he was usually drunk 'but sometimes you get sober'.[36]

It seems clear, from this sample at least, that location played an important role in the nature of robbery in eighteenth-century London. There were daring street robberies in the hinterlands of Islington as travellers made their way to and from the centre. Likewise, areas, which had notorious reputations for criminality, such as the St Giles rookery and Whitechapel, were infested with houses of ill repute where the unwary passer-by or sex tourist could expect trouble. In the smarter parts of town, householders were also at risk from more organized thieves, some of whom went to elaborate lengths to separate victims from their wealth.

Most robbery took place at night, or at least in the evening, but not in the small hours that we would normally associate with burglary. The cover of dark would have made the footpad's chance of escape more likely, despite the presence of the watch, simply because fewer witnesses would have been abroad after dark. However, almost all of those whose robbery was associated with prostitution fell victim at night because they had deliberately placed themselves in those areas at that time.

Women rarely used weapons – the occasional poker or stick or their teeth – and that supports what we know about female property crime. This is not to say they were not usually violent, although violence can involve all sorts of actions. Men *were* likely to commit robberies while armed. In five cases, a pistol was used to threaten (but was not discharged), and in seven others, a blade (a dagger, knife or hanger) was deployed. Victims were cut, stabbed, hit across the head, throttled, tied up, pushed about and knocked down as their assailants tried either to extract their valuable or more often, make their escape. On one occasion, a watchman was knocked to the ground and his pockets rifled while he made his rounds. Several victims chose to resist in ways that would horrify modern police officers. Criminals were chased, often into buildings, caught, struck with canes or otherwise overpowered. Bystanders not infrequently came to the assistance of robbery victims either when they saw a crime being committed or when they heard the cry of 'murder' or 'stop thief!'

Perhaps they did so because the policing of London at this time is perhaps best described as sporadic. The Watch patrolled the streets but individual watchmen varied considerably in how best they performed their duties. The Bow Street Runners were quite effective when they went in pursuit of criminals on information, but they were few in number and could not cover every street and highway. Thief-takers could be expected to follow up crimes for profit but were not a preventative force, and the same was true of the parish constables. All of these options will be explored in Chapter 10. The reward system may well have persuaded some people to prosecute and others to perjure themselves in the dock, however, by the latter years of the century, defence counsel like William Garrow were becoming adept at exposing 'blood money' witnesses in court. Henry Fielding was probably right in calling for a more joined up and professional state-funded police, but he was just as accurate in bemoaning the ease at which criminals could launder their stolen goods through the pawnbroker and second-hand networks.

Burglary and housebreaking

If robbery was the quintessential eighteenth-century crime, then burglary would appear to be the crime that best fitted the nineteenth. As one scholar has recently noted, 'no crime was more appropriate to late Victorian English society, when a "man's home was his castle" and the sanctity of domestic life was paramount.'[37] Burglars operated with stealth and skill rather than with violence (for the most part at least), and they employed a variety of tools that captured the imagination of an increasingly literate public. Newspapers began to carry advertisements for anti-burglary devices alongside its reportage of ever more elaborate and daring raids on homes and businesses. Above all, the Victorian burglar had become a *professional* criminal, and this fitted the prevailing discourse about crime and criminality of the second half of the 1800s.

Of course burglary was not invented in the nineteenth century; it had long been an offence that was punishable by death and did not cease to be a capital crime until 1837. This section will start by taking a broad view of burglary and housebreaking and defining the difference between them. It will then look at the way in which burglary became such a prominent crime in the Victorian psyche and concentrate on the depiction of burglars in the contemporary media and records of Old Bailey trials.

The laws surrounding burglary and housebreaking were complicated in the eighteenth century. There were variations depending on the value of goods that were stolen and whether anyone was 'put in fear' as a result of the break in. Technically, burglary happened at night and so carried the 'fear factor' of a home being invaded while the occupants slept. This continues to be seen as a very serious crime in modern Britain; no one wants to wake to find a masked man in their bedroom rifling through their property. But, while housebreaking (an offence that took place during the daytime) was seen as less serious, it was deemed to be just as grave if persons were in the property when the thieves broke in. Thus, it was *fear* that elevated this form of theft to one of especial concern.

Robbing someone's home or business could be more profitable than stopping them on the street simply because victims could only carry a limited amount about their persons, while their wealth was most likely to be held at their property. Thieves who broke into houses could hope to find jewellery, cash, plate and other expensive luxury items, and if they were well organized and had 'cased the joint', they might be able to carry off a considerable amount while the household slept or were elsewhere. Items stolen were easy to get rid of, either directly or via the networks of receivers and second-hand goods markets. Burglary and housebreaking were also less risky than highway robbery as intruders were better able to escape, and there was less chance of policing agents (such as the Watch or Bow Street Runners) catching them by responding to cries of 'murder' or 'stop thief'. Burglary remained a serious problem for householders into the nineteenth century, while robbery declined as the better organized professional police forces established themselves on the streets of English cities and towns. However, as William Meier has observed, 'criminals were beginning to adapt [to the new police] by the third quarter of the nineteenth century' and no more so than in burglary.[38]

In the second half of the nineteenth century, attitudes towards crime and criminals were undergoing a cultural change, and we can see some elements of these changing perceptions of criminality by looking at burglary and housebreaking as they were reported and commented upon in the popular press and periodicals of the day. In the period 1841–1900, there were 4,820 Old Bailey reported trials for burglary and 1,407 for the related offence of housebreaking with the highest percentage taking place in the economically depressed years of the 1880s (see Table 4.3 below).

Housebreaking could be quite opportunistic, especially as many premises were largely unprotected and left open most of the day – only being secured at night. Burglary could equally be a matter of trial and error – the trying of door handles or looking for open windows or a break in the fence – but it was more likely to be premeditated. In Henry Mayhew's *London Labour and the London Poor*, one of his researchers wrote:

> The expert burglar is generally very ingenious in his devices, and combines manual dexterity with courage. In his own sphere the burglar in manual adroitness equals the accomplished pickpocket, while in personal daring he rivals our modern ruffians of the highway.[39]

There was perhaps some perverse admiration in this description, reflecting conflicting views of criminals, as not only a danger to society but also a source of vicarious entertainment. The Victorians could read about the special tools and methods that members of the so-called 'criminal class' used to break into their homes and steal their valuables. In the reports of break-ins or the trials of criminals, the print media often informed their readers that 'burglars invariably possessed tools like the iron bar or "jemmy," various types of wedges, matches, knives and chisels, and a set of skeleton keys'.[40] Often, these were little more than common tools adapted or simply employed for an illegal purpose. If caught in the act or approached on suspicion by an alert police constable or security guard, thieves would often discard their tools – and they wrapped them in cloth in advance so as to make the least noise when they did so.

Table 4.3 Burglary and housebreaking trials at the Old Bailey, 1841–1900.

Decades	Burglary Number	As Percentage	Housebreaking	As Percentage
1840s	538	11.16	525	37.31
1850s	744	15.43	270	19.19
1860s	881	18.27	149	10.59
1870s	722	14.97	98	6.97
1880s	1,034	21.45	209	14.85
1890s	901	18.69	145	10.31
Total	4,820		1,407	

Source: www.oldbaileyonline.org

This technique did not help James Moore when he was seen, with a companion, by a policeman (PC 205 of M division), trying the doors of several houses on Horsemonger Lane, south London. Both men attempted to make a run for it, but Moore was captured after throwing away 'a jemmy, chisel and two keys'. He was also carrying candles and matches. At his examination, the defendant denied dropping the tools and claimed that he used the candles and matches in his trade as a house painter. The policeman was unimpressed and told the magistrate he 'had no doubt that he was a professional housebreaker. His hands were too soft'.[41]

The perception that professional criminals were raiding the property of the rich and not-so rich from the 1860s onwards was in some degree in conflict with the reality of property crime in the period. 'Property' observed *The Times* in 1881 'is safer than it has ever been against depredations of every sort'.[42] The explanation for this improvement in law and order was the gradual development of professional policing in the years from 1829. Middle-class fears about the working-class criminal had in some ways now been replaced by a concern with the 'expert' crook – the professional burglar and housebreaker. This in turn justified the continued funding and augmentation of the Metropolitan Police on the basis that society needed professional crime fighters to counter professional criminals.

When William Taylor was arrested for breaking into a room in a lodging house in 1841, he was searched and found to possess no less than nine skeleton keys.[43] Burglars could also fashion replica keys by making an impression of the lock they wished to open using wax moulds or similar items made especially for the purpose. This involved a level of planning and premeditation and an ability to not look too suspicious. John Binny remarked that crooks could adopt a pose that suggested they were doing nothing wrong: 'When looking into the lock they frequently strike a match on the doorway, and pretend to be lighting a pipe or cigar, which prevents passers-by suspecting their object.'[44]

As with eighteenth-century robbers, the targets of burglars and housebreakers were goods that could be easily disposed of. In robbing a wealthy home, intruders would look for jewellery, plate (silver goods), money and, failing that, clothes. All of these could find a ready market in the pawn shops and second-hand stalls of the capital, albeit for much less than their true value. Richard Robins, who was just seventeen, was convicted and transported for ten years for breaking into the home of James Watson in St Martin-in-the-Fields to steal clothes. Stolen clothes were easy to dispose of in London: they could be sold at market, exchanged, sold on to old clothes dealers or pawned. Any of these might have been Richard's intention, or he might simply have needed some decent apparel to secure work or a position in service.[45] The types of items stolen remained constant across the period 1841–1900 as thieves made off with silver thimbles and cutlery (spoons in particular), and on one occasion, a burglar made off with a portable writing desk. Rolls of cloth were stolen from drapers' shops, blankets from homes along with other textiles, and of course, handkerchiefs were popular with burglars and housebreakers. In August 1872, William Hastings and Sidney Pocock stole several cruet forks, a toast rack, mustard pot, wine strainer, saltcellars, eighteen forks and a flute, as well as some billiard balls, all from a house in Russell Square.[46]

On some occasions, household servants were complicit in the theft of their employer's property. Felons used servant girls in particular to gain access to homes or to locate goods that might be worth stealing. Maidservants were supposedly vulnerable to the charms of the more debonair members of the criminal class, and others (perhaps those with dark secrets or related by blood) may have been forced to help in some way. Whatever the motivations of domestic servants, the fact that it was they that secured the homes, *and* knew where valuable items were kept as well as having knowledge of the movements of the household, made them important allies for the would-be thief. Most burglaries took place in the early hours of the morning – between 2 am and 4 am, while the 'peak time for housebreaking offenses was in the early evening, between 7 pm and 9 pm – precisely when many inhabitants would be taking their dinner'.[47] Servants, of course, if they acted as accomplices, could let criminals know when the rest of the household would be out or otherwise engaged and act as decoys or lookouts.

In December 1861, Sarah Collett discovered that a friend had left her position as a maid at an elderly lady's house in Paddington and so applied for the vacant post. Three weeks later, she conspired to let in two masked men who threatened her mistress and then attacked her about the head before making off with eleven silver spoons, some forks, a ladle, sugar sifter, tongs, a butter knife and a gold watch and chain. The thieves were caught and, for such a violent robbery, were sent to prison for life. Collett received four years for her involvement in the crime.[48] This sort of violent burglary drew plenty of attention, but it was also unusual: 'In reality... violence as an aggravation of burglary was the exception rather than the rule'.[49]

Housebreakers must have expected to encounter servants or other members of the household if they attempted to enter property during daylight hours, but not all of them had such elaborate excuses as William Brown who entered the home of George Hopcraft in Sydenham at about one in the afternoon. One of the Hopcraft's servants discovered the housebreaker in the breakfast room, coming in through a window she had only recently closed. Brown scarpered, but the servant girl gave chase and raised the alarm. The footman caught Brown as he attempted to escape across the lawns and into the kitchen garden. Two days earlier, he had tried to steal from a house in Lewisham but had almost been caught red-handed there by another alert servant. At half past five the housemaid, Mary Ann Sandwell, had been passing the drawing room when she heard a window being opened. At first, she thought it was one of the other servants and called out to enquire who it was. When she received no reply, she opened the door and found Brown, half in and half out of the window. When she asked what he was doing there, he answered: 'Pray don't be alarmed. A canary bird has flown away, and I thought it flew up here.' On this occasion, he got away, but when he came before the magistrate at Greenwich Mary, Ann was able to identify him as the failed housebreaker from earlier in the week.[50] Again, the reporting of this reveals the multiple ways in which crime news could be used – as a caution to householders, to highlight the problem of crime and as an amusing anecdote to entertain readers.[51]

William Brown was only 17 when he attempted to burgle the Hopcraft household, and while the newspaper report was enjoying a laugh at the young man's expense, it was also downplaying the threat offered by this young criminal. By the last quarter of the nineteenth century, the cult of professionalism within Victorian society had, in the area of criminal justice at least, firmly begun to separate criminal deviance from the rest of normal society. Characters such as William Brown were somehow less responsible for their actions than the depredators of the first half of the century; they were less individual and less dangerous as a result. Charles Booth's study of poverty in the late 1880s relied on statistics rather than upon examples (as Binny and Mayhew had done at mid-century); Booth generalized the problem and so underpinned the need for professionals (the police and prison reformers) to solve it.[52] The declining fear of the criminal may not have been of much comfort to those whose homes were chosen for daylight or moonlight robbery, but it perhaps influenced *Punch's* humorous take on the discovery that some burglars had abandoned jemmies and pistols for chloroform and mercury. Remarking that criminals had embraced the progressive spirit of the day, it went on to add that if 'Mr Bill Sykes [a reference to Dickens' archetypal villain from *Oliver* Twist] paid us a nocturnal visit, we should certainly prefer to have our sense of feeling numbed rather than have our brains blown out'.[53]

William Meier has noted that after a period where the police seemed to gain the upper hand on criminals, the last quarter of the century saw a shift towards the crooks again.[54] By the 1880s (when there was a recognized increase in crime statistics), the failure of the police to effectively thwart burglars revealed itself in the satirical periodicals of the day, before emerging more forcefully in direct attacks on police competence in newspapers such as the *Pall Mall Gazette* and *Reynolds*. In February 1881, *Punch* reported the fictional meeting of the 'Association of Burglars' (presided over by 'Mr Matthew Arnold Sikes', with interjections from the floor by 'Mr Smashem' amongst others). Here the scientific nature of 'modern' burglary was praised, and it was remarked (by a retired felon) that it was a lot safer and less risky now than it had been in his days. The meeting, after the obligatory vote of thanks to the Chair, broke up with 'each member going to somebody else's house in the fashionable quarter now known as Burglaria'.[55]

At the same time, *Funny Folks* gently mocked the *Daily Telegraph* for advising its readers to take precautions against burglars by fitting electric door handles or keeping geese, and itself recommended the buttering of doorsteps and the distribution of orange peel – both presumably designed to cause intruders to slip and fall, to then be swept up by the maid servants in the morning![56] By 1887, the situation was apparently unchanged with *Moonshine* suggesting that Mrs Muggins would not have lost all her plate and Dresden ware if her husband had invested in a 'Patent Electric Burglar Detector'. While the article was satirical, it is indicative of a view that recognized the necessity of individuals protecting their homes (and the goods therein) by all means possible rather than simply relying upon the police to do so. This sense of personal responsibility or liability for protecting the home comes at a time that also saw the emergence of home contents insurance, and this may have had an effect on attitudes towards this form of property crime. Lloyds of London began to offer insurance for householders in 1887, and this may have increased the pressure on property owners to take careful precautions to protect their effects.

So what can we say about the nature of burglary and housebreaking in the Victorian period? First, that burglars, then as now, stole items they could easily exchange for ready cash – this is true of those that robbed private homes, public houses or workshops and warehouses. Some of these robberies were carefully planned, executed with almost military precision and sometimes with inside help. On other occasions, the thefts were opportunistic: a door that yielded to a gentle shove or a window left open just wide enough to tempt an intruder to try his luck. Some burglars used tools, some (like skeleton keys) being specially designed for the purpose, but others – chisels or jemmies – that would have been in common usage among the working classes. It was often the possession of these tools that occasioned the arrest of individuals who were caught and prosecuted even when they tried to ditch the items in making their escape.

The victims of burglary reacted in different ways to an intrusion into their homes and businesses. Some, including servants, chased or scared off thieves, while others may well have cowered in their beds, too frightened to find out what that noise in the night was. Servants and housekeepers would certainly have been annoyed to find their carefully maintained houses left in a state of disarray by unwanted night-time visitors. Were they also upset and scared by the violation of their employer's (and their own) home? We can agree that burglary, as a violation of the home, was and remains a potentially traumatic experience for anyone who is the victim of it. Personally, I have been burgled twice in my life. On the second occasion, I chased and caught the thief with the help of housemates and recovered my property. The burglar was sent to prison for twelve months. If he had been operating in the 1850s, he would have received a much harsher sentence, something that reflects the changes in our attitudes towards property crime and the punishment of offenders.

The gradual introduction of insurance from the late 1880s onwards and the availability of anti-burglar devices may also have changed the way in which such crimes were regarded: householders had always been expected to protect their properties because to some extent there was an acceptance that criminality was inevitable. But, while by the late nineteenth century the police had established themselves as the primary crime prevention agency, they could not be expected to prevent all break-ins. The introduction of insurance and alarms is perhaps evidence of the limitations of the police and an affirmation that the responsibility for preventing these unwanted visitors lies with householders and property owners, the victims of crime.

Robbery and burglary were considered, by the public and the courts, to be the most serious of property crimes, but alongside them, we should add forgery and coining.

Counterfeiting: Forgery, coining and uttering

In the twenty-first century, we have a very sophisticated monetary system, and banks and government are continually developing new systems to thwart attempts (by criminals and terrorist groups) to undermine the currency by flooding the market with counterfeit money. However, most money transactions are open to fraud, and there is a sophisticated international criminal industry involved in forgery and counterfeiting. While the monetary system has become more complex, the problem of forgery has been around for centuries. Forgery and counterfeiting today, according to the 1981 act is defined thus: 'A person is guilty of forgery if he makes a false instrument, with the intention that he or another shall use it to induce somebody to accept it as genuine'.[57] A 'false instrument' in this case means anything from credit cards or postal orders to a passport or share certificate.

Forgery and counterfeiting are crimes which have engaged historians for a number of reasons. Forgery covers a wide range of activities which involve some form of fraud, but the focus of historical work has been on the late eighteenth and early nineteenth century and on looking at the way in which the prosecution of forgery became central to wider debates about the application of the capital laws.[58] Coining (which is the specific offence of counterfeiting and distributing the metal coin of the realm) is an older offence which has more usually been used by scholars to look at aspects of 'social a crime' or within a wider discussion about the role of early policing agents (such as the Bow Street Runners).[59] There is now a considerable body of work on forgery and coining available, so what follows is a necessarily brief overview of some of this research and the debates it has spawned.

Let us start by emphasizing the point that coining and forgery, while not the same thing, were both considered to be offences against the monarch and therefore deemed to be treason. As such, they carried a more serious punishment than all of the other property offences discussed in this chapter. In the early modern period, traitors were drawn to the place of execution on a sledge (as a mark of ignominy), hanged until they were almost dead and then cut up (quartered) while still alive, and their bodies displayed to the public. Female traitors were saved this gruesome punishment and instead burned alive at the stake. By the late eighteenth century, men convicted of coining or forgery were simply being hanged, but some women still suffered an awful death by flames.[60] Let us look first at the nature of coining and what it involved before considering the crime of forgery, and how historians have explored the ways in which nineteenth-century penal reformers used this particular crime to argue for the removal of death penalty in the 1810s.

In the 1700s, Justice Buller defined forgery as 'the making of a false instrument, with intent to deceive'.[61] The offence could cover pretty much anything that related to paper transactions. In the eighteenth century, it usually referred to banknotes (or 'bills of exchange') but might also extend to other items such as a draft for a sailor's wages. However, before the late seventeenth century, the English did not use banknotes; instead, everything was exchanged with coin. Notes, or bills of exchange, began to appear from the 1690s, but these, along with banknotes, remained largely handwritten until the middle of the nineteenth century and so were quite easy to replicate. Coins, made from copper, silver or gold, were also relatively easy to 'clip'.[62] This involved cutting or shaving off some of the precious metals, which could then be melted down and cast as new coins or ingots.[63] Coiners could make considerable sums as the example of Joseph Wood shows. Wood bought up large amounts of gold coin and then filed these guineas down and re-milled them. The reworked coins were then exchanged for paper notes which were used to purchase fresh guineas. In just two years, Wood managed to make £2,000 profit, a huge sum in its day.[64] Others probably operated at way below Wood's level, but this was often a collective effort as early work on coining has demonstrated.[65]

Coins could also be forged; dies could be made and coins cast from them. Because there were multiple roles to perform, coining became something of a cottage industry, and coiners often worked as a group (or a gang) since clippings from metal coin had to be melted, and false coins had to be created and then redistributed (and this was often a task ascribed to women). The process of getting a coin or note into circulation was called uttering and was itself an offence. Thus, coining drew in craftsmen from traditional trades such as metal workers, tool makers and smiths, as these were the workers who had both the skills and the necessary tools to carry out the clipping and manufacture of counterfeit coins. As with many offences, the crime of coining has not entirely disappeared; today, the Royal Mint estimates that as many of 3.04 per cent of £1 coins in circulation are fake.[66]

As we noted above, counterfeiting was not only a crime against the person, it was also, and more importantly, a crime against the monarch. Money was issued (minted) in the name of the king or queen (after all it is the monarch's head that appears on our currency). So to attack the coin of the realm was to attack the sovereign and was therefore a form of treason. Coining, which had been a concern since the medieval period, was made capital during the reign of Elizabeth I. But, this and all subsequent attempts by Stuart and Hanoverian monarchs to prevent attacks on the coinage failed.[67] In part, this is explained by the reality that neither those that carried out the offence nor the wider general public saw coining as a crime in the same way that the state did; coining was viewed as a victimless crime despite attempts by the state to associate coiners with treason. Moreover, the quality of coin in circulation throughout the Tudor, Stuart and early Hanoverian period was so poor that coining was relatively easy to do and a much more lucrative crime, with less risk of prosecution, than other more direct forms of property offending.

In 1687, the grand jury of the City of London stated its concern about the increase of 'Clippers and False-coiners'.[68] False coins had to be exchanged for genuine currency, and here, women were often involved, using a larger denomination coin to buy something low in value and thereby coming away with a considerable amount of legitimate change. In June 1688, the Old Bailey saw the trial and conviction of a gang of coiners. Thomas Baily and Valentine Cogswell operated a press in Red Lion Fields, near Holborn. The pair was overseen by George Emmit who rented several properties for the purpose of making and passing false money. Two other men were employed as clippers, and four others were convicted for distributing (uttering) monies.[69]

In July 1695, Dorothy Goreing was convicted of clipping, filing and diminishing '20 pieces of Silver of Lawful Coyn of this Realm, called Shillings, and 20 other pieces called Sixpences… with Shears, Files, and other Iron Instruments'. Goreing was sentenced to death but spared on account of being pregnant.[70] Women appeared in considerable numbers in coining and forgery cases, and in the late eighteenth and early nineteenth century, the Bank of England was particularly rigorous in pressing prosecutions against them in its attempt to protect the currency.[71] The government acted against counterfeiters, and the late seventeenth century saw various acts passed to protect the coinage while the Mint attempted to improve methods of production to guard against counterfeiting.[72] However, as developments in minting coins progressed to thwart counterfeiting (such as milling or machine-struck coinage), so too did the coiners adapt themselves. They were given more opportunities for illegal profit by the creation of paper bills of exchange (the early form of banknotes) in the late 1600s as England developed into a truly global mercantile nation with trade based on credit and commerce.

As McGowen has noted, the changing nature of commerce opened up opportunities for dishonest individuals to exploit loopholes in the law.[73] There was recognition that in this new world of paper currency and bills of exchange the reality was that banking sector operated on the belief that an individual's word or their signature was sacrosanct. An infamous forgery case (that of Hales and Kinnersley) exposed this as a fiction and must have sent shockwaves through eighteenth-century society. The Chief Justice warned in 1729 that if forgery was not suppressed, it 'must tend to hinder all commerce by bills and paper-credit'.[74] A new forgery bill became law on the 14 May 1729, and it made forgery punishable by death. It was, as McGowen emphasizes, a piece of sweeping legislation quite in 'contrast to the specificity of most capital' statutes in the 1700s.[75] As Phil Handler has argued, hereafter forgery and the death penalty were interlinked because of the 'dangerous economic threat' [posed by the forgery of paper currency] which 'preyed on fears about authenticity and the security of exchange, a feature that had made the crime of forgery seem so subversive and serious in the eighteenth century'.[76] The skill of the forger meant that ordinary people, tradesmen and clerks alike could not distinguish genuine notes from fakes.

The whole nation was therefore put at risk by attempts to undermine the system of monetary exchange. Over the next 100 or so years, the Forgery Act sent very many individuals to the gallows or overseas and became bound up in early nineteenth-century debates about the harshness of the capital code. Among those prosecuted under the 1729 act was George Barber who, in 1760, walked into the offices of the bankers Honeywood and Fullers in Birchin Lane and changed a £50 note for cash. The clerk was not sure about the bill, suspecting that handwriting was forged, and he went to check with his colleagues. Barber may have panicked at this stage, and in his haste to get away, he confirmed the suspicions of the clerk. Barber was chased and captured before being committed for trial for forgery.[77] The unfortunate Barber was convicted and sentenced to death at the January session at the Old Bailey in 1761 after confessing his guilt and pleading for mercy at his arrest. He had two other forged notes on him when he was arrested, so the procession of witnesses that gave him a good character was not enough to save him, and he was hanged at Tyburn.[78]

Goreing and Barber represent just two examples of the crimes of coining and forgery tried at the Old Bailey, both of which involved some elements of individual skill, planning and bravado, while Emmet's case demonstrates that coining operations could involve groups of people. The risks if you were caught were considerable, but the potential for gain may well have outweighed the fear of prosecution. Nearly 25 per cent of the 2,033 people convicted of coining offences between 1674 and 1840 (over 500 individuals) were sentenced to death with a further 319 being ordered for transportation. The average chance of conviction over this long period was high (at 68 per cent) but particularly so in the early decades of the nineteenth century when 70–95 per cent of those tried were found guilty.[79]

This corresponded with a period in which the Bank of England was producing 'low value paper money, of poor quality, [that was] easy to forge'.[80] This situation had been caused by the suspension of gold payments during the wars with Revolutionary and Napoleonic France. The British government was acting to prevent withdrawals of gold as people panicked at the threat of a French invasion. In order to maintain the circulation of money, the Bank resorted to the production of a large number of banknotes, many of which were for small denominations (£1 and £2).[81] The low denomination notes were 'scarcely more than a printed form with a number, a date and a clerk's signature' which 'presented little challenge to the criminal entrepreneurs, many of them dealers in fraudulent coin, who now seized upon the new opportunity for easy profit'.[82] As a result, there was a surge in prosecutions across the country with over 2,000 offenders being convicted of coining-related crimes.[83] After 1797, the Bank of England adopted a strategy to combat the attacks on the currency. Using the law discretionarily, it allowed defendants to make plea bargains with their solicitors, Freshfields.[84] Many of those prosecuted by the Bank of England in the 1790s were encouraged to plead guilty to the lesser crime of uttering and accept a sentence of transportation in return for their lives and some financial support from the Bank while they waited in Newgate or set sail for Botany Bay. By contrast, the Bank's solicitors acted without mercy to those that refused their 'generous' offer.

In 1801, the Bank secured new legislation that allowed offenders to be prosecuted for either possessing the 'instruments for making Bank note paper' or forged notes themselves (and knowing them to be forged).[85] The penalty was transportation for fourteen years, which was severe, but not as terminal as hanging, and in this, the bank was responding to widespread distaste at the number of individuals that were being condemned to death as a consequence of the Bank's war on the forgers. The Bank's campaign against the forgers (many of whom worked out of Birmingham) was orchestrated by Freshfields, who employed hundreds of constables and policing agents. Their success relied on an extensive network of informants, the exploitation of the reward system and a determination to press charges and prosecute offenders. This attracted men like John Haddock, a constable from Bewdley, in Worcestershire, who arrested a man suspected of passing counterfeit notes and gathered evidence against him, for which he was rewarded with the considerable sum of £15 (enough money, in 1816, to buy a horse).[86]

In 1824, William Hill was tried at the Old Bailey for uttering forged £5 notes. He and an accomplice had tried to buy some cloth in a shop on the Strand using a fake £5 note. The cloth came to £3 9s. and Hill tendered the note, saying, 'give me change for this'. However, the shop keeper was suspicious, and when she asked him his name and address,

Hill gave her a false one. When the couple then left in a hurry, they were followed and arrested. Hill was convicted and sentenced to death, but the jury recommended him to mercy 'on account of his poverty […] and previous good character'.[87]

Forgery was one of the last property offences to remain capital as the reformers campaign to abolish the 'Bloody Code' gathered momentum in the early 1800s, and this reflects the determination of the Bank of England and the English state to fight any attempts at undermining the financial system. The Home Secretary (and the man credited with administering the move away from hanging) Robert Peel stated in 1830 that 'the crime of forgery had appeared to him to occupy a most important station in the list of offences', and he was reluctant to see it downgraded. McGowen has argued that 'forgery came to occupy an almost unique place in the minds of both those who demanded reform of the criminal law and those who defended the traditional legal order'.[88] In 1818, a crisis surrounding the legitimacy of paper currency had its repercussions in the Old Bailey. In December, two juries refused to convict any of those brought before them accused of forging banknotes. The juries refused to accept the evidence presented by the Bank which, according to Handler, 'derived from fears concerning the reliability of the currency', something that was the subject of a public debate instigated by radical journalists who were demanding a return to a cash-based system of monetary exchange.[89] The crisis excited considerable debate, and years later, the caricaturist George Cruikshank recalled how in 1818 he had witnessed the aftermath of an execution of two women for forgery and been appalled that 'a poor woman could be put to death for such a minor offence'.[90] The banknote crisis brought the whole criminal justice system into question because, as even *The Times* recognized, if Old Bailey juries could not determine whether paper notes were genuine or forgeries, it undermined the reliability of evidence. It would seem then that there are some grounds for believing that the public in all eras felt that forgery and coining were not offences that warranted the use of such excessive punishment, and in the early nineteenth century, this feeling gathered momentum among reformers who argued that the whole apparatus of the 'Bloody Code' was unfit for purpose.

In the early 1810s, a prominent campaigner against capital punishment, Thomas Fowell Buxton, used the banking crisis to denounce the use of the death penalty on the grounds that it had failed to deter forgers in the past and was now discouraging both prosecutions and convictions.[91] The 1819 parliamentary committee tasked with investigating the arguments for reforming the capital statues agreed with him and recommended that while hanging should be retained for persistent offenders (and those that forged Bank of England notes), it should be removed for all other forgery offences. However, the bill that resulted from the committee's report (the Forgery Punishment Mitigation Bill, 1821) was lost at its third reading. Cash payments were resumed in the same year, and penal law reform dropped off the agenda until 1823. For Handler, this demonstrates the vital importance of forgery to the debates around the abolition of hanging for property crimes. He argues that they 'became the battleground on which the dispute over the efficacy of capital punishment was fought'.[92]

Robert Peel continued to maintain that 'the death penalty on forgery did not need mitigation, and right up to 1830 he continued to think that forgers should die'.[93] Gatrell is scathing of both Peel and the Quakers who had lent their voice to demands for reform. After all, for many, forgery was a 'middle-class crime' committed by respectable clerks, not rough working-class criminals, something Gatrell noted in his critique of reformers' supposedly humanitarian attitudes towards forgers.[94] Forgery was finally removed from the capital statutes in 1830, but not before many men and women had gone to the gallows.

Theft: From grand and petty larceny to simple theft

While it was robbery and burglary that dominated the consciousness of eighteenth- and nineteenth-century commentators and the wider reading public, these crimes only accounted for a minority of property offences. There were far more shoplifters and pickpockets than highwaymen and burglars, but even these were eclipsed by the numbers of larcenies that were tried in the jury courts. Between 1660 and 1800, almost 70 per cent of Surrey property crime indictments were for simple grand larceny or petty larceny, ten times the proportion for robbery (the next highest category).[95]

The distinction between grand and petty larceny was drawn from the *value* of the goods stolen, not the method. As we have seen, if a theft took place in a specific place or involved the use of violence, it could be prosecuted under more specific legislation. Indeed, throughout the long eighteenth century, there were a plethora of statutes that covered all manner of thefts, and general legislation was rare.[96] Grand larceny was the theft of goods above the value of one shilling, and the penalty for this was death by hanging. For thefts below this value (petty larceny), the most the court could award was transportation. As with almost all property crimes in the period before the reform of the 'Bloody Code', grand larceny was therefore subject to a great deal of discretion from prosecutors and juries. Petty larceny was usually prosecuted in the lower courts of quarter sessions or before the justices of the peace because it was not always considered to be felonious (although there was some debate about this). In 1827, grand and petty larcenies were replaced by one category of offence: simple larceny. Simple larceny covered all thefts that did not include an aggravating circumstance, such as violence, breaking into property, stealing from a specified place and picking a pocket, and after 1855, this offence was dealt with entirely at the summary level.

Simple larceny (and its predecessors) covers such a wider variety of thefts that it makes any attempt to categorize it somewhat superfluous. So, it is perhaps more useful to look at three aspects of theft here: first, what sorts of goods were taken; second, who prosecuted larceny; and finally, to what extent did prevailing economic, political or social conditions affect the prosecution rate for larceny?

The nature of goods stolen

We have already seen that robbers and burglars stole slightly different things. The former were looking for purses of money or high-value jewellery. Prostitutes were adept at separating their clients from their watches, chains, cash and even their clothes. Burglars and housebreakers had more choice given that they robbed houses where more things to steal and where detection was less likely. Shoplifters were presented with a dazzling array of consumer goods in cities like London, Bath and Bristol, and pickpockets helped themselves to personal items such as watches, jewellery and handkerchiefs.

Theft was often opportunistic and thieves stole items that were easy to remove, use, eat or dispose of quickly. In May 1748, Anne Monk attempted to steal an agricultural tool from a barn as she tramped across the Northamptonshire countryside, but a sharp-eyed servant spotted her. When she was brought before a local JP, she had a straining cloth on her that she had taken from a washing line on her travels. Anne would have been able to exchange both items for money or food had she been successful, as it was all she gained was a short spell in the local bridewell and a stern instruction from the justice not to return to the parish.[97] In May 1740, Edward Nicholls, a shipwright, pinched a coulter (a part of a plough) from a barn in Chatham and tried to sell it to one of the local blacksmiths. The owner had reported the loss and alerted the smith, so poor Edward was caught, prosecuted at the quarter sessions and punished with a whipping.[98]

In the City of London, magistrates at the two summary courts at Guildhall and Mansion House presided over hundreds of hearings relating to theft every year. Most of the items taken could be described as personal property, often of low value but not always. In January 1785, Thomas Sawyer stole a shirt, scarf and handkerchief from a horse and cart, and the magistrate committed for trial at Old Bailey while no one was able to provide any evidence that Joseph Garlin had *not* found the coat he was accused of stealing.[99] George Shirley was not so lucky when he tried to persuade a local constable that he had been fortunate enough to find a side of beef behind a water pump. The meat had been stolen and Shirley was arrested.[100] We could add a multitude of other examples of the thefts of cheeses, tools, clothes, money, jewellery and (in London at least) pewter pint pots or tankards from the capital's numerous inns and alehouses.

The location of the crime would also affect the nature of the items taken. Theft by servants was a widespread and recognized problem.[101] Daniel Defoe complained about maids 'who beggar you inchmeal', by taking small amounts of household goods ('tea, sugar, wine etc.'), and quipped that 'some of these maids are mighty charitable, and can make a shift to maintain a small family with what they can purloin from their masters and mistresses'.[102] Servants were generally poorly paid, and those with wealthy employers must have been tempted to steal on a regular basis. Many of these thefts may well have been motivated by a desire to supplement leisure activities or to make a meagre salary stretch that little bit further by using the opportunities their service provided to steal small amounts of goods (such as the stubs of candles) that their rich masters would hardly notice.[103]

The same situation prevailed at other workplaces. The London docks saw plenty of pilferage as workers took home 'samples' of goods such as tobacco, dyes, alcohol and cotton. Some of this they regarded as legitimate perks of their trades (as is explained later in the section on 'social crime'), but as the eighteenth century unfolded, their employers were increasingly inclined to disagree. Prosecutions and increased private policing on dockyards and warehouses reflected the move towards a capitalist economic system and the end of workplace privileges.

Shops of course played into the hands of thieves as they displayed their wares in windows or outside. Even goods kept close by the counter were vulnerable to practised thieves who use diversionary tactics to get shopkeepers and their staff to look the other way. Crowded marketplaces, public executions and other social gatherings provided ample opportunities for pickpockets.

While all of the examples so far have been eighteenth-century ones, the pattern continued into the nineteenth. The idea of the juvenile pickpocket represented by Dickens' 'Artful Dodger' and his crew was a reality in the first decades of the 1800s. In 1830 (the first full year in which Peel's New Police operated), there are over 1,300 trials for simple larceny recorded in the *Proceedings*. Of these, 162 were for defendants aged 16 or under and almost invariably these were boys. James McGrath was just 9 years of age (the same age as the fictional Oliver Twist) when he appeared at the court accused (with an older lad) of stealing at hat.[104] James Green (also 9) pinched money out of Mary Dickinson's till while she fetched him some ginger for his toothache.[105] In both instances, the boys were whipped and let go. The same year, Thomas Roberts and two companions stole some shoes from outside a shop on the City Road. While the other escaped, Tom was not so lucky, and he too suffered a beating as a result.[106] However, most defendants appearing at the Old Bailey in the nineteenth century were older, and this is partly explained by the fact that younger thieves were more likely to be dealt with lower down the criminal justice system, at the summary level. During the nineteenth century, legislation that awarded more summary power to magistrates effectively removed all juvenile property criminals from the jury courts, but the practice preceded legislation, as was the case with much of the development of the criminal justice system.

Catherine Graham stole a coat from just inside a house while the servant was distracted by the weekly arrival of the dustmen.[107] William Collins pinched a hat that was hanging on a door knob[108] and Ann Read was taken as she tried to run off with a pair of boots from a workshop.[109] In the same year, thieves stole a pair of bellows, a leg of pork, onions, ham, more shoes, a hogshead of wine, a teakettle, feathers, all sorts of clothes, a gold pin, various types of jewellery, ribbon and cloth, and a portmanteau (a large travelling bag or suitcase, which may of course have come in use to transport all these plundered goods!). The point of this seemingly endless list of stolen items is that the crime of simple larceny after 1827 covered a vast range of depredations. People stole whatever they felt they could eat, use or sell on and exchange. This of course meant that there were plenty of victims of theft.

Other forms of specific property offending

Pocket picking and shoplifting will both be considered in Chapter 7, and so, there is little need to replicate that discussion here except to note that both these were offences that were committed by men and women and a considerable number of juveniles. They were also predominantly *urban* crimes and so are associated with the crowded streets of London and England's other major centres. Both of these forms of appropriation (along with robbery, burglary and in fact pretty much all grand and petty larceny) often required the tacit involvement of a network of 'fences' or receivers who would sell on, exchange or otherwise dispose of stolen items or produce.

Receiving stolen goods

Men like Ikey Solomons (supposedly, but probably not, the model for Dickens' 'Fagin') served a useful purpose for thieves. Solomon was a notorious character in the early decades of the nineteenth century. At his arrest in 1826, a search of his premises discovered somewhere between £18,000 and £20,000 in stolen goods and banknotes.[110] Receivers like the fictional Fagin were associated with the 'low lodging houses' and 'rookeries' in the metropolis' rougher areas (such as St Giles, the Borough and Whitechapel),[111] but such places also existed outside of London.[112] Young offenders who were interviewed on the hulk *Euryalus* revealed the extent and importance of the network of receivers (like the notorious William Sheen) they interacted with and the 'central role' they had in their lives.[113]

Receiving was a problem for the authorities because it was deemed to encourage thefts. This had been recognized well before the likes of Solomon rose to prominence. An act to prevent shoplifting in 1699 seems to have been aimed especially at the prosecution of receivers, as was a statute (in 1713) that made theft from a house punishable by death.[114] Other laws in the late seventeenth and early eighteenth centuries made receiving stolen goods a felony where once it had been merely a misdemeanour.[115] Henry Fielding, the Bow Street magistrate, complained about receivers and argued that they constituted a worse problem than the thieves that supplied them.[116] Catching receivers and prosecuting was made more difficult because in most instances, the thief had to have been caught and successfully convicted first. When Alexander Macarty [sic] was convicted by the Kingston assizes of stealing a large quantity of indigo and other dyes from his masters in Southwark, it opened the opportunity for the prosecution of Edward Griffin for receiving. Griffin was described as a victualler who kept a pub in Soho. Macarty claimed (when he was examined by Fielding) to have sold the indigo to him. Griffin at first attempted to deny all knowledge of the transaction but then admitted buying it and selling it on to a 'blue maker' (someone involved in whitening fabrics using dyes) in Oxford Street. Griffin was convicted and sentenced to be transported.[117] Almost exactly 100 years later, Charles Faulkner, a jeweller in Marylebone, was convicted of receiving thousands of precious stones that had been stolen from other jewellers in Clerkenwell Green. Faulkner had a brother-in-law who had served time in prison who made the acquaintance of a burglar called Rice. Rice had stolen the stones in question soon after his release from gaol. Faulkner was found guilty and given four years penal servitude.[118]

In 1910, Joseph Brandl, a hat shape manufacturer operating in the London's East End, sold thirty rolls of silk to a buyer for £119 (about £7,000 today). But the goods were stolen, having been taken en route to their intended purchaser in the City, a Swiss silk manufacturer. The value of silk was estimated to be £1,751 (or close to £100,000 in modern money), so Brandl's customer was right to think it was a 'fair price' to pay! Despite protesting his innocence, Brandl was sent to prison for six months.[119]

These three examples show how important receiving was to thieves, especially those taking items in bulk that were not so easy to dispose of. Smaller things could be traded directly or pawned, but unscrupulous dealers like Brandl or Faulkner were invaluable in understanding markets and having contacts within legitimate trading circles. Trade and exchange also created opportunities for another form of property crime, fraud.

Fraud and deception

Fraud is closely linked to forgery because it generally involves misrepresentation or impersonation (of someone or something). As a category of crime, fraud can also include bribery while deception might mean falsifying documents for personal use of private gain (e.g. creating a fake marriage certificate). As with counterfeit money, frauds have the capacity to undermine legitimate forms of business and so adversely impact upon social and commercial relations.

Some forms of fraud (still perpetrated today on unwary visitors to town centres up and down the country) were relatively low level and involved games of chance. These so-called 'Tricks of the Town' included games of dice or cards and examples of jugglers or other street performers who tricked their audience into handing over their coins. These sorts of fraudsters preyed on newcomers to the city who were often easy to spot because of their homespun clothes or rural accents. Gambling was as endemic among the pooper class (who could not afford it) as it was within the ranks of the elite (who, at least for the most part, could). The Court of Bridewell in London actively enforced laws against street gambling, and the authorities issued regular proclamations against 'illegal sports and pastimes'.[120] This sort of fraud was practised at the numerous fairs and markets across the country because there was always someone ready to take advantage of gullible individuals who hoped that they could 'beat the table'. In 1748, a seller of rags from Oundle was sent to the local house of correction for conspiring with an accomplice to trick William Winslowe, first out of his money, and then, when he attempted to win it back, his horse. The dice were loaded and Winslowe was duped.[121]

Fraudsters or 'confidence tricksters' as they came to be known in the twentieth century 'personified theft by means of skill and wits, rather than by manual labor [sic] (as in burglary) or with violence (as in robbery)'.[122] The fact that fraud often involves intelligence and a good deal of bravado has made it seem somehow different from these other forms of property offending. One modern TV drama even presents the protagonists of ever more elaborate frauds and tricks as somewhat heroic or at least admirable.[123] In 1695, Anne Hardy was fairly typical of fraudsters in the late seventeenth and throughout the eighteenth century in that she attempted to obtain the pay of a dead sailor by pretending to be his sister. Her punishment was to stand in the pillory and to be exposed to the anger of the London crowd.[124] Trying to gain a sailor's wages was a common fraud, and several men and women were prosecuted at Old Bailey or brought before the City justices at Guildhall and Mansion House. Christian Squires attempted the same ruse in 1744 and persuaded a court in Canterbury to grant her a letter of attorney for her brother that had died at the battle of La Guaira in 1743 during the war of the Austrian Succession. She was discovered when the man's real sister turned up to claim his wages. She too was pilloried near the Navy Office to deter others from following her example.[125]

Another seemingly popular eighteenth-century fraud was to cheat persons out of their lottery tickets or rather their insurance against their numbers not being drawn. This is what Jonathan Sheppard was accused of doing when he was brought before the sitting justice at Guildhall in 1775. Fortunately for him, the justice dismissed the case for a lack of evidence.[126] John Peter Mayaffree was not so lucky. He was convicted at the Old Bailey in 1746 of making and selling false lottery tickets. We are quite familiar with the concept of a National Lottery, and one existed in England throughout much of the 1700s. Contemporaries however had mixed views about it, believing it encouraged gambling and idleness and also that it attracted criminals and fraudsters and it was eventually banned in the early 1800s. Mayaffree's case was highly technical – as many modern frauds are – and it involved him buying some tickets and altering them and selling them on under a false name. The jury convicted him but recommended mercy 'on account of his excellent character and tender years', and perhaps a feeling that the people he attempted to cheat (the lottery office owners) were not above condemnation themselves.[127]

Passing oneself off as someone else – especially someone of wealth – involved a certain amount of playacting and preparation. In 1870, two 'lady swindlers' set themselves up in an up market lodging house in Scarborough and managed to persuade local tradesmen that they were descended from Robert the Bruce (the heroic medieval king of Scotland). Given that for much of the eighteenth and nineteenth century, monetary credit was given on the basis of appearance and a belief in your trustworthiness (literally one's 'credibility'), a confident and well-organized fraudster could get away with a lot. These two were caught and given eight months at hard labour.[128] The Victorians were aware that the increasingly complex world of business, with its transfer of deeds, titles, shares as well as money, created new possibilities for fraudulent activity (and worse). Maria Manning's motivation for arranging the murder of her lover, Patrick O'Connor, was to get her hands on his railway shares. She was arrested in Scotland when she tried to cash in on them.

One local paper in the north east of England reported the case of a woman who was supposedly using the new Married Women's Property Act (passed in 1870) to make 'fraudulent claims to furniture and effects, and even to real property, which owing to her improved status and power to enter into contracts are difficult to investigate and disprove'.[129] Changes to the laws surrounding bankruptcy and debt, particularly the Debtors Act (1869) that effectively ended the practice of imprisonment for debt, also involved penalties for those that tried to cheat the system. Henry Mason, a Bristol grocer, tried to avoid his debts by applying for bankruptcy and then removing all his goods before the receiver could assess and seize them. He and a team of men emptied his shop and sold on his merchandise. Despite his attempts to apologize to the court, the judge was not amused and sent him down for eight months.[130]

While some frauds were aimed at deceiving the general public or local businesses, others were the result of opportunistic employees, who saw ways to profit illegally from their employment. The advent of the railway offered just such an opportunity for private gain (as the infamous murderess Maria Manning realized). Two London booking clerks working for the London, Chatham and Dover Railway Company realized that they could resell used tickets.[131] This sort of small-scale fraud must have been very hard to detect, and businesses needed to improve their security and systems in order to thwart it. Attempts to improve the way money is exchanged or goods are sold can place obstacles in the path of some would-be thieves, while at the same time creating openings for others. The move towards electronic forms of exchange means that forging false signatures on bank cheques, for example, is made more difficult, but now identity theft is on the increase. Credibility remains at the heart of transactions in society, as anyone who has received an email promising them that there are huge sums of free money waiting for them in a foreign bank account if only they would provide some personal information can attest. Similarly, while fraud is ever present, so are attempts to steal from employers.

Embezzlement and theft from employers

Much of the property crime that has already been discussed did or could have involved theft from employers. Servants routinely stole their master or mistress' property be it small amounts of food, the stubs of candles or more valuable items such as linen, clothes and cutlery. Employment offered all sorts of opportunities for theft so 'common pilferers' lifted all manner of goods from the warehouses and wharfs that lined the eighteenth-century River Thames including dyes, tobacco, fuel and spirits. Many probably did so believing this sort of appropriation to be no more than a perk of their trade; employers increasingly saw this differently, and offenders were punished if caught.[132] However, there was a specific offence of embezzling that was prosecuted throughout the period we are interested in. What did this involve?

Embezzlement was generally dealt with summarily by the magistracy as a misdemeanour, rather than as a felony that needed to be heard before a judge and jury.[133] The eighteenth century saw the passing of several acts to make the embezzlement of property by employees a capital offence. While it was relatively rare for masters to use this legislation, the fact that it existed demonstrates the underlying concern that society had with this sort of activity, as it was a crime that suggested that even one's closest employees could not be trusted. This concern continued into the Victorian period where the fact that this sort of crime was 'hidden' to some extent undermined a prevailing confidence (brought upon by the establishment of professional policing) that crime was under control.[134]

In 1823, the law was tightened to specially cover employees who stole from their employers. Legislation that prosecuted thefts from a specific place had been used since the early 1700s, but this new act was created to respond to concerns about workplace appropriation that followed the rapid industrializing process of the late eighteenth century.[135] Most (76 per cent) of those successfully prosecuted for this offence at the Old

Bailey after the passing of the act were men, and most were subsequently sent to prison. The peak period for indictments was the 1830s and 1840s, which was also a time of widespread political and social unrest. In 1847 (the year which saw the highest number of guilty verdicts for these sorts of thefts), 351 men and 106 women were convicted at the Central Criminal Court for stealing from their employers. William Phillips took home copper from a factory where he worked with around fifty other men. His foreman suspected it was not the first time he had done so, just the first time he had been caught. Given his youth (he was just 17), the court were minded to be lenient. They were less inclined to show the same leniency towards Frederick Claus. Claus worked for the London and North Western Railway Company as a porter until May 1847. He was visited by a police superintendent (in the employ of the railway), who found a large amount of clothes belonging to the company. There were two dozen coats, trousers, waistcoats, buttons and boots, which were supposed to have been distributed to employees annually (or biannually in the case of boots and trousers). Claus claimed that he dealt in old clothes and had bought and paid for them legitimately. The court was not convinced, and a string of witnesses swore that the items were company issue or that they had missed them recently. Claus was sent to prison for a year.[136]

These examples could be supported by hundreds of other incidents in which metal, cloth, foodstuffs, fuel or tools were pilfered from the workplace. The routine prosecution of such offences was dwarfed by the amount of petty larceny (much of it from employers) that was dealt with summarily. The extension of summary powers to magistrates in the first half of the nineteenth century now meant that most young thieves and most petty thieves could be prosecuted more quickly before 'the beak' at a Police Court in any of England's towns and cities. Of course, many employers would not have bothered with the time and expense of taking an employee to court. Throughout the period 1660–1914, those who lost their employment were in a precarious position. The Poor Law offered some support for those without work, but after 1834, the imposition of the workhouse test meant that help came at a considerable price. Employers wielded a powerful weapon against any employee who chose to dip his or her 'fingers in the till'; they could simply be dismissed, without a hearing and without any references.

It is likely then that those who did choose to prosecute offenders did so at times of hardship (when thefts might be more prevalent) or industrial dispute (to exercise another layer of control of their workforce), or when it was clear that the offender had been 'at it' for some time or when an example was required. This situation probably persists to the present day. One sociological exploration of pilfering in the late 1970s concluded that ' "caught", for[137] the employee thief, rarely means "court" ', and thefts from the workplace were considered as economic rather than moral crimes. We should always remember that the victims of thefts did not always prosecute, and there were multiple reasons for this.

A short note on the victims of crime

Most of those who prosecuted as victims of these crimes were men. This is not at all surprising of course, because men owned most property. Women, for most of the period covered by this book, effectively lost control of any property they had when they married. Only 10 per cent of prosecutors bringing property offenders to the summary courts of the City of London were female, and the vast majority (68 per cent) were either tradesmen or merchants. The above sample from 1830 shows that at the Old Bailey, over 80 per cent of victims were men. They were tradesmen, like the prosecutors at the summary level in the late eighteenth century: butchers, cheese mongers, haberdashers, barbers, brokers, shoemakers, tobacconists and all manner of non-descript or general shopkeepers.

However, we should not discount the significant number of poorer victims that appeared as prosecutors in the summary court in the second half of the 1700s. Almost 13 per cent of these prosecutors were in occupations that offered what was at best irregular or sporadic employment, and a further 16 per cent can be seen as members of the labouring poor. Undoubtedly, some of them were appearing in court on behalf of their employers, but by no means were all of them.[138] The fact that grand larceny covered the theft of goods valued at over a shilling meant that it supposedly protected the possession of even the most humblest of Englishmen or women. The caveat here is that prosecution was a time-consuming and potentially expensive business, and so, it was more likely that prosecutors would be drawn from among those who were better off. This process may have begun to change in the 1800s with the advent of professional police forces. Now prosecutions started to be instigated by the police themselves, and many offenders were brought before the magistrates in Police Courts accused of committing minor property crimes.

In this chapter, I have tried to outline some of the key characteristics of property crime and how it was perceived. Stealing other people's property appears to continue to be a perennial problem for society, and the sister chapter to this one will look at some of the explanations surrounding the causes of theft. Naturally, people's motivations will differ according to the individual and the circumstances they find themselves in, but it is worth keeping in mind that over the course of the last 200–300 years, society has increasingly tried to understand property a little more and punish it a little less.

CHAPTER 5
THE CAUSES OF PROPERTY CRIME

What we will try to understand in this chapter is why people stole. What motivated considerable numbers of men, women and children to risk their lives or freedom to steal items and goods that were of relatively small value? This involves a discussion of what has been termed 'social crime'; whether this was taking apples from common land, game from the forests or the residue left behind after cargo ships had been unloaded at the docks, this pilfering of goods represents a blurred line between illegal activity and traditional custom. Trying to understand why people stole is difficult. Even with important advances in psychology and criminology, there are still strong disagreements about a criminal's motivation for theft. It is easy to condemn theft as borne out of greed or a reluctance to earn the money required to enjoy the latest consumer luxuries. Likewise, opportunistic theft (such as shoplifting) is sometimes dismissed as thrill-seeking behaviour. Some recent high-profile thefts by celebrities (such as the actress Winona Ryder or the TV chef Anthony Worrall-Thompson) have been explained as psychological reactions to problems in their lives with little to do with the items stolen at all. In other instances, there appear to be comparisons to be drawn with other forms of negative and addictive behaviour such as alcoholism. In the later 1800s, the term *kleptomania* emerged to explain the actions of women that stole items they did not need but simply felt compelled to take.[1] However valid these theories are, it is very hard to apply them retrospectively to larcenists in the past because court records and newspaper reports so rarely explain why people stole. We can reasonably speculate that some theft was occasioned by need, although this need might have been caused by a 'deviant' lifestyle. A modern example would be theft by drug users who have resorted to crime in order to support an expensive addiction to narcotics.

Economics and property crime: The effect of 'dearth'[2]

In the past, some people clearly stole to support themselves when times were hard, and historians have identified clear correlations between poverty and destitution, poor harvests and high food prices and increased levels of prosecutions. As William Cobbett wrote, 'Who is to expect morality in a half-starved man?'[3]

Throughout the period of this book, the typical English family relied on bread as the foundation of their diet, and so fluctuations in the price of wheat could easily tip communities into hardship and poverty, making it more likely that some might resort to theft. Historians have, however, cautioned against a direct correlation between high food prices and rising levels of crime. This may have been more apparent in the countryside when harvests were poor and labourers were unable to fund work. Indeed, it probably forced some to turn to rural offending such as poaching, or if they were near to the coast, smuggling, leading Eric Hobsbawm and George Rudé to conclude that people in rural areas stole to survive.[4] However, in reality, it is likely that there were multiple and overlapping causal factors behind theft in the countryside.

There were certainly years when the harvest failed and prices of basic commodities rose alarmingly. Historians of riot and social protest have explored the phenomenon of the food riot in Georgian England and the ways in which the labouring poor took action to counter attempts (by famers and dealers) to raise the price of wheat or corn, or to move goods around in order to profit from spiralling price increases. Magistrates were routinely called upon to intervene before rioting broke out or to regulate (or 'set') the price of bread.[5] One of the problems this causes for researchers is that during periods of riots and protests, some prosecutors opted to bring indictments against rioters for property offences rather than for rioting, because it was easier to secure convictions. As a result, property crime statistics might appear to rise at times of tension, but this may have more to do with prosecution strategies rather than with increased levels of theft. At the same time, statistics may also be affected by discretionary behaviour by justices, juries and prosecutors who, taking pity of poorer destitute defendants at times of dearth, declined to prosecute or find them guilty as charged. Nineteenth-century observers were aware of the links between poverty and crime, but that it was but one explanation among many.[6] One contemporary viewed criminals as gamblers who were forever 'employed in calculating the chances for and against them'.[7] John Binny, writing in the 1850s, blamed crime on immorality, vice and on individuals who were 'too lazy to work'.[8]

There were clear differences between the urban and rural experience of crime, and this was recognized by contemporaries. Charles Brereton, a critic of the scheme to introduce a rural police, argued that there were clear distinctions between criminals in towns and elsewhere.

> In cities the majority of thieves exist in gangs, practice fraud by profession, and live by a constant series of depredations…criminals in the country only occasionally once or twice a year steal a sheep, pig, corn, hay, wood, turnips, poultry as the case may be.[9]

In terms of the nature of things stolen, he was probably correct, but the motivations are less clear. Lynn MacKay has suggested there were multiple reasons behind thefts in London. Some of those tried attempted to excuse their behaviour by suggesting that they were incapacitated by alcohol and did not remember what they had done. Others claimed they had not intended to steal or had only done so at the behest of someone else, while some said they had 'found' items or had legitimate reasons to have them in their possession (such as having been employed to deliver them for example – even if the mysterious owner had subsequently disappeared without trace). Female offenders were more likely to steal from those they knew: from neighbours, friends or employers, and this reflected the relative restrictions on women by comparison to men. Women were also more closely connected in 'borrowing networks', where items of clothing and other goods would be pawned or lent as required. When someone abused this system (or there were other reasons for relationship breakdowns), this could result in an indictment for theft. This also suggests that a 'somewhat fluid notion of private property' existed among plebeian Londoners in the 1700s, quite different to the one outlined by John Locke.[10]

Thus, a whole host of variables affected the prosecution of property criminals and the motivations of those that stole. As a result, we are perhaps left to conclude that poverty and need, while clearly a factor in propelling some into crime, was not the only explanation. Modern criminology exhibits a number of conflicting theories for why people do (or did) commit crime.[11] These might range from what Croall terms the 'everyday' offender to 'young people having fun', unskilled opportunists up to the 'skilled and motivated property offender'.[12]

A second factor that historians have identified as affecting property crime rates was war. Throughout most of the eighteenth and some of the nineteenth century England was at war, either with France (and Spain) or in its colonies in America, India and Africa. As a general rule, historians have agreed that during wartime crime rates were reduced with fewer indictments being prosecuted, whereas a return to peace led to increased prosecutions. Let us explore this further.

War and its effects upon prosecution rates

Warfare in the long eighteenth century took thousands of Englishmen away from their country to fight in continental Europe, Canada and colonial America, as well as patrolling the seas and defending imperial possessions in the Caribbean and Australasia. While the numbers of men involved was not high by the comparison with the First World War, these conflicts stretched over a much longer timespan (the wars against Revolutionary and Napoleonic France lasted nearly twenty years, for example), and so the pressure for recruits was considerable. The need for troops affected crime rates in a number of ways. The simple fact that young men could sign up for (or be duped into joining) the army or the navy reduced the number of individuals competing for work. As a result, there were more opportunities for older men and women to take up the slack caused by the recruitments of soldiers and sailors. This eased the pressure of work and probably also slightly improved pay rates. By contrast, when peace returned, so did hundreds of demobilized men.

Not only that but the grim realities of war may have created or exacerbated criminal behaviour in some. Highwaymen, for example, had to be adept at riding horses and have a familiarity with guns and bladed weapons – these were also the skills required and developed by cavalrymen. Servicemen who returned home wounded, missing limbs or blinded had little opportunity to resume whatever employment they had pursued before the war and now faced the threat of poverty; it is likely that some of these resorted to crime as a result. However, once again historians have encountered a problem in trying to draw simple corollaries between war, peace and crime rates. This is partly because prosecutors and magistrates made use of the nation's need for troops, and second, because soldiers and sailors who committed crimes while in service but on home soil could be prosecuted by the military authorities and so do not appear in the records of the criminal justice system. So, some offenders were simply invited to enlist in the forces to avoid a trial altogether (thereby not only benefitting the state but also earning money for constables who were rewarded for finding 'volunteers'). Young offenders were often squirreled off into the Marine Society or the arms of the nearest recruiting sergeant. This alternative was not available in times of peace, and it is notable that following victory at Waterloo in 1815 and the final collapse of the French First Empire, there was considerable concern about the rising level of criminal activity, especially among the young.

After Waterloo, though Britain enjoyed a relatively long period of peace abroad, it experienced considerable upheaval and sporadic protest at home. The armed forces were not involved in a major conflict until the 1850s when troops were once again involved in action in the Crimea (1853–1856) and the Indian 'Mutiny' (1857–1858). Thereafter, small numbers of troops were almost constantly deployed protecting and expanding the British Empire until the next major conflict in South Africa from 1899 to 1902. There were concerns about youth and crime throughout the period from 1815 to the 1850s, and the last decades of the nineteenth century saw a considerable moral panic about delinquency and the lack of order and morality among young people.

The final issue that needs to be considered within the context of motivations of those committing property crimes is therefore age. Unfortunately, age is (unlike gender) almost impossible to glean from records of crime before the nineteenth century. Modern studies of criminality have revealed that while large numbers of individuals have committed a crime of some description by the time they reach their thirties, the peak age for offending is 18. There is also 'some evidence specialisation increased with age', and this – as far as records allow us to compare – is also true of the eighteenth and nineteenth centuries.[13]

Age and the importance of the life cycle

As I noted above, determining the age of offenders is difficult for much of the eighteenth century. Courts rarely recorded ages until the 1800s, but for a brief window between 1782 and 1787, the ages of offenders tried on the Home Circuit are available, and this reveals that two-thirds of offenders were aged under 30. The peak ages for offending were the 'late teens and early twenties' with half of all offenders being 18–25 years old.[14] This statistic aligns very neatly with modern research, and the data from the late 1700s also shows us that there were similar variations in the ages at which offenders were most likely to be charged with particular offences. Three-fifths of receivers were over 35 and one-fifth over 55 while only 15 per cent of frauds, forgers and coiners were under 25, suggesting that these sorts of crimes attracted older individuals. Highwaymen and footpads tended to be younger because such a violent crime required more agile, fit and energetic individuals (such as returning soldiers).

Teenage defendants in the early years of the nineteenth century were actually more likely to be convicted of crime than older prisoners who were brought to trial. Shore's work on London has shown us that 'younger people were less likely to be acquitted, and juveniles were the least likely to be acquitted'.[15] Therefore, teenagers and young adults were considered to be a problem throughout the late seventeenth to early twentieth centuries and as a result were at a greater risk of prosecution, conviction and punishment.

Women in late-eighteenth- and early nineteenth-century London were most vulnerable to prosecution when they were single (and often newly arrived in the capital) or when widowed or abandoned by their male partners. This would indicate that there is a connection not only between offending and economic hardship but also between offending and independence. However, it is important to remind ourselves (again) that patterns of offending are measured by the statistics of prosecutions, *not* by incidents of crime. Very young thieves, women with children or the elderly did not appear to offer the same threat to society as men in their late teens or early twenties, nor did they appear in such great numbers in court.

Figure 5.1 shows quite clearly the impact that age has on patterns of prosecution. The proportion of those aged 18–25 accounts for approximately 40 per cent of all defendants, even though this covers just eight years of the life cycle. Those aged 25–40 and 40–55 (a combined total of just thirty years) only amount to 43 per cent. This would seem to confirm that, in the period where we have reasonably good data for ages, it was the 18–25s that were most likely to appear in court.

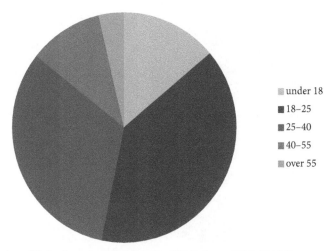

Figure 5.1 Age of defendants in all trials at the Old Bailey, c.1800–1913.[16]

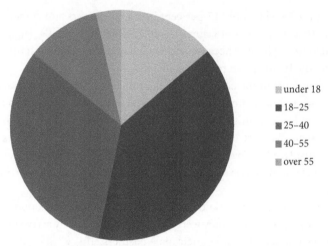

Figure 5.2 Age of male defendants in all trials at the Old Bailey, c.1800–1913.[17]

As we can see from Figure 5.2, the pattern remains almost identical when we look only at male defendants, but there is some variation for females (Figure 5.3). Here, while the age range 18–25 is still proportionally dominant (given that it only covers eight years), there is a significantly increased proportion of female defendants aged 25–40 and fewer under 18. This probably reflects differences in years of female independence and vulnerability as compared with men.

The statistics of crime are also affected by the prosecution strategies of those who fell victim to thefts and the survival of material that allows the historian to measure offending and its prosecution in the past. Much crime was dealt with summarily, without a jury trial and often left little record.

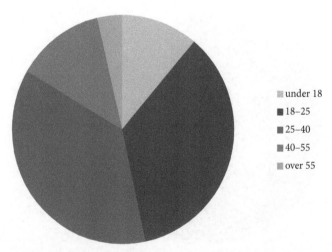

Figure 5.3 Age of female defendants in all trials at the Old Bailey, c.1800–1913.[18]

Property crimes prosecuted at the summary level

Historians are beginning to better understand how summary proceedings played out across the long eighteenth and early nineteenth centuries. By the middle of the nineteenth centuries, most juvenile offenders and petty thieves were appearing before JPs at petty sessions rather than being sent on to face a jury trial. There are differences here between rural crime, which was closely linked to agriculture, the theft of fuel and industries such as spinning and weaving, and urban crime, which was more likely to be associated with pilferage from warehouses and docksides.

Many of those working in the rural economy were employed as outworkers, meaning that they worked from home but for a central manufacturer. One example is the worsted spinning industry, which produced yarn that could be used in the manufacture of stockings, clothes and other goods. Various types of wool were spun to make worsted, and spinners were paid according to the weight of worsted that they produced. Outworkers would be given raw wool, and the finished product would be collected by the manufacturer's agent when completed.[19] This process was, however, open to fraud and embezzlement. The notebooks of the second Earl Spencer detail some of his justicing work surrounding his Northamptonshire estate in the late eighteenth century.[20] Within them are several prosecutions of women for the offence of false reeling, such as this entry in June 1793:

> Ann Miller brought on a summons for false reeling. The yarn produced. J Eddings, inspector, swears that it is short in the hank by several yards [...] Convicted and sentenced to pay 40s time given till next Saturday and if not paid then, a warrant of distress to be issued.[21]

Spencer was applying the law as he was entitled to do as a justice. Under legislation passed between 1777 and 1792, inspectors were employed to police the worsted industry. False reeling 'involved the yarn being deficient in the number of threads' but reeled onto a standard reel staff, while short reeling meant that the offender had used a 'a reel of less than the standard circumference'.[22] Either fraud meant that the spinner handed over less yarn than she was employed to spin, meaning she could keep some for herself and fractionally improve the wage rate she was being paid. The legislation to introduce worsted inspectors was the manufacturers' reaction to embezzlement within their industry, and justices were given powers to punish offenders on a sliding scale. First offenders faced a small fine (5–20s.) that was increased by a second or subsequent offence to between 40s. and £5. If the spinner was determined to continue to flout the laws, they faced a spell of imprisonment and a whipping for any further infractions.[23] The prosecution of other forms of rural appropriation also had their roots in the development of a new capitalist economic system but was far less straightforward than false or short reeling.

The taking of fruit and wood were both offences that could be punished summarily. Both were also actions undertaken as part of the 'economy of makeshifts' of rural society. As such, they had been seen, alongside gleaning (collecting the leftover wheat or corn from a field that has been harvested) and the grazing of cattle and pigs in woods and on common land, as a part of a range of customary 'rights' that had been claimed by the rural labouring for centuries.[24] As Thompson has described, these rights were increasingly contested and eroded as the English countryside was enclosed, and its populace turned off the land or forced to become waged labourers.[25]

The theft of wood was '[p]ossibly the most common way in which the law and rights of property were infringed' in eighteenth-century England.[26] The rural poor had long been accustomed to the practice of collecting kindling and branches to use for fuel. This practice was celebrated and affirmed as part of the ritual calendar of early modern and eighteenth-century England on May Day and at other festivals. However, in the process of taking 'dead wood' (that which came away easily), some gatherers took green wood (which was also useful for building) and that had the potential to cause damage to trees. Landowners increasingly objected to the 'snapping' of wood and legislators moved to remove customary rights from wood gathering and so make it illegal. In 1663, parliament passed an act 'for the Punishment of unlawful cutting or stealing or spoiling of wood'[27] that extended Elizabethan legislation. Offenders could be asked to make reparation to the landowner, be fined or imprisoned for up to a month in the nearest bridewell and whipped.

In the eighteenth century, as rural communities reacted to parliamentary enclosure and a widespread attack on customary practices, the penalties for offending were increased. Wood thieves now faced an increased fine (up to £20) for a first offence; a fine of £30 or 12–18 months in prison for second; and for a third offence, they could be formally indicted and, if convicted, transported for seven years.[28] As a result of these legislative changes (and landowners' determination to protect their property), offenders before their local justices charged with cutting or taking wood. Rob Breton was convicted on the evidence of a land agent, and as he did not have the money to pay 40s., he was committed to a house of correction for a month and sentenced 'to be once whipped'.[29]

The wide definition of what constituted 'wood' allowed for the summary prosecution of individuals who were protesting about the enclosure of land, by the pulling down and taking away of fence pales, thus making convictions easier to obtain. So, we should see the use of summary powers to punish wood thieves (as well as those that 'scrumped' apples, picked berries or stole all manner of woodland and hedgerow produce) as a part of a wider criminalization of custom in the long eighteenth century. The most famous of these ongoing battles between the labouring poor and the elites was the so-called 'long affray', the war between poachers and gamekeepers.

Poaching and the game laws

Under late seventeenth-century legislation, the hunting of game (deer, rabbits, wild birds, etc.) was effectively made an elite pastime, and anyone from even a fairly middling situation was barred from doing so.[30] In effect, if you did not meet the set property qualification, you could not hunt, even on your own land.[31] Until the eighteenth century, game cases were tried before a jury at quarter sessions, but thereafter, offenders were dealt with summarily before a local magistrate. Moreover, a 1722 law allowed prosecutors to take those they accused through a civil process (in the court of record), which could increase the financial penalties (although this carried its own risks as Munsche explains).[32]

The penalties for breaking the law were reinforced and increased in the early 1700s, so that offenders faced fines of between £5 and £30 as well as lengthy periods of imprisonment. The game laws were not simply there to protect game as property but also to 'protect the poor from their own idleness'.[33] Poaching continued despite the game laws, and parliament attempted to legislate to curb the practice. The law made a distinction between hunting during the day (which might be sport or an individual attempt to secure food) and at night (which suggested a less legitimate purpose such as poaching for commercial gain). In 1770, the punishment for night poaching was changed from a £5 fine to six months' imprisonment and a public whipping. This was raised in 1773 to a fine of £10 with imprisonment for three months if the fine could not be paid – and £10 was a huge sum for a rural labourer to find. Finally, in 1784, anyone hunting was required to have a certificate (which cost two guineas); without this they would incur a £20 fine or a term of imprisonment. Parliament was seemingly intent on preserving the privilege of hunting game for country gentlemen and no one else.[34]

Despite the risks of being caught, poaching remained a perennial problem for landowners and the magistracy. Landowners and farmers could simply withdraw employment (which could extend to the poacher's family and kin network), but this embedded rural discontent and undermined the 'bonds of deference' that underpinned social relations in the countryside. Munsche's analysis of those prosecuted for poaching in Wiltshire also shows that there were plenty who could afford the fines, suggesting that the trade in game was very profitable in the second half of the eighteenth century.[35] In fact, the game laws probably helped to encourage a trade in game rather than prevent it. There was an extensive black market for game and gangs of poachers, as well as individuals were able to exploit this. For example, a poacher in Staffordshire 'killed nearly eighty hares during the winter of 1764 and sold them in Lichfield at three shillings each, a return of some £12, which is probably as much as he earned in a year as a labourer'.[36]

Game offences were often prosecuted before the magistracy without the need for a jury. Given that many JPs were landowners and hunting men themselves, or moved within circles that cherished their right to hunt, it is evident that poachers could expect little sympathy when they came before them. Burn's manual for JPs for the year 1785 has no fewer than ninety pages dedicated to the game laws, which shows the importance and ubiquity (and complexity) of the laws.[37] However, throughout the long period covered by this study, life in rural England was tough: '[w]ork and wages, at the best of times, were barely adequate to sustain a labouring family'[38] and it is no surprise that some resorted to poaching to supplement a meagre existence. The numbers of prosecutions for poaching increased at times of social tension (such as in the immediate aftermath of the passing of the 1834 Poor Law Amendment Act or in 1846, when the potato crop was devastated by blight).[39] So, some authors have seen poaching simply as a necessary consequence of hard times, arguing that men poached 'to fill their children's empty bellies'.[40] But this is far too simplistic, as poaching could involve all sorts of people, not all of them poor or working class.

Poaching was a skilled activity, learned over time and practised by members of middle class as well as the labouring classes. It was hard to quantify; parliamentary returns of convictions for the 1800s almost certainly vastly underestimate the amount of illegal hunting that was going on, especially at night when poachers were harder to catch. Poaching could be a solitary practice, or it could involve gangs of armed men. The wars between poachers and their antithesis, the gamekeepers, could be both violent and deadly. Keepers homes were attacked and individuals were forced, 'on pain of death' to disable all the traps that had been set to catch unwary poachers.[41] By contrast, the gamekeepers were detested for their unscrupulous methods and callous disregard for the lives and well-being of those that attempted to steal game from their master's land. Lord Ellenborough's Act of 1803 made resisting arrest by a gamekeeper a capital crime if the offender was in possession of a loaded gun (regardless of whether he presented or fired it). In 1816 transportation was introduced for those taking game or rabbits with a net and further legislation in 1828 extended this up to fourteen years for poaching gangs. Bankes' Act of 1818 made it illegal to buy game, with financial penalties applied at £5 per animal.[42] But, despite the fact that some poachers were transported or imprisoned and that the law allowed such severe sentences, most poachers were dealt with summarily and fined.

The battles between gamekeepers and poachers have been described as a war, and its victims even, with more than a touch of hyperbole, likened to those of Nazi Germany. There were clear double standards applied to poaching: so a 'gentleman could not poach' even when caught red-handed, and there were flagrant examples of hypocrisy, so while the trade in poached meat was illegal, 'a judge (being a gentleman) would have no qualms in buying for his table'.[43] Poaching was not the only theft that involved animals, however.

Theft of animals and livestock

The stealing of horses, sheep and cattle were deemed to be particularly serious crimes. Horse theft had been a non-clergyable offence from the reign of Henry VIII. Stealing horses was a relatively easy crime to commit and can be likened to taking motor vehicles today; in stealing a horse, the thief had ensured a quick getaway and would find it easy to sell on afterwards. For this reason, and because horse thefts were often the work of organized gangs, horse thieves could expect little mercy from the courts if convicted. So, in eighteenth-century Essex, one set of assize judges chose to execute all of the horse thieves that they had convicted, sparing none, in an attempt to clamp down on the crime.

Traditionally, sheep stealing had not been seen to be as serious as horse theft, but it was made capital without benefit of clergy in 1741 after a wave of thefts prompted landowners and farmers to petition their MPs. There had been a poor harvest that forced up the price of wheat and caused distress in rural areas with a concomitant rise in property crime.[44] In 1801 ('a year of exceptional hunger'), four sheep thieves were hanged at the Salisbury assizes, emphasizing the determination of the authorities to clamp down on the crime to send a strong message to others tempted to supplement their meagre diets with illegally sourced mutton.[45]

There was a difference however in the ways in which the courts tended to approach theft of livestock. It was more usual for the courts to discriminate between those that stole one sheep (for food) and others that 'rustled' several animals to sell on for profit. The former were likely (if they had had no previous court appearances) to be released or, at the worst, treated more leniently, while those deemed to be 'professional' thieves could expect the gallows.[46] In 1822, Sir James Park, defending his decision not to hang a sheep thief, declared that he 'always distinguished between stealing sheep to sell and stealing a single sheep to eat', as one was clearly more worthy of severe punishment than the other.[47] There was a 'black market in mutton [which] was similar to that in game…and some butchers dealt in stolen meat just as poulterers bought poached pheasant or hare with no questions asked'.[48] Mutton, poultry and venison were all stolen by poachers and criminal gangs, and in 1730s Essex, there was a particular problem with the taking of deer from Waltham Forest. This is where Dick Turpin started his criminal career, by purchasing and reselling stolen venison for the Gregory Gang.

Poaching, along with wood theft, some forms of embezzlement and traditional practices like gleaning, sits in a grey area of property crime. These were considered by some (most often those that owned land) at times across the 1700s and 1800s to be *criminal* activities, while many of those committing them did not see them in that way. The rural poor saw them as legitimate and long-established 'rights' that had been enjoyed by their ancestors, and that were under threat from a new economic system. Historians have sought to explain this and other forms of criminal activity as representative of a struggle between established custom and the pressures and requirements of capitalist economics. In doing so, they have conceptualized them as 'social crimes', and the nature (and problems) of this term will be discussed next.

Social crime and banditry

The concept of 'social crime' had its origins in the work of Marxist historians such as Edward Thompson and Eric Hobsbawn.[49] The ideology underpinning the concept was that while 'crime' can be defined as actions that break the law, not all lawbreaking actions are seen as criminal by those perpetrating them. Moreover, the law can be seen as an artificial construct; something imposed on the majority by the minority to keep order or maintain an unequal distribution of wealth. The theory of *social crime*, therefore, was intimately linked to theories of history and class struggle. This was one of key reasons social historians such as Thompson and Hay embraced the history of crime in the first place. In recent years, social crime as an idea has all but disappeared from the historiography, as class-based interpretations of history have fallen out of fashion. However, in the absence of any dominant or more cohesive metanarrative, I think we should be careful about ditching class completely. Thus, an understanding and critique of social crime and banditry remains very useful.

In 1972, Hobsbawn wrote, 'Social criminality [...] occurs when there is a conflict of laws e.g. between an official and unofficial system, or when acts of law-breaking have a distinct element of social protest in them.'[50] This conflict is based in class relations and in the transitions from a society based on custom to one rooted in capitalist economics. Put simply, while almost all individuals in English society in the period 1660–1914 would have defined murder, child rape and violent robbery as acts they disapproved of and wanted to see punished, the same would not have necessarily been true about poaching rabbits or avoiding the duty payable on brandy or tea. Likewise, some sections of society would have been unlikely to condemn workers that took home 'perks' to supplement their low wages or rioters whose aim was to help the community avoid what they considered to be unfair road tolls or price rises in the food market.

The problem for historians or criminologists is that the term 'social criminality' is vague and can be used to explain and excuse a considerable amount of behaviour. However, before we dismiss the concept and illustrate its flaws, let us look at a structure that allows us to engage with what social crime is or was.

The first feature of a social crime is that perpetrator of the offence did not believe that they were committing a crime (even though the law was clearly broken). Like millions of tax evaders today, the smuggler did not see what they were doing as illegal. After all, they were harming no individual person and in fact were helping hundreds of people by supplying them with cheaper commodities. Second, the wider community (but crucially the community from within which offender lived, and *not* their social superiors the gentry and middling sorts) also viewed their actions as legitimate. The poacher that flouted the game laws to snare rabbits to feed his family broke the law but was unlikely to be condemned by his neighbours; the landowners and JPs from whom he took game, however, held a quite different view. Poaching, wood theft, gleaning and stealing apples from orchards all reflected the collision between the growing economic system of capital and property ownership against the long-established customary rights and 'economy of makeshifts' of the poor.

As a consequence, the third feature of social crime was that it was more difficult to prosecute. This was either because the community sheltered individual offenders from prosecution, or because large crowds committed such acts collectively and could not be stopped or arrested by the authorities. Coastal communities where smuggling was prevalent tended to close ranks when the excise men arrived looking for smugglers. Many felt a sense of solidarity with the offenders or feared the consequences of giving them away, as communities might ostracize those who did so. After all, smuggling 'was a business. Probably half of the three to four million pounds of tea consumed annually in Britain at the mid-century was contraband', and as Nicholas Rogers suggests, this business was borne out of the government's policy of charging a high tax on imported tea. It was also very difficult to prevent or prosecute as local people and organized gangs of smugglers were happy to use violence against the exercise men sent to close down the trade and catch the perpetrators.[51] In the early-to-mid-1700s, contraband tea 'passed through many hands – the smuggler, the dealer, the innkeeper – generally remaining near where it landed', and it quickly became 'big' business in eighteenth-century Sussex.[52] Given that the eighteenth-century state had limited policing and relied on deterrents to prevent crime, it was relatively easy to avoid arrest and prosecution if the community refused to give you up. Even if smugglers were captured, it was often hard to get a conviction. Many quarter sessions and assize juries contained men who might be in considerable sympathy with the offender. As was also true in many game cases for example, the farmers who often dominated juries themselves felt aggrieved that they could not hunt game on their own land so were not always inclined to convict their poorer neighbours for so doing.[53] Efforts to enforce legislation were hampered not only by local opposition from the labouring class (who could earn much more money aiding the landing of contraband goods than they could from more honest work) but also by the county magistracy. As Rogers noted, magistrates 'frequently winked at smuggling activities, especially when they knew they were condoned or even encouraged by local people whose livelihood depended on the trade'. Bribery was not unknown and revenue officers could be bought off or persuaded to look the other way.[54]

One example that is particularly interesting and revealing of the attitudes of communities towards smugglers is the prosecutions of those carrying out assaults on excise officers. These were the large force of coastguards and fleet-based men employed by the government to prevent smuggling. In Cornwall, those excise men pleading 'not guilty' to assaults were overwhelmingly convicted, showing that the petty jurors at the quarter sessions were quite clear whose side they were on.[55] In Sussex, it took ten years for the killers of a customs officer named Thomas Carswell to be brought to trial, despite a generous reward being offered. Contemporaries condemned smuggling gangs for using intimidation to prevent locals from informing on their activities, but communities may well have largely sympathized with the offenders.[56]

Here then is some evidence of a conflict of opinion on the rights and wrongs of the law and what constitutes a crime. As a result, the authorities were often forced to remove smuggling cases to areas where juries could be expected to be much less sympathetic or to convene special assizes to deal with the problem. Indeed, many of those convicted for smuggling in Sussex and Dorset in the 1700s were tried, not at local assizes, but at the Old Bailey.[57]

Some smugglers, like the Hawkshurst gang in Sussex, took on the revenue and boldly flouted the law, with their activities likened to civil rebellion rather than mere criminality.[58] In 1747, the gang apparently threatened to burn down the town of Goudhurst in Kent but was fought off by the militia.[59] In the end, the authorities hanged or transported around seventy-five members of the gang and fourteen 'were subjected to the further punishment of hanging in chains', so heinous were their crimes considered to be.[60] Some smugglers turned to other forms of crime such as burglary and highway robbery when smuggling dried up, and it would be inaccurate to see smuggling simply as a form of social crime – it was also an organized crime which involved serious violence. Moreover, despite the risks involved, 'smuggling was extremely profitable for large numbers of people'.[61] Perhaps as a consequence of this and a dislike of the authority that exercised such a ruthless system of punishment, smugglers could rely on considerable local support, and thus, we might also view such activity as an example of regional resistance to central rule, something that is also highlighted by recent work on the extent of the reach of the 'Bloody Code'.[62]

Historians have identified four different types of social crime: rioting, individual covert protests, rural appropriation of material goods and workplace (or industrial) appropriation. Rural crimes included wood theft, smuggling and poaching (that have already been discussed) and gleaning (which was the removal of corn or other crops that was left on fields and traditionally given to the poor but increasingly, and often unsuccessfully, claimed by the farmers as their property).[63] Here, custom and changing practices were in conflict, and developments in agriculture and the enclosure of land were at odds to traditional concepts of rights.

Changes to industrial practices also affected customary rights since most trades had perquisites ('perks') attached. Eighteenth-century workers were often paid piece rates for work completed and wages included supplements that directly related to the industry. Thus, carpenters and shipbuilders took home 'chips' – the wood left over when cutting up timber. They could use these to make other products either to sell or use for themselves. Weavers had traditionally been allowed the silk or cotton from the end of the loom, called 'thrums'. They went on strike in 1758 when the manufacturers tried to deny these to them. Coalheavers (those tasked with unloading cargos of the fuel from ships in dock) expected a bag or two of coal for themselves, and London dock porters believed they were entitled to small amounts of tobacco that they removed from the barrels they were unloading. Tailors took home remnants of cloth ('cabbage'), and hatters attempted to reduce their costs by substituting cheaper material for expensive beaver pelt, a practice called 'bugging'. Women working at reeling wool in rural Northamptonshire would soak the wool in water (to increase its weight) before returning it so that it concealed the fact that they had kept some for their own use.

Each of these forms of appropriation was social crimes in the sense that the perpetrators and the communities in which they were done felt them to be legitimate 'perks' of the job. They were therefore difficult to prosecute or convict. Often, special policing arrangements were needed (such as special constables on the London docks) along with an increased use of summary legislation to ensure offenders were both caught and punished. Only when factories replaced domestic or workshop located outwork did it become easier to prevent these forms of theft. Even after this however, nineteenth-century factory owners and shopkeepers continued to experience large-scale appropriation, as did newer trades. And of course, trying to prevent workplace appropriation in all its forms has continued to be a problem well into the twenty-first century as anyone that has used the office photocopier, phone or internet for their own personal use will testify.

Problems with the use of the term 'social crime'[64]

Trying to conceptualize certain types of property offending as 'social crime' is difficult because boundaries are often blurred. Indeed, the whole social crime thesis is problematic, which is probably why historians had distanced themselves from it in recent years (although there are signs that it is due for a revival). Early historians of crime were apt to see almost all property criminals as semi-heroic warriors against the inevitable onslaught of capitalism,[65] when the reality is that many thieves were simply individuals who stole for a variety of reasons. Social criminals are often portrayed to be 'good' criminals by contrast with the more ordinary 'bad' criminal, but this is hard to uphold under any close examination of so-called 'social' offending.

Not all smugglers or poachers were operating out of any sense of altruism, nor did they all eschew violence (as was very evident with the Hawkhurst gang, for example). Food rioters usually avoided violence, but if farmers refused to hand over grain, violence might ensue, mills were pulled down and traders did get assaulted. Coastal wreckers (those salvaging goods from ships that ran around) might focus on grabbing what they could rather than on saving the lives of those that had been shipwrecked. So, these were not all peaceful, quiet, non-violent groups.

Nor is it straightforward to argue that social criminals always had community approval because it is necessary to qualify what we mean by 'community' in different cases. In some sorts of social crime (smuggling and poaching, for example), the labouring poor and middling sort might have explicitly or tacitly approved of their actions, while in others only the labouring poor would support them; the middling sort would have opposed bread riots, gleaning and industrial pilfering, for example.

Nor were those involved in social crimes always individual semi-starving labourers eking out a living from perks. Some were well-organized groups of capitalist operators. Many sold the goods they appropriated for considerable sums. Poaching gangs could make big profits and came out of town to raid the countryside. Smuggling can be seen as a profit-making trade just like any other. It is difficult to see these groups as rejecting current notions of property and profit, and so, this is perhaps not the place to find anti-capitalist heroes.

Undoubtedly, communities were more likely to be sympathetic to smugglers, gleaners or poachers than they were to murderers, highway robbers or burglars, and so it is easy to exaggerate both the degree of social solidarity behind certain crimes and the extent to which social criminals might not also indulge in theft or violence. However, social crime *is* a useful concept in reminding us that 'the law' is not monolithic. Some parts of the law accord more with broader cultural norms than others. Some forms of lawbreaking are less acquisitive and more communally motivated. But the borders between normal and social crime were easily crossed, and the exact topography of both is difficult to map.

Property crime: Summary and a few conclusions

One of the problems in trying to write about property crime is the sheer variation and scope of this nature of offending. Arguably large amounts of this volume (the criminal courts and prosecution process, policing, punishment, youth crime and gender) are explicitly interlinked with the unlawful appropriation of other people's property. But, it is a topic area that has (as a whole), and for some of the reasons I have just stated, been largely avoided by historians of crime. There has been plenty of work on the prosecution of property crime and the punishment of offenders, particularly in the long eighteenth century. There have also been studies of crime (including property crime) in different areas or at different levels of the court system, and researchers have delivered excellent discursive work on the importance of gender, age and the life cycle to the prosecution of theft. We are also blessed with a large body of more popular histories that provide examples of highwaymen, thieves, pirates, poachers and conmen throughout the last 300 years or more. Nevertheless, we are not so well served by academic works that analyse the methods and practices of thieves and swindlers, especially those from the 1800s.

Property crime encompasses a tremendous range of offending from the very minor (collecting broken branches or the stubs of candles) to the major (bank robberies or elaborate frauds) and could be violent and direct or surreptitious and almost undetectable. What a study of property crime tells us is that offenders acted under multiplicity of often overlapping motives. Some stole because they were hungry or their families were. Others did so because they thought it presented a quicker and easier way of gaining the luxuries they desired than working legitimately did. In still other cases, there was a prevailing sense that it was not really criminal to take home produce or goods from work but rather a part of one's traditional, earned entitlement.

One thing seems very clear in the histories of property offending, and that is the gendered nature of theft and fraudulent behaviour. Men and women stole different things, and they stole in different ways. Young offenders may not have been as vulnerable to prosecution for serious offences, but tens of thousands of them were summarily convicted before magistrates. Punishments for property crime were reduced as the eighteenth century gave way to the nineteenth, with forgery being the last of the property statutes to have the capital element removed from it in the 1830s. Hereafter, England stopped executing thieves, but transportation and long prison sentences awaited those that were convicted of what were (by modern standards) relatively trivial episodes of lawbreaking.

We still have a lot to learn about property crime, especially at the level of the summary and Police courts. The extent to which magistrates acted as filters to the jury courts is beginning to be explored but requires more dedicated studies. The links between offending and the patterns or paths from petty crime to more serious offending have also been the subject of recent research for the nineteenth and early twentieth centuries; it would be good to see if this can be applied to earlier period where records allow. Mapping crime represents another welcome departure from county studies of crime, and new technologies allow historians to ask new questions about property crime and where and in what contexts it occurred. This and new methodologies to explore discourses of criminal behaviour offer the prospect of some interesting future research.

Ultimately, we are left with the conclusion that property crime, more than any other form of offending, is rooted in the unequal distribution of wealth in our past history. For all of the period between 1660 and 1914, England was, to a larger or lesser degree, characterized by a deep divide between the haves and the have-nots. The decline in property indictments from the 1850s may well have had as much to do with rising standards of living as better policing, but economic crisis in the 1880s saw levels begin to rise again. The link between theft and economic hardship can be overstated, but it cannot be dismissed. Most of those prosecuted for property crime in the late seventeenth, eighteenth, nineteenth and twentieth centuries (and we might add the 2000s as well) were young men aged 18–25 from (relatively) poor working-class backgrounds who were often unemployed or seasonally employed. Most (but not all) of those that prosecuted them were drawn from a class at least one if not several tiers above them. Theft then, while not an expression of class struggle, is a symptom of a society in which it is generally believed that it is acceptable for some people to be extremely wealthy while others are expected to live close to subsistence. From the middle of the twentieth century, the socialist government of Clement Attlee began to address the issue of welfare, but the basic tenet (that some are rich while most are not) has not changed fundamentally. Instead, we are left with what we might call relative poverty or deprivation; this was evident in the 2010 riots in London and elsewhere which affected areas of working-class domicile that have been poor for well over a century.

Given this observation, I would argue that while there are plenty of ways in which historians can view crime and property in particular, the recent tendency to ignore the concept of class as Marxist views has supposedly become redundant, meaning we are in danger of ditching one useful metanarrative and replacing it with nothing but a series of micro-studies than enlighten but do not explain why those in power placed the protection of property at the heart of their criminal justice strategy.

CHAPTER 6
GENDER AND CRIME IN THE CRIMINAL JUSTICE SYSTEM: WOMEN AS VICTIMS

Introduction: Gender history

While this chapter is headed 'Gender', it is really about the ways in which the operation of the criminal justice system affected the women caught up in it. There is a considerable body of work on women's (or gender) history, and I do not intend to spend time here discussing it.[1] However, it is important to understand that contemporary attitudes towards women directly and indirectly affected the way women were treated by the English courts in the period between the late seventeenth and early twentieth centuries.

We should begin by stating something that is *not* in dispute among historians, criminologists and criminal justice professionals, which is that *men commit most crime*. Women have always represented a minority of those that are accused, prosecuted, convicted and punished for crime. The questions that historians have set out to answer usually involve an attempt to explain *why* this is the case.

For example, Garthine Walker's study of those prosecuted at the courts of Great Sessions and Quarter Sessions of Cheshire and Chester in the late sixteenth to the 1660s shows that property was overwhelmingly a male dominated activity.[2] Likewise, in Surrey between 1660 and 1802, women only made up around 20 per cent of all offenders, the figure is similar (19 per cent) for London in the nineteenth century, and by the outbreak of the First World War, women only accounted for about 16 per cent of offenders in English or Welsh prisons.[3] Women also represent a minority of offenders who appeared before magistrates in the eighteenth, nineteenth and early twentieth centuries. Men dominated the statistics of those brought before the aldermen justices of the City of London in the period between 1750 and 1800, and the same was true for the less busy magistrate Edmund Tew in Boldon in the north-east of England.[4] In addition, a study of persistent minor offenders in Crewe between 1880 and 1940 shows that men outnumber women by 82 to 18 per cent.[5] That aside, there is also a great deal of research which suggests that women were treated with greater leniency by the courts than were men, but explanations for this differ. Finally, it is important to remember that the English criminal justice system, for all of the timescale of this book, was 'run exclusively by men'.[6]

Furthermore, it seems to be the case that the nature of female offending was different from men's. Peter King has stressed the importance that the life cycle[7] had on patterns of female property crime.[8] It also appears to be the case that in the period we are interested in women were much more likely to be involved in crime if they lived in London or one of England's other major urban centres. All these questions need answers, as does a suggestion that the nineteenth century saw a virtual collapse in the numbers of female criminals coming before the jury courts.[9] Was the idea of the 'vanishing female' a reality, or was it instead a result of changing prosecution practice that was tied to the nature of female offending?

Some of these questions will be tackled in the companion chapter to this one, because since gender is such an important topic, I have chosen to divide it in two. The second chapter will look at female offenders (as property criminals, prostitutes and murderers) and finish by offering some broad conclusions on the nature of female criminality. This first section will therefore deal with women as the victims of crimes of violence, usually perpetrated by men.

However, before we consider these broader questions in more detail, it is necessary to consider both the underlying ideology that affected women, and how they were viewed in the 200 or so years covered by this study. This is because, fundamentally, women were viewed as second-class citizens by the early modern, Hanoverian and Victorian state and society. This is not a revelation, of course, but a study of gender and crime is an ideal way to explore gender inequality in the past because it demonstrates both how patriarchy oppressed women and also reveals the agency of those women who attempt to subvert it or manipulate it to their advantage.

The position of women and the problem of patriarchy

Prior to the later twentieth century, most women were effectively considered to be non-persons under law. Women were, and to a certain extent remain, defined by their relationship to men; therefore, women were (and are) the wives, daughters or widows of men. Even today, it is still very common for married women to adopt their husband's surname instead of retaining their own. The wedding ring is an ancient symbol of bondage, not merely an aesthetically pleasing circle of gold, and in eighteenth- and nineteenth-century society, women were certainly deemed to be subordinate to men. Women promised, and were expected, to 'honour and obey' their husbands as the master of the house. This prevailing ideology, *patriarchy*, had its roots in religion. St Augustine, an early Christian theologian, wrote that 'woman ought to serve her husband as unto God, affirming that in nothing hath woman equal power with man... affirming that woman ought to be repressed'.[10] In Christian belief, Eve was given to Adam as his help mate, and it was Eve who brought about man's fall from grace in the Garden of Eden; her inequality was therefore enshrined as a Biblical 'fact'.

Patriarchy, then, represented women as second-class citizens behind men. A wife also became a man's property; she owned no property herself while married, and anything she took into the marriage effectively became her husband's property. She had no rights to her children, had almost no chance of divorce (until laws were amended in the late nineteenth century) and, if she was middle class, was not expected to work or have a career; her role was very much that of the homemaker and mother. The idea that women and men had very different roles in life is characterized as 'separate spheres' in that women's life was private and men's public.[11] However, there is a wide-ranging debate about the reality of separate spheres, and it is evident that in working-class households the division of labour was much less clear. Most lower-class women worked, particularly in England's larger towns, and many couples operated small businesses together, working as a team. Anna Clark has characterized the working-class marriage as part of a wider struggle for class power, agency and identity.[12] This struggle challenged the notions of patriarchy and the domestic division of labour, and Clark's work provides a useful counter to easy stereotypes of domestic bliss and female compliance. As we shall see, women in the eighteenth and nineteenth centuries did not always passively accept their position in the home or the unquestioned authority of their husbands.

Let us now return to the effects of patriarchy and the peculiar situation of women in law. The underlying principle here was coverture, which can be defined as the state or condition of a married woman.

In his comprehensive *Commentaries on the Laws of England*, the eighteenth-century jurist William Blackstone tackled the issue of coverture and noted that:

By marriage, the husband and wife are one person in law; that is, the very being or legal existence of the woman is suspended during the marriage, or at least is incorporated and consolidated into that of her husband.[13]

What Blackstone was arguing was that women effectively disappeared upon marriage, at least as far as the law was concerned. This had implications for women who either attempted to use the criminal justice system or found themselves accused of committing crimes. This will be explored further in Chapter 7 (which analyses female property crime) and below (when looking at women as the victims of male violence), but it is worth first addressing the issue of coverture in more detail.

The legal principle of 'femme couvert'

Female offenders who committed a crime in partnership with their husbands (or sometimes other men) were able to avoid conviction and punishment by claiming that they were only acting under the instructions of their husband (and master). This rule, termed *femme couvert*, protected married women (and some unmarried women who cohabited), from prosecution. Blackstone wrote, '[i]f a woman commit theft...by the coercion of her husband; or merely by his command;...she is not guilty of any crime: being considered as acting by compulsion and not her own will.'[14] As Peter King notes, this shows us that 'patriarchal assumptions were therefore institutionalized within both formal legal rulings and pre-trial practices',[15] and as a result, many married women who were charged as co-defendants with men were acquitted, thereby benefitting from a patriarchal system which usually repressed them. The same benefit was not extended to single women, and we should be wary of seeing *femme couvert* as some sort of 'get out jail free' card for female defendants. Carolyn Conley reminds us that in the Victorian era women '*might* be relieved of responsibility for thefts committed in the presence of their husbands *if* they could prove they were coerced. Married women had no such immunity in cases of murder, robbery, or treason, and authorities were divided over the status of misdemeanours.' Conley concludes that the defence was 'useless in the mid-nineteenth century', citing several examples from Kent where *femme couvert* was unsuccessful.[16]

Regardless of how useful *femme couvert* was in rescuing some women from the vagaries of the criminal justice system, patriarchy itself made life even more difficult for those who fell victim to male violence. This will be dealt with in more detail below, but it is necessary to reemphasize the reality that married women were considered to be the property of their husbands. In cases of domestic violence and rape, the position of women as chattels effectively removed their right to protection from the English legal system. Fathers, as we shall see, often prosecuted rapes as damage to their property, rather than violations of the bodies of young women. In some instances, cases were settled out of court, with marriage or offers of compensation being recognized as reasonable alternatives to a trial of the perpetrator. Patriarchy also ensured that it was invariably the character of victim of rape and not the alleged rapist that was on trial.

The rule of thumb

Figure 6.1 *Judge Thumb Or Patent Sticks for Family Correction: Warranted Lawful!*, by Gillray (1782).

Sometime in the 1780s, Francis Buller, a celebrated judge, is supposed to have declared that men had the right to beat their wives so long as they used a stick no thicker than their thumb (see Figure 6.1). As Elizabeth Foyster noted, there is little or no evidence that Buller ever said this, nor that it became a precedent for future cases.[17] However, the idea that a man could chastise his wife using reasonable force did have currency in the eighteenth and nineteenth centuries and was not effectively challenged until 1891. The underlying principle prevailed that, as master of his house, a man was both morally obliged and legally entitled to administer discipline to those beneath him and this included children, servants and his spouse.

So, while the so-called 'rule of thumb' may be a myth, for many women the reality was a life that involved regular violence within the home. Not all women accepted this with a passive turn of the cheek; some retaliated, while others fled, and a small but significant number took their partners to court. This will be explored later in this chapter, but it is suffice to say that contemporary notions of womanhood and a woman's place coloured the way the courts and wider legal system operated.

There were two other ways in which attitudes towards women affected the criminal justice system.

As the science of criminology developed in the second half of the nineteenth century, the idea emerged that female criminals were somehow worse than their male counterparts. This notion that women could be viewed as 'doubly deviant' arises from the belief that female offending is seen 'not merely as unusual, but in extreme cases...that it contradicts gendered assumptions about "caring" femininity, as well as threatening broader social norms through the act of law-breaking'.[18] We can see this idea manifest itself in media representations of notorious female criminals from Catherine Hayes (who murdered her husband for his money in 1726 and was burned at the stake) through Sarah Malcolm (who was termed 'an evil, barbaric and stubborn woman'[19] after her trial for the murder of three other women in 1733) to modern day killers such as Myra Hindley and Rosemary West. The idea of the female murderer as more morally corrupt than their male counterparts has also coloured attitudes towards women accused of killing their newborn babies and the history of infanticide (or 'new born child murder'), and how the legal system struggled to understand the causal factors will be discussed in Chapter 7.

Second, female property criminals were increasingly characterized as 'weak' in the nineteenth century. This was a change from representations of them in the late seventeenth and early eighteenth centuries, which depicted them as somehow imbued with a sense of devilish courage, in their attempt to use their charms to part male dupes and patsies from their possessions.[20] Popular print culture celebrated the lives of 'deviant' women, such as the pirates Anne Bonney and Mary Read, who existed successfully within a male-dominated world and seemingly shunned the yoke of patriarchy. Cross-dressing or otherwise mannish women were also the subject of contemporary pamphlets such as *Long Meg of Westminster*[21] whose actions threatened to turn the patriarchal rule of men 'upside down'.

But towards the end of the eighteenth century, there appears to have been an effort to close down all attempts at female independence. Perhaps the politically charged world of the late 1700s (which witnessed first rebellion in America and then revolution in France), and the prominence of the ideas of equality and freedom, linked to notions about women's rights (as expressed by Mary Wollstonecraft in 1792[22]), necessitated efforts to put women back in 'their place'. The moral panic caused by the so-called 'Monster' who terrorized women in London in the 1790s can also be viewed as part of an ongoing move to repress women's independence.[23]

Whether as a consequence of this prevailing concern about female independence or for other reasons, by the late eighteenth century femininity, at least for middle-class women, 'was being delineated in terms of purity and virtue'.[24] Now women who committed crime were no longer seen as strong but as weak-willed and morally corrupt. This can be seen most obviously not only in nineteenth-century characterizations of the prostitute but also in the idea that female thieves were suffering from a form of mental illness: kleptomania.[25] Women went from being deviant through choice to being deviant through moral or mental weakness. This discourse, therefore, allowed men to perpetuate and legitimize the dominant ideology of patriarchy well into the late nineteenth century and, indeed, far beyond.

Having provided an introductory framework for understanding the history of crime through the prism of gender, this chapter will now go on to look at a series of topics in which women's experience of crime and criminal justice is most of interest to historians.

Women as the victims of male violence and sexual assault

As I noted at the beginning of this chapter, the underlying philosophy of patriarchy affected the ways in which women were treated by the criminal justice system in different ways. While it may have protected some, it most definitely negatively impacted the lives of others. This is most obvious in the experiences of women who suffered violence of sexual assaults at the hands of men. In this next section, I will consider the crimes of rape and then domestic assault. For reasons of space, I do not intend to look at sexual assaults on children (something that is at the top of modern agendas of crime and punishment), nor am I going to discuss rape in the context of male victims. While these are both subjects worthy of study, they deserve more attention than this volume has time to allow.

Sexual violence against women

Rape, in law, is the 'carnal knowledge of a woman forcibly and against her will', but determining whether or not consent had been given made (and still makes) rape 'very difficult to prove'.[26] While rape was not exclusively perpetrated by men on women, this was (and is) the most common circumstance in which it was committed, and so it seems most appropriate to discuss it within a broader chapter that is focused on women's experience of the criminal justice system (rather than the chapter which deals with violence). Moreover, while rape and other forms of sexual assault represent violent attacks on the female body, historians have tended to see them as indicative of a wider repression of women in history. As a result, it is impossible to separate sexual assault from a broader gender history that has explored the social control of women within a patriarchal society.

Rape was not always viewed simply as an attack on a woman, for much of the period of history that concerns this book, rape was also seen as a violation of the property rights of the man that *owned* the body of the female concerned. If a man raped an unmarried girl, he 'ruined' her and thereby devalued her in the marriage market; it was an injury to her father as well as her person. The individual that raped another man's wife was liable to be prosecuted by the angry husband whose 'property' had, similarly, been damaged. As a result, prosecutors could offer compensation for their transgressions. Similarly, if a father was satisfied that the rapist was prepared to marry his victim, they would often overlook the fact that he had forced his intentions on his intended before the actual marriage had taken place.[27] Thus, it was not unusual for attackers to attempt to buy off their victims or their families. Not that many really needed to, defence counsel were quite adept at arguing that allegations of rape were unfounded, especially if the victim was a working-class girl and the accused a respectable man with a position to uphold. The idea that a woman (especially a young unmarried woman) was the property of a man led to families accepting compensation from those accused of raping their daughters or wives in return for them dropping legal charges, and if compensation had been accepted, judges would routinely dismiss cases that came before them.

Until 1841, rape was a capital offence, and many juries were reluctant to find men guilty given the sentence the judge was bound to hand down. The conviction rate for rape in Victorian Kent was just 41 per cent (as opposed to 74 per cent for other offences), and it was more likely that a grand jury would reject a rape indictment than any other type of accusation.

They were more likely to declare cases of attempted rape or indecent assault to be 'true bills', given that these carried a much lesser sentence on conviction.[28] When the victim of rape was a prostitute, or a convicted drunk (as many streetwalkers were), the conviction rate fell to just 10 per cent.[29] The difficulty of proving rape rested primarily on the reality that accusations were in effect one person's word against another's. It was easy, claimed many contemporaries, for a woman to cry 'rape' and so drag an innocent man through the courts. A victim's testimony was therefore frequently undermined by the prevailing belief that women lied about rape. A year before the outbreak of the First World War, a medical 'expert' cautioned that 'a girl who has had sexual intercourse is in possession of all the medical evidence necessary...to make a charge of assault against you'.[30] Early in the late nineteenth century, another expert declared that women who brought accusations of rape were '[e]xcept upon the strongest corroborating evidence...liars, plausible liars, cunning liars'.[31]

Victims were particularly suspect if they had enjoyed any kind of previous relationship (however platonic or innocent) with their assailant. In the 1800s, a greater emphasis was placed in court of proving that consent was (or was not) given by the victim. It was widely believed that a fit and healthy woman could not be forced to have sex without giving her consent. Nor was consent simply taken as a woman's final acquiescence to sex; if she had placed herself in a situation – by, for example, going for drink with a man – she would often be deemed to have consented.[32] In Victorian Kent, rape cases were dismissed because a victim had, for example, 'foolishly' entered a hop field with her assailant, or had, in other words, put *herself* in danger.[33] Other contexts placed women in vulnerable positions, because they either exposed them to the risk of being alone with men or made them vulnerable to assaults that they then found difficult or impossible to resist or report.[34]

Often the relative position of victim and attacker meant that it was very unlikely that she would press charges. Servants raped by their masters (or his sons) were scared of losing their employment or of being believed; they were equally afraid of screaming for help or fighting back. The failure to do either, or to bring charges at the earliest opportunity, undermined their attempt to prove the crime if and when they did go to law. The law required that victims come forward quickly and show that they had made an attempt to resist the attack. Until 1828, the victim had to declare (in open court) that her attacker had ejaculated and indeed describe the assault in lurid detail. This exposed the victim to an appalling secondary ordeal, that of describing the sexual violation of her body in front of an audience of men.

The law on rape was amended in 1828 as part of Robert Peel's broader reform of the criminal justice system. Ostensibly, this addressed contemporary concerns that rapists were getting away with assault because it was so hard to prove, but it has also been seen as an attempt to silence women in court. Popular opinion held that if a woman was able to speak knowledgably about the sexual act, she was 'immodest'; sex was not something that respectable women were to discuss at all, let alone in front of men. Women were placed in an all but impossible position with regard to rape. Their chastity or honour was sacrosanct, but if that was violated by the unwanted attentions of a man, she was not supposed to actively resist or complain and certainly not in public. According to Clark, the nineteenth-century 'rape victim who tried to gain redress violated this decorum with her anger, for she also broke the taboo on female speech about sex'.[35]

Rape victims, if they prosecuted at all, increasingly resorted to euphemism in court rather than setting out in graphic detail what had happened to them. Juries, without this detail, often found defendants not guilty, and judges, wishing to avoid language that might offend, sometimes dismissed cases on the grounds that it was not in the public interest to hear women talk about sex. There were well-established themes in nineteenth-century popular culture that related to women, and these seem to have influenced the way narratives of assaults on women were framed. Victims and witnesses described the events that they had experienced using a language (often imbued with euphemism) that their audience (i.e. the court) would understand. Thus, sexual and other assaults as described in the witness box met contemporary expectations of these sorts of 'outrages'; thus, victims reported that they were 'wronged' or 'ravished'. Women were attacked in the open air, or assaulted at home or work, by men who took advantage of their 'weakness' or vulnerability. These discourses were played out in court and in the newspaper reports of hearings and trials and followed clear chronological narrative patterns. Consistent repetition helped to validate the evidence presented, but women had to perform a role that was expected of them, to 'mind the story' as D'Cruze puts it.[36] Working-class women who used the language of the street (often the language of their assailants) found that their testimony was rejected on the grounds that they were too 'knowing' or uncouth; more 'respectable' women who chose to remain silent or say little (in order to preserve their modesty) were equally unsuccessful as judges directed juries to acquit because no evidence had been offered.

Even if they did choose to speak out and describe what had happened, victims faced another prevailing 'truth': that rape was virtually impossible anyway. Nineteenth-century forensic medicine (such as it was) generally agreed women could not be raped 'contrary to her desire, by a single man'.[37] Indeed, even under hypnosis, medical practitioners argued that the difference between 'virtuous' and 'non-virtuous' women was evident; and only the latter could be forced to engage in sexual intercourse under the power of suggestion, the former having some kind of innate sense of decency. If this viewpoint was extended, as seems likely, then it followed that most rape victims were not 'respectable'.[38] Rape victims had to report the assault as soon as possible and provide evidence of the attack. While this did not, by the late 1820s, mean emission, it did usually involve penetration.[39] But, as had been the case in the earlier period, the 'character and reputation of the woman was an essential object of enquiry'.[40] Consent was sometimes given, defence counsels argued, and then later denied as the woman attempted to remake her lost character. What Gatrell's micro-history of the rape of Elizabeth Cureton reveals is the reality that if a young and unmarried woman such allowed herself to be in the company of men, without supervision, then she risked any assault upon her being seen as understandable, accepted and deserved.[41]

There seems to be very little difference in the nature of rape trials in the period between the late seventeenth and late nineteenth centuries. The removal of capital punishment in 1841 may have made it slightly easier to gain convictions, but in practice, the courts rarely found men guilty, and class prejudice ensured that middling and elite men accused of assaulting working-class women would invariably gain the sympathy of the court. Most successful rape charges resulted from very clear evidence of violence, as this was where juries were most likely to be sympathetic towards the victim because as Conley puts it: 'Lust could be excused; gratuitous violence could not'.[42] D'Cruze's powerful study of the experience of working-class women who complained of sexual violence and other assaults against them reveals the ways in which they attempted to demonstrate the wrongs done to them (or their daughters) in a very direct and visible way. Black eyes, bruises and other injuries were openly displayed as evidence of male violence and torn or soiled clothes or undergarments were brought to court; mothers appeared with their babes in arms to underline their position.[43] It was also much better, as Anna Clark's work has shown, for women to bring a charge of attempted rape. This allowed her to demonstrate that she had defended her honour and a chaste woman was also a more credible witness.[44]

What is clear then is that the female victim had, for all of the period we are interested in here, been placed at a severe disadvantage within the criminal justice system. Women were expected to meet gendered stereotypes imposed, largely at least, by men. They had to appear passive, respectable and modest, and yet, in order to complain effectively about unwarranted sexual assaults made against them, they were required to provide detailed evidence that undermined their reputations and exposed them to the judgement of their communities. They were often disbelieved, blamed for leading on or otherwise inviting the assaults they had suffered or simply ridiculed and ignored. Men, by contrast, unless they exhibited very clear examples of behaviour considered reprehensible by their fellow men, were generally given the benefit of the doubt and even when convicted, treated very leniently by the courts.

As the work of Conley and Clark demonstrates, rape victims were doubly violated and then condemned for it, and it is worth concluding this section with Carolyn Conley's words:

> Rape victims were suspect on at least three counts: they were female, they had been at least temporarily outside the supervision of male guardians…and they were publically announcing their loss of sexual innocence.[45]

Domestic violence and women's experience

Chapter 3 dealt in some detail with the nature of assault and at how it was prosecuted. It discussed the gradual change that saw assault move away from being viewed less as a dispute between two parties, to something that the state was obliged to prosecute and punish. Assault was increasingly seen, especially in the second half of the 1800s, as a predominantly male activity, and there was a specific focus on stamping out fights that took place in public. One consequence of this was that violence became domesticized, moved off of the streets and into the home, where the main victims were women and children.[46]

Domestic (or marital) violence is perhaps the hardest form of interpersonal violence to quantify historically, as so much of it went unreported and unprosecuted. Many of those abused by husbands or common law partners chose not to report them for fear of suffering worse punishment, while others felt ashamed and blamed themselves for the attacks. Using the law (and thereby providing historians with an opportunity to investigate the nature and extent of such violence) was also fraught with difficulties. The eighteenth-century magistracy or later Police Courts fined or imprisoned wife beaters, and the impact on the family budget could be catastrophic.

As has been established already, the courts of early modern, Georgian and Victorian England did not recognize married women as persons in law. As Dobash and Dobash have written,

> The seeds of wife beating lie in the subordination of females and in their subjection to male authority and control. This relationship between women and men has been institutionalized in the structure of the patriarchal family and is supported by the economic and political institutions and by a belief system, including a religious one, that makes such relationships seem natural, morally just, and sacred.[47]

Patriarchy placed women in a subordinate position, and the so-called 'rule of thumb' supposedly legitimized violence towards women so long as it was not excessive. Indeed, men who failed to control or chastise their disobedient partners faced the same forms of community ridicule as the victims of adultery and were liable to be paraded in a *charivari* or subjected to 'rough music'.[48]

Historical studies of marital violence have shown that the motives for male violence included 'sexual jealousy, frustration or insecurity, concerns over money, or the management of economic resources' as well as 'excessive consumption of alcohol'.[49] The loss of control of men was increasingly viewed with disdain by the Victorian magistracy, but violent behaviour could be justified if it appeared that the victim had in some way 'deserved' her fate. Magistrates routinely dismissed accusation of abuse if they felt the victim had provoked the assault, by being 'bad wives', 'nags' or being in other ways 'irritating'.[50] A failure to please by, for example, not preparing meals on time or to a standard the husband expected could justify a beating, as could behaviour that was considered unfeminine, such as drinking or staying out at night. Thus, we need to be aware of how we view domestic violence through a modern lens; in the period between the late seventeenth century and at least as far as the late nineteenth (if not beyond), a certain level of violence and coercion in the home was expected or at least tolerated. This is often revealed by the language used in courts by justices which suggests that society believed that some responsibility lay with those who were beaten; that it was only therefore disobedient or 'bad' wives who were assaulted.

Class, as with rape, was an important factor, and by the middle of the nineteenth century, marital abuse was most often associated with the labouring classes. In 1878, Frances Power Cobbe, in an article entitled 'Wife-Torture in England', described male lower-class labourers and artisans as 'dangerous wife beaters devoid of self control and forethought of consequence'.[51] Anna Clarke has suggested that domestic violence was more common among independent artisans in traditional crafts (such as cobblers in

Northampton) than it was within the emerging new industrial trades, but Elizabeth Foyster has found no evidence that supports this from her research.[52] Given that men and women often worked closely together in plebeian relationships, there would have been plenty of opportunity for tensions to arise. This is not to discount the reality that spousal abuse still occurred in middle-class marriages, but the nature of that abuse was either different or was described differently. It was not the subject of public discussion in the way that working-class violence was. Cobbe herself accepted that wife beaters existed within the ranks of polite society but believed (probably naively) that 'it rarely extends to anything beyond an occasional blow of two, not of a dangerous kind'.[53] Middle-class abusers might have been more circumspect in their methods of inflicting violence on their womenfolk, and middle-class wives better able to hide their scars and bruises, since they were able to stay at home and conceal any marks under clothing and make-up.

Northampton's large population of shoemakers was tarnished with a reputation for domestic violence in the nineteenth century, which was epitomized in a graphic etching by Rowlandson which shows a cobbler sewing up his wife's lips.[54] The strong correlation between working-class culture, male drinking and notions of what constituted appropriate female behaviour meant that Friday or Saturday nights were potentially traumatic for many working-class women throughout the long nineteenth century. Wife beating was not then confined to the poorest (or seen as simply a product of economic tensions) but seemed to permeate working-class male culture. Both D'Cruze and Hammerton have found that a significant proportion of those men prosecuted for domestic violence were described as 'skilled' or 'semi-skilled' workers; men who were in this period supposedly influenced by middle-class tropes about 'respectability' and 'self-improvement'.[55]

Clark has described domestic violence as a facet of an ongoing power struggle within working-class relationships (what she terms the 'struggle for the breeches'). She argues that there was 'a contradiction between patriarchal ideals and the reality of the family economy' which created a 'struggle for power, resources, and freedom within the family'.[56] In many labouring families, marriage roles were not so easily delineated as they were for the wealthier classes, nor was marriage in the eighteenth century. Poorer couples living together in the urban sprawl of London may not have been that concerned to officially marry with all the expense that entailed, and secret marriages were not uncommon. As Tanya Evans has recently written, 'evidence suggests that marital and sexual relationships were necessarily fluid' in eighteenth-century London.[57] Within plebeian culture, there was certainly some room for informal divorce and remarriage.[58] Men and women worked as partners or held different employments, and both contributed to the family income and both wished to enjoy the fruits of their labour. Clark argues that while this had always been the case, it became a particular source of tension in the late eighteenth and early nineteenth centuries as the temptations of metropolitan living put increased pressure on couples.

What then were the responses to marital violence and how effective were they? There was plenty of advice available for women, but most of it was intended to reassert established notions of patriarchal rule and the 'correct' roles of men and women within marriage. Prescriptive literature 'taught wives the importance of obedience and submission, even to husbands who were violent and cruel'.[59] By submitting to male authority and obeying, women could present themselves as guiltless victims, and this was the most likely way in which they could earn the support of their communities and the sympathy of the courts. As Conley has noted, '[c]hivalry and fair play demanded that the weaker sex be protected from the stronger, but the same logic implied that women were inherently inferior and must be dealt with accordingly. In order to merit protection a woman had to be obedient, submissive, and incapable of defending herself'.[60] In one of her evangelical tracts, *The Wife Reformed*, the conservative social reformer Hannah More (1745–1833) urged women to be more submissive and suggested that male violence was caused by female neglect of duty or inappropriate behaviour.[61] There is evidence to suggest that some women followed this sort of advice or were at least careful to represent themselves as having complied with the ideals of feminine virtue, when presenting their cases in court. This was difficult, however, because while the law was supposed to protect those that both required and deserved it, in practice this meant middle-class women as working-class women were not seen to be 'delicate' in this way. If a woman stood up for herself or dared to strike back at her abuser, her use of violence was deemed more reprehensible and her actions less likely to be seen as justifiable. Once again a double standard operated, and patriarchy ensured that female victims were considered to be in some part responsible for whatever injury had been done to them.

Clearly, the most official action women could take was to turn to the Law, although this was – as we noted earlier – fairly problematic. The court (most often the summary or police court) offered both advantages and disadvantages for the victim of abuse. As Shani D'Cruze reminds us that the courtroom 'was also a performance space, framed for public observation'.[62] So, a woman could employ the law – in the person of the justice – as an arbiter of her dispute, and she could do this in front of witnesses. This meant that the outcome – perhaps a reconciliation and her husband's contrition – could be seen and heard, giving it gravitas and authority. This might then act as a restraint on a violent male who might not wish to risk the public opprobrium which accompanied a court appearance. However, the relationship could also be damaged irrevocably by such an action. Men would frequently resort to the threat of desertion as a way of controlling their wives. Offenders most often faced a fine and sometimes imprisonment, neither of which was really satisfactory for the victim.[63]

Hammerton suggests that women were often unwilling to go to law in Victorian and Edwardian Lancashire for this very reason, thus accepting by default that a certain level of marital violence was inevitable.[64] In the eighteenth-century City of London, women did use the law, but while there are numerous instances of women using the summary courts at Mansion House and Guildhall, this does not represent any real sense that the process was useful to them. Many probably used the law as a last resort and only after putting up with many months or years of abuse. Throughout the period, neither the magistracy nor, after 1829, the police were keen to get involved in what was considered to be a private matter. This reluctance reflected a wider underlying belief that domestic issues should not be aired in public, and that married women were, to some degree at least, the property of their husbands. The police would only get involved if the victims requested their help, or when violence was extreme or took place in public where it could not be safely ignored.

But, if battered wives adopted a passive approach to their husband's abuse, many women – notably those from the upper or middle classes – revealed the reality of their domestic situations through writing. Some wrote of their sufferings in letters or diaries, a form of catharsis and process of 'self-definition and preservation'. While this was unlikely to amend a wayward husband's behaviour, Foyster views it as a 'private act of resistance'.[65] It allowed women to assert their 'innocence' and the unjustified nature of the attacks upon them, and it might alert other family members or friends to their plight or simply provide a record of their suffering. Some women took solace in religion. These forms of passive resistance allowed women to maintain the 'moral high ground' and thus negate any sense of blame that attached to them for their spouse's aggression.

Women could also withdraw their labour or familial duties to express their resistance to abuse. This essentially avoided direct confrontation and demonstrated to the man how dependent he was on his partner. This was a dangerous strategy, however, as, along with the refusal to share the marital bed, it risked both further harm and accusations of disobedience. Women could also use their position as the managers of the household budget to fight back against abusers, by pawning his goods or running up debts in his name. While a wife that separated from her husband could not use his name to gain credit, a 'wife who had fled from a violent husband could continue to rely upon him for the payment of necessaries'.[66] It would be wrong then to see all victims of domestic violence as passive. The existence of plenty of examples within popular literature, chapbooks and ballads shows that the cartoon image of the enraged wife wielding a rolling pin, saucepan or other household implement is not without foundation; some women clearly did fight back. Indeed, in terms of non-lethal violence, Garthine Walker has found that in Cheshire women, 'like men, armed themselves with whatever was to hand: any household or agricultural tool, stones; one woman even threw boiling water in the face of a man who came to collect a debt', and she refutes any suggestion that women were simply passive victims, or that they only attacked other women (as was often the case in assault hearings in late eighteenth-century London). In Cheshire, at least, it seems that men represented the most likely victims of female attacks.[67] But of course this was a risky strategy as men could use evidence of female retaliation against them in court. As Walker noted, men's violence was somehow legitimate while women's could never be.[68]

Thus, female victims of male violence were hugely disadvantaged both by societal values and by the restricted legal opportunities open to them. Many would have opted not to use the law but to find alternative ways to respond. Communities might rally around a beaten wife, and men, particularly those with a poor reputation for violence or drunkenness, could find themselves on the receiving end of local retribution or condemnation.

There was little change in the operation of the law towards domestic violence throughout the eighteenth and nineteenth centuries, but there was a small measure of progress, at least in legislation, from the middle of the 1800s. Conley has stated bluntly that domestic violence 'was a serious problem that Victorian judicial authorities treated with ambivalence'.[69] The Act for the Better Prevention of Aggravated Assaults Upon Women (1854) supposedly made it easier for convictions to be obtained and for more severe sentences (of up to six months imprisonment) to be handed down, but in reality, it appears to have made little impression since most assaults on wives and common law partners never reached court at all. The 1857 Divorce Act and the creation of a divorce court brought many more women into court to complain at their treatment, and in 1858, a legal judgement made a small improvement in the situation for abused wives. Previously women who complained of violence or other forms of abuse were caught by legal rules concerning 'condonation'. If a wife who claimed her husband had abused her either explicitly 'forgave an act of cruelty (or adultery), or implicitly forgave it by cohabiting with the offender afterwards, was deemed to have *condoned* the offences' and so reduced its impact.[70] For most women, with nowhere else to go than the marital home, this was an impossible situation. In 1858, Sir Cresswell Creswell, presiding in the case of *Bostock vs. Bostock*, ruled that 'further cohabitation would be attended with danger to the party threatened' and so helped shift the emphasis from the nature of the offences committed – the violence and mental cruelty – to the effects they had on the victim. It made divorce on grounds of cruelty easier for women to achieve in the courts and recognized that men did not have an unrestricted licence to mistreat their spouses. A further ruling in 1869/1870 recognized that 'cruelty' did not have to mean actual physical violence.

Women (at least those from the middle classes) gained further independence with the passage of the Married Women's Property Act in 1870, and the subsequent Matrimonial Causes Act (1878) provided for the economic support of abused wives through maintenance and separation payments. Throughout the late Victorian period, literature and political writings (such as J. S. Mill's *The Subjection of Women* and Trollope's *He Knew He Was Right* – both published in 1869) highlighted the problems of marital violence and the rights of women. In 1886, more legislation made provision for the upkeep of women whose husbands had deserted them and the Summary Jurisdiction Act (1895) extended the separation and maintenance allowances to those who suffered 'persistent cruelty' from their husbands.

Gradually then the position of women within marriage was improved at the end of the nineteenth century, but it has to be recognized that this was a painfully slow process and the main beneficiaries were middle-class women. For working-class women and girls, male violence remained an everyday part of the relationship between the sexes. It was not until 1891 in a ruling in the case of *Regina vs. Jackson* that English law recognized that a woman had the right *not* to be beaten by her husband. It is worth noting that in the twenty-first century, domestic violence remains a problem with many of the same issues that affected women in the past.

Concluding remarks

The early modern and eighteenth-century justice system was far from friendly towards the female victims of male violence. The prevailing discourse of patriarchy effectively imprisoned women within the constraints of a male-dominated society. Men populated the entire justice system, from the parish constable, justice of the peace, to judge and jury at quarter sessions or assize courts; female voices were seldom heard and frequently dismissed as unimportant. This situation remained the case for much of the nineteenth century – indeed the presence of woman on the throne of England and the Empire did not lead to a dramatic overhaul of the status quo. There were small victories however, and by the end of the 1800s, perhaps an acceptance that women had a right to protection regardless of their social status or relationship to men. I would be very cautious, however, in seeing much in the way of effective legal reform until well into the modern age. The Suffrage movement that culminated in votes for women after the First World War owed much to a long struggle and the experience of women's roles in wartime Britain. A year after women were enfranchised, the Sex Discrimination (Removal) Act (1919) allowed women to practise law and serve as jurors. It still took until 1921 for the first women to be sworn onto a jury (when Mrs Taylor Bumpstead was elected foreman of the jury at the Old Bailey). Rose Heilbron became the first high court judge in 1965, after a stellar career as a barrister. Despite these advances, the justice system, legislature and civil service remain largely a male preserve, and there is considerable space for improvements in equality.

However, it is too easy to see women's place in the history of crime as one that is defined by passivity and victimhood. Gender historians have done much to rescue women from the 'condescension of history' (to borrow a phrase from E. P. Thompson), and while female assault and rape victims were severely hamstrung by a patriarchal court system, the evidence suggests that many of them were prepared to use the law and to stand up to the abuse of their partners and other menfolk. In the next chapter, we will explore the ways in which other women rebelled against the restrictions society's attitudes placed upon them or reacted to the pressures of survival in an economically and sexually unequal society. Women may have committed less crime than men, but they still appear in considerable numbers in court and other records as property offenders, prostitutes and murderers.

CHAPTER 7
GENDER AND CRIME: WOMEN AS PERPETRATORS OF CRIME

In Chapter 6, we looked at the ways in which the prevailing ideology of patriarchy affected the way women were treated by the criminal justice system. While it is dangerous to elide the early modern period with the Victorian, it is equally hard to see much progress towards equality in the way women were treated as victims of male violence. However, it is possible to see much more evidence of change rather than continuity in the way that women who committed property crimes were dealt with by the courts and penal system. There was also a definite improvement in the treatment of women who were accused of killing their newborn babies with a move towards understanding such crimes from a psychological perspective. Women who killed adults or children (other than infants) were widely held up as being the worst examples of their sex, as were those who resorted (often through economic hardship) to prostitution, and they will also be discussed in this chapter. But we will start with property offending and levels of female participation in it.

Female property crime and the issue of 'crime rates'

While there have been fluctuations in the numbers of women involved in property crime, it is reasonable to state that fewer women than men have always appeared in court. Beattie found that women accounted for just 24 per cent of all of those accused of property offences at the Surrey assizes between 1660 and 1800.[1] For a similar period, at the Old Bailey, the proportion is higher (35 per cent), but still significantly fewer women were sent for trial than men.[2] In Essex, in the second half of the eighteenth century the figure was smaller still; only 13 per cent were formally indicted at the assizes.[3] In late-seventeenth-century Cheshire, men also dominated property crime.[4] In the nineteenth century, a similar pattern is discernible; according to the official judicial statistics, women made up on average around 21 per cent of property offenders between 1860 and 1890, and this fell to around 17 per cent by 1910.[5] This pattern is repeated in the statistics at London's Central Criminal Court which shows that women make up just 19 per cent of defendants between 1800 and 1913 but also demonstrates a clear fall in indictments after mid-century.

However, these statistics conceal a great deal of female property crime, because a large proportion of offending was dealt with outside of the jury courts. There may also be regional variations in the numbers of prosecutions of women. In the north-east, for example, around a fifth of those accused of serious thefts were women and 'a much higher proportion of those accused of minor' ones.[6] Clearly, women did steal, but this is often overlooked or downplayed by a concentration on male offending. King suggests that the proportionally higher numbers of women appearing in the north-east of England may reflect the reality that when overall numbers of offenders appearing before courts was low, those exercising their discretionary power chose not to filter female offenders out of the process, as they clearly were doing elsewhere.[7] Women are often hidden in the records, but this does not mean they did not exist, and historians perhaps need to look more carefully for their presence. The law protected some married women, via *femme couvert*, while others probably played a more active role in crime than the records suggest. Early modern, Hanoverian and Victorian women were an integral part of the household and of family businesses, and so, while men dominate the statistics of property crime, we should not always take this at face value.

First, we will review one of the key debates surrounding the supposed decline in female property offending.

The 'vanishing female' thesis

In 1991, Malcolm Feeley and Deborah Little published a groundbreaking article that sought to explain what they saw as a dramatic change in patterns of female offending between the late seventeenth and early twentieth centuries. They found that by taking samples of cases reported in the Old Bailey Sessions Papers at twenty-year intervals, these showed a very clear fall in female offenders indicted to appear before the courts. They concluded that female offending dropped from around 45 per cent in the 1730s to less than 10 per cent by 1912.[8]

Using John Beattie's work on Surrey and Landau's on Middlesex, they concluded that:

> The evidence all points in the same direction, suggesting that in the past women were more heavily involved as defendants in the criminal process than they are today and that sometime in the eighteenth and early nineteenth centuries there was a real decline in the proportion of women involved in the criminal courts.[9]

The question, of course, was why?

They analysed and dismissed explanations relating to changing demographic patterns in London and more specific changes surrounding the prosecution of women for what can be viewed as gendered crimes such as newborn child murder and witchcraft. In addition, they explored the possibility that crime became increasingly seen as a male problem (something Martin Wiener has related to changing attitudes towards masculinity[10]). They also looked at the effects of women being charged *with* men (as accomplices), but the proportion of women appearing singly or with men remained constant across the period of their research. Finally, they considered the effect of war and peace on the statistics.

They argued that the decline in female offending was represented a real fall in female crime and not simply a statistical anomaly caused by changing patterns of prosecution and concluded that it was the result of changing attitudes towards the social control of women. They pointed to a long-term change in the role of women across the nineteenth century, which saw women being increasingly shunted into a restricted domestic role that effectively restricted their opportunities to commit crimes. Once again, the prevailing philosophy of patriarchy appears to have been an important factor in understanding the female experience of the criminal justice system.

While several historians appeared to embrace Feeley and Little's work, others have been keen to point out the flaws in their argument. Conley agrees that there does seem to have been a decline in female offending in Kent between 1859 and 1880 which echoes similar falls identified by Philips in the Black Country[11] and the broader survey conducted by Gatrell and Hadden.[12] However, in other studies, it quickly becomes apparent that the supposed decline that Feeley and Little identified in London was not repeated elsewhere. In Essex, the percentage of females indicted for property crime and other felonies in the period 1740–1847 remained steady except for a fall between 1834 and 1838. There is a slight reduction but nothing as dramatic as the decline they suggested.[13] In Somerset and Berkshire, similar patterns emerge; there are fluctuations in the proportion and numbers of women being sent for trial but nothing to indicate a significant falling off in the prosecution of female offenders.[14]

Feeley and Little had relied upon the records of the Old Bailey but had not included those indicted criminals that had been sent to the quarter sessions courts, while much of the work that has critiqued them does. This is significant because it speaks to the *nature* of female property offending, something that will be returned to shortly. It is also clear that the proportion of indicted females rose during periods of international conflict. War had an important effect on prosecution rates, and the absence of men would naturally cause the proportion of female offenders to rise. In Gloucestershire, between 1789 and 1793, 16.3 per cent of those indicted at assizes and quarter sessions were women, but this figure rose to 23.8 per cent in the period 1806–1811 when England was fighting a continental war in Portugal and Spain.[15] So, Feeley and Little, in presenting information from the capital, may have been relying on a partial record of female offending and prosecution patterns. While they looked at national figures for the thirteen years between 1805 and 1818 when there was a very marked *decline* (and this was, of course, in a period of war when proportion might have been expected to *rise*), they are perhaps guilty of taking a snapshot of prosecution patterns.[16] If a longer view is taken, a very different picture emerges. By looking at national statistics (using parliamentary returns), what can be shown is that while the percentage of female offenders declined from c.1805 to c.1815, it then began to *increase* again and steadily rose to reach a peak of around 22 per cent by 1853.[17] Moreover, Feeley and Little's thesis is predicated on the fall-off in female offending from the late seventeenth century, when the proportion of females being indicted was at its highest. What if that highpoint was actually an anomaly, as King suggests?[18]

The records of the City of London's two summary courts show that in the later eighteenth century, considerable numbers of women came before the courts accused of a wide range of property, violent and other crimes. The magistracy sent fewer women than men on to the jury courts, preferring to fine them or order brief periods of imprisonment in Bridewell or indeed dismissing the cases against altogether. This filtration process was not exclusive to women – many men also found that the accusations against them (sometimes for charges that were certainly felonious) were being dealt with summarily – but, it is likely that the City justices were more frequently releasing women or punishing them using summary powers than they were releasing or punishing male defendants. If this pattern were being repeated elsewhere in the capital (at Bow Street or other of the metropolis' justice rooms), then this would affect the numbers of women appearing at Old Bailey (just as it was to do after 1835 when magistrates were given official powers to deal with an increased numbers of property crimes summarily). Therefore, it is reasonable to argue that Feeley and Little, by concentrating on the Old Bailey, were not even getting an accurate picture of female criminality in London, let alone the rest of the country. As King so eloquently puts it, on 'closer inspection therefore, the vanishing female offender vanishes'.[19]

The nature of female property offending

Property crime is heavily gendered, both in the items stolen and the method of theft employed. Women were much more frequently prosecuted for stealing clothes, linen, food and other household goods, while men were more likely to take tools and goods from warehouses and docks. This is because a significant proportion of theft involved workplace appropriation or stealing from your employer. Given that large numbers of women found work as domestic servants, it is not surprising that they stole those items that they had easy access to. Contemporaries were well aware of this kind of theft in the eighteenth century; Daniel Defoe complained of servants who were 'light of finger...who beggar you by inchmeal'.[20] Servants pilfered food, the stubs of candles, linen and pawned their mistresses' dresses and occasionally more expensive consumer items. They did so because there was a ready market for second-hand goods in London and elsewhere, and female servants' wages were low. Women, of all ranks, knew the value of household items, and servants participated in the reporting of thefts from their masters and gave evidence of goods stolen. Therefore, women were well placed to make good use of the widespread second-hand market for clothes and household items and the 'ubiquity' of pawn broking.[21]

Not only were the goods stolen by women reflective of the domestic sphere, the methods they used to steal and the nature of thefts they undertook also met often contemporary expectations of female behaviour. So, while male property crime was often confrontational and involved violence, female offending was generally less direct and more covert. Women also acted as accomplices for men in burglaries and housebreaking, by identifying the location of valuable goods or opening doors and windows in the houses where they were employed as domestic servants. But, a woman was much more likely to be indicted for picking pockets or shoplifting than she was for robbery or burglary. Outside London (or in an earlier period), the situation may have been different, especially in the late 1600s. Walker found that theft was gendered in other ways, not simply in what was taken but also in the choice offenders made to act alone or with others. Here, women tended to commit burglaries alone or with other women, and not, as a reliance on Old Bailey records has suggested, as accomplices to men. This might be a reflection of regional difference or perhaps suggests greater female independence in the early modern period.[22]

However, let us persevere with the figures for the capital and look at a sample of property crimes selected from across the extent of the *Old Bailey Proceedings*. While this is not a complete record of all cases heard at the Old Bailey, and of course only covers offenders prosecuted in London, it is a useful indicator of gendered pattern of property offending.

Perhaps the first observation to make is that property crime is dominated by men. This supports Beattie's survey of Surrey between 1663 and 1802 which showed that 76 per cent of those indicted for a property crime at the assizes for the county were male.[23] But it also provides evidence of the gendered nature of female and male offending. The most serious property crime was highway robbery (or robbery). This offence, in all its guises, was overwhelmingly male; just 11–17 per cent of women were accused of this crime in this sample.

The same is true for burglary and housebreaking. While a higher proportion of women are involved in this crime in the earlier period, by the nineteenth century they have all but disappeared from the higher court. It would also appear that women were rarely, if ever, accused of stealing animals (which usually meant horses, cattle or sheep) because the use of animals (in particular horse and cattle) was predominantly male; a lower-class woman would draw considerable attention if she were seen riding or leading a horse through the capital's streets.

Men also dominate the statistics for more general forms of larceny, thefts from specified locations and receiving stolen goods, although women again appear to 'vanish' from these statistics as nineteenth-century criminal justice reforms removed many prosecutions to the summary courts. It was for stealing from shops, picking pockets and coining that women were seemingly most vulnerable to prosecution at the Old Bailey.

Stealing from shops (shoplifting)

As Figure 7.1 shows, shoplifting was a much less gendered crime in terms of the percentages of men and women committing it. The fall-off in the proportion of women being indicted for shoplifting at Old Bailey in the period after 1828 has probably more to do with a shift in judicial jurisdiction which transferred such crimes to the summary courts rather than being representative of a decline in the percentage of women that were charged with committing this offence. Shoplifting was also a predominantly urban

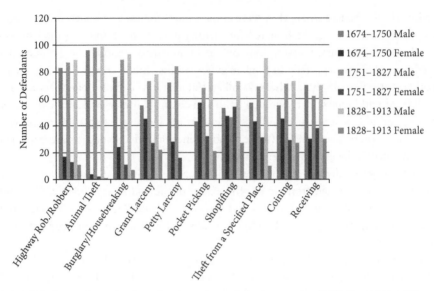

Figure 7.1 Proportion of male to female property defendants at the Old Bailey, 1674–1913.

crime, which is unsurprising given that shops were much more common in towns and cities. Women's involvement in shoplifting ('stealing privily from a shop') was a consequence of the freedoms, opportunities and dangers that manifested in English towns and cities. The city offered a 'wider opportunity for employment and a greater range of leisure and entertainment options', but at the same time, it was an unforgiving and unsupportive environment within which women, in particular, were exposed to poverty.[24] By contrast, the rural community offered a level of support and protection from the consequences of unemployment. Here, offenders were also more likely to be subjected to localized and community sanctions for petty property offending, and so, fewer women would face a jury trial.[25]

Urban centres (such as London, Bath and Bristol) were also well served by a growing retail trade, which, in the eighteenth century, placed a new emphasis on the fashionable display of luxury goods. London's shops were a revelation to both British and overseas visitors, and the extravagant window displays attracted shoppers from dawn till late at night. While 'going a shopping' had become an accepted cultural activity for the respectable, the opulent and conspicuous displays also attracted a less respectable 'customer', the shoplifter.

The problem of shoplifting, and especially shoplifting by women, was first identified in the late seventeenth century. Legislators, perhaps motivated by a desire to restrict the perceived independence of women in urban areas, or under pressure from London's growing retail traders, decided to clamp down on what was seen as 'private' (unseen) theft from shops. In 1699, shoplifting was made a capital offence in response to fears that the crime had mushroomed in the previous decades.[26] The theft of goods valued at 5s. and above, taken without the shopkeeper or any other witnesses *seeing* the theft, was now punishable by hanging. This was hard to prove in court, and as a result, many women were convicted of the lesser offence of larceny, while others walked free altogether. We can see the way in which the difficulties of proving guilt in shoplifting cases affected the prosecution of women in this case from 1786.

In late February, a journeyman haberdasher brought an accusation of shoplifting against two women at the Old Bailey. Sarah Lyon and Ann Gibson were charged with stealing nine yards of lace with a value of 20s. from a shop in the City of London. The women entered the shop with Ann's child, and they asked the assistant if they could look at some thread lace, supposedly to edge a cap for the child. They looked at a variety of items but could not agree a price with the assistant so made some small purchases and left. However, the assistant noticed that some lace was missing and chased and caught them. Both women denied taking anything but the assistant detained them until a constable arrived. He searched the women and found some lace in Lyon's pocket – 'half in and half out'. At the discovery, Sarah apparently said, 'Oh Lord! How came it here, I cannot think how it came here'; Gibson had nothing on her. Lyon blamed the theft on the child, saying that while they had been haggling over the price, the child was playing with the lace in the box and must have pinched some. The shop assistant said he had taken great care that the child 'did not touch a piece of lace'. So, it seemed that while Lyons was guilty of theft (given that the lace was found on her person), was she guilty of stealing it 'privately'? The court pressed the shop man on this: 'did you not see her take this lace, or touch it?' asked the judge; 'No, I did not' was his reply. Lyon was convicted but only sentenced to six months in a house of correction with a private whipping, escaping the death penalty because it was hard to prove that she had taken the lace under the terms of the act.[27]

The death penalty was removed from shoplifting in 1823, and thereafter those convicted faced the prospect of being transported. However, much of this theft was prosecuted merely as simple larceny as shopkeepers were reluctant to go to the expense and trouble of a jury trial and may well also have been concerned not to be seen to be pursuing a capital charge against what were often young women. In 1820, Parliament, under pressure from those determined to dismantle the 'Bloody Code', made it harder to hang shoplifters. As a result, 'indictments rose rapidly' thereafter.[28] Lesser charges were also more likely to secure a conviction (juries being less squeamish about finding women guilty if there was no chance of sending them to the gallows), and a visit to a nearby justice of the peace might have secured the return of the goods taken at considerably less expense.

Deirdre Palk has shown that the courts chose to make examples of notably 'troublesome' or 'unfeminine' women, those who were drunk, or used foul language, or who were associated with prostitution. Thus, Mary Palmer, who at 18 already had a baby, attracted the suspicions of the shop assistant who told the court, 'I did not much like her appearance, she looked like a girl of the town' (in other words, a prostitute).[29] These factors, along with the relatively larger numbers of women who appeared in court, go some way to explaining why the prevailing leniency of Old Bailey juries and judges towards female defendants is less apparent when it comes to shoplifting. In the period

1780–1823, large numbers of women were sentenced to death or transportation. As Palk notes, what we might term 'judicial paternalism may not operate to the same extent when women are no longer a minority in court'.[30]

In 1826, Maria Allen was convicted of stealing 54 yards of ribbon from a linen draper. Maria had bought a few things, but she had been acting suspiciously. The draper had observed her using her shawl to obscure her basket into which he noticed her putting her hands 'two or three times, very quickly'. When she left the shop he pursued her, searched her basket and found his missing ribbon. No one had seen her taking the ribbon, and she was only 18 years old. The judge handed down a sentence of seven years transportation.[31]

What about shoplifting in the later nineteenth century? After 1823, stealing from shops was no longer a capital offence, and as the century unfolded, attitudes towards female shoplifters became interwoven with a developing discourse that viewed the female criminal as 'weak' and subjected to uncontrollable urges. While lower-class women were still identified as the main culprits in the nineteenth-century diatribes against shoplifting in the press and among the victims – the traders themselves – there was a growing concern that shoplifting was attracting an altogether more 'respectable' well-heeled offender. As early as 1819, a parliamentary committee observed that some of the women involved were in 'better circumstances', meaning they perhaps had no *need* to steal.[32] Commentators also pointed out that the method of displaying goods was putting temptations into the path of women.

In the later 1800s, a new phenomenon emerged: the middle-class shoplifter who stole, not for profit or need, but because she desired this or that luxury item. This is a trope that twenty-first-century audiences are more familiar with, and it is often treated less as a crime and more as a sign of a weakened mental health.[33] It is certainly taken much less seriously than it was in the period between 1700 and 1900. It seems that on occasions when respectable women were accused of taking goods from shops, they attempted, quite successfully sometimes, to put the blame upon their accusers or to turn the tables and condemn them for bringing their reputation into disrepute. They deployed what Tammy Whitlock has called 'the absent-minded defence' and argued that while they might have placed goods in their pockets, they had fully intended to pay for them, but had experienced a momentarily lapse of memory, and had walked out of the store without doing so.[34] It also presented problems for the shopkeepers or managers of the emerging department stores in that public sympathy (and fascination) often rested with the middle-class women who stole, rather than with the targets of their crimes.[35]

In 1844, *Punch* responded to an apparent surge in middle-class shoplifting cases by ridiculing those involved and the defence they offered. However, the issue of middle-class women being accused of this crime had a much more disturbing aspect to it. Given the nature of shoplifting, women suspected of the crime were routinely searched by shop staff. This presented the unfortunate situation of working-class assistants searching their social superiors and, of course, accusing them of wrongdoing. The *cause celebré* was that of Mrs Jane Tyrwhitt, an extremely wealthy lady who was accused of stealing a small microscope from a stall in the Soho Bazaar. While the jury acquitted her, it seems quite certain that she had committed the crime and that her social status had saved her; it appeared that the law operated differently according to class.[36]

Therefore, it is hard for us to separate contemporary concerns about middle-class shoplifters from a wider discourse about respectable women in the public sphere. Once again, it is evident that underlying attitudes towards women in general affected attitudes towards female criminality in particular. As a result, such thieving was increasingly explained away as a peculiar manifestation of the female mind. By the mid-nineteenth century, a new defence, that of kleptomania (or the 'thieving madness'), had begun to be used regularly by counsel in courts across England. Doctors were being called as witnesses in a variety of trials, and from the middle of the nineteenth century, it seems that a diagnosis of 'brain fever' or kleptomania was being offered to account for the deviant behaviour of some women accused of stealing from shops. Kleptomania 'provided at long last a plausible explanation for why otherwise respectable women' stole.[37]

So, while shoplifting was often a female offence, the falling proportion of women appearing in court can in part be explained by the actions of prosecutors (in not bringing cases to court) and a developing discourse that viewed such behaviour as symptomatic of female weakness rather than female criminality. To what extent did this also affect another area of property crime, pocket picking, in which women featured in large numbers?

Pocket picking

Picking pockets was, like shoplifting, a difficult crime to prove. Much of the theft from the person that occurred in eighteenth- and nineteenth-century London was carried out by prostitutes and often went unpunished, either because their victims were too embarrassed to go to law or the courts took a dim view of the men that put themselves at risk. Picking pockets was a capital crime (from 1565 until its repeal in 1808) which meant that juries were reluctant to find women guilty. Theft had to take place without the victim's knowledge for this to be deemed capital under the terms of the statute, but by the 1780s, while this included goods taken while the victim slept, it pointedly *did not* include possessions pinched while the owner was intoxicated. The courts continued to find against men that accused women who robbed them when they had visited them for illicit sex.

Again picking pockets appears to have been a crime driven by the growing urban environment; cities such as Bath and London with their bustling streets and large crowds offered innumerable opportunities for light-fingered thieves to part unwary pedestrians from their valuables. The same skills of distraction that made women successful shoplifters also served them well as pickpockets. An ability to get close to victims and to appear unthreatening undoubtedly meant that many people were unaware that they had been robbed until it was too late to catch the perpetrator.

Picking pockets is closely associated with juvenile crime, but female pickpockets were more likely to take higher value items than their male (and often juvenile) counterparts.

This was directly related to differences in the ways in which men (or boys) and women stole; women operated in private, and this enabled them to get closer to their victims and so take items such as watches and money, while male pickpockets weaved in and out of the crowded streets using greater dexterity to remove handkerchiefs from back pockets. This is therefore one area in which female property crime was potentially more lucrative than the male equivalent.[38]

Again, it is useful to look at an example of female offending in the records of the *Old Bailey Proceedings*. In 1787, William Mulry, rather the worse for drink, was enticed into Mary Harris's room in Hedge Lane. He awoke to find that his silver watch, chain, seal, two keys and several coins were all missing. When Mary was searched, the watch was found on her. She claimed he had lent it to her and earned her living selling flowers; the jury did not believe her but only found her guilty of the theft, not of stealing *privately*. As a result, the judge sent her to gaol for a year.[39] This shows how hard it was to convict women of privately stealing from their clients.

In 1855, two women appeared at Old Bailey accused of picking the pockets of a woman newly arrived in London by means of a distraction. As Mary Parsons made her way towards London Bridge station, two women and a younger girl approached her to ask directions. As Mary tried to help them, one of the women picked her pockets removing two banknotes that were later traced back to them. Only one of the women was convicted (the evidence against the other was not sufficiently convincing), and she was sent to prison for twelve months.[40] The perils of the city were evident here and Mrs Parsons's assailants were well able to take advantage of unwary travellers.

Victorians were concerned about women who stole in this secret or private manner. New opportunities for theft arose both from the growing urban sprawl of nineteenth-century England and from new methods of transportation. The chaplain of Liverpool gaol, Reverend Clay, remarked that female pickpockets operated on the new omnibuses: as the bus pulled away 'they get into it, and being dressed like any gentleman's girls, [...] they get close beside a lady, and contrive to place their shawl or mantle over the lady's dress pocket, which shades their hands'.[41] Non-threatening, able to blend in with the society they inhabited, female thieves were ideally suited to this form of indirect offending.

In the later nineteenth century, pocket picking, along with other forms of less serious property crime, was being held up as less of a threat to society than violence. In this context, the female offender was also considered to represent less of a risk, and so, by comparison to men, fewer women were brought to court. Picking pockets, while still a prevalent form of criminal activity, diminished in part through the efforts of the New Police who patrolled the nation's streets and provided a visible deterrent to thieves. Public fear of pickpockets was reduced as the concern turned to more serious, violent and male offenders.[42] In consequence, much of this criminal activity was dealt with at petty sessions level, removing women from the jury courts.

Finally, this examination of gendered property crime will look at women's involvement in offences against the currency – coining, forgery and the related offence of 'uttering' false money.

Coining and forgery

Understandably, an offence which threatened the value of the nation's currency was taken very seriously. However, in a period before modern anti-forgery precautions could be applied to both minted coins and bank notes, it is equally understandable that many individuals resorted to illegal methods to exploit society's reliance upon a mechanism of monetary exchange despite the severe consequences of getting caught doing so.

As was shown in Chapter 4, forgery and coining were two separate offences; the former included all sorts of related attempts to defraud using paper 'instruments',[43] while the latter was specifically related to the illegal manufacture of metal coin. Women convicted of making false gold or silver coin were liable to be burned alive for their offences. Men convicted of coining in gold or silver were supposed to be hanged, drawn and quartered, but women were supposedly spared the indignity of having their bodies exposed by being cut up by the executioner. It was thought to be much better to burn them instead.

Women were most often accused of uttering (or passing) forged money. This was because women were less suspicious, more easily trusted and able to dispose of false coin in the networks of trade within which they operated. Just as women were able to use the second-hand market to get rid of stolen linen, clothes and other items they were ideally placed to recycle false coinage.

By the later decades of the eighteenth century, the Bank of England had become the most prominent (and determined) prosecutor of suspected coiners, forgers and utterers. The Bank set up a committee to investigate forgery cases and took a proactive role in prosecutions. Deirdre Palk found that women were most commonly involved in the distribution of forged notes, often as part of organized gangs. The Bank operated a particularly determined plea bargaining policy; plead guilty to the lesser offence of uttering and women (and men) were pretty much guaranteed to be transported. However, if defendants chose to place themselves at the mercy of the jury and plead their innocence, the Bank used its wealth to prosecute those accused for the more serious indictment of forgery. If the jury found against the defendant, the Bank then pressed for the death penalty without mercy. Of those tried between 1804 and 1834, only 6 per cent of women (and 8 per cent of men) were acquitted; thirty women (16 per cent) and ninety-six men (17 per cent) were sent to the gallows. This is one area in which capital punishment was applied equally to men and women, a most unusual statistic in gendered studies of criminality.[44]

Uttering also carried the death penalty between 1725 and 1832. The way uttering worked in practice is illustrated by a case from 1738. A witness saw Judith Murray 'utter' some forged shillings in a London tavern. She gave one genuine half-crown to her brother for him to buy drink that only cost sixpence, so he would get the balance. Judith then told the landlord she had change after all and swapped up all the good coinage with the bad, which was then returned along with what they owned, in return for the original half-crown. She could keep doing this time and time again because the small amount of the transactions meant it was unlikely to raise much suspicion.[45] Judith Murray was an active member of a coining gang, and she both uttered coin and forged it. She and co-defendants were all convicted and sentenced to death. Some shopkeepers were alert to forged currency: in 1840, Jane Blinkford (who had a previous conviction for uttering) tried to buy a saveloy sausage in a London butcher's shop with a false shilling. The assistant told her it was 'bad' and a policeman was called. Jane, aged just 20, was transported to Australia.[46] A month later, Ruth Miles, another young girl (17) with a record of previous offending, was sentenced to fifteen years transportation for a similar offence. The Old Bailey court was clearly taking an extremely dim view of offenders that attempted to profit by undermining the coin of the realm, regardless of their age or gender.

Of course, women committed many forms of property offending, albeit in smaller numbers than men, and their offending was also affected by their age and marital status.

The importance of the life cycle to female offending

Any consideration of female offending needs to take account of the importance of the life cycle to women's vulnerability to unemployment and poverty. In his study of female offending in London in the late eighteenth century, Peter King found that young unmarried women in London were almost four times as likely to be prosecuted as women in their thirties.[47] That unmarried women were more vulnerable to prosecution does not mean they necessarily committed more crime, but patriarchy and family networks perhaps protected married women better. The principle of *femme couvert*, while not a guarantee against prosecution, certainly seems to have saved some women from the terrors of facing a full jury trial if they could demonstrate that they were acting under the instructions of a male partner. However, of those women imprisoned in Newgate gaol in 1792, some 58.9 per cent were single, which was a higher proportion to the population in London as a whole. By 1801, approximately 45 per cent of women aged 9 or over remained unmarried, so the evidence that nearly 60 per cent of female prisoners in Newgate were unmarried suggests that this was a significant factor in these women's decision to commit some form of criminal activity. Marriage (or cohabitation) offered some protection from poverty as there were two potential breadwinners. Thus, women may well have been exposed to prosecution before marriage, or after a partner had deserted them, gone off to war or had died. For women in late eighteenth-century London, the most vulnerable periods of the life cycle were therefore in their late teens and early twenties or from their fifties onwards. In the Black Country, in the mid-Victorian period, the peaks were at 18–25 and 24–40 which reveal similar starting points for first offenders as the London evidence.[48] New research on female offenders in nineteenth-century London and Liverpool draws upon previous work and suggests that women started offending earlier than historians have previously thought and continued for longer across the life cycle.[49] This was especially true for persistent or repeat offenders.[50] As Lucy Williams argues, in the later nineteenth century at least, a 'woman's age at her first conviction could go on to determine the length, scale, and character of her criminal career'.[51]

London was also a magnet for migrant workers from all over the British Isles. Typically, most female migrants left home in their late teens and gained some experience of service prior to arriving in the capital city, and migrants of both sexes were extremely vulnerable to prosecution. Those unable to find work quickly would soon spend or lose their small capital and run the risk of turning to crime to avoid destitution.

In the period 1791–1793, the majority – some 58 per cent – of those of both sexes accused of property crimes at the Old Bailey gave their place of birth as being outside of London. Some 56 per cent of female defendants were migrant workers.[52] These figures therefore indicate that it was young single women in their early-to-mid-twenties that were most likely to find themselves on trial at the eighteenth-century Old Bailey as a result of the economic difficulties that they were exposed to on arrival in the capital. The same would appear to be the case in the nineteenth century; in Liverpool, many of those women prosecuted for property crime were Irish immigrants, driven abroad by the Potato Famine or its repercussions.

Women also became vulnerable to prosecution towards the end of their life cycle. Widows without family support could easily fall into crime as a survival strategy, and single women in London were particularly at risk when economic hardships occurred. Work was harder to come by, and they had no man to fall back on as wage provider, and in times of war, this vulnerability was even more marked. Economic need rather than greed was the most important factor in explaining property crime in the eighteenth and nineteenth century. For women at least, the exposure to poverty as a result of being single, widowed or abandoned by a male partner was the most significant causal factor in their descent into crime. Commentators rarely agreed with this explanation and continued to associate female crime with individual moral decay or weakness. These were both a consequence of seeing women as second-class citizens, and this could work in women's favour. However, in two significant areas at least, patriarchy condemned women to be treated very badly by the criminal justice system when arguably they needed the courts to support and protect them.

Newborn child murder and the concealment of birth

Infanticide (newborn child murder) or the killing of a baby at birth or very soon afterwards was an almost exclusively female crime. It was also a crime that was mainly focused on prosecuting the murderers of illegitimate babies.[53] As such, it is strongly interlinked with contemporary notions of how women should (and should not) behave, especially with regard to their sexuality.

In the eighteenth century, infanticide took two forms in law: 'If a married woman (or a man) was prosecuted for killing a new-born child, the charge would be [...] murder, and a conviction could only be obtained if there was evidence that the child had been born alive and that the accused had deliberately killed it.'[54] The mother was therefore presumed innocent until proven guilty. However, the situation for unmarried mothers was quite different. Under the terms of a 1624 act, the onus was on proving, with at least one witness, that any 'bastard' (illegitimate) child born dead had indeed been born dead, and not killed shortly afterwards.[55] This effectively shifted the burden of proof from the accuser to accused and meant that mothers who gave birth in secret (without witnesses) were severely disadvantaged. However, we should be careful about overemphasizing the implied removal of the presumption of innocence here. The presumption was not properly established until the nineteenth century. In addition, although the 1624 legislation 'presumed that a woman who concealed the death of her bastard had murdered it, concealment still had to be proven by evidence'. Regardless of the circumstances, the court would still make efforts to hear evidence from witnesses and experts (midwives or other medical practitioners) to determine whether a natural death might have occurred or not.[56]

Infanticide seems to have been aimed much more at the control of sexual activity and immorality than at any perceived problem with the killing of children. As Garthine Walker notes, the 1624 law 'defined poor unmarried women as precisely the sort of ungodly, dissolute persons who would perpetrate a heinous, "unnatural" deed'.[57] Under the bastardy laws (designed to control illegitimacy) women were obliged to tell the poor law officers the identity of the father of their child, so he could be made to support her, thereby ensuring that this expense did not end up being the responsibility of local ratepayers. If women refused to disclose this information, magistrates were empowered to send them to the local house of correction for up to a year, and infanticide should be seen in this context.[58]

The motives for infanticide were complex and, given the limited sources available to historians, difficult to unpack. Clearly, shame was a factor given that throughout the period from the early modern to the modern era, unmarried mothers were not considered to be 'respectable', and society offered them little real support. The bastardy laws effectively criminalized premarital sex if it did not lead to marriage. In reality, many of those accused of infanticide were young domestic servants terrified of losing their jobs if they were discovered to have had a child.[59] Some killed their babies because they could not afford to raise them; some through callous indifference and some out a misplaced sense that it was 'for the best'. Other women committed the offence for psychological reasons (and this was to become the most successful form of defence in the 1800s), and a small number probably killed deliberately for gain (as with some baby-farmers) or out of malice.[60] Many others were charged with the offence when no deliberate action had taken place; after all birth was a dangerous and unpredictable event in the past, especially when young mothers were concerned to hide their 'shame' from the prying eyes of neighbours, fellow servants or employers.

Throughout the seventeenth and into the early eighteenth century, many unmarried women were prosecuted and hanged under the terms of the 1624 act, reflecting society's distaste both of the act and a wider disgust about illegitimacy.[61] In 1708, Mary Ellenor, a London servant, had fallen pregnant without a husband and her dead baby was found where she left it, in an outside privy. Her mistress had suspected the girl was hiding something and refused to believe Mary's claim that she had miscarried. In court, Mary had little chance to defend herself given the conditions and the terms of the act, and she was sentenced to death.[62] Disposing of the child in this way was quite common, and it offered 'some privacy without creating too much suspicion',[63] but to a modern audience, it appears callous rather than practical.

As Figure 7.2 shows, proportionally more women were convicted in the late seventeenth and early eighteenth centuries than was the case as the century unfolded. In fact, while indictments for infanticide continued to be brought to English courts throughout the eighteenth century, convictions were rare by comparison to the early modern period.[64] By the middle of the 1700s, juries were insisting on proof of wrongdoing in infanticide cases rather than applying the law as it had been framed in 1624. If a woman could show that she had prepared for the birth, that she had collected linen or prepared a cot for example, this would significantly help her case.

So, when Ann Seabrook was charged with infanticide in 1756 (her dead child having been discovered by the river near her home), she claimed it was stillborn. She told the court that 'she had kept it to her warme for two hours, but during that Time it never stird a Limb nor open'd its Eyes, whereupon she threw it into the River in hopes the Tide would have carry'd it away and this she did in order to hide the shame from the Eyes of the World'.[65] A fellow servant said she had seen her making clothes for the baby while she was pregnant and the jury found her not guilty, and she was let off with a reprimand. Many women escaped capital punishment because juries were not prepared to convict them of killing and were more comfortable deploying a secondary (or partial) verdict of concealment, something that agitated commentators in the 1700s.

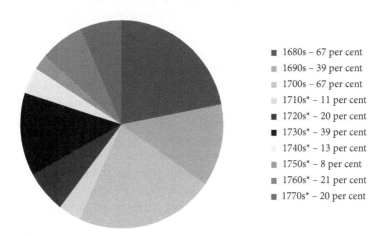

■ 1680s – 67 per cent
■ 1690s – 39 per cent
■ 1700s – 67 per cent
▨ 1710s* – 11 per cent
■ 1720s* – 20 per cent
■ 1730s* – 39 per cent
▨ 1740s* – 13 per cent
■ 1750s* – 8 per cent
■ 1760s* – 21 per cent
■ 1770s* – 20 per cent

Figure 7.2 Proportion of guilty verdicts in infanticide cases at Old Bailey, 1680–1780.

Note: *The records for 1710s are incomplete, so this may not represent such a dramatic fall in guilty outcomes.

A study of the sessions papers reveals a noticeable falling away of convictions for infanticide at the Old Bailey after about 1750, which probably reflects a widespread change in attitude towards infanticide in the second half of the century. Contemporaries were aware that the act penalized otherwise honest and 'innocent' servant girls, not the sexually wanton 'harlots' that the 1624 act had been aimed at. There were few alternatives for servants who found themselves carrying unwanted offspring, and while initiatives such as Sir Thomas Coram's Foundling Hospital, which opened in London in 1750, provided unmarried mothers with places where they could deposit their unwanted children, this only catered for a tiny minority.

Alongside with a measure of sympathy for defendants, there were other practical legal reasons for the decline in convictions. It was quite difficult for the prosecution to prove that a child had survived birth only to be killed afterwards, as medicine was divided on what constituted 'independent life' after birth. A crude 'lung test' had been devised in the seventeenth century which involved placing the lungs of the dead child in a bowl of water to see if they sank or not. This was based on the theory that aerated lungs would float when placed in water demonstrating that the child had breathed and so had been alive. Many medical men were sceptical however, and evidence based on this 'hydrostatic test' (and other tests that involved comparing the weight of the lungs to the mass of the deceased overall) was often discounted in the eighteenth century.[66] In 1768, when Ann Haywood was acquitted of killing her baby boy, a surgeon told the court that, 'I opened the thorax, and took out the lungs, in order to make the experiment usually made in these cases', and that while 'the lungs did swim [i.e. float],...I was of opinion that that experiment cannot be conclusive in this case, because the body had laid three days in the bog house, and I think such a fermentation might have been brought off, that it might gather air'.[67] In Ann's case, the crucial evidence was that she had made provision for the birth, something that helped to convince jurors that she had not intended to kill the child.

As a result of the complexity of the law and the reluctance of juries to send young mothers to the gallows, convictions were rare. This change of attitudes among the jury was formalized with new legislation in 1803 which saw infanticide treated just like any other murder, with the accused deemed to be innocent until proven guilty. This new statute (Lord Ellenborough's Act[68]) also allowed juries to deliver an alternative verdict of *concealment of birth* for unmarried mothers whose newborn babies had died, which carried a maximum sentence of two years in prison.

It seems that juries had effectively had the final word on infanticide with fewer and fewer convictions; most women charged with the crime were acquitted or found guilty of concealment. Those brought before the court were often young women, often servants desperate to keep their positions and their respectability, and jurors were well aware that some had been seduced by other servants or members of the household, often against their will.[69] Kilday argues that this change to the law, while motivated in part by a feeling that the 1624 act was both harsh and unfair, was driven more by a desire to 'shore up loopholes in the law' and ensure that genuine prosecutions succeeded than by any sympathy with those accused.[70] In 1828, a further amendment of the laws surrounding infanticide was passed making concealment itself an offence, rather than merely an alternative verdict. In addition, there was no longer a requirement for the prosecution (or defence) to prove that the child had been born alive (or dead) and the revised law now applied to both single and married mothers. The laws were tightened in 1861 to include accomplices and to extend concealment to cases where the child had not even died. These laws remained in place until important changes were made in 1922.[71]

There was a widespread moral panic about infanticide in Victorian England that encompassed several baby-farming scandals and brought infanticide to the forefront once again.[72] Contemporary commentators complained that 'the feeble wail of murdered childhood in its agony assails our ears at every turn', and newspapers suggested that the murder of new born children had become commonplace.[73] This led in turn to an increase in prosecutions and parliamentary returns records a sharp upturn in indictments from the late 1840s which peaked in the late 1860s.[74] However, most women still avoided the worst outcome (a capital sentence), and many escaped any sort of punishment by effectively pleading temporary insanity. The nineteenth century saw an increased emphasis on the mental state of the mother and a 'forensic interest concentrated on puerperal insanity', a process that arguably began in the late eighteenth century.

There was also a new emphasis on childhood and 'infant life preservation' at the end of the nineteenth century.[75] The Boer War and the parlous state of some of Britain's cities had placed motherhood at the heart of late Victorian and Edwardian society. In consequence, the twentieth century saw moves to alter the legislation surrounding infanticide and concealment; some commentators felt it was too easy for a murderous mother to escape the consequences of her actions and argued that the law needed to be improved. It was still very hard to prove that a child had been killed rather than been born dead, and very few women were ever executed for the offence, as most were granted clemency by the Home Secretary. In 1922, a new act placed most cases of infanticide on a level with manslaughter and allowed juries to find women guilty but insane or simply guilty of concealment.[76]

So, what are we to make of the prosecution of women for infanticide over this long period? Evidently, this was not simply an attempt to protect the newborn child. Movements to protect infants were under way in the nineteenth century, and increasingly, this did come to dominate debates. But, early infanticide legislation was aimed at controlling the bodies and sexuality of young unmarried (and for the most part, working-class) women. Clearly, married women *did* kill their newborns but were much less likely to be accused of doing so. They had the advantage of not having to conceal pregnancies, and the 1624 act did not place the onus of proof on them, but on the prosecutor instead. They could also rely a little more on accomplices, and so here it is possible to see some examples of infanticide as attempts at controlling family size. Even when they did get to court, prosecutions against married women often failed to gain convictions because juries accepted pleas of temporary insanity as they found it hard to believe that a woman 'in her right mind' could murder her own baby.[77] And it was this belief, coupled with the inability of medical science to come up with a definitive way of proving guilt, that led to so many women either being acquitted, found guilty of a lesser charge or having the sentences of death passed upon the quashed on appeal.

Infanticide could involve deliberate killing, and there were women (like the notorious baby farmer Amelia Dyer who was hanged in 1896) who murdered their children (or the children of others), but for most of those indicted, the act of infanticide was a reaction to a desperate situation or caused by the effort of giving birth on one's own, in secret. This is why infanticide and concealment need to be situated within a discussion of female offending and the gendered concepts of morality and not within a wider discussion of homicide.

Prostitution

Morality (or rather immorality) and attitudes towards female sexuality also informed debates about women who acted as prostitutes throughout the period of this study. However, prostitution was not a crime in the technical legal sense of the word; indeed it seems reasonable to argue that there has never really been a concerted effort to prohibit prostitution perhaps because there is a tacit acceptance that the so-called 'oldest profession' in the world[78] is impossible to outlaw completely. Instead, legislators and local authorities have attempted to control, contain or regulate the sex trade in order to minimize the disruption it causes to those not involved in it or (more recently) to protect the individuals who prostitute themselves. So, we have seen attempts to keep prostitution to certain areas of towns and cities or legislation that is aimed at preventing the exploitation of sex workers (such as efforts to combat people trafficking, for example). There have also been ongoing efforts across the last 300 years to reform, educate or otherwise help prostitutes to leave the profession or to take measures to stay safe if they choose to remain in it. While not all prostitutes are women, English law has generally maintained the position that clients are male and sex workers are female and that the burden of guilt rests with the latter.[79]

In the eighteenth century, efforts at regulating the sex trade were motivated by both moral *and* pragmatic factors. This duality can be seen quite clearly in the movement for the Reformation of Manners. While this movement (which started in 1689 and lasted until 1738, before resurfacing in the 1780s) was launched under the backdrop of a concern about the 'overflowing of vice', it was driven and maintained by 'concerns about the perceived growth of crime and disorder' in London and in particular concerns that related to the behaviour of the poor.[80] Problems of crime and immorality were interlinked in contemporary discourse, with the former being seen as an individual failing rather than a product of environmental factors. Efforts were coordinated to close down brothels and round up and prosecute the huge numbers of streetwalkers that operated in the capital. As a result, a small number of Westminster justices of the peace actively pursued the prosecution of prostitutes as 'loose [or lewd] idle and disorderly persons', sending more than 200 women to the local house of correction in six months alone.[81]

This approach to the problem of prostitution characterizes the Georgian period. There were attempts to close down brothels, but the trade survived and indeed prospered. Covent Garden was synonymous with the sex industry, and publications such as

Harris's List of Covent Garden Ladies not only acted as a gazetteer of individual tastes and proclivities, but also offered a defence of the 'oldest profession'.[82] London offered a range of related material from erotica to pornography, much of it consumed by the same class of person as those so concerned to protect the morals of the working classes.[83] Thus, prostitution continued to exist despite the periodic attempts at its suppression throughout the 1700s.

During the same period, there were also attempts made to save prostitutes and to begin a process of rehabilitation and reform. Within a year of *Harris's List* first appearing, an institution opened in London with the avowed purpose to rescue 'fallen' women. From 1758, the Magadalen Hospital for the Reception of Penitent Prostitutes opened and took in women for, on average, three years in the hope of turning their lives around.

The Reformation of Manners movement and the efforts of philanthropists such as Jonas Hanway were underpinned by a desire not to eradicate prostitution but to limit and regulate it. Contemporaries recognized that prostitution was a social problem, one with close links to poverty and crime. Most biographies of prostitutes echoed those of the thousands of male property criminals hanged at Tyburn in that they described a descent into vice and crime a fall from grace, but not always one of their own making. The typical story of the prostitute (as illustrated by William Hogarth in *A Harlot's Progress*[84]) was also a story of exploitation, misfortune and the consequences of bad, if sometimes unavoidable, life choices.

Figure 7.3 William Hogarth, *A Harlot's Progress* 1.

Figure 7.4 William Hogarth, *A Harlot's Progress* 2.

Hogarth's eponymous heroine, Moll Hackabout, was a country girl set on making her way to London to find a position as a domestic servant or seamstress. Unfortunately for Moll she was met from the stagecoach in Cheapside by a notorious procuress – a woman tasked with finding a fresh supply of young women for the capital's many brothels. Having been promised lodgings and a new set of more suitable clothes, Moll was inveigled into a fashionable bawdy house where a wealthy man fell for her charms and made her his mistress. Moll fell yet further and eventually ended up as a common whore in a cheap brothel.

When the brothel was raided by a Westminster magistrate, Moll was carried off to Bridewell. Her 'progress' was then completed as she finally dies from syphilis, a typical path for London's many whores.

The problems associated with prostitution were well understood, but given that the underlying cause was poverty and the demand for cheap sex, contemporaries realized that most efforts to tackle the trade were futile. This situation continued in to the nineteenth century, although attempts to control prostitution were now redoubled and imbued with a new urgency – underpinned by the emergence of a new and opinionated medical profession.

Victorian attitudes and the 'Great Social Evil'

By the mid-nineteenth century, prostitutes were lumped with the destitute poor and the 'criminal class' and discussed within a discourse that viewed them as a danger, both to polite society and to the industrious working class that had built and sustained the wealth of Victorian Britain. The term 'Great Social Evil' was applied to the problem of prostitution, and in the 1860s, debates surrounding the role of prostitution in the spread of disease led to the passing of the Contagious Diseases Acts.

While the eighteenth century had seen a number of initiatives aimed at controlling or regulating prostitution, it was the Victorian period that saw a concerted effort to deal with the consequences (if not the causes) of the trade. Middle-class attitudes towards prostitution were underpinned by a fear that it was a corrupting influence that would pollute respectable lives, wreck marriages, break-up the family home and destroy the very fabric of the nation. Attitudes towards prostitution seemed to have fluctuated across the century; in the early 1800s, a 'cult of sentimentality' described prostitutes as the 'helpless victims of seduction or social injustice'.[85] The mid-century saw the intervention of by medical professionals, philanthropic reformers and socialists. In 1857, William Acton published a study of prostitution that was to have considerable influence over contemporary attitudes towards the trade.[86] Acton's work was followed in 1871 by William Logan's *The Great Social Evil*, which echoed an earlier study of the problem by William Tait.[87] Both of these latter studies offered a more scientific and authoritative analysis of prostitution than Acton's as well as appreciating that the sex trade was often interlinked with poverty and the restricted opportunities for women to find legitimate paid employment.[88]

Social investigators scoured the slums of Britain as well as the music halls and pubs to explore the horrors of vice. Henry Mayhew and Bracebridge Hemyng collaborated to produce a detailed examination of the prostitution in London, complete with interviews, descriptions and an analysis of the trade.[89] This was a very different 'guide' to the eighteenth-century *Harris's List* that had celebrated prostitution. Prostitution remained high on the agenda for philanthropists, social reformers and newspaper editors and arguably the most dramatic campaign was that launched by W. T. Stead in 1885 when he exposed the problem of child prostitution to the shocked and disgusted readership of his *Pall Mall Gazette*.[90]

The Contagious Diseases Acts

But the campaigns that arguably best characterize Victorian attitudes towards prostitution were those surrounding the Contagious Diseases Acts (CDAs). The first CDA had been passed in 1864 and was followed by subsequent acts in 1866 and 1869. The acts were a reaction to the discovery of widespread venereal infection among members of the armed forces (around a third were said to have contracted one or other sexually transmitted infection) and the fear that this represented a threat to Britain's ability to defend the Empire. The solution to this was typically gendered and in keeping with contemporary attitudes towards men and women. Instead of attempting to prevent soldiers and sailors from visiting prostitutes (or indeed allowing them to marry), the passing of the CDAs initiated a targeted assault on the bodies of female sex workers.

The CDAs (which at first were only applied to garrison towns and ports) allowed local police to round up and arrest prostitutes and forcibly subject them to a medical examination. Women that resisted examination could be sent to prison. Once examined, if they were found to be infected with a sexually transmitted disease, the women were detained in a Lock Hospital until the infection had been 'cured'. They were then released with a certificate to demonstrate that they were 'clean' and allowed to continue to ply their trade. While men were also offered cures, they were not forced to undergo an examination; the legislation therefore effectively underlined the 'double standard' that applied to male and female rights in the nineteenth century.

The CDAs came under vociferous attack from several church groups (who condemned the hypocrisy of the state for punishing women but not men for what was a joint act of sexual illegitimacy) and some prominent women. Most notable was Josephine Butler, who started a campaign against the acts and established a newspaper (*The Shield*) to publicize her views. Butler and her supporters railed against an act that seemingly legitimized prostitution by statute and that 'brutalised and degraded the prostitute still further' rather than helping to save her or turn her away from her sinful existence.[91] Her organization, the Ladies' Association Against the Contagious Diseases Act, held meetings and rallies across the country and attracted a wide membership from both middle-class and working women. However, she met much opposition, not only from medical professionals such as Elizabeth Garrett Anderson and men who saw her as a dangerous campaigner for feminism, but also from prostitutes themselves, some of whom welcomed the CDAs believing that they had effectively legitimized their trade.

In 1886, the legislation was repealed. The CDAs represent the culmination of Victorian attitudes towards the threat posed by prostitution: a threat to the home, the nation and the Empire. In addition, they can be seen as an attempt at state regulation of an illegitimate trade that was impossible to eradicate. Butler went on to link up with William Stead (editor of the *Pall Mall Gazette*) in his campaign to force the passage of the Criminal Law Amendment Act which (along with raising the age of female consent from 13 to 16) introduced a 'summary (and effective) procedure for action against brothels', something which was to have a marked impact on prostitution in the capital in the last decades of the nineteenth century. But by clearing out the brothels, the police simply forced the women out onto the streets, creating a larger social problem and, in 1888, leaving prostitutes exposed in the East End of London to the threat of the world's most notorious serial killer, 'Jack the Ripper'.[92]

For the historical study of prostitution, there is a noticeable lack of almost any sources that offer a prostitute's first-hand perspective on the sex trade. While there are plenty of contemporary men (and some women) who were happy to write copious amounts about the 'Great Social Evil', we hardly ever get to hear from those that sold themselves. Even those few women that spoke to Mayhew and Hemyng have had their words filtered through a middle-class lens. As Stephan Slater observed, the Metropolitan Police targeted working-class street prostitution, not the activities of those that served the sexual fancies of the West End elite.[93] Historians can only attempt to estimate the numbers of women who prostituted themselves, and given that selling sex was often only a part-time or temporary strategy for poorer women, it increases the uncertainties underpinning this topic. Given that it was not actually a crime, prostitution was generally treated as a social problem, and women regarded and labelled as 'disorderly' or 'lewd', and it was only when they committed a secondary offence that we encounter them within the criminal justice system.

Concluding remarks: Women and the 'relentless logic of patriarchy'[94]

Sexual inequality is apparent in all walks of life from the early modern to the modern age, and the study of the history of crime and punishment is an ideal way in which to explore such gender inequality. Women who attempted to use the law to prosecute those that raped them were faced by a masculine wall of suspicion; one that challenged them to expose themselves to ridicule and humiliation and was often more interested in protecting the reputation of the accused man than in protecting the person of the wronged woman. Anna Clark's powerful study of rape in the eighteenth century also reveals the callous attitudes of men who saw the rape of women as something for which mere financial compensation was appropriate.[95] Abused wives faced similar problems in going to law. Patriarchy ruled that they were their husband's property to do with as he wished. Even if the courts did side with the victims of abuse, the consequences of pursuing an action for assault could leave a woman open to further violence, loss of a breadwinner or abandonment. It is hardly to be wondered at that so few cases reached the courts.

When it came to newborn child murder, it was the unmarried women of the servant class that appeared in courts accused of murdering their babies. Effectively denied the same the rights as other prisoners, they often found themselves in an impossible situation; a situation made worse by the illegitimacy of their pregnancy and thus their own fall from innocence. They were condemned for being pregnant, regardless of the reality that in many instances they had been seduced or raped by fellow servants, their employer or one of his sons. Once again patriarchy operated to ensure that women were considered as creatures less deserving of legal protection.

However, female property criminals may have benefitted from the legal interpretation of patriarchy. Coverture here protected wives who acted with their husbands; by treating them as 'non-persons' under law, they could hardly be blamed if they followed the lead of their menfolk. How effective this was is open to debate, and it would be interesting if we could see some more focused regional studies on female offending. Attitudes towards female offending certainly appear to have spared many women from the gallows and (alongside juveniles) drove debates about the removal of capital punishments from non-violent property crime. Women also benefitted from the retreat from judicial violence as forms of flogging were removed for women before men (in 1820). By contrast, of course, men were not burned alive as women were. Prostitution, like infanticide, should be seen not as a female *crime* but as a further example of the exploitation of women in a male-dominated society. Finally, Walker argued that by 'employing gender as an analytical tool, our definition of "criminality" must surely be redefined'. She was referring to property crime and to the networks that early modern women operated in.[96] Often these involved men, and so women can 'disappear' from the histories, but we should not be too quick to accept that plebeian women were passive participants in male-dominated crimes. As Walker and others have shown, women were quite a capable of acting independently of men and in confederation with other women.[97] They may often be 'hidden from history' but are certainly not absent.

CHAPTER 8
JUVENILE CRIME: FROM ARTFUL DODGER TO REFORMATORY BOY

The concept of the young offender, with all that it implies for penal policy, is a Victorian creation.[1]

It has been a long established fact that youth offending and concerns about juvenile crime have been at the centre of debates about the criminal justice system from the second half of the twentieth century.[2] What is less clear is whether this concern represents continuity in terms of attitudes towards young criminals or is a more 'modern' problem. In this chapter the issue of juvenile crime (or 'delinquency') will be explored using a variety of sources and perspectives. It will look at the changing characterization of youth crime and at the attempts of society to deal with young offenders. Before doing so we need to think a little about changing notions of youth and childhood in a broader context.

Preliminary thoughts on the history of childhood

It is very important to recognize that before the later medieval period very little distinction was made between adults and children. Children were generally considered to be small adults; they were dressed similar to adults, they lived as adults and shared the same food and drink; with the exception of the children of the elite, there was no attempt to provide them with education or a separate status. As soon as they could work, they did. Gradually, from the elites downwards, the concept of childhood and the obedient child emerged and became well established (at least in the minds and homes of middle classes) by the early eighteenth century. Thereafter, if children failed to behave properly or to live up to the moral standards that middling society expected of them, the fault was placed squarely at the feet of the parents or with educators.[3]

However, the notion of childhood remained very much the preserve of the rich and middling sorts. For the majority of families, children were a resource and were expected to contribute, from a very early age, to the family economy. Cruelty to children was widespread – Dickens' description of brutal workhouse overseers, masters and school teachers was no invention. Children were sent down mines, up chimneys and made to do back-breaking and dangerous work in mills and factories throughout much of the Victorian period. The Factory Acts (of 1819 and 1833) were the first attempts to legislate against the exploitation of very young children but, by modern standards, these did very little to distinguish children from other workers, and the majority of children aged over 8 were employed in some way and those that were not were very likely left to fend for themselves while their parents worked.

There was also little in the way of state schooling and so the children of the poor received little education until the second half of the nineteenth century.[4] Only in 1889 was parental cruelty recognized as a criminal offence. It was legitimate to strike, flog and beat children and adolescents well into the twentieth century, at home, at work and at school. Child protection, something that society places such a high cachet on today, only really emerged as a concern in the later Victorian period. Thus, any discussion of juvenile crime needs to take into account the context of childhood and attitudes towards it in the period covered by this book.

Doli incapax: Determining the age of criminal responsibility

Another crucial factor that needs to be considered here is the question of at what age do the actions of children become criminal? The age of criminal responsibility in England currently stands at 10; below that age children are not considered to be old enough to be held responsible for their actions. However, a further clause in law – doli incapax (Incapable of evil) – had until quite recently held that those aged under 14 were incapable of criminal intent. In practice this meant that in court the prosecution were obliged to demonstrate that the accused understood 'that their actions were "seriously wrong" and not merely mischievous'.[5] However, the Bulger murder case of 1993 (and the outpouring of anger it generated), led to the removal of that clause in 1998. As Muncie points out, this came at a time when the United Nations was recommending that the United Kingdom follow much of the rest of Europe in raising the age of criminal responsibility.

Venables and Thompson, the boys found guilty of killing James Bulger, were held up as examples of degenerate youth; set aside as 'the other', not part of 'normal' society. As Heather Shore has noted, this has echoes in past representations of child murderers (something that is extremely rare) such as Mary Bell (1968) and John Bell, no relation, in 1831.[6]

So how does the current age of criminal responsibility compare with previous centuries? From the early seventeenth to the nineteenth centuries children were deemed to be adults from the age of 7 and, while doli incapax existed in law up to the age of 14, it was not unheard of for children as young as eight or nine to be hanged. There were also further complications surrounding the notion of innocence and experience. Was a child that had committed a number of crimes and been convicted of them more culpable than one that was prosecuted for a first offence?[7] However, while the law made very little allowance for the age of an offender until the early 1800s (and indeed up to mid-century), the courts practiced a good deal of discretion in convicting and sentencing young offenders. This reflected contemporary concerns about what we term 'teenagers' and, by contrast, the supposed innocence and ability to reform of younger children. Thus, as King states: the 'very young and those in middle age were both likely to receive favourable treatment' while 'those aged in their late teens and early twenties were generally treated more harshly'.[8]

The age of criminal responsibility remained at 7 until 1933 when it was raised to 8 under the terms of the Children and Young Persons Act. In 1969 a similar act raised it to the current level of 10 years. This means that England and Wales have one of the lowest ages of criminal responsibility in the world.

Problems in researching the history of youth crime

The historian is presented with some fundamental problems in researching juvenile crime.[9] The further back one goes in history, the less material there is that we can use to discuss juvenile crime. Court records rarely refer to the age of defendants before the early nineteenth century and may only make oblique references to 'youth' or 'youthfulness' rather than stating that the offender is a child or juvenile. It was also only in the late eighteenth and early nineteenth centuries that newspapers began to be useful sources for the historian of youth crime. Newspapers did not exist before the late seventeenth century and rarely did they have any systematic discussion of crime, let alone youth crime in particular. The systematic recording of offenders' ages and annual publication of crime statistics in the nineteenth century encouraged the development of statistical analysis of crime and numerous special investigations into the causes of crime. As a result, concerns about youth offending led to the establishment of a society that was perhaps the first of its kind to be particularly interested in the rise of youth offending. However, before we look in detail at the so-called Alarming Increase Committee, it is important to recognize that there had been previous calls for something to be done about youthful bad behaviour.

In early modern England there was widespread concern with the behaviour of apprentices, leading to periodic injunctions for masters to 'take care and order' over them.[10] Apprentices were condemned for not attending church, for swearing, 'cursing and disturbing the peace' and for gambling in churchyards.[11] Traditionally, apprentice boys had been placed with masters (usually from the age of 14 but sometimes earlier) and lived as part of their households. They were fed and clothed by their masters and mistresses and learned the 'secret arts' (skills) of their trade. However, some apprentices found the restrictive nature of this relationship increasingly hard to cope with and there were frequent complaints about apprentices running away or refusing to work.[12] Apprentices skipped work to attend fairs or public executions, or they slipped out at night to meet with girls, to drink and generally to 'get up to no good'. Moreover, indoor apprenticeship was in decline towards the end of the eighteenth century, which raised new concerns about adolescent behaviour and the control of youth.[13] However, we should note that while one major historical study of youth crime has suggested that there is a long historical continuity in negative attitudes towards young offenders,[14] there are clear differences in the nature of the juvenile 'crime' described. In the early modern period, attention focussed on the disobedient apprentice.[15] In the eighteenth century, this continued and social commentators drew close attention to the links between unruly apprentices and the descent into more serious criminality, with Jack Sheppard being a clear example of how immorality and disobedience could go hand-in-hand and find a desperate end on the gallows.[16] William Hogarth epitomized this in his *Industry & Idleness* print series, where two apprentices tread divergent paths, one ending up as Lord Mayor and the other at Tyburn. As seen in Figure 8.1, in plate 3 Hogarth shows the idle apprentice playing at dice with his friends while the congregation enter church for the daily service.

From 1814, the decline in indoor apprenticeship, which had been caused in part by the prohibitive costs incurred by parents wishing to place their children, was undermined further by the repeal of legislation (the Statute of Artificers, 1562) that had required seven-year apprenticeships for skilled trades.[17] Thereafter, concerns about youth began to shift from unruly behaviour (although this was always a theme in concerns about young people) towards criminality, particularly in the urban environment where poverty, lack of education and parental neglect were often cited as causal factors for youth crime. This prompted a number of attempts at intervention and prevention.

Figure 8.1 *The Idle 'Prentice at Play in the Church Yard during Divine Service,* by William Hogarth (1747).

Early concerns about youth and crime

The Marine Society was founded in 1756 by Jonas Hanway and Sir John Fielding as a means to remove troublesome children from the corruption of their environment. It provided an opportunity for poor boys ('those most destitute'[18]) to go to sea at a time when the navy was in need of sailors at the outbreak of the Seven Years' War.[19] As Hanway wrote, sending children to the navy at an early age would accustom them to the service:

> If the children of the poor are sent to sea before their constitutions and turn of mind are formed, they will be habituated to a sea life, and the duties of a ship will become the less perilous and toilsome.[20]

In the first year of its establishment, the Marine Society clothed and prepared 1,868 boys for service at sea (and helped clear the capital's streets of delinquent boys[21]), but it was only ever a temporary solution to the problem of juvenile destitution and crime.[22] Bow Street magistrates had been sending vagabond boys into the navy for some time, making use of an act of Queen Anne, and for a while Fielding and Hanway's ideas dovetailed. The Bow Street office used some of the fines it levied on offenders to provide funds for the society, but Hanway's concerns about the use of the Society as a home for young offenders led to a falling out between the two men. By 1770, the Society was refusing to take delinquent boys and only finding spaces for those deemed poor but 'respectable'.[23]

In 1788 concerns about vagrancy and crime amongst the young led to the creation of the Philanthropic Society by William Young. The Society took in young boys and girls aged 8–12 and housed them in rented property where they were cared for and taught basic work skills. The Philanthropic Society included a system of rewards, offered as 'tickets for good or bad behaviour' alongside education and a set of exercises designed at testing each individual's resistance to temptation.[24] The aim was to send them on into apprenticeships and then into full-time work. Its intentions are set out in the opening lines of its first report, three years after it was founded:

> The Philanthropic Society aims at the prevention of crimes, by removing out of the way of evil counsel, and evil company, those children, who are, in the present state of things, destined to ruin.[25]

By 1792, the society had provided fifty places for children in homes and established its own property in Southwark, south London. The society expanded in the early nineteenth century, setting up a place in Bermondsey called 'The Reform', which operated under a strict disciplinary regime, and a manufactory in St George's Fields. However positive the Philanthropic's aims were, it was only ever able to cater for a very small number of young people. It was reliant on donations and received no help from the central government. As with the Marine Society, it concentrated its efforts on destitute children rather than criminal ones, who were considered too difficult to manage. At its height, it probably helped around 200 children, a very small percentage of London's destitute or criminal youth, and in 1849 the Society moved its main premises to Redhill, in Surrey, believing that the countryside offered a better environment for reform than the overcrowded metropolis.[26]

The third attempt to provide some form of intervention in the lives of those vulnerable to falling in to poverty and crime was the Refuge for the Destitute. The Refuge, formed in 1805, was used by magistrates in the capital as an informal punishment option for young offenders.[27] The Refuge (which took in adults as well as children) had many similarities with the Philanthropic. It operated as a sort of closed asylum type institution offering both temporary relief from poverty and a semi-permanent refuge with training for life beyond the institution. The Refuge provided space for both boys and girls and aimed to educate and then to place them in apprenticeships and service positions. It was much more closely associated with the rescue and reform of offenders than either the Marine or Philanthropic societies. Its annual report of 1819 stated that:

> The object of this institution is to provide a place of Refuge and Reformation for persons who have been discharged from Prison, or the Hulks [...] Within this asylum they are withdrawn from the paths of temptation and vice; they are taught to renounce their former habits of life; to pursue industrious employments; to form resolutions of penitence and reformation, and to return to society with renewed hearts and amended lives.[28]

The records of the Refuge have survived and so allow us to see the sorts of children that the organization was able to help. Take, for example, the case of Caroline Norvel, a 15-year-old from Hoxton, north-east London. Her mother was 'a paralytic' in the local workhouse and her father was 'at sea'. In 1819, Caroline had been brought before the City magistrate at the Guildhall accused of stealing from her mistress and he sent her to the Refuge instead of the Bridewell.[29] Caroline, effectively abandoned by both parents, was at risk of becoming a regular attendee before the courts, or one of London's many prostitutes. In 1819, the Refuge housed around 120 persons: men, women and children.[30]

The Refuge had clear advantages over the Marine and Philanthropic Societies. The fact that it offered long-term care meant that offenders now had a real opportunity to change their lives. Perhaps most importantly though, the government provided the Refuge with a small subsidy, meaning it was not totally reliant upon charitable donations. The subsidy was a reflection of the interest taken in the Refuge by key members of the government that included the Prime Minister, Spencer Percival. Soon after its creation, the Refuge became in effect an early juvenile reformatory, taking those aged over 13 that the Philanthropic Society had turned away. By the 1840s, when the laws of summary punishment were under discussion, it was clear that magistrates were committing young offenders to the Refuge for the Destitute despite there being no formal or official legislation that allowed them to do so.[31]

There were other attempts at providing alternative accommodation for young offenders amidst a growing consensus that prison was not the most appropriate or effective means to deal with delinquent youth.[32] But the eighteenth-century state lacked the resources and levels of administration to establish purpose-built separate institutions for offenders and so while the debate continued, efforts at reforms were largely piecemeal and ineffectual. The wars with France also hindered attempts to make significant changes to the treatment of young criminals and those at risk of falling into crime. However, the post-war 'crime wave' rekindled concerns about the rising numbers of young felons on London's streets and prompted an investigation that was to make an important contribution to changing attitudes towards youth offending and its prevention.

The 'Alarming Increase' committee

The term 'juvenile delinquency' appears in print in the widely publicized work of the 'Committee for Investigating the Alarming Increase of Juvenile Delinquency in the Metropolis' formed in 1815. The committee, concerned about perceived rising levels of youth crime, undertook an investigation into the causes of youth offending. This revealed that 'Juvenile Delinquency existed in the metropolis to a very alarming extent' and that youths, 'organized into gangs', frequented 'houses where they planned their enterprises' and shared out the proceeds of their crimes.[33] This report was followed by a parliamentary committee into policing in London which called on several of its members to give evidence.

Let us look at the findings of the committee's investigations in some detail. The investigators estimated that there were 'thousands' of young offenders under the age of 17 who were regularly involved in crime in the capital. Boys went on to commit more serious property offences as they grew up while the girls became prostitutes. They therefore developed a very gendered view of youth crime and located it within a wider discourse about criminality within society. The principal causes of youth crime were, in the opinion of the investigators, as follows:

The improper conduct of parents
The want of education
The want of suitable employment
The violation of the Sabbath, and habits of gambling in the public streets.

With perhaps the exception of the fourth explanation, these causes could be applied easily to discussions of juvenile crime throughout the period from 1816 to the present day. They recognized the connection between poverty and crime and noted that a lack of work forced some into crime. Parents unable to support their offspring turned to crime or turned their children out onto the street where the temptation to steal or to get involved with others who did, was almost irresistible. Parents who found themselves in poverty were also less inclined to send their children to school because they needed them to work to supplement the family income; a lack of education limited the children's chances to find work but it also meant that important lessons in morality were, in the minds of the gentlemen of the committee, missed.

The committee's members were driven by the same considerations and motivations that inspired the movements against capital punishment and cited three further causal factors in the perpetuation of the problem of youth criminality. These were the 'severity of the capital code', the lack of an effective police force and the state of the prisons. So we need to understand the efforts of these men within a wider context of reforms to the criminal justice system.

In the minds of prison reformers the juvenile offender was key; it was here that many felt that a real attempt to remould offenders could be successful. The *Report* quoted John Howard, who had complained about the state of prisons in the last quarter of the previous century. Howard argued that since juvenile and older offenders were not separated from each other, the corruption of the younger inmates was inevitable: 'the ferocious inspire others with their ferocity, the cunning with their cunning, and the debauched with their libertinism' he declared.[34] Howard wanted to see prisons that acted to reform those incarcerated within their walls and he and the committee could see precious little reformation taking place in the overcrowded and squalid gaols of London and elsewhere. The Society knew what was wrong – or what they felt was wrong – and had some sympathy for the young people who found themselves caught up in a cycle of poverty, neglect, crime and punishment. Indeed they were optimistic that many could be saved from the gallows or a life of idleness by what would later be called intervention. 'Small indeed is the number of those [boys] in whom the sense of virtue is wholly extinct', it argued.[35] Thus, the *Report* – while the first, and by no means the last, attempt to address the issues relating to juvenile offending – is perhaps the most important evidence we have of changing attitudes towards the punishment and treatment of youth crime in England. Much of what was to unfold over the next 100 years echoed its findings.

As we have seen, men such as Jonas Hanway had already recognized that separating young offenders from older ones was crucial if a new generation of thieves was to be prevented. This ideal was to come to fruition in the Reformatory movement of the later nineteenth century, but it is too easy to see the development of alternative forms of punishment for young offenders as a product of those mid-nineteenth century reforms; the next section will look at work that argues for a gradual evolution of separate institutions for the care and punishment of juvenile criminals.

The development of alternative forms of punishment

The evolution of alternative forms of punishment for young offenders has a long and complex history and was part of a wider rhetoric of reform for the punishment of *all* offenders, one that was part of a general retreat from physical punishments based on pain and public shaming. The movement for the reform of penal policy was also influenced by developments outside of Britain. For example, in France a 'family-style agricultural reformatory' was set up in 1839 at Mettray, near Tours. Mettray became an exemplar for a system of rehabilitating young offenders using 'houses' to 'foster supposedly "natural" social relations in a largely rural context', instead of locking children up in large, impersonal and foreboding prisons.[36] England had its own 'Mettray', at Stretton-in-Dunsmore, which had been set up in 1817 at the behest of the Birmingham magistracy. It suffered the fate of other early juvenile establishments in that it was unable to sustain itself financially and closed at mid-century. Alongside Stretton was Elizabeth Fry's Chelsea School of Reform which provided a refuge for 'viciously disposed and neglected female children' aged 8–13 and another similar institution at Chiswick, also in the capital.[37] While there was no formal or legislative procedure to send children to these institutions, it is clear that the courts were increasingly using these institutions as a way of providing an alternative and separate punishment for young offenders.

However, many of those young offenders convicted of crimes in the late nineteenth century were not sent to any establishment with as worthy intentions as these. Nor were they transported to Australia where they could, at least, hope to affect some positive change in their environment and future. Instead most of them ended on the hulks. These were floating decommissioned naval vessels, moored at Chatham on the Thames or in Portsmouth harbour where conditions were dreadful.

At first juveniles were confined (with adult offenders) below decks for sixteen hours a day where they were more or less left to their own devices. In 1825 juvenile prisoners were transferred to the *Euryallus* at Chatham so that they could be separated from other convicts. Not that conditions improved; rather they seemed to get worse. Locked below decks for twenty-three hours a day, 2,500 boys up to the age of 14 were forced to do manual work and 'half starved to death' on meagre rations, punished with the 'cat' (the cat of nine tails used to flog sailors in the navy) and all without the least attempt at reformation. In addition, observers complained that a subculture of gang violence and intimidation had been allowed to fester. There was an initial clear out to Millbank or transportation but the hulks remained operational until 1843; they were, as Radzinowicz and Hood declared, 'an unredeemed failure'.[38] The middle of the nineteenth century saw fresh concerns about rising levels of youth crime which engendered a new discourse about the need for tougher punishments.[39] The most obvious manifestation of this was the opening a new prison, specifically for the treatment of young criminals, at Parkhurst on the Isle of Wight.

Parkhurst prison and the transportation of young offenders

Parkhurst received its first intake of juvenile convicts in December 1838. Taken from Millbank and the hulks, some 146 lads made up the first cohort of prisoners in the converted hospital at Albany barracks.[40] The idea of Parkhurst was to provide a separate penal institution for offenders, many of whom would remain there until they could be transported to the Australian colonies. Discipline was harsh and there was a strict routine that boys had to adhere to. Boys were not normally transported until they reached 14 years of age but the prospects in Australia for young criminals were good; colonists favoured younger convicts over the older ones as they were seen to be more productive and more likely to be reformed. It was the role of the governor of the prison to recommend lads to the Home Office to be issued with a 'ticket of leave' on arrival, and they would then be sent out on the next available ship. This 'privilege' was reserved for those that knuckled down and embraced the regime at the prison without question or rebellion. One of the incentives for juveniles sent to Parkhurst to behave, therefore, was of early shipping to New South Wales or Tasmania with the prospect of work and a new future ahead of them.

At Parkhurst, inmates could expect to go through a period of isolation from other convicts in separate cells for their first four months, during which time they were largely expected to remain silent when in contact with others during work or schooling. The regime was relaxed slightly during breaks. Inmates were taught reading and writing and some mathematics, and were assessed as to their characters by the staff. Once they progressed to the general ward they continued to be educated and were employed in a variety of different forms of work, many of which echoed practices in adult prisons and the workhouse. So boys were employed in 'shoemaking, brickmaking, blacksmithing, gardening, painting, cooking and laundry work' as well as sewing and making stockings, all of which were useful trades that could form the basis of paid employment on their release.[41] Whilst inmates were trained for their lives after release, there appears to have been no attempt to maintain links with their families at home. It comes as no surprise that, isolated as Parkhurst was, there is 'no evidence of any family visiting' the prison but this also reflects a contemporary understanding of penal policies and the rehabilitation of offenders.[42] The intention of Victorian penal reformers was to separate young offenders from all negative influences on their development. The prison offered an ideal environment to remould young minds and set them on a path to being a useful member of Britain's expanding industrial and commercial future. Parkhurst prison and the transportation system offered these offenders a new start in life and the opportunity to escape from the contaminated environments in which they were born.

However, Parkhurst proved to be a short-term and unsuccessful experiment in youth detention. In 1852 the last boys were sent abroad as transportation came to an end and the prison was now limited in the opportunities that it could offer its inmates. Whilst boys continued to be trained, it was harder to place them in work upon release because domestic employers were much less willing than their counterparts in Australia to take those with a convict past. It was now imperative to find a new alternative to deal with the large numbers of young offenders that were being processed by the courts.

The reformatory and industrial school: The campaign of Mary Carpenter

By the 1840s the tide of opinion was beginning to move towards a potentially more compassionate 'reform' or welfare model for juvenile institutions. The relative success of the French experiment at Mettray inspired some English observers who believed that it was necessary to replace punishment-based regimes with reform-based ones. Mettray took in young boys under 16 years of age who were then subjected to constant surveillance within what we might describe today as an 'open' prison. The intention was to promote reform through a transformation of an individual's conscience.[43] Inspired by this, Mary Carpenter and other reformers mounted a huge campaign for a reformatory system in England based on the courts' right to sentence directly juveniles to a reformatory, as they were in France.

Carpenter was the daughter of a Unitarian minister and she had inherited his evangelical zeal.[44] Carpenter had set up a ragged school for poor children in Bristol in 1846 and had been doing charitable work for several years. She was particularly interested in the cause of child poverty and identified that particularly 'difficult' children could easily fall into criminal activity. In 1851, Carpenter published an important essay entitled *Reformatory Schools for the Children of the Perishing and Dangerous Classes and for Juvenile Offenders* and convened a conference to debate the problem of juvenile offending and the best means to tackle it. Her ideas attracted a good deal of support and a year later she and Russell Scott established a juvenile reformatory at Kingswood near Bristol. In 1854 she opened a girls' reformatory at Red Lodge nearby. Carpenter's essays[45] were influential and her explanations about the causes of juvenile crime were almost 'entirely social and environmental'.[46] She argued that children were not naturally vicious, and that it was instead their neglectful parents, lack of moral education, failed socialization, and poverty which had led them into crime in the first place. Thereafter, the cruel and corrupting experience of prison or the workhouse had 'demoralized them'.[47] For Carpenter, these juvenile criminals were not inherently 'bad'; their offences were trivial and certainly no worse than those committed by rich young men at boarding schools whose offending was often overlooked. Her belief was that the state had a role to play in addressing this neglect of proper upbringing through education and reform. Carpenter argued that reformatory training could reform even the worst examples of delinquent youths.

Carpenter's experiment at Kingswood was followed by other voluntary and independent schemes across the country in a piecemeal fashion that echoes previous attempts at finding alternatives to sending young offenders to conventional adult prisons. Following the gradual growth of more and more voluntary refuges and 'schools' for juveniles in the 1840s and early 1850s and Carpenter's extended campaign, two acts were passed. The Young Offenders Act (1854) permitted the setting up of reformatories to train and contain delinquents and then in 1857 another act established industrial schools on parallel lines for minor offenders. Industrial schools were establishments 'in which Industrial Training is provided, and in which children are lodged, clothed, fed, as well as taught'.[48] Magistrates could now send juvenile offenders to these institutions and money was provided by the state to support the voluntary bodies that ran them.

Any child sent to a reformatory had to serve a fourteen-day prison sentence beforehand, which went quite against Carpenter's philosophy of separation but was a necessary compromise for those that believed that reformatories would be seen as an attractive and 'soft' option. The proponents of the reformatory movement warned that by sending children to prison first they would be brought into contact with criminals who were more deeply rooted in their criminality, and that this would undermine and obstruct their rehabilitation. It was (and indeed remains) a very reasonable objection but Carpenter and Davenport Hill were operating within a society that demanded that some form of punishment be meted out to those that broke the law. Victorian social policy was underpinned by the principle of 'less eligibility' which argued that those who did not work, or those that stole or otherwise offended, should not enjoy a quality of existence that was in any way superior to those that attempted to live within the rules and lead honest, industrious lives. Under the 1854 act, magistrates could order a juvenile to a reformatory for a period of two to five years (the minimum tariff was set at two years because it was felt that no effective rehabilitation could take place in less time). If they ran away, then recapture would bring with it a period of three months at hard labour.

Reformatories were funded partly through state finances and partly by parental contribution (parents could be ordered to pay 'up to five shillings a week for the care and maintenance of the child'[49]). The same was true for the industrial schools to which children (aged 7–14) who found begging could be sent. Again, parents were liable (up to the cost of three shillings a week) for the upkeep of their children. As Muncie concludes, now there 'was a double incentive for parents to try to conform to the dominant morality and middle-class child-rearing practices: both the fear of losing their child and burden of maintenance that attended such separation. Parents who failed to provide such care in effect signed away their rights to their children'.[50] However, parents could (and did) use the system themselves to send their own offspring to industrial schools if they felt they were unable to cope with their behaviour at home (although in this case they had to cover the full costs of the child's care).

The industrial schools also took in children who had been categorized 'as "neglected" by their parents' after 1870 London School Board committee members were arguing for the use of these institutions as a form of intervention into the lives of children at risk of falling into crime and delinquency.[51] The industrial school was thus often the preferred destination for 'delinquent' girls where the fear was that vagrancy would lead inevitably to prostitution and thence to worse forms of crime.[52] If they could be educated and taught a trade or skills (such as sewing) and their morals 'corrected', they might yet lead a useful life.

Primary education had been made compulsory in 1870, but many working-class parents resisted the law that compelled them to send their children to school, believing instead that after the age of 5 or 6 they were 'useful' members of the family and saw their opportunity to work (and contribute) as more important than education. This resulted in conflicts between parents and local education authority, conflicts that frequently ended up in the summary courts.[53] After 1847 magistrates were given the formal right to send juveniles to reformatories and industrial schools, which they 'readily used'.[54] The use of reformatories, industrial schools and compulsory education can be seen, then, as part and parcel of a wider discourse that had long placed some of the blame for juvenile crime on poor parenting and a lack of formal education.[55]

It is quite difficult for historians to assess the effectiveness of these early reformatories or industrial schools because the records that survive are either largely administrative or are written from the perspective of the institutions' governors. A crucial missing element is the voices of those that were sent to them. We can however use the published works of Carpenter and others to look at the motivations and intentions of those behind the reformatory and industrial schools movements. In 1854 Carpenter and Scott published their first report on their Kingswood experiment. They explained that the school had been set up to offer education and training as a means 'to extirpate acquired habits of idleness and vice, and to replace them by habits of industry and a sense of moral responsibility'.[56] The rhetoric here clearly echoes that of previous commentaries on juvenile crime. By removing children from a corrupting environment and providing them with care, education and skills, Carpenter and her supporters believed that young criminals could be refashioned into useful members of society. The report championed the progress that had been made, even with some of the 'wilder' inmates:

> The pilfering propensities which at first shewed themselves strongly in the girls, and to a smaller extent in some of the boys, have now been so greatly subdued, that both are frequently trusted with money when sent on errands into the village, and the girls can be employed with safety in domestic occupations involving temptations which at first they could not resist.[57]

We might expect Carpenter to celebrate her successes but the early reformatories could only deal with a small number of those young persons sentenced for minor acts of criminality and the reformatories themselves were unable to cope with large numbers of inmates. Kingswood was quite small; the first report indicates that there were fewer than thirty children housed in it. The Red Lodge reformatory took just twenty-one girls aged from under 12 to 16 but specified that it would not take anyone who was 'a fit subject for a Penitentiary', suggesting that Carpenter was quite careful about selecting candidates she believed she had some chance of reforming.[58] Eventually, four reformatories were set up in the 1870s to deal specially with the problem of girls who had been involved in, or even associated with, prostitution or were otherwise sexually experienced. Carpenter argued that younger girls should be kept separate from the older ones, who she said were 'very precocious in knowledge'.[59] This again suggests a continuity of approach with Hanway's Marine Society and the Philanthropic Society, both of whom quickly adopted a position of trying to help what we might term the 'deserving' children of the poor rather than the very delinquent, but also to avoid the 'corruption' or 'pollution' of *less* delinquent youths.

The Reverend Sedgewick, writing in support of the creation of industrial schools in 1853, drew specific links between the reformation of juveniles and what he saw as the failure of the transportation system. Whilst transportation sent petty criminals across the seas to populate a growing empire by educating them, a new generation of skilled and useful citizens could be created:

> In these industrial schools we shall be training up a new, vigorous and well-skilled race of emigrants, instead of sending forth, as we do now, the dregs of our population, an illiterate, unskilful band, to people the vast possessions of this mighty kingdom.[60]

The problem with the 1854 act was its insistence that all of those sentenced to a reformatory should first serve a short period in a conventional prison. This undoubtedly served to allay the fears of those that felt that reformatories were a 'soft' option and that prison offered a reminder of what lay in store for those that failed to take up the opportunities that reformatory schools offered. However, by sending juveniles to gaol the act undermined one of Carpenter's key principles – that of avoiding the demoralizing effects of incarceration with other offenders. The Industrial Schools Act (1857) allowed convicted children aged 7–15 for vagrancy to be sent to an industrial school. This was extended in 1861 to include those aged under 14, who had been found begging, homeless or 'frequenting with thieves', or simply children whose parents were unable to control them, and those under 12 who had committed offences that would incur a custodial sentence. As a result, many juveniles could now be whisked off to industrial schools for relatively minor forms of offending or anti-social behaviour or indeed because their parents felt unable to cope with their care. Whether this really represented the march of progress or 'welfarism' in the treatment of young offenders is something that will be considered next.

We should also recognize that despite Mary Carpenter's aversion to the use of corporal punishment, children were still beaten in nineteenth-century England with what we would consider to be alarming regularity. Children were routinely flogged, by prison officers or the police, for all sorts of minor forms of crime. On occasions there was public outcry as the screams of children were heard emanating from within magistrates' court and other places, and crowds would sometimes intervene. Many policemen were reluctant to carry out floggings and some magistrates prided themselves on not handing down sentences of whippings on youngsters. Nevertheless, the whipping of juveniles was retained until well into the twentieth century. It even won the support of the Howard Association and the NSPCC and was eventually endorsed by the Children's Act (1908). It was not finally removed from the disciplinary armory of the criminal justice system until 1948.

As the nineteenth century went on, and budgets were increasingly tight, the reformatories struggled to fulfil Carpenter's bold ambitions for the reform of young offenders. They could rarely recruit suitable staff, and separate cottage units proved too expensive to maintain as the numbers of juveniles sentenced to them increased with the end of transportation. As a result, regimes became rigid and inmates often rebelled against them. The ability of the reformatories and industrial schools to offer the care and rehabilitation that their creators had envisaged were undermined by a lack of investment in much the same way that previous attempts at establishing alternative arrangements for juveniles had floundered.

However, by 1860 the country had forty-eight reformatories, and they were taking in 1,000 new inmates annually, contributing to an overall population of around 4,000 reformatory boys and girls. Industrial schools did not match the rapid growth of reformatories at first, but after 1866 there was a slow and incremental increase in numbers. By 1914 there were forty-three reformatories in England and Wales, and a further 132 industrial schools and twelve truant schools dealing with some 30,000 children, which represented 'one in every 230 of the juvenile population between five and 15 years'.[61] In 1908 older juveniles (those aged 16–20) were provided for by separate institutions – Borstals – which soon developed an even more punitive tone. Thus, even though the importance of the welfare of the child was increasingly recognized after 1945, the 1948 act allowed the setting up of detention centres to give persistent young offenders a 'short, sharp shock'.[62] We would have to suggest, therefore, that Carpenter's desire to see alternative reformatory and industrial schools helping to rehabilitate a generation of young offenders was only partially successful at best. That said, her principal philosophy, that children under the age of 16 should not be held responsible (or at least not solely responsible) for their criminal actions, foreshadowed future developments in the treatment of juvenile offenders. In stating her belief that children were less culpable than adult criminals she was able to argue that they should be punished differently, indeed not punished at all in a conventional sense. In the twentieth century there were ongoing attempts to remove juveniles from the adult penal system and find a different solution to the problem they posed.

1908 and all that: The Children Act and the birth of 'welfarism'

The Children Act has been hailed variously as a 'turning point' for childcare in Britain or as little more than a consolidation of existing practice in legislation. It is not necessary here to pursue a debate into the efficacy or otherwise of the act. Instead, we need to be clear about what the act did.

Part of the act was concerned with child protection. Thus, it now became illegal to sell cigarettes to those aged under 16 and the rules surrounding private child-minders were tightened up. It incorporated the Prevention of Cruelty to Children Act (1889) and added clauses relating to a concern about what we would now term 'cot deaths'. There were also some minor changes to the ways in which children in reformatories and industrial schools were treated and this included a provision for them to be boarded out if this was deemed appropriate by the authorities.

Significantly, the act established, for the first time, separate courts for the hearing of cases against juveniles. Cases against children were now to be held in separate buildings, the public was excluded and parents were obliged to attend. In addition, the law now proscribed that children under 14 could no longer be sent to adult prisons whilst awaiting trial and sanctioned the building of special remand centres to house them. Those aged 14–16 could also only be sent to prisons if they were declared to be too 'unruly' to be housed elsewhere.[63] Parents could be held responsible and fined for their children's behaviour or be required to find sureties for their future conduct. Finally, the act meant that no one under the age of 16 could be executed for any crime. The Children Act established in law the principle that young offenders were different from adult ones and thus required a special recognition. In effect, the 1908 act looked forward to a less punitive and more welfare-based policy as regards youth crime although this is a contested conclusion to draw.

Juvenile crime and the historian: Debates and discussion

Debates surrounding delinquent youth have shared common themes across Europe throughout the time period covered by this volume and beyond. Early histories of juvenile offenders and the development of separate institutions to house them have followed similar patterns to those that have described the retreat from the 'Bloody Code' and the arrival of the prison. These have taken a broadly positive view of the penal reformers and held them up as heroes and seen all reform as progressive. This view was challenged in the 1970s and 1980s by those who viewed the reformatory and industrial school as a part of the 'carceral archipelago'[64] of the rising 'policeman state'.[65] These institutions, far from being benign were instead part and parcel of a disciplinary process to mould the working classes to the needs of the rising industrial middle class. While accepting that argument is neither complete nor satisfactory, more recent work has looked instead at the ways in which the notion of 'juvenile delinquency' has emerged as a terminology and at the effects that this has had on practice and legislation. This is something that can be pursued now with more vigour given the advances in technologies such as data mining and word clouds. For example, if the term 'juvenile delinquency' is entered into an Ngram viewer such as Google's, we can see that the first use of the term appears in about 1815 (at the time of the Alarming Increase committee's report); there is a small but notable spike in the use of the phrase in the late 1840s and then a steady rise from about 1904 to the late 1950s.[66]

This reflects the fact that there have, as Shore and Cox have indicated, been several well-documented 'panics about urban culture, poor parenting, dangerous pleasures, family breakdown, national fitness and future social stability'.[67] We saw several of these themes in the rhetoric of the reformatory movement and the earlier report of the *Alarming Increase* committee. The problem of the family and in particular family breakdown is not a new phenomenon (despite what some modern British tabloid newspapers would have us believe). The decline of apprenticeships in the late eighteenth century led contemporaries to worry about issues of discipline within the home and on the streets.

To some extent the history of juvenile offending is interwoven with the history of the family and of changing attitudes towards youth and, in particular, adolescence. The changing nature of punishment for young offenders reflected, as Margaret May has argued, a recognition that children who appeared in court were not merely 'little adults' but 'beings in their own right' who 'were entitled to special care because they lacked full responsibility for their actions'.[68] The agenda of reform was partly set by the penal reformers who wished to separate young and vulnerable offenders from the corruption of others and in the belief that the new rhetoric of rehabilitation was most suited to those least corrupted by their exposure to the criminal justice system. One of the questions we might ask ourselves is how successful have attempts been to isolate juveniles from the environmental factors that have supposedly led to their descent into crime?

It is also clear that the notion of juvenile delinquency has a long but contested history. The term first appeared in the early nineteenth century but concerns about juvenile crime and anti-social behaviour were nothing new.[69] Instead of juvenile delinquency being 'invented' or 'legislated into existence' in the early nineteenth century, perhaps we should instead take a wider perspective and argue that the problem of youth was something that arose at particular 'moments' in history.[70] Griffiths noted the use of Bridewell to deal with unruly and troublesome apprentices in the early modern period and, while legislation to send juveniles to separate institutions is undoubtedly a product of the nineteenth century, it is possible to argue that a much longer gestation was in place. King's work on the Refuge for the Destitute demonstrates that the eighteenth-century courts were already finding alternative destinations for young offenders accused of committing petty property crimes.

What is perhaps different about the rise of alternative institutions from the 1830s onwards is the involvement of the state as opposed to the reliance on philanthropy and charitable donations. This movement also reflected a wide reengagement of the state in the building and maintenance of so-called 'total institutions' such as the penitentiary prison, workhouse and asylum.[71] Therefore, we need to understand the history of the treatment of juvenile offenders within the broader 'reforms' of the nineteenth-century state. There are also plenty of questions going forward for historians to engage with, not least what perspective histories of crime can offer to current debates about youth detention and offending. If we agree with Heindensohn that juvenile delinquency is the 'main form in which the problem of crime is conceptualized' then a debate that is informed by history is essential to future youth offending policies.[72]

On a more prosaic level the future historian is still hamstrung by the problem of a lack of source material. In particular it is extremely rare to hear the voice of the juvenile in any of these debates. The notebooks of William Augustus Miles remain one of the very few instances in which the opinions and motivations of child criminals (in this case juveniles imprisoned on the prison hulk *Euryalus*) are available for examination. Here, as with Mayhew's interviews later in the century, these views are filtered to some extent through the lens of penal or social reform.[73]

We still have much to understand then about the ways in which youth crime has been conceptualized and understood and the strategies that have been deployed to combat it. One important area, I would argue, is the way in which youth (or more properly adolescence) has been manipulated by print and other forms of media from every stage in our history. In an ever ageing population there is a tendency to view those aged 12–21 with a good deal of suspicion and some degree of fear. This is apparent in the panics about apprenticeship, the Alarming Increase committee, and the reaction to gang crime in the last quarter of the nineteenth century, to the Mods and Rockers and to 'feral youth' and 'hoodies' today. This 'panic' has also almost invariably been focused on working-class youth and it is important therefore to recognize that the debates about youth and crime have a very evident class agenda. There has been relatively little work on delinquency that falls outside of the usual working-class stereotypes. Nicola Phillips has noted that eighteenth-century commentators spoke of members of the elite using debtors prisons as a means of disciplining their wayward sons and, in at least one instance, taking more drastic action to try to correct delinquent or criminal behaviour, but we could do with more.[74]

Finally, although we have had some recent work on the problem of delinquent girls,[75] most of the studies that have been undertaken have been concerned with boys. We need more comparative work on female offending and on the institutions (such as Red Lodge) that were specifically set up to help young women caught up in patterns of offending in order to determine to what extent they offer an alternative history of youth crime.

This completes the first part of this study; Section Two will now follow the pathway of the offender from arrest and hearing, to committal, trial and punishment.

SECTION II
THE EVOLUTION AND DEVELOPMENT OF THE ENGLISH CRIMINAL JUSTICE SYSTEM

CHAPTER 9

FROM PARLOUR TO POLICE COURT: THE ROLE OF THE JP AND THE EMERGENCE OF THE MODERN MAGISTRATE

Most histories of crime and punishment since the 1970s have placed their emphasis on the jury courts of assize and quarter sessions, and with good reason. After all it was within those courts that most serious crimes were dealt with and the most severe punishments handed down. However, historians are now aware that this concentration on the higher courts is disproportionate. In reality, most people in the eighteenth and nineteenth centuries who encountered the criminal justice system would have done so at a level below the jury courts. Thus, for many people who had cause to either use the law or be caught up in the machinations of the criminal justice system, the most significant figure would have been the justice of the peace, or magistrate. Given that most histories have tended to overlook the important role that these largely amateur justices played in the administration of the law in the eighteenth and nineteenth centuries, this remains an area of the history of crime that still requires considerable research. However, it is now possible to offer an overview of the justice of peace for the long eighteenth century and to look briefly at the ways in which the role developed in the nineteenth.

This chapter will look at the nature of the justice of the peace (JP), the sorts of people that filled this role, the powers they had and at how they operated. There are clear differences in the way that JPs operated across the country in the long eighteenth century, especially in some parts of the capital where a more entrepreneurial system was in place. The chapter will also consider how our understanding of the importance of discretion as practised by the JP impacts the debate about the use or function of the criminal justice system in the period: a system described by Douglas Hay as a 'powerful tool of the ruling elites'.[1] It will also attempt to synthesize current research into summary proceedings, work that focuses on gender and the development of the magistracy in the nineteenth century. Finally, this chapter will suggest areas for future research and an attempt to pose some questions for future historians to answer, as this is potentially the richest area for researchers to mine in the following decades.

But let us start with a fairly straightforward question: who were the justices of the peace?

A typology of justices in the eighteenth century

For most of the long eighteenth century, rural and urban communities throughout England and Wales were served by justices of the peace who dispensed justice, settled disputes and dealt with a considerable workload of administrative business. Each county returned a list of JPs who held office, without remuneration, in a voluntary capacity. Justices were expected, but not compelled, to attend the quarter sessions (where they would sit as a bench of judges) and the assizes (where they might form part of the grand jury). But it is their work *outside* of the jury courts that is of most interest here. This is because justices represent the entry point for the Hanoverian criminal justice system. In a period before the creation of formal professional police forces the JP was the central figure of justice in his community; the person to turn to when you fell victim to a crime. However, as we shall see, he was much more than that. As well as dealing with crime the local justice was tasked with keeping order, maintaining good community relations, upholding the law of the land and regulating local commerce and employment relationships. It is not an exaggeration to argue that the eighteenth-century JP was *the* central figure in rural England. However, there were different types of JPs and some were more active than others.

JPs were, in rural and provincial England at least, drawn primarily from the patrician class. As members of the nobility and gentry they were ideally suited to a role as mediators within their communities. Men such as the 2nd Earl Spencer, who served as a JP in Northamptonshire in the 1790s, were well-known and well-respected local figures, who were used to dealing with people from across the social scale, be they minor servants, trusted lieutenants or members of the middling sorts. Operating as a JP was a part of the public life of men such as Spencer, a life that might include an interest in politics, the church or the local hunt. We should not think of these men as professional lawgivers, but more as administrators and counsellors who spent a part of their time (perhaps a few hours each week when they were at their country estates) dispensing justice. It is unlikely that such men had much formal legal training or practical experience. However, they would almost certainly have some familiarity with the law as a basic study of English law would have formed a part of their education. As collectors, many of them would also have owned one or more law books, and from the late eighteenth century, all justices on the county list were supplied with a copy of Richard Burn's manual for JPs.[2] It is also likely that they employed clerks who would have been tasked with checking the law for them. Indeed, in London recent research suggests that clerks played a role that was in many ways similar to that played by magistrates' clerks today.[3]

However, not all JPs in rural or provincial England were members of the ruling elite. Men such as Edmund Tew in the north-east were clergymen, and were well used to attending to the needs of their communities and well positioned to act as authority figures. Clergy JPs also attended the sessions of the peace and so played a full part in the criminal justice system of the counties they served. Clergymen were well educated and while they might, like their patrician colleagues, have been unfamiliar with the professional practice of the law, they shared their interest in the law as an intellectual exercise and as a part of the duty of a 'gentleman'. There were also members of the middling sorts or minor gentry who operated as justices and some of these had experience of practising as lawyers, locally and in the capital. Philip Ward (a Northamptonshire JP) had enjoyed a long career as a lawyer at one of London's prestigious Inns of Court before he retired to his family estate near to Oundle and served his community as a justice.[4]

Thus, in provincial England rural communities and small towns were served by a mixture of aristocrats, minor gentry and clergymen JPs, but how did they operate and what sort of business did they conduct?

The practice of summary proceedings in eighteenth-century England

Justices held irregular meetings (hearings) at their own homes or in local public houses. Philip Ward welcomed complainants to his Northamptonshire estate but also convened petty sessions in the nearby town of Oundle. Justices could adjudicate on most matters on their own, without a jury, but there were occasions or particular types of hearings that required the presence of additional magistrates, and these were most likely to take place in public spaces. Thus when JPs sat in pairs or threes it was often to deal with matters that required the presence of more than one magistrate. For example, when approached to adjudicate on a case of settlement,[5] a justice was obliged to consider the merits of the case with a fellow JP and there were several other occasions that necessitated the presence of more than one magistrate.

However, making contact with your local JP may have been quite a difficult or at least a protracted process, particularly if you lived in a small village some way from the nearest town or the local justice's house. In theory, a complainant only had to make his or her way to the magistrate's home to request an audience. It is entirely possible that locals would have been aware of when their local justice was available or not but that is hard to know for sure. In reality, anyone wishing to visit a magistrate would have had to make a journey to his house and hoped to gain admittance to his parlour. Of course, it would have been entirely possible that the justice would be otherwise engaged, out of the house, or indeed away from home for the day or longer. At certain times of the year the gentry decamped to London or Bath as men such as Earl Spencer had important political commitments that required them to spend many months of the year away from their estates, whilst lower gentry such as Philip Ward may well have continued to practise at law and visit his lodgings in the capital. Therefore, one of the first observations that can be made about JPs outside of London (where, as will become clear, the system functioned quite differently) is that their availability varied considerably.

Some JPs (such as Samuel Whitbread in Bedfordshire or William Ward in Northamptonshire) were clearly very dedicated to their duties – holding regular hearings, convening petty sessions and attending the sessions – while others (such as Earl Spencer) merely treated their magisterial role as a nominal one and in consequence hardly ever sullied their hands with judicial business. This had important consequences for those that sought the advice and help of JPs throughout the period but also for those magistrates that were active. In turn, this throws up some important issues for historians who have studied the work that these men undertook. Peter King has noted that those seeking to take their complaints before JPs would have been able to decide which justice to choose, and may have indeed made an *informed* choice based upon their knowledge of the office holders on offer.[6]

Thus, a labouring man who was in dispute with his employer may have chosen to go before a member of the aristocracy because he could have been known as someone with an innate dislike of the middling sorts. By contrast, a small landlord may have decided to choose a justice, perhaps one drawn from the minor gentry, who would have been more sympathetic to the needs of the growing consumer class. Others may have picked JPs based on their reputation for kindness, their morality (particular in the case of clergymen JPs) or indeed their intolerance of certain pastimes, crimes or forms of behaviour. King has argued that the ability to pick and choose between a number of magistrates allowed the labouring poor a greater degree of agency within the criminal justice system than has been previously suggested.[7] King's argument is persuasive but given that in some parts of the country access to justices was patchy at best, this thesis must be treated with care. Not everybody would have been able to seek out the justice that best suited their purpose when and where they needed him. Simple geography placed constraints on the operation of justice at this level; well-populated areas such as the home counties of Buckinghamshire and Surrey may have provided a greater access to 'justice' than the more sparsely populated regions of the north east or south west. This caveat is even more appropriate when the availability and natures of justices in the larger towns and cities of England is considered.

London and the 'trading justice'

One of the complaints lodged at the magistracy in the provinces throughout the later eighteenth century was that the quality of those putting themselves forward as JPs was falling. The result was the recruitment of lesser gentry, the clergy and some professional men. Nowhere was this situation more pronounced than in London and in Middlesex in particular. In Middlesex, justicing had become, as Norma Landau has written, 'a business'.[8] Here JPs touted for work outside their offices and charged customers for warrants and summonses. They drew criticism from contemporaries who labelled them 'trading justices' and deplored their activities for creating a culture of litigation in the capital.

At Bow Street in Covent Garden, the Westminster Justice De Veil, and his successors, the Fieldings (Henry and his half-brother John), had established a rotation office to provide an accessible venue for summary hearings. The Fieldings employed a number of men as officers (or 'Runners' as they came to be known) to help locate lost property and bring offenders into the court. Clearly, the presence of Bow Street allowed Londoners access to the law much more easily than those living in rural areas or even within the smaller towns of England and Wales. The same was true for those living and working within the City of London. Here two summary courts operated six days a week all year round.[9] The City had no problem with trading justices because it had met the challenge of a lack of magistrates by making its twenty-six aldermen serve as JPs in rotation. While the twenty-six sat for two or three days in turn at Guildhall, the lord mayor – as chief magistrate of the City – heard cases in the Mansion House.

The City's magistracy were unpaid and took no fees for their services, while those using their courts would have found it very convenient to take their complaints before them. However, they would also have presented what might be considered to be a united front as representatives of the capital's mercantile elite.[10] The City aldermen were all rich businessmen interlinked by marriage, commerce and politics, and it is unlikely that members of the labouring poor or lower middling sorts could have hoped to exploit any weaknesses within this group of powerful patricians. It may be then that in London while summary justice was much more accessible, it came at a price; both in financial terms and because of the limited opportunities for the triangulation between authority types that King has suggested was possible in provincial England.[11]

In Westminster, the Fieldings brothers pioneered their own form of entrepreneurial magistracy at Bow Street, employing a small team of 'runners' to help them investigate crime. A version of this model was eventually rolled out across the capital from 1792 as seven police offices were created. These new 'publick offices' [sic] were supposed to be self-supporting, drawing on the fees and penalties charged by the court. This income covered the expenses of the office including the 'wages of the six constables attached to each office, besides the salaries and even the pensions of the justices'.[12] Eventually, they were to form the basis of the police magistrate courts of the nineteenth century and of modern magistrate courts today.

What this brief typology reveals is that there was no uniform system of summary justice operating across England and Wales in the 1700s. As we have seen, JPs were drawn from a range of backgrounds and were largely amateur and untrained. Some, such as Philip Ward in Northamptonshire, would have had some legal background, while others, such as Edmund Tew in Boldon, would have relied on legal handbooks such as that produced by Richard Burn from the middle of the eighteenth century.[13] Part of the problem for historians of crime and legal history is that while justices were obliged to keep a record of their activities and judgements, there was no set form that this record was supposed to take and no obligation to leave a copy of their adjudications behind. So, unlike assize and quarter sessions records (which survived in large numbers across the eighteenth and nineteenth centuries in a fairly standardized form), the survival of summary records is at best partial and accidental. Much of what we do know, therefore, has come from a growing body of justices' notebooks and papers deposited in county record offices across England.[14]

The nature of the business of the eighteenth-century justice of the peace

From the research that has been undertaken so far, it is possible to say something about the nature of the business conducted by these amateur magistrates. And it is important to state from the outset that much of what they dealt with had very little to do with what we would understand as *criminality*. In fact, magistrates operating in provincial rural England and Wales, and in London and Middlesex, conducted settlement examinations, dealt with requests for poor relief,[15] interviewed bastard bearers and heard all sorts of issues relating to the application of the poor laws. Both rural and metropolitan justices also heard complaints about wages, employment conditions, badly behaved apprentices and unruly servants. It would appear that men and women of the lower classes felt that it was a legitimate and useful exercise to approach a JP for help in resolving these sorts of disputes.

Petty violence and the magistrate: Mediation and problem solving

In addition to the everyday business of poor law and master/servant, JPs across the country were hearing tremendous numbers of complaints about petty (and not so petty) violence. Assault was prosecuted at the quarter sessions (as Landau has shown[16]) but it was much more common for complaints of assault to be heard before individual JPs. Here the role of the magistrate was most clear: He acted as a mediator between the combatants, brokering settlements more often than not and occasionally dismissing cases that he found to be trivial or where guilt on both sides was apparent.

The realities of assault prosecutions at this level have been dealt with in Chapter 3 but here it is important to note that while levels varied throughout the period and across the county, roughly *one third* of the business of justices was taken up for assault, domestic abuse, slander or the use of threatening words. Clearly, the JP, as the head of his community, had a vested interest in resolving these interpersonal disputes quickly so as to calm local tensions because one of the principal duties of the eighteenth-century justice was to maintain order ('keep the peace') is his community. Assault accusations (which could and did vary enormously with regard to how serious they were) were generally treated as *civil* disputes between individuals and not as *criminal* actions that required the intervention of the state. In consequence, JPs generally attempted to broker reconciliations between the affected parties. It is also interesting to note that some magistrates offered female victims of domestic violence the opportunity to separate from their abusive partners by awarding costs and maintenance, rather than by simply punishing the abusers. While this might seem to be a negligent attitude towards violence, it also suggests a pragmatic approach to a perennial problem and a crime that was extremely hard to either prosecute or stamp out.

Naturally, a large proportion of justices' time was taken up with property crime and this falls into two, sometimes overlapping, areas: felonies and misdemeanours. A felony was an indictable crime; a crime that required a trial by jury and potentially carried the maximum sentence of death if it was capital (a grand larceny). Non-capital felonies (petty larceny) were also supposed to go before a judge and jury but would not attract the death penalty. Misdemeanours could be heard without a jury and so fell under the power and responsibilities of the JP. However, this situation is complicated because it was understood that the JP had a role in the process of bringing felonies before the courts.[17] As the central figure in the community and the effective representative of the criminal justice system, especially in provincial England and Wales, JPs were expected to act as a sort of filter to the wider justice system, weeding out cases that were trivial or had little chance of resulting in a successful prosecution at court. This was supposed to be the responsibility of the grand jury at quarter sessions and assize but it is evident from the notebooks of justices that have survived that JPs often provided the first step in felony cases. There also seems to be considerable difference between rural and urban (or indeed metropolitan) areas. Rural justices, such as Philip Ward near Oundle, had far less property crime to deal with than the City justices at Guildhall or the Fieldings in Bow Street. In part this reflects the fact that much rural pilfering would have been dealt with without the need for prosecution, whereas in towns inhabitants were both more exposed to poverty and need *and* presented with more opportunities to steal. What is perhaps most interesting is that in London the magistracy appears to have acted as a more obvious filter to the wider criminal justice system by rejecting many cases of petty theft without sending them on for trial. Strictly speaking, JPs did not have the authority to do this, but in the City of London at least this practice was both widespread and endemic. Men and women accused of committing petty larceny, and even, on some occasions, grand larceny, were routinely questioned, imprisoned, questioned again and then sent to the Bridewell (the City of London's house of correction) for short periods – all without the use of a jury trial as the law intended.[18]

The justice's role in property cases was twofold: In the first instance he was there to hear a victim's complaint (or to hear evidence presented by a policing agent such as a watchman or constable who had arrested someone on suspicion of committing a crime). He would listen to evidence and help in the early stages of what we might describe as the putting together of a case. This could lead to the next action, which was issuing a formal indictment against the accused and related documents such as recognizements to prosecute or give evidence in court, and warrants to arrest suspects or search premises.

The same role applied to justices in the countryside just as much as in the towns but we can discern some clear differences here. In rural areas it is evident that JPs more usually sent offenders on for trial at the sessions or assizes. It may be the case that, given that there were fewer incidents of reported property crime in rural areas (for the reasons stated earlier), justices were less obliged or inclined to act as filters when pre-trial hearings were convened. Alternatively, rural JPs may have been more comfortable with allowing the law to take its course and so routinely sent indictable cases up through the system. This is an area of the summary process that needs more work if we are to fully understand practice at this level.

There was one area of property offending that did fall directly within the responsibilities and power of the JP and that was the prosecution of certain misdemeanours such as wood stealing, some forms of embezzlement and the theft of certain crops or other produce. However, since this is clearly related to theft and to what historians have identified as 'social crime', it is dealt with in Chapter 5.

In summary then, throughout the long eighteenth century the justices of the peace in England and Wales operated as amateur lawmen serving their communities and maintaining order and good social relations as their first duty. They had multiple commitments on their time and they varied tremendously in how much of their time they were prepared to give up. There were clear rural and urban differences and the practice of summary justice in London was in many ways unique. We can look at the ways in which this system developed and how the powers of magistrates were increasingly extended in the nineteenth century.

The evolution of police courts and the modern magistracy

As the nineteenth century progressed, summary justice became more widespread. By 1831 there were 523 petty sessional divisions in England and from 1836 onwards more formalized Petty Sessions, with at least two justices sitting, were convened across the country. Here justices dealt with a range of criminal, civil and administrative business just as they had in the eighteenth century.[19] The 1792 Middlesex Justices Act had created seven public offices on the Bow Street model. The name changed from 'Public' to 'Police Office' and finally to 'Police Courts'; the term 'magistrate' was first officially used in 1839 when legislation was passed to regulate the courts.[20] The nine London courts (which were expanded to thirteen in London by the mid-century) were served by three magistrates, nearly all of whom had been qualified barristers. The 1839 act insisted that all subsequent appointments to the magistracy had to be barristers at law. In the capital they were empowered to sit alone, whereas elsewhere in the country magistrates continued to sit as benches of two or more. In London, and in the other towns and cities which convened police courts, the role of the justice of the peace as a worthy amateur had therefore been significantly changed.

Nineteenth-century police court magistrates dispensed justice for a host of minor crimes, misdemeanours and incidents of petty violence. They dealt with problems similar to those presented to their counterparts in the eighteenth century: common assaults, drunk and disorderly behaviour and vagrancy. Police courts cleared the cells of the local police stations and so magistrates would have seen the drunks, gamblers, beggars and prostitutes caught up by the patrols of the capital's police. The police courts had a reputation for harshness and cases were dealt with brusquely, most within minutes. There was no jury and little else to restrict the sitting magistrate from making decisions on the lives of those brought before him. Magistrates could examine offenders and acquit them if they felt there was insufficient evidence to convict, or find them guilty and then award punishment. Mr Lushington at Thames Police Court was infamous for his dislike of brawling drunks, particularly those that then assaulted the policemen that attempted to restrain them. Those brought before him could therefore expect a heavy fine, imprisonment or both.[21] Many other offenders were simply fined or warned against their future behaviour and released. In reality, police court magistrates had a range of options available to them and a tremendous ability to exercise their discretion.

However, it would be wrong to simply dismiss these courts as serving the needs of the authorities; police courts were more than just an extension of the disciplinary arm of the state. According to one contemporary writer the original purpose of the police courts was to provide a forum for quick and restorative justice for the poor of the capital.[22] Another author was at pains to point out how women used the courts to ask for advice, or to obtain summonses against their abusive or absent husbands. Others used the police courts as an alternative to the much more expensive divorce courts, to gain separation orders.[23] This civil, non-criminal role was a large part of the business of the courts and clearly important. Here we see the so-called 'people's courts' in action providing quick restorative 'justice' for the working classes. Thus, while the setting for the operation of summary proceedings may have become more formalized in the Victorian period, it functioned in much the same way that it had throughout the eighteenth century.

A brief look at the business of the Thames Police Court in the late 1880s reveals a pattern that is not dissimilar from the work of the Guildhall and Mansion House justice rooms in the late eighteenth century. Just under a fifth of the cases had nothing to do with crime, at least as the modern reader would understand it.[24] The Thames and the other metropolitan police courts heard prosecutions of parents who failed to ensure their children attended school; individuals who failed to pay their gas bills; landlords accused of letting or house building violations; commercial drivers for obstructing the streets, and all manner of petty infringements of local laws. A third of cases were for disorderly behaviour, and most of these of course were linked to drunkenness. A quarter were offenders brought in for violence, again often drink related. Finally, the remainder were minor property offenders who were remanded on suspicion or sentenced to short terms of imprisonment if found guilty.

To some degree, the police courts acted as a part of the disciplinary armoury of the middle class in Victorian London. Here workers were prosecuted for pilfering from their employers, drunks and street brawlers were admonished by their social superiors and prostitutes upbraided for their dissolute behaviour. However, as Jennifer Davis has argued, it would be wrong to simply dismiss the police courts as a lever of class control. Her research has shown that the working class used the police courts to prosecute each other and complain at poor treatment by employers, poor law officials and others.[25] Women certainly used the police courts to challenge legitimacy of the violence inflicted upon them by their drunken husbands and common law partners and, as Michelle Abraham has shown in research outside of the capital, often received considerable sympathy from the magistracy and local police.[26]

In 1848 the Jervis' Acts tightened magisterial procedures but also consolidated existing legislation of summary jurisdiction. These were three acts of parliament introduced by the sitting Attorney General Sir John Jervis. The first was designed to protect justices from being prosecuted by individuals unhappy with their decisions. Complainants could sue for damages in the civil court or even demand a re-trial if they felt that magistrates had overstepped their authority and while there is no consensus on how exposed justices were; the 1848 Justices Protection Act effectively prevented trivial attempts to undermine their authority. The Summary Jurisdiction Act and the Indictable Offences Act passed at the same time extended both the powers of justices to punish minor offenders and extended the range of offences that came under their purview.

Taken as a whole then, the Jervis' Acts fundamentally consolidated the role of the magistrate in the middle of the nineteenth century and established the importance of police courts throughout England and Wales. There would be no retreat from this process and further legislation later in the nineteenth and early twentieth centuries continued the move towards summary jurisdiction for an increasing number of what had formally been indictable criminal offences. In 1847 and 1850 changes to the law allowed magistrates at petty sessions to try juveniles aged 14 or under and then those under 16 who were accused of simple larceny. There was further reform in 1855 when the Criminal Justice Act (18 & 19 Vict. c.126) empowered magistrates to try cases of theft or embezzlement of goods to the value of less than five shillings so long as the accused was happy to subject himself to a summary trial.[27] Cases of the theft of goods valued at over five shillings could also be heard before magistrates if the defendant pleaded guilty and in 1879 the value of the stolen goods was raised to £2. Offenders convicted by the bench could then be imprisoned in a house of correction or common gaol, with or without hard labour for up to six months. This increase in the jurisdiction of the magistracy meant that by the late nineteenth century the summary courts were dealing with twenty times the amount of cases heard at the jury courts.

The process of extending summary jurisdiction was not confined to the capital. Outside of London the 1835 Municipal Corporation Act allowed boroughs to appoint their own stipendiary magistrates and towns such as Northampton now regularly convened petty sessions courts to deal with the same wide range of petty offences, complaints and regulatory business. Historians have been slow to look at the work of these provincial courtrooms but they are now beginning to be explored.[28] The pattern here was consistent with the metropolitan police courts and points towards what might be seen as the gradual evolution of uniformity in the English court system at this level. Future research needs to look much more closely at the police courts of London and elsewhere and at how they were used by and at the role of both the police and the emerging police court missionary service (the forerunners of probation officers) at the end of the century.[29]

Historians and the magistracy: An overview of research into the justice of the peace

Whilst there has been a neglect of the topic, a small but important body of work has emerged since the 1970s. Perhaps the most important starting point was Norma Landau's study of the Kent bench[30] which explored the nature of the justices themselves rather than the work that they undertook. In this respect the text is frustrating because it tells us relatively little about what duties the JPs of the county performed or how they reached their decisions. However, it is extremely valuable in providing a social background for the type of men that entered the county lists. Similarly, earlier works by Sir Thomas Skyrme[31] and Esther Moir[32] concentrate on law and procedure and do not engage with the nature of the role or duties that JPs performed. Neither their work nor Landau's allows us to really understand how summary proceedings operated or indeed how they might have been utilized by ordinary members of the labouring population.

However, more recently Peter King and others have made significant inroads into the subject and have identified a number of key themes for further research. King's pioneering essay on the role of summary proceedings brought together a range of research into justice's notebooks including JPs from Bedfordshire, Essex, the north-east of England and London. Using notebooks and justices' diaries, King argues that the magistracy had a flexible approach to the law and exercised considerable discretion in its application. JPs were influenced by their own social backgrounds and attitudes towards members of their community, which was reflected in their judicial decision-making. Those that used the magistracy to prosecute offenders or to settle disputes about employment or demands upon the poor laws were also adept at negotiating their way through this discretionary minefield. Thus, by carefully selecting which justice to take their complaint before members of the labouring poor (broadly defined) could exploit class divisions between the elite and middling sorts to their advantage.[33] More detailed work by Douglas Hay has also looked at how masters and servants utilized the summary process. Hay has argued that the outcome of these disputes in Warwickshire most frequently favoured the servants as plaintiffs.[34] Therefore, Hay and King's work would suggest that the labouring poor had considerable agency when it came to using the summary process, a finding that runs counter to Hay's own analysis of the criminal justice system at the jury courts which had concluded that it was an ideological tool of a ruling class.[35]

Most other research concerning the magistracy has consisted of case studies of either individual JPs or specific geographic locations. Thus, Robert Shoemaker studied the Middlesex bench in the late seventeenth and early eighteenth centuries. His concern was with how the summary process operated as a disciplinary mechanism for controlling the urban poor. Importantly, Shoemaker suggested that urban magistrates had a greater social and legal authority over their communities than their rural counterparts did.[36] This has been developed and sustained by the work of John Beattie and Drew Gray, both of whom have looked at the operation of the City of London's magistrates in the eighteenth century. Beattie noted that the aldermen of the City had no qualms about ignoring the letter of the law in the period to 1750 and frequently sent petty property offenders to the Bridewell house of correction rather than, as statute law demanded, indicting them as petty larcenists and sending before a judge and jury.[37] Gray has shown that this practice was continued throughout the second half of the century and therefore preceded much of the nineteenth-century legislation that enshrined this practice in law.[38] The difference between the urban and rural benches is interesting and illustrative of the different needs of the metropolis and the quite different nature of provincial class relations. Deference was easier to maintain in the countryside where opportunities for work were perhaps more restricted and traditions and social relations less under threat from new ideas about equality.

In the metropolitan sphere, social relations were more fluid and stretched than elsewhere. Crime was also of much greater concern and the contemporary news media continuously focused on the depredations of the capital's criminal elements and the poor, riotous and rowdy behaviour of the lower orders. In this climate it is understandable that a more detached magistracy may have felt the need to present a more united class front to those coming before them. How this manifested itself in practice is still an area that requires more research but one of the themes that has emerged from Gray's study of the City of London summary courts is that of a system that was less useful to the working population who were in dispute with their masters. Here the presence of a united mercantile elite may have hamstrung the attempts of some apprentices and servants to manipulate the summary process to their advantage.

Outside of London there have been a number of studies of individual justices based upon the handful of notebooks that have survived. In many cases these are little more than transcriptions of the notebooks with a short introduction or commentary.[39] A notable exception is an essay by Gwenda Morgan and Peter Rushton on the notebook of Edmund Tew JP from Boldon in the north-east. Here they examine Tew's role as justice, thematically looking at his work with the poor law, in dealing with violence and petty criminality, arguing that Tew was most concerned with maintaining good relations within his community and in acting against 'unneighbourly behaviour'.[40] Tew was first and foremost a negotiator or counsellor rather than someone attempting to act as an agent of social control. Tentative work on two of Northamptonshire's JPs in the period would also appear to echo this conclusion. Phillip Ward of Stoke Doyle in the north-east of the county and William Ward (no relation) of Guilsborough in the south-west both appear to have acted to maintain peaceful communities. One work by Dietrich Oberwitiler has attempted to look at a small number of justices to understand their operations but has been fairly limited in its focus.[41]

What is now required is a deeper analysis of the records of the various extant notebooks and summary court records from the long eighteenth century to both understand how summary proceedings operated and to explore a number of important themes. Through the work we have on London, we now have a better idea of how the City courts functioned and some suggestions of the ways in which JPs might have reached some of the decisions they took.[42] In the notebook of Philip Ward we have a rare insight into the workings of a JP who had, in the 1740s, no access to the 'bible' of later justices, Burn's *Justice of the Peace and Parish Officer*.[43]

However, while there is growing body of work outlining the work of the magistracy in the eighteenth century, there is much less on the development of police court magistrates in the Victorian period and at the gradual evolution of the modern magistrates court in the twentieth century.[44] Jennifer Davis' work on the London police courts is a notable exception here but her seminal essay of 1984 has surprisingly not led to detailed research in this area. Researchers are somewhat hamstrung by the lack of court records but there are a handful of memoirs and contemporary discussions of the police courts that could be utilized as well as extensive coverage in the London and national press. A detailed and extensive study of these courts would be of significant interest for historians of crime and those interested in social relations in the nineteenth century.

The English magistrate represents a continuous link between the medieval and early modern justice systems, that of the eighteenth and nineteenth centuries and the system that operates today. The role is amateur and people from all sorts of backgrounds and cultures are invited to become JPs; the requirements are 'good character, common sense and an ability to listen and be impartial'.[45] However, given that a candidate needs to provide three references of character, not have been convicted of 'serious' crime, not been declared bankrupt and be able to give up 26–35 days a year for unpaid work, I might suggest that the role is likely to be somewhat self-selecting.

Modern JPs sit in threes to deliver their judgements and nowadays they rely more heavily on the clerk of the court. They undergo some training and can, as indeed the likes of Phillip Ward did, rely on the advice of more experienced colleagues. Fundamentally however, they are still able to pass quite life-changing sentences on those that appear before them. Importantly, modern reforms have allowed defendants to be represented by professionals in court. Justices are also more accountable today and the process of summary justice has been divorced from the paternalistic rule of small county communities by the English gentry.

Perhaps the most noticeable change has been in the purpose of the JP. In the early to late eighteenth century he was tasked with keeping the peace in his community and in overseeing day to day life. As a result, justices such as Ward, Spencer and Whitbread heard a considerable amount of business that had nothing whatsoever to do with crime. Poor law claims, settlement inquiries, complaints about the state of the highways and disputes over wages or employment all came before the magistracy between 1660 and well into the 1800s. Now much of that role has been assumed by the councils of England and by other government departments such as health or social services; magistrates are largely left to deal with petty crimes. Finally, it is worth noting that magistrates only act as arbiters now; they have no investigative or preventative role; all such roles are left to the new keepers of the Queen's peace – the police, and the evolution of professional policing is the subject of the next chapter.

CHAPTER 10
DOGBERRY TO DETECTIVES: POLICING FROM AMATEURS TO PROFESSIONALS

The period covered by this book saw a great deal of change in the way in which England was policed and the nature of that change has been the source of considerable debate. In order to understand the changing landscape of policing it is necessary to chart its reality in the late seventeenth century and look at developments in the eighteenth and how these were finally to evolve into professional police forces in the nineteenth. It is important to stress that professional policing *evolved*, it did not suddenly appear in 1829 with Sir Robert Peel's Metropolitan Police. So, this chapter will look first at policing in the early modern period.

Policing early modern England

For much of England in the late seventeenth century the principal character in local policing was the parish constable. The term 'constable' had Norman origins and included both high and petty constables.[1] Medieval petty constables were elected locally and were answerable to the sheriff and the hundred courts.[2] The old titles of tithingman or headborough (headman in the village), survived into the early modern period and beyond, but they were increasingly known as *constables*. Parish constables were elected from amongst the ratepayers and expected to serve for a year or sometimes two. As well as being answerable to their communities they were directly responsible to the justices of the peace and so to part of the machinery of government. The creation of the office of JP effectively downgraded the social status of the constable – something that was to continue across the long period of this study.[3] Those performing the role of parish constable in early modern England were often the subject of ridicule, perhaps because they were seen as incompetent or symbolic of unwanted authority. However, Emsley warns against accepting contemporary criticism of constables at face value as evidence that such men were incompetent and corrupt. Parish constables had to fulfil a variety of functions for their local communities as well as serving as representatives of national government and the monarch. Given that the position was temporary, it is likely that some individuals would have come in for criticism for a lack of experience or for being inefficient or lacking motivation. This becomes clearer when the roles of these amateur constables are considered.

Parish constables were not salaried but they could claim expenses for the wide variety of tasks they performed. The constable's account book for a small Northamptonshire village lists disbursements for attending courts and coroner's inquests, fees for shooting birds and for collecting the Militia returns.[4] Constables could also claim expenses for escorting prisoners to and from court, and for removing vagrants to the parish borders. The evidence from this source and contemporary manuals such as William Lambard's reveals that a parish constable had to carry out a lot of different duties.[5] As well as being the local law enforcement officer he was a tax collector, a recruiting officer and had a role in supervising what crops were grown. In consequence, the position of parish constable was a difficult one because he was caught between his duty to the state and to the community. Laws passed by parliament might be held as unfair or unacceptable to village life and culture. By the same token the main desire of most villagers was to avoid trouble in their daily lives, lives that were open to many possible arenas of conflict. Constables were amateurs and, as ratepayers, were respectable property-owning men drawn from within the local community, often tradesmen with vested interests. Thus, maintaining local goodwill and neighbourliness was important because constables had to continue to work in the parish in which they served after their term of office had expired and, consequently, they were under a good deal of pressure. The role of the constable as a mediator in village affairs must have been important, especially as these individuals were, at least in the sixteenth and seventeenth centuries, drawn from amongst the more educated and better off of the populace. It is likely that, for the most part at least, they enjoyed the confidence and respect of the community, despite some of the Shakespearean references (to 'Dogberry' and 'Elbow') that suggest otherwise.

The specific *policing* duty of the constable was to assist the justices in keeping the peace and to arrest lawbreakers and so they had powers of arrest, search and could enter properties in pursuit of offenders.[6] Given that the early modern justice system was largely victim-led, the parish constable was (along with the JP) the first point of call for victims of crime. It is important to remember that given the parallel administrative nature of the role, and its temporary status, constables sometimes found themselves ensnared at the point where national legislative prescription and local customary norms clashed. Therefore, constables who tried to enforce laws that the community disapproved of risked not only loss of time and money but they were also likely to arouse the anger of the neighbourhood. This could lead to violence, abuse and if they were tradesmen, a loss of custom. On rare occasions constables could suffer directly from their efforts to enforce the law: in 1788 in Pattishall, Northamptonshire, a constable was shot dead while attempting to execute a warrant for assault.[7]

The parish constable in an urban environment

Much of the historical work on constables has looked at their role in rural communities but it is important to recognize that the petty constable was also a feature of urban law enforcement throughout the long eighteenth century. In the City of London constables were elected annually by the inhabitants of the twenty-six wards and served for a year. Wards were subdivided into precincts and each City precinct elected one or two constables to serve their community in much the same manner described earlier. These men were obliged, under the terms of the Statute of Winchester, 'to take a turn to police his community'.[8]

However, it appears that many of those elected as constables opted out of the responsibility. The duty of constable was likely to adversely affect an individual's business and family life.[9] One City constable asked to be relieved of his duty because he was 'troubled with two Ruptures', and was subject to bouts of 'faintness and weakness so much so that he is frequently obligated to lay down for two or three hours at a time'.[10] The City generally refused exemptions but sometimes allowed individuals to hire substitutes to serve in their stead. By paying a fine of around £7 or a hiring fee of around £5–15 it was possible to get someone else to take your turn for you, and this practice was quite widespread in the long eighteenth century.[11] Beattie, Gray and Harris have all shown that substitute constables regularly replaced elected ratepayers and many of these substitutes served for many consecutive years, becoming in effect semi-professional peace officers.[12] Substitutes were not exclusive to the City, and there is evidence of substitutes serving in Westminster and in rural communities (although not to the extent that they did in the capital). This further demonstrates the slowly developing nature of policing in the period before 1829 and, as I have noted elsewhere, these substitutes represent 'an historical bridge between the parochial constabulary and the nineteenth-century professionals'.[13]

Constables had, then, existed since medieval times, but in the eighteenth century there were small-scale attempts to improve the policing in England and Wales. Some of these initiatives may appear quite familiar to a modern readership that is used to self-help groups such as the Neighbourhood Watch.

Associations for the prosecution of felons

In 1789, *The Times* newspaper 'praised "the associations which are formed in numerous counties for the prosecution of felons" as excellent institutions'.[14] The costs of prosecuting could be prohibitive to the victim of crime even well into the nineteenth century, and historians have explored the development of privately funded subscription organizations (termed Associations for the Prosecution of Felons), which were created to assist their members in combatting crime and meeting the expense of prosecution. Prosecuting property crimes at the assizes might cost an individual £10–£20 (and even as much as £10 at quarter sessions) when all the associated costs of advertising stolen goods, apprehending suspects, paying witnesses' expenses, hiring lawyers and compensating for one's own time were factored in.[15] The private prosecution system put considerable obstacles in the path of the victim of crime and so prosecution associations can be seen as a mechanism to offset some of these costs. Historians have tried to see these associations as an attempt to improve a criminal justice system that was woefully inefficient and discretionary,[16] but Philips and King have suggested that they actually had very little effect on indictment rates and acted more as insurance clubs. So what do we know about prosecution associations and how they operated?

There were probably in excess of 1,000 prosecution associations operating in rural and urban England and Wales between 1750 and 1850, and quite possibly many more. Unfortunately, existing records do not allow us to be entirely accurate either about the numbers of associations or levels of subscriptions to them.[17] It would seem that most of them were made up of men who paid a regular subscription (sometimes annually or when the raising of funds was necessary). Most associations consisted of gentlemen and farmers as well as tradesmen (particularly in urban areas), but there were also JPs, clergymen and other prominent members of the local society. These were small, local organizations of between twenty and sixty members.[18] So, for example, in Essex the 'majority of urban subscribers were distributors, retailers, or food processors whose activities were particularly vulnerable to theft.[19] A rural/urban distinction can be seen in the sorts of offences these associations sought to prosecute. Rural associations brought prosecutions against those stealing animals (horse and livestock), crops, wood and fencing while those in towns concentrated on domestic thefts, workplace appropriation and those stealing from gardens and allotments. King noticed that the focus of associations in Essex shifted over time, so in the period before the 1780s associations concentrated 'most heavily on horse- and sheep-stealing, highway robbery, and housebreaking but during the 1780s an increasing proportion of associations became interested in minor crimes such as petty larceny, wood stealing, and vegetable theft as well as continuing their involvement in the prosecution of major felonies.[20] This suggests that associations were affected by national concerns about rising crime, fears most often circulated by the increasingly influential provincial newspapers.

It would certainly appear to be the case that while associations were recorded as early as the 1690s, their heyday was in the period after 1750 to the late 1780s. Whilst this can be attributed to fears about 'crime waves' Philips noted that this was also a period when the English legal system was becoming more expensive for prosecutors. Increasingly, offenders were being represented by counsel at assizes and quarter sessions and associations were under pressure to maintain funds to support their membership. Prosecution itself was not always the intention and simply joining an association might have been viewed as a form of pre-emptive counter to falling victim to crime. Prosecution associations are probably best viewed as self-support clubs for those worried about the rising costs of prosecution rather than as a form of ideologically driven crime prevention networks. They often worked with local petty constables and sometimes employed their own patrols or thief-takers but it is not accurate to see such associations as crime fighting organizations. They served their members, who were overwhelmingly drawn from the propertied class, and it would seem that they rarely helped non-members. As King argues, 'the associations very rarely had any intention of providing a general prosecution service although a few parochial initiatives may have had this aim'. [21]

Associations for the prosecution of felons flourished in the last quarter of the eighteenth century and many survived long into the nineteenth. They offered a level of financial support to their members at a time when the costs of prosecution were rising and in a climate when the fear of crime was being highlighted by increased media coverage. It is very hard to say how effective they were, either in preventing crime or in prosecuting criminals, but that was probably not the reason that individuals joined. Instead, it appears that they offered a level of insurance against falling victim to crime and were a product of the 'clubbable' culture of the age. However, despite their limitations they were a part of the evolutionary process of policing in England and Wales and have to be seen alongside the changing nature of the parish constables, substitution and a growing discussion about the best way to combat criminality. In towns in particular this debate was focused upon the limitations of two other forms of policing, watching networks and thief-takers.

The night watch and thief-takers

Urban areas of England employed watchmen to patrol along set beats at night and tasked beadles with their supervision. The night watch had its origins in the medieval period, with the Statute of Winchester impelling boroughs to create a watch patrol, drawn from amongst the householders in turn, from 1285 onwards.[22] Watchmen patrolled the streets equipped with a staff and lantern and could rest in their stand or shelter there from inclement weather. For much of their history watchmen, like parish constables, were subject to considerable criticism and abuse from commentators, press and public alike. Harris has noted that in the City of London watchmen (as well as constables) were systematically criticized for their lack of efficiency, decrepitude and corrupt practices.[23] The City Marshall (the effective head of policing in the square mile) was critical of watchmen for failing to bring in 'disorderly persons' and for taking bribes. In the aftermath of the 1780 Gordon Riots William Blizzard drew attention to the cosy relationship between constables and publicans, and in 1803 the campaigning magistrate Patrick Colquhoun cast similar aspersions about the links between the men of the watch and brothels of the capital.[24]

But it is too easy to accept contemporary criticism of watchmen at face value when a much more nuanced view is required. Elaine Reynolds has argued that the night watch in London underwent considerable reform and improvement in the long eighteenth century, beginning with Westminster in the 1730s.[25] In 1735, Westminster's vestrymen successfully petitioned for an act of parliament which allowed them to raise a tax to recruit a paid night watch. The City of London followed suit in 1737. Arguably, despite a host of contemporary critics, the City watch was already better regulated by the early years of the eighteenth century. The Common Council (which administered the city) had insisted on the building of watch houses and the establishment of beats and stands.[26]

Watchmen were an easy target, both for expressions of youthful excess and the sharp criticism of the press and others. Watchmen were verbally and physically abused, their lanterns stolen and their stands turned over, and they apparently received very little protection from the courts.[27] The newspapers highlighted incidents in which watchmen stood by as premises were burgled or victims were robbed, but such negative depictions can be balanced by more positive reports of their behaviour. Watchmen saved lives by spotting fires, prevented burglaries by warning householders of open doors or windows and chased and caught felons fleeing from the scenes of crime. They also arrested drunks, prostitutes and other 'suspicious characters' they found on the streets. Recent research has, for example, pointed to the proactive involvement of the watch and other policing agents after 1792 (and the creation of the police offices of the metropolis) in the arrest of those suspected of stealing metals.[28] The actions of watchmen were actually quite similar to those of the professional police after 1829 as the following example from 1771 demonstrates. Robert Cleghorn and Richard Aldrich were running away from a property in Cheapside with a bundle of stolen goods when they were spotted by James Wright, a City of London watchman. Wright gave chase and called for assistance. A second watchman joined the chase and despite the fact that the thieves separated to confound the chase both were arrested and taken back to the watch house and searched. The men were sent to trial, convicted and transported, with Wright giving evidence in court.[29] Even a casual scrutiny of the *Old Bailey Proceedings* reveals many more examples of watchmen acting bravely, diligently and effectively.

This is not, of course, to suggest that all watchmen were equally competent or above corruption. Certainly, many deserved the brickbats hurled at them by pamphleteers and the press but it would be inaccurate if not lazy to swallow every morsel of criticism without challenge. Eighteenth-century urban policing was evolving alongside other reforms to local government, such as improved paving and lighting, and attempts to 'civilize' the metropolis. Peel's reforms in 1829 therefore have to be considered in the context of the century of reform that preceded them. In his parliamentary report on policing in 1828 Edwin Chadwick called for a 'centralized, hierarchical police with a tremendous range of duties' able to 'prevent crime...[and] preserve public peace and order'. As Reynolds has argued, by the late eighteenth century the night watch of London 'met all but one of these criteria'; it may not have been centralized but its rationale was the prevention of crime and the preservation of the peace.[30] In many ways the watch was to be the model for the Metropolitan Police that replaced it; indeed many former watchmen were recruited into the ranks of the 'Peelers' (even if large numbers were dismissed in the first few years of the force's existence). However, in London policing was not just the preserve of the constabulary, beadles and watch; alongside and separate to them were less official crime fighters, the thief-takers who were the forerunners of modern detectives.

Government rewards and thief-taking in London

In 1692, in response to ongoing fears of rising crime, parliament passed an Act for Encouraging the Apprehending of Highway Men which rewarded those who successfully prosecuted such criminals with £40 on conviction. In addition, prosecutors could claim the condemned felon's horse, arms and any other possessions so long as they had not themselves been stolen in the course of the offence. Similar acts followed that offered rewards for apprehending shoplifters, counterfeiters, burglars and housebreakers and for receivers of stolen goods.[31] In the 1740s rewards were extended to cover the theft of cattle and sheep. The so-called 'Tyburn ticket', which excused the bearer from serving in a number of parochial offices, was given to those who successfully prosecuted horse thieves.[32] In 1720, amidst huge concerns about the frightening levels of street robberies, a royal proclamation augmented the £40 reward for the prosecution of highway robbery with an additional £100 for the conviction of felons within the capital. This was renewed several times over the next three decades.[33]

This was a significant incentive to pursue criminals but was also a clear invitation to corrupt practice, creating a climate within which a new sort of policing agent could prosper.[34] Those that took advantage of this new opportunity for enrichment were termed 'thief-takers' and their appearance and rise to prominence is an important part of the story of policing in England. Rewards were intended to encourage victims of crime to prosecute at a time when the costs and time involved in doing so was known to be onerous, but the unexpected consequence of the reward system was the creation of a market in the prosecution of offenders.

Rewards were usually divided between a number of individuals including the arresting constables, watchmen, witnesses and the victims of crime. The allocation of rewards was at the discretion of the judge and while large sums, sometimes well in excess of £100, were common, these had to be divided amongst several people (which may well have a deliberate ploy by the judges to check the corrupt behaviour of thief-takers).[35] Exactly how rewards were divided is not entirely clear but research has been able to establish that certain individuals crop up time and again in the records as the recipients of reward money. For the period 1730–1733 (where records exist) Beattie has found that in 'the majority of trials where rewards were paid… groups of between six and ten recipients shared' the proceeds.[36] Ruth Paley has been able to identify a list of names of over thirty persons as thief-takers who would have shared in reward money.[37] Despite the division of rewards the spoils were high; Beattie estimates the average individual that benefited from parliamentary rewards received £12 10s., an amount that equates to approximately £1,000 in modern money.[38]

Almost all the thief-takers that Paley has researched had some kind of criminal past, serious or otherwise.[39] As she puts it, these were men with a 'clear and unambiguous history of involvement in the world of professional crime'.[40] Even Bow Street (sometimes held up as an example of good practice), at least in its early inception, employed thief-takers such as Steven McDaniel and John Berry, who operated on the margins of legality. While there was no official link between thief-takers and more formal policing agents, research suggests that there were some loose connections.[41] So, while Paley's study showed that few mid-century thief-takers had ever worked as constables or watchmen, Beattie discovered that several former constables, sponging house[42] officers and turnkeys had gone on to work as thief-takers in an earlier period. Moreover, thief-takers (regardless of background) tended to inhabit environments associated with criminals such as brothels, low-lodging houses and taverns. Not only were they able to profit from the system of government and private rewards but they were also exploiting 'the debt laws, receiving, theft, intimidation, perjury and blackmail were all so lucrative in themselves that they provided the everyday business of the London thief-taker '.[43] In addition, thief-takers pocketed stolen goods and money from those they captured, often justifying this appropriation as a reasonable action to recover expenses. Overall, most of the criticism of thief-takers in the first half of the eighteenth century focused on the fact that they were corrupt and that they created as much crime as they solved or prevented. They were also widely criticized for sending hundreds of petty criminals to their deaths at the gallows, but this was, in part at least, an inevitable consequence of the reward system.

By providing a system of rewards the government had effectively encouraged a trade in 'blood-money' and thief-takers were accused, with good cause, of profiting from conspiracies to send others to the gallows. As Paley argues, 'There can be little doubt that thief-takers richly deserved the canting title of "traps" that contemporaries bestowed upon them and that they did indeed, as so frequently alleged, send decoys "out athieving to convict lads" '.[44] Importantly, thief-takers seem to have been able to manipulate the trial process by carefully selecting whom they sent there. Their experience of appearing at the Old Bailey on multiple occasions gave them a distinct advantage over defendants, and their careful construction of prosecutions meant that they offered a united and seemingly watertight case to London juries. Indeed, recent research has suggested that the specialist evidence offered by Bow Street Runners gave Fielding's men a more authoritative voice in court which influenced jurors in their favour.[45] When a thief-taker appeared in court to prosecute a vulnerable defendant – such as someone young, inexperienced and often newly arrived in the capital – the mechanics of the system worked to the advantage of the prosecution as trials were short, defendants often lacked any sort of legal advice or advocacy and there was scant regard for 'truth or the rules of evidence'.[46]

Wild's was not the only blood-money scandal to hit the capital in the eighteenth century: in 1754 members of the McDaniel gang 'were convicted of falsely accusing young men of robbery in order to collect the reward money'.[48] To some extent the development of Bow Street and the runners undermined the existence of such wilfully corrupt policing agents and while the Fielding brothers had employed former thief-takers with shady pasts (such as Steven McDaniel and John Berry), by '1751 or 1752 at the latest Fielding's force of thief-takers consisted of almost entirely new men'.[49] This was because thief-takers, 'as Fielding was only too aware, occupied a somewhat ambiguous position in society. They straddled the margins of the conventional and criminal worlds and formed, in effect, a sort of entrepreneurial police force, dependent on fees and rewards.'[50]

So, why did Georgian society allow thief-takers to operate, especially when it is evident that concerns about 'blood-money' scandals were widespread? The answer was that they were a necessary evil in an age before professional policing. In reality the whole criminal justice system was open to bribery and corrupt practice and so by exposing the activities of thief-takers such as Steven McDaniel the authorities would have opened a Pandora's Box of corruption and venality and undermined what little faith remained in policing in the metropolis. Rawlings concludes that while thief-takers garnered a considerable amount of opprobrium 'there was no mechanism for exposing them, partly because the criminal justice system was constructed around accusations brought by victims and was not designed to deal with the motivations which prompted thief-takers; and partly

Jonathan Wild: The thief-taker general

Figure 10.1 A gallows ticket to Wild's execution at Tyburn in 1725.

The archetypal and most famous of all thief-takers was Jonathan Wild, who was hanged at Tyburn in 1725 after a long career in which he earned somewhere in excess of £500,000 in today's money and sent at least sixty criminals to the gallows. Wild was not the first thief-taker to profit from the miscarriage of justice but he does appear to have been particularly rapacious in his desire to accumulate wealth and prestige through the office of a crime fighter. Wild, himself very familiar with the criminal underworld of early eighteenth-century London, started by approaching those that had recently suffered from the loss of goods to thieves, suggesting to them that he could help recover them. He then advertised in the press for the stolen goods, which indicated his goodwill, but also showed that he did not have them himself and alerted the thieves to the fact that the owner, via Wild, was ready to trade for them. This also served to spread Wild's name as the person to turn to when one was the victim of crime. His business grew and he established an office in the Old Bailey close by the sessions house and the nearby Blue Boar public house, so that victims would now come to him to ask for help. Wild helped capture and convict numerous felons, some (such as 'Blueskin' Blake and Jack Sheppard) who were certainly guilty, but he also sent many minor criminals and innocent parties to their deaths or transportation if they refused to come under his protection and tutelage. In effect, Wild ran a criminal network of thieves and prostitutes in Hanoverian London and it was probably only a matter of time before he himself fell victim to the justice system. Wild was finally caught, prosecuted and hanged on charges derived from new legislation that prescribed the death penalty for those found guilty of taking rewards for assisting the recovery of stolen goods, legislation clearly aimed at the corrupt practices of London thief-takers (see Figure 10.1).[47]

because they played a useful role for victims and the criminal justice system'.[51] However, as defence counsel began to impact the criminal trial towards the end of the eighteenth century, the evidence offered by thief-takers was more regularly challenged and exposed to scrutiny by the court. According to David Lemmings thief-takers 'broke new "law enforcement" ground. Although few were free from nefarious practices, in the course of their prosecuting activities during the 1690s they took on a detective role relatively unknown to the early modern constables and watchmen'.[52] They were certainly disliked by large sections of society: Witnesses and prosecutors at Old Bailey were increasingly at pains to point out that they were not there to benefit from the rewards system or in any way connected with the business of thief-taking. For some contemporaries, such as Bernard Mandeville, thief-taking was 'an acceptable activity and that thief-takers had an obligation to the public to be more than merely self-interested private bounty hunters'.[53] He may have been unduly optimistic in this view however, and it is clear that the use of rewards had created a private prosecution system that had been, since its inception, open to widespread corruption and abuse. The government finally abolished rewards in 1818.

Meanwhile, in 1749, Henry Fielding and his blind half-brother John founded their own group of thief-takers and these were to develop into one of the most celebrated crime fighting organizations and an important precursor of professional policing.

The Fieldings, Bow Street and the runners

The middle of the eighteenth century experienced a 'crime wave' and in response a parliamentary committee was established to investigate ways of improving legislation, which in effect entailed toughening up the laws relating to felonies. As a result, a plethora of bills emerged from the committee's report. These included the infamous Murder Act of 1752 and a move to reimburse victims for the costs of prosecution. There was also legislation that allowed magistrates to hold individuals who had been arrested on suspicion of theft for up to six days. This was designed to enable victims of robberies to attend court to hear their re-examination by justices (a practice common amongst London JPs). This is a useful foreground to the development of policing at Bow Street because it illustrates both how important the role of media-driven 'moral panics' about crime and disorder were to the process of police reform *and* how changes in practice were affected by individuals and legislative change. With this in mind we can now move forward to look at how the Bow Street Runners operated and at the legacy they left behind for future policing initiatives in London and the rest of the country.

Henry Fielding looms large in the history of crime and punishment because of his work as a London magistrate and the extensive self-publicizing of his efforts to improve policing. In response to the 1751 crime wave Henry Fielding set down his views on the criminal justice system and what was required to improve it. In the *Enquiry into the Causes of the Late Increase of Robbers*, Fielding adopted a position that was to be replicated many more times by many other writers and commentators across the eighteenth and nineteenth centuries – that of placing considerable blame for crime on the 'growing insubordination' of the poor, on vagrancy, the commercialization of society, drinking, gambling and the pursuit of luxury over good honest toil.[54] While Fielding was not particularly novel in his approach, he was in a position (as justice) to apply his ideas to policing the metropolis. Fielding had taken over as chief magistrate at Bow Street from Sir Thomas De Veil, who had drawn some criticism (perhaps undeserved) for the manner in which he acted as a so-called 'trading justice' during the period 1729–1748.[55] Fielding and his half-brother John were supporters of the office of thief-taker despite the criticism of it and established a justice business in Bow Street, Covent Garden (an area synonymous with prostitution, petty crime and drunkenness) with its own team of men whose principal occupation was to investigate crime and catch thieves. In the winter of 1748/1749 Henry Fielding appointed six men, all former Westminster constables, as the 'first quasi-official thief-takers'. These were men that could be engaged by the public to recover stolen goods but crucially were also 'available to Fielding to be sent at no cost to the victim to find and arrest offenders when he judged it in the public interest'. [56] This important distinction suggests a shift towards the creation of a professional, proactive police force in London, something quite different from the reactive constables and watchmen and the purely commercialized activities of other entrepreneurial thief catchers.

The men Fielding employed were entitled 'Principal Officers' rather than 'runners'. Indeed the term 'runner' was probably a derogatory one more usually applied to those that ran errands for the courts.[57] However, for our purposes the term Bow Street 'runner' will apply to the Principal Officers rather than any of the support staff that also served the justice office in the period. The Fieldings and their successors retained six 'runners' throughout the period to 1840 (when the force was disbanded) alongside paid clerks, more junior staff and a significant number of patrols. Importantly, runners were salaried, as the Fieldings had negotiated a small stipend from the government who were persuaded of the necessity of financing the policing of the capital in this small way.[58] The runners were able to earn money from rewards in the same way as other thief-takers and in the early years of the office many of the runners had other jobs – partly to supplement the income they derived from their policing activities, but also because the nature of them were often symbiotic with their role as Fielding's men. William Pentlow, for example, was a former parish constable who became keeper of the New Prison in 1751. Other members of Bow Street served as turnkeys (gaolers) in the capital's various prisons. These dual roles gave them valuable insight into criminal activities. The stipend also allowed the Fieldings to maintain the small team of clerks that processed and stored valuable information about crime and criminality in the capital. The keeping of records – of goods stolen, arrests made, examinations, convictions, suspicious persons and lists of those transported – appears to be the first real attempt to gather what we might term 'criminal intelligence'. Sadly, this had not survived, first being destroyed in the Gordon Riots and thereafter lost when the Bow Street office moved in the 1800s. But this 'detailed material about crime and suspected offenders was fundamental to Fielding's policing ambitions' and has led Beattie to describe Bow Street as the 'Scotland Yard of its day'.[59] The growth of business meant that by the 1760s the runners were no longer finding it necessary to undertake roles elsewhere, and by the 1780s runners were able to live comfortably on the salaries they earned.

The two other developments of Bow Street were the horse and foot patrols that helped to supplement the watch and constabulary (especially on the borders of the metropolis and in areas which fell between the jurisdictions of London parishes), and the publication of details of crime in the *Hue & Cry*. The Fieldings were very keen to get government support for their patrols and while a horse patrol was instigated, it was expensive and was withdrawn soon after its creation. According to David Cox, the Bow Street patrols were only ever meant to have a preventive role, 'whereas the role of the Principal Officers was from the outset considered to be fundamentally detective in nature'.[60] Both patrols can be seen, however, as forming important staging posts on the path to the creation of professional police in 1829. The foot patrol was uniformed after 1822; the horse patrol (created in 1805) was the 'first uniformed police force in England'.[61] The *Hue & Cry*, a newspaper published by Bow Street justices, provided useful information about crime, criminals, stolen goods and deserters, and was distributed to all JPs across the country after 1771. John Fielding sent out lists of those suspects his men had arrested and demanded that his fellow justices in the counties reciprocate; in doing so he was effectively attempting to gather criminal intelligence for the very first time.[62]

While primarily serving the capital, the runners were frequently sent outside of London to help local justices and constabulary. Cox argues that 'in several ways the utilization of Principal Officers in provincially instigated cases paved the way for important subsequent developments in policing, especially with regard to detective practices'.[63] Beattie agrees with this analysis, suggesting that we should see the runners as early detectives and as such credit them with significant impact on police history.

However, detection was not part of the remit of the early 'Peelers' (the nickname of the Metropolitan Police), as we shall see. Instead, other functions of the runners, and perhaps more importantly of the men that created them and guided their activities, were later continued by the Met. It is interesting that, as Beattie's study of Bow Street shows, under Sir John Fielding the runners were deployed to police working-class culture in much the same way as the Met were to do after 1829. This role, that Robert Storch has likened to that of 'domestic missionaries',[64] involved 'sending his men to shut down forms of popular entertainment that he and other middle-class men believed led working men into crime, like drinking and gambling, because they lost time and money and encouraged laziness and bad habits that led inevitably to bad companions and bad life choices'.[65] The Bow Street Runners have, until recently, been sadly neglected by academic historians. In part this is due to a paucity of records that allows us to recreate their activities, but the emergence of the *Old Bailey Online* and Beattie's creative use of what at first hand appear unprepossessing primary material have helped restate the importance of the runners to the early history of policing in London and further afield. How this then evolved, with the creation of the Metropolitan Police in 1829, is the subject of the next section of this chapter.

The coming of the professionals

So far this chapter has looked at the nature of policing in England in the period before the creation of professional forces in the nineteenth century. We have seen that England has a long history of amateur and semi-professional policing and that this was one that was based largely on community and locally organized and controlled police, rather than national policing. Despite the claims of early police historians, it is clear that England (and in particular London) was far from being *unpoliced* in the decades prior to 1829. Indeed, there was little that was revolutionary about Peel's reforms in 1829 – uniformed police already existed, as did individuals who earned their living from policing. Moreover, there was some degree of organization (if not at national level) and certainly a recognition that the problems of crime were caused by a range of economic, social and cultural factors. Thus, the questions we need to ask are: first, why did Robert Peel decide to reform the system that was in existence in London? Second, why did it take until 1829 to implement changes that had been in discussion for over fifty years? Third, how did the process of reform change the nature of policing in London and, thereafter, how did this spread to cover the rest of England and Wales? And finally, what was the impact of the so-called 'new police' on communities in England and how were they received by the population?

These are all important questions and historians have generally fallen into three broad camps of opinion with regards to them: orthodox (or Reithian), revisionist (or left-leaning/Marxist) and neo-Reithian (or pragmatist), and these differing views will be analysed and explained. Finally, this chapter will look at the ways in which policing has developed operationally since the creation of the Met in 1829, by looking at the evolution of detection and the limited use of forensics up until the outbreak of war in 1914.

Barriers to professional policing prior to 1829

England had a characteristic distrust of professional policing that was rooted in the legacy of the British Civil Wars and a sense of English political and social freedoms that contrasted sharply with the repressive nature of European states, notably revolutionary and Napoleonic France and Prussia.[66] The English people remembered that Cromwell had used his New Model Army as 'a domestic police' and that this 'evangelical constabulary' had closed down and prohibited many of the popular pastimes enjoyed by ordinary citizens.[67] In addition, her nearest continental neighbour, France, had a long-established system of centrally controlled state police that were anathema to the ideal of the 'free-born Englishman'. Thus, both of these cultural factors were important barriers to any attempt to create professional policing bodies in England. This view was neatly summarized by one writer in December 1811 who wrote (when commenting on a recent and highly publicized series of murders in east London): 'I had rather half a dozen people's throats should be cut in Ratcliffe Highway every three or four years than be subject to domiciliary visits, spies, and all the rest of Fouché's contrivances.'[68]

Alongside this was a prevailing view, outside of London at least, that there was no need for professional police and certainly not one that was controlled by Westminster and funded out of local taxation. Policing, in the form of the parish constabulary, and the Prosecution Associations may have been reactive and amateur but it was relatively inexpensive and was controlled by the local justices. There was, and there continued to be after 1829, considerable resistance to any scheme that would place an extra burden on ratepayers whilst at the same time removing power from prominent local landowners and authority figures. The situation in urban areas was similar; towns were expanding and their populations growing in the late eighteenth century but very few came anywhere close to the size of the capital. Crime and disorder were perennial problems but they had not reached the levels that caused commentators to despair of the existing means of dealing with them. London was different; its size, wealth and opportunities for various forms of property offending, coupled with its widespread poverty, large migrant population and relative lack of community support presented peculiar problems for the authorities. Its role as the seat of government also focused considerable attention on law and order in the capital. But even here there was resistance to change. Local metropolitan parishes petitioned parliament for bills allowing them to raise money to improve the watch and street lighting; the City of London similarly made important reforms of its police in the 1770s and the Fieldings at Bow Street provided a city-wide system of detection.

There were several 'moral panics' about crime across the 1700s culminating in 1780 with the Gordon Riots which saw much of the city devastated by rioting, looting and the destruction of property – including Bow Street and many of the capital's prisons. However, attempts at reform in the wake of the riots were stifled quite quickly by resistance from the City of London, which regarded any attempt at creating a uniform system of police as an infringement upon their authority. A parliamentary bill, introduced by Pitt the Younger's Tory government in 1785, had proposed a system of nine police divisions, comprising foot and mounted police, overseen by a hierarchical command structure that was to be ultimately responsible to the Home Office.[69] After this was defeated the proponents of the bill returned in 1792 with a revised and more limited version that excluded the City and was more closely modelled on Bow Street, and while criticisms resurfaced about the threats to English liberties, these failed to stop the legislation's passage. This bill, which became the Middlesex Justices' Act (1792), created seven 'police offices' across the capital,[70] each staffed by three stipendiary magistrates who were supported by six constables.[71] In 1798, further reform, initiated by Patrick Colquhoun (one of the stipendiary justices operating in the east of London) and West India merchants, established a private river police (which in 1800 became part of the government scheme as the Thames River Police) at Wapping with jurisdiction to police the river, including the stretch that ran through the City.[72] The river police was much larger than the other police offices and could be deployed to help out elsewhere when needed.[73]

While the 1785 bill failed in England, a similar bill was passed by the Irish parliament in Dublin. The Dublin Police Act (1786) created the Irish County Police fifty years before one was introduced to the mainland.[74] This was followed, in 1814, by Robert Peel's Peace Preservation Police and so, as G. A. Minto has suggested,[75] the idea of professional police was tested out on Ireland before it was introduced into England and Wales. The results of the experiment in Ireland no doubt helped persuade Peel of the benefits of introducing such an institution at home. Notwithstanding developments in Ireland, debate about the state of policing in the capital continued, notably with the publication of Colquhoun's *A Treatise on the Police of the Metropolis* (1796) and in the wake of the Ratcliffe Highway murders in 1811. Parliament convened no less than four separate committees to investigate crime and punishment in the capital during between 1812 and 1828 and the report of the 1812 committee resulted in an abortive attempt at passing legislation to improve minimum standards in the parish watch for Middlesex. Again this failed because of local resistance to the removal of individual parishes' own supervisory power.

However, in 1829 Peel managed to obtain parliament's assent to the Metropolitan Police Act, despite the misgivings of an 1822 parliamentary commission which had concluded that:

It is difficult to reconcile an effective system of police, with that perfect freedom of action and exemption from interference, which are the great privileges and blessings of society in this country.[76]

The act resulted in the abolition of the parish-based watching systems and the eventual (if not immediate) amalgamation of the stipendiary magistrates police and the Bow Street officers. This new force took on all the crime prevention roles that had been performed by parochial officers and (albeit much later) the detection roles played by the Bow Street Runners and the stipendiary magistrate's constables. Given the ongoing resistance to any scheme of centrally controlled police, how did Peel manage to convince parliament to pass this legislation and why did he want to in the first place?

Why 1829? Historians' explanations for the coming of the new police

Historians have fallen into three broad and sometimes overlapping camps when it comes to the question of police history. It is hard to improve on Robert Reiner's excellent synthesis of these views[77] but I will make an attempt to at least replicate them here.

The causal factors behind the introduction of the Peel's Metropolitan Police bill in 1829 can be broken down into the following themes: *personalities, events, politics* and *social and economic change.*

Traditional, or orthodox, historians of the police have stressed the importance of the role of Peel alongside a rise in levels of crime in London.[78] Critchley pointed to the state of crime in the capital in the eighteenth century and the reflections of contemporaries such as the Fieldings, Walpole and Colquhoun, all of whom were at pains to argue that London was an unruly, crime-ridden place.[79] From 1810 onwards the official statistics of crime were published (the numbers of individuals indicted for trial, not of course the actual levels of crime) and this appeared to show that offending was on the increase. By the mid-1820s crime rates were rising but, as has been noted earlier in this study, measuring statistics of crime is problematic. The 1820s had seen a major overhaul of the criminal justice system and a rationalization of statutes; so while more crime was being prosecuted it does not necessarily follow that more crime was being committed. However, in the last years of the 1820s there may have been an upsurge in property offending; at the very least the rise in prosecutions may have occasioned a growing concern about property owners' vulnerability to theft.[80]

Linked to this concern about rising levels of crime was a fear of disorder and political protest. The end of war with France in 1815 had brought political radicalism back into focus as well as plunging the nation into an economic downturn that was exacerbated by the return of thousands of demobbed servicemen to Britain. Broadly speaking, revisionist (or conflict) historians have argued that the creation of the police was a response to political radicalism, to the fear of protest from below, rather than a calculated strategy to combat rising levels of crime. This argument is worth exploring, particularly in the context of a series of events that affected England in the early decades of the nineteenth century. For example, Palmer makes an important and persuasive case for seeing the introduction of the new police in the context of a growing climate of unrest in the period 1812–1829.[81]

We have already seen how the Gordon Riots of 1780 unnerved contemporaries and led to calls for police reform. England and Wales have had a long history of popular protest which, for much of the eighteenth century, was tolerated by the authorities so long as it did not spill over into excessive violence or the wanton destruction of property.[82] Crowds in London and throughout the country rioted over grain prices, politics, religion, enclosure of common land, the installation of turnpikes and against community hate figures, and on occasion these protests were suppressed by the military and punished severely but more often were accepted as legitimate expressions of discontent. However, revisionists have argued that the new capitalist class of nineteenth-century England was increasingly uncomfortable with such an unruly populace and came to the conclusion that the rising population and the growing urban centres needed a more disciplined and disciplinary method of policing. Hence, as Storch has argued, the new police were intended to be used as 'domestic missionaries' to pacify and 'civilize' working-class neighbourhoods and the 'maintenance of order required by the new capitalist class'.[83]

England certainly faced a number of challenges in the period between 1812 and the advent of professional policing. In 1811, in east London two families were brutally murdered on the Ratcliffe Highway and the shock of these killings engendered new concerns about the ineffectiveness of the watch and constabulary.[84] This was followed in 1812 with the assassination of Prime Minister Spencer Percival in the lobby of the Houses of Parliament. Further incidents included the Corn Bill Riots in London in March 1815 which, while they were not on the scale of the 1780 disturbances, again exposed the weaknesses of the existing police presence. In addition, there were riots at Spa Fields in 1816 following a demonstration by political radicals, and in 1820 the Cato Street conspiracy was exposed as a group of radicals plotting to blow up the entire cabinet. Then in June 1821 crowds protested in support of Queen Caroline and the military had to be called out to disperse them. While Cato Street and the other incidents of popular protest were ultimately ineffectual, they clearly unnerved the authorities. When these are combined with Luddism (protests against the introduction of new labour saving machinery to textile manufacturing), popular 'risings' at Pentridge and Huddersfield in 1817 and finally, the so-called 'Peterloo massacre' in Manchester in 1819 it is possible to argue that the security of the English state was under strain, if not at risk, and that domestic policing was deemed inadequate without military support.

Here then the views of orthodox and revisionists overlap somewhat; both accept that contemporary concerns about policing underpinned a desire for reform but they explain it in different terms. Orthodox historians stress that it was rising levels of crime, and disorder, coupled with an inadequate and ineffectual system of police that occasioned the need for professional police. Revisionists, by contrast, refute arguments about rising crime and instead place the emphasis on the concerns of the ruling class of growing levels of popular disobedience. Both are linked to another central theme which is the growth of an industrial and urban population.

It is not a matter of dispute that the population of England and Wales was growing rapidly in the late eighteenth and early nineteenth centuries. Nor was the growth of cities something that was ignored by contemporaries: 'What can be stable with these enormous cities?' remarked Lord Liverpool, 'One insurrection in London and all is lost.'[85] But there is little evidence that those in positions of power were unduly concerned about it. Instead, Reiner suggests that reform is better seen as the result of the 'entrepreneurial activities of the reformers themselves, who became dominant in central government' rather than 'an automatic reflex of urbanization and industrial capitalism.'[86] Palmer also makes the important point that 'Conflict historians have tended to ignore or downplay the resistance within the elite to the establishment of a powerful police; hence, they view the propertied class as more unified than it was.'[87] As for crime itself, there is, as has been noted, considerable room for debate about the levels of criminality in the decades immediately preceding the introduction of the Metropolitan Police.

When Peel became Home Secretary in 1822, the need 'for a more effective, a more preventive, police in London was very much on the agenda' but this was confined to discussion about improvement to Bow Street and the operation of the police offices.[88] Work by Randall McGowen on the campaign against forgery in the early decades of the nineteenth century also offers an alternative view of police reform. The operation conducted by the Bank of England's solicitors between 1797 and 1821 'demonstrates' (in McGowen's view) just 'how much could be achieved by existing police arrangements'. By employing constables, thief-takers and informants to catch individuals and gangs involved in counterfeiting bank notes, he argues that the Bank of England 'came close to realizing the ambitions of Henry and John Fielding to create a more efficient police.'[89] At the same time, by using the reward system so effectively, they prompted reformers to call for a system of *public* rather than *private* policing; a system that did not rely on persuading policing agents to act by dangling financial incentives in front of them. Arguments about the quality of the existing policing raged but the notion of national police controlled by central government was not being seriously considered by anyone. So let us turn to the person of Peel himself; how much was he responsible for this major change in British society?

Sir Robert Peel and the creation of the Metropolitan Police

Traditional historians may have been wrong about many of the causes of police reform but the importance of Robert Peel would seem to have been somewhat neglected in the debates about social control and the effectiveness or otherwise of the old police. Peel replaced Henry Addington, Viscount Sidmouth, who had served as Home Secretary from 1812 to 1822 and had overseen a turbulent period in British history. Sidmouth has been described as an 'unimaginative Tory traditionalist' who was 'not the person to press for radical reform of cherished local institutions of the civil power.'[90] Peel, by contrast, was a younger man (just 34 when he took control of the Home Office), ambitious and on the way up. Sidmouth had a well-known reluctance to travel very far from the capital whereas Peel had served as Secretary of State in Ireland and frequently made the journey between London and Ireland. Peel involved himself directly in the policing of the metropolis, looking at the appointment of new constables and the decision-making of the stipendiaries before setting up two committees to look into policing in the capital. This was a man who appeared to buy into the rhetoric of the reformers and had seen the benefits of professional policing in Ireland. Recent work has offered an interesting perspective on Peel and his reforms, particularly with regards to his manipulation of crime rates in the run up to the passing of the 1829 legislation and in the reception of the 1822 committee report into policing. The 1822 report has a passage that has often been quoted in support of an argument that suggests there was no desire for a centrally controlled professional police force in London in the early 1820s. The quote reads as follows:

> It is difficult to reconcile an effective system of police, with that perfect freedom of action and exemption from interference, which are the great privileges and blessings of society in this country; and Your Committee think that the forfeiture or curtailment of such advantages would be too great a sacrifice for improvements in police, or facilities in detection of crime however desirable in themselves if abstractedly considered.[91]

However, Beattie argues that historians have misunderstood this statement – given in response to an 'isolated suggestion made to the committee for the creation of new powers "for the repression of particular abuses"' – because they have taken it out of its context. It was, he continues, 'essentially an aside. There is *not the slightest evidence that the committee stood in the way of an ambitious plan* [my italics] that Peel had hoped to have endorsed. Indeed, it seems clear that he had formed no such plan, that he had no ambition at this point to overturn the current structure.'[92] And perhaps this is key to understanding Peel; he was a pragmatist reformer, *not* a revolutionary. The Metropolitan Police bill passed easily through the Commons, partly due to Peel's skill as a parliamentarian, partly because the house was exhausted by the debates around Catholic emancipation, but also because Peel kept the details of the scheme deliberately vague and uncontroversial. As Palmer wrote, 'the most astounding feature' of Peel's 1829 Police bill was 'its lack of specificity'.[93] In addition, Peel was able to rely upon the support of the Prime Minister, the Duke of Wellington, who was also convinced of the need for an improved police for London, and, furthermore, Peel sensibly excluded the City of London and so avoided resistance from their vested interests.

Beattie's second point is that Peel was able to use the crime statistics to his advantage because he was speaking to 'an audience that did not have to be persuaded' that there was a serious problem with crime in the capital.[94] While the watch (as Reynolds has shown[95]) was much improved by the 1820s and the Bow Street Runners were providing a much improved level of policing throughout the capital, there were still areas of the metropolis that were neglected. As London expanded in the early years of the new century parishes on the outskirts were complaining to Peel that they lacked the funds to sustain a night watch and were consequently served by little more than one or two constables. It is Beattie's conclusion therefore that the 1829 act was passed because 'opposition to a centralized police force under the Home Office had been eroded by the experience of crime over the previous four years', experience that had been augmented by consistent and continued pressure for reform from the press and entrepreneurial reformers.[96] Palmer also noted a change in attitude at the top of society, expressed in support for the measure in the London press; 'The recognition of rising crime and the persistence of popular radicalism led the English ruling classes in 1829 to consolidate their collective interests', he argues.[97]

This debate needs to take account of developments in policing outside of London where resistance to the idea of a centrally controlled police continued well into the mid-1850s but before we return to this it is necessary to look at how the 1829 act changed policing in the capital.

The 1829 Metropolitan Police Act and the characteristics of the 'new police'

While crime prevention was stressed as the first duty of the new police constables, it was only a part of their brief. The new police were a multi-functional body – crime prevention was 'a means to an end'. Underpinning the rationale of the new police was, in the view of the force's earliest historian, Charles Reith, 'the security of the person and property [and] the preservation of the public tranquillity'.[98] And this undoubtedly included the control of a potentially rebellious population. Peel had seen the benefits of centrally organized controlled policing in Ireland and the new force on London's streets brought with it many of the policing practices developed there to deal with civil disobedience. These then were the twin aims of the Metropolitan Police, to prevent crime and to maintain order. What did these new constables look like and how did they operate?

The key features of the Metropolitan Police

Peel's new force was uniformed; this in itself was not particularly novel, the Bow Street Horse patrol and several parish watches wore some semblance of uniform. Care though was taken to distinguish this new civil body from the military – a clear acknowledgement of long-held English concerns about standing armies.[99] Thus, the new officers wore blue swallow tailed coats with little decoration – in marked contrast to the red tunics of the army with their colourful facings and badges.[100] The police wore top hats which served both to give them the presence they required on London streets and to identify them with the citizenry they were serving and policing. The top hat was maintained until 1864 when the more familiar modern style police helmet was introduced. Concerns about militarization were also uppermost in determining the arms and equipment that the new police were issued with. The early officers of the Met were armed with wooden truncheons, and not with side arms or sharp weapons (unlike the Bow Street Patrol who carried cutlasses) and the truncheon were deliberately concealed by their tail coats. Peel was taking a calculated risk in trusting the general public to respect policing without an armed force, but by doing so he made the acceptance of the new police much more likely. Thus, the principle was established (one that persists to this day) that the British policeman is unarmed, unlike forces in America or continental Europe. This also echoed the traditional antecedents of the police, the volunteer citizenry of the constabulary and watch, who carried staffs of office, truncheons and were occasionally issued with swords when necessary (Figure 10.2).

Operationally the 'new' police were very similar to the 'old'; the new officers of the Met did not have a detective role. Instead they were deployed in set 'beats', patrolling day and night and reporting back to watch houses and then, later in the century, to police stations. This meant that, despite the new uniforms, the first officers of the Met (many of whom were recruited from amongst the old watch and constabulary) were very similar to, and had an almost identical role to the old watchmen they replaced. However, the 1829 act did mark some significant breaks with the past.

The new force was salaried and this represented a departure from the old system which had allowed rewards to be paid to runners and constables. While Bow Street Runners had been able to subsist on their share of rewards and their stipend, and watchmen had received a small salary, the latter certainly needed to look for work elsewhere to supplement their wages from policing. The wage paid to the new police

PEELER

On Post.

Figure 10.2 The peeler and the later nineteenth-century policeman: note the differences in their headgear.

officers was initially low, and the intention was to recruit men from the lower classes. Indeed, the authorities were looking to recruit from a similar demographic to that of the armed forces: young, strong, fit and healthy individuals without dependent families that could be trained to follow orders without question. This effectively excluded many (but not all) of the old watchmen of the metropolis and encouraged men from the Bow Street patrols to enrol.[101] Shpayer-Makov concludes that while no 'special skill was demanded save that of a general ability to cope with the job at hand', the Met were careful in selecting recruits.[102] The force was expected to maintain strict rules of discipline. There was to be no drinking on duty, no socializing with the surrounding community and the constables were allowed very little discretion in the carrying out of their duties. In the first year of the force there was a rapid turnover of men as those unable to maintain these standards were quickly weeded out.

The second important way in which the new police differed from the old was in the rigid hierarchical system Peel created to oversee them. There were two Police Commissioners, one with a military background (Lieutenant-Colonel Sir Charles Rowan) and the other drawn from the law (Richard Mayne), both of whom reported to Peel. Below that there were eight superintendents, twenty inspectors, eighty-eight sergeants and 895 constables. This new force was, therefore, significantly smaller than the watch and constabulary it replaced; it was also much more carefully organized and was managed centrally from the Home Office, rather than being administered locally by the vestries or stipendiaries.

So, in summary, this was a quasi-military force which rejected notions of communal self-policing, had the discipline to be used against rioters, but did not have the arms to threaten or alienate the populace. In London the new police soon came under much criticism and opposition but they gradually established themselves as a part of British life. It is worth noting that the old thief-taker model survived in parallel until the stipendiary magistrate's police and the Bow Street Runners were amalgamated in 1839 and debates about the nature of policing continued well into the nineteenth century. Having looked in detail at the emergence of the Metropolitan Police, we can now move on to look at how this model was eventually rolled out across the rest of England and Wales in the next three decades.

The development of national policing

The creation of the Met in 1829 represented an important change in attitudes towards professional policing, but it was the result of a number of interconnecting factors coming together at a moment in history when the conditions were right. In many respects the story of the development of policing in provincial England is very similar. Here a long-established resistance to central interference in local matters, along with concerns about cost to ratepayers, was gradually eroded by a combination of events and changing perceptions about crime and policing.[103]

The coming of the new police to the Boroughs of England was, in contrast to the 1829 Metropolitan Police Act, an indirect by-product of a much larger project. Newly elected after the Great Reform Act of 1832 the Whigs set about attacking what they saw as the corrupt and outdated institutions of the old regime. Amongst the more obvious candidates were the municipal corporations which were thoroughly reformed in 1835. A small part of this reform related to their policing and watching arrangements that had previously often been uncoordinated under various authorities such as the town corporation, the improvement and lighting commissions and private subscription associations (the prosecution associations that were discussed earlier).[104] The new incorporated boroughs were now legally obliged to raise a police force that was to be overseen by a watch committee.[105] The effects of the act varied but it saw the old beadles and watchmen amalgamated into one uniformed police force. Outside of London there was considerable reform of policing going on in the 1820s and 1830s, but pattern of progress towards any semblance of a national police force was piecemeal and the subject of continual and fierce debate. No uniform system of police was established until 1856.

Throughout the period there were multiple outbreaks of rural discontent, (the most serious being the so-called Captain Swing protests in the 1830s in which cattle, horses, hay ricks and farm buildings were the targets of acts of violence and arson) and the system of substitution was coming under considerable criticism.[106] In addition, antipathy towards the new poor law of 1834 manifested itself in attacks on officials and workhouses meaning that, as Rawlings notes, the rural gentry, worried by this unrest, became 'increasingly convinced of the need for a reform of policing'.[107] This move towards reform was driven along without much impetus from the national state and systems of policing were improved by closer supervision by magistrates or vestries.[108] Meanwhile, the position of the parish constable was being called into question more frequently. Not only was the constable ill-equipped to deal with the problems of rural unrest and anti-poor law rioting, but he was also the focus of a power struggle between the vestries and the county bench of JPs. The next central move towards a coordinated system of police outside the capital was the establishment of a parliamentary committee and the distribution of a questionnaire.

This committee was headed by Edwin Chadwick (1800–1890), the individual largely responsible for the Poor Law Amendment Act of 1834 and someone well known to favour a national, centrally run police force.[109] Chadwick sent questionnaires to all quarter sessions divisions in England and Wales asking them a series of (in some respects fairly loaded) questions about their policing arrangements and about crime and disorder in their areas. Respondents were asked to comment on levels of policing, the number of constables, whether they employed substitutes and whether they were deemed adequate. He asked about crime and the ability of the local constabulary to deal with it, and about any outbreaks of arson or other forms of rural protest. Having collected the data Chadwick prepared a report that arguably ignored a prevailing opinion that the provinces rejected the idea of a national police force. In short, the report concluded that crime was on the increase, that criminals were targeting areas where policing was perceived to be weaker, that the parish constabulary were not fit for purpose and that there was no clear correlation between crime and poverty. The commission's recommendations were not translated into legislation because of the ongoing issues surrounding costs and local politics. The bill that emerged from the commission, the County Police Act (or Rural Constabulary Act), was passed fairly quickly because it was a compromise. It opted for a reform model that was permissive rather than compulsory and Chadwick's dreams of a centralist police force were rejected. Instead, county police forces were to be placed under the authority of county quarter sessions. Each quarter session could decide whether to continue with its old arrangements or introduce a new county police force.[110] And this is reflected in the way that police reform happened in the counties.

Because the 1839 act was only *permissive*, not all counties rushed to create police forces. Twenty-one counties adopted the new system for all or part of its jurisdiction, while twenty-four others declined to adopt it at all. There were a variety of reasons that helped explain why some chose to do so. Some counties suffered from outbreaks of rural protests but, as Rawlings makes clear, there 'was no simple connection between rural unrest and the rural police.'[111] Chartism prompted some counties to press for a police force while others reacted to incidents of serious crime, such as a particularly brutal murder; in other places party and local politics played an important role in decisions to adopt the act or not.[112] This came back to concerns about control and the nature of policing outside of the capital. So, objections were based on practical concerns that London-style preventative policing – the beat system – was simply inappropriate for rural areas and was decried as 'watching and suspecting'; or that the reforms shifted control away from the petty sessions, where individual magistrates held sway, and towards the quarter sessions, where the influence of wealthier and landed interests was likely to be more decisive.[113] So, this was not a simple battle between central and local governments but had more to do with struggles within competing authorities at local level, and an avoidance of what can be termed 'county centralization'. [114]

While some counties plumped for a new police and others did not, this did not mean that there was no change in provincial policing before 1856. Some areas took advantage of other legislation or continued with private forms of policing initiatives. The Lighting and Watching Act (1833) allowed vestries to appoint inspectors to hire watchmen and supervise their activities.[115] This kept control of policing in local hands and away from the larger landowners who controlled the quarter sessions. Some rural areas took to the act with enthusiasm as did some unincorporated towns such as Braintree in Essex. However, it does not seem to have been widely adopted. Police could also be funded from the poor rates if justices saw fit to do so, but this was often simply used as a temporary measure to appoint extra constables to deal with outbreaks of trouble associated with opposition to the new poor law. Finally, local areas could create their own private police by raising subscriptions, and this was often done in connection with the prosecution associations.[116]

In 1842, an act more in line with the needs of the gentry and local magistrates was passed. This was used considerably in counties which had not adopted the 1839 act. This act, the Parish Constables Act (1842), had three elements to it. First it required magistrates to draw up lists of those who could be sworn as constables (these men had to be aged

25–55). Second, all substitute constables now had to be approved by the magistrates and finally, parish constables were now to be supervised by paid superintendent constables appointed by the quarter sessions and salaried from the county rate. In 1850, further legislation allowed quarter sessions to appoint these officers for every petty sessions division. The advantage of the act was that it was cheaper; the disadvantage was that parish constables saw little reason to take any notice of these paid superintendents. All these initiatives show, therefore, that the idea of some degree of professional policing was now widely accepted by rural as well as urban elites and helped to pave the way for the 1856 act which brought policing to the whole country.

These new county police operated in much the same ways as their colleagues in London, dealing with petty crime (often poaching and the theft of crops, apples, wood and so forth) but also supervising and regulating popular pastimes (drinking, fairs, gambling and cruel sports), activities that brought them into conflict with the local labouring population.[117] But in doing so they demonstrated their usefulness to the rural property-owning class and the utility of professional policing went some way to overcoming concerns about a loss of local authority over them. In 1853, another parliamentary committee was established to again consider the question of a national police. This committee recommended that county police be mandatory and that the government should be expected to pick up some of the costs of policing. An initial bill was dropped amidst fears that it would provoke local resistance but in 1856 the County and Borough Police Act passed into law. This legislation made it compulsory for all counties and all boroughs to introduce the new police. It was made more palatable by offering to pay a quarter of the expenses of the new force from central government funds. It also left local police forces under local government control but at the same time created a central inspectorate; only if the force demonstrated its efficiency to the inspectorate would it receive this funding.[118]

Why did the 1856 legislation succeed where other attempts had failed? It would seem that again many factors combined to create an atmosphere of acceptance. There were the old arguments about the efficiency or otherwise of the parish constable and a general consensus, born of witnessing the successful application of policing in London, that it was better to have professional detached men to police communities rather than those who were all too deeply involved with it. In addition, Britain was at war with Imperial Russia and troops that had been billeted throughout the countryside were needed to fight in the Crimea. Government let it be known that no longer could counties rely on the military to put down popular unrest, an alternative, civil force, had to be found. As Steedman has noted: 'To many county chief constables, the entire justification for the existence of a rural police was its ability to face a riot and, armed – not always with cutlasses but certainly with batons and the military discipline bestowed by drilling – put down that riot.'[119] There were criminal justice concerns as well: debates surrounding the Penal Servitude Act (1853) – which allowed prisoners to be released early from gaol for good behaviour – were highlighted in the press and this helped to create a widespread concern about 'ticket of leave' men being foisted onto the population, and this was exacerbated by the growing discussion about the end of transportation to Australia.

Britain could no longer export its 'criminal class' and the necessity for a professional crime fighting body had perhaps never before appeared so apparent.

Thus, the widespread acceptance of compulsory policing by 1856 can be attributed to a range of factors including the end of transportation, the withdrawal of troops from northern English counties and the growth of the railways, but Storch and Philips argue that there was also an ideological shift in thinking about police. The year 1856 marked, they argue, a watershed in 'a long and complex process of both ideological change and practical experiment' in which the ruling provincial class had been persuaded of the utility of such a force.[120]

Historians have clashed over the effect that the police have had on British society and on the reactions of the newly policed population, in particular the working classes. Before looking at the development of the police in the late nineteenth and early twentieth centuries, we will look briefly at this historiographical debate.

Reaction – a plague of blue locusts?

The 'new police' constituted the most important innovation in law enforcement in the first half of the nineteenth century.[121]

Perhaps unsurprisingly, given their dismissal of the old system of policing as inefficient and outdated, the early historians were unashamedly positive about the effect that the new force had on British society. Reith was particularly eulogistic, stating that wherever 'the police appeared, they brought with them a new era and new standards of individual liberty'.[122] Critchley dismissed early opposition to the new police, not in terms of the conflicting interests of different social groups that the revisionists were later to do, but as irrational and reactionary and led by professional criminals. Radzinowicz notes that even members of parliament who had opposed the formation of professional police forces in the 1820s had, by the middle of the following decade, been persuaded to change their minds by the 'admirable manner in which [the police] performed its duties'.[123] Opposition faded away, this account tells us, when the police established themselves and demonstrated their fairness towards all classes. For orthodox historians then, the impact of the new force was in solving the problems of order and lawlessness. The new police protected private property, and often this was the property and persons of the poor, and they did not subject the working class to processes they did not deserve. So, everyone gained and the police were seen as an unequivocally beneficial institution.

It is easy to dismiss this rosy analysis of the new institution of professional policing but it is probably worth recognizing that by the outbreak of war in 1914 the police had largely come to be accepted as a part of daily life in Britain.[124] However, this process had taken much longer than Reith and Critchley suggested and arguably, resistance to the police from some sections of society (and not simply from criminals) continued well into the twentieth century (and indeed still continues in the twenty-first).

The revisionist attack on this consensus model of history began in the 1970s. Robert Storch saw opposition to the new police as having a direct link with Marxist theories of class conflict. He also gave this opposition a much higher profile than Reith had, and argued that it persisted. According to Storch and Philips, the gentry were reluctant to let go of their power over policing (particularly in the provinces) but this faded as they began to see the usefulness of the police as a bulwark against popular radicalism. Instead, the bulk of opposition came from the working classes – to them the police were a 'plague of blue locusts'.[125] Importantly, it was not simply the criminal of 'rough' element that opposed the police, nor just those radicalized by Chartism or the campaign for parliamentary representation.[126] The working class, particularly in the north of England, opposed, rioted against and assaulted the new police when they attempted to interfere with their leisure activities, street life and their drinking habits. For example, the 'statistics suggest that, during the 1860s, a Middlesborough policeman might expect an assault twice a year'.[127] Clashes between workers and police were notably more frequent during industrial disputes as the police were sent in to break up strikes and marshal demonstrations.[128]

For revisionists the long-term impact of the introduction of the new police was the transformation of England into a policed society – a 'policeman state' as Gatrell has termed it.[129] The result, as Alan Silver has argued, is 'that central power exercises potentially violent supervision over the population by bureaucratic means widely diffused throughout civil society in small and discretionary operations that are capable of rapid concentration'.[130] Thus, for the revisionists the impact of the must be analysed in class terms. The penetration of the political and moral authority of the dominant elite into working class life pictured the policeman as a 'domestic missionary',[131] who took the values of the central authorities with him into the communities of the poor.

While the revisionist critique of early police history is persuasive, it is itself open to criticism. In its attempt to define police history in purely class terms, it has failed to appreciate the ability of the police to win over the majority of the population, albeit reluctantly at first, so that opposition tended to be partial and driven by events. As Phillips (for the Black Country) and Davis (for London) have shown, the working class, while resenting some of the activities of the police (largely in relation to their attempts to police morals or to interfere in employment disputes), were prepared to use the police when it suited them.[132] As Reiner puts it, many 'working-class people accepted the basic legitimacy of the laws protecting property, and the agents who enforced them, however much they may have resented certain specific aspects of property law which were clearly class-biased in intent and practice'.[133] There have also been a series of case studies of policing across the country that have demonstrated that reactions to the introduction of a more formalized and professional system of policing were affected by local conditions and initiatives.[134] Moreover, we need to be careful about seeing opposition in simple class terms because it is very hard to argue that the elite, middle or working class can ever be described as united or as presenting a group ideology. There were factions within elite society who both opposed and welcomed police reform, and we have seen the divisions between smaller property owners and the larger landowners who dominated quarter sessions. The working classes were equally split over issues such as politics, race and religion and it would be hard, if not impossible, to try and argue that there was one *working-class* view of policing. More realistically, it would seem that members of society at all social levels saw the new police as a necessary 'evil', useful when needed, a financial burden at times, and a nuisance or oppressive force at others.

So far this chapter has charted the development of policing in England from the late seventeenth to the mid-nineteenth century, and has considered some of debates that have surrounded it. In closing we need to look at later developments and in particular at the role of detection.

The rise of the detective

We should remember that one of the fundamental objections to the creation of professional police forces was a concern that this might echo continental experiments with state run police who operated surveillance networks for their monarchs and governments; and Robert Peel famously declared, *God forbid that [I] should mean to countenance a system of espionage*.[135] Hence, when the new officers of the Met took to the streets in October 1829, there was no detective branch and no detectives. As Beattie has shown, this represented a continuation of the watching and patrolling functions of the 'old' police rather than that of the more investigative and proactive approach of the Bow Street Runners.[136] Bow Street had been the model for the creation of the seven London police offices in 1792 but by 1829 the necessity of detection seems to have disappeared. It took a little while for detection to become rooted within everyday police work and its development was, as with much of police history, piecemeal and driven by events. Historians of the police have, until recently, had relatively little to say about the rise of the detective, but this has begun to change in recent years, notably with the publication of Haia Shpayer-Makov's major study of the English detective.[137]

Antipathy towards any form of policing that hinted at continental systems of espionage resurfaced soon after the creation of the Metropolitan Police. Between February 1832 and March 1833, Sergeant William Popay infiltrated the working-class National Political Union, posing as a 'militant member who supported violent tactics'.[138] Regardless of claim that Popay was acting independently of any instruction from his superiors, the negative reaction that this revelation of supposed spying by a serving officer (acting as an 'agent provocateur'[139]) engendered in the press and public did little to advance the beneficial nature of detection to a wider audience.[140] Thereafter however, a series of incidents began to change attitudes within, and outside of Westminster. The first of these was the murder of Lord William Russell in May 1840. Russell was killed at his home in what at first appeared to have been a burglary but it was later discovered that the killer was his manservant, Francis Courvoisier. Two days after the murder *The Times* criticized the police for its failure to solve the mystery, or even find any clues, and called for the reinstatement of the Bow Street Runners who had been disbanded a year earlier. The case of Daniel Good in April 1842 caused further consternation in the press. Good had murdered his wife, escaped from custody and had gone on the run for fifteen days, only being caught by chance. In the same month there was the first of several attempts on the life of Queen Victoria. In consequence, as Shpayer-Makov argues, 'the press served as a pressure group lobbying for improved detection'. And this seems to have worked because both incidents prompted the establishment of the Detective Department in August 1842 at Scotland Yard, with a compliment of two inspectors and six sergeants. This was of course a very small step forward and the new department actually consisted of fewer detectives than had operated out of Bow Street until 1839, but it was start.[141]

While the Met's two Commissioners, Mayne and Rowan, expressed concerns in public about the use of disguises in detective work, they acknowledged its usefulness in private. This reflects the underlying battle between public policing and any hint of spying. However, the idea of detection gained ground within the public in the 1860s because of a number of incidents that suggested the need for a more intelligence-based form of policingrather than simple patrolling, and because of a related growth in popular fiction that championed and romanticized the science of detection.

In 1862, the so-called 'garrotting panic' suggested that the streets of London and other major urban centres were unsafe and infested with violent robbers[142]; the end of transportation to Australia and the Penal Servitude Acts (1853 and 1864) raised concerns about ticket-of-leave men, while the Clerkenwell prison bombing of 1867 heightened fears of Fenian terrorism. The result of all these factors was the establishment of a new committee to look into the state of policing and detection in the capital. The Clerkenwell bomb had also prompted the resignation of Commissioner Mayne and his replacement, Colonel Edmund Henderson, undertook a thorough overhaul of the Met's detective branch. Henderson placed 'anticipatory action' at the heart of Scotland Yard's detective strategy and set his men to undertake a greater surveillance of criminals and to intelligence gathering on a larger scale than had been seen previously. As Shpayer-Makov has noted, to some degree 'this strategy was a sequel to that initiated by the Fieldings of gathering criminal intelligence not only for immediate purposes but with a view to storing it for future use'.[143] Again we can see that the Bow Street operation had in many ways been ahead of its time. Henderson's detectives were able to use the Habitual Criminals Act (1869) and the Prevention of Crimes Act (1871), both of which were predicated on a need to gather more criminal intelligence of former convicts including using the new science of photography.

Thus, detection seemed to be progressing well towards becoming an established part of police work. There were still relatively small numbers of detectives and most 'detection' was being carried out by ordinary uniformed policemen, albeit sometimes in plain clothes.[144] Then in 1877, an event hit Scotland Yard that threatened to undo all the progress that had been made so far. The Turf scandal of 1877 undermined confidence in the detective department and ultimately led to a change of name and a reorganization. Three chief inspectors were accused of fraud and the subsequent trial 'left a stigma on the reputation of all detectives'. A parliamentary committee – The Departmental Commission on the State, Discipline, and Organisation of the Detective Force of the Metropolitan Police (1878) – recommended a reorganization of the detective force, and even a national detective agency.[145] Instead, the Criminal Investigation Department (CID) was founded, which did not, notably, include the name 'Detective'. CID was headed by Howard Vincent, someone who did not have a background in policing and so was untainted by the scandal of the turf fraud. The first superintendent CID was Fredrick Adolphus 'Dolly' Williamson, who had survived the turf scandal, and who was eventually to rise to the rank of Chief Constable.

In 1880, a Convict Supervision Office was established at Scotland Yard that could coordinate criminal intelligence gathering and distribute or make available this information to all police forces throughout the country. In addition, from 1883 the Met took over the publication and distribution of the *Police Gazette*, which reported details of crime and criminals. These developments 'contributed to the emergence of Scotland Yard as an informal national resource'.[146] CID officers were regularly sent out to help provincial forces (as indeed had the old Bow Street Runners before and after the Met's creation[147]), which while it might have helped solve crimes was not unproblematic. The growing reputation of Scotland Yard created tensions both within the Met and with provincial forces. But it was the use of London officers in provincial investigations, and the publicity given to particular individuals (such as Detective Inspector Whicher) that helped to cement the idea of the detective in the public mind.[148] The public began to warm to the idea of the detective, and characters in popular fiction such as Dickens's Inspector Bucket in *Bleak House* (based on the real-life Detective Inspector Field) helped glamourize the role. Sgt Cuff in *The Moonstone* and then Sherlock Holmes firmly established the detective in the public psyche in the last decades of the 1800s. The short stories of Conan Doyle, while representing a critique of the police in the character of 'that imbecile Lestrade' demonstrated the value of detection in the capture of criminals and the prevention of crime. Acceptance of the detective now began to overtake the negative view of them as undercover spies. This in turn was strengthened by the development of the concept of the 'criminal class' and so the need to counter this threat with professionals adept at catching them. In short, 'a new, widely disseminated image of the criminal as a professional implied the necessity for more sophisticated skills on the part of crime fighters'.[149]

Indeed this process would appear to have been completed with the creation of Special Branch as a subdivision of CID in 1883. Special Branch (or the Special Irish Branch as it was originally titled) was formed as a counter to increased Irish Republican terrorism in the 1880s.[150] The government and press began to accept that some sort of covert policing might be necessary to fight a different sort of criminal, the politically motivated and indiscriminate terrorist. Special Branch moved on from surveillance of Fenians to other political targets such as anarchists and socialists and immigrant groups suspected of being involved in plots to murder European monarchs and ministers.

The failure to capture the elusive 'Jack the Ripper' in 1888 again prompted widespread criticism of the police and its methods of detection but the resources at their disposal were limited. Forensic detection was in its infancy and with no clear links between victims and the killer it would have taken a piece of luck to have caught the murderer. There were relatively few developments in forensics in the late nineteenth century that could help these new detectives but in 1894 Scotland Yard began to use Alphonse Bertillon's anthropometric system for the identification of criminals by 'measuring certain parts of the body of the criminal to form a unique portrait'.[151] In 1901, a fingerprint bureau was established at the Yard and the first investigation to successfully utilize fingerprinting was in 1902 in the trial of Henry Jackson for burglary. However, the principle of detection, in London at least, was well established and the position of Scotland Yard at the centre of this was equally important. As Shpayar-Makov concludes, 'By the outbreak of war [in 1914], it had long been assumed that, even if private detection had a role to play in society, when crime called for a professional response, official detectives became essential.'[152] Thus, by the end of the period covered by this book policing had gone from an amateur victim-led and reactive system to a well-established, public and professional vocation with specialized individuals and a clear hierarchical structure.

Concluding remarks on policing

In concluding, all that remains is to note that the police were still finding their feet in late Victorian England; while they were largely accepted as part and parcel of British life they still had some way to go to reaching the esteemed status of the 'great British bobby' (as represented by the character of PC Dixon of Dock Green[153]) in the so-called 'golden age of policing' in the 1950s. Popular culture still denigrated the beat bobby, as the music hall ditty 'If you want to know the time, ask a P'liceman' (which first emerged during the Whitechapel murders) shows. As Emsley noted, the 'implicit joke for the knowing working-class audience, was that the "p'liceman" would have acquired his watch and chain from the drunk he had rolled out of the road'.[154] Police in-house journals, such as the *Police Service Advertiser* (launched in 1866) functioned as both a debating forum and self-help organ. By changing its name to the *Police Guardian* in 1872 it reasserted its position as the voice of the ordinary policeman. In 1893 the *Police Review and Parade Gossip* arrived packed with news and opinion on police work and conditions as well as stories and even poems from serving officers. The aim was to create a positive image of policemen and police work and to redress what the editors saw as:

> a tendency, all too prevalent, as evidenced on the stage and in the comic Press, as well as on the public footpath, to treat a policeman with less regard for his own self-respect than should prevail amongst men towards their fellow-men in all ranks of life.[155]

Publications such as this helped in the 'process of constituting "policeman as a class"'.[156]

Historians looking at the police have embraced new disciplines and initiatives with historical research to explore policing. One of these has been recent work that considers the place of the policeman in the history of masculinities and in contrast to the European and colonial development of policing. European and English police forces developed quite differently but there are also clear overlaps and shared experiences.[157] We also have seen the recent publication of research that has examined the way that the individual policeman has operated on the 'front line' and the effect that the changing nature of policing institutions have had on those tasked with policing communities.[158] While there has been the beginning of work on the role of the detective and the development of forensic science and 'modern' methods of policing, there is still much we need to learn about this. Too often histories of policing have been parochial or administrative and more research needs to be done to explore the reasons for the piecemeal introduction of forces after 1839.[159] There is also probably room for some more work on the Prosecution Associations and the extent to which they continued into the nineteenth century.

Finally, I would like to suggest that the fundamental change in policing is similar to the change in prosecution: The state has increasingly taken over a role that was performed by what might loosely be termed a collective male citizenship. We have lost the participatory aspect of the criminal justice system as we have distanced ourselves from the process itself. Eighteenth-century Londoners routinely assisted victims of crime by helping to capture thieves; now we are strongly advised to avoid such displays of bravado lest we get injured or expose ourselves to a counter prosecution by the criminal himself. As McGowen has noted, this was very different in the past when the 'fact that so much of law enforcement was carried on by private initiative meant that knowledge of what to do, as well as the willingness to undertake it, were shared by many more people than would be true after the introduction of a "reformed" police'.[160] As a consequence the police have assumed, for some at least, the position of our keepers rather than our servants; increasingly, the police represent the state rather than serving its people. I think the police themselves have recognized this and the reintroduction of amateur volunteers (in the shape of the special constabulary and Police Support Volunteers) as well as local liaison officers, all reflect attempts by the police to operate as a part of their communities. The 1980s perhaps represent the nadir of public/police relations and greater accountability, and a desire to distance themselves from whichever home secretary is in power has probably meant that modern police officers are intent on being loved and respected more. To some extent of course, our relationship with the police is very personal and coloured by experience and there is little the police can do about that. It is worth remembering how policing evolved in England, and recognizing that historically the public have always played an important role in combatting crime and criminals as well as challenging the worst excesses of organized police.

CHAPTER 11

REMOVING THE VICTIM? THE CHANGING NATURE OF PROSECUTION IN THE COURTS IN ENGLAND

The court system

It is useful to conceptualize the eighteenth-century criminal justice system as operating as a two-tier system. At the base was the summary process and above that a layer of jury courts. The summary process was operated by the magistracy – the justices of the peace (JPs) who acted alone or in pairs, without juries but with a wide range of powers and discretion as we saw in Chapter 9.

It might be helpful here to imagine the path of any given criminal act and its prosecution in the eighteenth century, just as we did with the theft of my bicycle in the twenty-first. Figure 11.1 shows a potential route for anyone accused of an offence in this period.

In the first instance, the victim of a pick-pocketing in the 1700s had a number of decisions to make. First, he or she might be expected to attempt to catch the perpetrator immediately if, say, he was aware of the theft as or soon after it happened. He could raise the 'hue and cry' and give chase, as bystanders were expected, indeed duty bound, to come to his aid. The Hanoverian criminal justice system was a victim-led system; before 1829 there were no professional trained policemen (although help with the apprehension of criminals was available, as Chapter 10 demonstrated). The process was also time consuming and potentially expensive, so for a minor loss the victim may have decided to do nothing. However, let us assume the culprit was detained, maybe with the assistance of a volunteer policing agent such as a parish constable, and an upstanding member of the public.

The victim's next move would be to take the culprit before a JP, perhaps after having had them confined to a lockup gaol (a compter) or watch house overnight. The JP would hear the complaint of the victim, listen to witnesses and the accused and then determine what to do next. According to the law, if there was any evidence of theft, the JP was then obliged to commit the accused to gaol to await trial or take sureties against his appearance there (bail). However, in London and possibly elsewhere, many cases simply dropped out of the system at this stage. Why was this? The answer is that on many occasions JPs appear to have dismissed cases on the grounds that there was insufficient

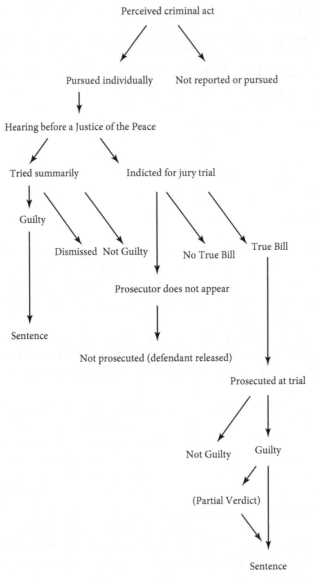

Figure 11.1 The defendant's possible pathway through the justice system.

evidence to proceed to a jury trial. Alternatively, the victim reached an agreement with the thief that ensured they got their goods back, perhaps with some compensation. This would end the matter at this early stage. However, if neither of these scenarios played out then the justice would formally indict the offender and the case would proceed to trial.

The ecclesiastic courts of England: A very brief overview

Before we look at the operation of the jury courts, it is important to acknowledge that England had another layer of courts that were a legacy of the medieval and early modern period.[1] Without wishing to dwell on this at any length there were a series of church courts that had dealt with many offences that were later heard by justices in or out of sessions. Early modern people appear to have been very litigious, using the law to sue one another and to bring private prosecutions for all manner of wrongs. Many of these came before the ecclesiastical courts where the church acted (or attempted to act) 'to control crime and disorder and to regulate many aspects of social life'.[2] Church courts had several functions, including licensing, determining issues of doctrine and administration, but the one that most links them to the later role of the JP was in the control of morality and behaviour. So consistory courts (church courts) acted to correct 'bad' behaviour; this correction had to do with religious law, with spiritual nonconformity, but also defamation, drunkenness, swearing and many other issues. In fact, the 'corrective powers of the church extended, therefore, over a wide range of human behaviour, taking in not only spiritual concerns but communal discord, martial arrangements and sexual misbehaviour' (which might include adultery, fornication or even incest).[3] From the late seventeenth century onwards, as the desire to prosecute religious dissent waned, many of these functions were assumed by parochial officers (such as church wardens) and later groups such as the Reformation of Manners movements took prosecutions before the justices and not the church courts. As a result, the ecclesiastical courts faded before nineteenth-century statutes removed their power to deal with divorce, defamation and the regulation of probate.

Let us return then to our defendant and his path through the judicial system.

The jury courts: Quarter sessions and assizes

If the accused were committed, they would appear before either the quarter sessions or assizes courts (see Figure 11.2); if they were in London they would take their trial at the Old Bailey which operated as a sort of amalgam of both quarter sessions and assize (and so will be treated separately here).

Both quarter sessions and assizes shared some common characteristics: both had two juries – Grand and Petty – presided over by a judge (or judges) and both were able to hear an extensive variety of offences and hand down a wide range of punishments. Both sat in public and were highly ritualized affairs. But they also had important differences; most notably, the assize was the only court with the power of life and death and so it tended to deal with the more serious offences throughout the eighteenth century.

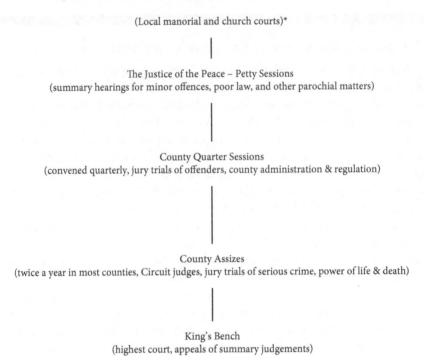

(Local manorial and church courts)*

|

The Justice of the Peace – Petty Sessions
(summary hearings for minor offences, poor law, and other parochial matters)

|

County Quarter Sessions
(convened quarterly, jury trials of offenders, county administration & regulation)

|

County Assizes
(twice a year in most counties, Circuit judges, jury trials of serious crime, power of life & death)

|

King's Bench
(highest court, appeals of summary judgements)

* largely in decline throughout the 1700s

Figure 11.2 The eighteenth-century court system.

Quarter sessions was the lesser court and, outside of the capital at least, each county convened quarter sessions, as the name suggests, four times a year. Sessions met at Epiphany, Lent (or Easter), Summer and Michaelmas and the judges were drawn from the registered JPs on the county list. JPs (whose commitment to their judicial work varied enormously) were expected to attend at least one sessions in each quarter although it seems likely, from the records that have survived, that a handful of men sat regularly in each county and took on most of the judicial work there.[4] The quarter sessions court dealt with a wide range of offending as well as a considerable amount of what might be described as civil and administrative business. Before the reformation of local government in the nineteenth century the quarter sessions was the effective governing authority in English counties, where power was exercised 'in the name of the king but in the interest of the locality'.[5] So the courts heard cases of petty theft, particularly petty larcenies (the theft of goods valued at under a shilling) or thefts that, in other words, did not demand the death sentence for those convicted. This could also involve other forms of property crime, such as receiving stolen goods or fraud, which did not attract the death penalty. However, all these cases could be (and were) heard at the assizes. It is important to note as well that the victim could also bring a case directly to the jury courts without going before a justice in the first instance. Occasionally the presiding county justices at quarter sessions would also leave cases, especially those that seemed more complex, to the more experienced (professional) judges that sat at the assizes.[6]

As well as minor property crime the quarter sessions also dealt with petty violence. Accusations of assault (a term that, as we saw in Chapter 3, covered a wide range of violent actions) were heard here and punished by fines and, more rarely, short periods of imprisonment. Most assaults were handled at summary level, so the ones that came to quarter sessions may have been those considered more serious or those that were unable to be resolved by the justices. The quarter sessions bench and juries also sat in judgement on riotous behaviour (although riot, as a capital offence, was more likely to be taken to the assizes); some other forms of disorderly or antisocial behaviour; sexual offences such as bigamy, as well as a tremendous amount of business that was largely non-criminal that involved infringements of tax law, trading violations (such as selling goods at short weight or selling alcohol without a licence) and various offences relating to the maintenance of, or driving on, the highways and byways. The quarter sessions bench (the magistrates) also reported on the operation of the poor laws, the state of the county gaols, set prices for bread and in effect carried out much of the business we would now associate with a borough or county council or municipal authority.

Criminal offenders found guilty at the quarter sessions could expect to be sentenced in the main to a short spell of imprisonment (in the local gaol or house of correction), or to be fined (anything from a shilling to larger sums of several pounds); some were also sentenced to be physically and publicly whipped and (after 1718) more serious property offenders were ordered to be transported to the colonies. Thus, we should see the quarter sessions as an integral part of county life rather than merely as an arm of the criminal justice system. Indeed, for both quarter sessions and assizes this represented a coming together of the 'county community'; the wealthy landed elite who exercised power.[7] This was even more evident in the biannual assizes.

The official term for the assize was: *The Commission of the Peace, and Oyer and Terminer, and Gaol-Delivery, held for the County of [wherever]*. This was because the assizes judges arrived in the county town twice each year (except in certain specific counties which held only one assize[8]) and *delivered* the local gaol. This meant they heard the trials of all those held in the goals who may have been waiting there for six months (or sometimes more) for the courts to convene, having been indicted for trial and unable to obtain bail. *Oyer and terminer* simply means 'to hear and determine' and is taken from the Norman French, so the preamble at the beginning of all assize (and Old Bailey) sessions indicates that the presiding judges were formally commissioned and appointed to adjudicate on the trials of those formally indicted for felonies.[9]

The judges were drawn from the high courts in London and arrived in the county with great 'pomp and circumstance', proceeded by javelin men in a colourful parade. The county elite would gather and there would be balls, banquets and an opportunity for networking and display.[10] Before the assize opened a local cleric would read the assize sermon and set the tone for the forthcoming trials of offenders. David Eastwood sums up the importance of the assizes very well in this passage:

This weaving of show and parade with the power of life and death at the Assizes demonstrated unequivocally the interconnectedness of symbolic and substantive power which was wholly characteristic of the public culture of Hanoverian England.[11]

The peculiarity of London and Middlesex: The Old Bailey sessions

The City of London and the County of Middlesex were separate jurisdictions in law. However, trials for both were held at the Old Bailey in the City. The City's chief magistrate was the Lord Mayor, and he and his fellow City justices were entitled to sit on the Old Bailey bench 'if they chose'.[12] The Old Bailey sessions (after 1669) met eight times a year 'between the four law terms and the two assize circuits', meaning that they sat in January, February, April, May, June, August, October and December. As Beattie points out, the sessions of the peace in the City and Middlesex 'sat at the same time' because unlike the jury courts outside of the capital (which operated independently) London's were closely interconnected. The capital had two jurisdictions, the City and Middlesex, and each held its own sessions of the peace. Two days before the Old Bailey court convened, the capital's magistracy opened the sessions of the peace at the Guildhall in the City of London. In Middlesex the justices sat at Hicks Hall. Those accused of petty offences (misdemeanours) were brought up and put on their trials before a bench of JPs and a jury. After two days the sessions were adjourned and the senior figures from the City of London (the Lord Mayor and the Recorder) joined three high court judges at the Old Bailey for what was in effect the capital's assizes. Middlesex justices were not included (Middlesex justices were considered to be beneath those of the City in social status) and so the grand jury at Hicks Hall continued to sit and send 'true bills' to the Old Bailey in the meantime. Thus, there was a similar, if different, symbiotic relationship between the Middlesex sessions and those of the City. This has implications for researchers: while outside of London quarter sessions and assize records are quite separate, those produced by the London courts are contained in 'one composite file' and 'a single Minute Book' for each jurisdiction (i.e. one for the City and one for Middlesex).[13]

The judges that sat at the Old Bailey were a mix of common law (high court) judges, City JPs, the Lord Mayor (the City's chief magistrate), the Recorder of London (the principal legal officer for the City) and the Common Sergeant (who advised the ruling council of the City on legal matters). In practice the senior common law judges took the most serious cases, leaving the more minor trials to the other magistracy.

In effect this close cooperation between the courts of London and Middlesex explains why it was 'possible for them to leave all property offences to the Old Bailey and to reserve for their own sessions of the peace the large majority of misdemeanours'.[14] It would also help explain the actions of City justices who frequently dealt with minor property offences themselves, choosing not to formally indict offenders for trial at the Old Bailey; after all they were, as regular attenders at Old Bailey, well aware of the large workload of the court and might have considered themselves able to filter out cases that were unlikely to be deemed 'true bills' by the grand jury.

The first purpose-built sessions house at the Old Bailey was erected in 1539. The building was named after the street in the City of London on which it was situated and it stood adjacent (and connected) to Newgate gaol. The original sessions house was burned down in the Great Fire of 1666 and replaced by a new one in 1673, and part of the courtroom was open to allow the air to circulate. This was designed to prevent infection but in 1737 the court was enclosed (possibly because the City wanted to limit the numbers of spectators).[15] When, in 1750 and 1752, a reoccurrence of 'gaol fever' (or more properly, typhus) in Newgate killed many prisoners as well as a number of justices and other officials, the architect George Dance was appointed to rebuild the gaol and the adjacent sessions house.[16] The new sessions house was completed in 1774. A second courtroom was added in 1824 before Newgate was demolished to make way for the Central Criminal Court in 1907, which (with some modern repairs and alterations) stands to this day.

Before we continue let us look at the three key components of the eighteenth-century trial (judge, jury and legal counsel) in a little more detail.

The eighteenth-century jury trial

The eighteenth-century trial was a very formal affair but it was also public and a much less sanitized occasion than is the case with modern trials. Before the legal profession fully took over the procedures of the court (a slow process that began in the late eighteenth century) the accused, the prosecutor (who was also the victim in most cases) jury and the audience (if we can call them that) all played an active part in the proceedings. John Langbein has described the early modern and eighteenth-century trial as 'an altercation' between the victim of crime as prosecutor and the defendant. The former could, but seldom did, employ the services of a lawyer while, except in certain circumstances, the latter was formally prohibited from doing so.[17] Throughout, there appears to have been relatively little emphasis on evidence (something which continues to surprise twenty-first-century observers) and the exercise of a great deal of discretion.

Judges and the judiciary

The integrity of the English judiciary had been questioned in the aftermath of the restoration of the monarchy (1660) as a result of the actions of prominent judges such as the notorious George Jeffreys and William Scroggs.[18] These judges represent the worst excesses of the judiciary at a period in time in which the courts acted as a political tool, with scant regard for evidence or any semblance of the principle of a 'fair trial'.[19] Their careers remind us that the judiciary and politics were not considered separate or unconnected worlds in the early modern period.[20] William, Lord Mansfield, who served as Lord Chief Justice from 1756 to 1788, had trained as a barrister at Lincoln's Inn before entering politics. He rose to the position of Attorney General and then Lord Chief Justice and carved out a reputation as a reformer. In contrast with Jeffreys and Scroggs, Mansfield appears to represent Enlightenment thinking and is credited with reforming the way the law operated, notably commercial law, and with smoothing the legal path for the abolition of the slave trade. But of course Lord Mansfield also presided as a judge at the Old Bailey, passing sentences of death on numerous property criminals.[21] Anyone that appears in a modern crown court or attends the Old Bailey today can hardly fail to notice that these courts appear to operate with a strange meshing of modern technology and quite ancient tradition; witnesses can be examined via video link by barristers dressed in robes before a judge wearing a wig that would not look out place in an eighteenth-century costume drama. So, without wishing to go into great detail about the make-up of the judiciary, it will be helpful to have a brief overview of its structure and roles.

Judges were drawn from the three common law courts of King's (or Queen's) Bench, Common Pleas and Exchequer. The most senior judges in eighteenth-century England were the Lord Chancellor and the Chief Justice of the King's Bench. In addition, there was the Chief Justice of Common Pleas ('Common Bench'), who presided over the court of Common Pleas (or 'Common Bench') that dealt with actions between subjects (in other words, those that did not concern the monarch). In effect this meant civil cases (recovery of debts or property) that were heard at Westminster Hall in London, rather than criminal ones.[22] The Court of Exchequer, alongside Chancery (which superseded it in 1841) dealt with equity matters and its head was the Chief Baron. The most senior position in Chancery was held by the Master of the Rolls (who today is the second most senior judge in England).

The judges sat in rotation in London, aided by the chief magistrate of the City of London (the Lord Mayor) and its chief legal officer, the Recorder of London. The county assizes were presided over by judges from the high courts in London who travelled around the country in *circuits* (hence the name, 'circuit' judge) 'delivering' the county gaols.[23] They were wealthy men who had carved out careers at the bar in London before being appointed as judges; many served as MPs and 'several were given peerages'.[24] These men therefore had a great knowledge of the law but when they came up across a case that presented complex legal questions they felt unable to rule upon, they could refer judgments to the Twelve Judges of England. The 'Twelve' were formally appointed by the Prime Minster and Lord Chancellor. Whilst there was no formal appeal process in criminal trials, if a judge on circuit felt that issues of law raised by a conviction might be unsafe he could turn to the Twelve.[25] This was a rare occurrence however, on average only eight cases were sent to the Twelve per annum and of these only 'about 40 per cent of convictions were overturned or amended as a result'.[26] Eighteenth-century judges therefore operated with relatively little scrutiny (if not to the excessive degree characterized by Jeffreys and Scroggs) and reflected the patrician nature of their society. Judges also tended to be selected after a period of service at the bar, so most were old (by the late 1800s the average age at appointment was 57). They rarely retired and so they tended to die in office, and no English judge has *ever* been removed from office. Again, it is worth noting that the men that presided over the trials (and who handed down sentences of death and transportation) on prisoners up and down the country (prisoners who were predominantly young working-class males) were rich, well educated and aged members of the English elite.

The role of the judge was to conduct the trial; to summarize the evidence presented and direct the jury on points of law. The judge therefore had an important relationship with the unpaid members of the jury both as the gatekeeper to the law and as grand foreman of court procedure. Ultimately, judge and jury needed to work together if the process of justice was to run smoothly. But at the same time the judge was also there as the first advocate of the accused, at least until the gradual emergence of defence counsel in the later 1700s. This curious contradiction (in the sense that the defendant was largely reliant in court upon the person who held the power of his life and death in their hands) is further highlighted by the great social distance that existed between elite judges and impoverished defendants.[27] This distance was a crucial element in what one historian has argued was the function of the criminal justice system as means of preserving the hegemony of the ruling class.[28]

As was noted earlier, the arrival of the assizes judges in a county town was highly ritualized and was accompanied by considerable pomp; once in court, 'the judges' every action was governed by the importance of spectacle'.[29] Douglas Hay describes a process by which the local populace was awed by the presence of the capital's judiciary and captivated by the theatre of the assizes. The judge sat at the apex of the criminal trial – literally raised above the commons – representing the 'majesty' of the Law. However, the reality seems a little different, many courtrooms were in fact crowded, rowdy and boisterous spaces where judges struggled to keep order.[30] Linebaugh has described the 'counter-theatre of the Old Bailey' Yard where pockets of 'an Idle and Disorderly Crew' maintained a hubbub of commentary on the doings of the court.[31]

The extent to which the crowd within the Hanoverian courtroom actually influenced the judges that presided there is hard to say because following sentencing, decisions concerning mercy and clemency were taken behind closed doors. It is much easier to believe that the crowd were able to influence the jury however, and their role and composition will be considered next.

The trial juries: Grand jury and petty jury

The legal principle that underpinned the trial in the eighteenth century was that every man had a right to be judged by his peers. This had been emphasized by the struggles of the British Civil Wars and had emerged as 'the sacred bulwark of the nation'.[32] In reality however, very few people were tried by their social equals. As we shall see, juries were made up of persons of property whilst the majority of those that they sat in judgment upon were members of the labouring poor. This had not always been the case; in the period before the English Civil Wars it seems that larger numbers of people served as jurors and these were likely to have represented a wider spectrum of society. But from the 1650s onwards the numbers called forward was reduced and the social status of jurors was raised.[33] That change reflects broader changes in English government and society; changes that one recent study has argued saw the law become less participatory and more centralized.[34] We need to remember that unlike many of the judicial systems of the European continent the English legal system was predicated on the jury. As Hay pointed out, jurors were 'ubiquitous' in eighteenth-century English society; they sat in the high courts of London, at assize and quarter session. Coroners' juries sat in judgement on the bodies of the deceased, while others adjudicated in manorial, county and hundred courts up and down the land. The English juror was then an essential element of the participatory English criminal (and civil) justice system.[35] For Peter King the 'trial before the petty jury, was the principal public moment in the long chain of individual and collective choices and interactions that determined the fate of the accused'.[36]

Historians have used the study of the jury as part of a wider debate about the utility and function of the criminal justice system in the long eighteenth century. That debate will be considered at the end of this chapter, in the meantime let us look at the jury and the individuals that served on them. Both assizes and quarter sessions courts were served by two sets of jurors – grand and petty. The composition of this was to some extent different but overlapping. They had a different function however.

Grand juries were tasked with assessing the indictments that were presented to the court before trials could take place. Thus, in effect they scrutinized the paperwork of the quarter session or assize (or the Old Bailey) to make sure that details were correct and that trials could proceed. Eighteenth-century prosecutions could fail if names were incorrectly recorded or a mistake was made with the occupation or trade of the defendant.[37] Grand jurors might also determine that there were insufficient grounds to continue with a prosecution, that the evidence was too weak or the charge inappropriate. Grand jurors could also examine witnesses to find out what they intended to say but were not allowed (at least until 1838 at the Old Bailey) to see the depositions that had been taken.[38] Before trials could take place then, the grand jury sat in judgement on the indictments and sent them back as either 'true bills' or 'no true bills'. The sizes of grand juries varied; in the counties twenty-three or more members was not uncommon and it seems that the county elite were keen to be selected, it being seen as a recognition of their social status. In London, where more jurors were available and class distinctions less closely drawn, it was usual for there to be seventeen grand jurors. A petty jury was always empanelled of twelve 'good men and true'.

The role of the trial (or petty) jury was to hear the case in court and to determine the defendant's guilt or innocence. This process of decision-making was not simply one of determining whether the prisoner had committed the crime or not, juries had an effective role in sentencing, albeit in an indirect manner. Eighteenth-century juries frequently mitigated the severity of the 'Bloody Code' by bringing in partial verdicts against defendants accused of capital property crimes. By downgrading the value of items stolen they effectively removed the ability of judges to pass death sentences on those accused of picking pockets, shoplifting and a variety of other non-violent or threatening thefts. By contrast, they rarely acted to save the lives of highway robbers or gang-related burglaries. It would seem their overriding judgements were based on the 'seriousness of the offence' and 'the conduct and character of the accused'. The performance of the defendant was therefore crucially important and the trial itself was also, in this way, part of the process of sentencing. John Langbein has argued that partial verdicts (or what Blackstone referred to as 'pious perjury') were only necessary so long as the criminal justice system operated under the aegis of the capital code. Once imprisonment had replaced the options of death or transportation, juries were no longer required to temper the severity of sentencing.[39] So, according to Langbein, the practice of *pious perjury* was unique to the long eighteenth century and to what was termed the 'Bloody Code'. However, it would be interesting to see whether the practice of downgrading was more prevalent in certain parts of the country than others (especially in the light of King and Ward's revelations about the reluctance of courts to hang offenders on the peripheries).[40] It would also be useful to discover more about the how discretionary role of the jury affected debates around the dismantling of the 'Bloody Code' in the early decades of the 1800s. We know that Old Bailey juries in a number of forgery trials in 1818 refused to convict those accused of forging Bank of England notes but how widespread was this and are there other instances which might have supported the efforts of reformers?[41] Equally, we are surely overdue a detailed analysis of jury decision-making in the nineteenth century, research that might suggest that jurors continued to have a highly discretionary role to play in sentencing beyond the 1830s.

Contemporaries were apt to complain about the behaviour of jurors, especially the petty jury, and some appear to have seen their actions as tantamount to an undermining of the rule of law. Some suggested that jurors were drawn from the 'meaner sort' of folk prompting historians to look in detail at the social make-up of juries. Langbein argued, in his counter to Hay's polemic essay on the Hanoverian elite's use of the law as a class tool,[42] that jurors of the period represented a much broader cross section of English society than had been suggested.[43] Jurors were occasionally described as 'labourers' and tradesmen and this suggested that they were much closer in social status to those in the dock than Hay allowed. Detailed research on the jury in London and several English counties has now left us in a position to argue that the eighteenth-century petty jury was overwhelmingly constructed of men of property. Officially, jurors had to own freehold land valued at £10 per year (or leasehold at £20) and they had to be aged 21–60. There were also a variety of other qualifications, all based on property. Thus, naturally this tended to exclude the working class who did not appear on juries until well into the late nineteenth century (and even then not in great numbers).

The situation was different at the lower levels of the court system. The picture that emerges from King's analysis of Essex is that quarter sessions jury membership varied. Here juries were often made up of farmers or yeomen, although there were also some tradesmen and artisans appearing. It seems that the 'poorer trades' were better represented amongst petty jurors at quarter sessions whilst at the assizes 'more prosperous' tradesmen dominated.[44] In 1780s Staffordshire gentlemen 'never sat on petty juries', and, as in Essex, the majority of jurors were farmers with the rest being drawn from amongst artisans and tradesmen.[45] In Northamptonshire in the 1770s, somewhere between a conservative estimate of 55 per cent and a possible 75 per cent of men were effectively barred from jury service on the grounds of having insufficient wealth. If we add the fact that women were excluded from jury service until 1919 this demonstrates that while jurors (petty jurors at least) were not members of the elite, they did represent a highly selective minority of the population; defendants in trials were clearly *not* being judged by their peers.

But this does not mean that they necessarily represented the views of the ruling elite. As King points out, the 'grand jury at the assizes obviously reflected gentry interests, but the approaches of the other three criminal trial juries reflected both the fissures and solidarities of what may broadly be called... the middling sort. This was not a monolithic group, but there were growing signs in Essex during the second half of the eighteenth century that they saw their interests as often very separate from those of the gentry'.[46] Nor can the eighteenth-century middling sort can be described as a united class. These men were, of course, closer in terms of age and education to the judges that sat at assizes and quarter sessions than they were to the defendants that crowded the gaols and lockups. The petty jurors of England resembled the judiciary in that they were predominately made up of men in their forties and fifties. Jurors were more likely to be literate and they were also often connected to local government, charities and other organizations making them well-informed members of their communities with perhaps a more than working knowledge of the law.[47] Many Essex jurors would have served on multiple occasions and gained 'considerable experience' of the workings of the assize or quarter sessions court.[48] As a result jurors often intervened in trials; they asked questions and had a much greater participatory role than they do today. Lemmings has described them as 'effectively expert witnesses'.[49] This was even truer of London juries. The familiarity of London jurors (both grand and petty) with the court system must have influenced their decision-making. They knew the courts, the judges and each other and they had probably formed their own understanding of what constituted an 'honest' or 'dishonest' defendant. In addition, since most were drawn from amongst those that owned at least some property they may well have seen themselves as a class distinct from most of those upon whom they sat in judgement.

And this situation may well have deepened in the course of the long eighteenth century. Hay argues that the jury was 'becoming more rather than less exclusive' and more representative of the moneyed class.[50] I think this can best be seen by means of a comparison, in wealth terms, between the petty juror and other players in the criminal justice system. An eighteenth-century juror was required to own freehold land rated at £10 per annum (this represented about thirty-five acres in the last quarter of the 1700s, a substantial amount of property). However, to serve as a JP one had to have an annual income from land of £100, and to be an MP the requirement was *three* times this amount. Thus, while jurors may not have shared in the conspicuous wealth of those that sat as justices and judges, they certainly *did* share their wider concerns about the rule of law and the importance of disciplining the vast majority of people that were excluded from the justice system. Here Langbein's claim that the criminal justice system served the interests of the poor as much as it did the wealthy seems far from credible.[51] It also helps to explain some of the derogatory comments expressed by contemporaries that juries were made up of the 'meaner sorts'; to the landed elite of the eighteenth century, the relative wealth of the £10 freeholder was paltry by comparison to their own, but they represented less than 5 per cent of the nation's population. The idea then that the average defendant in eighteenth-century England could expect to be judged by his or her peers is frankly risible. A tremendous amount of discretion was available to the jury but that discretion was applied from a position of considerable distance from the accused. What safeguards did the prisoner possess? Who spoke up or represented them in court? Modern courts are dominated by the legal profession and the principle is enshrined in law that all defendants are entitled to legal support in challenging accusations levelled against them. This was not the case in the 1700s.

Procedure: How did the trial function in practice?

The morning after the assize judges had arrived in town, they rose early and met with the local JPs at a convenient venue. A variety of formal business would begin and the calendar of prisoners (those waiting their trials) would be read out.[52] The formal process of a session of *oyer* and *terminer* and gaol delivery began with the clerk of the court. It was his role to draw up the bills of indictment that were then presented to the Grand jurors. The indictment was the charge – the allegation against the defendant – and it contained the details of the offence committed. This could be quite detailed like this one from 1783 at the Old Bailey:

THOMAS COMPTON otherwise COLEMAN, and ANN his wife, otherwise called ANN COMPTON, otherwise COLEMAN spinster, were indicted for burglariously and feloniously breaking and entering the dwelling house of Joseph Clarke, on the 28th of March last, about the hour of twelve in the night, and feloniously stealing therein, ninety-eight yards of printed cotton, value 12 l. ninety-eight yards of printed linen and cotton, value 11 l. forty-two yards of other printed linen, value 31 l. 10 s. two hundred thirteen yards of Irish linen, value 13 l. thirteen yards of diaper cloth, value 19 s. sixty-nine silk handkerchief, value 14 l. one cotton half handkerchief, value 15 d. forty-three cotton handkerchiefs, value 5 l. twenty-four linen handkerchief, value 3 l. fourteen yards of plain lawn, value 40 s. twenty-four pair of worsted stockings, value 40 s. sixty-nine yards of figured lawn, value 10 l. thirteen stuff petticoats, value 4 l. 17 s. sixteen pair of mens leather shoes, value 4 l. six pair of womens shoes, value 21 s. eighteen yards of flannel, value 1 l. 7 s. one hundred and thirty yards of silk ribbon, value 3 l. 5 s. thirty-four yards of black lace, value 4 l. ninety-eight yards of white thread lace, value 10 l. one hundred and twenty-eight yards of worsted gartering, value 16 s. and four pounds weight of worsted, value 8 s. the property of the said Joseph Clarke in his dwelling house.[53]

While others were fairly straightforward as this example, from the same sessions of Old Bailey shows:

> JOHN BURTON and THOMAS DUXTON otherwise DUCKSTON were indicted for burglariously and feloniously breaking and entering the dwelling house of Robert Symonds, Esq; about the hour of three.[54]

The clerk was careful to draw up the indictment using the committing JP's notes along with the recognizances[55] of the witnesses and the prosecutor, as well as the details submitted to the gaol calendars (the formal list of prisoners awaiting trial which hold details of their crime, the prosecutor and the magistrate that committed them for trial[56]). Once the grand jury had considered the indictments, some prisoners would be discharged. In some cases the jury decided that there was no case to answer or that the indictment was unsafe or contained mistakes. If an indictment was badly drawn or wrong name or date was used, a grand jury could reject it.[57] They would send the indictment back marked 'no true bill' or 'ignoramus' (literally 'we do not know') and the accused would be set free. But others avoided trials (or at least had them delayed) because the prosecutor (or a witness) failed to appear in court. Indeed it was not uncommon for prosecutors to press for formal indictment, so that the accused was thrown into gaol for weeks or months (especially outside of the capital where the high court judges sat only every six months), only to fail to appear against them. This allowed prosecutors to effectively punish suspected offenders without having to undergo the expense (in money and time) of a jury trial. The eighteenth-century court system therefore encouraged the practice of false (or malicious) prosecution.[58] Some prisoners escaped from gaol before their trial came up whilst others died of disease or neglect, so not all those appearing on the gaol calendars actually made it to trial. What of those that did?

The clerk then called each prisoner forward in turn to answer to their name and to hear the indictment against them. It was at this point that they were required to plead 'guilty' or 'not guilty'. If one was accused of a felony in the eighteenth century it was (in most circumstances at least) very foolish to plead guilty. Most property crimes until the 1820s carried a death penalty and whilst a considerable degree of discretion was available to judges, juries and the prosecutor, it was unwise to place the noose around your own neck. So most defendants pleaded 'not guilty'.

If one chose not to plead at all the Hanoverian law had a peculiarly brutal way of encouraging you so to do. Offenders who were convicted of felonies and sentenced to death effectively forfeited their estates (if they had them) to the crown. However, if a defendant refused to enter a plea they could be subject to the punishment of *peine forte et dure* (from the French, meaning 'hard and forceful punishment'). Those refusing to plead would be tortured by having weights piled upon them until they either acquiesced or their chests collapsed and they died of suffocation. Andrea McKenzie has suggested that these offenders who opted to undergo such a dreadful torture rather than submit to the court's demand for a plea reflects their attempt to regain some agency and demonstrate their 'resolution and courage – attributes that were always at a premium, but never more than in the face of death [...] At the heart of such displays of bravura was the rejection of a tribunal apparently calculated to undermine or to supress such performances'.[59] This barbarous practice was formally abolished in 1772 and thereafter anyone refusing to plead was effectively judged to be guilty and dealt with accordingly. After 1827 this was reversed and those refusing to offer a plea were simply tried on the basis that they had presented themselves as 'not guilty' as charged. The English criminal justice system therefore managed to find a way around the problem of defendants who simply refused to acknowledge that a trial was happening regardless of their desire to participate or not.

Having pleaded 'not guilty', prisoners at the bar (literally a physical barrier behind which the defendant stood) waited while the clerk swore in a petty jury to hear the case. Prisoners could, but rarely did, object to up to twenty of those selected as jurors; with the jury having been sworn in, trials then went forward at a tremendous speed by modern standards.[60] We are also used to a system that assumes that the defendant in court is innocent and tasks the prosecution with *proving* that they have committed the crime they are accused of, *beyond reasonable doubt*. This was not the case in the seventeenth and eighteenth centuries and change did not really occur (at least formally) until well into the nineteenth century. In the words of John Beattie, if an 'assumption was made in court about the prisoner' it was:

> [N]ot that he was innocent until the case against him was proved... but that if he were innocent he ought to be able to demonstrate it for the jury by the quality and character of his reply to the prosecutor's evidence.[61]

As this was a victim-led system it generally fell to the prosecutor to open the trial and to set out the case against the accused. He did this with the help of his witnesses, who were called upon to provide supporting evidence (on oath) of the defendant's guilt. There were no opening statements from prosecution and defence as there were to be in the nineteenth century and, as we have seen, there was little recourse to barristers until the later 1700s. Even then this was probably largely a pattern of trials at the Old Bailey in London.

The accused was clearly at a considerable disadvantage in this situation. He was only allowed to call upon professional legal help to argue points of law, and only on occasions when the law was deemed to be particularly complicated.[62] He was not sworn and could not give evidence himself, nor could he ask his wife to do so. He had the right to cross-examine witnesses but was unlikely to be very good at it. Defendants could make a pre-trial statement, but few did and at the end they could offer an unsworn statement. This could often be disastrous: 'most, if they attempted to speak at length, descended into rambling irrelevance'.[63] Even if prisoners in Newgate or county gaols were able to find people to speak for them the system still worked against them. The costs involved with attending trials prevented (or at best restricted) the appearance of defence witnesses. The accused could not even see the case before him until the formal charge was read to him in court and he had the opportunity to plead, so he had no idea what evidence was going to be presented, or even exactly what he was accused of.

Defendants were entitled to challenge the evidence presented against them but often they would have found themselves in a situation where they were simply gainsaying accusations levelled against them. We need to be aware that evidence (that is, forensic or material evidence as we understand it) was much less important in a Hanoverian courtroom.

In reality the defendant's main advocate was the court itself, in the person of the judge and the jury. The judge played a vital role here because it was his duty to see that the law was being upheld. The judge offered further scrutiny of the indictment and represented the interests both of the crown and the accused. Contemporaries saw no conflict of interest in this situation, at least for much of the century. As William Blackstone noted in 1769, the role of the judge was to 'be counsel for the prisoner; that is, shall see that the proceedings against him are legal and strictly regular'.[64] Clearly, this was an unsatisfactory situation for those that found themselves on trial for their life. The judge might question prosecutors and their witnesses, sometimes quite aggressively as a defence barrister might do, but he would also sum up and could direct the jury to find defendants guilty and then hand down severe sentences upon them. In the absence of any prosecuting counsel it also fell to the judge to take up *that* role, which – given that they were also advocate for the defence – was fraught with difficulties.

At the end of the evidence when all witnesses had been examined the judge would turn to the prisoner and ask them to explain themselves. Most would say very little more than to protest their innocence. In London from mid-century some of those accused at the Old Bailey were able to call upon defence counsel and they would declare that they left their defence 'to my counsel' (you can see this increasingly in trials by consulting the *Old Bailey Online*). Those accused of serious felonies were further disadvantaged having often been locked up in county gaols or Newgate prison for several weeks or months in debilitating conditions.

Eighteenth- and early nineteenth-century gaols, compters and lock-ups were unpleasant places, run by entrepreneurial wardens and one's experiences a as prisoner was entirely dependent upon person wealth or the support of family or friends. Conditions were awful and there was no segregation or sanitation, and it is hardly likely that defendants held in them were in any real state to offer a thorough defence in court. Most had come straight from gaol, were dirty, sick and suffering from a lack of sleep. They would have looked disheveled by comparison to those appearing against them, further distancing themselves from the good opinions of the jury. Defendants would have had little or no time to prepare themselves to counter accusations from the prosecutor nor would they have been able to arrange for witnesses to appear on their behalf. The best they could hope for was to persuade friends or employers to appear as character witnesses.

Trials were quick, most lasting just a few minutes. Even murder trials rarely lasted that long and jurors would usually sit in adjudication on several trials, one after the other (unlike today when a new jury is empanelled for each case). In London, prior to 1738, jurors would hear several cases and then withdraw to pronounce judgments on them all.

After then pressure on the deliberations meant they had little time to leave court and so they did not withdraw at all, but simply went into a huddle to confer. All of this took place in the presence of the public, witnesses, prosecution and the accused, all of whom might attempt to influence their decision-making. In all probability, given the fact that certain jurors made multiple appearances (especially at the Old Bailey), experienced jurors and foremen probably wielded disproportionate influence over the other members. Even by the early decades of the nineteenth century, jurors often remained in court to reach their verdicts, only retiring to the jury room if they could not agree quickly. There they would 'be kept without fire, food or drink'. The poet Alexander Pope quipped that many 'wretches hang so that jurymen may dine'.[65] This archaic rule was not abolished until the passing of the Juries Act in 1870.

At the end of this process the jury would give its verdict and the prisoners would either be convicted or acquitted. If found guilty, the eighteenth-century felon could expect little mercy from the judge but he would have to wait to find out what fate awaited him. Until the 1840s sentences were delivered at the close of the session or assizes with those convicted being told their fate in groups and then taken back to the cells or off to the nearby county gaol.[66] The range of punishments available included (in different periods) branding, whipping, the pillory, transportation and death (in a small variety of forms); imprisonment was not generally used as a punishment option until the nineteenth century. As a result, a guilty verdict at the assizes was likely to mean that the convicted offender was sentenced to death (or transportation). Given that this outcome was preceded by what appears to have been a hearing heavily weighted in favour of the prosecution, it is hard not to conclude that the eighteenth-century criminal justice system was far from fair.

The gradual emergence of counsel (lawyers/barristers)

The speed of the eighteenth-century trial comes as a shock to the twenty-first-century reader that is used to the detailed challenges that prosecution and defence counsel make to every nuance of presented evidence in the modern crown courtroom. We are also familiar, thanks to the regular news reporting of trials at the Old Bailey and elsewhere (and the handful of fictional representations of the law), with an adversarial trial system where two barristers trade legal points such as boxers going toe-to-toe. The fact that they are wearing wigs and robes merely adds to the sense of drama and theatre. The English trial would appear to be more about the skill of an individual barrister in presenting an argument than it is about establishing truth or the defendant's guilt or innocence. But, as has been shown earlier, the eighteenth-century trial did not resemble the modern one in anything but the costumes worn. So how did the trial change and at what point did the legal profession begin to take over proceedings?

Prior to 1836 a defendant on a felony charge had no right to defence counsel unless he was facing a charge of treason (the law there had been changed after 1695). Gradually this began to change across the century as judges permitted defence counsel to examine and cross-examine witnesses but not to address the jury. In reality this was fairly academic as the vast majority of prisoners would have lacked the funds to hire a barrister anyway. As we have seen, the principle was that the accused should be able to defend themselves and the court would be able to tell whether they were being truthful by the means in which they did so. Points of law could be clarified by a professional and that role was played by the judge, who was there to ensure that the defendant was given a fair hearing under law. Curiously (to modern eyes at least), defendants in civil cases or those accused of minor offences (termed misdemeanours) *were* entitled to legal representation and one scholar has suggested that the gradual transition to the lawyer-led criminal trial may have started in the lower courts.[67]

The revolution (if we can use that term) in the criminal trial is usually associated with the career of one man, William Garrow, who seemingly single-handedly transformed court practice in the late eighteenth century.[68] But revolution *is* probably far too dramatic a term for something which happened slowly and over a long period. In reality the emergence of defence counsel had its roots, not simply in the actions and personality of one individual, but in the changing nature of prosecution from the early decades of the 1700s. John Langbein has argued that it was the emergence of prosecution lawyers and the availability of government rewards for prosecutors that may have forced the hands of the judiciary. As he puts it, '[t]he use of prosecution solicitors was associated with a perceptible increase in the use of counsel to prosecute felony cases at trial, further exaggerating the imbalance between the unaided accused and the lawyer-conducted prosecution.'[69] Judges became increasingly uncomfortable about the motivations of prosecutors and witnesses who sought to profit from the reward system. Rewards allowed the emergence of thief-takers, entrepreneurial policing agents and prompted an outpouring of criticism over 'blood money' scandals leading to the arrest, trial and execution of Jonathan Wild in 1752. Rewards were so valuable that witnesses were quite prepared to perjure themselves in order to gain the £40 that was payable for the successful conviction of highway robbers or horse thieves. In consequence, judges were, from the 1730s onwards, increasingly happy to allow defence counsel to interrogate witnesses and challenge their 'evidence'.

The government was also turning to professionals to prosecute in areas where it had particular concerns (such as the undermining of the currency by forgers). Thus, the period saw the Mint, Post Office and Bank of England all turn to the criminal bar in order to ensure convictions.[70] Prisoners in Newgate were also approached by lawyers offering to act for them for a fee. But 'Newgate solicitors' was a derogatory term for corrupt or otherwise disreputable legal operators who attempted to bribe jurors, witnesses and others to get defendants convicted so that they, or their clients, could profit from rewards. There was a ready supply of 'straw men' who 'promenaded up and down outside the Old Bailey with straw tucked into their shoes, advertising their willingness to accept a bribe in return for giving false evidence'.[71] In addition, there was the well-established practice of defendants turning king's (or queen's) evidence thereby avoiding prosecution (or gaining a reduced sentence), by giving damning prosecution testimony against their confederates. With all of these considerations it is perhaps easy to see why some judges (and it is clear that the practice surrounding defence counsel was far from uniform) were prepared to allow defendants to employ barristers if they could afford to do so. In the 1760s William Blackstone commented that judges were now so aware of the potentially imbalanced nature of the jury trial that 'they seldom scruple to allow a prisoner counsel to stand by him at the bar, and instruct him what questions to ask, or even to ask questions of him, with respect to matters of fact'.[72] Considerable restrictions still applied nevertheless.

Barristers could examine witnesses but they could not address the jury. Nor could they offer an opening address. And there were not very many of them, probably because the business of the criminal law was far less lucrative than pursuing civil suits in Chancery. From 1715 the courts began to see the occasional appearance of lawyers for the prosecution but this was probably only one or two a year. Research using the *Old Bailey Proceedings* reveals that defence counsel appeared in just nine trials at the Old Bailey in 1736. So they were becoming more 'common if not numerous'.[73] By 1788 one in eight of those accused of a property crime were represented and by 1800 it was between 25 and 33 per cent.

The emergence of defence counsel had a concomitant effect on the rules surrounding evidence. Until the mid-eighteenth century hearsay evidence (evidence that is indirect, e.g. 'I was told by a friend...') was still allowed but with the arrival of a more robust system of defence hearsay was increasingly challenged. Confessions remained important, especially those confessions given before JPs at pre-trial hearings, but even these were beginning to be considered to be inadmissible by courts in the middle of the eighteenth century. And as we have seen king's evidence, or the evidence of those who were suspected of lying to gain rewards or a bribe, was increasingly treated with scepticism. According to Allyson May, William Garrow and the new breed of Old Bailey barristers 'succeeded in many cases in exposing false or malicious prosecutions and perjured testimony'.[74] However, eighteenth-century barristers still represented the propertied interest. While the eighteenth-century bar was 'more solidly drawn from the middle classes' after the 1760s – by comparison to the seventeenth century – they were still supposed to be 'gentleman of strictly polite accomplishments and elite association'.[75] Thus, the social distance between those on trial and those prosecuting or defending was (and in many cases remains) considerable.

Important changes in the nineteenth century and early twentieth century

The eighteenth- and early nineteenth-century trial largely remained an adversarial confrontation between the prosecutor (usually the victim of the crime) and the defendant. Since there was little financial help for prosecutors (and none for defendants) there was relatively little recourse to professionals. Judges would usually assign counsel to poor defendants in murder cases but counsel was unpaid and frequently unbriefed. As we have seen, this situation was in the process of change towards the end of the 1700s but while practice was being altered it took much longer for these changes to be enshrined in legal reforms. The first important reform was the passing of the Prisoner's Counsel Act.

The 1836 Prisoner's Counsel Act

This effectively confirmed what had been the practice of the law (at the Old Bailey if not elsewhere in the country) since the early decades of the nineteenth century. The act 'granted defendants the right to make "their full Answer and Defense" by "Counsel learned in the Law"'. This also included those appearing before magistrates at summary level.[76] From this point onwards then, defendants had the *right* to be represented by a barrister in court but this did not mean that most were. There was no legal aid (no financial support for those accused of felonies) and as a consequence most trials continued to be conducted as they had been previously, without counsel. The right was hard won, with debates in parliament in the 1820s and 1830s and a gradual move towards entitlement to representation. Opponents of change argued that the trial was all about establishing the truth by 'calm and dispassionate enquiry'.[77] If defence counsel were allowed to make speeches on behalf of their clients, the prosecution would respond in kind and the truth would be lost in the cacophony, opponents claimed. Supporters of change argued that by allowing a professional trained in the law to thoroughly investigate the evidence presented, the truth would emerge. So, in effect both sides of the argument turned on how best to get at the truth. There were also arguments as to how it would work, and who had the important 'last word', as well as the role of the judge in summing up. Underlying all of this, according to at least one scholar, was the end of the conceit that the law was somehow infallible. The act became law in October 1836 and included clauses that entitled prisoners to see what evidence was going to be used against them and, in the words of David Cairns, 'transformed the rough-and-ready procedure of the eighteenth and early nineteenth centuries into the scrupulous adversarial trial of today'.[78]

That adversarial encounter between two learned counsels supposedly operated on the basis that each represented a cause they believed to be just. But in reality defence barristers were sometimes placed in the position of defending a client they knew (or suspected) was guilty. Barristers 'faced with a confession of guilt' from their client were unable to get professional guidance (as counsel can today) and had to continue to represent defendants they knew were guilty. This is most famously illustrated by the case of François Courvoisier in 1840 who admitted to his brief (Charles Phillips) that he had murdered his master (Lord Russell) but insisted that Phillips continue to try and get him off.[79] Neither could barristers refuse to represent people on the grounds of disliking their opinions; David Lemmings has dubbed this the 'cab-rank rule' and cites the example of Thomas Erskine who defended the radical Tom Paine (who had been accused of sedition and was tried in absentia in 1792).[80] Both Phillips and Erskine were the subject of criticism for their actions although both believed they were serving the higher cause, that of the integrity of the law and criminal justice.

The 1879 Prosecution of Offenders Act

The next reform that made a significant move towards the modern criminal trial was the creation of a system of public prosecution. Nowadays we are familiar with a system of state justice – the Crown Prosecution Service (CPS), created in 1986, that brings prosecutions on our behalf. This is a very different situation for most of the period covered by this book, where the onus of prosecuting rested with the victim of crime. As late as the 1790s more than 80 per cent of criminal prosecutions were brought by the victims themselves. There were areas in which the state (in the name of the Crown or government) or institutions (such as the Bank of England) took on the role of prosecutor – notably in treason, murder or coining trials – but the fundamental responsibility rested with the victim. As a result, there was a marked reluctance by some to prosecute, caused in part by costs and the time involved in bringing cases to court. Under Queen Anne rewards were introduced to encourage prosecution and gradually legislation was passed that allowed prosecutors to recover their costs.[81] After 1829 the new police began to play a more active role in bringing cases to court, but there was no public prosecutor in the majority of cases.[82] A public prosecution system had been recommended by reformers such as Jeremy Bentham (the originator of the panopticon prison); Patrick Colquhoun (a London magistrate who argued for the creation of a professional police force); Samuel Romilly (who campaigned tirelessly for the reform of the so-called 'Bloody Code'); and Robert Peel (the Home Secretary that created the Metropolitan Police in 1829). Peel declared that 'I would have a public prosecutor acting in each case on principal, and not on the heated and vindictive feelings of the individual sufferer.'[83] This went to the heart of the issue but change was still resisted until the last quarter of the century. In 1879, parliament passed the Prosecution of Offenders Act and created the position of the Director of Public Prosecutions. Its first incumbent was Sir John Maule but he dealt with very little business, leaving most prosecutions to the police or Treasury Solicitor.[84] In 1884, the roles of the DPP and the Treasury Solicitor (the other government official able to bring prosecutions) were merged.

The 1898 Criminal Evidence Act

The next change continued the process of allowing the accused a full and fair participation in his own defence. As we have seen, the defendant had no right to speak on oath; indeed, this was deliberate as contemporaries argued it exposed him to the risk of perjuring himself. Reformers argued for change but only piecemeal changes were secured. However, by 1885 several specific acts had allowed the defendant to give evidence and speak in his defence and the passing of the 1898 Criminal Evidence Act allowed the accused to speak on oath in *all* trial situations. Now, and 'for the first time [...] accused persons and their spouses were [considered] competent witnesses in criminal trials'.[85] Bentley has noted that with this change in law the 'shape of the criminal trial was decisively and dramatically altered, and with it both the trial system and law of criminal evidence entered the modern age'.[86] There were three other changes that supported this move towards the creation of the 'modern' criminal trial.

The Poor Prisoner's Defence Act (1903), Criminal Appeal Act (1907) and the Costs in Criminal Cases Act (1908)

The first of these reforms dealt with the problem of representation by counsel when the defendant was poor (as of course, most were). There was no 'statutory provision for legal aid' (although under certain circumstances judges might assign barristers to the defence, in murder cases for example) until this legislation in 1903. Now courts were able to grant limited legal aid to those in need if it was considered 'desirable in the interests of justice'. The act was amended in 1930 to include those pleading guilty.[87] There were subsequent improvements in the legal aid system for defendants in legislation passed between 1949 and 1960, which made the process a much more effective tool for those accused of offences. Sadly, those hard won reforms appear to be under attack in the early twenty-first century.

The Criminal Appeal Act (1907) allowed appeals on law and on facts (previously there had been no effective system of appeal against a verdict unless there was a dispute about the interpretation of the law). This was significant and has been followed in the later twentieth century by legislation that has allowed for appeals against sentences (both from the defence and prosecution). Finally, the Costs in Criminal Cases Act (passed in 1908) brought to an end the practice of judges prosecuting defendants in court.[88]

The court of King's (or Queen's) Bench

The criminal law has evolved over centuries and it is quite easy to forget that it has its roots in the person of the ruling monarch. Without wishing to delve too deeply into medieval history it is necessary to establish that the courts of King's Bench, Exchequer and Common Pleas have developed over time but that at one point King's Bench and Common Pleas had equal jurisdiction and existed in parallel. By the eighteenth century King's Bench had become the 'most important' of the high courts. King's Bench was the only court that heard cases brought by criminal information (i.e. those that have been brought without seeking an indictment first). These were either presented by the master of the Crown Office on behalf of private individuals or by law officers of the Crown on behalf of the government. However, both 'could be brought only for serious misdemeanours'. These were different from indictments, being 'speedy, expensive' and offering 'some significant opportunities and dangers for both parties'.[89] King's Bench was also a court of review; indeed it was the Supreme Court of criminal review and all summary convictions, along with indictments at quarter sessions and assizes, could be removed here by writ of certiorari if you had the money to do so (which most complainants did not). Finally, the court's pre-eminence was enhanced by the fact that it was the King's Bench judges (which included the lord chief justice) 'who most often made criminal law as well as enforced it'.[90] The history of King's Bench has largely been left to legal historians because the process of this court was notoriously complex and its records extremely hard to understand. Nevertheless, it would be useful if future scholars were able to turn their attention to try and unpack its histories.

The medieval court system was divided between Crown and Common Pleas; between matters that touched the concern of the monarch and those presented on behalf of commoners. This and the principle of the right to a trial by one's peers (as enshrined in Magna Carta as *habeas corpus*) are the keystones of the criminal justice system. However, as we have seen, most of those brought before the courts (whether at quarter sessions or assizes) were, for much of the period covered by this study, judged by men who represented a small minority of the property owning class; the accused were denied what we would consider to be amongst the most basic of human rights: that is, a fair trial. Without entitlement to legal representation until well into the nineteenth century and without effective legal aid until the mid-twentieth or later, defendants were reliant on the judge, jury and their own wits to avoid the gallows, transportation or imprisonment. When change came it was not largely as a result of pressure from those championing the rights of the accused but as a consequence instead of changing practices within the legal profession and the wider criminal justice system. It would be incorrect to see the evolution of the modern adversarial trial as part of a Whiggish march of progress when instead it is better viewed as a consequence of entrenched attempts to preserve the status quo in the face of the arrival of new methods of policing and prosecution.

The massive change was in the role of the prosecutor. For most of the period from 1680 onwards prosecution was victim-led (except in cases of homicide and some specific offences such as forgery) and this persisted until almost the end of the nineteenth century. The police increasingly played an active role here but it was not until the 1880s that the Director of Public Prosecutions really began to influence criminal proceedings. One of the features that might surprise our ancestors would be the relative unimportance of the victim in the criminal justice system today. Many other things they would recognize; the court system of assize and quarter session was not overhauled until 1971, jurors remained predominantly male and propertied until well after the First World War and judges and counsel continue to wear wigs and gowns to this day. However, in a very real way the reforms of the law and criminal justice system have made strides to ensure that the system is fairer than it was. The issue of whom the law served in the eighteenth (and nineteenth) century is the final area this chapter will consider before we move on to look at policing and punishment in subsequent chapters.

A subtle instrument of class rule? Douglas Hay and the use of the law debate

In 1975, a group of historians associated with the Centre for the Study of Social History at the University of Warwick published what has become the seminal text in the history of crime. In a series of essays on topics such as poaching, smuggling and public execution they argued that the ideology of rule had 'its visible and material embodiment above all in the ideology and practice of the law', and that at the 'heart of this ideology' stood the gallows, as the symbol of elite power and authority.[91] This thesis has been challenged since but remains a useful paradigm for understanding the function and purpose of the criminal justice system in the long eighteenth century. Let us look at how Douglas Hay, whose essay[92] opens the volume, commenced this debate before turning to those scholars (notably John Langbein and Peter King) that have attempted to contradict or amend the Warwick school's conclusions.

Having established that the period saw a tremendous rise in the number of offences that could be punished by death (there were over 200 statutes that decreed the use of hanging), Hay set out to answer two key questions: first, why was there not a proportionate increase in the number of people being executed? Many more people were being sentenced to death and then pardoned or reprieved (by being given a secondary punishment such as transportation) than were actually being killed by the state. Second, why, given that contemporaries frequently questioned the efficacy of hanging as a deterrent for crime, was the ultimate sanction of capital punishment retained as long as it was? Reformers argued that threatening to execute petty thieves put victims of crime off prosecuting and caused jurors to acquit guilty criminals. Simply put, the property of the 'haves' was not being protected from the depredations of the 'have-nots'. Hay's conclusion was that the criminal justice system was not simply concerned with crime but instead was about preserving the hegemony of the ruling class in a society without a system of professional police or a standing army, or, as Edward Thompson put it:

> The hegemony of the 18th century gentry and aristocracy was expressed, above all, not in military force, not in the mystifications of a priesthood or of the press, not even in economic coercion, but in the rituals of the study of the Justices of the Peace, in the Quarter sessions, in the pomp of the Assizes and in the theatre of Tyburn.[93]

Hay then went on to describe how the law combined 'imagery and force, ideals and practice' in its successful oppression of the vast majority of 'unpropertied Englishmen'.[94] It did this through the use of 'Majesty', 'Justice' and 'Mercy'.

Majesty was represented by the assize circuit and the pomp and ceremony that accompanied the arrival of the high court judges in the county towns of England and Wales. The procession of the assize judges, with heralds and javelin men to escort them; the glamour of the nobility, who turned the biannual assizes into a social occasion; and the drama of the court (which included the dreaded black cap that signalled a death sentence), were all carefully orchestrated events designed to awe the populace and reinforce the authority of the elites. Hay likened it to the importance of religion in the previous centuries: 'The labouring poor knew more of the terrors of the law than those of religion' he wrote, 'When they did hear of Hell, it was often from a judge.'[95]

The law had to be magnificent but it also had to be fair, and seen to be so. This of course was a legal *tromp d'oeil*, a deceit, because for the Warwick school the criminal law served the interests of those in power, the propertied class. Here was where the importance of observing legal niceties (such as the Grand jury's scrutiny of indictments to filter out those where names had been misspelt) and the occasional conviction of someone other than a member of the labouring classes were crucial. So, both Reverend Dodd (a former chaplain to the royal family) and Lord Ferrers (who murdered his steward) went to the gallows to show that no one was above the law. The defence (albeit in absentia) of Tom Paine by Erskine showed the public that the law had no prejudices; it supposedly protected the property of everyone regardless of class, and tried everyone regardless of their political views. This was not the summary tyranny of Scroggs and Jeffreys, it was the measured justice of an enlightened age and it contrasted sharply with both the earlier century and the worst excesses of revolutionary France. However, this was a fiction in that those sitting in judgement on the majority of defendants were, as we have seen, representative of a small minority of the population. Moreover, while rich men committed crime, the offences they preferred were harder to prosecute, with fraud and the embezzlement of expenses in government being harder to detect.

Third, Hay noted that the 'prerogative of mercy ran throughout the administration of the criminal law'.[96] Many of those sentenced to death were spared the gallows by the intervention of a judge, an elite connection or the request of the prosecutor. The National Archives at Kew contains reams of petitions for pardon or clemency from hundreds of persons who were condemned to die for a variety of property offences.[97] The mystery of how pardons were granted were part of the ritual of terror and mercy, and since the outcome was uncertain the gratitude of the condemned or their friends and family when a reprieve came through helped reinforce paternalistic bonds in Georgian society. As Hay noted, the use of discretionary pardons 'allowed a prosecutor to terrorise the petty thief and then command his gratitude, or at least the approval of his neighbourhood as a man of compassion'.[98]

Majesty, Justice and Mercy were supplemented by what Hay termed 'Delicacy' and 'Circumspection'. By this he meant that the terror of the gallows had to be tempered, because the rule of law was based (if in limited terms) on the consent of the people. Underneath its confident exterior the ruling class realized that its grip on the reins of government was actually fairly insecure; the trick was never to let the majority realize how powerful they really were. So capital punishment had to be used with caution, excess had to be avoided and the targets of the gallows had to seem reasonable. It was better to hang the ringleaders of a riot and spare many others, or to execute a violent highwayman rather than a starving pickpocket. This sent a message that the law was just. All of this was necessary, Hay argues, because the elite were attempting to govern without 'a police force and without a large army', and so the 'ideology of the law was crucial in sustaining the hegemony of the English ruling class'.[99]

Hay's thesis has inspired much of the work on the history of crime that has come after it, indeed my own interest in the subject was prompted by the debate surrounding the use of the law. While Hay offers us a seemingly plausible explanation, his essay is based on quite a partial view of the criminal justice system. Hay was looking at the operation of the law at the county assizes (with some London sources), while the other contributors to the Warwick school focused on poachers in Hampshire and the West Midlands, and smuggling in Sussex. Hay suggested that the criminal law served the interests of those with property and that discretion (and with it the power to be merciful) largely rested with the wealthier classes. But when historians began to look at the criminal justice system of the eighteenth century in more detail they began to find ways to challenge this.

John Langbein took issue with Hay's attempt to present the criminal law as an ideological tool. It was instead, Langbein argued, a system which 'existed to serve and protect the interests of the people who suffered as victims of crime', and most of those were not members of the ruling class.[100] For his research Langbein drew upon the records of the Old Bailey and one particular judge (Dudley Ryder) as well as Peter King's study of the Essex quarter sessions.[101] Langbein critiques Hay's essay on a number of grounds, arguing that he concentrated too much on offences which demonstrate the move away from a society based on customary rights and towards one based on a capitalist understanding of the ownership of property.[102] However, most of those prosecuted at the Old Bailey were accused of forms of theft that are hard to associate with what historians have termed 'social crime', nor were they stealing because they were destitute.

Moreover, they were stealing from individuals who 'were not much better off'.[103] The fact that government rewards existed to encourage people to prosecute suggested to Langbein that this was a system that served the majority and not simply a small minority of 'self-serving gentlemen'.[104] Discretion was available to more people than Hay allowed, and crucially in Langbein's view, this included the petty jury. Jurors frequently returned 'partial verdicts', downgrading the value of goods stolen so that judges were unable to apply the death penalty to those convicted. Where jurors did capitally convict it was in cases of the most serious forms of violent property crime or where there was clear evidence of gangs at work. While Hay saw the petty jury as a part of the ruling class conspiracy, Langbein argues that they were overwhelmingly non-elite, and motivated by understandable notions of respect for private property rather than some ideological determination to oppress the poor.

Langbein also argues that judges had relatively little discretion, at least in sentencing. Where they did have a role was in the pardoning process, and where Hay sees this as part of a careful conspiracy, Langbein opts for pragmatism. In his view those recommended to mercy were those deemed less criminal, or where the evidence was less reliable. He downplays the value of elite connections; Hay had argued that an ability to marshal persons of character to plead for mercy had the dual benefit of saving lives and cementing social ties of deference. One recent study has shown, however, that in some circumstances even connections to the highest in the land was not always enough to save you from the gallows.[105]

I have deliberately left King's analysis (used by Langbein) for separate consideration and before I look at Langbein's final (and very useful) point about the growth of legal statutes, let us turn to King's work on decision-making and the use of the law in the eighteenth century.

As King noted, '[p]eople from almost every group in eighteenth-century society took others to court'.[106] Discretion was available to a much wider group of persons than Hay suggested in his original essay, and while women and the young had the fewest opportunities to exercise it, the opportunities for those at the top of the social ladder were also restricted. This is because, in a victim-led system, the decision-making of the prosecutor was key. It was he who had the power to prosecute (or not), to prosecute at summary level or press for a full jury trial; thus, 'individual victims could, and did, end the vast majority of criminal processes well before they reached the courts and this lower, but vastly more extensive, form of pardoning was mainly in the hands of the middling sort and the laboring poor'.[107] Many of these same individuals could also influence sentencing by helping to frame the indictment and by recommending mercy at the end of the trial (or afterwards). Judicial decisions to pardon were made, King demonstrates, not simply on the grounds of class but on factors such as previous good character, youth, a lack of previous convictions and poverty. Those sent to hang were those where an example was required to deter others; where violence was used; bad character or previous convictions was evident, or there were gang associations. In short, judges and supporters of petitions of mercy were informed by the circumstances of the crime and its perpetrator, not by an imperative to uphold the rule of a minority class.[108]

Thus, the ability of a wider cohort of persons to use and influence the law has encouraged historians to rethink Hay's thesis. John Brewer and John Styles have suggested that the eighteenth-century criminal justice system is best seen as 'a multiple-use right available to *most* Englishmen' [my italics].[109] There is of course a difference between use and effective use; it was relatively easy for individuals of almost all classes to go to law in the 1700s, but some were more successful than others. As we have seen, the costs (both financial and in terms of one's time) were prohibitive and contemporaries recognized this (and so created a system of rewards and expenses). In addition, since most of those that prosecuted at the jury courts prosecuted those that had stolen from them, it is somewhat inevitable that prosecutors were drawn from amongst the ranks of those that had property to steal. This did not have to be that much however; the theft of goods valued at over a shilling carried the possibility of death in certain circumstances.

Likewise, jury service was based on a property qualification and so it is likely that those that determined guilt or innocence were closer in social class to those prosecuting than to those in the dock. But this does not mean that we should conclude that they automatically sided with the victims, nor that their decisions were made from an ideological standpoint. The criminal trial was heavily weighted in favour of the prosecution (or at least it was weighted *against* the defendant) and jurors had to make decisions based on what was presented to them. That so many chose to return partial verdicts (and so save the lives of thousands of petty thieves) suggests they had considerable sympathy for the plight of those accused of crime (and this might have been more pronounced outside of London and the Home Counties, where the power of government was weaker).[110] That they cheerfully condemned gangs of highway robbers and horse thieves to death perhaps reflects not a confederacy with the ruling elite but a pragmatic and understandable distaste for organized crime.[111] We should always be wary of judging our ancestors' punishment system by that of our own; hanging was prescribed for a huge number of offences so it is not surprising if jurors and prosecutors made decisions that spared many but not all from the rope. This brings us back to Langbein's point about statutes, and his explanation for the supposedly peculiar paradox of the Hanoverian justice system.

Hay asked why, given that the numbers of laws that prescribed the death penalty rose in the long eighteenth century, did the relative numbers of executions fall? His answer was that it was a conspiracy on behalf of the ruling elite to maintain their authority over the labouring population, but Langbein offers an alternative explanation. His argument is, not surprisingly for a legal historian, based on the deficiencies of the criminal law in the period. He says that the 'English did not have 200 separate crimes in the modern sense that could be punished with death. Rather, they lacked general definitions, especially for larceny and embezzlement, with the result that they were constantly having to add particulars in order to compensate for the want of generality.'[112] As a result, the law contained statutes that decreed death for specific offences relating to specific places (such as stealing linen from bleaching yards) because these laws were often brought as private member's bills on behalf of patrons. Most offenders continued to be prosecuted, tried and convicted under long-established capital statutes (such as highway robbery, horse theft and burglary). Therefore, in Langbein's analysis Hay's question is founded on a false assumption.

So, what is the student to make of this long and protracted debate; have historians successfully undermined Hay's thesis? You must draw your own conclusions but I would offer the following amendment to the debate as it stands. Both Hay and Langbein concentrated their attention on the jury courts of Old Bailey and the county assizes, while King used the records of the quarter sessions. These represent but a part of the wider criminal process of the period and neglect to consider where most people encountered the law, which was at the summary level. Here justices (often but not always members of the elite) operated with very little sanction or scrutiny.[113] Members of the labouring poor, artisans, farmers, women, masters and servants, all took their complaints to the magistracy and achieved varying levels of success. However, most of those that were disciplined by the JPs at summary level belonged to the poorer classes; here were vagrants, idle and disorderly, bastard-bearers, petty thieves and pilferers that represented the lower rungs of the social level. So, we see that the same social class of defendants appeared before justices at petty sessions, quarter sessions and assizes; being admonished, imprisoned, whipped and escorted out of the parish at the lower courts or transported and hanged in the higher courts.

One final thought: just because the criminal justice system was *used* by labouring people, it does not follow either that they accepted its legitimacy or that it was a system which represented everyone equally. It may be going too far to argue that the Hanoverian justice system was an ideological tool of the ruling class but it is surely naïve in the extreme to see it as a system which sought merely to 'protect the people, overwhelmingly non-elite, who suffered from crime'.[114] The debate is far from closed however. We are learning more about the role of justices in the pre-trial process and the types of case loads they dealt with. We need to move the debate into the nineteenth century and see how the emergence of professional policing and the collapse of capital punishment might affect it. This study attempts to bridge a considerable span of history but within that the targets of the criminal justice system have remained the same. Indeed, they remain the same in the early twenty-first century. Most of those prosecuted at courts in the late seventeenth, eighteenth, nineteenth, twentieth and twenty-first centuries were young men aged 18–24, drawn from the less educated, unskilled and poorer classes of society. The criminal justice system may not be (or have been) an ideological weapon but it is (and was) a useful tool of control that helps to maintain societal inequalities.

CHAPTER 12

THE DECLINE AND FALL OF THE 'BLOODY CODE': THE CHANGING NATURE OF PUNISHMENT POLICY IN THE LONG EIGHTEENTH CENTURY

The history of punishment in the years between 1660 and 1914 can too easily be viewed as a simple journey of progression, from the brutality of the gallows to the relative calm and ordered world of the penitentiary. In reality, of course, the story is much more complicated than that, and historians continue to research and debate the changing nature of state punishments in this period.

This chapter will look briefly at the punishments that were inherited from the early modern criminal justice system before moving on to look at how these were reformed or developed in the first half of the eighteenth century. It will then consider the rise and fall of the so-called 'Bloody Code' and its impact on Hanoverian attitudes towards execution. With growing concern about the utility and effect on the public of hanging came a search for alternative sanctions to deter and punish criminals, which included transportation overseas to English colonies in America and the gradual use of prison as a form of punishment. There will also be a detailed exploration of transportation to Australia and the historical debates surrounding it. Chapter 13 will then look in detail at the rise to prominence of the prison in the nineteenth century and at arguments of reforms concerning the nature of prison regimes. Finally, it will end with a short discussion about the development of non-custodial sentencing in the early years of the twentieth century.

Defining punishment

However, we need to foreshadow this discussion with some sort of definition of what we mean by 'punishment' and think a little about what it is for. This might seem fairly straightforward but is actually quite problematic. Nicola Lacey reached the conclusion that legal (i.e. state) punishment is

> the principled infliction by a state-constituted institution of what are generally regarded as unpleasant consequences upon individuals or groups adjudicated [...] to have breached the law.[1]

If this is what punishment *is*, then our next question must ask what is it *for*? The obvious answer would be that punishment is applied to offenders to deter others from committing crime. However, punishment can also be viewed as a form of retribution, a means for society to 'avenge' itself on the criminal on behalf of the victim of crime. Modern debates about, for example, the restitution of the death penalty, or the quality of prisoners' lives, often turn around questions of justification and intention.

Again, this might seem self-explanatory; criminals deserve to be punished because they have committed a crime, they should expect nothing less than their 'just deserts'. Therefore, it follows that the state has a right to punish anyone that violates its laws. But determining what form of punishment is fitting or appropriate (or indeed will most effectively meet the needs of society or persons that have been offended against) is far less clear. The ancient, biblical principle of 'an eye for an eye'[2] informed early punishment, but its impracticality is evident. If 'someone kills they are killed' makes a crude sort of sense but if a man steals my car am I supposed to steal his? What about theories of punishment that stress culpability? In essence this means that some crimes justify more severe forms of punishment than others or that some offenders are more morally culpable than others. Thus, the murderer is clearly deserving of punishment; but what about the person whose offence causes no harm to anyone else, but (like the private consumer of an illegal drug) still breaks the law?

According to Durkheim, punishment, as well as being a tool to control crime, is a means for the governing authority to demonstrate that they are in charge. But punishment draws its strength from its legitimacy; it reflects a sense of morality that most people subscribe to. Thus, certain crimes – in particular murder, rape or child abuse, for example – trigger feelings of moral outrage in us and we expect the state to punish offenders. Therefore, in Durkheim's view, the 'existence of strong bonds of moral solidarity are the conditions which cause punishments to come about, and, in their turn, punishments result in the reaffirmation and strengthening of these same social bonds'.[3]

Jeremy Bentham, who was to devise one of the most 'rational' solutions to the problem of punishment – the panopticon 'inspection house' – stated that punishment 'whatever shape it may assume, is an evil'[4]; he argued that the purpose of punishment had to be married to the needs of society, not to some desire for revenge. As we shall see, contemporary commentators struggled with the justifications and purposes of state punishments throughout the long eighteenth century, and how they should be applied.

Early modern punishments and their justification

The early modern period had a plethora of non-capital and capital punishments which were characterized by three elements: they were public, physical and most were intended to shame the individual. They also need to be seen within the context of a society that can arguably be said to have toughened up on crime and offenders. Offenders were flogged, set in the stocks or pillory, branded, ducked, hanged, tortured, burned, beheaded and their bodies displayed in public. Minor offenders were fined and imprisoned, although imprisonment was not commonly used to punish criminals. Let us look in some detail at the nature of these punishments and the justifications for their use.

Some of the more outlandish (to modern eyes at least) punishments of the period, such as the ducking stool and scold's bridle, appear to have been employed only occasionally.[5] The stocks were used to punish individuals but were also deployed locally to restrain offenders that were due to be taken to the county gaol when no lockup or alternative was available. A variant of the stocks was the pillory which seems to have been used more extensively in London but not as much elsewhere. Offenders were set in the pillory, their head and hands restrained by the mechanism, on a platform that could be turned so that the crowd could see them and, if it wished, throw things at them. Being pilloried was a potentially lethal experience; those found guilty of acts that the public particularly abhorred (such as paedophiles, sodomites or procurers) were sometimes killed in the pillory. Others might have additional punishment decreed by the courts, such as bodily mutilations (ears or tongues cut off or nailed to the pillory). However, some would have suffered little more than the unpleasantness of being on public display and the discomfort of being restrained in this way.

Offenders that might be viewed as those transgressing moral codes of sexual conduct, such as brothel keepers and prostitutes, were treated in a similar way to those offending against community values (such as adulterers, scolds and henpecked husbands) by being 'carted'; literally paraded about in an open cart. This echoed the *skimmington* or *charivari* that continued long into the eighteenth and nineteenth centuries.[6] The purpose of all of these forms of punishment was to publicly shame a person and hold them to account for their actions. It also served to purify the offender and to begin the process of their rehabilitation within society. In doing so it reflected punishments meted out by the church courts which proscribed public displays of penance such as standing outside church or processing through villages or towns dressed in white carrying a candle, often with a notice detailing their offence.

More often offenders were submitted to punishments that were to remain in place well into the eighteenth century. Many petty property criminals were whipped for thefts not exceeding a shilling ('petty larceny'). Flogging took place in public spaces (such as market places) or near to the scene of the crime and offenders were often tied to a post or to the back of a cart (flogged 'at the cart's tail'). There was no distinction between the sexes; both women and men were whipped in public.

Fines were also deployed as a form of punishment and these were usually small and used for minor property crime (pilfering) or non-lethal violence (assault). Some minor offenders from the 1550s onwards were imprisoned in houses of correction which served as institutions to deal with vagrants, prostitutes, petty thieves and the disorderly. The first of these was the Bridewell in London (founded in 1553), which gave its name to similar gaols up and down the country. Most of those sent to bridewells were committed by justices of the peace acting summarily, and for short periods of up to a year with hard labour. Griffiths' work on the London Bridewell has shown that a tremendous range of offenders were punished by a spell inside its walls, including runaway or disobedient servants, bastard-bearers, fornicators, drunkards, blasphemers, scolds, those guilty of assault or abuse language or making threats, the idle and disorderly, beggars, street walkers, unlicensed porters, fraudsters and pilferers – indeed pretty much anyone the justices wanted to lock up without needing to prove guilt before a judge and jury.[7] The author of an early manual for justices, Michael Dalton, urged JPs to commit all sorts of petty offenders to houses of correction but with little legal justification for doing so. The house of correction became a commonplace institution in the early modern state and continued to receive beggars, vagrants, petty thieves, and prostitutes for short periods of 'hard labour'. Inmates were set to work; indeed work seems to have been at the heart of these penal institutions. Bridewell keepers were part jailer and part master and Innes has described houses of correction as a form of 'small enterprise' which were intended to be largely self-sustaining. There are clearly close ties between the Bridewell and the workhouses that developed from the first quarter of the eighteenth century. Both were predicated on the need to discipline and control the labouring poor, and in particular those 'that would not work'.[8] Given that other gaols were used merely to hold prisoners until they could be either tried and released or condemned and then executed, the house of correction represents an important bridge between early modern punishments and the use of the prison as a form of rehabilitation in the nineteenth century.

The early modern period also saw the extension of capital punishment within the criminal justice system and a reduction in the number of offences that were afforded the benefit of clergy.[9] Under Henry VIII and then Elizabeth I the number of offences which carried the death penalty increased after a period of virtual stagnation with regards to capital crimes. So, benefit of clergy was removed from highway robbery, treason, murder, witchcraft, the theft of horses or goods from masters (valued at over 40s.), sodomy and some forms of arson.[10] The period also appears to have established the principle of the 'last dying speeches' of the convicted felon at the gallows (see Chapter 2), as part of the process of justification for the capital sentence and the preparation of the condemned man's passage in to the afterlife. Thus, 'execution became not just a simple demonstration that crime did not pay, but rather a more sophisticated underpinning of that ideological control to which contemporary regimes aspired'.[11] Bound up with this was an increased role for the clergy, who now routinely administered to the executed felon in a way that does not seem to have been so common in the earlier medieval period. Execution could take different forms; nobles could be beheaded and traitors subjected to forms of torture in addition to death. Those convicted of treason would be drawn to the place of execution on a sledge and then hanged. Before they were dead however, their bodies would be taken down and further tortures inflicted on them. They would be cut open, their intestines removed and burned. Some would have died during the process but others must have endured awful pain before the executioner finally brought their suffering to an end. Some of those condemned to death (for coining, petty treason or heresy) were burned alive at the stake. All of these punishments took place in public before crowds that, by the seventeenth century, were generally well behaved and relatively subdued.

The archetypal symbol of early modern period and eighteenth-century punishment was the gallows, and particularly the 'fatal tree' at Tyburn in London. By the early 1700s the execution of offenders was imbued with rituals 'that were both well established and elaborate'.[12] This ritual relied on the participation of the crowd. It began with a religious service at the gaol, where the condemned were secured, after which the prisoners were taken to have their 'irons' (their fetters and chains) removed. With their hands then tied in front of them, they were taken on a cart through the streets to the place of execution. In London and other towns and cities we know that large crowds gathered to witness these processions. The procession could be solemn or riotous, depending on the status or infamy of the person being executed. It is said that as he was processed to Tyburn Jack Sheppard was showered with flowers and goodwill messages, whilst the despised thief-taker Jonathan Wild was pelted with mud and excrement. Officers (marshals or constables) accompanied the cart; they were there to protect the condemned and ensure no escapes occurred. In the early eighteenth century it was customary for the cart to stop at various inns along the route so that the prisoners could be treated to a drink to stiffen their courage but this was later abandoned because commentators complained that it contributed to a sense of carnival that was inappropriate. When they arrived at the gallows there were often huge crowds, particularly in London, waiting to see the 'show'. People jostled for better vantage points and 'stands and other impromptu structures [were] erected to afford spectators a better view'.[13] Nowhere is this better illustrated than in William Hogarth's final panel of his *Industry and Idleness* series (see Figure 12.1), which shows the idle apprentice arriving at the 'triple tree' amidst a mighty throng of people, eager to watch him be 'turned off'.

In Hogarth's image crowds gather around the cart (which is finding it hard to make progress through them); there are already other bodies hanging from the gallows.

Figure 12.1 *Industry and Idleness: The Idle Prentice Executed at Tyburn*, by William Hogarth (1747).

Pickpockets and beggars operate amongst the assembled masses and the 'last dying speeches' of the condemned are sold as both valedictions and mementos of the event.

The atmosphere was often carnivalesque, something that attracted plenty of criticism from those that witnessed it. But the public nature of the execution was vital to early modern and eighteenth-century society: here justice was seen to be carried out on the body of the criminal. Before offenders were hanged they made a short statement (their 'last dying speech') and formally accepted their fate, forgave the hangman and entrusted their soul to God. This operated to justify the criminal justice system in front of the community that had been offended by the felon's criminal actions.

There was little that was swift about the hanging itself however. The condemned were hauled up on to the gallows by ropes pulled by the carthorses and then left to slowly strangle to death. Heavier individuals would die more quickly and it was common for the friends of those being executed to pull on their legs to end their suffering. Alternatively, one could pay the hangman to do this for you, hastening the end. We should be under no illusions that those that were hanged died quickly, for they did not – this was a painful and very public humiliation, often for offenders who had committed relatively trivial property crimes.

Concern about the effect on the sensibilities of the crowd or the potential for disorder caused by the Tyburn procession in London led to the removal of executions from Tyburn in 1783. Hereafter, public hangings took place outside Newgate prison (or at others of the capital's various gaols). The so-called 'new drop' introduced in the early nineteenth century was designed to quickly break the neck and so avoid the pain and suffering associated with the gallows. At first these were fairly ineffectual but gradually the science of execution improved. Indeed, by the middle of the twentieth century the famous executioner Albert Pierrepoint was proud of his ability to despatch his charges in seconds, almost painlessly. After 1868 there were no more executions in public and the image of justice switched from the gallows to the prison. Thus, as the period of our main interest opened, the key punishments of hanging, burning, pillory, whipping, fines and imprisonment were all in place. Over the next 200 years there was to be considerable reform of the penal system.

Benefit of clergy

In the medieval period, clergymen were only subject to the jurisdiction of the church, and not the secular courts. By the 1300s, this principle had been effectively extended to mean that ordained clerks of the church, if convicted by secular courts, could escape capital punishments by claiming 'benefit of clergy'. What did benefit of clergy mean and how did it operate? In reality it was to become a literacy test. Condemned convicts were required to prove their literacy by reading a psalm (Psalm 51 – the so-called 'neck verse') and thereby have their sentence of death suspended. In 1487, benefit was extended to non-ordained convicts but could be used once only; offenders were branded on the thumb with an *M* (for murder) or *T* (theft) and if convicted subsequently, the death sentence would be carried out.

However, it is far from clear whether this rule was actually applied and it seems more likely that sentencing decisions remained at the discretion of the presiding judge. From 1623 benefit was extended to include women and after 1476 the link with the ecclesiastical courts was removed completely. In effect, those granted benefit of clergy were, by the early seventeenth century at least, simply released without further punishment and by 1660 Beattie argues that the literacy test was largely ignored as well.[14] In 1706 the literacy was abandoned altogether and from 1717 nearly everyone who applied for benefit was transported to the English colonies in America.[15] Thus, benefit of clergy, by the early years of the eighteenth century, had become a way in which the justice system could apply discretionary mercy to sentencing; and that discretion rested largely with the judge at assizes. Indeed, as Beattie reminds us, for those unable to read 'all felonies were potentially capital before 1706', when the requirement to pass a literacy test for benefit of clergy was removed.[16]

The 'Bloody Code' and its collapse

The seemingly indiscriminate use of the death penalty in the period between the late 1680s and the early 1830s has come to be seen as the defining characteristic of the Hanoverian criminal justice system. From 1689 onwards, as parliament sat more regularly it was able to pass more laws – laws that frequently had very specific and localized intentions. These were laws that protected the property of those with influence within parliament, the small numbers of men that were entitled to vote and their representatives. The creation of new statutes also reflected the changing nature of commerce and the development of a capitalist economy in eighteenth-century England. For some historians, the expansion of the capital code in the 1700s can be explained as an attempt to cover loopholes in the law caused by 'issues of definition' in the existing legislation.[17] Alternatively, it can be seen as a reaction to the increased use of benefit of clergy. For others, it reflected the needs of the propertied elite to protect its interests (its wealth) from the property-less majority, the labouring classes. After all, as the philosopher John Locke recognized, government 'has no other end but the preservation of property'.[18] This surge in new statutes criminalized many activities formally seen as customary rights or perquisites ('perks') attached to common lands, woods, game, industrial practices and trade. Thus, an act in 1753 made the theft of shipwrecked goods punishable by death, one in 1764 prescribed death for those stealing or destroying linen, another in 1769 made the act of destroying a mill a capital offence, and perhaps most significant of all, new legislation protected the new paper currency that was symbolic of England's burgeoning commercial expansion.[19] In all the capital code expanded from 50 to over 200 separate statutes that decreed the death penalty for those that broke them. In reality most of those executed continued to be condemned under legislation enacted in the medieval and early modern periods.

The Waltham 'Black' Act

In 1723, parliament passed, almost without debate, an act which created 'at a blow some fifty new capital offences'.[20] This act, according to Edward Thompson, 'signalled the onset of the flood-tide of eighteenth-century retributive justice'.[21] The Black Act (more properly titled 'An Act for the more effectual punishing of wicked and evil-disposed person going about in Disguise etc.'[22]) considered a person to be a criminal if he or she was found to be armed and disguised on the highways or within the royal deer parks, and made the penalty for this death. In addition, there were a host of related offences that also prescribed the death sentence. Ostensibly the act was aimed at preventing poaching and attacks on gamekeepers around Waltham in Hampshire but has come to be seen as an example of the Hanoverian regime's brutal repression of the labouring class. Even such a conservative voice as Radzinowicz recognized that the extent of the act signalled a dramatic extension of the power of the eighteenth-century state. He noted that 'There is hardly a criminal act which did not come within the provision of the Black Act [...] the Act constituted in itself a complete and extremely severe criminal code'. [23]

The act allowed prosecutors to choose where in the country to prosecute and it gave them more time (three years) to bring a prosecution. This meant that individuals could be tried before judges and juries where they might be less likely to benefit from the sympathies of locals. For example, smugglers and those accused of attacks on the revenue men who policed the illegal trade in alcohol and tobacco along the southern coast were often acquitted by sympathetic juries who either approved of their actions or had been bribed or coerced into so doing.[24] By moving offenders to assizes in 'neutral' areas, and allowing more time to bring cases to trial, prosecutions were more likely to succeed. The Black Act, therefore, needs to be seen as a draconian piece of legislation that undermined some of the basic principles of the English criminal justice system.

In exploring the reasons for the act, orthodox or traditional historians have argued that the government was responding to an emergency or crisis; a sudden rise in incidents of deer stealing and violence directed towards the game keepers that policed the royal forest. But Thompson suggests instead that it was the challenge to authority that required the creation of such a brutal piece of legislation. Indeed, he argues, it 'was neither necessary, nor especially effective, in dealing with the particular "emergency" which served as its excuse'.[25] Others have suggested that the act was linked to fears about the Jacobite rebellion and so had a wider political motivation beyond the protection of property in Georgian England.[26] However we choose to understand the motivations behind the passing of the Black Act, it was a fairly clumsy piece of legislation. Nevertheless the act remained useful for the authorities because contained within it were specific clauses such as that concerned with 'shooting at the person' and the sending of threatening letters. Many of those tried in the eighteenth century for attempted murder were indicted under the terms of the Black Act for 'maliciously shooting at' their victim; this remained the case until Lord Ellenborough's 1803 act (the Malicious Shooting Act) and possibly for some time afterwards. Thus, while the Black Act was a temporary measure, it remained on the statute until 1828 although Peel had repealed many of its provisions by then.[27]

The Black Act was not the only notably harsh piece of legislation passed in response to a perceived crisis. In 1752, following a 'crime wave' that had been widely discussed in the newspapers and by contemporaries such as Henry Fielding, parliament passed the Murder Act.

The 1752 Murder Act

As Richard Ward's recent work has demonstrated, contemporaries at mid-century were extremely worried about what they saw as rising levels of violent crime, notably street or 'highway', robbery. This fear of crime was driven more by distorted newspaper reports and by pamphlets 'dedicated to the recent crime problem' than by reality, but it served to create an atmosphere of anxiety that required the attention of those in authority.[28] This heightened anxiety about crime led to the passing of the Murder Act which introduced new penalties for those convicted of murder. The act allowed for the execution of convicted killers within three days of sentencing, effectively limiting any real chance of achieving a pardon or commutation of sentence to transportation. It also prescribed that the bodies of executed murderers be handed over to surgeons for anatomization and dissection. While it is arguable that murderers were unlikely to escape death anyway (and the act did actually allow judges the option of overriding the 2–3-day rule if they saw fit), the introduction of anatomization was an attempt to ramp up the fear of execution and appease contemporary concerns that hanging was failing to deter criminals. In discussing the awful practice of *piene forte et dure* (the pressing of those that would not enter a plea) Andrea McKenzie has noted the bravado of robbers who were caught and indicted; for young men such as those immortalized in Gay's *Beggar's Opera*, the gallows perhaps offered little to fear and even a reputation to win.[29] By removing the option of a Christian burial in an age in which most people (even those steeped in criminality) believed in God and the afterlife, the existence of the soul, and the hope of resurrection, anatomization must have been an especial horror. This is evident in the lengths to which some went to save their loved ones and friends from such an indignity.[30] There is a postscript to this discussion of anatomization based on recent work by Elizabeth Hurren and her study of the practice after the passing of the Murder Act. She reveals that there were 'three distinct penal stages: first, a death penalty (legal death, to be hanged); second, a sentence to be anatomised (medical death) to look at the major organs expiring; and finally, dissection (post-mortem punishment)'. She suggests then that this reflected the reality that 'sometimes those executed for homicide did not expire on the gallows'.[31] Anatomization, then, was not simply the dissection of the criminal corpse and many of those facing this awful sentence must have realized this.

The extent of executions in London and the provinces

Given that the Bloody Code contained so many potential opportunities to deploy the death penalty, we might reasonably ask ourselves – just how many people met their death on the gallows? An important new research is very revealing: it shows that levels of executions varied considerably across the country. Indeed, some areas hardly saw an execution at all (something that has implications for the debate surrounding Hay's seminal thesis that the criminal justice system was an elite tool).[32] Gatrell used figures from an 1819 parliamentary select committee which allows an overview of capital convictions and executions from 1699 to 1818.[33] A lack of detailed information for all areas outside of London means that figures for provincial England are estimated and these results should be treated with caution, however it is possible to map what was happening in London.

Broadly speaking, the early eighteenth century witnessed 'relatively low' execution rates in London, with later peaks that coincided with periods of 'crime waves' (such as the 1780s) or the end of wars (i.e. after 1815).[34] Here the figures from the 1819 committee reveal that from the 1760s onwards more than half of those sentenced to death were pardoned or had their sentences commuted (to transportation or some form of imprisonment). Indeed, it was only in the period 1751–1760 that pardons fell below 50 per cent. In the early nineteenth century well over 80 per cent of those sentenced to death were reprieved but large numbers were still being capitally convicted (so, in the period 1826–1830 there were 857 capital convictions at the Old Bailey and eighty-nine hangings, still more than twice as many executions as there had been between 1801 and 1805). Gatrell has argued that far from there being a 'squeamishness about bringing people to court under capital law', there was actually a massive increase in prosecutions between 1805 and 1830 (when hanging was almost entirely reserved for the punishment of murderers). This led Gatrell to conclude that the retreat from hanging in the 1830s was a reaction to the high numbers being sentenced to death and the impossibility of hanging them all without provoking a popular revolt against the criminal justice system. Before the reform of capital statutes in the 1820s and 1830s there were, as has been noted, over 200 offences which carried the death penalty. But after 1837 execution was reserved for murder and attempted murder, rape and some forms of child abuse, sodomy, burglary or robbery with violence, some forms of arson, treason and a small number of other serious but rare offences. Further legislation in 1861 restricted the use of the gallows to murder or treason although, as Gatrell notes, in 'practice, after 1837 only murderers were hanged'.[35] In 1868, hanging moved behind closed doors and the spectacle of the gallows – such a feature of the Hanoverian justice system – became a thing of the past.

Before we look at the reasons behind the supposed 'collapse' of the use of the death penalty in England in the early nineteenth century, we need to pause and consider whether our understanding of the use of the gallows has been overly influenced by histories that concentrate on London and the Home Counties. Similarly, we have wonderful qualitative resources for London for the long eighteenth century but the use of the Old Bailey Proceedings is apt to produce a London-centric discourse on crime and punishment. Peter King and Richard Ward have recently argued that while executions were frequent in

London, the picture was very different elsewhere in England and Wales. Using a range of sources previously underexploited by historians (the accounts – or 'cravings' – of county sheriffs) they have noted the 'refusal of many areas on the periphery [such as Cornwall, Westmorland, Durham and Wales] to implement the Bloody Code'.[36] While large numbers of felons were being sent to the gallows in London and the Home Counties, hardly anyone was being capitally convicted let alone executed in these areas. So, in the period that King and Ward have looked at, the third quarter of the eighteenth century, executions per annum in London were 'over fifty times higher (at 3.85/100,000) than the average rate (of 0.07) for the ten counties with the lowest'.[37] Even if we accept Simon Devereaux's caveat that the third quarter of the century may have been an 'exceptionally quiet time' for executions, even in London, this still represents a massive difference in penal policy and a sobering reminder to historians that when we consider the 'Bloody Code' we need to be quite careful of making generalizations based on the centre.[38]

King and Ward offer an interesting set of explanations for the stark difference in the use of capital punishment. There was less of an inequality gap within societies on the periphery than was the case nearer the centre and as a result prosecutors and jurors were likely to have been closer, in a socio-economic sense, to those that were accused of offending. Jurors had a great deal of discretion available to them, not least in being able to downgrade the value of goods stolen so as to prevent judges from handing down sentences of death. If jurors on the periphery were uncomfortable with sending property offenders to the gallows, it is quite likely, King and Ward argue, that local prosecutors would also have been 'more reluctant to prosecute, and more reluctant to use capital charges' both of which help explain why indictment and execution rates for property criminals were so low.[39] Murderers were still executed but property crime was not punished by death on the periphery.

The actions of jurors and prosecutors were echoed by those of the sheriffs, the men tasked by the courts with carrying out executions. It is evident that they tried very hard *not* to hang convicts, on one occasion even conspiring with the local magistracy to allow a convicted felon to escape. It was also hard to find hangmen to carry out executions. Petitions demonstrate that some areas were very proud of their record of not hanging offenders and the idea emerges, strongly, that 'their county's reputation was on the line, and that the convict was in a real sense the victim, thus putting the judges increasingly on the defensive' when it came to sentencing.[40] It seems then that the further removed from London and the centre of government, the less the Bloody Code operated as a mechanism of fear and control. King and Ward suggest that communities may have seen the justice system as alien to their culture; it was carried out in English, which for the Welsh (and maybe for some other regions) was not widely understood and certainly not the language used in daily life. There were religious differences as well. Both Cornwall and Wales were hotbeds of non-conformity, and dissenting clergymen opposed use of the death penalty for property offenders on the grounds that it contravened 'God's law'. This reflects early nineteenth-century evangelical opposition to the death penalty, which used religious scripture to campaign against the hanging of all but the most serious violent offenders.[41]

So, we need to be cautious of understanding the retreat from hanging in England in the 1830s as something that happened suddenly or indeed that it had not occurred to people earlier that 'capital punishment for relatively trivial crimes was an inhumane way of dealing with crime'[42] as Gatrell suggests. Instead, it would seem that outside of the centre and away from the reach of the state, regions on the periphery found other ways to keep safe their property and deter criminals. Future historians of crime might like to explore what these alternatives were; my view is that we need to look at the ways in which JPs operated here and explore the practice of restorative justice more closely on the peripheries. King and Ward have opened up the debate here and I would hope and expect this will drive new research over the next few years because their important findings require us, as they say, to 'rethink some of our core assumptions about the foundations of elite's hegemony, about attitudes to the abolition of capital punishment, and about the reach of the state in the long eighteenth century'.[43] It is to the second of those points, the abolition of the death penalty, that this chapter will now turn.

Historians' explanations for the collapse of the Bloody Code

The Bloody Code was at its height in the period just before its collapse in the 1820s, at least in London and the Home Counties. A rising population, and a greater concentration of people in urban areas, contributed to growing concerns about crime. When this was combined with financial support for prosecutors and some improvement in policing (in the capital at least) the rate of prosecutions rose. Inevitably, since so many offences carried the death penalty, the number of capital convictions rose accordingly. Therefore, as Gatrell says, the 'implications could not be evaded for long. A consistent proportion of the condemned could not be hanged if the land were not to be covered in gallows'.[44] Gatrell's explanation for the retreat from hanging as a primary form of punishment for property crime is therefore structural; the system simply could not support the numbers of convicted criminals that were sentenced to death. However, there are several alternative viewpoints that need to be considered here.

Contemporaries were themselves uneasy about the Bloody Code. Critics condemned the theatre of the gallows and argued that far from deterring criminals the large crowds that watched executions drew gangs of pickpockets. Apprentices avoided work to watch hangings and drunkenness and debauchery were features of the spectacle. Far from being solemn affairs the execution had degenerated into festivals of death. One foreign commentator was shocked at how sanguinary the English justice was; 'the smallest thief is punished with death' wrote Meister during his visit between 1789 and 1792.[45] The reality that hanging was applied to a huge range of crimes, seemingly regardless of differing levels of seriousness, led others to conclude that the code was indiscriminate. After all, a murderer was treated in much the same way as a highway robber, burglar or even a relatively minor petty thief.

In this way the fairness of the system was being called into question and this, according to one historian, had a political significance in the period. Randall McGowen has argued that criticism of the criminal justice system was a legitimate way for opposition (Whig) politicians to attack the Tory government.[46] Whigs claimed that the system was uncertain and tyrannical; whether one was hanged or pardoned was arbitrary, and this meant that 'justice' resembled a lottery. This manifested itself in the marked reluctance of victims of crime to prosecute and so threatened to undermine the criminal justice system. Put simply, prosecutors were reluctant to bring charges against those that had stolen small amounts from them because of the risk that they would be the cause of their death on the gallows, and this situation was particularly apparent in prosecutions against female thieves. Contemporaries also noted that criminals were well aware of the discretionary nature of the lottery and of calculating that they had a more than evens chance of escaping the noose. The Bloody Code was, therefore, a poor deterrent. Samuel Romilly, an ardent campaigner against the death penalty, declared that 'certainty of punishment rather than its severity' was crucial for the prevention of crime. Sir William Meredith complained that 'the cruel exhibition of every execution day is proof that hanging carries no terror with it'. Meredith agreed with Romilly that 'it is not the mode, but the certainty of punishment that creates terror'.[47] In short, the criminal justice system was inefficient and was failing in its purpose, which was to protect property. The subject was returned to time and again in parliamentary debates and the Whigs argued that an inefficient and unfair justice system put both property and national stability at stake.

McGowen has suggested that what really lay behind the humanitarian rhetoric of the Whig reformers was not efficiency but a concern for what he terms the 'image of justice'. Given that the public too often identified with the condemned rather than the victims of crime, the system was sending the wrong message and needed to be reformed. This was very apparent in the debates surrounding the 1819 select committee that investigated the reform of the criminal law. Phil Handler noted that the committee set out a new model of punishment which 'had to be certain, proportionate and in harmony with public feeling' as opposed to one that advocated 'harsh, discretionary punishment'.[48] By reducing the number of capital statutes the government had the opportunity to re-legitimize the justice system. Not surprisingly, Tory ministers did not agree. They argued that the use of discretion helped to cement the importance of paternalist rule and that by unravelling the code the reformers would in effect unravel the machinery of monarchical government. It was discretion that allowed the law to be flexible: by imposing a less arbitrary system a more rigid and, by implication, a harsher system might be created. So, while the Whigs condemned 'tyranny' and urged reform, the Tories counselled against jettisoning the severe punishments that existed. This was, in McGowen's view, part of a wider attack on the *ancien regime* and an attempt by the middling class to exert their rights to be a more important part of government.[49] Handler stresses the centrality of the arguments surrounding the hanging of forgers and utterers after the bank crisis of 1818 to the debate about abolition. Radicals used the bank note crisis to criticize both the system of paper currency exchange and to 'bring the inadequacies of the criminal justice system into sharp relief'. In doing so he offers another interesting and nuanced view of McGowen's 'image of justice' thesis.[50]

McGowen's is a sophisticated and complex explanation which uses a traditional narrative of reform as expressed by writers such as Radzinowicz, but interprets it quite differently. However, those writers that favour a Marxist or social control interpretation of events have suggested that the Bloody Code came to an end because it no longer served the interests of those in power. Michel Foucault has linked the end of the Bloody Code with the rise of capitalism and a greater determination by those in power to observe, discipline and control the working classes. In his brilliant thesis, *Discipline and Punish*, Foucault outlined a change from public physical punishments in the eighteenth century to private incarceration in the nineteenth.[51] The former demonstrated the power of the monarch over the individual while the latter reclassified the offender as a deviant who had transgressed society's norms.

However, the growth of the state also allowed for the creation of bureaucracies and the establishment of state institutions such as the police. The latter clearly helped to make arrest and therefore prosecution more certain, and went some way to meeting concerns about the efficiency of the justice system. A bigger state with larger tax gathering powers also allowed for the building of prisons as alternatives to hanging and these structural explanations, alongside Gatrell's, are plausible alternatives to Foucault's social control paradigm. Historians have explored the collapse of the Bloody Code from other angles, looking at the effect on the crowd, the role of evangelical religion and enlightened 'rational' reformers.[52] Follett covers the importance of evangelical Christians to the debate on hanging at length. In his view strongly held religious views were brought to play in the parliamentary debates on the amelioration of the death penalty. The protagonists were men (such as William Wilberforce) who had previously campaigned successfully against slavery and who were able to present 'rationalistic arguments for proportionality and certainty in punishment with religiously-based notions of justice and mercy'.[53] The debates blended the views of evangelicals (such as Thomas Fowell Buxton) with utilitarians (e.g. Jeremy Bentham). There was considerable agreement between them but the evangelicals provided the philosophy which underpinned the drive for reform. This came down to debates about how a Christian society should treat those that offended against it, and in doing so made a case for a penal system that would inculcate reform and redemption.[54] Jeremy Bentham (who was no evangelical, but a man steeped in Enlightenment reason) opposed the death penalty (except for murder) on pragmatic and philosophical grounds. Hanging had no economic benefit; better surely to make the criminal work for the good the community he had offended than kill him. Using execution for both property *and* violent offences was, he contended, irrational and made it unpopular with the public, and this undermined the rule of law. Juries, witnesses and prosecutors all realized this and used the discretion available to them to prevent judges from sending many offenders to their deaths. Furthermore, Bentham was worried that in the hands of 'evil judges' or a 'tyrannical government' the death penalty was a dangerous weapon of power, much better then to restrict its use and find an alternative way to deal with crime.[55] So, despite some differences between evangelical and utilitarian viewpoints Follett suggests that their positions were not as far apart as some historians have suggested.

Several scholars (McGowen, Ignatieff and Emsley in particular) have questioned the motivation of Evangelical reformers and seen them as 'bent on social control'. However, Follett suggests that this is not really *that* important a point since the reformers themselves would hardly have challenged this or seen it as a criticism. The criminal law 'by definition was, and always has been, about social control. It has always concerned the protection of persons and property from those who, wilfully or out of necessity, choose to attack these objects for personal gain, survival, or political protest'.[56] Both sets of reformers opposed the death penalty and argued that there were better ways to punish; methods that offered the hope of rehabilitation and redemption through repentance. These were widely held Christian values amongst the burgeoning middle classes of England who believed in the importance of respecting private property. So, while Follett and McGowen might disagree about the differences between conservative and evangelical views on the use of hanging, there was a gradual move to make property crime non-capital in the nineteenth century.

Whether we use Gatrell's structural explanation, or Foucault's social control thesis, it is clear from the work we have on evangelicalism, or the reshaping of the British political makeup in the 1830s, that there is no simple or short answer to the question of why the Bloody Code was abandoned in the 1820s and 1830s and of course, recent work on execution on the periphery as we have seen[57] necessitates a thorough reassessment of what has been argued up until now. But statute by statute (starting with picking pockets) all the laws that involved property crime were made non-capital in this period. As Earl Grey said in support of Sir Samuel Romilly's 1832 bill to remove the death penalty from the crime of shoplifting: 'Is it no evil that one individual should have it in his power to visit another with such capital punishment, or to exempt him from it, at his discretion?'[58] Once the reformers had successfully removed the death penalty for all property crimes, it was only retained for a handful of offences, and in effect only used for murderers. Thereafter, the debate turned from hanging to the public spectacle and eventually that too was abolished. After the execution of the unfortunate Fenian 'terrorist' Michael Barrett for blowing up Clerkenwell Gaol in 1868 all subsequent hangings took place behind closed doors.[59] In the meantime the English state set about to find an alternative to the practice of strangling its unwanted criminals to death; ultimately the alternative it decided upon was the penitentiary prison that had been championed by those reformers who had so vehemently opposed hanging.

The search for alternative, intermediate punishments

From the beginning of the period covered by this book all the existing early modern punishments remained in place. Moreover, the early to mid-1700s saw the extension of capital punishment to more and more offences as well as additional humiliations being added to execution for some offenders; there was little real change in the options open to judges sentencing those found guilty of felonies. As a result, many of those convicted at the assizes were sentenced to death and then had to hope that, through benefit of clergy or the pardoning process, they would be spared the noose. Benefit of clergy allowed those convicted of capital crimes to take a literacy test at the end of trials and before sentencing. Whilst clergy was almost always granted the judges 'retained a discretionary power that was virtually uncontrollable to decide whether a man had read well enough to save his life'. This power was removed in 1706 and Beattie sees this as 'profoundly important' because it brought a certain level of equality to sentencing.[60]

We are now used to the idea that most of those convicted of crime will be fined, given a community punishment or a probation order, while those deemed worthy of a more serious punishment will be committed to prison. However, the prison was largely a nineteenth-century phenomenon and while there were experiments with custodial sentences and long-established institutions for the disciplining of the immoral, petty thieves, vagrants and servants (the houses of correction or 'bridewells' that were discussed earlier), society was still wrestling with the problem of what to do with those found guilty of felonious (capital) property crime. So, before we turn to the subject of gaols and how they began to rise to prominence it is necessary to consider the alternatives to execution that existed in the seventeenth and early eighteenth centuries. This discussion will largely confine itself to criminal transportation to the Americas because in effect this was to remain the only real alternative to hanging until the 1770s.

Transportation to America and the 1718 act

We more usually associate the export of criminals from Britain with the birth and growth of Australia but the transportation of convicted criminals has a long history in England. Even before the 1718 Transportation Act (which provided official sanction for the practice) the English state had banished offenders to various destinations. Most were transported to the new colonies in America (such as Maryland and Virginia). These were usually capital convicts whose sentences had been commuted, but it seems likely that significant numbers of petty thieves were also being sent abroad even though there was no legal framework for doing so. There was some enthusiasm for transportation after the Restoration of the monarchy in 1660 but this was not sustained. Even after 1718, when transportation became an official option for the courts, not all counties used it in the same ways: some utilized it for offenders at all levels of the court system while others restricted it those tried at assizes.[61] While there were principled objections to the use of transportation as a punishment the main reasons behind its marginal use were practical. As Beattie points out, the system was poorly run and unpopular amongst the colonists. In addition, it was organized by merchants who selected only those convicts they thought they could sell as indentured servants, as a result older convicts and women were often left to rot in gaol. Moreover, the colonists objected to having criminals dumped on them and some (notably Virginia and Maryland) passed local laws to prohibit the practice. Later attempts to send felons to the West Indies met similar local resistance.[62] Some of the problems associated with transportation were addressed by the 1718 act that allocated government money to the scheme; merchants were now paid to transport offenders, either directly from the treasury or from the county rates. The growing colonies were also better equipped to receive a new influx of criminals and the English government more determined in the 1720s than it had been in the late seventeenth century to impose its will. Estimates vary but perhaps as many as 50,000 British criminals were forcibly migrated to the continent. This then, to some extent, explains the relatively slow development of imprisonment in eighteenth-century England because in the colonies the English justice system possessed a viable alternative to hanging and one that still achieved, at an affordable price, the removal of felons from its shores.[63]

Problems remained however, and the system was predicated on the sale of felons at the docks where the ships disembarked to colonists who would use them as indentured labour on their farms and plantations. As Morgan and Rushton have described, 'Shiploads of a hundred or more felons were not unusual' and in 1774 'the *William* left the Bristol Channel with ninety-nine convicts, drawn from fifteen counties from as far north as Cheshire and as far east as Northampton, as well as most of the western Midlands, Monmouthshire and the South West'.[64] But each English region varied, and in other examples ships sailed with many more voluntary migrants than convicts on board.

The system was also open to corruption. Some convicts bribed their way home almost as soon as they had arrived, and if they were former seamen they had plenty of chances to find a returning ship; if one could bribe the ship's captain or crew and slip away at port then the likelihood of making it back to England was significantly increased. Those unable to work (the sick and elderly) were perhaps less likely to be transported and certainly less able to find a position when they arrived, so the system had some important flaws.

At mid-century there was plenty of press criticism of transportation and alarm at the perceived numbers of those escaping and returning to England. In reality this was probably exaggerated by the print media and used as part of wider debate about penal policy (which influenced the passing of the Murder Act in 1752). Relatively few of those that were placed with colonial masters were able to escape because the colonies possessed the mechanisms of surveillance to control these workforces and the ability to recapture anyone who attempted to run away.

Nor would everyone sentenced to transportation have been unhappy with the situation. Transportation offered a new start away from the crowded cities and towns of England and in a potentially much improved climate. Convicted criminals petitioned the king to be transported instead of being hanged, and judges could use their discretion to reprieve others at the end of trials (in what Beattie has termed 'administrative pardons'). Before 1718 some would have had to arrange their own transportation, and so 'consented' to be transported rather than suffer a worse fate. Given that the alternative was branding on the hand or death, it is not surprising that the New World looked attractive to some. Not to all, though; despite contemporary criticism that it was 'soft option', there was considerable depiction of the process in contemporary print culture to the extent that 'the imagery of virtual slavery in the colonies' was 'deeply imbedded in popular consciousness'.[65]

The transportation of convicts to British America offered the motherland a real alternative to capital punishment and undoubtedly ameliorated the 'Bloody Code' in the

1700s. It removed felons from sight and continued a tradition from the early modern period of expelling the unwanted, non-useful members of society (such as beggars and vagrants). But it was not without its problems, not least for the colonists who increasingly resented being a dumping ground for Britain's criminals. This position was to eventually undermine the practice (as indeed it was to do later on in the mid-nineteenth century with criminal transportation to Australia). Morgan and Ruston identify the tensions that arose as a result of transportation in the years before the outbreak of the American Revolution. They argue that

> The convicts became a source of bad blood between the 'mother country' and her colonies. To the British they furnished proof of the polluted – hence illegitimate – society demanding independence. This dismissive image had racial overtones, in the sense that a criminal class could be conceived as a kind of hereditary difference, an 'other' whose stigma could not be removed.[66]

These same themes emerged in debates about returning convicts from Australia and in concerns about what were termed 'ticket-of-leave' men in the 1850s and 1860s. It would seem then that criminal transportation, whilst offering an important alternative to hanging, could only ever operate as a temporary measure; it was no panacea for the justice system. Things came to a head in 1775 and while the British government initially set about finding a new destination (the West Indies seeming the obvious one) English prisons began to become overcrowded with convicts who could not now be sent overseas. After the war it seems there were hopes that the trade in convict labour could be recommenced, almost as if nothing had changed. Of course the situation had changed fundamentally and efforts to ship convicts to the United States in the early 1780s floundered. Thus, the outbreak of war with the American rebels in 1775 brought transportation there to an end and produced something of a crisis in the criminal justice system. The crowded insanitary nature of British gaols forced the government to look elsewhere, first to West Africa and then to Botany Bay. The experience of transportation to the American colonies no doubt influenced policy making in what was to become Australia. That of course is an important story and it will be addressed later but for now we need to think a little about late seventeenth- and eighteenth-century prisons and what they were used for and how this changed across the 1700s.

The eighteenth-century prison

Prisons existed in the eighteenth century but they were far removed from the highly regulated institutions they were to become in the late 1800s. The Hanoverian gaol was privately run and intended to be self-supporting or profit-making. In this they were fundamentally similar to the network of houses of correction that existed across England and Wales by the early 1700s. In 1706, an act of parliament 'authorised the sentencing of people convicted of simple felonies at quarter sessions or assizes for terms in bridewells of between six months and two years' and this probably encouraged magistrates to use these institutions for the punishment of petty thieves, poachers and those embezzling their master's goods or stealing wood.[67] As was noted earlier, those confined to the house of correction for short sentences (generally under a year and often merely for a few weeks or months) were set to work. Inmates might unpick oakum (the tarred rope used by the navy) or be tasked with breaking rocks, but individual bridewell masters could utilize their inmates as they wished. The situation was similar in the county gaols and those of the major cities, such as London.

The keeper (governor) of the gaol employed turnkeys (warders) to run the day-to-day business of the gaols and there was little interference from outside. The county quarter sessions bench was tasked with overseeing conditions in their local goals but this appears to have been done lightly if at all. Secondly, it is clear that there was little, if any, separation of different sorts of inmate. As a result debtors, remand prisoners and the condemned were often mixed in together despite there being a presumption that, as they had different privileges, they should be kept apart. Likewise, male and female prisoners and the young were often allowed to associate with each other.

The entrepreneurial nature of prisons in the 1700s and the lack of separation of inmates horrified reformers such as John Howard and Elizabeth Fry. Prisons were dangerous places because there was very little control over those imprisoned in them. In Newgate, London's largest gaol, around 200 prisoners were contained and their financial situation largely determined the conditions they experienced. Wealthier inmates could rent rooms on the 'Master's side' where they could enjoy almost unlimited access to the outside world. Prisoners could have their friends and family visit at any time or allow them to stay, they could purchase food and drink, entertain and even have prostitutes brought to their rooms. More importantly, they could perhaps pay the turnkeys not to shackle them in irons. In most gaols irons and fetters were the main means to prevent escape given that the regimes were so lax and many prison walls were low or crumbling.[68]

The situation on the 'Common side' was much less attractive; here a lack of money meant prisoners suffered in appalling conditions. Gaols had no obligations to provide food and drink for inmates, regardless of the reason for their imprisonment, and so many handed out the barest minimum of sustenance – bread and water, and even this was limited. Prisoners were able to beg for alms from passers-by, or were brought food by their families and friends. Starvation, disease and death were common as sanitary conditions were atrocious. In the Poultry Compter at the heart of the City of London the deaths of three inmates in 1786 from disease, starvation and neglect prompted a concerned philanthropist to petition the Common Council for an improvement in conditions.[69] The stories of these inmates could have been repeated across the city and the rest of the country as the letters of prisoners confined in Newgate between 1781 and 1827 for offences against the Bank of England testify.[70]

Thus wealth, not the nature of one's offence or status (debtor, convict or remand prisoner) determined one's experience of gaol in the 1700s. Turnkeys unashamedly exploited richer prisoners for every shilling they could and neglected the poorest who had little to offer. And the exploitation of the situation extended to the prisoners themselves; so new inmates were charged 'garnish' (a small fee that allowed them to buy food and other comforts) by established ones. The extraction of money did not stop at the end of a sentence either – turnkeys charged a release fee and if prisoners could not afford to pay then they would be forced to remain in gaol despite being acquitted in court or completing the length of their sentence.

All of this shocked prison reformers who viewed prisons as centres of contamination within which any new inmate was exposed to disease, vice and corruption. If that was not bad enough prisons were also largely run by the prisoners themselves, who created their own rules and laid on their own forms of entertainment. Gambling, drinking, prostitution and violence largely went unchecked; prisoners even staged their own mock trials in Newgate, appointed 'judges' and 'juries', accepted bribes, handed down sentences and carried out punishments. This creation of an inmate subculture was of particular concern to reformers because it meant that any attempt at the control and rehabilitation of inmates was critically undermined; meaning, as Ignatieff has observed, that eighteenth-century prisons did 'not enforce a "discipline" in the nineteenth-century sense of the term'.[71] As a result, the gaols of the 1700s were fetid, unregulated and dangerous places to be incarcerated within.

Efforts were made in the later 1700s to address these problems. John Howard made a survey of English and Continental gaols. He noted the poor conditions and published his findings in his *The State of Prisons in England and Wales... and an Account of Some Foreign Prisons* (1777). Robert Turnbull visited the Pennsylvania State penitentiary in Philadelphia and was impressed by the industry he saw there. It 'was with difficulty' he wrote, that 'I divested myself of the idea that these men *surely were not convicts*, but accustomed to labour from their infancy'.[72] The Philadelphia prison (now the Eastern State Penitentiary, preserved as a museum and tourist attraction) offered a model of what a prison could be like, and it drew heavily on the writings of reformers and penologists such as Beccaria, Bentham, Howard and George Onesiphorous Paul, the keeper of Gloucester gaol. Paul argued that convicts should be separated from each other. In 1809, he wrote:

> In a Penitentiary House, I conceive it as absolutely necessary to reformation, that the prisoners should generally, as a class, be secluded from intercourse with all persons without the walls of their prison; and that they should individually be separated in all their hours of occupation.[73]

What Paul established in his report was the importance of separating prisoners from each other (while at the same time noting in passing that complete isolation in solitary confinement was not beneficial and could be harmful – something not always recognized by later penal theorists). The majority of prison reformers accepted this in the late eighteenth and early nineteenth centuries and separation underpinned efforts to improve prison conditions. However, the process of prison reform is characterized by grandiose ideals coming into sharp conflict with the harsh realities of funding and concerns about making prisons too 'soft'. Indeed the same complaints that are routinely levelled at the twenty-first-century penal system have been aimed at governments for centuries.

We started this exploration of the history of punishment with the public and physical infliction of pain in the early modern age. The 1700s saw the continuation of hanging alongside flogging and the pillory, as thousands of men and women (and in some cases children) were sent to their deaths for a wide range of offences, most of which related to the theft of property. There was a growing acceptance that execution was neither effective in deterring crime nor was it reasonable to treat all criminals in the same way. Juries were increasingly reluctant to convict and prosecutors shied away from bringing charges against petty thieves they had no wish to see dangling from a rope.

As a result the state sought alternatives to the gallows and increased the numbers of felons it exiled abroad, making transportation statutory punishment after 1718. In the meantime it continued the largely local and entrepreneurial experiment with imprisonment at hard labour that had been started in the Tudor and Elizabethan periods. The next chapter will take the story of punishment forward into the nineteenth century and discuss the second wave of transportation and the arguments for different forms of prison regime. If the Hanoverian epoch was the 'age of the gallows' then the Victorian period must surely be seen as the 'age of the prison'. However, how much more civilized or successful the prison was as a form of punishment is something that has exercised historians of crime for many years, and this will be discussed in the next chapter.

CHAPTER 13
THE RISE AND FALL OF INCARCERATION

In the previous chapter we saw how ideas about reformation and qualms about the discretionary use of the 'Bloody Code' had engendered a deep sense of unease about the criminal justice system. Experiments with alternatives to hanging had been brought to an abrupt end in 1775 with the outbreak of war with the American colonies. Despite attempts to utilize old naval vessels as floating prisons (the hulks), there was an awareness that a new destination had to be found for Britain's unwanted felons lest the gallows become overburdened under the weight of thousands of robbers, burglars and horse thieves. This chapter will look at how this problem was initially solved by the discovery of Australia and the recommencement of criminal transportation to Botany Bay after 1787.

Australia was to be a temporary measure, albeit of long duration. The real alternative to hanging was imprisonment and this chapter will concentrate for the most part on the rise of the prison. By the middle of the 1800s the key issue for the state was not whether to transport or imprison, rather it was to what sort of regime of discipline should convicted criminals be subjected to. This in turn reflected changing attitudes towards crime and criminality and was affected by the belief in the existence of a 'criminal class' in Victorian society. Arguments turned on how best to treat these 'habitual' criminals and whether efforts to rehabilitate them were desirable or effectual. By the 1860s the experiment with reform had largely been discarded and a new system, based in part on the experiences of officials working in the penal colony at Norfolk Island, was deployed in English prisons.

Eventually, reformers again cried foul and at the very end of the nineteenth century (and then after the First World War) there was a move to rethink the nature of punishment and whether all persons were suitable objects to be placed inside the walls of Pentonville and the nation's other convict and local prisons. We will start however, with the return to criminal transportation, this time to the newest addition to the growing British Empire.

Transportation to Australia – convict workers

As we have seen, the curtailment of transportation to the American colonies after 1775 necessitated a search for alternatives and various options were explored. Many of those sent to the hulks died, prisons were not unable to absorb the increased numbers and the gallows could only hang so many 'examples' without risking a popular reaction against it. In 1779, a parliamentary committee recommended that alternative destinations for transportation be explored, and these included Africa and the new colony at Botany Bay in Australia. As pressure on the creaking justice system grew in the 1780s, finding a new transportation destination became an imperative for government and in 1786 after rejecting Africa, Canada, the West Indies and other places, the cabinet decided on Australia.[1]

The first fleet landed its cargo of 736 convicts (548 men and 188 women) in Botany Bay in 1788, just eighteen years after Captain Cook had first set foot there. As Robert Hughes has written:

> Now this coast was to witness a new colonial experiment, never tried before, not repeated since. An unexplored continent would become a jail. The space around it, the very air and sea, the whole transparent labyrinth of the South Pacific, would become a wall 14,000 miles thick.[2]

What set Australia apart was that 'from the outset it was a penal colony in which labour was regulated by government' and not by the colonists as had been the case in America.[3] Botany Bay and New South Wales were then to become a penal colony for the next thirty-five years where the main settlers were convicts, marines and the wives of marines. Throughout the early years of the nineteenth century convicted criminals were also sent to other destinations on the Australian continent: Norfolk Island, Van Diemen's Land, Port Macquarie and Moreton Bay.

Convicts were set to work, in effect to develop and extend the colony under the supervision of the British navy. Convicts (a term disliked by those transported, who referred to themselves as 'government men' or prisoners[4]) formed the majority of the colony's population for the first few decades, and by 1821 there were a growing number of freed convicts who were appointed to positions of trust and responsibility as well as being granted land. The possibility of reform and of starting a new life seems to have been a part of the vision of some, like Sir Samuel Romilly, who advocated the use of transportation over the death penalty. By the time the last prisoners arrived in Western Australia in 1868, some 162,000 men and women had been taken out of Britain and relocated in the new colony, brought there in over 800 ships in just less than eighty years.

In recent years the history of Australian convict migration has undergone something of a transformation as historians such as Hamish Maxwell-Stewart and Deborah Oxley have opened new areas of research into the lives of those that were forcibly transported to the other side of the world.[5] Traditional histories of Australia had tended to paint a picture of either a group of heroic individuals, often transported for their political beliefs (the Tolpuddle Martyrs or the Chartists), or of a criminal class of professional thieves and prostitutes cast out of their homeland for a refusal to conform to the strict rules of the British criminal justice system.[6] Australians have thus grown up with conflicting interpretations of their nation's history either as something to be proud of – something that defines their independence and their 'natural' antipathy to England – or with the shame of the stain left on the so called 'Fatal Shore'.[7] Realistically, neither of the positions are accurate representations of the men and women who were transported for seven or fourteen years, or for life.

In the late 1980s, a new perspective on transportation emerged which challenged both positions and offered a fresh analysis. *Convict Workers: Reinterpreting Australia's Past* (1988) set out a manifesto for a new paradigm of convict history. Stephen Nicholas, Peter Shergold, Oxley and others suggested instead that the 'convict settlers were Australia's first migrants'.[8] Rather than viewing transportation simply as a means of punishing criminals or of expelling an unwanted deviant population, the *Convict Workers* School has argued that transportation represented an attempt by the British state to export a working population to colonize and build this new addition to the empire.

They compared the policy of transportation with that of other states such as France and Spain, arguing that it needs to be 'located within the comparative literature of "unfree" labour migration'.[9] The Spanish used a system of galley slaves until 1748 when it established penal colonies (*presides*) in North Africa, Puerto Rico and Cuba. In France proposals to send offenders to French Polynesia or the South Atlantic were rejected in the 1780s but by the mid-1800s political prisoners, convicts and the unemployed were being sent to colonial destinations such as Algeria. The Russian state also sent millions of its people into exile in Siberia, a process that continued well into the twentieth century.[10] For Nicholas and Shergold then, 'Convictism, like indenture, represented a half-way stage between a slave and free labour system.'[11]

Their second point was that the convicts sent to Australia were not professional criminals or members of a criminal class: they were ordinary working-class men and women drawn from across the British Isles. Whilst they had all committed (or been found guilty of committing) felonies deemed punishable by transportation, in reality this meant the majority were guilty of stealing relatively small amounts of property. So, most of these were opportunistic petty thieves using crime as part of their struggle to survive. In addition, many of those transported to Australia were themselves migrants to (or within) England and so were especially suited to this new role as colonists. They brought a useful cross-section of skills from a range of working-class labouring backgrounds and they were young – around 80 per cent were aged 16–25 – in marked contrast to the free migrants to the colony. Most convicts were single males and so 'the age-sex structure of the convicts provided a unique workforce upon which to build economic growth'.[12]

These migrants were relatively fit and well-educated; the majority could read and write and those unlikely to survive the long sea journey were left behind. Maxwell-Stewart is currently researching the health and physical status of the convict population and has been able to demonstrate that those transported in many ways benefitted from the experience compared to the extended families that remained in Britain and Ireland.[13] Finally, the *Convict Workers* School rejects the idea that the convict system wasted the lives of those caught up in it. There were brutal punishment regimes within the colony, notably at Norfolk Island, but the majority of convicts were well treated and set to work. The system of public labour used was well organized and reflected the free labour market, and this was not a 'society terrorised by the lash'. Convicts were well fed, medically looked after and housed in better conditions than their counterparts in Britain. Overall then, this book views the transportation system not simply as a way of ridding England of its desperate villains and whores, but also as a successful and calculated example of empire building.

But just as had been the case in the America, the Australian colony increasingly came to resent being a depository for British and Irish criminals. They were not the only discordant voices that were raised in opposition to the practice. An anonymous writer in the mid-1830s condemned transportation as 'an evil in every sense of the word'. He argued that in turning Australia into one giant prison society England was condemning its children to grow up in a world where 'the infant is educated among convicts, and the clanking of chains is a music to the ear – the cry of the unfortunate, suffering under the lash of flagellator, it becomes accustomed to – in fact, its education is commenced, continued, and finished in the a gaol'.[14] The author was correct in identifying some aspects of the convict experience as abhorrent. The harsh regime endured by those convicts that did not submit themselves to authority of the colony's governors was qualitatively worse than anything they might have experienced in England. Norfolk Island was the destination for those that broke the rules 'down under' and it was an unforgiving place. Discipline bordered on the brutal and inhumane and except for a brief period in the 1840s, when Captain Alexander Maconochie was in charge, the island was a place of dread. Maconochie was more enlightened and pioneered the Mark System (later adopted in part in English prisons). This allowed convicts to gain credits that could be used towards their eventual release, through work and good behaviour. This notion that freedom could be earned chimed with the ideas around reform and redemption. Maconochie attested that there 'is no greater mistake in the whole compass of existing penal discipline [...] than its studied imposition of degradation as a portion of punishment. It destroys every better impulse'.[15] Not everyone involved in the penal system (in Australia or England and Wales) shared this view however, and in many gaols inmates were treated in ways that would have shocked the early proponents of prison reform.

Elsewhere in the colony transported felons could hope to swiftly get placed with a colonist as a servant or labourer and from there work their ways towards a 'ticket-of-leave' and their freedom. If they survived the journey from England and made a good fist of it on arrival, those sent half way around the world had a decent chance of forging a new and arguably better life than the friends and families they left behind in England's crowded and polluted towns.

However we view transportation, as an alternative to hanging it was fundamental to the English criminal justice prior to the abolition of most capital statutes in the 1820s and 1830s. It allowed the authorities to remove offenders without risking the adverse reactions of crowds witnessing a rising numbers of executions at a time when crime rates were increasing. Transportation to Australia came under pressure for the same reasons as it had done in America; the settled colony began to object to its use as a dumping ground and from the 1850s onwards the numbers sent across the seas declined until the policy was abandoned in the mid-1860s. That left the criminal justice system with just one serious alternative, that of imprisonment.

The process of prison reform from 1750 onwards

As we have seen, there was a general move to improve the fetid, overcrowded and corrupt gaols of eighteenth-century England and Wales. However history wishes to view prison reformers such as Howard, Hanway, Bentham and Fry, it is clear that they influenced an important change in prison conditions towards the end of the 1700s. One of the first and important reforms was driven by Howard. The Gaols (Discharged Prisoners) Act (1774) gave magistrates the power to pay the gaol fees of those who had been held on remand but acquitted when they came for trial. Conditions in eighteenth-century gaols were appalling and institutions were run for private profit. So, a gaoler was at liberty to keep prisoners incarcerated beyond the period of their conviction and even once they had been found not guilty by a jury, if they did not have the funds to pay their fees. Clearly, this was an inhumane practice and added to the overcrowding of local prisons. Howard was also the orchestrator of a second act that year, the Health of Prisoners' Act, which required gaols to be 'ventilated, regularly cleaned, provided with sick rooms, baths and a surgeon'.[16] Henceforth, prisons were supposed to be safe and clean environment.

The move towards building more prisons and using imprisonment as a form of punishment in its own right (rather than as a temporary measure ahead of trial or other sentence) was in part prompted by the outbreak of war with the American colonists in 1775. As a result of the American Revolution (and subsequent War of Independence) convicts could no longer be transported overseas and thus an important alternative to hanging had been removed. The Hard Labour Act (or 'Hulks Act' 1776) allowed for the forcible employment of convicts in work schemes along the Thames, and their confinement to hulks (decommissioned naval vessels) at other times. However, the hulks were not suitable for female convicts nor was it thought that inmates could be imprisoned on them for long periods, given the poor conditions on board. The hulks were used to house juvenile offenders however, often with detrimental effects, as Shore's detailed study of the youths confined on the *Euryalus* shows.[17]

As debates continued about what to do with convicted criminals Jeremy Bentham, along with Charles Bunbury, Gilbert Elliot and William Eden were engaged in the drafting of the Penitentiary Act of 1779, which proposed the building of two national prisons in and around London. The act has been described as the 'most forward-looking English penal measure of its time' but it was significantly watered down by the time of its passage into law.[18] In 1778, after the Hulks bill had been extended for another year (despite some concern over conditions onboard), Eden and William Blackstone set out plans to build 'Houses of Hard Labour' throughout the country.[19] As Devereaux's careful analysis of the debates surrounding penal practice in the late 1770s shows, while Eden appears to have been convinced of the ideal of imprisonment, others were committed to a return to transportation either after the war against the rebels had been won or once an alternative destination for convicts could be found. The plan to build more local prisons floundered and Eden and Blackstone set about drafting a new bill that incorporated both imprisonment and transportation. Two new 'national' penitentiaries were proposed, one 'to house 600 men and other 300 women', which was only a very small proportion of those convicted.[20] This, then, was an experiment in penal practice, not a wholesale change or revolution. The two proposed penitentiaries were not built, at least not for many years (Milbank was to open in 1819 as the first 'national' prison), but the 1780s saw an extensive prison-building programme across the country in a 'self-conscious emulation of the system outlined in the Penitentiary Act'.[21] The act is therefore an important marker on the move towards the systematic imprisonment of offenders that was to characterize penal policy in the second half of the nineteenth century.

While the act did not lead to the building of the proposed national prisons, the idea that such institutions should be built and the notion that prison regimes had the potential to reform criminals continued to be disseminated, notably by Paul and Bentham. Paul completed the building of Gloucester gaol in 1791 and instilled a regime based on solitude and discipline alongside work with the aim of reformation.[22] Bentham's vision far exceeded Paul's and was less consciously based in religion than any of his fellow reformers. In 1791, Bentham submitted his final design for a prison that would impel prisoners to conform to its regime by submitting them to constant surveillance, this was the panopticon.

Jeremy Bentham and the panopticon[23]

Bentham was a philosopher and a jurist (someone who studies the law) and is most commonly associated with Utilitarianism; the philosophy that espouses the principle of the 'greatest happiness of the greatest number'. Bentham looms large in any history of imprisonment in England and his brainchild, the panopticon or 'inspection house' is often used to illustrate the principle of late eighteenth- and early nineteenth-century prison reformers. But what exactly was the panopticon and what did Bentham intend it to do?

Bentham believed that punishment should reform as well as punish offenders. He opposed the death penalty on the basis that it offered no hope of reform and was therefore ineffectual.[24] He also advocated setting prisoners to work so that their labour could benefit society. Thus for him, executing felons was also inefficient because it removed the value of their labour from the wider community. Instead, Bentham argued that convicted criminals should be locked up in secure and humane gaols where they could be instilled with a sense of purpose through work and thus rehabilitated so as to become useful members of society on their release. He saw punishment as a social necessity but he rejected the idea that it should be based on retribution. So, instead of being 'an act of wrath or vengeance' it should be carefully calculated to benefit 'the social and the offender's needs'.[25]

His panopticon envisaged a prison where every moment of the inmates' lives was scrutinized by the warders, who were in turn to be watched by inspectors; 'inspection was to be the watchword of the new authority'.[26] Bentham's sketch of his model prison from 1791 shows a central inspection tower with individual cells radiating out from it, allowing those in the tower to see everything that occurs in the gaol without themselves being observed. Inmates were to be set to work which Bentham saw as the real measure of an individual's reformation. Indeed Bentham's intention was 'to change habits not to seek an internal change of character'[27] and it was here that it differed most clearly from Howard and Hanway. Bentham fundamentally disagreed with these religious reformers because while for Hanway and Howard 'salvation was the primary end of punishment as it was of human existence', Bentham 'saw no way of judging a man's moral improvement except by measuring the improvement in his work' (Figure 13.1).[28]

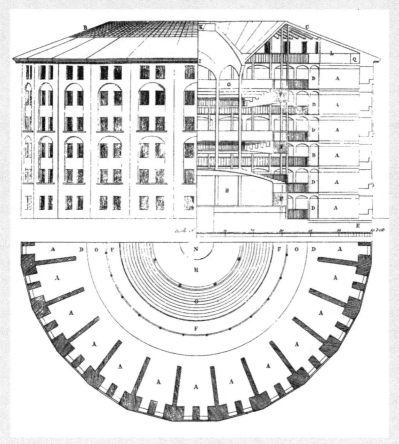

Figure 13.1 Bentham's sketch for an inspection house (panopticon). from the UCL's Bentham Project.

Bentham has been, perhaps a little rudely, sidelined in debates about the development of the prison and Semple's study offers us a much more nuanced and careful appraisal of his contribution. However, as Semple herself recognizes, if his scheme had been adopted it would have made him extremely rich. But of course Bentham's vision was never realized in England although both Millbank (where Bentham intended it to be built) and Pentonville contained elements of his design, but owed more to Howard than to the father of utilitarianism. The panopticon was just too expensive for England and Bentham, despite his involvement in discussion on penal reform, was one of several and not even the most influential figure in penal policy in the 1790s. Versions of his design were built however, in Italy, Portugal and the Netherlands as well as in the Americas.

The panopticon remains then, as a vision of how the ideal prison *might* have been, and not an example of the reality of such institutions in the nineteenth century. The reality was much less idealistic and much more mundane.

Prison regimes: The emergence of the ideal of reformation

The underlying principle of early nineteenth-century penal reform policy was that prisoners could be reformed, or, if that was not possible, they should at least not become worse offenders. To achieve this convicts had to be divided into distinct classes (remand prisoners from long term ones, young from old and men from women) and either separated from each other (kept in solitary confinement) or subjected to a silent routine (where communication between prisoners was forbidden). As we shall see, all of these lofty ideals were beset with ideological and practical problems, which (along with the perennial problem of funding) were ultimately to undermine all efforts at reforming criminals.

This reformatory process was, for some reformers (such as John Howard), underpinned by religion. Others, notably Jeremy Bentham, argued that reforming prisoners was beneficial to society and that was more important than any benefit to the felon's immortal soul. Punishment, Bentham believed,

should tend to reform the criminal, not encourage him in his vices; it should prevent him repeating his crime; it should be convertible to profit to compensate for the wrong; it should be popular to avoid public resistance to the law; it should be simply described and easily understood; and it should be remissible for those unjustly convicted.[29]

There was a distinction then, between 'Benthamites [who] were primarily interested in example' and deterrence, and evangelical reformers who wanted to effect 'the reformation of the criminal himself'.[30] Prison offered the opportunity to differentiate between criminal acts and their punishment in a way that hanging and transportation did not. Different sorts of prisoners could be separated and could be treated differently and for differing periods of time. All reformers appear to have agreed that removing prisoners from their environment was the first step in reforming or rehabilitating them, but they disagreed about how this was best achieved.

Prison regimes: Silent or separate?

Throughout the nineteenth century two competing and sometimes overlapping regimes of punishment were advocated, the silent and the separate systems. The silent system meant that prisoners were kept separate at night but allowed to associate together during the day – for work, exercise and chapel – but not allowed to communicate with each other. The silent regime was informed by a contemporary belief that convicted criminals were inherently corrupt and would corrupt those around them. Thus, old offenders would adversely influence younger ones, and first-time offenders would learn 'new tricks' from more experienced ones; prisons were, as Thomas Buxton noted, 'nurseries, schools, and colleges of vice'.[31] The silent system was 'based on a profoundly pessimistic view of the offender as corrupt, deviant, and lacking self-control'.[32] Nevertheless, this system appealed to the keepers and funders of local prisons because it was relatively inexpensive and easy to administer. There was a necessity in some places for more staff to police it but no need for new buildings or excessive modification to existing ones and so it is hard to judge how effectively it operated. As Helen Johnston notes, a parliamentary committee report in 1835 revealed 'considerable diversity in the number of staff, and therefore the operation', of many local prisons in England and Wales.[33]

However, not everyone believed the silent regime was appropriate for all prisoners. Women, it was thought, lacked the 'self-discipline to maintain silence' and forcing working-class women to refrain from everyday conversation was unnecessarily cruel.[34] As we have seen, even such a champion of the separate system as Sir George Onesiphorous Paul (who designed a new penitentiary prison at Gloucester in 1791) recognized that solitary confinement had its limits. 'I am convinced' he wrote, 'that secluded or solitary confinement must not be adopted, without occupation to soften and relieve the mind from the pressure of reflection without an object.' The risk was that inmates would, without anything to do or anyone to talk to, go slowly mad.[35] There were other problems with the silent system; it was very hard to ensure it operated completely as prisoners were adept at finding ways to circumvent the imposed silence. Inmates used code, corrupted hymn verses or found other ways to beat the system. And so an alternative system was proposed, a system pioneered in Pennsylvania's State Penitentiary that isolated prisoners from each other completely.

As one of the early pioneers of the separate system in England Paul argued that prisoners should be separated for most of the time they were in prison. Jonas Hanway agreed; he proposed a prison building with separate cells where prisoners would lose their names in favour of a prison number and through 'solitude in imprisonment' come to a 'right sense of their condition'.[36] Hanway was a 'passionate' advocate 'of the crushing of the evil in the criminal between the anvil of solitude and the hammer of religion'.[37] He advocated a prison where the convicts 'may learn to be cleanly in person, pious and laborious; and by the salutary potency of solitude and proper treatment, deprecate the vengeance of Heaven for offences past'.[38]

In practice separation meant that inmates were as far as possible isolated from each other; the only human contact they were to have would be prison warders and the chaplain. When the prison regime required inmates to be removed from their separate cells – for recreation or work – they wore masks to cover their faces or were placed in purpose-built separate stalls in the prison chapel. The idea was that this would reform the criminal by 'inducing a profound spiritual transformation subject to the weight of isolation from all but beneficial influences' (Figure 13.2).[39]

Separation had its critics, especially by the later nineteenth century as it became clear that the process had failed both to deter criminals and had adversely affected the mental health of inmates. One commentator remarked that separation, 'by night and day, speedily produces madness and imbecility, or at best renders the mind morbid and flabby'.[40] As Ignatieff's powerful description of a day in Pentonville prison so vividly shows, the separate system drove some to suicide and many others to the asylum.[41] Despite attempts to regulate prisons with external inspectors, abuses were common and

CONVICTS EXERCISING AT PENTONVILLE PRISON.

Figure 13.2 The separate system at Pentonville Prison . Mayhew and Binny, *London Labour and the London Poor* (1861).

hidden from the public in a way that had not been the case in the more open gaols of the previous century. But perhaps more important than any humanitarian concerns were criticisms of the efficacy of the separate system and of the extent to which rehabilitation was held to be more important than punishment. Not for the first or last time, prisons were being described as being too soft on their inmates. Between 1857 and 1863 this criticism intensified and was fuelled by concerns over rising levels of crime and the end of the transportation to Australia. Both were exacerbated by the garrotting panics in the mid-1850s and 1860s and were followed by a move away from reformism with the passing of the Prison Act (1865). This new system relied on separation of prisoners at night and hard labour by day, the premise being to break the spirit of convicts and make prison something to be feared.[42]

The later nineteenth-century prison and the move away from reformation

In 1835, prison inspectors were appointed to look into regimes and conditions in local gaols and the reports of two of these inspectors, William Crawford and the Rev. Whitworth Russell helped persuade government of the need to introduce the separate system as the preferred penal regime. Crawford had been impressed by what he had seen in America and was vocal in his criticism of the silent regime in England, which he believed was too easily circumnavigated by prisoners. He believed in setting inmates to work but not necessarily in reskilling them for a future life; he noted that it 'should never be forgotten that a gaol is not a school for the instruction of artisans, but a place of punishment'.[43] The separate system was enshrined in the Prison Act of 1839; however while Crawford and Russell's desire to implement it was apparent, they recognized that it was not always practical. Thus, it should come as no surprise that the system was not universally adopted. Instead, although the 'government pressed for such regimes, local magistrates were slow to implement and practice varied widely across the country'.[44]

Crawford and Russell were also influential in increasing the role played by the prison chaplain as a crucial element in the successful rehabilitation of convicts under the separate system. This was evident at Millbank on the Thames. However, the regime at Millbank was causing problems and inmates were suffering from the mental pressures of isolation; in 1842 the separate system was suspended and a year later Millbank ceased to be a convict prison and became instead a holding depot for transportees. By then a new prison had been constructed in London – Pentonville – which opened in 1842. Pentonville was, in the words of Ignatieff, 'the culmination of three generations of thinking and experimentation with penitentiary routine'.[45] However, Pentonville was yet another failure in a succession of misguided attempts to 'grind men good'.[46] It was supposed to be a model for future national prisons but very quickly it exposed the flaws inherent within the separate system. The regime was far too rigid and caused prisoners to suffer from mental and physical health problems that undermined any hope of reintegration within Victorian society. Eventually, like Millbank before it, the authorities were forced to concede that their ambitions for Pentonville were unlikely to reap the rewards they hoped for. As McConville has argued, Pentonville 'sank under the weight of public disapproval, its own unfulfilled promises', and, just seven years after it opened, 'the reformatory experiment was effectively abandoned'.[47]

Later nineteenth-century developments

The later Victorian period saw a change in emphasis in viewing the offender. While the final decades of the long eighteenth century had been dominated by ideas about the reformability of criminals, by the second half of the nineteenth century opinions were hardening. Increasingly, a perception gained ground that there 'was little point in attempting the reformation and education of those who the social Darwinian and positivist thinkers were describing as innately criminal and inferior'.[48] The growing bureaucratic state allowed for much better record keeping, and the techniques of social investigation led to more analysis of statistics and the increased classification of criminals. Prisoners were photographed, measured and interviewed to determine what made them criminal. Their physiognomy was the subject of debate in the same way that other outsiders – immigrant foreigners and native peoples – were. The keeping of records meant that criminal convictions carried more weight than they had previously.

After 1864 the sentence of Penal Servitude gave judges and magistrates the power to hand down severe sentences on relatively minor, if annoying, offenders. Persistent offending could now be rewarded with long periods of incarceration. And, as was noted earlier, the effective end of transportation and the perceived rise in levels of crime in the 1860s had placed greater emphasis on making prison a deterrent to crime rather than a means to rehabilitate offenders.

In 1865, parliament passed the Prison Act and took control of prisons out of the hands of local authorities and into those of a national inspectorate. It required each prison authority to provide separate cells and stipulated that inmates should be set to hard labour at 'the tread-wheel, shot-drill, crank, capstan, stone-breaking and "such other like description of hard body labour".'[49] This also included the picking of oakum, which was tiring, filthy work that lacerated convicts' fingers.[50] Inmates were also tasked with sewing coal sacks, mail bags or stockings, all of which could be seen as productive work that Bentham would have approved of.

However, the real image we have of Victorian prisons is of lines of uniformed convicts relentlessly climbing giant treadmills like so many caged lab rats. The treadmill (or wheel) meant that prisoners were forced to spend hours upon hours climbing anything from 6,000 to 20,000 feet a day, depending on age, health and the individual prison regime. It was dangerous and convicts were injured, crippled and even killed by accidents caused by falling off or into the mechanism.[51] The use of the treadmill was not abolished until 1895. The crank was an equally unpopular form of hard labour amongst prisoners. Inmates were required to turn a handle of a machine which could be adjusted by a prison warder to increase or decrease resistance by means of screw (hence the name 'screws' used as a slang term for prison officers). Again, the inmate was set a certain number of turns and punished if he did not complete them. Finally, there was the shot drill which simply involved 'stooping down (without bending the knees) and picking up a thirty-two pounder round shot [a cannon ball], bringing it up slowly until it is on a level with chest, then taking two steps to the right and releasing it on the ground again'.[52] All these forms of hard labour were open to abuse by those controlling them.

In some respects the Victorian period demonstrates the ongoing problems the authorities had in trying to standardize the treatment of offenders. In 1865 the Prison Act amalgamated the old houses of correction and county jails.[53] In 1867, there were 126 local prisons, controlled by county and borough magistrates, paid for from the rates and used to house petty criminals serving sentences of no more than two years alongside debtors, convicts awaiting execution and those awaiting trial. Also, by 1867 there were nine state financed convict prisons, including the following specialist institutions: Millbank (which operated as a transportation depot after 1843), Pentonville (where the separate system was practised), Portsmouth and Portland (where prisoners were employed in public works), Parkhurst (which housed juveniles), Brixton (a women's prison) and Dartmoor (reserved for invalids).[54] In addition, there was an asylum for criminal lunatics at Broadmoor from 1863. These institutions were used to finally replace transportation to Australia as a penal option. In all of these prisons, separation, silence and hard labour were practised in some or the other form.

However, prisoners in the larger national gaols, who were serving longer sentences, were more likely to be deployed in productive work or in public works such as road building, strengthening naval or military defences or land reclamation. This was similar to the system employed in Australia and another idea born in the new colony formed a part of penal policy in England and Wales.

The 1865 act had defined a regime based on behaviourist principles and uniformity: all convicts would be treated equally wherever they were in the country. It was a system based on 'hard labour, hard board and hard fare'. The *de facto* head of the prison service, Edmund Du Cane, determined diets, work and living conditions to meet this overarching theory of punishment and confinement. The experience of the convict was of progression, even in his diet. In the early weeks or months the food allowed was barely subsistence, what McConville has termed 'scientific starvation'.[55] Du Cane argued that abstinence from food was a good thing for an individual's health but also that if prisoners were too well fed, others might be encouraged to commit crime in order to get a good meal; the principle of 'less eligibility' in practice. However, with a considerable number of habitual offenders coming in and out of prison and existing on poor diets the effect on them was devastating, as was the denial of sleep, not as a torture but simply from the practice of sleeping on a hard board. Depriving convicts of company and of reading material – excepting the Bible – was also supposed to help focus the mind of the individual on reformation.

As prisoners progressed through the system, they could improve their conditions – diet, work, bedding, association, leisure and so on. This principle had been pioneered at Norfolk Island by Andrew Maconochie. Maconochie believed that inmates needed an incentive to improve and to behave rather than simply being given a length of time to serve. In 1847 he wrote that it is 'that instead of Criminals being sentenced to so many months or years of labour in a penal condition, they be required to earn so many hundred or thousand marks of approval'.[56] Prisoners worked to earn benefits, benefits that could easily be revoked if they misbehaved or slackened in their work. It was a system that encouraged discipline and the work ethic but it had a devastating effect on prisoners' lives.

This operated on the principle that prisoners could earn their early release through good behaviour, and prisoners with something to aim for or with something to lose were more easily controlled. Thus, the prisoner went through a series of stages: he started life in the separate system (the softening up process) before being transferred to a public works prison, where he had limited association with others. A detailed record was kept of each convict's progress and sentences 'were converted into marks, and prisoners were informed of the total number standing between them and liberty'. Bad behaviour not only lost 'marks' but it also incurred physical punishments (floggings) and harsher living conditions. Release was not unconditional and those set at liberty on a 'ticket-of-leave' could be recalled at any point and for the slightest infringement. As McConville says, 'Energy, commitment, and complete submission were the supposed prerequisites of early release.'[57]

However, much of this did not apply in the local prisons where men served short sentences, and were not entitled to any remission for good behaviour: if you were sentenced to two years, you served two years – there was no remission for good behaviour. When he became chair of the Directors of Convict Prisons in 1863, Du Cane set about the nationalization of the local prison system, a system he knew very little about. The result was a disaster for any hopes of reform or rehabilitation as Du Cane's mantra was uniformity regardless of how appropriate a response that was to the needs of the penal system at a local level. For most of those confined in local prisons the mark system was almost pointless; they still suffered from the harsh regime but had no time to earn improved conditions as most were there only for a month or two.

As a result, the 1860s witnessed a retreat from any real attempt at reformation.[58] Du Cane's rationale was that the sentences imposed on inmates in local prisons were so short that reformative efforts were wasted. Since it was futile to attempt reform in the local prisons, it was misguided to distract them from their principal task, which was to deter petty offenders. There was a certain ruthless logic here: by treating petty local offenders to a taste of the brutal prison regime, Du Cane believed he could effectively deter lesser criminals from graduating into more serious ones.[59] But the reality was that most of those convicted of an indictable offence were being sent to prison, placing increasing strain on the system and at the same time undermining any thoughts of rehabilitation.[60]

Life in the convict gaols was grim and uncompromising, with unrealistic work targets that forced prisoners, malnourished and lacking in sleep, to work till they dropped in chain gangs. The picture that emerges is one of an unbending punitive system of imprisonment that met Foucault's concept of deepening discipline. The prison allowed for the exact measurement of sentencing that fitted the crime in a way that transportation and execution did not. Once in prison, convicts had to keep to a narrow path in order not to fall foul of the disciplinary system. In doing so, they were observed at every turn, continually measured and examined to make sure they abided to the process of reformation. Du Cane increased the use of punishment beatings and had little sympathy for those that disapproved of his methods: 'A person can always avoid being flogged', he argued, 'by avoiding committing the offence.'[61]

Some inmates were considered to be unsuited for the harsh conditions of incarceration set down by Du Cane: juveniles, women and political prisoners all presented 'exceptions' to the regular hardened criminal. Female prisoners and the young had previously been identified as needing or deserving different treatment by the penal system,[62] but in the last quarter of the nineteenth century the complaints of Irish political prisoners, 'gentlemen' fraudsters and those imprisoned, such as Oscar Wilde, for 'moral' offences, began to raise serious concerns about the treatment of individuals in English gaols. It was argued that there should be distinctions drawn between the working-class 'career' criminal (who repeatedly offended) and first-time offenders and those whose crime was less heinous. Critics, who called for an end to the universal application of 'hard bed, hard work, hard fare', echoed late eighteenth-century critiques of the lack of separation in unreformed gaols.[63]

Medical officers had been introduced to prisons following the 1865 act and gradually began to have more involvement in the arguments around prison conditions. At first the main intention of medical officers seems to have been to spot those inmates who were trying to secure better conditions or avoid work by shamming (in other words, pretending to be ill). But gradually doctors could also determine genuine cases of physical or mental illness and some were prepared to accept that the penal system was, at least in part, a causal factor in the deterioration of those committed to it.

This quote, from one inmate who left us his memoirs, gives a sense of how he saw his incarceration (for fraud):

An English prison is a vast machine in which a man counts for just nothing at all. […] The prison does not look on him as a man at all. He is merely an object which must move in a certain rut and occupy a certain niche provided for it. There is no room for the smallest sentiment. The vast machine of which he is an item keeps undisturbed on its course. Move with it and all is well. Resist, and you will be crushed as inevitably as the man who plants himself on the railroad track when the express is coming. Without passion, without prejudice, but also without pity and without remorse, the machine crushes and passes on. The dead man is carried to his grave and in ten minutes is as much forgotten as though he never existed.[64]

Unfortunately, this did little to rehabilitate individual convicts and prepare them for a normal existence outside of prison. Recidivism was high, as was mental illness and physical degradation amongst offenders. Du Cane's reforms failed to provide an effective punishment policy in the nineteenth century. Conflicting ideas about how prisoners should be treated; arguments over local or national control; spiralling costs; and a lack of uniformity and of a body to oversee the reforms, all contributed to this failure. As with the police the prison system was beset with a number of problems that compromised its role and purpose, and many of these same problems are still with us over a century later.

The problems with the prison system were largely unreported until late in the century as Du Cane effectively operated without any supervision. Nineteenth-century prisons were closed institutions, quite unlike the chaotic local gaols of the eighteenth century. Du Cane had complete unfettered control of the prison system and he preferred (and was mostly allowed) to operate without interference from outside. Things did begin to change in the last quarter of the century, first in the 1870s and then gradually over the next decades as light was shone into these closed institutions.

In 1879, a new Royal Commission (the Kimberley Commission) was set up to investigate. This came into being at a time when confidence in society's ability to win the war on crime was at a relative high. Crime rates were low and there was a growing acceptance of the new police. The commission heard evidence from some selected convicts and those that had served 'time', and accepted the 'need to distinguish between types of offenders' such as juveniles, political prisoners and what might be termed 'real' criminals.[65] Further criticism of the system resurfaced in the late 1880s and in 1891 the Penal Servitude Bill made several improvements to the prison regime (including making it easier to gain some remission). In the same year, the Humanitarian League was established and it campaigned for, amongst other things, better treatment for prisoners. While progress was piecemeal and slow, it appears that the last quarter of the 1800s witnessed a shift in attitudes towards prisons and those detained within them.

The 1890s saw a change in attitudes towards prison regimes, a change that was occasioned not by their failure but instead by their perceived success. The professionalization of policing and the rest of the criminal justice system meant that criminals were more likely to be caught, prosecuted and punished and there was a widespread feeling of confidence that crime was falling. As a result, more questions were asked about the way in which the state treated its criminals – what Wiener calls an 'emerging discomfort with the infliction of suffering [...] for ends that were now seen as less urgent and less clear' began to merge and questions were asked.[66]

In 1895, the Gladstone report highlighted some of the worst aspects of the penal system. This followed a series of articles in the *Daily Chronicle* newspaper a year earlier, which had exposed conditions in English prisons. The same paper also published two letters from Oscar Wilde who served two years in Reading gaol in conditions the committee deemed 'more than a man could endure'.[67] In 1898, a new Prison Act made some attempt to overhaul the worst excesses of Du Cane's regime. The treadmill and crank were abolished, the length of solitary confinement reduced and the remission of up to a sixth of a person's sentence was allowed. The bill had a troubled passage through parliament with some attacking it for offering little in the way of reform whilst others suggested it went too far towards making life comfortable for prisoners. Herbert Asquith worried that it might make things too humane and so dilute the deterrent nature of imprisonment. He told parliament that the aim should be to 'keep our prisons empty, and not to make them full, and there ought to be in no stage of prison discipline any inducement to any part of the population to come under it'.[68] Real change had to wait until after the First World War. The experience of hundreds of conscientious objectors, locked up and subjected to what was still a Victorian prison regime, led to an outpouring of criticism in the post-war years. Far fewer individuals were sent to prison in the aftermath of peace in 1918 but wider change to the system was still slow and piecemeal.

The nineteenth-century prison can be seen as a success or as a failure; it is entirely down one's perspective. For the authorities of Victorian England the prison system was relatively successful in that it removed thousands of unwanted felons from society and housed them at minimal cost. It engaged them in public work and probably deterred some (if only the minority) from ever breaking the law again. However, from the standpoint of society the system was a crushing failure; prisoners were swept up inside a huge machine, broken and brutalized, before being spewed back into their communities unfit and unable to contribute in any useful way. Many returned to crime or ended up in the workhouse, or succumbed to disease and died as a result of their treatment at the hands of Du Cane's system. The Webbs' opinion was stark:

> The reflection emerges that, when all is said and done, it is probably quite impossible to make a good job of the deliberate incarceration of a human being in the most enlightened of dungeons [...] We suspect that it passes the wit of man to contrive a prison which shall not only be gravely injurious to the minds of the vast majority of prisoners, if not also to their bodies. [69]

The prison needs to be considered alongside other institutions (as both Foucault and Ignatieff have recognized) that have been considered as agents of social control. The sociologist Erving Goffman offered a powerful critique of incarceration in his 1961 *Asylums*.[70] He presented the notion of the 'total institution' and before we look at the ways in which Edwardian society began to take the first tentative steps towards real alternatives to imprisonment it is worth us briefly looking at what Goffman's thesis has to say.

The total institution

What is a total institution? The phrase was coined by Erwin Goffman and defined as follows:

> A total institution may be defined as a place of residence and work where a large number of like-situated individuals, cut off from the wider society for an appreciable period of time, together lead an enclosed, formally administered round of life.[71]

The nineteenth century witnessed the building of a series of total institutions designed to house a range of different deviant types. The most obvious and typical of these were the penitentiary prisons that held criminals securely and isolated them from the outside world. As we have seen, this isolation was essential to reformers' hopes of 'curing' convicts of their criminal instincts and rehabilitating them to the world of industry. This principle was applied equally to other deviant types, each of whom had their own purpose-built, total institution.

As Foucault noted, deviants were subjected to a crude 'binary division and branding (mad/sane; dangerous/harmless; normal/abnormal)' after which they were sent to the appropriate institution.[72]

So the 'mad' went to the insane asylum, the 'sick' to the lock hospital, the 'delinquent' to the juvenile reformatory and the 'pauper' to the workhouse. Each inflicted a particular routine on its inmates and each operated almost independently of the society outside the institution. In all of these total institutions the inmates were kept under surveillance, often separated from each other, and were 'treated' for their conditions. The creation of such institutions has been explained by Foucault and others as part of the process of social control exerted by the newly emerged capitalist class; as Ignatieff stated, its was no accident 'that these state institutions so closely resembled the factory'.[73]

The 'total institution' is a useful way in which to understand Foucault's social control thesis and his idea of a 'carceral archipelago' but it is not the end of the story of penal reform in the period covered by this book. The early twentieth century witnessed a gradual move towards decarceration – the removal of offenders from prisons and a new search for an alternative. In part this was helped by the onset of war in 1914, which cut swathes into the usual demographic of the prison population – the young male working-class criminal – but also exposed Du Cane's legacy to the critical eyes of the intelligentsia. Significant numbers of conscientious objectors had been imprisoned in what was a Victorian prison system and their accounts of the brutality of the system shocked post-war society. The most innovative change, however, came about not as a result of policy making at the centre but instead, as was so often the case in the history of our criminal justice system, from the efforts of a small band of dedicated reformers at a local level. The result was the creation in 1908 of the probation service.

The move towards probation

The notion that punishment could be deferred or withheld has a long history in English law. Offenders could be required to find others who would provide security (in the form of money) that they would not break the law again and/or be required to do so themselves. Those found to have committed acts of petty violence or immorality could be bound over (to keep the peace) and after 1861 this could in effect be applied to any offence short of murder.[74] From the mid-1860s at least one Middlesex judge, Sir William Cox, had been allowing some of those convicted before him to walk free from court with no formal punishment. This practice had also been pioneered in Birmingham by the Recorder, Matthew Davenport Hill, who preferred to send young first-time offenders into the care of 'suitable guardians' who might be relatives, friends or employers. It was becoming widely recognized that once young offenders entered the walls of a prison or reformatory, it was much more difficult to keep them out of them in the future. Hill noted that his experiment in finding alternatives to incarceration resulted in far fewer reconvictions in the future.[75] This system was already well established in Massachusetts, USA where 'state agents' were employed to investigate the case of every juvenile up to the age of 17 that came before the courts, whereupon they 'advised on the best course of action'. In some circumstances the Massachusetts state agents recommended that offenders, while not being incarcerated, should be put 'on probation' and monitored. Again, the results were very positive as the levels of recidivism were much lower than for those that were sent through the prison system.[76]

In London the Church of England Temperance Society (hereafter CoETS) began to appoint a small number of persons as Police Court Missionaries (PCMs) to visit the courts and prisons of the capital to try to intervene in the lives of those accused of drunkenness to get them to sign the pledge of abstinence. The misuse of alcohol was considered to be a social problem and a major causal factor in the committal of crime. It was believed that by tackling drinking, many of the social ills of society could be prevented. Addressing a sermon at Aylesbury, the Clerical Superintendent of the CoETS told the congregation that the statistics produced by the PCM showed that large numbers of those appearing at police courts were charged with 'offences connected with "drunkenness," etc.,' and complained that intemperance was 'a sin which not only kept a man from doing his duty to his wife and family, but it robbed his employer of that industry and proper work which he had a right to expect'.[77] One missionary, Thomas Holmes, wrote an account of his experiences and condemned the 'evil' of drinking and poor parenting. At Lambeth Police Court he quoted the sitting magistrates who complained that 'If I were to sit here from Monday morning till Saturday to protect women that had got drunken and brutal husbands, I should not get through half of them.'[78]

By the middle of the 1880s there were eight PCMs operating at the London courts. These PCMs were keen to help those that were willing to sign the pledge, but the magistracy began to utilize them to perform a similar role to the state agents in Massachusetts, that of advising which defendants were suitable objects for release on recognizance. Some of the cases with which their involvement drew notice in the newspapers of the day demonstrate the motivations behind this missionary work. The concentration was on the young, on women and on the vulnerable. In 1889, *Reynold's Newspaper* reported the case of a policeman who had nearly drowned whilst rescuing a young woman from the Regent's Park canal after she had thrown herself in. She was charged with attempted suicide at Marylebone Police Court and given into the care of Mr Harris, a PCM, so she could find a safe home as she 'had frequently threatened to destroy herself'.[79] The *Daily News* reported that one missionary 'alone had rescued during last year seventy-eight young girls, and succeeded in getting homes for them or restoring them to their families'; the role of the PCMs was 'to get hold of men and women, especially young women, on their first appearance before a magistrate on charges of drunkenness, and to stop them on what too often proves a downward course'.[80] In 1890, when William Midson and his wife and children were charged with begging, the impoverished cabbie told the magistrates that he would rather 'go to gaol for six months than go to the workhouse for a fortnight'. The justice referred the case to the PCM, who inquired into the circumstances and reported that it was his belief that the case was genuine. It did not save the family from the workhouse but no fines or imprisonment followed.[81]

In 1886, the Home Secretary, Sir William Harcourt, concerned with the ill effect of imprisoning juveniles, began an enquiry into the possibility of using probation as an alternative to imprisonment. The Howard Association pointed to the example of Massachusetts. There was considerable discussion of the pros and cons of probation for first offender. This led to the passing of the Probation of First Offenders Act (1887), which 'enabled courts to release "on probation of good conduct" any first offender convicted of larceny, false pretences or any other offence punishable with not more than two years imprisonment' – this did not include provision for supervision however, so it differed somewhat from the American model, but it was the start of a route to something different.[82]

In principle the idea of probation, as it was employed in Massachusetts, seemed sound and in 1907 the Liberal Government introduced a bill to create an English probation system.[83] The bill became law in August 1907 and the first probation orders began to be imposed upon offenders in the following year. Those considered fit for release were placed on probation orders of up to three years and officers were appointed to supervise them by the petty session's bench. It was intended that probation would help rehabilitate the criminal and encourage reform. As one recent history of probation has noted: 'The essence of the new order was that it was not a punishment and not a sentence, even though the charge was proved'; instead the 'probationer had to give a signed undertaking to be of good behaviour' and the order could 'include various conditions as to residence, avoiding alcohol, or other matters the court deemed necessary to prevent re-offending'.[84]

Probation officers were there to support the offender and help them find work, or if they were juveniles, to assist in placing them in education. A distinction was made between the probation officer and the police so as to build up levels of trust between officers and those they supervised; these were not 'police' agents but agents of the court and 'friends' of the offender. They need to be seen in the context of social workers rather than enforcement officers. The early officers also belonged to other voluntary organizations such as the CoETS, the Police Court Mission, Salvation Army or the NSPCC. All of these reflect the underlying ethos of those working in probation in the early twentieth century; these were social workers not criminal justice officers, and very many of them were inspired by their religious beliefs to play an active role in the care and resettlement of offenders.

Probation developed after 1908 and came to play a very significant role in the penal system of the twentieth century (if not at first[85]). It reflected that branch of penal theory which had long argued for the rehabilitation of criminals and the prevention of crime by intervention not simply by deterrent. Sadly, the probation experiment has barely survived for a century and the modern 'force' is quite far removed from the principles that underpinned the original Police Court Missionaries in that it has become much more closely aligned with the penal system and further removed from social work than its founders envisaged.

Before we conclude this study of punishment let us turn to the ways in which historians have characterized the changes in penal policy from the early modern period onwards.

Understanding the rise of the prison: The historical debate

Historical explanations for the rise of the prison generally fall into three, sometimes overlapping camps: orthodox, revisionist and counter-revisionist. Let us look at these arguments in turn.

Orthodox explanations

Until the 1970s historical writing on penal reform was dominated by a narrative of reform and progress. This history was keen to stress the vital role played by philanthropic reformers such as John Howard, Jonas Hanway and Elizabeth Fry, all of whom campaigned for better prison conditions and new forms of confinement and treatments for prisoners. Their views derived in part from Enlightenment theorists like Cesare Beccaria and William Eden, who had questioned the value and morality of capital punishment. In the later 1770s these reformers (driven by new humanitarian ideals and strong religious beliefs, as well as by a new set of concerns relating to rising levels of crime, the end of transportation to America and a growth in the numbers of people claiming poor relief) set out to convince legislators and criminal justice practitioners that cruel and arbitrary punishments should be replaced by imprisonment in hygienic, well-built prisons that would be both reformative and punitive.[86] They were assisted in this by a growing sensibility within society that was increasingly revolted by physical cruelty in all its forms. These reformers, it is argued, were gradually able to make English society, and in particular its governing elite, see the need for change; the result of this move was the eventual decline and fall of hanging, the abolition of public whipping and other physical non-lethal punishments and the rise of the prison penitentiary.

However, these historical accounts have made a number of assumptions about the historical process that created penal change and so have come under scrutiny and criticism from subsequent historians of crime and punishment. Underpinning this explanation is the notion that change was driven by a new humanitarian consciousness; the idea that capital punishment was somehow wrong and understood to be wrong in a newly enlightened society which placed a greater emphasis on the value of the human body. Interwoven with this was a belief, or indeed an assumption, that the intention of Howard and the other reformers was to create more humane institutions to house and rehabilitate offenders and that their proposals were indeed offering something qualitatively better (better for the inmate that is) than was in existence at the time. Most of those that have written this early orthodox history of penal reform have concentrated on institutions and how they had changed over time, but from the records of their *administration* rather than the *experiences* of those that were subjected to their regimes. They reached the conclusion that these reformers helped to change the face of the English penal system for the better and, therefore, deserve to be held up as heroes of reform, in much the same way as William Wilberforce is credited with the abolition of slavery.

However, there is a different way to view the drive for reform. Instead of simply seeing the act of philanthropy as having a humanitarian or religious focus, it is possible to argue that it is also political and ideologically driven. This view has been most effectively set out by Michael Ignatieff, who regarded the actions of the reformers as being motivated by a social crisis caused by rising crime and poverty, which were in themselves a product of the changing economic and social structure of late eighteenth-century English society.[87] Howard emerges not as a champion of humanitarian reform, but instead as a heroic figure for the new bourgeoisie, the class that was on the rise in the late 1700s. Ignatieff's argument, in his seminal work *A Just Measure of Pain*, offers us a distinct and theoretical model of changing penal policy and builds on the work of other writers who offered what has been termed a 'revisionist' perspective of changing punishment policy.

The revisionist viewpoint

As we have seen with the history of the police, historians from the 1970s onwards have critiqued the consensual view of history that has regarded the move towards professionalism as a simple teleology of reform. Instead of seeing prison reform and the move from hanging to incarceration as a product of enlightened humanitarianism, the revisionists argued that:

> The motives and programme of reform were more complicated than a simple revulsion at cruelty or impatience with administrative incompetence – the reformers' critique of eighteenth-century punishment flowed from a more, not less, ambitious conception of power, aiming for the first time at altering the criminal personality.[88]

Let us explore this idea a little further by reference to the work of Foucault and Ignatieff. Foucault, who looked primarily at France not England, saw the move towards imprisonment as part of a wider process of 'social control'; arguing that 'prison does not control the criminal, it controls the working class by creating criminals – and this…is its real function and the reason for its retention'.[89] Foucault's book starts with a comparison of the execution of the regicide Damiens and the prison regime at Mettray. The full force of physical punishment was inflicted upon the body of the unfortunate Damiens who was publically hanged, burned, disembowelled and torn apart by horses to demonstrate the power of the French king and state and the consequences of the offender's symbolic attack on it. By contrast, the prison regime at Mettray was ordered, silent and private. Foucault's argument is that the nineteenth century saw a move away from the punishment of the body of the criminal to a punishment of his mind. The ideal tool for this purpose was the penitentiary prison because this allowed the authorities to remould the prisoner – the deviant criminal – into a more useful member of society.[90] Not only did it allow for the reform and remodelling of the criminal, but also the prison, alongside a series of complementary institutions (such as the workhouse, asylum and lock hospital), which better enabled the disciplining of the working class.

Ignatieff's approach in *A Just Measure of Pain* was similar to Foucault's. Ignatieff contrasted the model penitentiary at Pentonville with Newgate gaol. By demonstrating that the ordered prison regime at Pentonville failed to reform offenders and was instead more likely to send them mad, Ignatieff aligned himself with Foucault's social control model. However, there are some subtle differences between the two works. Ignatieff's work concentrates on the role of the reformers (in particular Howard), who he saw as the architects of the new penal system. Foucault focused more on the regimes and institutions and was, it must be said, much less concerned with evidence than Ignatieff. Thus, while Ignatieff's model 'of the reform of character is one of symbolic persuasion; Foucault's is of disciplinary routinization'.[91] But, for both, the adoption of imprisonment as punishment and the panopticon penitentiary as the method of delivery had less to do with the prevention of crime and more to do with power.

Foucault and Ignatieff were preceded by Rusche and Kirchheimer, who approached the changing nature of punishment from a Marxist perspective. Marxists saw the prison and the factory as a part of the transformation of Western society to capitalism. In addition, the use of transportation, galley slavery (by the French and Spanish) and the introduction of hard labour as a form of punishment within gaols are all examples of the imposition of the capitalist economic system into the lives of the working classes. While these new prison regimes were just as ineffectual as the old ones had been, they could now fall back on the 'rhetoric of reform and religious ideology' to justify their existence.[92]

The revisionist, or 'social control', thesis provides us with a useful framework with which to study the move towards imprisonment as a universal punishment in England and elsewhere. When we look at prisons alongside other contemporary institutions, such as the asylum, school, workhouse, factory and hospital, it is possible to construct a viable argument of a determined effort to deal with deviancy in all its forms. For Ignatieff, the late eighteenth century witnessed a rising concern with the problems of society – and this was followed by a series of social crises in the early nineteenth. He sees the ideology of reformation in penal policy manifested in all sorts of ways:

> The social anxieties of the middle class in the 1790s ensured that this hard faith in human malleability soon received operational formulation at the hands of the medical profession, in asylums for the insane, Houses of Industry for paupers, hospitals for the sick, and penitentiaries for the criminal. In each environment, the poor were to be 'cured' of immorality, disease, insanity, or crime, as well as related defects of body and mind, by isolation, exhortations, and regimens of obedience training.[93]

The counter-revisionist challenge

However, there are other ways to see the reform of punishment within society than as either a crude implementation of capitalist ideology or as a heroic attempt to improve the conditions of prisoners. We need perhaps to return to an attempt to understand what punishment is for. According to Durkheim, punishment is there to reinforce society's values; it is 'a means of conveying a moral message'. In order to be effective in this aim, it is important that the penal sanctions that are applied are not disproportionate or seen as illegitimate. So, Durkheim would argue that penal sanctions 'cannot help but be unpleasant, but this aspect of suffering should be reduced to a minimum'.[94] In this way, punishment becomes something other than 'an instrument of crime control', it is a demonstration that the authorities are *in* control.[95] It is evident when looking at history that those states that experienced stable government with (albeit limited) extensions of freedom and the franchise have adopted less extreme forms of punishment.

A more telling criticism of the revisionists is that they have placed far too much emphasis on the written works of the reformers – in many respects it can be argued that they were taken in by the rhetoric and failed to appreciate the difference between policy and practice. More recent work has revealed a much more disparate and complicated story of prison reform and the adoption of penal change. Thus, for example, in Lancashire, as Margaret De Lacy's work has shown, a lack of resources made any attempt to impose the reformists' ideals impossible.[96] If prison is to be seen as part of a drive towards creating a disciplined workforce to fulfil the needs of a new industrial class, then we might have expected the new reformed prisons to emerge in the emerging industrial heartlands of England, not as they did, in the relatively unchanged agricultural districts such as Gloucestershire and Norfolk.

And here it is possible to argue that the revisionists have characterized the ruling classes as much united and determined to impose a unified vision. This was, however, far from the truth. As we have seen elsewhere, there were many competing interests for power and, as with police reform, change in punishment policy was gradual and piecemeal and affected by mundane factors such as costs and bureaucracy. Nor were the ruling elite allowed to impose their will without challenge; policies were debated, contested and amended. Ultimately, penal policy has to remain legitimate in the eyes of the many, not just the few. And this is crucial because the so-called target of Foucault's 'carceral archipelago', the working classes, consistently used and legitimized the criminal justice system.

While he does not accept the counter-revisionist position completely, Ignatieff does recognize that the arguments expressed by himself and Foucault 'contained three basic misconceptions: that the state enjoys a monopoly over punitive regulation of behaviour in society, that its moral authority and practical power are the major binding sources of social order and that all social relations can be described in the language of subordination'.[97] It is more complex than that and the ongoing history of the prison show us that regimes can be subverted, challenged and overthrown. We might end by noting that Foucault and Ignatieff's models of 'social control' are predicated on the notion that institutions such as the prison *work* when clearly they do not. Indeed as Ignatieff himself reflected, 'the prison is perhaps *the* classic example of an institution which works badly and which nonetheless survives in the face of recurrent scepticism as to its deterrent or reformative capacity'.[98]

Unfortunately, the counter-revisionist position offers no overarching thesis with which to understand changing penal policy. It has successfully questioned the value of seeing the move towards imprisonment for most offenders either as part and parcel of a move towards a capitalist economy – since this can be shown to be well underway before the nineteenth century – or as an effective system of social control. It demonstrates a degree of continuity that is often absent from the revisionist viewpoint and a variety that belies any attempt to impose a uniform system (before the late 1800s). It is in danger, however, of a return to the institutional history of the early twentieth century, which failed to offer any rationale for penal reform beyond that of good intentions. The revisionists have succeeded in undermining those early histories of the triumph of reform and perhaps now we need a new paradigm to replace the failed rhetoric of social control.

Conclusion: Some final thoughts on the shift from pain to penitentiary

We started this section on punishment with a warning that it is too simplistic to see the move from hanging, the pillory and whipping to incarceration in a highly regulated Victorian prison as a straightforward journey of enlightened reform. The path itself was winding and uneven with many twists and turns along the route, but more importantly the destination and goal seems far from certain. It is not at all clear whether the reforms of the late eighteenth and early nineteenth centuries actually improved the situation for the many thousands of inmates of British prisons. While we can be clear, of course, that the retreat from the public hanging of selective petty property criminals represents an advance for a 'civilized' country, it is much less clear that civilization was the driving force behind that change.

In the early modern period brutal physical punishments, carried out in public, were a regular feature of life. All manner of offenders were hanged, burned at the stake, beheaded, tortured, pressed, flogged and pilloried in front of their communities as examples of what happened to those that transgressed the laws of God and the monarch. The intention was part deterrence and part purification; bodies were literally scourged of sin and pain was used to bring about repentance and, ultimately, redemption. By the early eighteenth century the number of those being executed was falling but most forms of physical punishment were retained. Across England and Wales the public execution and the gibbet represented a striking visual image of the power of the Hanoverian state and its 'Bloody Code' of laws, which prescribed death for over 200 separate offences.

However, recent work has demonstrated that the reach of the state seems to have been limited. An 'unbloody code' appears to have operated on the peripheries; in Wales, Scotland, the North West and Cornwell there were hardly any executions at all, for decades.[99] So, the story of the rise and fall of the 'Bloody Code' has to be seen within this context, as a story of the limited power of the state. This requires further study to see whether the elegant thesis put forward by King and Ward for the late eighteenth century can be supported in other regions or time periods. We also need some stronger answers to the questions raised by this new concept; why were so few sent to the gallows in Cornwall and Wales? Can this be explained by a different legal culture, by language or religion? Given that there were notable differences in the way the 'Bloody Code' operated in the 1700s, how does this affect the competing explanations for its demise in the early nineteenth century?

Gatrell's structural thesis would seem to be problematic given these new findings but if we consider that the real battleground for change was the centre, then the rise in executions just before the code collapsed still retains a certain credibility. Likewise, McGowen's arguments surrounding the debates in parliament and the 'image of justice' are more persuasive when viewed from a London-centric position.[100] Many of those arguing for a reform of the penal laws were driven by strong non-conformist religious beliefs (beliefs that were already prevalent on the peripheries) and in our modern secular age we need to be aware that past societies placed a much greater importance on religious morality than we do today. Others played a more pragmatic card, arguing that hanging was ineffectual and counterproductive; that the best way to deal with crime was to employ criminals in useful tasks that benefitted society. Others preferred a system that forced offenders to reflect on the crime they had committed and in so doing affect a change on their personality, and believed this was best achieved by the imposition of silence, separation from others and non-productive, physical forms of labour (such as the treadmill).

In between these arguments, for and against the abolition of hanging and the differing systems of imprisonment, there was a campaign to improve the squalid conditions in English gaols and a search for some alternative to execution that still allowed the state to rid itself of its unwanted felons. The result was a much greater use of transportation (to the American colonies and then to Botany Bay), which have to be seen within the context of the growth of Empire. Australian academics have persuasively argued that those sent to the new continent after 1787 are best seen as 'convict workers' rather than the offloaded dregs of the mother country. Those left behind were increasingly imprisoned in the old gaols and houses of correction that were run as entrepreneurial fiefdoms by the prison keepers. Reformers such as John Howard and Elizabeth Fry railed against the conditions within these institutions and in the nineteenth century change gradually began to occur.

The nineteenth century saw the seemingly inexorable rise of the prison. While Bentham's panopticon ideal was never realized and the first national prison, Millbank, was a failure, the Victorian period saw the building of a system of institutions aimed at disciplining the so-called 'criminal classes'. Pentonville, Portland, Parkhurst and Broadmoor all rose up as penal edifices to cater for different sorts of inmates. Competing ideas about different regimes were influenced by experiments in Australia and the reductionist 'mark' system was applied to British gaols. The drive for uniformity meant that prisoners suffered the brutality imposed on them regardless of whether they were serious offenders or petty ones and once Du Cane had control of local gaols, those serving short sentences were caught in a system that crushed them.

So, we might well ask: Where was the enlightened progress that had started in the late eighteenth century? What would Bentham, Romilly or Howard have made of Pentonville? More to the point, would those convicted of a property crime in the last quarter of the nineteenth century (when transportation had been abandoned) have been worse off than those tried in the first quarter? Indeed, would they not rather have taken their chances with the vagaries of the 'Bloody Code', when only around a tenth of those sentenced to death had those sentences carried out? The aims of the reformers in abolishing capital punishment and improving the state of the prisons may have been couched in good intentions but it seems far from certain that the effects were beneficial, for those convicted or for society. So when we talk about 'progress' we need to be quite careful of what we mean. Foucault and Ignatieff's arguments about the need to punish more effectively, not to punish less, deserve careful consideration when the long history of penal reform is examined.[101]

By the end of the nineteenth century questions were beginning to be asked about conditions in prisons, despite the best efforts to keep the public out. The imprisonment of Oscar Wilde, a growing number of 'gentlemen' criminals and a handful of political prisoners exposed the 'hard work, hard bed, hard board' regime as unsuitable for all but the most unredeemable of convicts. Change was slow and piecemeal and real progress had to wait until well into the new century. There were also some innovations, the adoption of probation for example, or the alternative provisions for young offenders but for most convicted criminals, prison remained the most likely outcome.

The history of punishment is a quite depressing one in my opinion. The arguments of the reformers – that criminals can be rehabilitated by forceful intervention in some form or another – echo down the centuries. But they are also hamstrung by the reluctance of the state to either spend the necessary money on rehabilitation or risk the wrath of public opinion by being seen to be 'soft on crime'. Successive home secretaries and justice ministers compete with each other to talk tough on penal policy and little real change is affected in the lives of those caught up in the system. Howard and his fellow reformers recognized that the key motor of rehabilitation was education; for them this meant religious education and the development of an appropriate morality. Nowadays we are more inclined to allow prisoners to engage in distance learning or develop craft skills in the prison workshops, or to undergo drug rehabilitation programmes. But this works only for those who are in prison for long enough for these schemes to have an effect. Given that most of the prison population is incarcerated for periods of up to two years, we are repeating the mistakes of our Victorian ancestors; little rehabilitation can take place in cash-strapped prisons where there is a culture of drug use, violence and intimidation. Meanwhile the experiment with probation appears to have been largely abandoned in exchange for a more penal system of 'offender management'.

Finally, it is worth noting that modern prisons are filled with the same sorts of inmates as Victorian ones: young, working-class males, from poor social backgrounds and with low educational skills. For them their first experience of prison is rarely their last and release into the community without support often simply means that the cycle of crime, arrest and imprisonment is just a matter of time. We have patently failed, then, to learn the lessons of the past and so are doomed to repeat the same mistakes in the future.

CONCLUSIONS AND SUGGESTIONS
FOR FURTHER RESEARCH

I have tried to cover a very long period of English history in this book – from the restoration of the monarchy in 1660 to the outbreak of the First World War. Those 250 years saw the coronations of eleven different monarchs; the rise of political parties; wars with the Netherlands, France and Spain; the loss of the American colonies and the establishment of Empire in India; war with Tsarist Russia, and then a series of colonial wars, the South African (Boer) war; and finally, the catastrophe of the 1914–1918 conflict. During this time, Britain witnessed the full flowering of the industrial age: the invention of steam power, the railway and the motor car. The population, whilst remaining predominately rural and agrarian for much of the period, grew massively and began to be concentrated in a handful of major urban areas. London, which was always the largest city in England, expanded to become the greatest capital in Europe. There were advances in science; the extension of the parliamentary franchise; the creation of daily newspapers; education and rising literacy; increasing life expectancy, along with changes to the family and the beginnings of feminism; and an acceptance of the changing nature of youth and childhood.

In short, a lot changed in ten generations and this was as true for the criminal justice system as it was for society as a whole. At the beginning of the 1700s, the symbol of justice in England was the gallows and by the middle of the eighteenth century there were over 200 separate offences that carried the death penalty. Indeed, there were so many that no one has ever been able to determine exactly how many there were. As we have seen though, this was largely meaningless as a statistic as most individuals who faced execution had been convicted of crimes, such as murder, highway robbery, burglary and animal stealing, that had been capital since Tudor times. We have also learned that the administration of hanging was used with calculated discretion rather than extreme force; except for periods when crime rates topped the agenda, very few of those sentenced to death were actually killed.

Regardless, the overriding theme of punishment in the eighteenth century is one of a search for alternatives to hanging, punctuated by the occasional retreat to brutality when the state felt it needed it (such as the introduction of anatomization under the 1752 Murder Act). Experimentation with exile – the transportation of convicts overseas – began in the late 1600s and was formalized in legislation in 1718. But it took war with the American colonists and the subsequent colonization of Australia to offer the real long-term alternative that the Georgian authorities sought. In the meantime they continued to explore the alternative of imprisonment, something that had been pioneered in the early modern age. Hanoverian gaols were fearsome places where neglect and disease were the results of venality and entrepreneurship. It is hard to imagine anyone surviving conditions in London's Newgate or any of the many local gaols where prisoners were confined for months before trial, reliant entirely on their friends and family or the depths of their own pockets.

Early historians of crime wanted us to see the reform of penal policy in the nineteenth century as evidence of the march of progress. This was an era in which heroes of reform such as Hanway, Bentham, Romilly and Howard strove to abolish execution for all but the heinous offenders and to clean up the nations prisons. Decrepit and unsanitary lockups were replaced with austere, but safe, state penitentiaries. These were well run and prisoners were properly fed and set on a course of rehabilitation. Later scholars have argued that this reform, such as it was, had less lofty intentions. The prison was equated with the workhouse, the asylum and the factory and seen as an integral part of a process of social control. Prison regimes, which either forced inmates to remain silent for almost the entirety of their incarceration or worse, to be separated completely from their fellows, were supposed to bring about a crisis of conscience and to lead to the reformation of the individual. In many cases they simply entrenched deviant behaviour or sent the poor recipient insane, and they did very little to rehabilitate offenders. With the end of transportation and other media-driven panic about crime, the 1860s saw the virtual abandonment of any real ambition to reform offenders and the introduction of even harsher prison regimes. It seems to be axiomatic that penal policy runs in circles but never actually manages to achieve its goal, the prevention of crime. By the end of the nineteenth century, England had built several national prisons and was locking up thousands of criminals and thoughts began to look again for alternatives. The relative success of the Police Court Missionaries, a body of well-meaning amateurs in the best tradition of Christian penal reformers, led to the creation of the probation service and the first non-custodial sentence since the abolition of whipping in the late 1700s. This is one area of the history of punishment that requires much more work, especially at a time when the modern probation service has been going through a tremendous change in its structure and function.

Arguably, punishment saw more creative reform for young offenders. Here attempts at finding new ways to deal with juveniles had developed in the middle of the eighteenth century although this again had early modern antecedents. The Marine Society, the Refuge for the Destitute and the Philanthropic Society all attempted to offer alternatives to sending young people through the adult punishment system. But ultimately these were all merely partial success stories and helped very few juvenile criminals. They lacked state support and, most importantly, the money and resources required to function effectively. Mary Carpenter's campaign to establish Juvenile Reformatories (in the second half of the 1800s) was able to garner much more support from the centre. Despite this, the reformatory movement was still largely a failure, hamstrung as it was by a lack of funds and poor levels of staffing. We still have much to learn about reformatories and the industrial school system, particularly in the ways in which it served girls.

The most important change to the treatment of juveniles within the criminal justice system was activated after 1908 and the Children's Act. This heralded the proper separation of young offenders from adult ones and the recognition that youth offending needed to be dealt with by specialists in dedicated youth courts and offender institutions. One might see then that the greatest reform of the late Victorian and early Edwardian age was in the way in which society dealt with young offenders but an important caveat needs to be recognized here: late nineteenth-century society also began the process of demonizing teenagers and of identifying them as a 'social problem'. The hooligan panic of the 1890s was the first of several 'moral panics' surrounding youth that have continued to this day. While we have now had several case studies of gang crime from the 1860s onwards, we still await a comprehensive study of youth offending after the 1830s. There are also questions to be answered about the effectiveness of early institutions in the rehabilitation of young criminals.

As well as changes to punishments, the long period studied here saw tremendous change in policing, although change was not as dramatic as early historians of the police would have us believe. Broadly speaking, policing went from being something largely undertaken by 'respectable' citizens on behalf of their communities to something organized and carried out by professionals drawn from amongst the working class. Between this, there were several important experiments and a very gradual change of attitudes amongst those in power. The much maligned night watch was reformed, thief-takers, prosecution associations and parish constables all overlapped with the creation of the Metropolitan Police in 1829. Private and amateur policing did not end in 1829 or 1839 and even after 1856 residual elements of all of these survived. I would like to see the continuation of the work we have on watch reform and thief-takers in particular to continue to develop the history of police. Beattie's excellent study of the Bow Street Runners has challenged previous understandings for the introduction of the police in London and some more research might finally answer the question of why they were founded in 1829 and not earlier (or indeed later).

While Shpayer-Makov has recently done much to enlighten our knowledge of detectives, this is yet another area where we are only just beginning to understand the early history of the police. Forensic science is increasingly popular but more research is needed here, and in the development of the early twentieth-century 'bobby'. Storch's fierce attack on the policing of the north of England in the early years of the professionals has been met with a series of case studies; what we now require is someone to draw this work together and offer a new thesis on policing and its impact on Britain.

This study has looked at the importance of gender to histories of crime and this is an area where women's history has done much to set the agenda. It is now clear that women were treated differently by the criminal justice system for much, if not all, of the time period under consideration here. Female offenders were to some extent protected by a patriarchal system but perhaps more importantly, society simply did not view most female property criminals as a threat (an exception might be those that participated in the networks of forgers and coiners, or who used violence). However, if women were served quite well by patriarchy here they suffered for it elsewhere; the victims of domestic abuse and rape were almost invariably female and they had limited success when they went to law. Women were also more likely to be demonized by society if they stepped over the boundaries of what was considered appropriate female behaviour. Female murderers were anathema, especially in Victorian England. To some extent the prosecution of women needs to be understood not only within the discourse of patriarchy but also the emerging challenge of feminism and women's rights in the long nineteenth century. This is very evident in Clark's work on the 'struggle for the breeches' but also Walkowitz's in observations on the independence of Victorian prostitutes. Here is another topic, prostitution, which offers tempting possibilities for future research. If sources can be found then we need to know more about the ways in which prostitutes viewed themselves as well as how they were seen by working-class people. Too much of what has been written is gleaned from the thoughts and opinions of their 'social betters' rather than the sex workers themselves and their communities.

The history of violence has given us a grand thesis – the decline of homicide – with which historians have now grappled for several decades. Have we reached a unanimous conclusion? I don't think we have. But we do at least now know that while Elias' paradigm remains a useful starting point, it is not without challenge. Middle-class values may well have become more civilized over the course of the early modern period and eighteenth century but can we really argue that this applied to society as whole? Our modern society remains very violent, at least in its popular culture, and there are many more questions to be answered here. We know more about non-lethal violence but can we really agree with Wiener that the Victorian period saw petty violence become the concern of the state rather than the individual? What implication does the research here have on the wider picture of a decline of violence? Despite Spierenburg's excellent history of murder in Europe, we still lack a stand-alone volume dedicated to the history of homicide in England and Wales.

In this book I have included two chapters on property crime. This topic seemed to be missing from similar publications and at first I wondered if we really needed it. After all, most crime is related to property and nearly all of those imprisoned, transported or hanged from the 1700s onwards had been convicted of stealing something. Historians have largely abandoned 'social crime' as a topic but this seems to be undergoing a welcome revival and, given the new ways in which we can search primary material, there is certainly scope for more work here. Indeed, it is here – in looking at property offending – that the richness of trial records is really able to tell us a great deal about how people valued possessions in the past. Here crime history interacts with the history of consumption and fashion and historians should talk to each other more to gain a better understanding of the impact of commerce and capitalism in the 250 years studied here. Perhaps we know all we need to about highwaymen but there is more to discover about burglars and about more 'modern' criminals, such as those that preyed upon the unfortunate railway travellers or stole mail. There is also plenty of work that needs to be done in mapping crime; modern technology allows this new approach which can teach us about an area that seemed to be replete. Recent work on criminal networks is a welcome addition to our understanding of how groups and gangs of criminals operated and have been characterized in the past.[1]

While we know a lot about the way the court system developed or evolved, we still have much to learn about the informal nature of summary proceedings. Eight years after I was awarded my PhD I am somewhat surprised that we have not had more research work on the justice or the peace and the summary process.[2] The records are hard to find and harder to interrogate but we need to better understand how justice was done at the lower reaches of the criminal justice system. This was where most people encountered the law and Lemming's recent suggestion that English people were retreating from using the law after the Glorious Revolution seems problematic given what we do know about the summary process.[3] Lemming's is a persuasive argument and historians need to engage with it head on and the continued exploration of the role of the JP is probably the best way to do this.

Leaving the Hanoverian justice behind, we also need to have a thorough study of the police magistrate. Aside from Jennifer Davis and a handful of other articles, there is a paucity of scholarship on these forerunners of modern magistrate courts. How were they used, and who used them? Were they simply there to discipline the poor or could they be effective arenas of negotiation for men and women in Victorian England?

This brings me back to one of the biggest questions that the history of crime has struggled with: who could use the law in the past and whom did it serve? Hay's brilliant 1975 essay was my entry point into this field of history and it continues, for me at least, to be a relevant and enlightening thesis. But clearly it is flawed and the work of several historians has served to revise it. Most recently, King and Ward's intriguing analysis of executions on the periphery surely requires a fresh look at this debate. Does the fact that the 'Bloody Code' was effectively a dead letter in much of England negate Hay's thesis? I'm not sure it does but it might mean that the rule of law was expressed in a much more nuanced way that E. P. Thompson's famous conclusion suggests. I have a hunch that the truth is somewhere to be found in the role of the justice of the peace.

We come back also to the importance of class and class conflict. I am no Marxist but it seems to me that to dispense with class as a way of understanding history, especially the history of crime is problematic. Crime, as more than one historian has observed, is about power.[4] Fundamentally the law exists to protect property and persons, but most law is actually concerned with the former. Looking back through history this was even more apparent in the long eighteenth century. There were over 200 statutes protecting property by threatening death by hanging; highwaymen were hanged in chains and their bodies opened for the benefit medical science – all to deter the property thief. In the nineteenth century the thief was transported or locked up for time periods modern society would not even consider. All of this was supposed to protect the property of the few from the filthy paws of the many, in a society where the gulf between rich and poor was immeasurable and no system of welfare existed. Why do people steal? That is a hard question to answer but one that historians have a duty to engage with if history has any lessons to impart to contemporary society.

This brings me to my final thoughts, which concern the media. This book starts with a discussion of the criminal and the way in which he (and it was usually a 'he') has been characterized by society. Whilst the law is made in parliament and decisions about individual lives are often influenced by a multitude of individual actors (prosecutors/ victims, witnesses, jurors, judges, the crowd), underlying all of this is society itself. Crime does not happen in a vacuum; prosecutions follow patterns and trends that sometime shave very little to do with the crime itself. The Murder Act (1752) came about after a crime wave in London; the Habitual Offenders Act (1869) followed the garrotting panic. These are just two examples amongst many of the ways in which the focus of media attention has helped to shape penal policy. One consistent development can be seen in the period from 1660 to 1914 and that is the rise of the print media, and of the popular newspaper. Driven by competition and the need to print news that people want to read, often with scant regard for the truth, the newspaper came to dominate national views and politics in the period of this book. Arguably this has remained so ever since and it is only in the last few decades that the internet and the development of social media has begun to wrest the control of opinion from the media.

I would suggest that we need to pay much more attention to print media of the past and to the way in which it presented crime and the criminal. In depictions of the sturdy beggar, the dandy highway, the juvenile delinquent and the whole family of the 'criminal class', we can see the hand of the newspaper magnet, investigative journalist and the social commentator, very few if any of whom shared a common social class with those they wrote about. Newspaper sources remain a rich vein for students of crime but we must never forget to eye them critically before we swallow the rhetoric they espouse. Too many popular histories of crime have made that mistake. Recently there has been a trend towards researching the individual lives of criminals and of criminal networks and criminal environments.[5] Scholars have begun to use the digital medium to look at crime and punishment history in ways that previous historians could not even imagine. Moreover, histories of crime have increasingly attracted attention from amateur researchers and family historians; having criminal ancestors is no longer a mark of shame but a veritable badge of honour it seems.[6] Modern technologies and a fresh review of archival material especially for the nineteenth and early twentieth centuries means we are now beginning to build up a less prejudicial view of the criminal than the one presented by Fielding, Mayhew and the newspaper industry. More of this research needs to be undertaken.

Overall then this study has attempted to make sense of 250 years of crime and punishment history and inevitably it can only hope to skim the surface in some places. There is plenty more to read, plenty more to discover and hopefully the next decades will continue to offer new opportunities for research.

NOTES

Chapter 1

1   There is an online bibliography where you will find an extensive list of books and articles relating to this topic area.

2   F. M. L. Thompson, 'Social Control in Victorian Britain', *The Economic History Review*, second series, XXXIV:2 (May 1981), 189.

3   Michel Foucault, *Discipline and Punish: The Birth of the Prison* (Vintage Books, London, 1977); Michael Ignatieff, *A Just Measure of Pain: the penitentiary in the industrial revolution, 1750–1850* (University of Chicago Press, Chicago, 1978).

4   E. P. Thompson, *Whigs and Hunters: The Origin of the Black Act* (Penguin, London, 1975); Douglas Hay et al. (eds.), *Albion's Fatal Tree: Crime and Society in Eighteenth-Century England* (Penguin, London, 1975).

5   Douglas Hay, Peter Linebaugh, E.P. Thompson (eds), *Albion's Fatal Tree: Crime and Society in Eighteenth-Century England* (Allen Lane, London, 1975).

6   Leon Radzinowicz, *A History of the English Criminal Law and Its Administration from 1750* (Stevens & Sons, London, 1948).

7   E. P. Thompson, 'The Moral Economy of the English Crowd in the Eighteenth Century', *Past and Present*, 50 (1971), 76–136.

8   See, for example, John Rule's 'Wrecking and Coastal Plunder' in Hay et al. (eds.), *Albion's Fatal Tree* (Penguin, 1975). For other work on social crime, see E. J. Hobsbawm, *Bandits* (1972); John Rule, 'Social Crime in the Rural South in the Eighteenth and Early 19th Century', *Southern History*, 1 (1979), 35–53; Peter Linebaugh, *The London Hanged: Crime and Civil Society in the Eighteenth Century* (Penguin, London, 1991).

9   V. A. C. Gatrell, 'Crime, Authority and the Policeman-State', in F. M. L. Thompson (ed.), *The Cambridge Social History of Britain, 1750–1950, Volume 3; Social Agencies and Institutions* (Cambridge UP, Cambridge, 1990), 246

10 Barry Godfrey, *Crime in England, 1880–1945: The Rough and the Criminal, the Policed and the Incarcerated* (Routledge, London, 2014); The IHR (Institute of Historical Research) at the University of London has a seminar series dedicated to Digital History, and this area is opening up exciting new methodologies with history (www.history.ac.uk/events/seminars/321) [last accessed 15 March 2015].

11 Peter King and Richard Ward, 'Rethinking the Bloody Code in Eighteenth-Century Britain: Capital Punishment at the Centre and on the Periphery', *Past & Present*, 228 (2015), 159–205.

12 See, for example, the *Data Mining with Criminal Intent* project that Hitchcock and Robert Shoemaker contributed to. Tim Hitchcock, 'Text Mining the Old Bailey Proceedings', *History Spot* (June, 2011) (http://historyspot.org.uk/podcasts/digital-history/text-mining-old-bailey-proceedings) [last accessed 15 March 2015].

13 See http://www.locatinglondon.org; http://www2.le.ac.uk/departments/archaeology/research/projects/criminal-bodies-1 [last accessed 15 March 2015].

14 Stanley Cohen, *Folk Devils and Moral Panics. The Creation of the Mods and Rockers* (MacGibbon, London, 1972).

15 John H. Langbein, *The Origins of the Adversary Criminal Trial* (Oxford UP, Oxford, 2003).

16 A full bibliography and some suggested seminar or research exercises are available on Bloomsbury's website.

17 J. J. Tobias, *Crime and Industrial Society in the Nineteenth Century* (Penguin, London, 1972), 25.

18 V. A. C. Gatrell and T. Hadden, 'Criminal Statistics and Their Interpretation', in E. A. Wrigley (ed.), *Nineteenth Century Social History: Essays in the Use of Quantitative Methods for the Study of Social Data* (Cambridge UP, Cambridge, 1972).

19 Chris X. Williams, 'Counting Crimes or Counting People: Some Implications of Mid-Nineteenth Century British Police Returns', *Crime, Histoire & Sociétés/Crime, History & Societies*, 4:2 (2000).

20 Howard X. Taylor, 'Rationing Crime: The Political Economy of Criminal Statistics since the 1850s', *Economic History Review*, 51 (1998), 588.

21 For an excellent guide to material, see David T. Hawkings, *Criminal Ancestors: A Guide to Historical Criminal Records in England and Wales* (The History Press, Stroud, 1992).

22 TNA ASSI series; for the calendars, see PCOM 2/300-460.

23 www.oldbaileyonline.org.

24 TNA HO27.

25 TNA PCOM 2/404 and MEPO 6/1-24.

26 TNA PCOM 3 and PCOM 4.

27 TNA PCOM 5.

28 TNA PCOM 2/84-471.

29 Hulks are at TNA HO 8 and HO 9; county prisons under HO23 while national prisons are to found at HO 24/1-29. Lists of those convicts bound for Australia are within the series HO 11/1-19.

30 TNA E 370/35-51 and T 64/262.

31 Peter King et al., *Harnessing the Power of the Criminal Corpse* (Wellcome Trust funded project 095904/Z/11/Z).

32 King and Ward, 'Rethinking the Bloody Code in Eighteenth-Century Britain'.

33 J. A. Sharpe, *Crime in Early Modern England, 1550–1750*, 2nd edition (Longman, Harlow, 1999), 243.

34 Michael R. Weisser, *Crime and Punishment in Early Modern Europe* (The Harvester Press, Hassocks, 1979), 56.

35 Malcolm Gaskill, *Crime and Mentalities in Early Modern England* (Cambridge UP, Cambridge, 2000), 294.

36 Martin Ingram, 'Shame and Pain: Themes and Variations in Tudor Punishments', in Simon Devereaux and Paul Griffiths (eds.), *Penal Practice and Culture, 1500–1900: Punishing the English* (Palgrave MacMillan, Basingstoke, 2004), 43–7.

37 Paul Griffiths, 'Bodies and Souls in Norwich: Punishing Petty Crime, 1540–1700', in Simon Devereaux and Paul Griffiths (eds.), *Penal Practice and Culture, 1500–1900: Punishing the English* (Palgrave, Basingstoke, 2004), 86.

38 Gaskill, *Crime and Mentalities*, 309.

39 See, for example, David Lemmings, *Law and Government in England during the Long Eighteenth Century: From Consent to Command* (Palgrave, Basingstoke, 2011); Martin

Ingram, *Church Courts, Sex and Marriage in England, 1570–1640* (Cambridge UP, Cambridge, 1990); R. B. Outhwaite, *The Rise and Fall of the English Ecclesiastical Courts, 1500–1860* (Cambridge UP, Cambridge, 2006).

Chapter 2

1   John Locke, *Two Treatises on Government* (London, 1689).

2   Cesare Beccaria, *On Crimes and Punishments* (London, 1764).

3   Peter King, *Crime, Justice and Discretion in England 1740–1820* (Oxford UP, Oxford, 2000).

4   Janet Semple, *Bentham's Prison: A Study of the Panopticon Penitentiary* (Clarendon Press, Oxford, 1993), 152.

5   David Garland, *Punishment and Welfare: A History of Penal Strategies* (Gower Publishing, Aldershot, 1985), 84–9.

6   Martin J. Wiener, *Reconstructing the Criminal: Culture, Law, and Policy in England, 1839–1914* (Cambridge UP, Cambridge 1990), 172.

7   Herbert Spencer, *Principles of Biology* (Williams and Norgate, London, 1864).

8   Henry Mayhew, *London Labour and the London Poor, Those That Will Work, Cannot Work, and Will Not Work* (Charles Griffin, London, 1851).

9   Cesare Lombroso, *Criminal Man*, translated and edited by Mary Gibson and Nicole Hahn Rafter (Duke UP, Durham, NC 2006).

10   J. Bruce Thomson, 'The Psychology of Criminals', *Journal of Mental Science*, 16 (1870).

11   Wiener, *Reconstructing the Criminal*, 357.

12   James Sharpe, *Dick Turpin: The Myth of the English Highwayman* (Profile Books, London, 2004), 216.

13   Peter King, 'Newspaper Reporting and Attitudes to Crime and Justice Late-Eighteenth and Early-Nineteenth-Century London', *Continuity and Change*, 22 (2007); Esther Snell, 'Discourses of Criminality in the Eighteenth-Century Press: The Presentation of Crime in the *Kentish Post*, 1717–1768', *Continuity and Change*, 22 (2007); Robert Shoemaker, 'Print Culture and the Creation of Public Knowledge about Crime in Eighteenth-Century London', in Paul Knepper et al. (eds.), *Urban Crime Prevention, Surveillance, and Restorative Justice* (CRC Press, London, 2009).

14   Norma Landau, 'Gauging Crime in Late Eighteenth-Century London', *Social History*, 35 (2010).

15   Richard M. Ward, *Print Culture, Crime and Justice in 18th-Century* (Bloomsbury, London, 2014), 35.

16   Snell, 'Discourses of Criminality in the Eighteenth-Century Press'.

17   Andrea McKenzie, *Lives of the Most Notorious Criminals: Popular Literature of Crime in England, 1675–1775* (University of Toronto PhD thesis, 1999), 458 (see note 2).

18   Phillip Rawlings, *Drunks, Whores and Idle Apprentices: Criminal Biographies of the Eighteenth Century* (Routledge, London, 1992), 2.

19   Robert B. Shoemaker, 'The Old Bailey Proceedings and the Representation of Crime and Criminal Justice in Eighteenth-Century London', *Journal of British Studies*, 47 (July 2008).

20 Rawlings, *Drunks, Whores and Idle Apprentices*, 4.

21 Ward, *Print Culture*, 41.

22 McKenzie, *Lives of the Most Notorious Criminals*, 459–60; 467.

23 Shoemaker, 'The Old Bailey Proceedings', 565.

24 Ward, *Print Culture*, 42.

25 For example, Henry Fielding, *An Enquiry into the Late Increase of Robbers, etc.* (London, 1751).

26 Andrea McKenzie, *Tyburn's Martyrs: Execution in England 1675–1775* (Hambledon Continuum, London, 2007).

27 Rawlings, *Drunks, Whores and Idle Apprentices*, 4–6.

28 www.oldbaileyonline.org t17240812-52.

29 Ignatieff, *A Just Measure of Pain*.

30 *Where's Jack?* (D. by James Clavell, 1969).

31 A. Ash and J. E. Day, *Immortal Turpin: The Authentic Account of England's Most Notorious Highwayman* (Staples Press, London, 1948).

32 Dereck Barlow, *Dick Turpin and the Gregory Gang* (Phillimore & Co., Chichester, 1973), 87–9.

33 Sharpe, *Dick Turpin*, 113.

34 Gillian Spraggs, *Outlaws & Highwaymen: The Cult of the Robber in England from the Middle Ages to the Nineteenth Century* (Pimlico, London, 2001), 178–9.

35 Sharpe, *Dick Turpin*, 135.

36 Ibid., 136.

37 Spraggs, *Outlaws & Highwaymen*, 252.

38 Sharpe, *Dick Turpin*, 20.

39 Barlow, *Dick Turpin and the Gregory Gang*.

40 Harrison Ainsworth, *Rookwood* (London, 1834), 63.

41 Ainsworth also wrote *Jack Sheppard*, which was serially published (as many novels were) in 1839–1840, accompanied by dramatic illustrations by the artist George Cruickshank.

42 D. Gray, *London's Shadows: The Dark Side of the Victorian City* (Bloomsbury, London, 2010).

43 Andrea McKenzie, 'The Real MacHeath: Social Satire, Appropriation, and Eighteenth-Century Criminal Biography', *Huntingdon Law Quarterly*, 69:4 (2006).

44 McKenzie, *Lives of the Most Notorious Criminals*, 459.

45 Ward, *Print Culture*, 36.

46 Ibid., 205.

47 Lincoln B. Faller, *Turned to Account: The Forms and Functions of Criminal Biography in Late Seventeenth- and Early Eighteenth-Century England* (Cambridge UP, Cambridge, 1987).

48 Rawling, *Drunks, Whores and Idle Apprentices*, 11.

49 Faller, *Turned to Account*, 178.

50 McKenzie, *Lives of the Most Notorious Criminals*.

51 Ibid., 471.

52 McKenzie, *Tyburn's Martyrs*, 252–3.

53 John Archer and Jo Jones, 'Headlines from History: Violence in the Press, 1850–1914', in Elizabeth A. Stanko (ed.), *The Meanings of Violence* (Routledge, London, 2003), 18; see also Philippe Chassaigne, 'Popular Representations of Crime: The Crime Broadside – A Subculture of Violence in Victorian Britain', *Crime, History and Societies*, 2 (1999); Charles Elkins, 'The Voice of the Poor: The Broadside as a Medium of Popular Culture and Dissent in Victorian England', *Journal of Popular Culture*, 2 (1980).

54 John Ashton, *Chapbooks of the Eighteenth Century* (Chatto & Windus, London, 1882).

55 John Springhall, *Youth, Popular Culture and Moral Panics: Penny Gaffs to Gansta-Rapp 1830–1996* (MacMIllan, Basingtoke, 1998), 39.

56 Springhall, *Youth, Popular Culture and Moral Panics*, 46.

57 http://www.bl.uk/reshelp/findhelprestype/news/barryono/barryono.html [last accessed 9 September 2014].

58 Alan Lee, 'The Structure, Ownership and Control of the Press, 1855–1914', in Boyce, Curran and Wingate (eds.), *Newspaper History: From the Seventeenth Century to the Present Day* (Constable, London, 1978), 117.

59 Lee Perry Curtis, Jr., *Jack the Ripper and the London* Press (Yale UP, New Haven, CT and London, 2001), 57.

60 Robert Sindall, *Street Violence in the Nineteenth Century* (Leicester UP, Leicester, 1990), 32.

61 Archer and Jones, 'Headlines from History', 17.

62 Cohen, *Folk Devils and Moral Panics*.

63 Ibid., 1.

64 J. Davis, 'The London Garrotting Panic of 1862: A Moral Panic and the Creation of a Criminal Class in Mid-Victorian England', in V. A. C. Gatrell et al. (eds.), *Crime and Law: The Social History of Crime in Western Europe since 1500* (Europa, London, 1980).

65 Cohen, *Folk Devils and Moral Panics*, 11.

66 Davis, 'The London Garrotting Panic of 1862', 191.

67 Ibid., 198.

68 *Spectator*, 17 July 1862.

69 *The Times*, 30 December 1862; *Observer*, 23 November 1862.

70 Sindall, *Street Violence*.

71 Davis, 'The London Garrotting Panic of 1862', 204–5.

72 Ibid., 205.

73 Ibid., 209; see also Victor Bailey, 'The Fabrication of Deviance: "Dangerous Classes" and "Criminal Classes" in Victorian England', in J. Rule and R. Malcolmson (eds.), *Protest and Survival: The Historical Experience. Essays for E. P. Thompson* (Merlin Press, London, 1993).

74 Archer and Jones, 'Headlines from History', 26.

75 Geoffrey Pearson, *Hooligan: A History of Respectable Fears* (MacMillan, Basingstoke, 1983).

76 Daniel Statt, 'The Case of the Mohawks: Rake Violence in Augustan London', *Social History*, 20:2 (1995).

77 John Pitts, *Reluctant Gangstas: The Changing Face of Youth Crime* (Willan, Cullompton, 2008).

78 Drew Gray, 'Gang Crime and the Media: The Regent's Park Murder of 1888', *Social and Cultural History*, 10:4 (2013).

Notes

79 John E. Archer, *The Monster Evil: Policing and Violence in Victorian Liverpool* (Liverpool UP, Liverpool, 2011); Andrew Davies, 'Youth Gangs, Masculinity and Violence in Late Victorian Manchester and Salford', *Journal of Social History*, 32:2 (1998); Stephen Humphries, *Hooligans and Rebels: An Oral History of Working-Class Childhood and Youth 1889–1939* (Wiley-Blackwell, Oxford, 1995); Heather Shore, *London's Criminal Underworlds, c. 1720–c. 1930: A Social and Cultural History* (Palgrave, Basingstoke, 2015).

80 John Pitts is a notable exception with his *Reluctant Gangstas* (cited above).

81 Gray, 'Gang Crime and the Media'.

82 Owen Jones, *Chavs: The Demonization of the Working Class* (Verso, London, 2011).

83 Humphries, *Hooligans and Rebels?*, 175.

84 H. French and M. Rothery, *Man's Estate: Landed Gentry Masculinities, 1660–1900* (Oxford UP, 2012), 125.

85 Judith Flanders, *The Invention of Murder: How the Victorians Revelled in Death and Detection and Created Modern Crime* (Harper Press, London, 2011).

86 Rosalind Crone, *Violent Victorians: Popular Entertainment in Nineteenth-Century* (Manchester UP, London, 2012).

87 Crone, *Violent Victorians*.

88 Flanders, *The Invention of Murder*.

89 John Carter Wood, *Violence and Crime in Nineteenth-Century England; The Shadow of Our Refinement* (Routledge, London, 2004), 10.

90 Crone, *Violent Victorians*, 67.

91 Katherine Watson, *Victims Poisoned Lives: English Poisoners and their Victims* (Hambledon Continuum, London, 2004).

92 Ian Burney, *Poison, Detection, and the Victorian Imagination* (Manchester UP, Manchester, 2006), 20; P. W. J. Bartrip, 'A "Pennurth of Arsenic for Rat Poison". The Arsenic Act, 1851 and the Prevention of Secret Poisoning', *Medical History*, 36 (1992).

93 Burney, *Poison, Detection, and the Victorian Imagination*, 25.

94 Harriet Martineau, quoted in Burney, *Poison, Detection, and the Victorian Imagination*, 28.

95 Burney, *Poison, Detection, and the Victorian Imagination*, 6.

96 Steve Chibnall, *Law and Order News* (Tavistock, London, 1977).

97 Deborah Gorham, 'The "Maiden Tribute of Modern Babylon" Re-examined: Child Prostitution and the Idea of Childhood in Late-Victorian England', *Victorian Studies*, 21:3 (Spring 1976); Alison Plowden, *The Case of Eliza Armstrong, A 'Child of 13 Bought for £5'* (BBC Publications, London, 1974).

98 Curtis, *Jack the Ripper and the London Press*, 68.

99 Archer and Jones, 'Headlines from History', 25.

100 Michael Diamond, *Victorian Sensation: Or the Spectacular, the Shocking and the Scandalous in Nineteenth-Century Britain* (Anthem Press, London, 2003), 184; see also the collection of essays on the media coverage in Alexandra Warwick and Martin Willis (eds.), *Jack the Ripper: Media, Culture, History* (Manchester UP, Manchester, 2007).

101 Curtis, *Jack the Ripper and the London Press*, 115.

102 *Daily Mail*, Friday, 15 July 1910.

103 *Devon and Exeter Daily Gazette*, 18 July 1910.

104 *Daily Mail*, 29 July 1910.

105 *The Times*, 1 September 1910.

106 Emsley, *Crime and Society in England*, 34.

107 J. Sharpe, ' "Last Dying Speeches": Religion, Ideology and Public Execution in Seventeenth-Century England', *Past & Present*, 107 (1985), 162.

108 Ward, *Print Culture*, 82.

109 Ibid., 216.

110 These are just two of many ex-convicts that have written or published their life stories; any 'true crime' section of your local bookshop will offer a plethora of alternatives.

Chapter 3

1 ONS, 'The likelihood of becoming a victim of crime', July 2013.

2 Martin J. Wiener, *Men of Blood: Violence, Manliness, and Criminal Justice in Victorian England* (Cambridge UP, Cambridge, 2004).

3 Norbert Elias, *The Civilizing Process*, translated by E. Jephcott (Urizen Books, New York, 1978).

4 Including: Lawrence Stone, 'Interpersonal Violence in English Society 1300–1980', *Past & Present*, 101 (1983); James A. Sharpe, 'Debate: The History of Violence in England; some observations', *Past & Present*, 108 (1985); Manuel Eisner, 'Modernization, Self-Control and Lethal Violence', *British Journal of Criminology*, 91 (2001), 618–638; Robert Shoemaker, 'Male Honour and the Decline of Violence in Eighteenth-Century London', *Social History*, 26 (2001), 190–208; Carter Wood, *Violence and Crime*; Pieter Spierenburg, *A History of Murder: Personal Violence in Europe from the Middles Ages to the Present* (Cambridge UP, Cambridge, 2008).

5 J. Carter Wood, 'Criminal Violence in Modern Britain', History Compass, 4:1 (2006), 78.

6 G. Morgan and P. Rushton, 'The Magistrate, the Community and the Maintenance of an Orderly Society in Eighteenth-Century England', *Historical Research*, 76 (2003), 191; Peter King, 'Punishing Assault: The Transformation of Attitudes in the English Courts', *The Journal of Interdisciplinary History*, 27:1 (Summer, 1996), 43–74; Drew D. Gray, 'The Regulation of Violence in the Metropolis; the Prosecution of Assault in the Summary Courts, c. 1780–1820', *London Journal*, 32:1 (2007).

7 *Homicide* means the killing of human beings. In this sense, we are referring to *unlawful* killing.

8 Ted Gurr, 'Historical Trends in Violent Crime: A Critical Review of the Evidence', *Crime and Justice: An Annual Review of Research*, 3 (1981), 295–353; see also J. A. Sharpe, *Crime in Seventeenth-Century England: A County Study* (Cambridge UP, Cambridge, 1983).

9 See Manuel Eisner, 'What Causes Large-Scale Variation in Homicide Rates?', in Juergen Heinze and Henning Kortuem (eds.), *Aggression in Humans and Primates* (de Gruyter, Berlin, 2012).

10 Peter King, 'The Impact of Urbanization on Murder Rates and on the Geography of Homicide in England and Wales, 1780–1850', *The Historical Journal*, 53:3 (2010), 687.

11 Stone, 'Interpersonal Violence in English Society'.

12 Barry Godfrey and Paul Lawrence, *Crime and Justice, 1750–1950* (Willan, Cullompton, 2005), 104.

13 See Jonathan Fletcher, *Violence and Civilization: An Introduction to the Work of Norbert Elias* (Polity Press, Cambridge, 1997).

14 Steven Pinker, *The Better Angels of Our Nature: The Decline of Violence in History and Its Causes* (Allen Lane, London, 2011), 78.

15 Wood, 'Criminal Violence in Modern Britain', 78.

16 Clive Emsley, *Hard Men: Violence in England Since 1750* (Hambledon Continuum, London, 2005), 73.

17 Stone, 'A Rejoinder', *Past & Present*, 108:1 (1985), 216–224.

18 Sharpe, 'Debate. The History of Violence in England'.

19 See, for example, King, 'The Impact of Urbanization'; Taylor, 'Rationing Crime'; M. Emmerichs, 'Getting Away with Murder: Homicide and the Coroners in Nineteenth-Century London', *Social Science History*, 25 (2001), 93–100; P. Fisher, 'Getting Away with Murder? The Suppression of Coroners' Inquests in Early Victorian England and Wales', *Local Population Studies*, 78 (2007), 47–62.

20 Spierenburg, *A History of Murder*, 167.

21 King, 'The Impact of Urbanization', 690, see also P. King, 'Urbanization, Rising Homicide Rates and the Geography of Lethal Violence in Scotland, 1800–1860', *History*, 96 (2011), 323.

22 Emmerichs, 'Getting Away with Murder?', 96–9.

23 King, 'The Impact of Urbanization', 676, see also J. Harvard, *The Detection of Secret Homicide* (MacMillan, London, 1960) and Watson, *Poisoned Lives*.

24 John E. Archer, 'Mysterious and Suspicious Deaths: Missing Homicides in North-West England (1850–1900)', *Crime, History & Societies*, 12:1 (2008) 45–63.

25 Archer, 'Mysterious and Suspicious Deaths', 11.

26 Notably Manuel Eisner, see 'Modernization'.

27 Ibid.

28 Manuel Eisner, 'Long-Term Historical Trends in Violent Crime', *Crime and Justice: A Review of Research*, 30 (2003), 88.

29 James Cockburn, 'Patterns of Violence in English Society: Homicide in Kent 1560–1985', *Past & Present*, 103 (1991), 70–106, Cockburn started his study in the sixteenth century because after 1487 all coroners were required by law to bring all their inquests into the court records. As a result, he was able to get data for a very long period (from the 1550s to 1985); King, 'The Impact of Urbanization'.

30 Shoemaker, 'Male Honour'.

31 King, 'Urbanization', 259.

32 Robert B. Shoemaker, 'The Taming of the Duel: Masculinity, Honour, and Ritual Violence in London, 1660–1800', *The Historical Journal*, 45:3 (2002).

33 Shoemaker, 'Male Honour'.

34 Ibid., 195.

35 Ibid., 203 see also Shoemaker, 'The Taming of the Duel'.

36 V. G. Kiernan, *The Duel in European History: Honour and the Reign of the Aristocracy* (Oxford UP, Oxford, 1988).

37 See Anthony Simpson, 'Dandelions on the Field of Honour; Dueling, the Middle Classes, and the Law in Nineteenth-Century England', *Criminal Justice History*, 9 (1998), 99–155.

38 Eisner, 'Modernization'.

39   King, 'The Impact of Urbanization', 685.

40   Eisner, 'What Causes Large-Scale Variation', 13.

41   Gregory Hanlon, 'Review Article. The Decline of Violence in the West: From Cultural to Post-Cultural History', *English Historical Review*, CXXVIII:53 (2013), 386.

42   Antonio Palumbo and Alan Scott (ed.), *Classical Social Theory I: Marx and Durkheim* (Oxford UP, Oxford, 2005).

43   Randolf Rolf, *American Homicide* (Cambridge, Cambridge, MA, 2009) quoted in Eisner, 'What Causes Large-Scale Variation', 20.

44   Manuel Eisner, 'Modernity Strikes Back? A Historical Perspective on the Latest Increase in Interpersonal Violence (1960–1990)', *International Journal of Conflict and Violence*, 2:2 (2008), 290.

45   Eisner, 'What Causes Large-Scale Variation', 19.

46   Fiona Brookman, *Understanding Homicide* (Sage, London, 2005), 3.

47   Louis Blom-Cooper and Terence Morris, *With Malice Aforethought: A Study of the Crime and Punishment for Homicide* (Hart Publishing, Oxford and Portland, Oregon, 2004), 15–6.

48   Quoted in Shani D'Cruze, Sandra Walklate and Samantha Pegg, *Murder: Social and Historical Approaches to Understanding Murder and Murderers* (Willan Publishing, Cullompton, 2006), 3.

49   For example, in the case of women that killed their husbands or masters, which until 1828 was treated as 'petty' treason, or infanticide.

50   For studies that consider this particular form of punishment, see Ruth Campbell, 'Sentence of Death by Burning for Women', *Journal of Legal History*, 5 (1984), 45–59; Simon Devereaux, 'The Abolition of the Burning of Women in England Reconsidered', *Crime, History & Societies*, 9:2 (2005), 73–98.

51   Gaskill, *Crime and Mentalities*, 210.

52   Ibid., 246.

53   D. Gray and P. King, 'The Killing of Constable Linnell: The Impact of Xenophobia and of Elite Connections on Eighteenth-Century Justice', *Family & Community History*, 16:1 (2013), 3–31.

54   Emmerichs, 'Getting Away with Murder?', 97.

55   Jeremy Horder (ed.), *Homicide Law in Comparative Perspective* (Hart Publishing, Oxford and Portland, Oregon, 2007), 12.

56   Gray and King, 'The Killing of Constable Linnell'.

57   Regina v. M'Naghten, 8 Eng. Rep. 718 [1843]; Philip Carlen, Lisa S. Nored, Ragan A. Downey, *An Introduction to Criminal Law* (Jones & Bartlett Publishers, Sudbury, MA 2011), 150.

58   www.oldbaileyonline.org t18560204-263.

59   Spierenburg, *A History of Murder*, 170–1.

60   Gaskill, *Crime and Mentalities,* 259.

61   D. Gray, *London's Shadows: The Dark Side of the Victorian City* (Bloomsbury, London, 2010), 224.

62   Anon, *Murder Will Out, or the Heinous Guilt of Murder and Assassination Laid Open in a Sermon upon the 5th November 1717* (London, 1717).

63   Henry Fielding, *Murders. True Examples of the Interposition of Providence, in the Discovery and Punishment of Murder* (London, 1799).

64   Gaskill, *Crime and Mentalities*, 206–7.

65   Blom-Cooper and Morris, *With Malice Aforethough*, 61–2.

66   Quoted in Horder (ed.), *Homicide Law in Comparative Perspective*, 7–8.

67   See Table 2.14 in Brookman, *Understanding Homicide*, 50.

68   See Gray, 'Gang Crime and the Media', but also Andrew Davies, 'Youth Gangs, Masculinity and Violence in Late Victorian Manchester and Salford', *Journal of Social History*, 32:2 (Winter 1998), 349–369; John E. Archer, *The Monster Evil: Policing and Violence in Victorian* (Liverpool UP, Liverpool, 2011). The wider problem of gang crime is discussed in the media and crime chapter.

69   Brookman, *Understanding Homicide*, 146.

70   Eisner, 'What Causes Large-Scale Variation', 11.

71   For a detailed analysis of the duel in a European context, see Spierenburg, *A History of Murder*, 71–96.

72   Emsley, *Hard Men*, 41.

73   Brookman, *Understanding Homicide*, 124.

74   Blom-Cooper and Morris, *With Malice Aforethought*, 19.

75   Richard A. Fletcher, *Bloodfeud: Murder and Revenge in Anglo-Saxon England* (Oxford UP, Oxford, 2004).

76   There is an excellent online collection of broadsides held by the Bodleian Library in Oxford and another at Harvard.

77   James Stannup, *The Whole Tryal, Life and Conversation [sic] Birth, Parentage, and Education, of the Lady Aberganey, Who Was Burnt at East Grinsted in Sussex* (London, 1712).

78   www.oldbaileyonline.org t18880109-215.

79   www.oldbaileyonline.org t18880730-773.

80   www.oldbaileyonline.org t18880130-291.

81   Cockburn, 'Patterns of Violence in English Society'.

82   www.oldbaileyonline.org t18880319-407.

83   www.oldbaileyonline.org t18881022-955.

84   www.oldbaileyonline.org t18880109-226.

85   www.oldbaileyonline.org t18880730-759.

86   www.oldbaileyonline.org t18880423-481.

87   www.oldbaileyonline.org t18880702-691.

88   www.oldbaileyonline.org t18880109-232.

89   The Offences against the Person Act 1861 (24 and 25 Vict c 100).

90   The Offences against the Person Act 1828 (9 Geo.4 c.31).

91   Richard Burn, *Justice of the Peace and Parish Officer*, Volume 1 (London, 1785), 111.

92   William Blackstone, *Commentaries on the Laws of England*, Volume 3 (London, 1765–1769), 120.

93   Michael Dalton, *The Countrey Justice* (London, 1618), 10.

94   Drew Gray, *Summary Proceedings and Social Relations in the City of London, c.1750-1820* (UCN PhD) data relates to examinations before the Guildhall and Mansion House Justices 1784–96.

95   King, 'Punishing Assault', 46.

96   www.oldbaileyonline.org Tabulating decade against verdict category where offence category is assault. Counting by verdict, 1674 to 1800.

97   Gray, *Summary Proceedings and Social Relations*, 94.

98   King, 'Punishing Assault', 46.

99   Michelle A. Abraham, 'The Summary Courts and the Prosecution of Assault in Northampton and Nottingham, 1886–1931' (Unpublished PhD, University of Leicester, 2011).

100 *Police Code Book* 1870 (Northamptonshire Record Office).

101 Quoted in V. A. C. Gatrell, 'The Decline of Theft and Violence in Victorian and Edwardian England' in Gatrell et al. (eds.), *Crime and the Law. The Social History of Crime in Western Europe since 1500* (Europa Publications Limited, London, 1980), 285.

102 Drew D. Gray, *Crime, Prosecution and Social Relations: The Summary Courts of the City of London in the Late Eighteenth Century* (Palgrave, Basingstoke, 2009), 20, 93.

103 P. King, 'Summary Courts and Social Relations in Eighteenth-Century England', *Past & Present*, 183 (2004), 170.

104 E. Crittal (ed.), *The Justicing Notebook of William Hunt, 1744–1749* (Wiltshire Record Society, Devizes, 1982).

105 Morgan and Rushton, 'The Magistrate'.

106 King, 'The Summary Courts and Social Relations'.

107 R. Shoemaker, *Prosecution and Punishment: Petty Crime and the Law in London and Rural Middlesex, 1660–1725* (Cambridge UP, Cambridge, 1991), 7.

108 Norma Landau, 'Indictment for Fun and Profit: A Prosecutor's Reward at the Eighteenth-Century Quarter Sessions', *Law and History Review*, 17:3 (Fall, 1999), 507–536.

109 LMA/MJR/M53 December 1789.

110 *The Observer* 1815.

111 Gray, *Summary Proceedings and Social Relations*, see Table 6.2, 151.

112 Morgan and Rushton, 'The Magistrate', Table 6.

113 R. S. Neale, *Bath: A Social History, 1680–1850* (Routledge & Kegan Paul, London, 1981) Table 3.8, 90.

114 REF to Shoemaker.

115 King, 'Summary Courts and Social Relations', Table 3, p.143.

116 E. Foyster, *Marital Violence: An English Family History, 1660–1857* (Cambridge University Press, Cambridge, 2005), 23; See also Anne-Marie Kilday, 'Just Who Was Wearing the Trousers in Victorian Britain? Violent Wives and Violent Women', in N. Vanfasse (ed.), *Social Deviance in England and France c. 1830–1900*, special issue of *Cahiers Edouardiens et Victoriens*, 61 (April 2005).

117 Gray, *Summary Proceedings and Social Relations*, Table 6.2, 151.

118 Ibid., 165–6.

119 T. Meldrum, 'A Woman's Court in London: Defamation at the Bishop of London's Consistory Court, 1700–1745', *The London Journal*, 19 (1994), 1–20.

120 Wiener, *Men of Blood*, 22.

121 Gray, *Summary Proceedings and Social Relations*, 182.

122 Landau, 'Indictment for Fun and Profit'.

123 Jennine Hurl, ' "She Being Bigg with Child Is Likely to Miscarry": Pregnant Victims Prosecuting Assault in Westminster, 1685–1720', *The London Journal*, 24:2 (1999), 18–33.

124 P. King, *Crime and Law in England, 1750–1840: Remaking Justice from the Margins* (Cambridge UP, Cambridge, 2006), see Table 7.1, 232.

125   Emsley, *Hard Men*, 12.

126   Wiener, *Men of Blood*; Wood, *Violence and Crime*.

127   Shoemaker, 'Male Honour'.

128   Carter Wood, *Violence and Crime*, 140.

129   Wiener, *Men of Blood*, 12.

130   Spierenburg, *A History of Murder*, 167; see also Hanlon, 'Decline of Violence', 383.

131   Wiener, *Men of Blood*, 21–2.

132   Ibid.

133   Gatrell, 'The Decline of Theft and Violence', 292.

134   Barry Godfrey, 'Counting and Accounting for the Decline in Non-Lethal Violence in England, Australia and New Zealand, 1880–1920', *British Journal of Criminology*, 43 (2003), 340–353.

135   John E. Archer, '"Men Behaving Badly?" Masculinity and the Uses of Violence, 1850–1900', in Shani D'Cruze (ed.), *Everyday Violence in Britain, 1850–1950* (Longman, London and New York, 2000), 49.

136   Gatrell, 'The Decline of Theft and Violence', 291.

137   Office for National Statistics [ONS] (2012), 'Crime Statistics, Nature of Crime Tables, 2011/12'.

138   http://www.bbc.co.uk/news/uk-17482035 [last accessed 4 April 2014].

139   Carter Wood, *Violence and Crime*, 140.

140   Godfrey, 'Counting and Accounting', 345.

141   Ibid., 345.

142   Gatrell, 'Decline of Theft and Violence', 296.

143   Pieter Spierenburg (ed.), *Men and Violence: Gender, Honor; and Rituals in Modern Europe and America* (Ohio State UP, Colombus, 1998).

144   Archer, 'Men Behaving Badly?', 42.

145   Carter Wood, *Violence and Crime*, 138; see also Godfrey, 'Counting and Accounting', 346.

146   Spierenburg, *A History of Murder*, 175–6.

147   Ibid., 175.

148   Carter Wood, *Violence and Crime*, 139.

149   Wiener, *Men of Blood*, 6.

150   Carter Wood, *Violence and Crime*, 143–4.

151   Abraham, 'The Summary Courts'.

152   For a separate discussion of domestic violence, see Chapter 6.

153   King, 'Punishing Assault', 53.

154   Lucy Williams, *'At Large': Women's Lives and Offending in Victorian Liverpool and London* (Unpublished PhD, University of Liverpool, 2014).

155   Raphael Samuel, *East End Underworld: Chapters in the Life of Arthur Harding* (Routledge, London, 1981).

156   Crone, *Violent Victorians*.

157   Spierenburg, *A History of Murder*.

158   We do have Vanessa McMahon's *Murder in Shakespeare's England* (Hambledon and London, London, 2004) which covers the early modern period.

Chapter 4

1   A shilling in the mid-1700s would have had the approximate buying power of £5 in the early 2000s, but this figure was falling across the eighteenth century; by 1800, a figure of around £1.60 in modern money is more realistic. This calculation was made using the National Archives' Currency Converter http://apps.nationalarchives.gov.uk/currency/ [last accessed 23 June 2014].

2   Stephen Buckle, *Natural Law and the Theory of Property* (Clarendon Press, Oxford 1991),10–11.

3   Richard Ashcraft, 'Locke's Political Philosophy', in Vere Chappell (ed.), *The Cambridge Companion to Locke* (Cambridge UP, Cambridge, 1994), 247.

4   John Dunn, *Locke* (Oxford UP, Oxford, 1984) 38–9.

5   Gerrard Winstanley, *The True Levellers Standard Advanced* in Vanfasse (ed.), *Social Deviance in England and France c. 1830–1900* (London, 1649).

6   William Blackstone, *Commentaries*, Volume 1, 134–5, 140–41.

7   For county or regional studies that address property crime outside of London, see, for example, J. M. Beattie, *Crime and the Courts in England, 1660–1800* (Princeton UP, Princeton, NJ, 1986); Carolyn A. Conley, *The Unwritten Law: Criminal Justice in Victorian Kent* (Oxford UP, Oxford, 1991); Hay et al. (eds.), *Albion's Fatal Tree*; King, *Crime, Justice and Discretion*; Gwenda Morgan and Peter Rushton, *Rogues, Thieves and the Rule of Law: The Problem of Law Enforcement in North-East England, 1718–1800* (UCL Press, London, 1998); David Phillips, *Crime and Authority in Victorian England: The Black Country 1835–1860* (Crook Helm, London, 1977); Sharpe, *Crime in Seventeenth-Century England*; Garthine Walker and Jenny Kermode, *Women, Crime and the Courts in Early Modern England* (UCL Press, London, 1994); Williams, "*At Large*"; Lucia Zedner, *Women, Crime and Custody in Victorian England* (Clarendon, Oxford, 1991:1994).

8   Shoemaker, 'The Old Bailey Proceedings and the Representation of Crime'.

9   Gatrell, 'The Decline of Theft and Violence'.

10   Ibid., Table III, 282.

11   McKenzie, *Lives of the Most Notorious Criminals*; Rawlings, *Drunks, Whores and Idle Apprentices*.

12   J. M., *The Traveller's Guide and the Country's Safety Being a Declaration of the Laws of England against Highway Men, or Robbers upon the Road* (British Library, London, 1683).

13   Beattie, *Crime and the Courts*, 148.

14   Paul Langford, *A Polite and Commercial People: England 1727–1783* (Oxford UP, Oxford, 1992).

15   J. M., *The Traveller's Guide*, 4.

16   Ibid., 68–9.

17   Anon, *Hanging not Punishment Enough for Murtherers, High-Way Men, and House-Breakers* in Vanfasse (ed.), *Social Deviance in England and France c. 1830–1900* (London, 1701), quoted in Beattie, *Crime and the Courts*, 149.

18   Beattie, *Crime and the Courts*, 148.

19   Fielding, *An Enquiry*, 68.

20   Ibid.

21   Richard Ward, 'Print Culture, Moral Panic, and the Administration of the Law: The London Crime Wave of 1744', *Crime, History & Societies*, 15:1 (2012); see also Richard Ward (ed.), *A Global History of Execution and the Criminal Corpse* (Palgrave, Basingstoke, 2015).

22   Beattie, *Crime and the Courts*.

23 www.oldbaileyonline.org, t17540424-52; J. M. Beattie, *The First English Detectives: The Bow Street Runners and the Policing of London, 1750–1840* (Oxford UP, Oxford, 2014).

24 www.oldbaileyonline.org, t17941111-49 and t17970111-42.

25 www.oldbaileyonline.org, t17840526-20.

26 www.oldbaileyonline.org, t17500425-38.

27 www.oldbaileyonline.org, t17921215-15.

28 www.oldbaileyonline.org, t17940716-7.

29 www.oldbaileyonline.org, t17871212-17.

30 www.oldbaileyonline.org, t17660219-42.

31 Gray, *Crime, Prosecution and Social Relations*.

32 *Fielding, An Enquiry*, 75.

33 Beattie, *The First English Detectives*.

34 www.oldbaileyonline.org, t17800913-57.

35 www.oldbaileyonline.org, t17931030-69.

36 www.oldbaileyonline.org, t17861025-72.

37 William M. Meier, *Property Crime in London, 1850–Present* (Palgrave MacMillan, Basingstoke, 2011), 15.

38 Meier, *Property Crime in London*, 13–14.

39 Mayhew, *London Labour and the London Poor*, 209.

40 Meier, *Property Crime in London*, 37.

41 *Morning Chronicle* (15 January 1861).

42 *The Times* (8 August 1881).

43 www.oldbaileyonline.org, t18410104-451.

44 Mayhew, *London Labour and the London Poor*, 211.

45 www.oldbaileyonline.org, t18410614-1601. An individual named Richard Robins appears in numerous trials for various property crimes in the period and we might expect offenders to have plenty of previous convictions.

46 www.oldbaileyonline.org, t18720819-609.

47 Meier, *Property Crime in London*, 37.

48 www.oldbaileyonline.org, 18620106-186.

49 Meier, *Property Crime in London*, 39.

50 *Pall Mall Gazette*, 22/2/1868.

51 Judith Rowbotham, Kim Stevenson and Samantha Pegg, *Crime News in Modern Britain. Press Reporting and Responsibility 1820–2010* (Palgrave Macmillan, Basingstoke, 2013).

52 Wiener, *Reconstructing the Criminal*, 230.

53 *Punch* (30 August 1873).

54 Meier, *Property Crime in London*, 13–14.

55 *Punch* (19 February 1881).

56 *Funny Folks* (8 September 1881).

57 Forgery and Counterfeiting Act 1981, c.45.

58 See, for example, Randall McGowen, 'The Bank of England and the Policing of Forgery 1797–1821', *Past & Present*, 186 (February 2005), 81–116; Randall McGowen, 'From Pillory to Gallows: The Punishment of Forgery in the Age of the Financial Revolution', *Past and Present*, 165:1 (1999); V. A. C. Gatrell, *The Hanging Tree: Execution and the English People 1770–1868* (Oxford UP, Oxford, 1994); Phil Handler, 'Forging the Agenda: The 1819 Select Committee on the Criminal Laws Revisited', *The Journal of Legal History*, 25:3 (December 2004), 249–268; Phil Handler, 'Forgery and the End of the 'Bloody Code' in Early Nineteenth-Century England', *The Historical Journal*, 48:3 (2005), 683–702.

59 J. M. Beattie, *Policing and Punishment in London, 1660–1750: Urban Crime and the Limits of Terror* (Oxford University Press, Oxford, 2001); Beattie, *The First English Detectives*.

60 Campbell, 'Sentence of Death by Burning for Women'; Devereaux, 'The Abolition of the Burning of Women'.

61 A. Hammond, *The Criminal Code, Forgery* (London, 1826). Note that the *intent* was important here.

62 Clipping copper coins was very common and not considered to be high treason, merely a felony, and so carried the death penalty by hanging.

63 John Styles, '"Our Traitorous Money Makers": The Yorkshire Coiners and the Law, 1760–83', in Brewer and Styles (eds.), *An Ungovernable People: The English and Their Law in the Seventeenth and Eighteenth Centuries* (Hutchinson & Co., London, 1980), 192.

64 Ibid., 180.

65 Ibid.

66 http://www.royalmint.com.

67 Gaskill, *Crime and Mentalities*, 127.

68 *London Gazette* (19 December 1687).

69 *London Gazette* (31 May–4 June 1688); www.oldbaileyonline.org, t16880531-24; t16880531-22; t16880711-29.

70 www.oldbaileyonline.org, t16950703-15.

71 Deirdre Palk (ed.), *Prisoners' Letters to the Bank of England, 1781–1827* (London Record Society, London, 2007).

72 McGowen, 'From Pillory to Gallows', 111.

73 Ibid., 111.

74 Ibid., 130.

75 Ibid. (see note 44), 128.

76 Handler, 'Forging the Agenda', 255; see also McGowen, 'From Pillory to Gallows', 133.

77 *Lloyd's Evening Post and British Chronicle* (5–8 December 1760); *Gazetteer and London Daily Advertiser* (8 December 1760).

78 *London Chronicle* (January–3 February 1761); www.oldbaileyonline.org, t17610116-9.

79 www.oldbaileyonline.org [last accessed 16 July 2014].

80 Deirdre Palk, *Gender, Crime and Judicial Discretion 1780–1830* (Boydell Press, Woodbridge, 2006), 89.

81 Palk, *Prisoners' Letters to the Bank of England*, viii.

82 McGowen, 'The Bank of England and the Policing of Forgery', 85.

83 Palk, *Gender, Crime and Judicial Discretion*, 89–90.

84 Handler, 'Forging the Agenda', 252.

85   Palk, *Prisoners' Letters to the Bank of England*, x.

86   McGowen, 'The Bank of England and the Policing of Forgery', 102.

87   *The Morning Chronicle* (19 February 1824).

88   McGowen, 'From Pillory to Gallows', 109.

89   Handler, 'Forging the Agenda', 253.

90   Quoted in Gatrell, *The Hanging Tree*, 187.

91   Handler, 'Forging the Agenda', 258.

92   Ibid., 262.

93   Gatrell, *Hanging Tree*, 581.

94   Handler, 'Forging the Agenda', 688; Gatrell, *The Hanging Tree*, 408–16.

95   Beattie, *Crime and the Courts*, see Table 4.1, 147.

96   Douglas Hay, 'Property, Authority and the Criminal Law', in D. Hay et al. (eds.), *Albion's Fatal Tree: Crime and Society in Eighteenth-Century England* (Penguin, London 1975).

97   Drew Gray, 'Making Law in Mid-Eighteenth-Century England: Legal Statutes and their Application in the Justicing Notebook of Phillip Ward of Stoke Doyle', *The Journal of Legal History*, 34:2 (2013), 224–5.

98   Elizabeth Melling (ed.), *Kentish Sources: VI Crime and Punishment* (Maidstone, 1969), Q/SB 1740, 68.

99   Gray, *Crime, Prosecution and Social Relations*, 73.

100 Ibid., 57.

101 King, *Crime, Justice and Discretion*, 178.

102 Daniel Defoe, *Everybody's Business Is Nobody's Business*, in Vanfasse (ed.), *Social Deviance in England and France c. 1830–1900* (London, 1725), Preface.

103 King, *Crime, Justice and Discretion*, 179.

104 www.oldbaileyonline.org, t18301028-195.

105 www.oldbaileyonline.org, t18300916-290.

106 www.oldbaileyonline.org, t18301209-165.

107 www.oldbaileyonline.org, t18300114-155.

108 www.oldbaileyonline.org, t18300114-165.

109 www.oldbaileyonline.org, t18300114-246.

110 J. J. Tobias, *Prince of Fences; The Life and Crimes of Ikey Solomons* (Valentine Mitchell, London, 1974), 49.

111 Heather Shore, *Artful Dodgers: Youth and Crime in Early 19th-Century London* (Boydell Press, London, 1999), 76.

112 Kellow Chesney, *The Victorian Underworld* (Maurice T. Smith, London, 1970), 112–113.

113 Shore, *Artful Dodgers*, 77; see also Shore, *London's Criminal Underworlds*.

114 Beattie, *Policing and Punishment*, 39.

115 Ibid., 250–51.

116 Henry Fielding, *Further Observations on the Buyers or Receivers of Stolen Goods*, in Vanfasse (ed.), *Social Deviance in England and France c. 1830–1900* (London, 1756); *An Enquiry*, 341.

117 www.oldbaileyonline.org, t17560915-56.

118 www.oldbaileyonline.org, t18561027-991.

119   www.oldbaileyonline.org, t19101011-26.

120   See Tim Hitchcock, *Down and Out in Eighteenth-Century London* (Hambeldon, London, 2004), 86–7.

121   The notebook of Phillip Ward of Stoke Doyle (Lincoln's Inn Library, Misc. MS. 592) Saturday 22 October 1748.

122   Meier, *Property Crime in London*, 89.

123   BBC's *Hustle*, 'a drama series about a team of con artists', http://www.bbc.co.uk/programmes/b007gf9k [last accessed 29 July 2014].

124   www.oldbaileyonline.org, t16950508-39.

125   www.oldbaileyonline.org, t17440728-43.

126   LMA/GJMR4, 14 December 1775.

127   www.oldbaileyonline.org, t17460226-36.

128   *The Bristol Mercury* (1 January 1870).

129   *The North-Eastern Daily Gazette* (3 January 1890).

130   *The Bristol Mercury and Daily Post* (3 July 1880).

131   *Lloyd's Weekly Newspaper* (7 January 1883).

132   Gray, *Crime, Prosecution and Social Relations*, 74–5; see also Peter D'Sena, 'Perquisites and Pilfering in the London Docks' (MPhil thesis, Open University, 1986) for a detailed analysis of pilfering in eighteenth century docklands.

133   Beattie, *Crime and the Courts*, 269.

134   Wiener, *Reconstructing the Criminal*, 246.

135   http://www.oldbaileyonline.org, [last accessed 30 July 2014].

136   www.oldbaileyonline.org, t18470510-1268.

137   Jason Ditton, *Part-Time Crime: An Ethnography of Fiddling & Pilferage* (MacMillan, Basingstoke, 1977), 183.

138   Gray, *Crime, Prosecution and Social Relations*, 73.

Chapter 5

1   See Meier, *Property Crime in London*, 77.

2   Dearth in this context means a lack or scarcity of food or other things necessary for survival and has often been associated with famine and poor harvests.

3   Quoted in John G. Rule, 'The Manifold Causes of Rural Crime: Sheep-Stealing in England, c.1740–1840', in John G. Rule (ed.), *Outside the Law: Studies in Crime and Order, 1650–1850* (Exeter UP, Exeter, 1982), 102.

4   Eric Hobsbawm and George Rudé, *Captain Swing* (Lawrence & Wishart, London, 1969), xxii.

5   For the debate surrounding food rioting, see Thompson, 'The Moral Economy of the English Crowd in the Eighteenth Century'; J. Stevenson, 'Food Riots in England, 1792–1818', in R. Quinault and J. Stevenson (eds.), *Popular Protest and Public Order* (London, 1974); Dale Williams, 'Were "Hunger" Rioters Really Hungry?', *Past & Present*, 71 (1976), 70–75; J. Bohstedt, *Riots and Community Politics in England and Wales, 1790–1810* (Harvard UP, Cambridge, MA, 1983). Note that this is not an exhaustive list.

6   Tobias, *Crime and Industrial Society in the Nineteenth Century*, 51.

7   Quoted in J. J. Tobias, *Nineteenth-Century Crime: Prevention and Punishment* (David & Charles, Newton Abbot, 1972), 39.

8   John Binny, 'Thieves and Swindlers', in H. Mayhew (ed.), *London Labour and the London Poor*. Republished in *The London Underworld in the Victorian Period* (Dover Publications, Mineola, NY), 122.

9   C. D. Brereton, *A Refutation of the First Report of the Constabulary Force Commissioners* (1840), 72–3.

10 Lynn MacKay, 'Why They Stole: Women in the Old Bailey, 1779–1789', *Journal of Social History*, 32 (1999), 626–30.

11 See, for example, the work of Jock Young and Jack Katz and debates about left realism and cultural criminology.

12 H. Croall, *Crime and Society in Britain* (Longman, Harlow, London, 2011), 304.

13 John Tierney, *Criminology: Theory and Context* (Longman, Harlow, 2010), n.247–8.

14 King, *Crime, Justice and Discretion*, 170.

15 Shore, *Artful Dodgers*, 116.

16 Tabulating where defendant gender is male, age is at least 8 and at most 100 counting by defendant. www.oldbaileyonline.org

17 Ibid.

18 Ibid.

19 For a detailed analysis of the worsted industry and its regulation, see John Styles, 'Spinners and the Law: Regulating Yarn Standards in the English Worsted Industries, 1550–1800', *Textile History*, 44:2 (2013), 145–70.

20 These notebooks are held by the British Library and cover the period 1787–1793.

21 BL/ADD 76340 Spencer Notebooks, Saturday 15 June 1793.

22 Styles, 'Spinners and the Law', 150.

23 Alfred P. Wadsworth, *The Cotton Trade and Industrial Lancashire, 1600–1780* (Manchester UP, Manchester, 1965), 396.

24 For gleaning, see Peter King, 'Legal Change, Customary Right, and Social Conflict in Late Eighteenth-Century England: The Origins of the Great Gleaning Case of 1788', *Law and History Review*, 10:1 (Spring, 1992), 1–31.

25 King, 'Legal Change, Customary Right'; E. P. Thompson, *Customs in Common* (Penguin, Middlesex, 1991).

26 Bob Bushaway, *By Rite: Custom, Ceremony and Community in England 1700–1880* (Junction Books, London, 1982), 208.

27 15 Chas II c.2.

28 6 Geo III c.48; see also Richard Burn, *Justice of the Peace and Parish Officer* (London, 1787), 'Wood'. v.4, 399.

29 BL/ADD76337 Spencer Notebooks, 2 February 1788.

30 Hay, 'Poaching and the Game Laws', in Hay et al., *Albion's Fatal Tree*, 189.

31 P. B. Munsche, 'The Game Laws in Wiltshire, 1750–1800', in J. S. Cockburn (ed.), *Crime in England, 1550–1800* (Princeton UP, Princeton, NJ, 1977), 210.

32 Ibid., 212.

33 Hay, 'Poaching and the Game Laws', 191.

34 Munsche, 'The Game Laws in Wiltshire', 214.

35 Ibid., 225.

36 Hay, 'Poaching and the Game Laws', 203.

37 Burn, *Justice*, v. II, 247.

38 John E. Archer, *'By a Flash and a Scare': Arson, Animal Maiming, and Poaching in East Anglia 1815–1870* (Clarendon Press, Oxford, 1990), 47.

39 Ibid., 229.

40 Harry Hopkins, *The Long Affray: The Poaching Wars in Britain 1760–1914* (Secker & Warburg, London, 1985), 25.

41 Archer, *'By a Flash and a Scare'*, 237.

42 Hopkins, *The Long Affray*, 306.

43 Ibid., 298.

44 Beattie, *Crime and the Courts*, 170.

45 Rule, 'The Manifold Causes of Rural Crime'.

46 Ibid., 107–10.

47 Gatrell, *The Hanging Tree*, 528–9.

48 Hay, 'Poaching and the Game Laws', 205.

49 Eric Hobsbawn, *Bandits* (Weidenfield & Nicolson, London, 1969, 2000).

50 Eric Hobsbawm 'Social Criminality: Distinctions between Socio-Political and Other Forms of Crime', *Bulletin of the Society for the Study of Labour History*, 25 (1972), 5.

51 Nicholas Rogers, *Mayhem: Post-War Crime and Violence in Britain, 1748–53* (Yale UP, London, 2012), 120–1.

52 Cal Winslow, 'Sussex Smugglers', in Hay et al. (eds.), *Albion's Fatal Tree: Crime and Society in Eighteenth-Century England* (Penguin, London, 1975), 126.

53 King, *Crime, Justice and Discretion*, 247.

54 Rogers, *Mayhem*, 121; Winslow, 'Sussex Smugglers', 141–2.

55 King, *Crime and Law*, 267.

56 Winslow, 'Sussex Smugglers', 129–30.

57 Zoe Dyndor, 'The Gibbet in the Landscape: Locating the Criminal Corpse in Mid-Eighteenth-Century England', in Richard Ward (ed.), *A Global History of Execution and the Criminal Corpse* (Palgrave, Basingstoke, 2015), 138.

58 Rogers, *Mayhem*, 123.

59 Winslow, 'Sussex Smugglers', 133.

60 Dyndor, 'The Gibbet in the Landscape', 135.

61 Winslow, 'Sussex Smugglers', 147.

62 Peter King and Richard Ward, 'Rethinking the Bloody Code in Eighteenth-Century Britain: Capital Punishment at the Centre and on the Periphery', *Past & Present,* 228 (2015); for more work on smuggling, see F. F. Nichols, *Honest Thieves* (Heinemann, Birkenhead, 1973); Frank McClynn, *Crime and Punishment in Eighteenth-Century England* (Oxford UP, Oxford, 1989); C. McCooey, *Smuggling on the South Coast* (Amberley Publishing, Stroud, 2012). There is also work on the practice of coastal wrecking which (for reasons of space) I do not

intend to discuss here. For those interested, see John Rule, 'Wrecking and Coastal Plunder', in Hay et al., *Albion's Fatal Tree*; Cathryn Pearce, *Cornish Wrecking, 1700–1860: Reality and Popular Myth* (Boydell Press, Woodbridge, 2010).

63 King, 'Legal Change, Customary Right'.

64 For further reading on the concept, see Sharpe, *Crime in Early Modern, 1550–1750*; John Lea, 'Social Crime Revisited', *Theoretical Criminology*, 3 (1999), 307–325; D. Jones, 'Rural Crime and Protest in the Victorian Era', in G. Mingay (ed.), *The Unquiet Countryside* (Routledge, London, 1989); J. Archer, 'Poaching Gangs and Violence: The Urban-Rural Divide in Nineteenth-Century Lancashire', *British Journal of Criminology*, 29 (1999).

65 For example, Peter Linebaugh, *The London Hanged: Crime and Civil Society in the Eighteenth Century* (Penguin, London, 1993).

Chapter 6

1 Of which a sample are: – Jane Purvis (ed.), *Women's History, Britain 1850–1945* (UCL Press, London, 1995); Kathryn Gleadle, *British Women in the Nineteenth Century* (Palgrave, Basingstoke, 2001); Bridget Hill, *Women, Work and Sexual Politics in Eighteenth-Century England* (Routledge, London, 1989); Pat Hudson and W. Lee (eds.), *Women's Work and the Family Economy in Historical Perspective* (Manchester UP, Manchester, 1990); Carole Smart, *The Ties that Bind: Law, Marriage and the Reproduction of Patriarchal Relations* (Routledge, London, 1984); Jeffrey Weeks, *Sex, Politics and Society: The Regulation of Sexuality Since 1800* (Longman, London, 1981).

2 Garthine Walker, 'Women, Theft and the World of Stolen Goods', in Garthine Walker and Jenny Kermode (eds.), *Women, Crime and the Courts in Early Modern England* (UCL Press, London, 1994), see Table 4.1, 80.

3 Beattie, *Crime and the Courts*; OBSP; BPP Research Paper, 'A Century of Change: Trends in UK Statistics since 1900', Table VI Prison Population.

4 Gray, *Summary Proceedings and Social Relations*; Morgan & Rushton, 'The Magistrate'.

5 B. Godrey and S. Farrall, *Criminal Lives: Family Life, Employment, and Offending* (Oxford UP, Oxford, 2012), 35–6.

6 Conley, *The Unwritten Law*, 68.

7 By which I mean the passage of a woman life – from childhood to adulthood, including (potentially) domestic service, marriage, motherhood and being widowed.

8 Peter King, 'Female Offenders, Work and Life-Cycle Change in Late-Eighteenth-Century London', *Continuity and Change*, 11:1 (May, 1996), 61–90.

9 Malcolm M. Feeley and Deborah E. Little, 'The Vanishing Female: The Decline of Women in the Criminal Process, 1687–1912', *Law & Society Review*, 719 (1991), 719–57.

10 St. Augustine, *Against Faustus*, c.7.

11 Nancy Cott, *The Bonds of Womanhood: 'Women's Sphere' in New England, 1780–1835* (Yale UP, New Haven, CT, 1977); Rosalind Rosenberg, *Beyond Separate Spheres: Intellectual Roots of Modern Feminism* (Yale UP, 1982); Leonore Davidoff and Catherine Hall, *Family Fortunes: Men and Women of the English Middle Class 1780–1850* (Routledge, London, 1987, 1992).

12 Anna Clark, *The Struggle for the Breeches: Gender and the Making of the British Working Class* (University of California Press, Berkeley, 1997).

13 Blackstone, *Commentaries*, Volume 1.

14 Ibid., Volume 4, Ch. 2.

15 King, 'Female Offenders', 67–8.

16 Conley, *The Unwritten Law*, 69.

17 Foyster, *Marital Violence*, 12.

18 Shani D'Cruze and Louise A. Jackson, *Women, Crime and Justice in England since 1660* (Palgrave MacMillian, Basingstoke, 2009), 15.

19 Tim Hitchcock and Robert Shoemaker, *Tales from the Hanging Court* (Hodder Arnold, London, 2006), 129–30.

20 D'Cruze and Jackson, *Women, Crime and Justice*, 45.

21 Ashton, *Chapbooks of the Eighteenth Century*.

22 Mary Wollstonecraft, *A Vindication of the Rights of Woman: With Strictures on Political and Moral Subjects* (London, 1792).

23 Jan Bondeson, *The London Monster: A Sanguinary Tale* (De capo Press, Boston, MA, 2002); Gray, *London's Shadows*.

24 D'Cruze and Jackson, *Women, Crime and Justice*, 45.

25 Meier, *Property Crime in London*.

26 Conley, *The Unwritten Law*, 81.

27 Anna Clark, *Women's Silence Men's Violence: Sexual Assault in England, 1770–1845* (Pandora Press, London, 1987), 129.

28 While 2013 saw a record rise in successful convictions in rape trials (63 per cent), critics still argue that only a minority of cases actually make it to trial in the first place. Rape is, therefore, still underreported, and one in two cases of rape is not pursued by the CPS. http://www.theguardian.com/society/2013/apr/23/rape-conviction-rate-high [last accessed 7 August 2014].

29 Conley, *The Unwritten Law*, 83, 90.

30 Joanna Bourke, *Rape: A History from 1860 to the Present* (Virago, London, 2007), 28.

31 Charles Routh (1886), quoted in Emsley, *Crime and Society in England*, 110.

32 Clark, *Women's Silence Men's Violence*, 72.

33 Conley, *The Unwritten Law*, 84.

34 In July 2014, the NUS (National Union of Students) criticized a poster campaign intended to raise awareness of the risks of drinking alcohol. The NHS poster, which carries the legend 'One in three reported rapes happens when the victim has been drinking', suggests that even in twenty-first-century Britain the responsibility of rape victims is still considered to be a significant factor to be taken into account. http://www.nusconnect.org.uk/news/article/nus/NUS-criticises-Know-Your-Limits-rape-poster-campaign/ [last accessed 7 August 2014].

35 Clark, *Women's Silence Men's Violence*, 59.

36 Shani D'Cruze, *Crimes of Outrage: Sex, Violence and Victorian Working Women* (Northern Illinois UP, DeKalb, IL, 1998), 147–69.

37 Bourke, *Rape*, 25.

38 Ibid., 66.

39 The statute removing the necessity to prove emission was 9 Geo. IV. C.31, s.18.

40　Gatrell, *The Hanging Tree*, 471.

41　Ibid.

42　Conley, *The Unwritten Law*, 94.

43　D'Cruze, *Crimes of Outrage*, 140–1.

44　Clark, *Women's Silence Men's Violence*, 48.

45　Conley, *The Unwritten Law*, 95.

46　Weiner, *Men of Blood*, 6; It is worth noting that the figures for domestic violence almost certainly underrepresent the number of male victims assaulted by their wives, simply because men would have found it a source of shame to admit to have been beaten by a woman, Garthine Walker, *Crime, Gender and Social Order in Early Modern England* (Cambridge UP, Cambridge, 2003), 81.

47　R Emmerson Dobash, *Violence Against Wives: A Case Against the Patriarchy* (Free Press, New York, 1979) 34.

48　For a discussion of these forms of customary community displeasure, see Thompson, *Customs in Common*, Chapter 8 'Rough Music', 467–533.

49　Foyster, *Marital Violence*, 3.

50　Conley, *The Unwritten Law*, 74–5.

51　Frances Power Cobbe, 'Wife-Torture in England', *Contemporary Review* (1878), 58.

52　Clarke, *The Struggle for the Breeches: Gender and the Making of the British Working Class* (University of California Press, Berkeley, CA, 1995), 74–6; Foyster, *Marital Violence*, 5.

53　Cobbe, 'Wife-Torture in England', 58.

54　Thomas Rowlandson, *The Coblers [sic] Cure for a Scolding Wife* (British Museum).

55　D'Cruze, *Crimes of Outrage*, 65; A. James Hammerton, *Cruelty and Companionship: Conflict in Nineteenth-Century Married Life* (Routledge, London, 1992), 37–8.

56　Clarke, *The Struggle for the Breeches*, 87.

57　T. Evans, *'Unfortunate Objects': Lone Mothers in Eighteenth-Century London* (Palgrave, Basingstoke, 2006), 3.

58　Thompson, *Customs in Common*.

59　Foyster, *Marital Violence*, 86.

60　Conley, *The Unwritten Law*, 71.

61　Hannah More, *The Wife Reformed* (London, 1795).

62　D'Cruze, *Crimes of Outrage*, 137.

63　Jennifer Davis, 'Prosecutions and Their Context: The Use of the Criminal Law in Later Nineteenth-Century London', in D. Hay and F. Snyder (eds.), *Policing and Prosecution in Britain 1750–1850* (Clarendon Press, Oxford, 1989), 419.

64　Hammerton, *Cruelty and Companionship*.

65　Foyster, *Marital Violence*, 93.

66　Ibid., 113.

67　Walker, *Crime, Gender and Social Order*, 79–80.

68　Ibid., 140.

69　Conley, *The Unwritten Law*, 74.

70　Hammerton, *Cruelty and Companionship*, 126.

Chapter 7

1   Beattie, *Crime and the Courts*, Table 5.3, 239.

2   www.oldbaileyonline/org statistics, counting all thefts from 1674 to 1800.

3   King, *Crime, Justice and Discretion*, 196.

4   Walker, 'Women, Theft and the World of Stolen Goods'.

5   Quoted in Zedner, *Women, Crime and Custody*, 304–5.

6   Morgan and Rushton, *Rogues, Thieves and the Rule of Law*, 67.

7   King, *Crime and Law*, 68.

8   Malcolm M. Feeley and Deborah L. Little, 'The Vanishing Female: The Decline of Women in the Criminal Process', *Law & Society Review*, 25:4 (1991), 720–3 (see figure 1).

9   Ibid., 732.

10 Wiener, *Men of Blood*.

11 Phillips, *Crime and Authority*, 148 (see figure 1).

12 Conley, *The Unwritten Law*, 70.

13 King, *Crime and Law*, 201.

14 R. Williams, 'Crime and the Rural Community', quoted in King, *Crime and Law*, 202.

15 King, *Crime and Law*, 205.

16 Feeley and Little, 'The Vanishing Female'.

17 Ibid., 206.

18 Ibid., 211.

19 King, *Crime and Law*, 220.

20 Defoe, *Everybody's Business Is Nobody's Business*.

21 Walker, 'Women, Theft and the World of Stolen Goods', 90–1.

22 Ibid., 85.

23 Beattie, *Crime and the Courts*.

24 Russell Dobash, *The Imprisonment of Women* (Blackwell, Oxford, 1986), 28.

25 Beattie, *Crime and the Courts*, 240.

26 Palk, *Gender*, 40.

27 OBO t17860222-63 trial of Sarah Lyon and Ann Gibson for theft/shoplifting 22/2/1786.

28 Peter King and Joan Noel, 'The Origins of the "Problem of Juvenile Delinquency": The Growth of Juvenile Prosecutions in London in Late Eighteenth and Early Nineteenth Centuries', *Criminal Justice History*, 14 (1993), 32.

29 Quoted in Palk, *Gender*, 52.

30 Palk, *Gender*, 53.

31 OBO t18260216-135 trial of Maria Allen for theft/shoplifting 16/2/1826.

32 BPP, *Report on Criminal Laws* (1819), 27.

33 Elaine S. Abelson, *Middle-Class Shoplifters in the Victorian Department Store* (Oxford UP, Oxford, 1989).

34 Tammy C. Whitlock, *Crime, Gender and Consumer Culture in Nineteenth-Century England* (Ashgate, Farnham, 2005) 41.

Notes

35   Abelson, *Middle-Class Shoplifters*, 150.

36   Whitlock, *Crime*, 143–4.

37   Ibid., 191.

38   Palk, *Gender*, 81.

39   www.oldbaileyonline.org, t17870711-76.

40   www.oldbaileyonline.org, t17860222-63.

41   Dobash, *The Imprisonment of Women*, 91.

42   Wiener, *Reconstructing the Criminal*, 282.

43   Hammond, *The Criminal Code, Forgery*.

44   Palk, *Gender*, see Table 19, 107.

45   www.oldbaileyonlie.org, OBO t17380412-11.

46   www.oldbaileyonlie.org, OBO t18400302-817.

47   King, 'Female Offenders'.

48   Phillips, *Crime and Authority*, 161.

49   Williams, '*At Large*', 100–1.

50   B. Godfrey and S. Farrall, *Criminal Lives: Family Life, Employment, and Offending* (Oxford UP, 2012), 39.

51   Williams, '*At Large*', 106.

52   King, 'Female offenders'.

53   Anne-Marie Kilday, *A History of Infanticide in Britain, c.1600 to the Present* (Palgrave Macmillan, Basingstoke, 2013), 6.

54   Beattie, *Crime and the Courts*, 113.

55   Mark Jackson, *New-Born Child Murder: Women, Illegitimacy and the Courts in Eighteenth-century England* (Manchester UP, Manchester, 1996), 33–4.

56   Walker, *Crime, Gender and Social Order*, 151.

57   Ibid., 148.

58   Burn, *Justice*, Volume 1, 214; legislation to tackle 'bastard bearers' in the secular courts was introduced 'in 1576 and then revised in 1610'. Kilday, *A History of Infanticide*, 17.

59   Mark Jackson, 'The Trial of Harriet Vooght: Continuity and Change in the History of Infanticide', in Mark Jackson (ed.), *Infanticide: Historical Perspectives on Child Murder and Concealment 1550–2000* (Ashgate, Aldershot, 2002), 8.

60   For a detailed exploration of the motives of infanticides, see Kilday, *A History of Infanticide*, 151–82.

61   Jackson, 'The Trial of Harriet Vooght', 6.

62   www.oldbaileyonline.org t17081013-1.

63   Kilday, *A History of Infanticide*, 63.

64   Ibid., 41.

65   Beattie, *Crime and the Courts*, 120.

66   Lionel Rose, *The Massacre of the Innocents: Infanticide in Britain 1800–1939* (Routledge & Kegan Paul, London, 1986) 72.

67   t17621208-26.

68   43 Geo. III c.58.

69   Elaine Farrell, 'A Most Diabolical Deed': Infanticide and Irish Society, 1850–1900 (Manchester UP, Manchester, 2013), 251.

70   Kilday, A History of Infanticide, 114.

71   Ibid., 118.

72   Ann R. Higginbotham, ' "Sin of the Age": Infanticide and Illegitimacy in Victorian London', in Kristine Ottesen Garrigan (ed.), Victorian Scandals: Representations of Gender and Class (Ohio UP, Stanford, OH, 1992), 257–88; For a discussion of baby-farming, see Rose, Massacre of the Innocents.

73   Kilday, A History of Infanticide, 119.

74   Ibid., see Fig. 5.1, 122.

75   Rose, Massacre of the Innocents, 175.

76   Daniel Grey: 'Women's Policy Networks and the Infanticide Act 1922', Twentieth-Century British History, 24:4 (2010), 441–63; ' "More Ignorant and Stupid than Wilfully Cruel": Homicide Trials and "Baby-Farming" in England and Wales in the Wake of the Children Act 1908', Crimes and Misdemeanours: Deviance and the Law in Historical Perspective, 3:2 (2009), 317–71.

77   Dana Rabin, 'Bodies of Evidence, States of Mind: Infanticide, Emotion and Sensibility in Eighteenth-Century England', in M. Jackson (ed.), Infanticide: Historical Perspectives on Child Murder and Concealment, 1550–2000 (Ashgate, Aldershot, 2002), 74.

78   According to Rudyard Kipling (writing in his 1888 short story On the City Wall), Lalun was a 'member of the most ancient profession in the world'.

79   D'Cruze and Jackson, Women, Crime and Justice, 74.

80   Shoemaker, Prosecution and Punishment, 239–40.

81   Ibid., 238; see also F. Dabhoiwala, 'Sex and Societies for Moral Reform, 1688–1800', Journal of British Studies, 46:2 (2007), 290–319.

82   See Hallie Rubenhold, The Covent Garden Ladies; Pimp General Jack & The Extraordinary Story of Harris's List (Tempus, London, 2005); Janet Ing Freeman, 'Jack Harris and "Honest Ranger": The Publication and Prosecution of Harris's List of Covent-Garden Ladies, 1760–95', The Library, 14: 4 (December 2013).

83   Barry Reay, Popular Cultures in England, 1550–1750 (Longman, London, 1998).

84   William Hogarth, A Harlot's Progress (1731–1732).

85   Linda Mahood, The Magdalenes. Prostitution in the Nineteenth Century (Routledge, London, 1990), 55.

86   W. Acton, Prostitution, Considered in Its Moral, Social and Sanitary Aspects, in London and Other Large Cities: With Proposals for the Mitigation and Prevention (London, 1857).

87   William Logan, The Great Social Evil; Its Causes, Extent, Results and Remedies (London, 1871); W. Tait, Magdalenism: An Inquiry into the Extent, Causes, and Consequences of Prostitution in Edinburgh (Edinburgh, 1841, 1852).

88   F. Finnegan, Poverty and Prostitution: A Study of Victorian Prostitutes in York (Cambridge UP, Cambridge, 1979), 6–7.

89   Mayhew, London Labour and the London Poor.

90   W. T. Stead, 'The Maiden Tribute of Modern Babylon', Pall Mall Gazette (1885).

91   Finnegan, Poverty and Prostitution, 9.

Notes

92 R. Hyam, *Empire and Sexuality: The British Experience* (Manchester UP, Manchester, 1990), 65–8.

93 Stephan Slater, 'Prostitutes and Popular History: Notes on the "Underworld", 1918–39', *Crime, History and Societies*, 13:1 (2009), 34.

94 King, *Crime, Justice and Discretion*, 200.

95 Clark, *Women's Silence, Men's Violence*.

96 Walker, 'Women, Theft and the World of Stolen Goods', 98.

97 Janice Turner, '"*Ill-Favoured Sluts*"? —The Disorderly Women of Rosemary Lane and Rag Fair', *The London Journal*, 38:2 (2013), 95–109.

Chapter 8

1 Leon Radzinowicz and Roger Hood, *A History of the Criminal Law and Its Administration from 1750: Volume Five – The Emergence of Penal Policy* (Stephens & Sons, London, 1986), 133.

2 Frances Heidensohn, *Crime and Society: Sociology for a Changing World* (MacMillan, Basingstoke, 1989).

3 John Muncie, *Youth & Crime*, 3rd edition (Sage Publications, London, 2009), 49.

4 Elementary education was tentatively established with the Forster (Education) Act in 1870. See Sascha Auerbach, '"Some Punishment Should Be Devised": Parents, Children, and the State in Victorian London', *The Historian*, 71:4 (2009), 757–79.

5 Muncie, *Youth & Crime*, 275.

6 Shore, *Artful Dodgers*, 67–8.

7 Ibid., 8–9.

8 King, *Crime and Law*, 62.

9 See King and Noel, 'The Origins of the "Problem of Juvenile Delinquency"'.

10 Paul Griffiths, *Youth and Authority: Formative Experiences in England, 1560–1640* (Clarendon Press, Oxford, 1996), 126.

11 Llana Krausman Ben-Amos, *Adolescence & Youth in Early Modern England* (Yale UP, New Haven & London, 1994), 189.

12 See Joan Lane, *Apprenticeship in England, 1600–1914* (Routledge, London, 1996).

13 Shore, *Artful Dodgers*, 22; King and Noel, 'The Origins of the "Problem of Juvenile Delinquency"', 25–6.

14 Pearson, *Hooligan*.

15 Griffiths, *Youth and Authority*.

16 Rawlings, *Drunks, Whores and Idle Apprentices*.

17 Shore, *Artful Dodgers*, 41.

18 Jonas Hanway, *Motives for the Establishment of the Marine Society, by a Merchant* (London, 1757), 8.

19 Richard Woodman, *Of Daring Temper: 250 Years of the Marine Society* (Marine Society (Seafarers' Libraries), London, 2006).

20 Hanway, *Motives for the Establishment of the Marine Society*, 5–6.

21 Radzinowicz and Hood, *A History of the Criminal Law*, Volume 5, 134.

22 The Marine Society, *To the Marine Society, in Praise of the Great and Good Work They Have Done* (London, 1757).

23 Woodman, *Of Daring Temper*, 24.

24 Radzinowicz and Hood, *A History of the Criminal Law*, Volume 5, 135.

25 Anon, *A Short Account of the Philanthropic Society* (London, 1791), 2.

26 The records of the Philanthropic Society are held by the Surrey RO (see http://www.surreycc. gov.uk/recreation-heritage-and-culture/archives-and-history/archives-and-history-research-guides/the-royal-philanthropic-school-at-redhill).

27 King, *Crime and Law*.

28 Refuge for the Destitute, annual report 1819 (1 January 1820), 1.

29 P. King (ed.), *Narratives of the Poor in Eighteenth-Century Britain; Volume 4 Institutional Responses: The Refuge for the Destitute* (Pickering Chatto, London, 2006), 262.

30 Refuge for the Destitute, annual report 1819 (1 January 1820).

31 P. King 'The Origins of Informal Juvenile Court Practices and of the Juvenile Reformatory in England, 1815–55' (unpublished article).

32 Such as, *The British Settlement founded on Tilgate Forest, Sussex for the Reform and Self-support of the Criminal and Destitute poor* (1795).

33 *Report of the Committee for Investigating the Causes of the Alarming Increase in Juvenile Delinquency in the Metropolis* (London, 1816), 5.

34 Ibid., 25.

35 Ibid.

36 Felix Driver, 'Discipline Without Frontiers? Representations of the Mettray Reformatory Colony in Britain, 1840–1880', *Journal of Historical Sociology*, 3:3 (September 1990), 273.

37 Shore, *Artful Dodgers*, 98.

38 Radzinowicz and Hood, *A History of the Criminal Law*, Volume 5, 143–4.

39 King, 'Origins', 21.

40 Jeannie Duckworth, *Fagin's Children: Criminal Children in Victorian England* (Continuum, London, 2002), 91–2.

41 Ibid., 99.

42 Ibid., 105.

43 Driver, 'Discipline Without Frontiers?', 276.

44 Radzinowicz and Hood, *A History of the Criminal Law*, Volume 5, 162.

45 Mary Carpenter, *Reformatory Schools for the Perishing and Dangerous Classes & for the Prevention of Juvenile Delinquency* (1851) and *Reformatory Schools for Juvenile Delinquents* (1853).

46 Radzinowicz and Hood, *A History of the Criminal Law*, Volume 5, 165.

47 Ibid., 166.

48 Quoted in Ibid., 180.

49 Radzinowicz and Hood, *A History of the Criminal Law*, Volume 5, 177.

50 Muncie, *Youth & Crime*, 60.

51 Auerbach, ' "Some Punishment Should Be Devised" ', 769.

Notes

52 Michelle Cale, 'Girls and the Perception of Sexual Danger in the Victorian Reformatory System', *The Historical Association*, 78:253 (1993), 201–17.

53 Sascha Auerbach, '"The Law Has No Feeling for Poor Folks Like Us!": Everyday Responses to Legal Compulsion in Working-Class Communities, 1871–1904', *Journal of Social History*, 45:3 (2012), 686–708.

54 Radzinowicz and Hood, *A History of the Criminal Law*, Volume 5, 178.

55 Margaret May, 'Innocence and Experience: The Evolution of the Concept of Juvenile Delinquency in the Mid-Nineteenth Century', *Victorian Studies*, 17:1 (September 1973), 7–29.

56 Russell Scott and Mary Carpenter, *First Report of the Kingswood Agricultural Reformatory School* (Kingswood, 1854), 1.

57 Ibid., 4.

58 Mary Carpenter, *Principles, Rules and Regulations of the Red Lodge Reformatory School with the First Report of Its Management* (Bristol, 1855), 2.

59 Quoted in Cale, 'Girls and the Perception of Sexual Danger', 211.

60 Rev. John Sedgwick, *Hints on the Establishment of Public Industrial Schools for the Working Classes* (London, 1853), 18.

61 Radzinowicz and Hood, *A History of the Criminal Law*, Volume 5, 181–2.

62 A phrase borrowed from Gilbert and Sullivan and usually associated with Willie Whitelaw, Home Secretary in Margaret Thatcher's Conservative government in the 1980s.

63 I. Pinchbeck and M. Hewitt, *Children in English Society* (Routledge and Kegan Paul, London, 1973), 144.

64 Foucault, *Discipline and Punish*.

65 Gatrell, 'Crime, Authority and the Policeman-State'.

66 http://books.google.com/ngrams/graph?content=juvenile+delinquency&year_ start=1800&year_end=2000&corpus=15&smoothing=3&share= [last accessed 30 August 2013].

67 Heather Shore (with Pamela Cox), 'Re-inventing the Juvenile Delinquent in Britain and Europe, 1650–1950', in Pamela Cox and Heather Shore (eds.), *Becoming Delinquent: British and European Youth, 1650–1950* (Ashgate, Dartmouth, 2002), 2.

68 May, 'Innocence and Experience', 7.

69 Paul Griffiths, *Lost Londons: Change, Crime and Control in the Capital City 1550–1660* (Cambridge UP, Cambridge, 2008).

70 Shore, 'Re-inventing the Juvenile Delinquent', 6.

71 REF to Ignatieff, *A Just Measure of Pain*; E. Goffman, *Asylums. Essays on the Social Situation of Mental patients and Other Inmates* (Penguin, London, 1961) etc.

72 Heidensohn, *Crime and Society*.

73 Miles' notebooks are held at the National Archives and discussed at length in Shore, *Artful Dodgers*.

74 Nicola Phillips, 'Parenting the Profligate Son: Masculinity, Gentility and Juvenile Delinquency in England, 1791–1814', *Gender & History*, 22:1 (April 2010), 102–3.

75 Pamela Cox, *Gender, Justice and Welfare: Bad Girls in Britain, 1900–1950* (Palgrave, Basingstoke, 2003); see also Cale, 'Girls and the Perception of Sexual Danger'.

Chapter 9

1   Hay, 'Property'.

2   Richard Burn, *Justice of the Peace and Parish Officer* (London, 1755 onwards); King, *Crime, Justice and Discretion*, 87.

3   Greg T. Smith (ed.), *Summary Justice in the City: A Selection of Cases Heard at the Guildhall Justice Room, 1752–1781*, London Record Society, 48 (Boydell & Brewer, Woodbridge, 2013).

4   Gray, 'Making Law'.

5   Settlement was an integral part of the poor law apparatus in the eighteenth century. There is a large literature on settlement and those interested in finding out more should start with Steve Hindle, *On the Parish?: The Micro-Politics of Poor Relief in Rural England, c.1550–1750* (Oxford UP, Oxford, 2004); Keith Snell, *Parish and Belonging: Community, Identity, and Welfare in England and Wales, 1700–1950* (Cambridge UP, Cambridge, 2006).

6   King, *Crime, Justice and Discretion*, 362.

7   Ibid.

8   Norma Landau, 'The Trading Justice's Trade', in Norma Landau (ed.), *Law, Crime and English Society, 1660–1830* (Cambridge UP, Cambridge, 2002).

9   See Beattie, *Policing and Punishment*; Gray, *Crime, Prosecution and Social Relations*; Smith, *Summary Justice in the City*.

10 N. Rogers, 'Money, Land and Lineage: The Big Bourgeoisie of Hanoverian London', *Social History*, 4:3 (October 1979), 442.

11 King, *Crime, Justice and Discretion*.

12 Henry Turner Waddy, *The Police Court and Its Work* (Butterworth, London, 1925), 39.

13 G. Morgan and P. Rushton (eds.), *The Justicing Notebook (1750–64) of Edmund Tew, Rector of Boldon* (Publications of the Surtees Society, Woodbridge, 2000).

14 For a list of available justicing notebooks see Gray, 'Making Law', 210; for further reading on the role of the JP in the eighteenth century see: King, 'Summary Courts and Social Relations in Eighteenth-Century England'; Gray, *Crime, Prosecution and Social Relations*; Morgan and Rushton, 'The Magistrate; N. Landau, *The Justices of the Peace, 1679–1760* (University of California Press, Berkeley, CA, 1984).

15 Once someone had established their entitlement to a settlement in any given place the parish was supposedly obliged to support them when they were sick or otherwise unable to gain employment. However, this help – or poor relief – was often negotiated between the parish (represented by the overseers of the poor), the person in need and the local justice of the peace.

16 Landau, 'Indictment for Fun and Profit'.

17 Smith, *Summary Justice in the City*.

18 Beattie, *Policing and Punishment*; Gray, *Crime, Prosecution and Social Relations*.

19 David Eastwood, *Government and Community in the English Provinces, 1700–1870* (MacMillan, Basingstoke, 1997), 97.

20 Waddy, *The Police Court*, 48.

21 Gray, *London's Shadows*.

22 Waddy, *The Police Court*, 1.

23 Anon, *The Justice of the Peace and His Functions On and Off the Bench. By a Middlesex Magistrate* (J. M. Dent & Sons, London, 1911).

24 Gray, *London's Shadows*, 174–85.

25 Jennifer Davis, 'A Poor Man's System of Justice: The London Police Courts in the Second Half of the Nineteenth Century', *The Historical Journal*, 27:2 (1984), 309–35.

26 Abraham, 'The Summary Courts'.

27 Edward William Cox, *The Practice of Summary Convictions in Larceny under the Criminal Justice Act (18 & 19 Vict. c.126) and the Juvenile Offenders Acts (10 & 11 Vict. c.82 and 13 & 14 Vict. c.37) with the Law of larceny, so far as it relates to these statutes; notes and forms* (London, 1856).

28 Abraham, 'The Summary Courts'.

29 There has been some work outside of England and Wales in this area; see, for example, David Barrie and Susan Broomhall, 'Public Men, Private Interests: The Origins, Structure and Practice of Police Courts in Scotland, c.1800–1833', *Continuity & Change*, 27:1 (May, 2012), 83–123, while others have explored aspects of the work of the police court: A. Croll, 'Street Disorders, Surveillance and Shame: Regulating Behaviour in the Public Spaces of the Late Victorian Town', *Social History*, 24:3 (1999), 250–68; W. McWilliams, 'The Mission to the English Police Courts, 1876–1936', *The Howard Journal of Criminal Justice*, 22:1–3 (1983), 129–47.

30 Landau, *The Justices*.

31 Thomas A. Skyrme, *A History of the Justices of the Peace* (in 3 volumes) (Barry Rose Law Publishers Ltd, Chichester, 1991).

32 E. Moir, *The Justice of the Peace* (Penguin, London, 1969).

33 King, 'The Summary Courts'.

34 D. Hay, 'Patronage, Paternalism and Welfare: Masters, Workers and Magistrates in Eighteenth-Century England', *International Labor and Working Class History*, 53 (1998), 27–47.

35 Hay, 'Power, Authority and the Criminal Law'.

36 Shoemaker, *Prosecution and Punishment*.

37 Beattie, *Policing and Punishment*.

38 Gray, 'Summary Proceedings and Social Relations'.

39 See, for example, A. F. Cirket (ed.), *Samuel Whitebread's Notebooks, 1810–1, 1813–14* (Bedfordshire Historical Record Society, Ampthill, 1971); Crittal, *The Justicing Notebook of William Hunt*; Morgan and Rushton, *The Justicing Notebook of Edmund Tew*; R. Paley (ed.), *Justice in Eighteenth-Century Hackney: The Justicing Notebook of Henry Norris and the Hackney Petty Sessions Book* (London Record Society, Boydell and Brewer, London, 1991); E. Silverthorne (ed.), *Deposition Book of Richard Wyatt, JP, 1767–1776* (Surrey Record Society, Guildford, 1978).

40 Morgan and Rushton, 'The Magistrate', 30.

41 Dietrich Oberwitiler, 'Crime and Authority in Eighteenth-Century England: Law Enforcement on the Local Level', *Historical Social Research*, 15:2 (1990), 3–34.

42 Beattie, *Policing and Punishment*; Gray, *Crime, Prosecution and Social Relations*; Smith, *Summary Justice in the City*.

43 Gray, 'Making Law'.

44 See, for example, Nell Darby, 'Rural Society and the Summary Process in England, 1685–1834' (PhD, Northampton, forthcoming).

45 http://www.communityhelpers.co.uk/how-become-jp.html [last accessed 29 August 2014].

Chapter 10

1 Clive Emsley, *The English Police: A Political and Social History* (Longman, London, 1996), 8.

2 Joan R. Kent, *The English Village Constable 1580–1642: A Social and Administrative Study* (Oxford UP, Oxford, 1986), 15.

3 T. A. Critchley, *A History of Police in England and Wales* (London, Constable, 1978), 15–16.

4 NRO: L(C) 1692, Account book of Cottesbrooke constables from 22 April 1802 to 30 March 1836.

5 William Lambard, *The Duties of Constables, Borsolders, Tythingmen, and Such Other Lowe and Lay Ministers of the Peace* (London, 1599).

6 Kent, *The English Village Constable*, 25.

7 Gray and King, 'The Killing of Constable Linnell'.

8 Beattie, *Policing and Punishment*, 114.

9 Defoe, quoted in Emsley, *The English Police*, 12.

10 Quoted in Gray, *Summary Proceedings and Social Relations*, 65.

11 Elaine Reynolds, *Before the Bobbies: The Night Watch and Police Reform in Metropolitan London, 1720–1830* (Stanford UP, Redwood City, CA, 1998), 66.

12 Beattie, *Policing and Punishment*; Gray, *Summary Proceedings and Social Relations*; Andrew T. Harris, *Policing the City: Crime and Legal Authority in London, 1780–1840* (Ohio State UP, Colombus, OH, 2004).

13 Gray, *Summary Proceedings and Social Relations*, 73.

14 P. J. R. King, 'Prosecution Associations and Their Impact in Eighteenth-Century Essex', in D. Hay and F. Synder (eds.), *Policing and Prosecution on Britain 1750–1850* (Oxford UP, Oxford, 1989) 206.

15 David Phillips, 'Good Men to Associate and Bad Men to Conspire: Associations for the Prosecution of Felons in England 1760–1860', in D. Hay and F. Synder (eds.), *Policing and Prosecution on Britain 1750–1850* (Oxford UP, Oxford, 1989), 116.

16 A. Shubert, '"Lest the Law Slumber in Action": Associations for the Prosecution of Felons' (MA thesis, Univ. Of Warwick, 1978).

17 Phillips, 'Good Men to Associate', 120.

18 Ibid., 134.

19 King, 'Prosecution Associations', 176.

20 Ibid., 174.

21 Ibid., 202.

22 Emsley, *The English Police*, 9; Reynolds, *Before the Bobbies*, 9.

23 Harris, *Policing the City*, 10.

24 Ibid., 10.

25 Reynolds, *Before the Bobbies*, 11.

26 Beattie, *Policing and Punishment*, 189–7.

27 Gray, *Crime, Prosecution and Social Relations*, 41.

28 B. Smith, 'The Myth of Private Prosecution in England 1790–1850', *Yale Journal of Law & the Humanities*, 29 (2006), 153.

29 www.oldbaileyonline.org t17710515-8.

30 Reynolds, *Before the Bobbies*, 163.

31 Gerald Howson, *Thief-Taker General: The Rise and Fall of Jonathan Wild* (Hutchinson, London, 1970), 37.

32 Beattie, *Crime and the Courts*, 52.

33 Ibid., 52.

34 Howson, *Thief-Taker General*, 37.

35 Beattie, *The First English Detectives*, 20.

36 Beattie, *Policing and Punishment*, 402.

37 Ruth Paley, 'Thief-Takers in London in the Age of the McDaniel Gang, c. 1745–1754', in D. Hay and F. Snyder (eds.), *Policing and Prosecution in Britain 1750–1850* (Clarendon Press, Oxford, 1989), see appendix 341.

38 Beattie, *Policing and Punishment*, 403.

39 Paley, 'Thief-Takers in London', 304.

40 Ibid., 304.

41 Beattie, *Policing and Punishment*, 406.

42 This was a place where debtors could be confined temporarily by their creditors in the hope that it would swiftly bring about a promise to pay what they owed.

43 Paley, 'Thief-Takers in London', 306.

44 Ibid., 323.

45 Beattie, *The First English Detectives*.

46 Paley, 'Thief-Takers in London', 328.

47 Philip Rawlings, *Policing: A Short History* (Willan, Cullompton, 2002), 80.

48 Rawlings, *Policing*, 83.

49 Paley, 'Thief-Takers in London', 314.

50 Ibid., 302.

51 Rawlings, *Policing*, 87.

52 Lemmings, *Law and Government in England*, 116.

53 Beattie, *Policing and Punishment*, 415.

54 Beattie, *The First English Detectives*, 17; see also F. Dodsworth, 'Police and the Prevention of Crime', *British Journal of Criminology*, 47 (2007), 439–454.

55 For trading justices see Norma Landau (ed.), *Law, Crime and English Society, 1660–1830* (Cambridge UP, Cambridge, 2002).

56 Beattie, *The First English Detectives*, 3; David J. Cox, *A Certain Share of Low Cunning: A History of the Bow Street Runners, 1792–1839* (Routledge, London, 2012), 28.

57 Cox, *A Certain Share of Low Cunning*, 2.

58   Gilbert Armitage, *The History of the Bow Street Runner, 1729–1829* (Wilshart & Co., London, 1932), 129.

59   Beattie, *The First English Detectives*, 30, 36.

60   Cox, *A Certain Share of Low Cunning*, 36.

61   Armitage, *History of the Bow Street Runners*.

62   Morgan and Rushton, *Rogues, Thieves and the Rule of Law*.

63   Cox, *A Certain Share of Low Cunning*, 5.

64   Robert Storch, 'The Policeman as Domestic Missionary: Urban Discipline and Popular Culture in Northern England, 1850–1880', *Journal of Social History*, 9:4 (1976).

65   Beattie, *The First English Detectives*, 42; see also Dodsworth, 'Police', 449–50.

66   Emsley, *The English Police*, 21; Stanley Palmer, *Police and Protest in England and Ireland, 1780–1850* (Cambridge UP, Cambridge, 1988), 71; D. Philips, 'A "Weak" State? The English State, the Magistracy and the Reform of Policing in the 1830s', *English Historical Review*, CXIX: 483 (2004), 877.

67   Palmer, *Police and Protest*, 73.

68   Quoted in Emsley, *The English Police*, 22. Fouché had been Napoleon I's Minister of Police in Paris.

69   Emsley, *The English Police*, 20–21.

70   Queen's Square, Great Marlborough Street, Worship Street, Lambeth Street, Shadwell, Union Hall and Hatton Garden.

71   Leon Radzinowicz, *A History of the Criminal Law and Its Administration from 1750: Volume 3, Cross-Currents in the Movement for the Reform of the Police* (Stevens & Sons, London, 1956), 123–30.

72   Leon Radzinowicz, *A History of the Criminal Law and Its Administration from 1750: Volume 2, The Clash between Private Initiative and Public Interest in the Enforcement of the Law* (Stevens & Sons, London, 1956), 529.

73   Emsley, *The English Police*, 21.

74   Palmer, *Police and Protest*, 28.

75   G. A. Minto, *The Thin Blue Line* (Hodder & Stoughton, London, 1965).

76   *Committee of the Police of the Metropolis* (1822), 11 quoted in Beattie, *The First English Detectives*, 238.

77   Robert Reiner, *The Politics of the Police*, 3rd edition (Oxford UP, 2000), 15–45.

78   Leon Radzinowicz, *A History of the Criminal Law and Its Administration from 1750: Volume 4, Grappling for Control* (Stevens & Sons, London, 1968), 159–60.

79   Critchley, *A History of Police*; Radzinowicz, *A History of the Criminal Law: Volume 3*.

80   See Gatrell and Hadden, 'Criminal Statistics and Their Interpretation', 336–96.

81   Palmer, *Police and Protest*, 163–91.

82   E. P. Thompson, *Customs in Common*; John Stevenson, *Popular Disturbances in England 1700–1832* (Longman, Harlow, 1979, 1992).

83   Reiner, *The Politics of the Police*, 50–1; see Storch, 'The Policeman as Domestic Missionary'.

84   P. D. James and T. A. Critchley, *The Maul and the Pear Tree: The Ratcliffe Highway Murders, 1811* (Constable, London, 1971).

85   Quoted in Palmer, *Police and Protest*, 163.

86   Reiner, *The Politics of the Police*, 60.

87   Palmer, *Police and Protest*, 8.

88   Beattie, *The First English Detectives*, 235.

89   McGowen, 'The Bank of England and the Policing of Forgery', 110–11.

90   Palmer, *Police and Protest*, 191.

91   Quoted in Beattie, *The First English Detectives*, 238.

92   Beattie, *The First English Detectives*, 238.

93   Palmer, *Police and Protest*, 292.

94   Beattie, *The First English Detectives*, 246.

95   Reynolds, *Before the Bobbies*.

96   Beattie, *The First English Detectives*, 253.

97   Palmer, *Police and Protest*, 293.

98   Charles Reith, *A New Study of Police History* (Oliver & Boyd, London, 1956), 135–6.

99   Radzinowicz, *A History of the Criminal Law: Volume 4*, 162.

100   Palmer, *Police and Protest*, 297.

101   Ibid., 300; for a detailed analysis of the selection criteria for those joining the Met see Haia Shpayer-Makov, *The Making of a Policeman: A Social History of a Labour Force in Metropolitan London, 1829–1914* (Ashgate, Aldershot, 2002).

102   Shpayer-Makov, *The Making of a Policeman*, 42.

103   Philips, 'A "Weak" State?', 889.

104   Radzinowicz, *A History of the Criminal Law: Volume 4*, 208.

105   Rawlings, *Policing*, 129.

106   Ibid., 125; Philips, 'A "Weak" State?', 887.

107   Rawlings, *Policing*, 125.

108   David Philips and Robert D. Storch, *Policing Provincial England 1829–1856. The Politics of Reform* (Leicester UP, Leicester, 1999), 35.

109   Radzinowicz, *A History of the Criminal Law: Volume 4*, 227.

110   Ibid., 263.

111   Rawlings, *Policing*, 135.

112   Radzinowicz, *A History of the Criminal Law: Volume 4*, 231.

113   Philips, 'A "Weak" State?', 884.

114   Carolyn Steedman, *Policing the Victorian Community: Formation of English Provincial Police Forces, 1856–80* (Routledge & Kegan Paul, London 1984), 19.

115   Philips, 'A "Weak" State?', 889–90.

116   Rawlings, *Policing*, 128.

117   Philips and Storch, *Policing Provincial England*, 225.

118   Radzinowicz credits Sir George Grey with 'breaking the deadlock and helping forward the expansion of the police'. Radzinowicz, *A History of the Criminal Law: Volume 4*, 294.

119   Steedman, *Policing the Victorian Community*, 23.

120   Philips and Storch, *Policing Provincial England*, 233.

121   Spierenburg, *A History of Murder*, 169.

122   Charles Reith, *Police Principles and the Problem of War* (Oxford UP, Oxford, 1940), 55.

123   Radzinowicz, *A History of the Criminal Law: Volume 4*, 201.

124   David Taylor, *The New Police in Nineteenth-Century England: Crime, Conflict and Control* (Manchester UP, 1997), 124.

125   Robert D. Storch, 'The Plague of Blue Locusts: Police Reform and Popular Resistance in Northern England, 1840–57', *International Review of Social History*, 20:1 (1975).

126   Taylor, *The New Police*, 124.

127   Clive Emsley, *The Great British Bobby: A History of British Policing from the 18th Century to the Present* (Quercus, London, 2009), 149.

128   Ibid., 151.

129   Gatrell, 'Crime, Authority and the Policeman-State'.

130   Quoted in Reiner, *The Politics of the Police*, 30; A. Silver, 'The Demand for Order in Civil Society', in D. Bordua (ed.), *The Police* (Wiley, New York, 1967), 8.

131   Storch, 'The Policeman as Domestic Missionary'.

132   Phillips, *Crime and Authority*; Davis, 'A Poor Man's System of Justice'.

133   Reiner, *The Politics of the Police*, 40.

134   Stephen Inwood, 'Policing London's Morals: The Metropolitan Police and Popular Culture, 1829–1850', *London Journal*, 15:2 (1990); John Field, 'Police, Power and Community in a Provincial English Town: Portsmouth 1815–1875', in V. Bailey (ed.), *Policing and Punishment in Nineteenth-Century Britain* (Croom Helm, London, 1981); David Taylor 'Conquering the British Ballarat: The Policing of Victorian Middlesbrough', *Journal of Social History*, 37 (2004), 3.

135   Quoted in Rawlings, *Policing*, 168.

136   Beattie, *The First English Detectives*.

137   Haia Shpayer-Makov, *The Ascent of the Detective: Police Sleuths in Victorian and Edwardian England* (Oxford UP, Oxford, 2011).

138   Shpayer-Makov, *The Ascent of the Detective*, 31.

139   Radzinowicz, *A History of the Criminal Law: Volume 4*, 186.

140   Taylor, *The New Police*, 99.

141   Shpayer-Makov, *The Ascent of the Detective*, 31–3.

142   Davis, 'The London Garrotting Panic of 1862'.

143   Shpayer-Makov, *The Ascent of the Detective*, 36.

144   Clive Emsley, *The Great British Bobby*, 167.

145   Shpayer-Makov, *The Ascent of the Detective*, 38–9.

146   Ibid., 49.

147   Cox, *A Certain Share of Low Cunning*.

148   Kate Summerscale, *The Suspicions of Mr. Whicher: or the Murder at Road Hill House* (Bloomsbury, London, 2009).

149   Shpayer-Makov, *The Ascent of the Detective*, 48.

150   Gray, *London's Shadows*, and K. R. M. Short, *The Dynamite War: Irish-American Bombers in Victorian Britain* (Gill & MacMillan, Dublin, 1979); Alex Butterworth, *The World That Never Was: A True Story of Dreamers, Schemers, Anarchists, and Secret Agents* (Vintage, London, 2011).

151   Shpayer-Makov, *The Ascent of the Detective*, 50.

152   Ibid., 61.

153   PC Dixon first appeared in *The Blue Lamp* (1950, d.Basil Deardon) played by Jack Warner. Warner went on to develop the popular role of Dixon in Ted Wills' BBC TV drama, *Dixon of Dock Green*, between 1955 and 1976.

154   Emsley, *The Great British Bobby,* 155.

155   Ibid., 101.

156   Francis Dodsworth, 'Men on a Mission: Masculinity, Violence and the Self-Presentation of Policemen in England, c. 1870–1914', in David Barrie and Susan Broomhall (eds.), *A History of Police and Masculinities, 1700–2010* (Routledge, London, 2010), 125.

157   See Clive Emsley, *Crime, Police, & Penal Policy: European Experiences 1750–1940* (Oxford UP, Oxford, 2007).

158   Chris A. Williams, *Police Control Systems in Britain, 1775–1975: From Parish Constable to National Computer* (Manchester UP, Manchester, 2014).

159   A county study that is an exception is B. J. Davey's excellent *Lawless and Immoral: Policing a Country Town 1838–1857* (Leicester UP, 1983).

160   McGowen, 'The Bank of England and the Policing of Forgery', 115.

Chapter 11

1   Lemmings, *Law and Government*, 18.

2   Ingram, *Church Courts*, 28.

3   Outhwaite, *The Rise and Fall of the English Ecclesiastical Courts,* 6.

4   King, *Crime and Law*, 49–50.

5   Eastwood, *Government and Community*, 10.

6   Beattie, *Crime and the Courts*, 15.

7   Eastwood, *Government and Community*, 100.

8   These were Cumberland, Durham, Northumberland and Westmoreland.

9   The City sessions of the peace were convened at Guildhall while the Middlesex justices sat at Hicks Hall in Clerkenwell; both met eight times a year and dealt with a similar range of business to that of county quarter sessions. The most noticeable difference, as Beattie notes, was that they 'did not deal with many charges of theft' (Beattie, *Policing and Punishment,* 21). This was because very many petty larcenies and some more serious incidents of property crime were filtered out of the system at the summary level. Beattie says it was because the sessions left 'virtually all charges involving the taking of property […] to the courts presided over by the judges of the high courts' (Beattie, *Policing and Punishment,* 12). See also Gray, *Crime, Prosecution and Social Relations.*

10   Hay, 'Property, Authority and the Criminal Law', 27.

11   Eastwood, *Government and Community*, 102.

12   Beattie, *Policing and Punishment,* 6.

13   Beattie, *Crime and the Courts*, 16; these records are held at the London Metropolitan Archives (LMA) which (perhaps confusingly) also houses the records of the City of London.

14 Beattie, *Policing and Punishment*, 16–17.

15 http://www.oldbaileyonline.org/static/The-old-bailey.jsp#a1673 [last accessed 17 April 2014].

16 Albert Crew, *The Old Bailey. History: Constitution: Functions. Notable Trials* (Nicholson and Watson, London, 1933), 10.

17 Langbein, *The Origins*, 10–11.

18 Scroggs, as Lord Chief Justice, presided over the trials of those accused of fermenting the so-called 'Popish plot' in 1678–1679. Jeffreys was Lord Chancellor under James II and conducted the trials of over 1,300 persons accused of treason in the wake of the Duke of Monmouth's rebellion. The trials, dubbed the 'bloody assizes' resulted in between 160 and 170 defendants being sentenced to death.

19 Theredore F. T. Plucknett, *A Concise History of the Common Law* (Little Brown, Boston, MA, 1956), 245.

20 Or indeed later in the eighteenth century. As David Lemmings argues, the late 1700s saw judges increasingly place 'a greater stress on order and obedience to the state' when previously they had been at pains to emphasize the 'consensual nature of government'. Lemmings, *Law and Government*, 181–2.

21 For example, at the April 1757 sessions of Old Bailey (where Mansfield sat for Middlesex and the lord mayor sat for London), nine defendants were sent to the gallows, two branded and thirty-four sentenced to transportation. www.oldbaileyonline.org, t17570420.

22 There were also three to four justices of Common Pleas until 1880. We no longer have a court of Common Pleas; it was merged with King's Bench in 1880.

23 The circuits were Home, Midland, Northern, Oxford, Western and Wales. Douglas Hay notes that the twelve judges of England (the twelve common law judges of Westminster Hall) 'went on six routes or circuits throughout England during the vacations between the law terms, to clear the gaols and hear and determine at trial ("oyer and terminer") the most serious criminal cases, including capital felonies'. See Douglas Hay (ed.), *Collections for a History of Staffordshire. Fourth Series, Volume 24. Criminal Cases on the Crown Side of King's Bench: Staffordshire, 1740–1800* (Staffordshire Record Society, 2010), 2.

24 King, *Crime, Justice and Discretion*, 245.

25 The Twelve judges also considered civil cases; see James Oldham, 'Informal Law-Making in England by the Twelve Judges in the Late 18th and Early 19th Centuries', *Law and History Review*, 27 (2011), 8.

26 Gray and King, 'The Killing of Constable Linnell', 13.

27 King, *Crime, Justice and Discretion*, 245.

28 Hay, 'Property, Authority and the Criminal Law'.

29 Ibid., 27.

30 King, *Crime, Justice and Discretion*, 255.

31 Linebaugh, *The London Hanged*, 87.

32 Blackstone, *Commentaries*, Volume 4, 344.

33 J. S. Cockburn, 'Twelve Silly Men? The Trial Jury at Assizes, 1560–1670', in J. S. Cockburn and Thomas Green (eds.), *Twelve Good Men and True: The Criminal Trial Jury in England, 1200–1800* (Princeton UP, Princeton, NJ, 1988), 165–6.

34 Lemmings, *Law and Government*.

35   D. Hay, 'The Class Composition of the Palladium of Liberty: Trial Jurors in the Eighteenth Century', in J. S. Cockburn and Thomas Green (eds.), *Twelve Good Men and True* (Princeton UP, Princeton, NJ), 308–9.

36   P. J. R. King, '"Illiterate Plebeians, Easily Misled": Jury Composition, Experience, and Behaviour in Essex, 1735–1815', in J. S. Cockburn and Thomas Green (eds.), *Twelve Good Men and True* (Princeton UP, Princeton, NJ), 254.

37   Hay, 'Property, Authority and the Criminal Law', 33.

38   David Bentley, *English Criminal Justice in the Nineteenth Century* (Hambledon Press, London, 1998), 132.

39   Langbein, *The Origins*, 59–60.

40   King and Ward, 'Rethinking the Bloody Code in Eighteenth-Century Britain'.

41   See Chapter 12.

42   Hay, 'Property, Authority and the Criminal Law'.

43   John H. Langbein, 'Albion's Fatal Flaws', *Past & Present*, 98 (February, 1983).

44   King, '"Illiterate Plebeians, Easily Misled"', 279.

45   Hay, 'The Class Composition of the Palladium of Liberty', 330.

46   King, '"Illiterate Plebeians, Easily Misled"', 304.

47   Ibid., 277.

48   Kind, *Crime, Justice and Discretion*, 245.

49   Lemmings, *Law and Government*, 123.

50   Hay, 'The Class Composition of the Palladium of Liberty', 311.

51   Langbein, 'Albion's Fatal Flaws'.

52   Louis A. Knafla, *Kent at Law 1602: The County Jurisdiction: Assizes and Sessions of the Peace* (Public Record Office, London, 1994), xviii.

53   www.oldbaileyonline.org t17830910-29: trial of Thomas and Ann Coleman, 10 September 1783.

54   www.oldbaileyonline.org t17830910-1: trial of John Burton and Thomas Duxton, 10 September 1783.

55   A recognizance was a formal legal document and, in this situation, obliged someone to attend court (whether to prosecute or appear as a witness). If you failed to attend, you could forfeit your sureties – money pledged by your or someone else (and often both) against your non-compliance. In reality many people failed to appear in court but the authorities did not routinely penalize them for it.

56   These exist in large numbers in county record offices and have been extensively used by historians of crime to count the numbers of offenders appearing in court.

57   Hay, 'Property, Authority and the Criminal Law', 32–3.

58   Douglas Hay, 'Prosecution and Power: Malicious Prosecution in the English Courts, 1750–1850', in D. Hay and F. Snyder (eds.), *Policing and Prosecution in Britain 1750–1850* (Oxford UP, Oxford, 1989).

59   Andrea McKenzie, '"This Death Some Strong and Stout Hearted Man Doth Choose": The Practice of Peine Forte et Dure in Seventeenth- and Eighteenth-Century England', *Law and History Review*, 23:2 (2005), 312.

60   Beattie, *Crime and the Courts*, 340.

61   Ibid., 341.

62 Langbein, *The Origins*, 26.

63 Bentley, *English Criminal Justice*, 151.

64 Blackstone, *Commentaries*, 349.

65 Bentley, *English Criminal Justice*, 275–6.

66 By 1840 most sentences were being delivered at conviction and in the 1890s allowance was made for the police to inform the court of any other offences they wished to be 'taken into consideration' before sentencing was passed.

67 Langbein, *The Origins*, 37.

68 John Hostettler and Richard Braby, *Sir William Garrow: His Life, Times and Fight for Justice* (Waterside Press, Sherfield on Loddon, 2010); J. M. Beattie, 'Garrow for the Defence', *History Today*, 41:1 (1991), 49–51; J. M. Beattie, 'Scales of Justice: Defence Counsel and the English Criminal Trial in the Eighteenth and Nineteenth Centuries', *Law and History Review*, 9:2 (1991); Allyson May, *The Bar and the Old Bailey, 1750–1850* (University of North Carolina Press, Chapel Hill, NC, 2003); David Lemmings, *Professors of the Law: Barristers and English Legal Culture in the Eighteenth Century* (Oxford UP, Oxford, 2002).

69 Langbein, *The Origins*, 109.

70 May, *The Bar and the Old Bailey*, 23.

71 Lucy Moore, *Con Men and Cutpurses: Scenes from the Hogarthian Underworld* (Penguin, London, 2004), xvii.

72 Blackstone quoted in Lemmings, *Professors of the Law*, 207.

73 Beattie, *Crime and the Courts*, 357.

74 May, *The Bar and The Old Bailey*, 240.

75 Lemmings, *Professors of the Law*, 311.

76 May, *The Bar and The Old Bailey*, 197.

77 David J. A. Cairns, *Advocacy and the Making of the Adversarial Criminal Trial, 1800–1865* (Clarendon Press, Oxford, 1998), 69.

78 Cairns, *Advocacy*, 176.

79 David Mellinkoff, *The Conscience of a Lawyer* (West Publishing Company, St Paul, MN, 1973); Cairns, *Advocacy*; May, *The Bar and the Old Bailey*.

80 Lemmings, *Professors of the Law*, 307.

81 In 1752 and 1788.

82 B. S. Godfrey, 'Changing Prosecution Practices and Their Impact on Crime Figures, 1857–1940', *British Journal of Criminology*, 48:2 (January, 2008).

83 Quoted in May, *The Bar and The Old Bailey*, 194.

84 Bentley, *English Criminal Justice*, 86.

85 Crew, *The Old Bailey*, 36.

86 Bentley, *English Criminal Justice*, 204.

87 Howard Levenson, 'Legal Aid for Mitigation', *The Modern Law Review*, 40:5 (January 2011), 523.

88 Bentley, *English Criminal Justice*, 72.

89 Hay (ed.), *Collections for a History of Staffordshire*, 7.

90 Ibid., 1.

91 Hay et al. (eds.), *Albion's Fatal Tree*, 13.

92   Hay, 'Property, Authority and the Criminal Law'.

93   Thompson, *Whigs and Hunters*, 262.

94   Hay, 'Property, Authority and the Criminal Law', 26.

95   Ibid., 30.

96   Hay, 'Property, Authority and the Criminal Law', 40.

97   These are held in the HO47 series of the TNA records; see also Gatrell, *The Hanging Tree*.

98   Hay, 'Property, Authority and the Criminal Law', 48.

99   Ibid., 56.

100 Langbein, 'Albion's Fatal Flaws', 97.

101 P. J. R. King, 'Decision-Makers and Decision-Making in the Eighteenth-Century Criminal Law, 1750–1800', *The Historical Journal*, 27:1 (1984).

102 See here E. P. Thompson's *Customs in Common*.

103 Langbein, 'Albion's Fatal Flaws', 101.

104 Ibid., 105.

105 Gray and King, 'The Killing of Constable Linnell'.

106 King, *Crime, Justice and Discretion*, 357.

107 Ibid., 357.

108 See Table 3, Ibid., 43.

109 J. Brewer and J. Styles (eds.), *An Ungovernable People; The English and Their Law in the Seventeenth and Eighteenth Centuries* (Hutchinson & Co., London, 1980), 20.

110 King and Ward, 'Rethinking the Bloody Code in Eighteenth-Century Britain'.

111 Or perhaps more properly for 'networks' of criminals. See Shore, *London's Criminal Underworlds*.

112 Langbein, 'Albion's Fatal Flaws', 118.

113 See Hay (ed.), *Collections for a History of Staffordshire*; Gray, 'Making Law'; King, 'The Summary Courts'.

114 Langbein, 'Albion's Fatal Flaws', 105.

Chapter 12

1   Nicola Lacey, *State Punishment: Political Principles and Community Values* (Routledge, London, 1988), 11–12.

2   The full quote is 'Life for life, eye for eye, tooth for tooth, hand for hand, foot for foot, Burning for burning, would for wound, stripe for stripe'; Exodus 21.23.

3   David Garland, *Punishment and Modern Society: A Study in Social Theory* (Clarendon, Oxford, 1991) 28.

4   Quoted in Janet Semple, *Bentham's Prison: A Study of the Panopticon Penitentiary* (Clarendon, Oxford, 1993), 25.

5   James Sharpe, *Judicial Punishment in England* (Faber, London, 1990); see also Ingram, 'Shame and Pain'.

6   E. P. Thompson, 'Rough Music', in *Customs in Common* (Penguin, London, 1993), 467–533.

7   Paul Griffiths, *Change, Crime and Control in the Capital City 1550–1660* (Cambridge UP, Cambridge, 2008).

8   Joanna Innes, 'Prisons for the Poor: English Bridewells, 1555–1800', in Francis Synder and Douglas Hay (eds.), *Labour, Law, and Crime: An Historical Perspective* (Tavistock Publications, London & New York, 1987), 71.

9   There is an explanation of Benefit of Clergy on pages 280–1.

10 Sharpe, *Judicial Punishment*, 28.

11 Ibid., 33.

12 McKenzie, *Tyburn's Martyrs*, 6.

13 Ibid., 13.

14 Beattie, *Crime and the Courts*, 142.

15 Langbein, 'Albion's Fatal Flaws', 117.

16 Beattie, *Crime and the Courts*, 452.

17 Langbein, 'Albion's Fatal Flaws', 119.

18 Hay, 'Property', 18.

19 Ibid., 21.

20 Thompson, *Whigs and Hunters*, 21.

21 Ibid., 23.

22 9 Geo. I, c.22 (1723).

23 Radzinowicz, *A History of the English Criminal Law and Its Administration from 1750*, 1, 77.

24 See, for example, Cal Winslow, 'Sussex Smugglers', in Hay et al. (eds.), *Albion's Fatal Tree: Crime and Society in Eighteenth-Century England* (Penguin, London, 1975).

25 Thompson, *Whigs and Hunters*, 191.

26 Lemmings, *Law and Government*, 132; E. Cruickshanks and H. Erskine-Hill, 'The Waltham Black Act and Jacobitism', *Journal of British Studies*, 24 (1985), 358–65.

27 Radzinowicz, I, 78–9.

28 Ward, 'Print Culture and Responses to Crime', 95 (see also 74–5).

29 Andrea McKenzie, '"This Death Some Strong and Stout Hearted Man Doth Choose": The Practice of Peine Forte et Dure in Seventeenth and Eighteenth-Century England', *Law and History Review*, 23:2 (2005), 279–313.

30 Peter Linebaugh, 'The Tyburn Riot Against the Surgeons', in Hay et al., *Albion's Fatal Tree*.

31 Elizabeth Hurren, 'The Dangerous Dead; Dissecting the Criminal Corpse', *The Lancet*, 382 (27 July 2013), 302.

32 King and Ward, 'Rethinking the Bloody Code in Eighteenth-Century Britain'.

33 Report from the select committee on criminal laws (8 July 1819).

34 Gatrell, *The Hanging Tree*, table 1, 616.

35 Ibid., 619.

36 King and Ward, 'Rethinking the Bloody Code in Eighteenth-Century Britain', 2.

37 Ibid., 8.

38 Simon Devereaux, 'England's "Bloody Code" in Crisis and Transition: Executions at the Old Bailey, 1760–1837', *Journal of the Canadian Historical Association*, 24:2 (2013), 71–113.

39 King and Ward, 'Rethinking the Bloody Code in Eighteenth-Century Britain', 22.

40   Ibid., 29.

41   See Richard R. Follett, *Evangelicalism, Penal Theory and the Politics of Criminal Law Reform in England, 1808–30* (Palgrave, Basingstoke, 2001).

42   Gatrell, *The Hanging Tree*, 241.

43   King and Ward, 'Rethinking the Bloody Code in Eighteenth-Century Britain', 47.

44   Gatrell, *The Hanging Tree*, 20.

45   Radzinowicz, *A History of the English Criminal Law*, 720.

46   Randall McGowen, 'The Image of Justice and Reform of the Criminal Law in Early Nineteenth-Century England', *Buffalo Law Review*, 32:1 (1983), 89–125; see also Randall McGowen, 'The Body and Punishment in Eighteenth-Century England', *Journal of Modern History*, 59 (1987), 651–79.

47   Sir William Meredith, 13 May 1777, *Series of Speeches* (1831), BL.

48   Phil Handler, 'Forging the Agenda: The 1819 Select Committee on the Criminal Laws Revisited', *The Journal of Legal History*, 25:3 (December 2004), 250.

49   McGowen, 'The Image of Justice'.

50   Handler, 'Forging the Agenda', 262.

51   Michel Foucault, *Discipline and Punish: The Birth of the Prison* (Vintage Books, London, 1977).

52   See Beattie, *Crime and the Courts*; Follett, *Evangelicalism*; Harry Potter, *Hanging in Judgement. Religion and the Death Penalty in England from the Bloody Code to Abolition* (SCM Press, Norwich, 1993); Randell McGowen, 'Revisiting The Hanging Tree: Gatrell on Emotion and History', *British Journal of Criminology*, 40:1 (2000), 1–13; J. A. Sharpe, 'Civility, Civilizing Processes, and the End of Public Punishment in England', in Peter Burke, Brian Harrison, and Paul Slack (eds.), *Civil Histories: Essays Presented to Sir Keith Thomas* (Oxford UP, Oxford, 2001).

53   Follett, *Evangelicalism*, 18.

54   Ibid., 80.

55   Semple, *Bentham's Prison*, 29.

56   Follett, *Evangelicalism*, 107.

57   King and Ward, 'Rethinking the Bloody Code in Eighteenth-Century Britain'.

58   Earl Grey and Lord Grenville (House of Lords, 2 April 1832) *Series of Speeches* (1831), BL, 13.

59   Barrett was unfortunate in that he probably had little or nothing to do with the bombing, he was just the person the authorities chose to make an example of.

60   Beattie, *Crime and the Courts*, 452.

61   Morgan and Rushton, *Eighteenth-Century Criminal Transportation*, 11–12, 19.

62   Beattie, *Crime and the Courts*, 479–81.

63   Gwenda Morgan and Peter Rushton, 'Running Away and Returning Home: The Fate of English Convicts in the American Colonies', *Crime. History and Societies*, 7:1 (2003), 61–2.

64   Gwenda Morgan and Peter Rushton, *Eighteenth-Century Criminal Transportation: The Formation of the Criminal Atlantic* (Palgrave, Basingstoke, 2004), 23.

65   Morgan and Rushton, 'Running Away and Returning Home', 127.

66   Ibid., 153.

67   Innes, 'Prisons for the Poor', 88–9.

68   Ignatieff, *A Just Measure of Pain*, 35.

69   Gray, *Crime, Prosecution and Social Relations*, 1–2.

70   Deirdre Palk (ed), *Prisoners' Letters to the Bank of England, 1781–1827* (London Record Society, London, 2007).

71   Ignatieff, *A Just Measure of Pain*, 39.

72   Robert J. Turnbull, *A Visit to the Philadelphia Prison* (London, 1798), 4–5.

73   Sir George Onesiphorous Paul, *Address to His Majesty's Justices of the Peace for the County of Gloucester on the Administration and Practical Effects of the System of Prison Regulation, Established in that County* (Gloucester, 1809), 76.

Chapter 13

1   Beattie, *Crime and the Courts*, 599.

2   Robert Hughes, *The Fatal Shore: The Epic of Australia's Founding* (Vintage, New York, 1988), 1.

3   Morgan and Rushton, *Eighteenth-Century Criminal Transportation*, 162.

4   Ian Duffield and James Bradley, *Representing Convicts: New Perspectives on Convict Forced Labour Migration* (Leicester UP, Leicester, 1997), 9.

5   Maxwell-Stewart, Hamish, 'Convict Transportation from Britain and Ireland 1615–1870', *History Compass*, 8:11 (2010), 1221–1242; Deborah Oxley, *Convict Maids: The Forced Migration of Women to Australia* (Cambridge UP, Cambridge, 1996).

6   M. Clark, 'The Origins of the Convicts Transported to Eastern Australia, 1787–1852', *Historical Studies: Australia and New Zealand*, 7 (1956), 314–27; M. Clark, *A Short History of Australia* (MacMillan, Melbourne, 1963,1982), 9.

7   Hughes, *The Fatal Shore*, xi–xv.

8   Stephen Nicholas et al., *Convict Workers: Reinterpreting Australia's Past* (Cambridge UP, Cambridge, 2007), 43.

9   Duffield and Bradley, *Representing Convicts*, 2; see also E. Christopher and H. Maxwell-Stewart, 'Convict Transportation in Global Context, c.1700–88', in Alison Bashford and Stuart Macintyre (eds.), *The Cambridge History of Australia: Indigenous and Colonial Australia* (Cambridge UP, Cambridge, 2013), 68–90.

10   Nicholas et al., *Convict Workers*, 34.

11   Ibid., 38.

12   Ibid., 8.

13   Christopher and Maxwell-Stewart, 'Convict Transportation'.

14   Anon., *The History of Van Dieman's Land from the Year 1824 to 1835 Inclusive to Which Is Added a Few Words on Prison Discipline* (London, 1835), 274–5.

15   Capt. Maconochie, RN, KH (Late superintendent of Norfolk Island), *The Mark System in Prison Discipline* (London, 1847, updated in 1855), 6.

16   Christopher Harding, *Imprisonment in England and Wales* (Croom Helm, London, 1985), 117.

Notes

17 Shore, *Artful Dodgers*.

18 Simon Devereaux, 'The Making of the Penitentiary Act, 1775–1779', *The Historical Journal*, 42:2 (1990), 405.

19 For a detailed examination of this act (the Hard Labour Act 1778) see Devereau's 'The Making of the Penitentiary Act'.

20 Devereaux, 'The Making of the Penitentiary Act', 429.

21 Ibid., 432.

22 Harding et al., *Imprisonment in England and Wales*, 122–4.

23 For a very thorough and detailed analysis of Bentham's panopticon and his contribution to penal reform in the long eighteenth century, see Janet Semple's excellent study, *Bentham's Prison* (1993).

24 Semple, *Bentham's Prison*, 27.

25 Ignatieff, *A Just Measure of Pain*, 77.

26 Ibid., 77.

27 Harding et al., *Imprisonment in England and Wales*, 128.

28 Semple, *Bentham's Prison*, 93.

29 Ibid., 27.

30 U. R. Q. Henriques, 'The Rise and Decline of the Separate System of Prison Discipline', *Past& Present*, 54 (1972), 64.

31 Thomas Fowell Buxton, *An Inquiry Whether Crime and Misery Are Produced or Prevented, by Our Present System of Prison Discipline* (London, 1818), 73.

32 Zedner, *Women, Crime and Custody*, 105.

33 Helen Johnston, *Punishment and Control in Historical Perspective* (Palgrave MacMillan, Basingstoke, 2008), 80.

34 Zedner, *Women, Crime and Custody*, 106.

35 Paul, *Address to His Majesty's Justices of the Peace*, 75.

36 Quoted in Henriques, 'The Rise and Decline of the Separate System of Prison Discipline', 65.

37 Semple, *Bentham's Prison*, 87.

38 Quoted in Henriques, 'The Rise and Decline of the Separate System of Prison Discipline', 65.

39 Zedner, *Women, Crime and Custody*, 109.

40 William Tallack, *Humanity and Humanitarianism with Special Reference to the Prison System of Great Britain and the United States. The Question of Criminal Lunacy and Capital Punishment* (The Howard Association, London, 1871), 20.

41 Ignatieff, *A Just Measure of Pain*, 9.

42 William James Forsythe, *The Reform of Prisoners, 1830–1900* (St. Martin's Press, New York, 1987).

43 Crawford quoted in Harding et al., *Imprisonment in England and Wales*, 148.

44 Johnston, 'Moral Guardians?', 84.

45 Ignatieff, *A Just Measure of Pain*, 3.

46 Margaret De Lacy, 'Grinding Men Good? Lancashire's Prisons at Mid-Century', in V. Bailey (ed.), *Policing and Punishment in Nineteenth-Century Britain* (Croom Helm, London, 1981).

47 Sean McConville, *A History of English Prison Administration Volume 1 1750–1877* (Routledge and Kegan Paul, Henley on Thames, 1981), 209.

48 Emsley, *Crime and Society in England*, 278.

49 Edmund Du Cane, *The Punishment and Prevention of Crime* (MacMillan & Co., London, 1885), 61.

50 Philip Priestley, *Victorian Prison Lives: English Prison Biography, 1830–1914* (Methuen, London, 1985), 121–3.

51 Ibid., 125–9.

52 Ibid, 130–1.

53 Sean McConville, 'The Victorian Prison. England, 1865–1965', in Morris and Rothman (eds.), *The Oxford History of the Prison: The Practice of Punishment in Western Society* (Oxford UP, 1998), 119.

54 Forsythe, *The Reform of Prisoners*, 44.

55 Sean McConville, *English Local Prisons 1860–1900, Next only to Death* (Routledge, London, 1995).

56 Maconochie, *The Mark System in Prison Discipline*, 4.

57 McConville, 'The Victorian Prison', 123.

58 Victor Bailey, 'English Prisons, Penal Culture, and the Abatement of Imprisonment, 1895–1922', *Journal of British Studies*, 26:3 (1997), 286.

59 McConville, 'The Victorian Prison', 137.

60 Wiener, *Reconstructing the Criminal*, 308.

61 Radzinowicz and Hood, *A History of the Criminal Law and Its Administration from 1750: Volume Five – The Emergence of Penal Policy* (Stephens & Sons, London, 1986).

62 Zedner, *Women, Crime and Custody*.

63 Wiener, *Reconstructing the Criminal*, 311.

64 Arthur Bidwell quoted in Priestley, *Victorian Prison Lives*, 229.

65 Wiener, *Reconstructing the Criminal*, 323.

66 Ibid., 259.

67 Bailey, 'English Prisons', 289.

68 Quoted in Radzinowicz and Hood, *A History of the Criminal Law*, 582.

69 Sidney and Beatrice Webb, *English Prisons Under Local Government* (John Cass, London, 1922), 247.

70 Goffman, *Asylums*.

71 Ibid., xxi.

72 Foucault, *Discipline and Punish*, 199.

73 Ignatieff, *A Just Measure of Pain*, 215.

74 Radzinowicz and Hood, *A History of the Criminal Law, Volume 5*, 633.

75 Martin Page, *Crime Fighters of London: A History of the Origins of and Development of the London Probation Service, 1876–1965* (Inner London Probation Trust, London, 1992), 4–6.

76 Radzinowicz and Hood, *A History of the Criminal Law, Volume 5*, 635.

77 *The Bucks Herald* (25 October 1884).

78 Thomas Holmes, *Pictures and Problems from the London Police Courts* (London, 1900), 62.

79 *Reynold's Newspaper* (31 March 1889).

80 *Daily News* (19 October 1889).

Notes

81   *The Sheffield Daily Telegraph* (28 August 1890).

82   Page, *Crime fighters of London*, 18–19; see also Dorothy Bochel, *Probation and After-Care: Its Development in England and Wales* (Scottish Academic Press, Edinburgh and London, 1976), 15.

83   Radzinowicz and Hood, *A History of the Criminal Law, Volume 5*, 642.

84   Philip Whiteread and Roger Statham, *The History of Probation: Politics, Power and Cultural Change 1876–2005* (Shaw & Sons, Crayford, 2006), 26.

85   Godfrey, *Crime in England*, 157.

86   Harding et al., *Imprisonment in England and Wales*, 110.

87   Ignatieff, *A Just Measure of Pain*.

88   Michael Ignatieff, 'State, Civil Society, and Total Institutions: A Critique of Recent Social Histories of Punishment', *Crime and Justice*, 185.

89   Garland, *Punishment and Modern Society*, 165.

90   Foucault, *Discipline and Punish*.

91   Ignatieff, 'State, Civil Society and Total Institution', 195.

92   Garland, *Punishment and Modern Society*, 103.

93   Ignatieff, *A Just Measure of Pain*, 213.

94   Garland, *Punishment and Modern Society*, 44–5.

95   Ibid., 59.

96   Margaret De Lacy, *Prison Reform in Lancashire, 1700–1850: A Study in Local Administration* (Stanford UP, Stanford, CA, 1986).

97   Ignatieff, 'State, Civil Society and Total Institution', 185

98   Ibid., 202.

99   King and Ward, 'The Bloody Code and the Unbloody Code'.

100 Gatrell, *Hanging Tree*; McGowen, 'Image of Justice'.

101 Foucault, *Discipline and Punish*; Ignatieff, *A Just Measure of Pain*.

Conclusion

1   Shore, *London's Criminal Underworlds*.

2   Gray, *Summary Proceedings and Social Relations*.

3   Lemmings, *Law and Government*.

4   Gatrell, 'Crime, Authority and the Policeman-State'.

5   Godfrey and Farrall, *Criminal Lives*.

6   Godfrey, *Crime in England*.

SELECT BIBLIOGRAPHY

John E. Archer, '"Men Behaving Badly"? Masculinity and the Uses of Violence, 1850–1900', in Shani D'Cruze (ed.), *Everyday Violence in Britain, 1850–1950* (Longman, 2000)

John E. Archer, 'Mysterious and Suspicious Deaths: Missing Homicides in North-West England (1850–1900)', *Crime, History & Societies*, 12:1, 45–63 (2008)

John E. Archer, *The Monster Evil: Policing and Violence in Victorian Liverpool* (Liverpool, Liverpool UP, 2011)

Victor Bailey (ed.), *Policing and Punishment in Nineteenth Century Britain* (Croom Helm, London, 1981)

Victor Bailey (ed.), 'English Prisons, Penal Culture, and the Abatement of Imprisonment, 1895–1922', *Journal of British Studies*, 26:3 (1997)

J. M. Beattie, *Crime and the Courts in England, 1660–1800* (Princeton UP, Princeton, NJ, 1986)

J. M. Beattie, *Policing and Punishment in London, 1660–1750: Urban Crime and the Limits of Terror* (Oxford UP, Oxford, 2001)

J. M. Beattie, *The First English Detectives: The Bow Street Runners and the Policing of London, 1750–1840* (Oxford UP, Oxford, 2014)

David Bentley, *English Criminal Justice in the Nineteenth Century* (Hambledon Press, London, 1998)

J. Brewer and J. Styles (eds.), *An Ungovernable People; The English and their Law in the Seventeenth and Eighteenth Centuries* (Hutchinson, London, 1980)

Anna Clark, *Women's Silence Men's Violence: Sexual Assault in England, 1770–1845* (Pandora Press, London, 1987)

Anna Clark, *The Struggle for the Breeches: Gender and the Making of the British Working Class* (University of California Press, Berkeley, CA, 1997)

J. S. Cockburn (ed.), *Crime in England 1550–1800* (Princeton UP, Princeton, NJ, 1977)

J. S. Cockburn and Thomas Green (eds.), *Twelve Good Men and True: The Criminal Trial Jury in England, 1200–1800* (Princeton UP, Princeton, NJ, 1988)

J. S. Cockburn and Thomas Green (eds.), 'Patterns of Violence in English Society: Homicide in Kent 1560–1985', *Past & Present*, 103 (1991)

Stanley Cohen, *Folk Devils and Moral Panics. The Creation of the Mods and Rockers* (MacGibbon, London, 1972)

Carolyn A. Conley, *The Unwritten Law: Criminal Justice in Victorian Kent* (Oxford UP, Oxford, 1991)

David J. Cox, *A Certain Share of Low Cunning: A History of the Bow Street Runners, 1792–1839* (Routledge, London, 2012)

Pamela Cox and Heather Shore (eds.), *Becoming Delinquent: British and European Youth, 1650–1950* (Ashgate, Dartmouth, 2002)

Pamela Cox, *Gender, Justice and Welfare: Bad Girls in Britain, 1900–1950* (Palgrave, Basingstoke, 2003)

T. A. Critchley, *A History of Police in England and Wales* (Constable, London, 1978)

Rosalind Crone. *Violent Victorians: Popular Entertainment in Nineteenth-Century London* (Manchester UP, Manchester, 2012)

Shani D'Cruze, *Everyday violence in Britain, 1850–1950* (Longman, London, 2000)

Shani D'Cruze and Louise A. Jackson, *Women, Crime and Justice in England since 1660* (Palgrave MacMillian, Basingstoke, 2009)

Select Bibliography

Andrew Davies, 'Youth Gangs, Masculinity and Violence in Late Victorian Manchester and Salford', *Journal of Social History*, 32:2 (Winter, 1998)

Jennifer Davis, 'The London Garrotting Panic: A Moral Panic and the Creation of a Criminal Class in Mid-Victorian England', in V.A.C Gatrell, B. Lehman and G. Parker (eds.), *Crime and the Law: The Social History of Crime in Western Europe since 1500* (Europa Publications, London, 1980)

Jennifer Davis, 'A Poor Man's System of Justice: The London Police Courts in the Second Half of the Nineteenth Century', *The Historical Journal*, 27:2 (1984)

Jennifer Davis, 'Prosecutions and their Context: The Use of the Criminal Law in Later Nineteenth-Century London', in Douglas Hay and Francis Synder, *Policing and Prosecution in Britain, 1850–1750* (Clarendon Press, Oxford, 1989)

Margaret De Lacy, 'Grinding Men Good? Lancashire's Prisons at Mid-Century', in V. Bailey (ed.), *Policing and Punishment in Nineteenth Century Britain* (Croom Helm, London, 1981)

Simon Devereaux, 'England's "Bloody Code" in Crisis and Transition: Executions at the Old Bailey, 1760–1837', *Journal of the Canadian Historical Association*, 24:2 (2013), 71–113

Simon Devereaux, 'The Making of the Penitentiary Act, 1775–1779', *The Historical Journal*, 42:2 (1990)

Simon Devereaux, 'The Abolition of the Burning of Women in England Reconsidered', *Crime, History, and Societies*, 9:2 (2005)

Simon Devereaux, 'Recasting the Theatre of Execution: The Abolition of the Tyburn Ritual', *Past & Present*, 202 (2009)

Ian Duffield and James Bradley, *Representing Convicts: New Perspectives on Convict Forced Labour Migration* (Leicester UP, Leicester, 1997)

Manuel Eisner, 'Modernization, Self-Control and Lethal Violence', *British Journal of Criminology*, 91 (2001)

Manuel Eisner, 'Long-Term Historical Trends in Violent Crime', *Crime and Justice: A Review of Research*, 30 (2003)

M. Emmerichs, 'Getting Away with Murder: Homicide and the Coroners in Nineteenth-Century London', *Social Science History*, 25 (2001)

Clive Emsley, *The English Police: A Political and Social History* (Harvester Wheatsheaf, Hemel Hempstead, 1991)

Clive Emsley, *The Great British Bobby: A History of British Policing from the 18th Century to the Present* (Quercus, London, 2009)

Clive Emsley, *Hard Men: the English and Violence since 1750* (Hambledon, London, 2005)

Clive Emsley, *Crime and Society in England, 1750–1900*, 4th edition (Longman, London, 2010)

Clive Emsley, Graeme Dunstall and Barry S. Godfrey, *Comparative Histories of Crime* (Willian, Cullompton, 2003)

Lincoln B. Faller, *Turned to Account: The Forms and Functions of Criminal Biography in Late Seventeenth- and Early Eighteenth-Century England* (Cambridge UP, Cambridge, 1987)

Malcolm M. Feeley and Deborah E. Little, 'The Vanishing Female: The Decline of Women in the Criminal Process, 1687–1912', *Law & Society Review*, 719 (1991)

Richard R. Follett, *Evangelicalism, Penal Theory and the Politics of Criminal Law Reform in England, 1808–30* (Palgrave, Basingstoke, 2001)

Michel Foucault, *Discipline and Punish: The Birth of the Prison* (Vintage Books, London, 1977)

E. Foyster, *Marital Violence: An English Family History, 1660–1857* (Cambridge UP, Cambridge, 2005)

David Garland, *Punishment and Welfare: A History of Penal Strategies* (Gower Publishing, Aldershot, 1985)

David Garland, *Punishment and Modern Society: A Study in Social Theory* (Clarendon Press, Oxford, 1991)

Malcolm Gaskill, *Crime and Mentalities in Early Modern England* (Cambridge UP, Cambridge, 2000)

V. A. C. Gatrell et al., *Crime and the Law. The Social History of Crime in Western Europe since 1500* (Europa, London, 1980)

V. A. C. Gatrell, 'Crime, Authority and the Policeman-State', in F. M. L. Thompson, *The Cambridge Social History of Britain 1750–1950* (Cambridge UP, 1990)

V. A. C. Gatrell, *The Hanging Tree: Execution and the English People 1770–1868* (Oxford UP, Oxford, 1994)

Barry Godfrey, 'Counting and Accounting for the Decline in Non-Lethal Violence in England, Australia and New Zealand, 1880–1920', *British Journal of Criminology*, 43 (2003)

Barry Godfrey, 'Changing Prosecution Practices and Their Impact on Crime Figures, 1857–1940', *British Journal of Criminology*, 48:2 (January, 2008)

Barry Godfrey, *Crime in England, 1880–1945: The Rough and the Criminal, the Policed and the Incarcerated* (Routledge, London, 2014)

B. Godfrey and S. Farrall, *Criminal Lives: Family Life, Employment, and Offending* (Oxford UP, Oxford, 2012)

Drew D. Gray, *Crime, Prosecution and Social Relations: The Summary Courts of the City of London in the Late Eighteenth Century* (Palgrave, Basingstoke, 2009)

Drew D. Gray, *London's Shadows: The Dark Side of the Victorian City* (Bloomsbury, London, 2010)

Drew D. Gray, 'Making Law in Mid-Eighteenth-Century England: Legal Statutes and their Application in the Justicing Notebook of Phillip Ward of Stoke Doyle', *The Journal of Legal History*, 34:2 (2013)

Drew D. Gray, 'Gang Crime and the Media: the Regent's Park Murder of 1888', *Social and Cultural History*, 10:4 (2013)

Drew Gray and Peter King, 'The Killing of Constable Linnell: The Impact of Xenophobia and of Elite Connections on Eighteenth-Century Justice', *Family & Community History*, 16:1 (April, 2013)

Daniel Grey, ' "More Ignorant and Stupid than Wilfully Cruel": Homicide Trials and "Baby-Farming" in England and Wales in the Wake of the Children Act 1908', *Crimes and Misdemeanours: Deviance and the Law in Historical Perspective*, 3:2 (2009)

Paul Griffiths, *Youth and Authority: Formative Experiences in England 1560–1640* (Clarendon Press, Oxford, 1996)

Paul Griffiths, *Lost Londons: Change, Crime and Control in the Capital City 1550–1660* (Cambridge UP, Cambridge, 2008)

Ted Gurr, 'Historical Trends in Violent Crime: A Critical Review of the Evidence', *Crime and Justice: An Annual Review of Research*, 3 (1981)

Phil Handler, 'Forgery and the End of the 'Bloody Code' in Early Nineteenth-Century England', *The Historical Journal*, 48:3 (2005)

Gregory Hanlon, 'Review Article. The Decline of Violence in the West: From Cultural to Post-Cultural History', *English Historical Review*, CXXVIII: 53 (2013)

Andrew T. Harris, *Policing the City: Crime and Legal Authority in London 1780–1840* (Ohio State UP, Colombus, 2004)

Douglas Hay, 'Property, Authority and the Criminal Law', in Douglas Hay et al. (eds.), *Albion's Fatal Tree: Crime and Society in Eighteenth-Century England* (Penguin, London, 1975)

Douglas Hay, 'Patronage, Paternalism and Welfare: Masters, Workers and Magistrates in Eighteenth-Century England', *International Labor and Working Class History*, 51 (1998)

Douglas Hay (ed.), *Collections for a History of Staffordshire. Fourth Series, Volume 24. Criminal Cases on the Crown Side of King's Bench: Staffordshire, 1740–1800* (Staffordshire Record Society, 2010)

D. Hay and F. Snyder (eds.), *Policing and Prosecution in Britain 1750–1850* (Oxford UP, Oxford, 1989)

Tony Henderson, *Disorderly Women in Eighteenth-Century London: Prostitution and Its Control in the Metropolis, 1730–1830* (Longman, London, 1999)

Select Bibliography

Tim Hitchcock, *Down and Out in Eighteenth-Century London* (Hambeldon Press, London, 2004)

Tim Hitchcock and Robert Shoemaker, *Tales from the Hanging Court* (Bloomsbury Academic, London, 2006)

Eric Hobsbawn, *Bandits* (Weidenfield & Nicolson, London, 1969, 2000)

Michael Ignatieff, *A Just Measure of Pain: A Just Measure of Pain: The Penitentiary in the Industrial Revolution, 1750–1850* (University of Chicago Press, Chicago, 1978)

Joanna Innes, 'Prisons for the Poor: English Bridewells, 1555–1800', in Francis Synder and Douglas Hay (eds.), *Labour, Law, and Crime: An Historical Perspective* (Tavistock Publications, London and New York, 1987)

Joanna Innes, *Inferior Politics: Social Problems and Social Policies in Eighteenth-Century Britain* (Oxford UP, Oxford, 2009)

Stephen Inwood, 'Policing London's Morals: the Metropolitan Police and Popular Culture, 1829–1850', *London Journal*, 15:2 (1990)

Mark Jackson, *Infanticide: Historical Perspectives on Child Murder and Concealment 1550–2000* (Ashgate, Aldershot, 2002)

Joan R. Kent, *The English Village Constable 1580–1642: A Social and Administrative Study* (Oxford UP, Oxford, 1986)

Anne-Marie Kilday, *A History of Infanticide in Britain, c.1600 to the Present* (Palgrave Macmillan, Basingstoke, 2013)

Peter King, 'Decision-Makers and Decision-Making in the Eighteenth Century Criminal law, 1750–1800', *The Historical Journal*, 27:1 (1984)

Peter King, 'Prosecution Associations and their Impact in Eighteenth-Century Essex', in D. Hay and F. Synder (eds.), *Policing and Prosecution on Britain 1750–1850* (Oxford UP, 1989)

Peter King, 'Punishing Assault: The Transformation of Attitudes in the English Courts', *The Journal of Interdisciplinary History* 27:1 (Summer, 1996)

Peter King, 'Female Offenders, Work and Life-Cycle Change in Late-Eighteenth-Century LONDON', *Continuity and Change*, 11:1 (May, 1996)

Peter King, *Crime, Justice and Discretion in England 1740–1820* (Oxford UP, Oxford, 2000)

Peter King. 'The Summary Courts and Social Relations in Eighteenth-Century England', *Past & Present*, 183 (May, 2004)

Peter King, *Crime and Law in England, 1750–1840: Remaking Justice from the Margins* (Cambridge UP, Cambridge, 2006)

Peter King, 'Newspaper Reporting and Attitudes to Crime and Justice Late-Eighteenth and Early-Nineteenth-Century London', *Continuity and Change*, 22 (2007)

Peter King, 'The Impact of Urbanization on Murder Rates and on the Geography of Homicide in England and Wales, 1780–1850', *The Historical Journal*, 53:3 (2010)

Peter King and Joan Noel, 'The Origins of the "Problem of Juvenile Delinquency": The Growth of Juvenile Prosecutions in London in Late Eighteenth and Early Nineteenth Centuries', *Criminal Justice History*, 14 (1993)

Peter King and Richard Ward, 'Rethinking the Bloody Code in Eighteenth-Century Britain: Capital Punishment at the Centre and on the Periphery', *Past & Present*, 228 (2015)

Norma Landau, *The Justices of the Peace, 1679–1760* (University of California Press, Berkeley, CA, 1984)

Norma Landau, 'Appearance at the Quarter Sessions of Eighteenth-Century Middlesex', *The London Journal*, 23:2 (1998)

Norma Landau, 'Indictment for Fun and Profit: A Prosecutor's Reward at the Eighteenth-Century Quarter Sessions', *Law and History Review*, 17:3 (Fall, 1999)

Norma Landau (ed.), *Law, Crime and English Society, 1660–1830* (Cambridge UP, Cambridge, 2002)

John H. Langbein, 'Albion's Fatal Flaws', *Past & Present*, 98 (February, 1983)

John H. Langbein, *The Origins of the Adversary Criminal Trial* (Oxford UP, Oxford, 2001)

David Lemmings, *Law and Government in England during the Long Eighteenth Century: From Consent to Command* (Palgrave, Basingstoke, 2011)

Peter Linebaugh, *The London Hanged: Crime and Civil Society in the Eighteenth Century* (Penguin, London, 1993)

Sean McConville, 'The Victorian Prison. England, 1865–1965', in David J Rothman and Norval Morris (eds.), *The Oxford History of the Prison: The Practice of Punishment in Western Society* (Oxford UP, Oxford, 1998)

Randall McGowen, 'The Image of Justice and Reform of the Criminal Law in Early Nineteenth-Century England', *Buffalo Law Review*, 32:1, 89–125 (1983)

Randall McGowen, 'The Body and Punishment in Eighteenth-Century England', *Journal of Modern History*, 59, 651–679 (1987)

Randall McGowen, 'Revisiting the Hanging Tree: Gatrell on Emotion and History', *British Journal of Criminology*, 40:1 (2000)

Randall McGowen, 'The Bank of England and the Policing of Forgery 1797–1821', *Past & Present*, 186 (February, 2005)

Andrea McKenzie, '"This Death Some Strong and Stout Hearted Man Doth Choose": The Practice of Peine Forte et Dure in Seventeenth and Eighteenth-Century England', *Law and History Review*, 23:2 (2005)

Andrea McKenzie, 'The Real MacHeath: Social Satire, Appropriation, and Eighteenth-Century Criminal Biography', *Huntingdon Law Quarterly*, 69:4 (2006)

Andrea McKenzie, *Tyburn's Martyrs: Execution in England 1675–1775* (Hambledon Continuum, London, 2007)

Hamish Maxwell-Stewart, 'Convict Transportation from Britain and Ireland 1615–1870', *History Compass*, 8:11 (2010), 1221–1242

Henry Mayhew & John Binny, *The Criminal Prisons of London: And Scenes of Prison Life* (Griffin, Bohn, and Company, London, 1862).

Allyson May, *The Bar and the Old Bailey, 1750–1850* (University of North Carolina Press, Chapel Hill, NC, 2003)

William M. Meier, *Property Crime in London, 1850-Present* (Palgrave MacMillan, Basingstoke, 2011)

Gwenda Morgan and Peter Rushton, *Rogues, Thieves and the Rule of Law: The Problem of Law Enforcement in North-East England, 1718–1800* (UCL Press, London, 1998)

Gwenda Morgan and Peter Rushton, 'The Magistrate, the Community and the Maintenance of an Orderly Society in Eighteenth-Century England', *Historical Research*, 76 (2003)

Gwenda Morgan and Peter Rushton, *Eighteenth-Century Criminal Transportation: The Formation of the Criminal Atlantic* (Palgrave, Basingstoke, 2004)

Morris and Rothman (eds.), *The Oxford History of the Prison: The Practice of Punishment in Western Society* (Oxford UP, Oxford, 1998)

Robert Muchembled, *A History of Violence: From the End of the Middle Ages to the Present* (Polity Press, Cambridge, 2011)

P. B. Munsche, 'The Game Laws in Wiltshire, 1750–1800', in J. S. Cockburn (ed.), *Crime in England, 1550–1800* (Princeton UP, Princeton, 1977)

Stephen Nicholas et al., *Convict Workers: Reinterpreting Australia's Past* (Cambridge UP, 2007)

Ruth Paley, 'Thief-Takers in London in the Age of the McDaniel Gang, c. 1745–1754', in D. Hay and F. Snyder (eds.), *Policing and Prosecution in Britain 1750–1850* (Oxford UP, Oxford, 1989)

Ruth Paley (ed.), *Justice in Eighteenth-Century Hackney: The Justicing Notebook of Henry Norris and the Hackney Petty Sessions Book* (London Record Society, London, 1991)

Deirdre Palk, *Gender, Crime and Judicial Discretion 1780–1830* (Boydell Press, Woodbridge, 2006)

Deirdre Palk (ed.), *Prisoners' Letters to the Bank of England, 1781–1827* (London Record Society, London, 2007)

Stanley Palmer, *Police and Protest in England and Ireland, 1780–1850* (Cambridge UP, Cambridge, 1988)

Geoffrey Pearson, *Hooligan: A History of Respectable Fears* (MacMillan, London, 1983)

David Phillips, *Crime and Authority in Victorian England: The Black Country 1835–1860* (Croom Helm, London, 1977)

David Phillips, 'A "Weak" State? The English State, the Magistracy and the Reform of Policing in the 1830s', *English Historical Review*, CXIX: 483 (2004)

David Philips and Robert D. Storch, *Policing Provincial England 1829–1856. The Politics of Reform* (Leicester UP, Leicester, 1999)

Harry Potter, *Hanging in Judgement. Religion and the Death Penalty in England from the Bloody Code to Abolition* (SCM Press, Norwich, 1993)

Leon Radzinowicz, *A History of the Criminal Law and Its Administration from 1750: Volume 1–4* (Stevens & Sons, London, 1948–1968)

Leon Radzinowicz and Roger Hood, *A History of the Criminal Law and Its Administration from 1750: Volume Five – The Emergence of Penal Policy* (Stephens & Sons, London, 1986)

Philip Rawlings, *Drunks, Whores and Idle Apprentices: Criminal Biographies of the Eighteenth Century* (Routledge, London, 1992)

Philip Rawlings, *Policing: A Short History* (Willan, Cullompton, 2002)

Robert Reiner, *The Politics of the Police*, 4th edition (Oxford UP, Oxford, 2010)

Elaine Reynolds, *Before the Bobbies: The Night Watch and Police Reform in Metropolitan London, 1720–1830* (Stanford UP, Redwood City, 1998)

Nicholas Rogers, *Mayhem: Post-War Crime and Violence in Britain, 1748–53* (Yale UP, New Haven, 2012)

John G. Rule (ed.), *Outside the Law: Studies in Crime and Order, 1650–1850* (Exeter University Press, Exeter, 1982)

Janet Semple, *Bentham's Prison: A Study of the Panopticon Penitentiary* (Clarendon, Oxford, 1993)

J. A. Sharpe, *Crime in Seventeenth-Century England: A County Study* (Cambridge UP, Cambridge, 1983)

J. A. Sharpe, *Crime in Early Modern England 1550–1750* (Longman, London, 1984)

J. A. Sharpe, 'Debate: The History of Violence in England; Some Observations', *Past & Present*, 108 (1985)

J. A. Sharpe, '"Last Dying Speeches": Religion, Ideology and Public Execution in Seventeenth-Century England', *Past & Present*, 107 (1985)

J. A. Sharpe, *Judicial Punishment in England* (Faber, London, 1990)

J. A. Sharpe, 'Civility, Civilizing Processes, and the End of Public Punishment in England', in Peter Burke, Brian Harrison and Paul Slack (eds.), *Civil Histories: Essays Presented to Sir Keith Thomas* (Oxford UP, Oxford, 2001)

J. A. Sharpe, *Dick Turpin: The Myth of the English Highwayman* (Profile Books, London, 2004)

Robert B. Shoemaker, *Prosecution and Punishment: Petty Crime and the Law in London and Rural Middlesex, 1660–1725* (Cambridge UP, Cambridge, 1991)

Robert B. Shoemaker, 'Male Honour and the Decline of Violence in Eighteenth-Century London', *Social History*, 26 (2001)

Robert B. Shoemaker, 'The Taming of the Duel; Masculinity, Honour and Ritual Violence in London, 1660–1800', *The Historical Journal*, 45:3 (2002), 525–545

Robert B. Shoemaker, 'The Old Bailey Proceedings and the Representation of Crime and Criminal Justice in Eighteenth-Century London', *Journal of British Studies*, 47 (July, 2008)

Robert B. Shoemaker, 'Print Culture and the Creation of Public Knowledge about Crime in Eighteenth-Century London', in Paul Knepper et al. (eds.), *Urban Crime Prevention, Surveillance, and Restorative Justice* (CRC Press, London, 2009)

Robert B. Shoemaker, *London's Criminal Underworlds, c. 1720 - c. 1930: A Social and Cultural History* (Palgrave, Basingstoke, 2015)

Heather Shore, *Artful Dodgers: Youth and Crime in Early 19th-Century London* (Boydell Press, London, 1999; 2002)

Haia Shpayer-Makov, *The Making of a Policeman: A Social History of a Labour Force in Metropolitan London, 1829–1914* (Ashgate, Aldershot, 2002)

Haia Shpayer-Makov, *The Ascent of the Detective: Police Sleuths in Victorian and Edwardian England* (Oxford UP, Oxford, 2011)

Robert Sindall, *Street Violence in the Nineteenth Century* (Leicester UP, 1990)

Esther Snell, 'Discourses of Criminality in the Eighteenth-Century Press: The Presentation of Crime in the *Kentish Post*, 1717–1768', *Continuity and Change*, 22 (2007)

Pieter Spierenburg (ed.), *A History of Murder: Personal Violence in Europe from the Middles Ages to the Present* (Cambridge UP, Cambridge, 2008)

John Springhall, *Youth, Popular Culture and Moral Panics: Penny Gaffs to Gansta-Rapp 1830–1996* (MacMIllan, Basingtoke, 1998)

Carolyn Steedman, *Policing the Victorian Community: Formation of English Provincial Police Forces, 1856–80* (Routledge & Kegan Paul, London, 1984)

Lawrence Stone, 'Interpersonal Violence in English Society 1300–1980', *Past & Present*, 101 (1983)

Robert D. Storch. The Plague of Blue Locusts: Police Reform and Popular Resistance in Northern England, 1840–57', *International Review of Social History*, 20:1 (1975)

Robert D. Storch, 'The Policeman as Domestic Missionary: Urban Discipline and Popular Culture in Northern England, 1850–1880', *Journal of Social History*, 9:4 (1976)

Francis Synder and Douglas Hay (eds.), *Labour, Law, and Crime: An Historical Perspective* (Tavistock Publications, London & New York, 1987)

David Taylor, *The New Police in Nineteenth-Century England: Crime, Conflict and Control* (Manchester UP, Manchester, 1997)

Howard Taylor, 'Rationing Crime: The Political Economy of Criminal Statistics since the 1850s', *Economic History Review*, 51 (1998)

E. P. Thompson, *Whigs and Hunters: the Origin of the Black Act* (Penguin, London, 1975, 1990)

E. P. Thompson, *Customs in Common* (Penguin, London, 1993)

F. M. L. Thompson (ed.), *The Cambridge Social History of Britain, 1750–1950, vol. 3; Social Agencies and Institutions* (Cambridge UP, Cambridge, 1990)

J. J. Tobias, *Crime and Industrial Society in the Nineteenth Century* (Penguin, Harwondsworth, 1972)

J. J. Tobias, *Crime and Policing in England 1700–1900* (Gill and Macmillan, Dublin, 1979)

Garthine Walker and Jenny Kermode, *Women, Crime and the Courts in Early Modern England* (UCL Press, London, 1994)

Garthine Walker, *Crime, Gender and Social Order in Early Modern England* (Cambridge UP, Cambridge, 2003)

Richard M. Ward, 'Print Culture, Moral Panic, and the Administration of the Law: The London Crime Wave of 1744', *Crime, History & Societies*, 15:1 (2012)

Richard M. Ward, *Print Culture, Crime and Justice in 18th Century London* (Bloomsbury, London, 2014)

Richard M. Ward (ed.), *A Global History of Execution and the Criminal Corpse* (Palgrave, Basingstoke, 2015)

Tammy C. Whitlock, *Crime, Gender and Consumer Culture in Nineteenth-Century England* (Ashgate, Farnham, 2005)

Martin J. Wiener, *Reconstructing the Criminal: Culture, Law, and Policy in England, 1839–1914* (Cambridge UP, Cambridge, 1990)

Martin J. Wiener, *Men of Blood: Violence, Manliness, and Criminal Justice in Victorian England* (Cambridge UP, Cambridge, 2004)

Select Bibliography

Chris Williams, 'Counting Crimes or Counting People: Some Implications of Mid-Nineteenth Century British Police Returns', *Crime, Histoire & Sociétés/Crime, History & Societies*, 4:2 (2000)

Chris Williams, *Police Control Systems in Britain, 1775–1975: From Parish Constable to National Computer* (Manchester UP, Manchester, 2014)

John Carter Wood, *Violence and Crime in Nineteenth-Century England; The Shadow of Our Refinement* (Routledge, London, 2004)

John Carter Wood, 'Criminal Violence in Modern Britain', *History Compass*, 4:1 (2006)

Lucia Zedner, *Women, Crime and Custody in Victorian England* (Clarendon, Oxford, 1991; 1994)

INDEX

Note: Locators followed by the letter 'n' refer to notes

Index

Index

Index